NEWPORT, R.I.

Dear M? Browell,

In reply to your

I beg

Greetings to

? all.

Edith ?

we do ?

spring

STATION: LEE

TELEGRAMS: LENOX

Dear

THE
LETTERS OF
EDITH WHARTON

THE
LETTERS OF
Edith Wharton

EDITED BY

R. W. B. LEWIS

AND

NANCY LEWIS

C. 1

CHARLES SCRIBNER'S SONS

NEW YORK

Copyright © 1988 by R. W. B. Lewis, Nancy Lewis,
and William R. Tyler
All rights reserved. No part of this book may be reproduced or
transmitted in any form or by any means, electronic or mechanical,
including photocopying, recording, or by any information storage
and retrieval system, without permission in writing
from the Publisher.

Charles Scribner's Sons
Macmillan Publishing Company
866 Third Avenue, New York, NY 10022
Collier Macmillan Canada, Inc.

Library of Congress Cataloging-in-Publication Data
Wharton, Edith, 1862–1937.
The letters of Edith Wharton, 1874–1937.
Includes index.
1. Wharton, Edith, 1862–1937—Correspondence.
2. Authors, American—20th century—Correspondence.
3. Authors, American—19th Century—Correspondence.
I. Lewis, R. W. B. (Richard Warrington Baldwin)
II. Lewis, Nancy.   III. Title.
PS3545.H16Z48   1988   813'.52 [B]   87-23526
ISBN 0-684-18585-7

Macmillan books are available at special discounts
for bulk purchases for sales promotions, premiums, fund-raising,
or educational use. For details, contact:
Special Sales Director
Macmillan Publishing Company
866 Third Avenue
New York, NY 10022

Design by Janet Tingey

10 9 8 7 6 5 4 3 2 1

PRINTED IN THE UNITED STATES OF AMERICA

FOR OUR CHILDREN

The editors are happy to acknowledge a special debt of gratitude to Nathaniel Lewis for his devoted and painstaking involvement over many months in the drafting and printing of the manuscript, and for a range of invaluable editorial and stylistic suggestions.

Contents

Illustrations

❀

THE
LETTERS OF
EDITH WHARTON

❈

Introduction

✺

EDITH WHARTON's long life—1862 to 1937—passed through and well beyond the great age of letter writing in America. In one perspective, that age may be seen as coming to an end with the death of Henry James in 1916 and of Henry Adams two years later. A different portent of the art's demise was offered by Edith Wharton herself in a letter of early 1914 to Corinne Robinson, the sister of Theodore Roosevelt, apologizing for not writing during a recent visit to New York and explaining that she had become so addicted to telephoning and telegraphing that she had lost the ability to express herself on paper. She soon recovered the ability, needless to say. Edith Wharton belongs to the American company of prolific and eloquent letter writers; and there are special qualities, special intensities of personal involvement and exposure, that set her letters apart from those of most others in that company.

Scarcely a day passed, in her maturity and in good health, when she did not compose and dispatch half a dozen letters, many of them carrying forward ongoing conversations. (Returning once from a short trip, in 1924, she found sixty-five letters awaiting her: the incoming mail over three days.) There are extant about four thousand letters from Edith Wharton that might be suitably drawn upon for a collection such as this one. At least as many more exist and are accessible—mainly in Beinecke Library, Yale—but these deal largely with routine business matters, and were dictated to and in some cases probably written by one or another of Mrs. Wharton's secretaries.

Of the usable four thousand, we have, after an elaborate and always fascinating process, chosen a little less than four hundred, about one in ten. We could well wish the number were higher, and could in fact, without much difficulty, have included up to one hundred more, but at some risk of repetition and perhaps an occasional slackening of appeal. The letters selected are intended to show Edith Wharton at her epistolary best and most characteristic, and in the striking variety of her voices, her changeable states of being, the modes and phases of her major relationships. One source of frustration to us, it might be added, was Edith Wharton's habit, in her later years, of embedding a passage of great charm or wit in an otherwise rather desultory letter. An anthology of these gemlike moments might be in order at some future date.

The largest surviving correspondences, as it happens, are those beginning in 1893 with the several editors at Charles Scribner's Sons (now held at Firestone Library, Princeton); and with Bernard Berenson, the distinguished Italian Renaissance art connoisseur and historian, and Mary Berenson. There are more than six hundred of the latter: happily for the rest of us, Berenson, with the help of his longtime associate Nicky Mariano, kept and catalogued every letter ever written to him by anyone of importance over the better part of a century. There are also about 360 letters, from the early 1900s, to Gaillard Lapsley, the astute Rhode Island–born don of medieval history at Cambridge, who would eventually be Edith Wharton's literary executor and the initiator of the Wharton archive at Yale. To swell the archives unexpectedly, there came into view a few years ago at the University of Texas in Austin—we will look more closely at this event—three hundred letters from Edith Wharton to her sometime lover, the Paris-based American journalist William Morton Fullerton.

The survival of letters is a chancy affair. Edith Wharton was thirty-eight years old, had been publishing fiction for nine years, and was the author of a book on house decoration and a well-received volume of short stories before someone other than her Scribners editors thought her letters worth retaining. This was Sara Norton, the literate and discerning daughter of Charles Eliot Norton, Harvard professor and scholar; among the 240 letters held on to—and, where necessary, dated—by Sara Norton are some of the finest Edith Wharton wrote before the First War. Some correspondences known to have existed have vanished: like that with Percy Lubbock, the gifted English writer with whom, after years of friendship and patronage, Edith had a falling-out; and Geoffrey Scott, the author of *The Architecture of Humanism*, who was, unwittingly, one of the causes of the falling-out.

Henry James burned all but a handful of the many letters (170?) Edith Wharton wrote him between 1902 and 1915. But Edith Wharton was the one to destroy her letters to Walter Berry, the American lawyer who was her adviser and companion for thirty years. She went to Berry's apartment in Paris after his death in 1927, retrieved her letters to him, and burned them. At a reasonable calculation, there must have been four hundred letters and more to be consumed. Most collections of letters in the modern period suffer from deprivations of this sort, and it is well to remember that the self-portraits emerging in the letters are inevitably limited or distorted by the simple phenomenon of what has survived, not to mention what has been editorially selected therefrom.

Edith Wharton's family clan—Stevenses, Rhinelanders, Joneses, New Yorkers all—were not themselves much given to letter writing as a serious exercise. In this they differed, for example, from the Jameses (William, Henry, Alice), who were brought up with a high regard for the practice and who regularly congratulated one another on the brilliance or vivacity of a letter just received. The American ancestry of Edith Jones reached back to the early eighteenth century, to Ebenezer Stevens, a gallant artillery commander and a fellow officer of the Marquis de Lafayette during the Revolutionary War, and to William and Frederick Rhinelander, who built a flourishing business in sugar and shipbuilding in the 1780s. It included assorted wealthy and influential Schermerhorns, among them Edith's second cousin Caroline Schermerhorn, who married William Backhouse Astor and managed to establish herself as *the* Mrs. Astor. What it did not include, as far as one can make out, was anything like a literary or artistic energy, any sustained interest in letters in both the broad and the literal meaning of the word.

The closest one gets to such an interest is with Edith's father, George Frederic Jones, a Columbia College graduate of upper-middle-class background whose comfortable income derived from city landholdings. George Frederic read with some diligence in history and philosophy, and he had a genuine if baffled fondness for poetry—a tendency, so his daughter was to feel, that had been stifled by her mother, Lucretia Rhinelander Jones. "I imagine there was a time," Edith Wharton wrote, looking back, "when his rather rudimentary love [of poetry] might have been developed had he any one with whom to share it. But my mother's matter-of-factness must have shrivelled any such buds of fancy." It was George Frederic, anyhow, who taught Edith to read, led her at a very young age to memorize and recite *The Idylls of the King*, and encouraged any symptom she might display of literary enthusiasm.

But the prevailing atmosphere in the Jones household and in the society—the old guard, the "good old families" of lengthy lineage and cautious habits—to which the Joneses belonged was one of indifference to literary expression and even suspicion of it. Edith's mother apparently did see to the private printing of her daughter's verses in 1878, but this was a solitary gesture. Neither Lucretia nor Edith's brothers—the remote Freddy, the kindly but unimaginative Harry—seem to have lent any significant support to Edith's shy efforts at literary composition in any form.

All the more, in after years, did Edith Wharton respond with pleasure if anyone spoke admiringly of one of her letters. In the winter of 1912, Bernard Berenson, writing from his Villa I Tatti outside Florence, remarked casually that he had received a "good letter" from her. Edith was much gratified. Her "epistolary art," she wrote in reply, had "never before been commended"; and as one result she found herself consciously striving to emulate the praised performance. "Beginning a letter to you," she went on, "has the excitement of a literary adventure as well as the joy of communicating with a friend." In typical fashion, she then deprecated: "Unluckily for literature, I always forget the former, and only remember the latter pleasure when I'm under way." As though to illustrate the point, she veered off into an inquiry about some trifling accident Berenson had suffered, and wondered whether he had incurred it while trying to scale a wall.

Early and late, the letters of Edith Wharton oscillate between the literary and the friendly: between the more or less consciously composed and the gracefully expressed at one moment, and the gossipy, the querying, the commiserating at another. One of her last letters, to Mary Berenson, concludes a lyrical outburst about her unabated pleasure in "this wonderful adventure of living"—"I'm an incorrigible life-lover & life-wonderer"—with a sympathetic reference to the illness of a sister of one of Berenson's Italian associates. In this respect, the letters mirror the life. A comparable alternation was indicated in a remark to Sara

Norton in September 1902. "Zwei Seelen wohnen, ach, in meine[r] Brust," Edith said, quoting from Goethe's *Faust* ("Two souls, alas, do dwell within my breast"); "& the Compleat Housekeeper has had the upper hand for the last weeks." Stories and articles by Edith Wharton were appearing everywhere in American periodicals; her novel *The Valley of Decision* was winning accolades on all sides and was selling briskly (thirty-five thousand copies by the end of the year); she had just finished the translation of a play by the German dramatist Sudermann. But her literary life had to slow down for a period while she devoted her energies to settling herself, her husband, Teddy Wharton, and the staff of servants and gardeners in The Mount, the new home in Lenox, Massachusetts.

The reflection of the two souls in the shifting rhythm of Edith Wharton's letters suggests what has been argued elsewhere, that letters by American women, and among them the literarily gifted, tend to give much more attention to the human concerns of daily life than do those of their male counterparts. For the attuned reader, this is always part of the attraction: in this case, the spectacle in letter form of Edith Wharton moving between a vigorous play of mind and imagination or of highly charged feeling and the horde of demanding and sometimes harrowing practical problems, professional and domestic, with which she had to cope virtually unaided.

Edith Wharton, as one might say, was nothing if not a dialectical personality. In the fall of 1907, she received from Robert Grant, the Boston judge and a novelist whose work she esteemed, a long and balanced analysis of her novel *The Fruit of the Tree*. She was happy, she replied, that he had liked the construction of the book, but agreed with him that in the interest of firm construction, she had allowed her characters to remain little more than "mere *building-material*." She then drew a distinction—a trifle muddled in formulation, but clear and compelling in essence—between *conceiving* a novelistic subject like a man, "that is, rather more architectonically & dramatically than most women," and *executing* the subject like a woman, via a marshaling of "small incidental effects" and a technique of "episodical characterisation."

One could go far into Edith Wharton's fiction writing by tracing within it the deployment of these two narrative modes: the masculine and the feminine, the dramatic and the accumulative. In her letter writing as well, we can observe the alternation and the mingling. A letter to Berenson from North Africa in April 1914, as an example, moves naturally from the evocation of an atmosphere like that of an "unexpurgated page of the Arabian Nights" and the delineation of "effeminacy, obesity, obscenity or black savageness" in the native populace to a moment of almost shattering drama: the sheer sexual terror Mrs. Wharton experienced when she awoke in the darkness of her Timgad hotel room to find a strange man bending over her. The letters to Henry James about visits to the battlefronts in the winter of 1915 are dramatic enough in all truth, and at the same time are enlivened by a succession of incidental effects. In the 1920s and later, as Edith Wharton's taste in fiction grew to favor less the tightly composed Jamesian mode and more the Victorian novel, and especially the gossipy narratives of Anthony Trollope, her letters became looser, more leisurely and spacious, more filled with solicitous inquiries, reports about friends, random anecdotes and musings.

The "masculine" and the "feminine" sides of Edith Wharton in her letters can be detected in other ways, but a clarifying word should be offered in advance. It is, of course, woefully misleading to say of her, as one or two onlookers have been tempted to do (for example, Janet Malcolm in a *New York Times* article on the Library of America volume of Edith Wharton's fiction), that she hated, feared, and distrusted women. Such an idea could derive only from an ignorance of her character and personal life, and from a doctrinaire misreading or simple nonreading of the work. As to the work, one could compile a list of female characters, from Fulvia Vivaldi in *The Valley of Decision* to Laura Testvalley in the posthumous novel *The Buccaneers*, whom Edith Wharton depicts with a sad and protective admiration. Among her personal relationships, one does remark the unrelenting and deepening rancor toward Lady Sybil Cutting, after her successive marriages to Geoffrey Scott and Percy Lubbock. But this was without parallel elsewhere, and it always had a touch of the darkly comic and hyperbolic.

On the other hand, it would be hardly less misleading to suggest that Edith Wharton was a feminist, at least in the current understanding of the term. She had no interest or belief in institutional reform, and rather shied away from literary women who did, like the English novelist May Sinclair. The latter, almost exactly Edith Wharton's age, was indeed an active supporter of women's suffrage as well as an intelligent propagandist for psychoanalysis. Mrs. Wharton managed twice not to meet May Sinclair, despite pressing invitations, during the London social whirl of December 1908; and on a later occasion alluded to May Sinclair's recent novel as pantingly didactic.

What Edith Wharton did, obviously, as a superb and intuitive social historian, was to dramatize the condition of women, which usually meant the repression and the entrapment of women, in the social worlds she lived in. Narrative after narrative culminates in the settled pathos or, as sometimes, the tragedy of that condition; but, again, the letters also testify to the informing vision. To Sara Norton, who wrote in October 1908 to ask whether she might not have done more over the years for her father, then on his deathbed, Edith replied in a gust of impatience: "Alas, I should like to get up on the house-top & cry to all who come after us: 'Take your own life, every one of you!' " A few months later, when her English friend John Hugh Smith spoke severely about a play, recently seen, which (he thought) weighted its plot too heavily on the side of the discontented wife, Edith Wharton rallied to the cause. She mentioned "a few other neurotic women who were discontented with their husbands & relations," naming Clytemnestra, Phaedra, Iseult, Pia Tolomei (in Dante's *Purgatorio*), and Anna Karenina; and went on to contend that "among all the tangles of this mortal coil," none contained "tighter knots to undo" and suggested "more tugging, & pain, & diversified elements of misery, than the marriage tie." Her point claimed to be literary: that the marriage tie with its tugging and pain was peculiarly " 'made to the hand' " of the dramatist; but the expression was of a woman whose compassion for the marital misery of women in general had been sharpened by her own wretched marriage and her adulterous relationship with Morton Fullerton.*

So much being said, it can be remarked that Edith Wharton had a

---

* The victimization of women continued to be an important theme in Edith Wharton's fiction to the end; but the compassionate attitude rather disappears from the *letters* in the later years. Occasionally, indeed, an acerbic note can be heard creeping into her comments in this area. Elizabeth Ammons, in her sensitive study *Edith Wharton's Argument with America* (1980), suggests that it was the overwhelming impact of the war and its threat to the traditional values she cherished that brought on Edith Wharton's conservatism—in general, and with regard to women—during her final decades.

decided masculine strain in her, even if the adjective be taken in a largely metaphoric and associational sense. Witness her keen interest in science and her self-declared role as the priestess of reason. During the early days in Paris, her letters are sprinkled with allusions to books on Darwinism, heredity, new developments in biology. She denounced William James's skepticism about the scientific mentality and what she called (it is wittily unfair) his "psychological-pietistic juggling." The phrase occurs in a letter to Sara Norton in February 1906, after she had read a philosophical tome "with a 'foreword' by le dit James." With the first page, she said, she was in the midst of "the familiar jargon," and she quoted a sentence: " 'Humanity will never be satisfied with scientific knowledge to explain its inward relation to reality.'—What other kind of knowledge is it capable of receiving? Oh, dear—oh, how slowly the wheels turn."

Edith Wharton's view of William James was no doubt colored by a possessive resentment at Henry James's devotion to his older brother. The feeling erupts when she writes to Morton Fullerton in 1910, after visiting with the suicidally depressed Henry James, that all the James family had been "the victims of the neurotic, unreliable Wm James," and that Henry's breakdown was "very different ... from the chronic flares and twitches of the other brother—William o' the wisp James." But along with the jealousy, there was a more purely intellectual aversion: the Enlightenment side of Edith Wharton was offended by William James's modernist philosophical flexibility.

Something of the same found expression in the message of warning she sent to Berenson in February 1922, when her young friend and protégée, the delightful Philomène de Lévis-Mirepoix, was about to join the Berensons for a trip to Egypt. They would both like Philomène, she said, and they could help greatly in the mental training she so badly needed. Her "charming eager helpless intelligence" had been filled with "third-rate flashy rubbish." Above all, Mary Berenson was not to befuddle Philomène "with Freudianism and all its jargon. . . . What she wants is to develop the *conscious*, & not grub after the sub-conscious. She wants to be taught first to see, to attend, to reflect."

All this bespeaks the aspect of Edith Wharton that Fullerton took cognizance of when he slyly addressed her as "Cher Ami." But the opposite aspect was always present, or always ready to be summoned up: what we may perhaps define as "the feminine-mystical mind," borrowing the phrase from *le dit* William James, who (in an essay of the 1890s) contrasted it with "the scientific-academic mind." And this aspect, this mind, was never more evident than in the letters to Morton Fullerton.

The very existence of these letters is a cause for astonishment, it having long been assumed that Fullerton yielded at last to the entreaties of his former mistress and burned the lot of them. Morton Fullerton died in 1952, in Paris, at the age of eighty-six. Some time before his death, he sold twenty-two letters from Edith Wharton (and a great many from Henry James) to Houghton Library at Harvard; these date from 1916, at least five years after the end of the love affair proper. It was the letters known to have been written during the peak of the affair, in 1908–1910, that were thought to have been destroyed. (A sizable batch of Fullerton documents from other sources, including passionate communications from the Ranee of Sarawak, turned up in the late 1960s, but it contained nothing from Edith Wharton.) Then, in 1980, some three hundred letters from Edith Wharton to Morton Fullerton—written between 1907 and 1915, and the great bulk of them during the critical period—were offered for sale by a Dutch firm of booksellers acting for an antiquarian bookdealer in Paris.

The collection was purchased by the Harry Ransom Humanities Research Center at the University of Texas in Austin. The university's *Library Chronicle* devoted a special issue in September 1985 to this new holding, printing twenty-six letters selected and splendidly edited by Professor Alan Gribben. This is the only instance, before the present volume, of the publication of letters by Edith Wharton. But precisely where the precious Fullerton papers lay hidden or forgotten for nearly three decades, and how and why they happened to come into sight just when they did: these questions remain shrouded in the intriguing mystery that attends other aspects of the Fullerton story. The Paris antiquarian, be it said, seems not to have had the letters in his possession very long, nor to have quite understood what they amounted to.

The relationship with Fullerton, as we watch it being enacted in the letters, passed recurrently through several distinct phases. The first cycle, to call it that, covered about eleven months, from February through

December 1908. The friendship had begun the previous spring in Paris, when Fullerton, working out of the Paris office of the London *Times* and drawing on his extensive knowledge of the Paris literary world, helped secure magazine publication for a French translation of *The House of Mirth*. It deepened appreciably during Fullerton's visit to The Mount in October 1907; and soon after the new year, in Paris again, it moved into intimacy. The affair was sanctified, so to say, by a quotation from Emerson: "just the phrase for you—and *me*," Edith wrote: " 'The moment my eyes fell on him I was content.' " There were carefully arranged assignations: "at the Louvre at one o'c, in the shadow of Jean Gougon's Diana"; at 7 P.M. in the Invalides station, but *inside* the station, so that Cook, her chauffeur, would not espy them meeting. There were hangings back ("At first—yes—I hesitated, because I thought it, for you, not very real") and surgings forward ("And if you can't come into the room without my feeling all over me a ripple of flame . . ."). There were occasions of great happiness, like the one signaled after a visit to Beauvais by the underlined phrase from the *Paradiso: quella allegrezza*; and others of despair, like that recorded two weeks after the Dante quotation: "Sometimes I feel that I *can't* go on like this: from moments of such nearness, when the last shadow of separateness melts, back into a complete néant of silence, of not hearing, not knowing." But when she left Paris in late May to return to The Mount, Edith Wharton, to paraphrase her own words, was almost beside herself in the excitement of her love.

Her first letters to Fullerton from Lenox are the most vibrant and openhearted she was ever to write. The one dated over three days from June 8 to 11, in fact, may almost be reckoned a masterpiece; it is certainly brilliant, and it reveals an evolving form, if only a half-conscious one—something approaching Emerson's "frolic architecture"; and can be scrutinized and enjoyed as if it were a wholly imaginative literary text. It begins with a ripple of happy memories, among them their first lunch together in Paris, "with the kindly prognathous lady-in-waiting, & the moist hippopotamous American with his cucumber-faced female." That memory contrasts with the dismal mood she had just barely overcome, and during which she almost cabled him a single word: "*Inconsolable.*" (But had she done so, Fullerton might have cabled back; telegrams to The Mount were telephoned from the village, and Teddy might have been the one to answer the phone. "Si figuri!") She is better now, and has finished three more chapters of her new novel, *The Custom of the Country*, an announcement she compares to a casually bragging message from the King of Spain to the Queen, his wife, in Hugo's *Ruy Blas*.

The images of the slant-jawed waitress at Duval's and the two American diners, affiliated respectively with the animal and the vegetable kingdoms, lead to (as they were probably evoked *by*) her current reading in studies of ancient forms of life, evolution, and Mendel's theories of heredity. She confesses to being dumbfounded by some of the phenomena described—the biophors and determinants (units of germ plasm that convey heredity, and units made up of these); but she gains control by converting them into comic cartoon figures: "the biophors . . . small and anxious to please, the determinants loud and domineering, with eyeglasses." More awesome to her inventive imagination is "that monstrous animal the heterozygote," a hybrid form she had encountered in a text on Mendelism. "Oh, dear—what nonsense to send three thousand miles."

She turns from the playfully literary and intellectual to the more than friendly; to the closely personal. "Do you want to know some of the things I like you for?" She lists Fullerton's capacity for discrimination in people and things, and his concern for the important trifles, the "green worms" of life—a waitress being deprived of a tip, a taxi driver of a fare. Most of all, she likes Fullerton for something that (she says) she and Fullerton are virtually alone in sharing: "a 'radiant reasonableness.'" She describes this paradoxical quality as talent for feeling "the 'natural magic,' au-delà, dream-side of things," even while insisting on "the netteté [clearness or sharpness] . . . in thinking, in conduct—yes! in feeling too!" In a superb small literary maneuver, and by way of concluding the June 8 portion of the letter, she quotes Milton's *Comus* on "that poor dear maligned Goddess of Reason":

> *"How charming is divine philosophy!*
> *Not harsh and crabbèd, as dull fools suppose,*
> *But musical as is Apollo's lute."*

With the Miltonic notion of musical philosophy, Edith Wharton has in effect married the *netteté* and the *au-delà*, dream-side, the scientific and the "feminine-mystical."

Taking up the letter two days later, Edith Wharton proceeds, with a certain hardening of tone, to castigate the sorry familiar tendency of lovers "to bargain and calculate, as if it were a game of skill played between antagonistics." A phrase from an obscure text thought to be by Pascal is drawn upon: "Il faut de l'adresse pour aimer"—*adresse* being skill or dexterity; a noble saying, she argues, if it means the exercise of sympathy and self-effacement; but "the most sordid of counsels if it appeals to the instinct to dole out, dissemble, keep in suspense." For herself, she wants no gaming, no winning: "I want to lose everything to you!"

The tone modulates again the next day, from the impassioned to the gently lyrical, with the news that against all belief she had heard a cuckoo calling from the woods near her garden: a sound thought to be unheard in New England; sweet and insistent, bring back the birdsong she and Fullerton had listened to in Montmorency.*

The entire letter is an expanding dance of opposites: Paris and Lenox, inconsolable and high-humored, the anxious biophor and the domineering determinants, love as gaming and love as self-giving. Finally, in an afterthought, Edith offers a contrast between novelistic possibilities: the ability "to do justice to the tender sentiment in fiction"—a quality she suspects that Fullerton's fiction-writing sister would accuse Mrs. Wharton of lacking—and her own "low & photographic order of talent qui a besoin de se documenter." So ends a letter that has been sufficiently documented and photographic, and which has not been remiss in the language of feeling, both tender and intense. Fusing and harmonizing the diverse aspects of Edith Wharton's nature, the letter has indeed made her during the time of its utterance a fully, one could say joyfully, integrated being.

In retrospect, we recognize the letter of June 8–11, 1908, as marking a moment of well-nigh perfect poise and balance in Edith Wharton's sense

---

* This is one of several moments when one wishes ardently that Edith Wharton had known the poetry of Emily Dickinson—in particular, here, "The Robin's my Criterion for Tune." That poem continues: "Because I grow—where Robins do—/ But, were I Cuckoo born—/ I'd swear by him—..." The only indication of an interest on Edith Wharton's part in her New England predecessor comes in July 1934, when she sent a $7.00 check to the *Yale Review* for one year's subscription and (as the bonus) *The Life and Letters of Emily Dickinson*, by Martha Dickinson Bianchi.

of the affair. The moment did not outlast the summer, partly because it was to a dangerous degree self-deceptive, and it would never be entirely recovered. A nakedly personal voice is heard in letters like that of August 26, 1908—a scant ten weeks later—which begins: "Dear, won't you tell me soon the meaning of this silence?" and goes on to say "how I dreaded to be to you, *even for an instant,* the 'donna non più giovane' who clings and encumbers"; and ends: "My last word is one of tenderness for the friend I love—for the lover I worshipped." Needless to say, it was not the last word. His silence remaining unbroken, Edith Wharton wrote icily to "Dear Mr. Fullerton" from London, in December, asking him to return to her at once "a few notes & letters of no value to your archives," but which could fill a lacuna "in those of their writer."

Over the next two years, the pattern repeated itself at intervals, with Edith Wharton constantly moving from the exhilarated to the apprehensive, from the hopeful to the wretched. A peak of erotic consummation and emotional fulfillment was reached in the summer of 1909, beginning with a "long secret night together" (in Edith's poetic account of it) at the Charing Cross Hotel in London and going on through a month of traveling in England. "During that month," Edith writes on August 12, "I have been completely happy. I have had everything in life that I ever longed for." A fortnight or so after that, she is saying how impossible it is that "our lives should run parallel much longer," and how much she dreads that her love may blind her to the facts when the time of separation arrives. In November, she again solicits the return of her letters.

Early in 1910, she starts to press for an end to the sexual part of their relationship—for "an easy transition to amitié," as she puts it in one letter—now calmly, now with a touch of frenzy beseeching Fullerton to take the step that she in herself seems not ready to take. Along with these confusing messages are expressions of pain and incomprehension at Fullerton's cavalier forgetfulness, his small-minded deceits, his erratic behavior. It is a humiliating period, lightened by only an occasional declaration that she—that "a woman like me"—deserves something rather better. Things come to a head after her return from a visit to London and Henry James. Fullerton writes her regularly while she is away, and, one gathers, in a most outspokenly loverlike manner; in Paris, he subjects her to the old familiar treatment, arriving on her doorstep unannounced, then disappearing, to leave her without a signal for days. The experience draws from her a statement at once desperate and forceful about the intolerable ambiguities of desire and identity that afflict them. "I am sad & bewildered beyond words": such is the opening of the mid-April letter. "Ballottée perpetually between one illusion & another ... I can't any longer find a point de repère. I don't know what you want, or what I am! You write me like a lover, you treat me like a casual acquaintance!"

She begs him to send her no more false or misleading letters like those she received from him in England, and comes to what is intended as an ending once and for all.

> I have had a difficult year—but the pain within my pain, the last turn of the screw, has been the impossibility of knowing what you wanted of me, & what you felt for me. . . . My life was better before I knew you. That is, for me, the sad conclusion of this sad year. And it is a bitter thing to say to the one being one has ever loved d'amour.

The affair continued in a sporadic manner for another season or two (perhaps half a year more than had been thought before the letters to Fullerton showed up), but, on Edith Wharton's part, with diminishing conviction and dwindling passion. By 1911, they had become "companions," in Edith's oft-invoked word, and were acting as one another's literary adviser. A note of astringency enters Mrs. Wharton's letters of counsel to Fullerton, as in the one of October 1912 about his work-in-progress, in which the professional writer tells her friend that, while the argument ought to be couched in a manly, energetic style, he had "hung it with all the heavy tin draperies of the Times jargon—that most prolix & pedantic of all the dead languages. . . . Read Emerson," she enjoins him, "read Tyndall, read Froud[e] even, read Arnold—get away from . . . all the scientific-politico-economic charabia [gibberish] of your own specialists into the clear air of the born writers."

The recurring expressions of subservience in the letters to Fullerton, with what seems to be a felt need for sexual nagging, cannot but strike a disquieting note for a reader in the late 1980s; and especially when, *through* these letters, we receive a clearer and far less appealing picture of Morton Fullerton than had hitherto been available. He was loved by many women, and liked and thought well of by a number of men.

Theodore Roosevelt, for example, is quoted as having a high opinion of him. He had undoubted graces of mind and speech; and for a space of time, as we know from other sources, the sexual relation between the lovers was vigorous and imaginative. But Fullerton was curiously insubstantial on the human side; he seems to have had almost no impulse to engage another person to the full of the other's being, no capacity for genuine human love. The slackness of conduct that caused Edith Wharton such torment derived, one comes to think, not only from a kind of smiling selfishness, but from a sheer slackness of nature. In allying herself to Fullerton, Edith Wharton (though she was slow to realize it) was acting out a theme she had dealt with in her earlier fiction, in *The Fruit of the Tree* and in novellas like *The Touchstone* and *Madame de Treymes*: the larger and finer spirit subdued and even defeated by the smaller and cruder one.

At the same time, the record of that poignant process, in the letters, is quite remarkably human. It is the disclosure of enormous emotional arousal and then of emotional bruising and grief not easily matched in our epistolary annals. Nor is Edith Wharton's revealed vulnerability limited to the Fullerton papers. This woman, whose public image was that of the austerely self-contained (and who could be exactly that in her formal correspondence), was in fact extraordinarily open to experience, immediately responsive to the here-and-now of life. She lived so close to the quick of things, was so urgently caught up in them, that sometimes, reading her letters, one feels that the prose is about to break through the page. This was true whether she was speaking of the vagaries of a lover, the dangerous illness of a friend, the exhilarating view from a mountaintop in Sicily, the march of the German armies, or the street riots in Paris. In her most personal communications, she was surprisingly unguarded; and so, she was vulnerable to a degree. We may think of the winter and spring of 1913, when she was nearly brought down by a series of unsettling events: a grave though short-lived misunderstanding with Henry James ("I can never get over this," she told Lapsley in the course of it); an estrangement from her brother Harry; the ugliness of the divorce proceedings.

She testified to her own grief at these times; and she was invariably responsive to the grief of others: of Sara Norton during the last illness and after the death of her father; of Dr. Beverley Robinson, on the death

of Anna Robinson, his wife of forty-six years and a friend of Edith Jones
in her Newport days. The last letter Edith Wharton wrote, a week before her own death, was a message of loving condolence to Matilda Gay
on the loss of her husband. Death is a major element in these letters
because it was accepted as such, as a central event in human experience,
by Edith Wharton in her life. Among her finest and most touching letters are those about the deaths of Henry James and Walter Berry, and
later of Catharine Gross, her lifelong friend and housekeeper; and to
these one must add the obituary, in June 1908, of the Norton family's
dog Taffy:

> His artless but engaging ways, his candid enjoyment of his dinner, his
> judicious habit of exercising by means of those daily rushes up & down
> the road, had for so many years interested & attracted us that he occupies
> a very special place in our crowded dog-memories.

The learning displayed in Edith Wharton's letters—the close acquaintance with texts literary, artistic, scientific, historical, philosophic,
religious, in five languages, from medieval to modern, from European
to American—is of sometimes awesome proportions. The letter to Fullerton on June 8, 1908, with its range and variety of allusions and quotation, is far from exceptional. To the same correspondent, and writing
in May 1911 from the tedious confines of the spa at Salsomaggiore, she
listed some of the books she had brought with her to while away the
hours: Richard Wagner's *My Life* (which had saved *hers*, she said), a
posthumous work by Victor Hugo, an historical essay by Ernest Renan
on Averroës, the twelfth-century Arabian philosopher and commentator
on Aristotle, an early novel by Flaubert (*Novembre*), a history of philosophy by George Henry Lewes ("which I love & haven't read for years"),
some Emerson, Sir Joshua Reynolds's *Discourses on Art* ("*such* a mixture
of drivel & insight"), Dostoievsky's *The Idiot*, Melville's *Moby Dick* ("do
you share my taste for Melville?"), an account of Germans in France, a
French translation of *Leaves of Grass* (" 'When lilacs last' is unbelievably
well done"), and a life of Whitman by the translator. She did not often
roam quite so broadly; but typically, in a letter to Berenson from Hyères
just before Christmas 1920 as she was about to take possession of her
new Riviera home, she mentioned a recent life of Blake, a reminiscent

essay by Max Beerbohm about a visit in 1899 to the London home of
Algernon Charles Swinburne and the lawyer-writer Theodore Watts-
Dunton, Santayana's *Character and Opinion in the United States* ("oh, what
a tone, what standards!"), a book ("brilliant yet impartial") about Mme.
de Maintenon—the mistress and then the extremely influential wife of
Louis XIV—by Edith Wharton's friend Mme. St.-René de Taillandier,
a "dull & laboured" study of George Sand, Barrett Wendell's *The Traditions of European Literature from Homer to Dante* ("terribly pre-masticated
and primaire"), and a review of a new biography of Goethe.

Only the accessibility of one of the world's great libraries, that of
Yale, and of a great humanities faculty, made it possible for us to track
down many of these references. But it was as desirable as it was necessary to show Edith Wharton forth, whenever the occasion demanded,
in the full panoply of her remarkable cultivation. What one discovers,
after this has happened a few times, is not merely that Edith Wharton
was learned, but that her learning was for her a vital and shaping presence.

Dante, for example, supplied her not so much with quotations as with
ways of focusing herself at key moments: she drew from the *Inferno* to
disavow an interest in argumentation ("*Non ragionam*"), the *Purgatorio*
to point to a disastrous marital situation (Pia Tolomei), and the *Paradiso*
to convey the blessed beauty of her postwar Mediterranean surroundings ("cielo della quieta"). Later in the 1920s, when what she described
to Fullerton as "the au-delà dream-side of things" took stronger possession of her, we find Edith Wharton talking to her old friend Margaret
Terry Chanler, a devout Catholic, about a life of St. François de Sales
and the saint's posthumous *Traité de l'amour de Dieu* (1626), the monumental ongoing work by Abbé Henri Bremond (her "beloved author"),
Histoire littéraire du sentiment religieux en France, and Henry Vaughan's poem
"The World," from which she quotes: "I saw Eternity the other night."

Edith Wharton read whatever book fell into her hands, from whatever
source and of whatever vintage; but what she *retained* from her reading
tended to gather into patterns. Her relation to German literature was
characteristic. We hear her tell Sara Norton of "rummaging" amid the
"metaphysical lumber" of Schopenhauer; and six years later—in the
summer of 1908, when she is meditating the import of the affair with
Fullerton—of reading Nietzsche's *Beyond Good and Evil* and warmly en-

dorsing its attack on Christian attitudes. A few years after that, as though by a natural sequence, she is reveling in Wagner's autobiography; and in Berlin in 1913, escorted by Bernard Berenson, she attends the cycle of *Der Ring des Nibelungen.*

Meanwhile, in a volume of German poetry given her by Berenson, she rereads the medieval songs of Walther von der Vogelweide, long a favorite of hers, and the verse of Goethe and Hugo von Hoffmansthal. Then, in the winter of 1917, she goes back to Walther and to the Icelandic sagas contemporary to him, the Edda, reading those tales of gods and men in an English version of the German translation from which Wagner drew his materials for the Ring cycle. Commenting on this to Berenson, she tells of quoting—to a hapless dinner companion who did not understand a word of it—a line from the dark story of Helgi and Sigrun: *"More powerful at night are the ghosts of the dead heroes than in the light of day."* All of her German reading and remembering resonated in the stirring passage, and at this sombre and perilous moment in the Great War.

"Goethe always Schillered when he wrote to Schiller, didn't he?" The observation was made to Berenson in the letter preceding the one about rereading the Edda. Edith had been going through the correspondence between the two German writers, and she continued: "That's the reason why, generally, transcribed talks are so much more satisfactory than letters. People talk more for themselves, apparently, & write more for their correspondents." The judgment arose from having simultaneously delved into the third volume of *With Walt Whitman in Camden,* Horace Traubel's record of conversations with her favorite American poet. To an extent, Edith Wharton did adjust her letter style to the person she was addressing: a somewhat different voice can be heard talking to Berenson and to Henry James, to Margaret Terry Chanler and to Minnie Jones, to her young English protégé John Hugh Smith and her American academic friend Gaillard Lapsley. Yet it is unmistakably, in every letter, the distinct and recognizable voice of Edith Wharton.

She could write Berenson a painterly letter, as she did from the palace of the Resident General of Morocco in October 1917: "Imagine, after a flight across the bled, passing through battle-mented gate after gate, crossing a dusty open space with mules, camels, story-tellers, & the usual 'comparses,' & passing through a green doorway into a great court full of flowers," and on through more flowers, orange groves, streams, fountains, yellow jasmines, and pomegranate trees. Yet something about Berenson drew from Edith Wharton an impish and teasing strain, as when agreeing to meet him in Rome (in April 1910), she declared her intention *not* to go to the kind of luxury hotel to which Berenson was addicted: "I'm still a slave to the picturesque, & want a Trasteverina dancing the Tarantella in front of a Locanda to the music of a Pifferaro." We find her, in like humor, writing Mary Berenson while traveling across Germany with B.B., that the latter was learning "several useful things" on the trip: among them, "getting out of the motor to ask the way of an intelligent-looking person on the corner, instead of calling out to the village idiot or a deaf octogenarian from one's seat; & abstaining from shallow generalizations such as: 'You'll find it's always safe in Germany to follow the telegraph poles.' "

To Margaret Terry Chanler, she spoke as one who belonged to the same richly be-cousined venerable American society, and to the same community of the extremely well read; to her sister-in-law Minnie, of whom she was enormously fond, her tone was a trifle impatient, as to one whose thought processes were never as rapid or as lucid as they might be. In the early letters to John Hugh Smith, there is an engaging air of flirtatiousness not unmixed with tenderness, of the admired and pursued older woman cautioning the impetuous younger male. With Lapsley she strikes a worldly adult note without the faintest hint of the erotic. Perhaps her most unchanging voice was to her editors and publishers: professional, businesslike, insistent, never missing a trick. In the wake of her first volume of fiction in 1899, she complains with some vehemence at the failure (as she alleges) of Charles Scribner's Sons to advertise the book, though it had (she said) been most favorably reviewed; and a few months afterward, responding to a "kind note" from William Crary Brownell reporting a sale of three thousand copies, she remarks pointedly: "I knew, from the number of letters I have received from publishers, that it must be doing well." Thirty-five years later, she is announcing to her editor at D. Appleton and Company that its advertising of *A Backward Glance* had been so deplorably sparse, and so far behind the practice of all the other major American publishers, that she wishes to be released from the contract for her next novel.

Only a scattered few of Edith Wharton's letters to Henry James have survived: some postcards in 1911, a literary chat in 1912, and a small batch during the early period of the war. The others were presumably destroyed in the ritual bonfire with which James, some time in the 1900s, did away with most of his incoming mail. The loss may well be a major one for literary history. There are about 170 letters extant from James to Edith Wharton, and one may suppose that she wrote that many to him. The few items that have slipped down to us suggest what we have been deprived of.

The two letters written in the winter of 1915 after successive visits to Verdun and neighboring points in the war zone are particularly dramatic and colorful, and made a profound impression on their recipient. From a hotel in Verdun on February 28, Edith Wharton describes some actual fighting she had witnessed.

> From a garden we looked across the valley to a height about 5 miles way, where white puffs & scarlet flashes kept springing up all over the dark hillside. It was the hill above Vauquois, where there has been desperate fighting for two days. The Germans were firing from the top at the French trenches below (hidden from us by an intervening rise of the ground); & the French were assaulting, & *their* puffs & flashes were half way up the hill. And so we saw the reason why there are to be so many wounded at Clermont tonight!

After a second little tour eleven days later, Edith sketched a scene on the Meuse River, west of Verdun:

> Picture this all under a white winter sky, driving great flurries of snow across the mud-and-cinder-coloured landscape, with the steel-cold Meuse winding between beaten poplars—Cook standing with Her [the Mercedes] in a knot of mud-coated military motors & artillery horses, soldiers coming & going, cavalrymen riding up with messages, poor bandaged creatures in rag-bag clothes leaning in doorways, & always, over & above us, the boom, boom, boom of the guns on the grey heights to the east.

"Those big summing-up impressions meet one at every turn," she added, as she went on to offer several more. Edith Wharton was well aware that she was addressing the American writer, in her literary epoch, who was the supreme collector, designer, and conveyer of impressions: the chief summer-up, so to say, of places and persons. Henry James was quick to acknowledge the achievement. He regularly treated Edith Wharton's letters with ceremonial enthusiasm, and sometimes provides us with a hint of what the lost missive may have contained. He had "revelled and rioted" in her letter from Munich in December 1909, he told her: "You are indeed my ideal of the dashing woman, and never dashed more felicitously or fruitfully, for my imagination, than when you dashed, at that particular psychologic moment, off to dear old rococo Munich. . . . Vivid and charming and sympathetic *au possible* your image and echo of it all." There, as often, mockery mixes audibly with admiration. The Jamesian response to what Edith had called her "*sensations de guerre*" was unmodified.

He would not, he says, attempt to expatiate on his failure to reply sooner to her "inexpressibly splendid bounties."

> The idea of "explaining" anything to *you* in these days, or of expatiation that isn't exclusively that of your own genius upon your own adventures and impressions! I think *the* reason why I have been so baffled, in a word, is that all my powers of being anything else have gone to living upon your two magnificent letters, the one from Verdun, and the one after your second visit there; which gave me matter of experience and appropriation to which I have done the fullest honour. Your whole record is sublime, and the interest and the beauty and the terror of it all have again and again called me back to it. . . . I know them at last, your incomparable pages, by heart.

Absorbing the Jamesian voice into her own, Edith Wharton had never expressed herself more handsomely. Henry James's tribute to the epistolary art of his friend and fellow writer ("Chère Madame et Confrère," he had called her), so much more cogent and elaborate than Berenson's, was warmed by a quality that must have made it especially endearing: a kind of generous envy, not only at Edith Wharton's powers of description but at the grand historic adventures that had called them into being.

PART ONE

Years of the Apprentice
1874, 1893–1902

Introduction

✺

EDITH NEWBOLD JONES was twelve years old when she wrote the first letter in this collection. She was in Newport with her family—her parents, George Frederic and Lucretia Rhinelander Jones, and two much older brothers, Freddy and Harry—in the Jones's summer home, Pencraig. Since their return from Europe in 1872 after six years of travel and residence, the family had been dividing the year between the old brownstone on West Twenty-third Street in New York City and the multigabled Pencraig on Harrison Avenue in Newport; and the young Edith was already beginning to feel, dimly, the differing pulls of Europe and America, and in the latter of the urban and the rural. Suitably enough, the oldest surviving letter of the future novelist of manners touches, and with a hint of mockery, on the engagement and forthcoming marriage of a young woman friend.

Almost twenty years must pass before another letter by Edith Wharton comes into view. She has indeed become Edith Wharton, Mrs. Edward R. Wharton, in the long interval; has been publishing poems since 1889 and short stories since 1891; has inherited large sums of money, and has spent a good deal of it in the purchase of a town house on upper Park Avenue and recently, in Newport, of the quietly elegant home called (for its position overlooking the Atlantic) Land's End.

Most of Edith Wharton's surviving early correspondence is with Scribners people: Edward L. Burlingame, the editor at *Scribner's Magazine*, and William Crary Brownell, the courtly and cultivated literary consultant for the publishing house of Charles Scribner's Sons. It was Burlingame, in November 1893, who proposed that the firm bring out a volume of Edith Wharton's stories. The self-confidence thereby engendered in the apprentice writer gave way a few months later when

Burlingame rejected one of her minor efforts. After a letter from Florence in late July 1894 about meeting the gifted English writer Vernon Lee and telling of an artistic find in a Tuscan monastery, Edith Wharton fell silent for sixteen months.

She was passing through what later parlance would call a severe crisis of identity. It was brought on (one speculates) by the emotional and sexual inadequacy of her marriage combined with the challenge to her creative self by the Scribners offer. A comparable challenge was provided by the first appearance on her literary horizon by already accomplished literary figures—Vernon Lee, and others, like Paul Bourget, not mentioned in the early letters. The symptoms of the prolonged malaise were extreme exhaustion, recurring fits of nausea, and paralyzing melancholia. She was sufficiently recovered by the summer of 1896 to begin work on a book about house decoration, which she wrote in collaboration with the young Boston architect Ogden Codman, and with helpful advice from her friend Walter Berry. *The Decoration of Houses* was published in December 1897.

Edith Wharton's sustained literary career may be dated from the spring of 1898, when she wrote several of her most enduring stories, among them "The Muse's Tragedy" and "Souls Belated." The effort led to a stretch as an outpatient in the rest-cure program in Philadelphia devised by the neurologist (and novelist) S. Weir Mitchell. But her first volume of fiction, the collection entitled *The Greater Inclination*, duly made its appearance in March of 1899; none of the items written before 1898 was included. To the Harvard professor Barrett Wendell, who sent her a word of congratulation, Mrs. Wharton said that the "poor little stories have been reclaimed, as it were, inch by inch, from almost continuous ill-health and mental lassitude." To Brownell at Scribners, meanwhile, she launched the first of a long series of complaints about the poor advertising of her well-reviewed book.

The first of Edith Wharton's private correspondents to preserve her letters was Sara Norton, a woman of considerable literary taste and knowledge, and the daughter of Charles Eliot Norton, the distinguished professor of fine arts at Harvard, and an internationally renowned scholar and man of letters. Sara Norton wrote in February 1900 to voice her admiration for Edith Wharton's novella *The Touchstone*. After a year's exchange, the two had proceeded at a measured New England pace to first names ("Affly yrs—Edith or Pussy as you please" was the signature

of the first letter addressed to "Sally"*). With Sally, the talk turned often
to Henry James, a very old friend of the Norton family, with Edith
displaying in her earliest recorded comments on James clear signs of a
restiveness of influence.

While writing the stories that went into her second collection, *Crucial
Instances* of 1901, Edith Wharton, now fully in command of her literary
energies, regularly turned aside to get ahead with her novel-in-progress,
The Valley of Decision. As publication date approached, she had severe
criticisms to make about the title page and the format; but when she
had penned the novel's last line, she sent an exultant message to Brownell: "The end at last!"

To Pauline Foster Du Pont[1]

Pencraig
September 23, 1874

My dear Pauley

Feeling myself bound to report the exact mental & moral condition
of Anna, since Doctor Robinson's[2] flying visit last Saturday, as well as
everything which occurred during that eventful period of her existence,
I think I can do no better than write to you, for I am the only good
correspondent of our family & you really ought to know something
about the general excitement, besides what Anna writes you. Besides, I
hope that some time you may send me an answer to my letter, telling
me about some of the jolly things you have seen & done since that
memorable Fourth of July when we threw torpedoes at Colonel Du
Pont's hat & set off a pan of fire crackers in the rain!—Anna is looking
out very anxiously for a letter from you & when she gets it I don't
know what she will do for joy. Today, she & Maggie Wingate, who is
staying here, were driven into town & took a walk around the cliffs.
They came back of course in perfect raptures & it must have been a
very pleasant recreation for poor Anna who spends her days in writing

---

*This may be the place to remark that, in these introductions, we refer to Edith
Wharton or Edith or Mrs. Wharton, but never simply to Wharton. The author of the
novels and stories may perhaps be alluded to by her surname. But the living individual,
the figure being treated here for the most part biographically, should surely be named
as she was by those associated with her.

letters to announce the great event of the season. It was such a disappointment to me that I was rather unwell while Doctor Robinson was here & as my illness was not serious enough for him to prescribe or pay professional visits, I only saw him for a moment on Sunday night before he went down to New York in the boat. Poor Anna! Can't you just imagine how that wretched infant Harry[3] teased her? But she was & is so sweet about it all & everybody was so delighted to have seen Doctor Robinson that although we still declare that there is no man *quite* good enough for her, she is left in peace otherwise, & now that Harry has gone to New York to be a shop keeper, we don't torment her very much & I think she may possibly manage to live through the visit without being made an absolute martyr of! Yes, Harry has gone to be a shop keeper—that is to make purchases for Fred's[4] grand "Miscellaneous Shop" up at the works & to poke all day in Fred's Office down town! Papa[5] was of course very unhappy at his departure & we have all, Anna & Bessie Bininger included, inundated him with long letters & postal cards. Of course we have a great many jokes about buying candy & cabbages & standing behind the counter but he has not yet dropped the "Esquire" from his name & is not absolutely a tradesman, so you need not be horrified at the announcement. But the grand addition to the family at Pencraig, is Crumpet's four puppies who were born about four or five weeks ago & who have lately absorbed everybody, but Harry in particular. He is perfectly delighted with them, is sure one of them is going to be like Grip & I believe he measures their noses everyday to see which has the shortest. Now that he is in New York, however, the state & condition of the new comers have to be duly reported by post every day. But I must stop now, for this is the first time I have been out of bed for several days & I dare not write too long a letter. Hoping, dear Pauley, that you will find time to answer this letter, I remain with much love from all to all, yours very affectionately

Edith Newbold Jones
Doyle[6] sends her best regards—

Copy: BL, of ms. letter in Eleutherian Mills Historical Library, Greenville, Delaware

1. Mary Pauline Foster (1849–1902) was the wife of Colonel Henry A. Du Pont, a West Point graduate who had seen extensive service with the Union Army during the Civil War. Edith Jones's poem of April 4, 1876, "She is not dead but sleepeth," was written after the death of the Du Ponts' eldest child.

2. Anna Foster, Pauline's younger sister, was engaged to Dr. Beverley Robinson, who had recently begun practice in New York City. They would be married in April 1875.

3. Henry Edward Jones (1850–1922), the younger of Edith's two brothers.

4. Frederic Rhinelander Jones (1846–1918), Edith's older brother. His small business—which included a shop, a warehouse, and an office—was of short duration.

5. George Frederic Jones (1821–1882), Edith's father.

6. Hannah Doyle, Edith's Irish nurse.

To Edward L. Burlingame[1]

Land's End
Newport, R.I.
November 25, 1893

Dear Mr Burlingame,

I need hardly say how much I am flattered by Messrs. Scribner's proposition to publish my stories in a volume.

I have several more, which you have not seen, & also the longer one called "Bunner Sisters"[2] which you may remember my sending you a year or two ago. You then pronounced it too long for one number of the magazine, & unsuited to serial publication, but you spoke otherwise very kindly of it, & though I am not a good judge of what I write, it seems to me, after several careful readings, up to my average of writing. I will therefore send it to you, if you approve, with the shorter stories you have not read. Shall I send them all at once?

We close our house here on Nov. 27th & go to Boston for a fortnight, where my address is 127 Beacon Street. After Dec. 10th we shall go to New York for two or three days, & then sail for Europe.

I hope that I shall see you when I am in New York, & shall write beforehand to ask when you are to be found "at home" at 743 Broadway.

Yours Sincerely
Edith Wharton

Ms:FL

1. Edward Livermore Burlingame (1848–1922), editor of *Scribner's Magazine* from its first issue in January 1887 until his resignation in 1914.
2. Edith Wharton had written *Bunner Sisters*, a thirty-thousand-word novella, in 1892. It would not in fact be published until it made part of the collection called *Xingu* in 1916.

To Edward L. Burlingame

Florence
March 26 [1894]

Dear Mr. Burlingame,

I have just received your letter of March 13th, in which you tell me you don't like the story which I called "Something Exquisite."[1] Pray, by the way, have no tender hearted compunctions about criticizing my stories— Your criticism is most helpful to me & I always recognize its justice. While I think that an inactive dilettantism produces just such maudlin over-sensibility as my poor heroine is afflicted with, I see perfectly that the contrast is too violent between her "schwärmerei"[2] in pink satin & the ensuing squalor.

I did not suppose that you would care at present for any more stories for the magazine—, & I sent "Something Exquisite" & the other story called "Judged"[3] only to see if you approved of them for the volume. I am therefore going to suggest detaching the *squalid* part of "Something Exquisite" from the prelude & epilogue, which have nothing to do with the story & including it in the volume in that shape. I should like to do this, unless you distinctly disapprove, for it seems to me that the sketch of the two schoolteachers, if it stands by itself, will no longer appear exaggeratedly squalid, & may perhaps do fairly well among the other stories.

I should like to bring out the book without adding many more stories, for I seem to have fallen into a period of groping, & perhaps, after publishing the volume, I might see better what direction I ought to take and acquire more assurance (the quality I feel I most lack). You were kind enough to give me so much encouragement when I saw you, & I feel myself so much complimented by the Messrs. Scribners' request that I should publish a volume of stories, that I am very ambitious to do better, & perhaps I could get a better view of what I have done & ought to do after the stories have been published. I have lost confidence in myself at present, & if you think "Judged" a failure I shall feel I have made entirely "fausse route." Pray don't regard this as the wail of the rejected authoress—it is only a cry for help & counsel to you who have been so kind in giving me both.

I didn't intend to withdraw the Carducci Sonnet,[4] but merely to ask you to publish it after the others—but if you have too many pray don't hesitate to return it.

When you next write will you tell me how many stories are needed for the volume? You spoke of ten, but perhaps a smaller number would do.

Yours sincerely
　　Edith Wharton

Ms:FL

1. "Something Exquisite," revised and renamed "Friends," appeared in the *Youth's Companion* in the issues of August 23 and 30, 1900. It is reprinted in *The Collected Short Stories of Edith Wharton.*
2. Rapture.
3. No story of this title was ever published.
4. "Life," a "sonnet after Carducci": i.e., in the manner of the nineteenth-century Italian poet Giosuè Carducci, upon whom EW's friend Paul Bourget had simultaneously based a poem.

To Edward L. Burlingame
Thusis [Switzerland]
July 30, 1894

Dear Mr. Burlingame,

I meant to thank you long before this for your long & helpful criticism of my last story. I appreciate greatly your giving so much time & thought to so trifling a subject, when you have so much to occupy you

& what you say will be of great help to me in the future. If Messrs. Scribners still want to publish a volume of my stories, however, I should rather have another six months in which to prepare it, for I haven't a sufficient number ready now for the autumn—

Meanwhile I send you by this mail a little article which should have gone to you before now. It is an account of some rather remarkable terra-cottas which I found last spring in a small place in Tuscany— The article speaks for itself,[1] I will therefore only add that I was so fully persuaded of the importance of the terra-cottas that I determined to have them photographed by Alinari at my own expense, on the chance that Scribner's or one of the other magazines would like to publish an illustrated account of them. Professor Ridolfi's verdict, which I quote in my article, so completely confirms my judgement that I think the subject cannot fail to be of interest to the public, especially as the terra-cottas are *entirely unknown*, even Miss Paget[2] (Vernon Lee) who has lived so long in Italy & devoted so much time to the study of Tuscan art, never having heard of them or of San Vivaldo.

I do not enclose Professor Ridolfi's letter, as I quote it so fully in my article, but will send it to you with pleasure if you wish to see it.

I send you Alinari's photographs with the article. If you do not care to publish the latter, will you kindly keep it & the photographs until you hear from me, as I fear they may be lost if you return them while we are on our wanderings.

Yours sincerely
Edith Wharton

The superior of the monastery, who kindly gave me permission to have the terra-cottas photographed, assured me that they had never been photographed before, except one or two, which were photographed by an amateur living in the neighborhood. I saw these photos which were absolutely worthless—Alinari had never even heard of the place.

Ms:FL

1. The rest of this letter speaks of EW's visit to the monastery of San Vivaldo in the hills southwest of Florence, and the article she had written about it. The

twenty-odd little chapels dotted amid the monastery woods housed a series of terra-cottas that were reputed to be crude imitations of seventeenth-century works. EW, after inspecting them, became convinced that half a dozen were superior originals from the late fifteenth and early sixteenth century. In Florence, she persuaded Signor Alinari, the famous photographer, to take pictures of these six. She showed the results to Professor Enrico Ridolfi, director of the Royal Museum in Florence, who declared them to have been done around the turn of the sixteenth century by "an artist of the school of the Robbias." They are now attributed to Giovanni della Robbia. EW's article, "A Tuscan Shrine," which appeared in *Scribner's Magazine* later in 1894, was included in the volume *Italian Backgrounds* in 1905.

2. Violet Paget (1856–1935), the author of many brilliant and scholarly studies of Italian history and art; she wrote under the name of Vernon Lee. EW had met her in the spring of 1894 at Miss Paget's villa, Il Palmerino, in Maiano, outside of Florence.

To Edward L. Burlingame

Land's End
Newport, R.I.
December 14, 1895

Dear Mr. Burlingame,

Since I last wrote you over a year ago, I have been very ill, & am not yet allowed to do any real work. But I have been scribbling a little & I have sent you a few pages which I hope you may like.

Pray don't trouble yourself to answer this—I only write it because it is such a distress to me to send such a waif[1] instead of the volume that Messrs. Scribner were once kind enough to ask for, that I cannot do so without a word of explanation. And I still hope to get well & have the volume ready next year.

Yours sincerely
Edith Wharton

Ms:FL

1. "The Valley of Childish Things and Other Emblems," ten brief fables on assorted topics. It is included in *The Collected Short Stories*.

To Edward L. Burlingame

Land's End
Newport, R.I.
July 10 [1898]

Dear Mr. Burlingame,

Your argument is irrefutable. I supposed that the Pelican[1] would take flight two weeks from now, & that it would therefore be within the bounds of possibility to bring out the Muse's Tragedy in October;[2] but I quite agree with you that at least two of the stories should appear in the magazine before the volume comes out, as it is so long since I have published any short stories, & if they are delayed in coming out, why, the book must wait too.—None of the stories on my list have been published in any other magazine; in fact I have never sent any story to any one but you, so you can of course take your choice for the magazine, if the remaining ones are finished in time.—

I agree with you in not caring for any of the titles I suggested. How do you like "The Ways of Men," from Pope's line?[3]—I should like "Mortals Mixed of Middle Clay,"[4] if it were not so long; & I fear that "Middle Clay" tout court would be classified as a manual of geology by the librarian who put Mill on Liberty & Mill on the Floss in the same category. Each of the stories is really a study in motives, but "Motives" is too short & jerky. "The Ways of Men" is easy to say.—As to the old stories of which you speak so kindly, I regard them as the excesses of youth. They were all written "at the top of my voice," & The Fulness of Life is one long shriek.[5]—I may not write any better, but at least I hope that I write in a lower key, & I fear that the voice of those early tales will drown all the others: it is for that reason that I prefer not to publish them. The list I sent you would furnish about 65,000 words: if that is not sufficient, I shall insist upon that lazy Defaulter's getting shaved & dressed & joining the party. He is still en déshabille.

Yours sincerely
        Edith Wharton

I send by express "Souls Belated" & "The Twilight of the God."[6]

Ms:FL

1. "The Pelican," written in March 1898, was the third story in EW's first volume of stories, *The Greater Inclination*, published in March 1899.

2. "The Muse's Tragedy," of June 1898, was the first story in the forthcoming collection.

3. Probably the line from Pope's "Chaucer: January and May": "And study'd Men, their Manners, and their Ways."

4. The first line of Emerson's poem "Guy" (*Poems*, 1847), with the word "Mortal" in the singular.

5. "The Fulness of Life" appeared in the December 1893 issue of *Scribner's*. Burlingame similarly urged in vain the inclusion in the new volume of "The Lamp of Psyche," which *Scribner's* had published in October 1895.

6. The story "Souls Belated" and "The Twilight of the God," a two-scene playlet, were included in *The Greater Inclination*.

To William Crary Brownell[1]

1329 K. St.
Washington
April 25, 1899

Dear Mr. Brownell,

I have been unwell or I should have replied sooner to your letter of April 18th. I am much obliged to you for allowing me ½ royalty on the first 500 of Mr. Lane's edition of my book.[2]

At the same time, you will pardon my saying that I do not think I have been fairly treated as regards the advertising of "The Greater Inclination." The book has now been out about six weeks, & I do not think I exaggerate in saying that it has met with an unusually favourable reception for a first volume by a writer virtually unknown. The press-notices have been, almost uniformly, not only approving but very flattering; & such papers as the Springfield Republican, the N.Y. Times, Literature, &c, have given a column of commendation, while I hear the Bookman is to publish an article in the coming number. In addition to this, the book was taken by an English publisher within a fortnight of its appearance here.

So much for *my* part in the transaction: now as to Mr. Scribner's.[3] I have naturally watched with interest the advertising of the book, &

have compared it with the notices given by other prominent publishers of books appearing under the same conditions. I find that Messrs. McMillan, Dodd & Mead, McClure, Harper, etc., advertise almost continuously in the daily papers every new book they publish, for the first few weeks after publication, giving large space to favourable press-notices; in addition to which, they of course advertise largely in the monthlies. So far, I have seen once, in a Sunday paper, I think, an advertisement of the Greater Inclination, with a line or two from the "Sun" review, which appeared among the first. Even that notice I have not found since, till it reappeared in the same shape in the new "Scribner" for May, without the addition of any of the many notices that have since come out.

In calling your attention to these facts I don't, of course, flatter myself that there is any hope of modifying the business methods of the firm; but I think myself justified in protesting against them in my own case.

If a book is unnoticed or unfavourably received, it is natural that the publisher should not take much trouble about advertising it; but to pursue the same course towards a volume which has been generally commended, seems to me essentially unjust. Certainly in these days of energetic & emphatic advertising, Mr. Scribner's methods do not tempt one to offer him one's wares a second time.

Sincerely Yours
Edith Wharton

Ms:FL

1. William Crary Brownell (1851–1928) joined Charles Scribner's Sons as a "literary consultant" in the mid-1880s. *French Traits*, the first of his estimable and influential volumes of criticism, appeared in 1899.

2. John Lane was the representative of John Murray, the English publisher of *The Greater Inclination*.

3. Charles Scribner (1854–1930) was the second in the line of the New York publishers bearing that name, and the founder (in 1887) of *Scribner's Magazine*, the outstanding literary periodical that would last until 1930.

To Barrett Wendell[1]

13, East 35th Street
New York
May 15, [1899]

My dear Mr. Wendell,

My husband has given me your letter & I have claimed the privilege of answering it myself.

I don't know if you still remember the pleasure with which one hears one's first endeavours commended by those who know; but if you do I needn't tell you what a kind thing it is to let me know what you think of my book.[2]

The poor little stories have been reclaimed, as it were, inch by inch, from almost continuous ill-health & mental lassitude, & my chief effort has naturally been to preserve, amid such limiting conditions, the same broad outlook on life. It is therefore specially pleasant to hear that you get glimpses of that big outer world through my writing; I don't mind being called "cynical & depressing" by the sentimentalists, as long as those who see the "inherences" recognize my ability to see them too.

We are just sailing for Europe, but I hope we may be in Boston next winter, & then I shall find the earliest opportunity of telling you de vive voix how much such a letter helps.

Sincerely Yours
    Edith Wharton

If there is any chance of meeting you abroad, send us a line to Munroe & Co. I have heard of you from so many friends that I feel as if I knew you.

Ms:HL

1. Barrett Wendell (1855–1921) had been a teacher of English at Harvard since 1880, and professor since 1898. He was becoming an increasingly forceful figure in the American academic world. His groundbreaking *Literary History of America* would appear in 1900.

2. *The Greater Inclination.*

To William Crary Brownell

Land's End
Newport, R.I.
September 26 [1899]

Dear Mr. Brownell,

Many thanks for your kind note. I am very much pleased with the sale of "The Greater Inclination"[1] though I knew, from the number of letters I have received from publishers, that it must be doing well. I didn't think it would have a popular success & I hope I shall make as good an impression next time—

I am much better, thanks, or rather I was till our return to Newport; but the dampness here—we are having mid-summer fogs—is making me as unhappy as usual.

With many messages to Mr. Burlingame.

Sincerely Yours
Edith Wharton

Ms:FL

1. About three thousand copies of the volume had been sold.

To Robert Grant[1]

Lenox, Mass.
July 25, 1900

Dear Mr. Grant,

May I say what pleasure I am having in reading "Unleavened Bread"? I have not waited to finish the book before telling you this because I have come across so many good things that I am impatient to express my appreciation of them; & there is an underlying sense of consecutiveness & logical development which make me feel sure I shall like the whole as much as the parts. There is, of course, no recipe for writing a good novel, & each "method" is worth just what the writer can make out of it; but I am so great a believer in the objective attitude that I have specially enjoyed the successful use you have made of it; your consistent abstinence from comment, explanation & partisanship, & your confidence in the reader's ability to draw his own conclusions. As for

Selma, I think her as good in her way as Gwendolen Grandcourt.[2] Every stroke tells, & you never forget the inconscient quality of her selfishness; you never fall into the error of making her deliberately false or cruel. The lesser characters seem to me admirably differentiated, from Mrs. Margaret Rodney Earle to the incomparable Mr. Lyons, whose speech to the Benham Institute on the nomination of Mrs. Luella Bailey is a masterpiece of American rhetoric!! Poor Babcock's downfall, too, is admirably indicated with so few touches, & Selma's reflection on her return to Benham, that "what she had learned" (of Babcock's career) "had tended merely to demonstrate the wisdom & justice of her action," is a masterstroke of characterization. "Unleavened Bread" in fact seems to me one of the best American novels I have read in years, & though you must be weary with the reiteration of its praises, I can't help adding my note to the chorus, & thanking you for the pleasure you have given me.

Sincerely Yrs
    Edith Wharton

Ms:BL

1. Robert Grant (1852–1940) was a novelist, short story writer, and distinguished Boston jurist. His first novel appeared in 1883. *Unleavened Bread* of 1900 is his most powerful and durable work. EW's comments touch on Selma White, the novel's hard-driving heroine, and two of her three husbands, Lewis Babcock and James Lyons. EW's *The Custom of the Country* (1913) owes more than a little to *Unleavened Bread*.
    2. The spirited figure in George Eliot's *Daniel Deronda* (1876).

To William Crary Brownell

Lenox, Mass
August 19, 1900

Dear Mr. Brownell,

Thanks for your note of the 17th. I fancy Mr. Morris feels that, having struck terror to the hearts of Scribner, Wharton & Co, he can afford to be magnanimous & publish the story next month.[1]

And now I have a confession to make. I set to work to finish the uncompleted tales as soon as we got back from Europe, but two or three weeks ago I took up "The Valley of Decision"[2] as a kind of interlude, as I often do; & now the thing has taken hold of me so that I can't get away from it, & I don't see how I can possibly have the short stories ready for this autumn. I am very sorry, but it is just as unexpected to me as to you, & the "Valley" is growing so rapidly & seems to me to be turning out so well that, even if I could, I shouldn't want to drop it now. I hope at this rate it may be finished by the Spring & I trust you will like it well enough to think me justified in dropping the other work. I have XV chapters done, & events are going at a great pace now.

Please accept all the proper excuses, & believe me ever

Sincerely Yrs
        Edith Wharton

I hope the stories will be ready for next Spring at any rate.

Ms:FL

1. The story in question was "The Line of Least Resistance," published in *Lippincott's Magazine* (of which Mr. Morris was editor) in October 1900. EW sent the tale to Henry James in London; after James's friendly but critical response, EW decided not to include it in her next collection. It can be found in *The Collected Short Stories*.

2. EW had been at work on her first novel, *The Valley of Decision*, since early in 1900.

To William Crary Brownell

Lenox, Mass.
November 7, 1900

Dear Mr. Brownell,

Don't think me a monster of inconsistency if I begin my letter about "The Valley" by talking of the postponed volume of short stories!

The last two or three weeks have brought about what seems an inevitably recurring thing with me—the necessity of dropping one kind of work & taking up another. After doing over 40,000 words of "The Valley" without a break I suddenly found the tank empty. I turned back to my short stories, & the change of air at once renewed my activity. I have finished one & sent it to Mr. Burlingame, on the chance that he may like it for the magazine; another will be finished in a day or two, making *six* with those already published; & if I write a seventh this month, as I expect to do, would not this make a sufficiently fat volume (the stories averaging about 6000 words)?[1]

I thought possibly *you* might think that the publication of this collection in February would not interfere with bringing out "The Valley" about June, supposing it to be finished then. The fact that I have not been able to touch "The Valley" for nearly a month makes me less confident about predicting its conclusion, & yet I have always found, after a break of this kind, that I am able to take up the interrupted work with fresh energy.

In this state of doubt it seemed to me that the stories might as well be used—I could even do an eighth (how queer that looks!) if seven are not enough. Let me know what you think of this. I have a good name, I think:—

Crucial Instances.

Being a term in philosophy, it keeps a sort of connection with "The Greater Inclination," doesn't it?

Don't think me a quite inexcusable nuisance—

& believe me Yrs Sincerely E Wharton

Mr. Murray, writing me about The Valley, mentioned that 2000 Touchstones had sold in England.[2]

Ms:FL

1. As EW here informs Brownell, the new volume would be called *Crucial Instances*; it was published in April 1901.

2. *The Touchstone*, a short novel, originally appeared in the April and May 1900 issues of *Scribner's*. It was published in England by John Murray.

To Sara Norton[1]

884 Park Avenue.
February 28 [1901]

Dear Sally,

I was so sorry not to see you again! We are so "far from today" up in this suburb that I think it a special compliment when my friends try to find me as perseveringly as you did— Yes, I should be delighted to see Mr. Harrison.[2] Do give him a letter, but with the proviso that we *may* not be here; for we had rather bad news of Teddy's mother[3] yesterday & unless she improves we may have to sail in a fortnight.

Still, I hope he will take the chance of finding us.

I believe my play[4] is really "going through," but I don't look forward to the result with any enthusiasm.

I am much more interested in my Italian novel, to which I return with fresh ardour after every temporary estrangement. I wish I could get some one else to write it for me, though!

The little vol. of stories will be out in two or three weeks & you shall have your copy more promptly than last time, I hope.

Affly Yrs—Edith or Pussy as you please.

Ms:BL

1. See introduction to this section.
2. Probably J. B. Harrison, editor of a small-town Indiana newspaper, a life-long friend of Charles Eliot Norton, with whom he was associated in many efforts to influence public opinion on political and other matters.
3. The former Nancy Spring of Boston. Her home was in Lenox, Massachusetts, but she was visiting in England at this time, when she fell ill.
4. "My play" was *The Man of Genius*, a drama of manners in English literary and social life. EW completed two acts of it before any thought of production had to be abandoned.

To Sara Norton

884 Park Avenue.

March 12 [1901]

Dear Sally,

We are awaiting Mr. Harrison with open arms, & perhaps when he discovers that I am a rabid Imperialist the shock may strike a few sparks out of him. But I don't see why you don't think that cut-and-dried Comte culte isn't a fit for him.

Mrs. Wharton is much better, & comes home in May, so we have decided not to go abroad this spring, & though I know you won't believe me I really think we shall go to Boston for a week toward the end of April. We hear the Somerset is comfortable, & I suppose by that time the steam heat will be turned off.

We have bought the Sargent farm at Lenox—I think when you were here we were "negotiating" for it, as Miss Sargent herself would say—& we are going to begin building in April.[1]

I was delighted with your application of Omar to the Sacred Fount![2] (I wish so fine a title had not been attached to so ignoble a book.) For my opinion of it I refer you to the last number of the Athenaeum, where there is an admirable review, which it is a thousand pities Mr. James should not read. I could cry over the ruins of such a talent. It reminds me, somehow, of the description of M. Valdemar's liquefaction in Poe's story.[3] (I mean the break up of Mr. James's talent, not, of course, the donnée of his book.)

Don't always apologize for writing me anything in excess of a note of one page. I enjoy so much talking over books with you.

Yours affly,
Edith W

There is also an excellent review of The Fount in the Spectator.

Ms:BL

1. Georgiana Sargent sold Laurel Lake Farm, as it was then known, to EW for the sum of $40,600. The deed was signed on June 29, and construction soon began on The Mount, as it came to be called.

2. Henry James's novel *The Sacred Fount* had appeared recently. Sara Norton evidently quoted from *The Rubáiyát of Omar Khayyám* as a way of deprecating it.

3. "The Facts in the Case of M. Valdemar."

To Sara Norton

Lenox, Mass.
Monday May 20 [1901]

Dear Sally,

My husband is sailing for England on Saturday, as the reports of his mother's condition are not satisfactory & he thinks he ought to bring her home if she is able to attempt the voyage. This has all been decided rather suddenly, & hence the abruptness of my telegram. I shall be all alone for the next ten days or so, & it would be a real act of philanthropy on your part to come & cheer me up. I seldom ask people to stay because I am obliged to lead such a quiet & systematic kind of life that the house is a dull one for visitors; but as you know Lenox & feel at home here I do not feel so shy about inviting you, especially as I think there are many things we enjoy talking of together.—At all events, it will be a great pleasure to me if you will come, & I hope you will remain till the 31st, when I have an old friend & her daughter coming for a few days. Teddy hopes to sail for home on June 6th, but if he is not able to do so I shall go over early in July & join him. He goes to New York on Thursday the 23rd to attend to some business before sailing, so after that date I shall have no company but my own unless you will take pity on me. The country is beautiful & the apple-blossoms are just showing themselves. Do be persuaded!

Affly Yours
Edith Wharton

If you are fond of riding, bring a habit & I will give you a mount.

Ms:BL

To Sara Norton

Lenox Mass.
November 25 [1901]

Dear Sally

So charmed am I with Mr. Santyana—the volume of him[1] that I may not keep—that I am going to ask you to get me two copies of the same. The sonnets are fine—full of ideas, of imagery, of expression. Some of the single lines are beautiful. But why doesn't he keep to sonnets? He ought to shun the lyric & the ode. Taken altogether—idea & execution—I like the Death of the Metaphysician[2] best—I send back the little book with a faint scratch here & there to show you the detached things that struck me. A little India-rubber will restore the pages to their first state, & this is the nearest approach to talking over a book together.

Affectionately Yrs,
    Edith

Please put this *a* in the Santyana on page 1.
Will you send the two copies here this week—or, if later than Dec. 1st, then to 884 Park Ave? Don't be in any haste about getting them. One can wait for anything so good.

Ms:BL

1. *Sonnets and Other Verses* by George Santayana (1863–1952) appeared in 1894.
2. "On the Death of a Metaphysician" is in *Sonnets* (2d ser.).

To William Crary Brownell

884 Park Avenue.
January 4 [1902]

Dear Mr. Brownell,

Words fail to express how completely I *don't* like it.[1] In the first place, I think the lettering of the title should be about three times as large.

Secondly, the quotation,[2] which is the motto of the book, should be completely separated from the title, & be printed in small italics. Thirdly, there should be some kind of an ornamental design in the space I have marked in red pencil (I forget the technical name of the thing)—&, fourthly, I think when the title page is plain it looks better to have the lettering partly red instead of all black. There are "lots more" criticisms to be made, but perhaps these will suffice for once!—

I have been thinking over the two-volume question, & I am more & more regretful about it. You said you had the impression that the book would not be more than 120,000 words long; but, even so, was it not a mistake to choose so small a page? I think at least I ought to have been consulted about it. The "make-up" of the book seems to me as inappropriate for the style of the story as for its length. As I told you, I counted on Mr. Updike's[3] showing you the page & type I had selected at his office, & my not hearing from the Messrs. Scribner confirmed me in the idea that he had done so, & that the matter had been settled accordingly.

As you say, it is spilt milk now, but I don't think the spilling is any fault of mine. Would it not be possible, by way of mending matters, to sell the book for a little less than $2? If it could be sold for $1.75 it seems to me that it would make a great difference.

Pardon this long letter.

Yrs Sincerely
    Edith Wharton

Ms:FL

1. The design for the title page of *The Valley of Decision*.
2. "Multitudes, multitudes in the valley of decision," from Joel, 3:14.
3. Daniel Berkeley Updike (1860–1941), founder (in 1893) of the Merrymount Press in Boston. He printed half a dozen of EW's earlier books, and was in the process of becoming the best commercial printer the country had known.

To William Crary Brownell

884 Park Avenue.
January 7, 1902

The end at last![1]

E.W.

Ms:FL

1. *The Valley of Decision* was finished.

PART TWO

Withdrawal from America

1902–1907

Introduction

❀

The Valley of Decision, an expansive novel set amid the political and ecclesiastical intrigues of later-eighteenth-century Italy, established Edith Wharton at a stroke as a major American writer. A Boston reviewer said that the work placed its author "side by side with the greatest novelists," and a Chicago commentator saw it as "the most distinguished performance yet accomplished on this continent." One consequence of the book's success was an invitation from the editor of the *Century* magazine to do a series of articles on Italian villas and their gardens, and in January 1903, Edith and Teddy took ship from Boston to Genoa to begin the necessary explorations.

It was on this trip that Edith had her first experience of an automobile when George Meyer, the American Ambassador to Italy, drove the Whartons from Rome to Caprarola and back, a one-hundred-mile trip, in an afternoon. The following winter, once again in Europe, the Whartons bought their own car, a Panhard-Levassor. In it, with Teddy driving, they made a tour of southern France, stopping at Hyères to visit the celebrated French writer Paul Bourget and Minnie Bourget; and in the English spring, they motored down from London to Rye, in Sussex, to call on Henry James.

Writing from Hyères, Mrs. Wharton told Brownell that she was "still sunk in that state of 'abrutissement' [stupefaction] which always overcomes me when I first come to Europe." Her immediate reaction on returning to America from these European forays was one of nearly complete estrangement. "My first few weeks in America are always miserable," she tells Sara Norton in June 1903, "because the tastes I am cursed with are all of a kind that cannot be gratified here.... *We* are none of us Americans, we don't think or feel as the Americans do, we are the wretched exotics produced in a European glass-house." Edith Wharton was of course one of the most American women of her time, and never more so than when giving vent to such utterances; or to the outburst elicited the following summer after a night in a Petersham, Massachusetts, hotel, the European "abrutissement" still lingering in her consciousness: "Such dreariness, such whining sallow women ... such crass food, crass manners ... What a horror it is for a whole nation to be developing without the sense of beauty, & eating bananas for breakfast."

Even so, once the settling-back process was gotten through, the return to America in these years had a gratifying aspect. This was the new home in the Berkshires of western Massachusetts, named The Mount after the home of an illustrious ancestor. Edith Wharton kept a close eye on the construction of the house, the installation of plumbing and lighting, and the laying out of the gardens; and the entrance into The Mount in September 1902 was an occasion for immense pride and pleasure. The place came fully to life at last in the summer of 1904, with an unbroken series of houseguests culminating in the arrival, in October, of Henry James and his friend Howard Sturgis.

Edith Wharton and Henry James had met in London—there had been a series of earlier failed possibilities—in the last days of 1903; and though each expressed a certain initial wariness about the other, the long friendship began almost at once. In an important manner of speaking, it was Henry James who turned Edith Wharton back from the European to the American scene in her fiction. In a letter of fulsome praise for *The Valley of Decision*, James urged her to address herself, now, to "the American subject. Don't pass it by—the immediate, the real, the only, the yours, the novelist's that it waits for. *Do New York!*"

In fact, Edith Wharton had been working with native materials for her next novel; but in the light of James's vehement advice, she shifted her focus to another topic she had been mulling for a year or two, fashionable society in New York. *The House of Mirth*, which came out in October 1905, dealt, as its author accurately told one admirer, with the species of idle rich that occupied only a corner of New York, but was more conspicuous there than "in an old civilization" and more harmful because in America, as against Europe, wealth tended to be disconnected from responsibility. The novel's enormous and instantaneous success became an element in the publishing-house lore: "the most rapid sale of any book ever published by Scribner," Brownell informed Mrs. Wharton; 140,000 copies had been sold within three months of publication. In the summer of 1906, Edith Wharton and Clyde Fitch, the popular American playwright, put together a stage version of *The House of Mirth*. It opened in New York on October 23, was greeted by the *Times* as "a doleful play," and promptly closed.

The Whartons passed the spring of 1906 in France and England, making extensive motor tours in both countries. During her stay in France, Mme. Wharton (the French faintly emphasized the last syllable) was introduced for the first time into the Parisian literary circles—they were social and aristocratic as well—by the Academician Paul Bourget. The latter instructed his young protégé, the exceedingly literate Charles Du Bos, to begin a French translation of *The House of Mirth*. The work was completed by the time the Whartons came back to Paris the next January. On this occasion, the Whartons rented the apartment of the George Vanderbilts at 58 Rue de Varenne, in the storied Faubourg St. Germain on the Left Bank. Edith Wharton's French residence had begun.

To Sara Norton

884 Park Avenue
January 24 [1902]

Dear Sally,

How did you know anything about the "old-established" anniversary[1] I am celebrating today? At any rate, your knowing, & your taking the trouble to send me that note, have given me more pleasure than anything else the day is likely to bring—I excessively hate to be forty. Not that I think it a bad thing to be—only I'm not ready yet!

Don't I know that feeling you describe, when one longs to go to a hospital & *have something cut out*, & come out minus an organ, but alive & active & like other people, instead of dragging on with this bloodless existence!! Only I fear you & I will never find a surgeon who will do us that service.

On Wednesday, at Mrs. Pat Campbell's[2] play, I saw Mrs. Whitridge, who said she expected Miss Ward[3] the next day. I hope I may see her, but I think it doubtful, as I go about so little.

Mrs. Campbell struck me the other night as a great ranting gawk. How I hate English & American acting! It's like an elephant walking on the keyboard of a piano.

While I had the "floo" I read Schopenhauer;[4] not "en bloc," but the chapter on the ascetic life, which Mrs. Winty Chanler[5] had spoken of as a marvellous analysis of the état d'âme of the saint. (In "Die Welt als Wille und Vorstellung.") How strange it is rummaging in all that old metaphysical lumber!—As for the sainthood, I prefer it as I find it in Pascal & St François de Sales—

I wish you were here & we could have a nice long talk.

Yr. devoted
    E.W.

Ms:BL

1. EW's fortieth birthday.
2. The celebrated English actress (1865–1940, born Beatrice Stella Tanner), known by her married name. She made her American debut in 1902 in *Magda*, the English version of Hermann Sudermann's play *Heimat*.
3. Mrs. Frederick Whitridge, the wife of an American lawyer, was the former Lucy Arnold, the older daughter of Matthew Arnold. Miss Dorothy Ward (born 1874) was the oldest child of Lucy Arnold's cousin Mary Augusta Arnold, the highly successful novelist known as Mrs. Humphry Ward, her husband being the Oxford don and journalist T. Humphry Ward.
4. *The World as Will and Idea*, in its English title, was the magnum opus of Arthur Schopenhauer (1788–1860).
5. See letter to Margaret Terry Chanler, May 17, 1902.

To Sara Norton

New York
February 13 [1902]

Dear Sally

Here I am, like a mother rushing to the defence of her deformed child! I hoped, when I sent you the advance sheets,[1] that you might be interested enough to tell me just where you thought I had made mistakes— & I rather expected you to put your finger on what is undoubtedly the weak spot from the novel-reader's point of view. Undoubtedly there is too much explanation, too much history &c, for the proper perspective of the novel; but then I must plead in extenuation.

1st that the period (in Italy) is one so unfamiliar to the reader that it was difficult to take for granted that he would fill out his background for himself;

& 2d, I meant the book to be a picture of a social phase, not of two people's individual history, & Fulvia & Oddo[2] are just little bits of looking-glass in which fragments of the great panorama are reflected. But I imagine the real weakness of the book is that I haven't fused my facts sufficiently with the general atmosphere of the story, so that they stick out here & there, & bump into the reader. I knew from the start that this would be the fault—the great fault, I mean—of the book. It is sure to bore people who don't care for Italy—

I know so well the value of a day in bed that I am glad to think of you being able to permit yourself such an interlude. I hope it means *only* that you are resting, though?

I am thinking of going to Mrs. Wharton's on March 1st, for a week, while Teddy is in North Carolina, & I want to see just as much of you as I can.

Yr affte   E.W.

I don't know Turgeniev's "Un Bulgare."[3] What volume is it in?—I can't get hold of the Punch with his humorous poem.

Ms:BL

1. Of *The Valley of Decision*.
2. In the published text, the male protagonist's name was spelled Odo.
3. The French title for the novel known in English as *On the Eve* (1860).

To *William Crary Brownell*

884 Park Avenue
February 14 [1902]

Dear Mr. Brownell

I hate to be photographed because the results are so trying to my vanity; but I would do anything to obliterate the Creole lady who has been masquerading in the papers under my name for the last year, & I will see if I can get myself done today or tomorrow—providing, always, the photographer agrees to finish me in time for the Tribune. I rather quake, by the way, at the thought of being "done" fundamentally by that sheet, for its superficial investigations have not been exactly caressing—

As to a paragraph about "The Valley," I could sooner write another 2 vol. novel! I can give you the "Grund-idee" of the book, but I am afraid you must add that undefinable Wanamaker[1] Touch that seems essential to the booming of fiction nowadays. (The Valley, then is an attempt to picture Italy at the time of the breaking up of the small principalities at the end of the 18th century, when all the old forms & traditions of court life were still preserved, but the immense intellectual & moral movement of the new regime was at work beneath the surface of things. This work, in Italy, was intellectual rather than political, & found little active expression, owing to the heterogeneous character of the Italian states & the impossibility of any concerted political move-ment. I have tried to reflect the traditional influences & customs of the day, together with the new ideas, in the mind of a cadet of one of the reigning houses, who is suddenly called to succeed to the Dukedom of Pianura, & tries to apply the theories of the French encyclopaedists to his small principality. Incidentally, I have given sketches of Venetian life, & glimpses of Sir Wm Hamilton's circle at Naples, & of the clerical milieu at Rome, where the suppression of the Society of Jesus, & the mysterious death of Ganganelli, had produced a violent reaction toward formalism & superstition. The close of the story pictures the falling to pieces of the whole business at the approach of Napoleon.)

There! It has taken me an hour's hard work to tell you that. I ought to add, though, that as far as I know, no novelist has ever dealt with this particular period of Italian life. "La Chartreuse de Parme" is, of course, after Waterloo.—I wish I could have given you a better résumé.

Yrs Sincerely,
Edith Wharton

Ms:FL

1. The popular department store.

To Sara Norton

New York
February 24 [1902]

Dear Sally

I am dismayed at the idea of Mr. Norton's wading through those tattered sheets—but there is no need for it, happily, as the book is out & a copy on its way to you. I hope this one won't go to "Shady Hill, Mass", like the last opus I sent you; but with Scribner one can never tell!

I think I shall go to Boston on March 2d or 3d, but I am still obliged to put it conditionally as the Dr. has not yet decided what Teddy is to do. We shall know this evening & I will send you word.

Have you read "Ulysses"[1] & what do you think of it?—If I am not as enthusiastic as you are about Tourgeneff—as you seem to suspect—it is probably because I am familiar with fewer of his stories. I am always handicapped, in reading the Russian novelists, by an inability to enter into the Slav consciousness; but the people in Fumée all seem to me very much alive. I never could find much vitality in the highly praised Gemma of Spring Torrents. The short stories I hardly know, but you must introduce me to Un Bulgare when I am in Boston.—I am childishly pleased by a review of my book in "The Mail & Express," in which the writer says that the book should be regarded as the picture of a period, not of one or two persons, & that Italy is my hero—or heroine, if you prefer. I would rather have had that said than any number of undiscerning compliments, because American & English reviewers of fiction are so disinclined to recognize that novels may be written from a dozen different standpoints, & that the "heart-interest" need not always predominate.

A bientôt, I hope,   E.W.
Please throw away the sheets—

Ms:BL

1. A poetic drama by the English writer and former actor Stephen Phillips (1864–1915), published in 1902 to considerable acclaim. As to his earlier work, *Paolo and Francesca*, see the letter to William Dean Howells of May 7, 1902.

To Sara Norton

884 Park Avenue
April 2 [1902]

Dear Sally

How nice of you to find time to cut out that flaming advertisement &
send it to me! It is a beautiful spectacle, that of our great country from
Maine to California joining in a chorus of praise over the Valley! The
advance orders are ahead of the second edition, which is not yet out, &
the "Department Stores" say they cannot keep up with the demand for
the book. Who will ever be able to forecast the fate of an American
novel or to unravel the psychology of the average novel-reader?—I
thought it would take "The Valley" a year to make itself known.

Where are you going for ten days, & why? I fear because you are
still not well. I am sure a change—any change—will do you good, for
we have been in Washington for ten days, & spite of bad food at the
wrong hotel I have come back feeling made over new, as I always do
after a breath of different air.—

I do hope you will be back in Boston by April 20th. We are going
there about that time. *Don't* go away then.

Affly Yrs Edith W.

P.S. I have a letter from Dr. Weir Mitchell,[1] whom I know very
slightly, but who had read "The Valley" & wanted to tell me that he
liked it; & he began thus:—

"I have just written to Charles Eliot Norton: *Read that book.*"
Poor Mr. Norton! He will have his fill of the Valley!

Ms:BL

1. Silas Weir Mitchell (1829–1914), the distinguished Philadelphia nerve specialist who was also a practicing novelist and poet. When EW, after a series of
nervous collapses, came to Philadelphia for treatment in October 1898, she was
given the "rest cure" devised by Dr. Mitchell for his patients in the Orthopedic
Hospital. As an outpatient, however, EW was lodged in the Stenton Hotel and
looked after by a Dr. McClellan.

To Charles Eliot Norton

Boston.
May 3 [1902]

Dear Mr Norton,[1]

I am sure Sally has already told you how much pleasure the record of poor Camilla Vinati's "ratto"[2] has given me; chiefly, of course, because of the thought to which I owe it, but in a lesser way also because it so quaintly corroborates certain statements in "The Valley" which some of my Catholic friends have questioned. It will be a great satisfaction to be able to prove, by producing this formidable document, that my Fulvia was not the only nun carried off by an enterprising lover, & that the real convent-doors were as easily unlatched as my fictitious ones.

I wish I could have thanked you de vive voix for thinking of me in this way, dear Mr Norton, but in June I hope we may be able to come over & spend a day with you in Ashfield, & by that time I expect to see you afoot again, & ready to lead me up that beautiful little hill on which the pyrola grows.

Teddy sends his kindest regards, & I am ever

Sincerely Yours,
Edith Wharton

Ms:HL

1. Charles Eliot Norton, whose knowledge of medieval Italy was extraordinary (he had translated Dante's *Divine Comedy*), had been of great help to EW, with books and advice, while she was writing *The Valley of Decision*.

2. Evidently a document recording the kidnapping ("ratto") of a nun, Camilla Vinati, during the period described in EW's novel.

To William Dean Howells[1]

884 Park Avenue
May 7, 1902

Dear Mr. Howells,

I should like to write an article on the three Francescas now before the public—Mr. Phillips's,[2] Mr. Crawford's[3] & d'Annunzio's[4]—of which the two latter, at least, seem to me worth discussing.

I had thought of offering the article to the North American, but as I do not know Mr. Harvey, & am not sure if he condescends to such frivolities as a dramatic criticism by a woman, I venture to approach him obliquely by begging you to transmit my suggestion if you think such an article would be acceptable.

My reason for making the proposition in advance is that I have to economize my strength, & that the article is not likely to get itself written unless it is likely to be taken by the North American.[5]

I wish *you* would write something about Mrs. Fiske,[6] who seems to me, from what I saw last night, worthy of being singled out by some one whose good opinion counts with our poor muddled "doped" theatrical public.

Sincerely Yours
    Edith Wharton

I have been wishing to call on Mrs. Howells this winter, but illness & repeated absences have made my social efforts few & spasmodic—I hope to make a spring visit instead.

Ms:HL

1. Howells was sixty-five at this time, an editor of *Harper's Magazine* and the author most recently of *Literature and Life*.

2. Stephen Phillips's *Paolo and Francesca*, published in 1900 and performed in 1902, was received with enormous enthusiasm, and its author was compared to Shakespeare.

3. *Francesca da Rimini*, a play of 1902 by the prolific novelist F. Marion Crawford (1854–1909), was written for Sarah Bernhardt and hence translated into French.

4. *Francesca da Rimini*, the most recent (1902) work for the stage by Gabriele d'Annunzio (1863–1938), the Italian poet, novelist, and playwright.

5. "The Three Francescas," by Edith Wharton, appeared in the July 1902 issue of the *North American Review*.

6. EW was stirred by the performance of the American actress Minnie Maddern Fiske in *Tess of the D'Urbervilles*.

To Margaret Terry Chanler[1]

884 Park Avenue
May 17 [1902]

Dear Mrs. Chanler

I must tell you at once how much I appreciate your finding the time & energy to write me that nice long letter. The sound of your voice—which I always hear in your letters—makes me regret more than ever that I could not pay you that little visit in March; but I was too unwell to be fit company for anyone, & if I go to Newport later I hope I shall be able to see you under more satisfactory circumstances—certainly it will not be "Society" that prevents!—

I shan't pretend to dissemble my pleasure at what you say of my book. I was very nervous about your verdict, I own, for it must seem presumptuous to anyone who knows Italy as you do that I should have attempted to write of it—& not even of the Italy I have seen, but of that vanished civilization which is fading away in the Longhi pictures & in the pages of eighteenth century travellers. It delights me to hear that I produced an illusion to you, but I know you must have detected many mistakes & anachronisms, & some day I hope you will point them out to me.

I am much interested by your account of "The Prisoner," for though I am such a persistent prowler among books I have never even heard of it, & "Brewster"[2] does not convey anything to me. I wish it would come! And thank you for thinking of me.

By the way, Mr. Crawford sent me about ten days ago the French version of his Francesca, & I am so emballée about it that I am writing for the North American an article on the three Francescas. It seems to me a very strong & simple play, & quite different in quality from anything he has ever written. I wonder if you agree with me? I wonder also if you have read d'Annunzio's Francesca. I am not an admirer of the great man's, but in his case too, the theme seems to have inspired him, & though the play is absurd *as* a play, it is full of beauty as a romantic poem, & as mediaeval as a gothic tapestry. If you haven't seen this, I will send you my copy, as I am sure Newport will not furnish one.

I wish I could join one of those prelatical afternoons at your bedside! I haven't seen Mr. Spring Rice[3] for years, & then I met him just once, for an afternoon on a yacht, but I was foudroyée, & have always hoped for another meeting. Is there any chance of his being here within the next ten days? If so, please send him to me. He told me such wonderful stories, I remember.

I don't know whether I wrote you that I saw a great deal of Bay Lodge[4] when we were in Washington about six weeks ago. He is one of the satisfactory people who are the same colour all through, like linoleum. So many are just oil-cloth!

He is to be here on Monday with Mrs. Bay for a day or two, en route for Nahant, & we shall have a talk about you, as we always do.

I enclose a letter which may amuse you—but is it a hoax, or is it possible that there are "educated" (even in the American sense) Italians, who cannot translate Leopardi?

Goodbye, & thanks again for your letter. I am going to send you a line now & then this summer just to sfogarmi, but you will be busy & you mustn't bother to answer. In the autumn I hope our new house will be ready for visitors, & that we may persuade you & Mr. Chanler to come to us for a few days.

> Affly Yours
> Edith W.

I am ashamed of this "smeary" letter, but I am breaking in a new pen which is particularly sulky.

Ms.BL

1. Margaret Terry Chanler was born in Rome, the daughter of the expatriate American painter Luther Terry. She and Edith Jones first met in 1866, when the Jones family was staying in Rome. In 1886, Margaret Terry married Winthrop Astor Chanler, sportsman and traveler, and a member of a clan that included William Backhouse Astor, Caroline Schermerhorn, Sam Ward and his sister Julia Ward Howe, Lewis Rutherfurd, and assorted Armstrongs and Livingstons. Margaret and Winthrop Chanler had seven surviving children. On the christening of their infant son Theodore, named for his godfather Theodore Roosevelt, see letter to Sara Norton, August 29, 1902.

2. Henry Bennet Brewster (1850–1908) was a longtime resident of Rome. Henry James described Brewster in *Notes of a Son and Brother* as "the clearest case of 'Cosmopolite culture' I was to have known." *The Prisoner*, which had a

brief vogue after its appearance in 1891, was a fictional allegory relating the reactions of various individuals of different beliefs to a document of a prisoner condemned to death.

3. Cecil Spring-Rice (1859–1918), the English diplomat, would become Ambassador to the United States in 1912 and be knighted in 1916. EW's meeting with him on the afternoon yachting party at Newport in the late 1870s is recounted by her in *A Backward Glance*, where she also offers two of the "wonderful stories"—tales of magic and the supernatural—that Spring-Rice had told her.

4. George Cabot ("Bay") Lodge (1873–1909), the son of the Massachusetts Senator Henry Cabot Lodge and an aspiring and ambitious poet; his second volume of poetry had just appeared. In 1900, he had married Matilda Elizabeth Frelinghuysen ("Bessie") Davis.

To Annie Adams Fields[1]

Somerset Hotel
Tuesday afternoon
[Summer 1902]

My dear Mrs. Fields,

I have just received your kind invitation for Friday, & I am going to reply by making a proposal which I trust you will think a pardonable one under the circumstances. My husband is going out on a bicycling expedition that afternoon & Mr. Updike & I were planning to go & see Mr. Le Moyne; so that I hope perhaps you will let me bring Mr. Updike instead of my husband, & thus not miss the pleasure of seeing you & Miss Jewett.[2] Mr. Updike assures me that you will allow him to act as a substitute, & my husband begs me to say, with his kindest regards, how sorry *he* is to give any one else an opportunity he would so greatly have enjoyed himself!

With many thanks for your kind thought,

Sincerely yours
Edith Wharton

Ms:HL

1. The widow of the Boston publisher James T. Fields (1817–1881). Annie Fields (1834–1915) became a well-known figure in her own right, and her home a literary meeting place.

2. Sarah Orne Jewett (1849–1909), the author of *The Country of the Pointed Firs* (1896) and many other volumes. She often stayed with her close friend Annie Fields when visiting Boston from her native Maine.

To Sara Norton

Lenox, Mass.
June 7 [1902]

Dear Sally

Thank you for sending me that fine notice from the Herald. I feel quite inflated since reading it!—I was so glad, too, to get your last letter, & to hear that Mr. Norton is so much better. I suppose you have both been scolding at this cold weather, but wait a little longer & you'll be wanting some of it back.

Lenox has had its usual tonic effect on me, & I feel like a new edition, revised & corrected, in Berkeley's best type. It is great fun out at the place, now too—everything is pushing up new shoots—not only cabbages & strawberries, but electric lights & plumbing. I really think we shall be installed—after a fashion—by Sept 1st.

Well—I'll resign myself to having you in July—& if we can charter an auto at Pittsfield perhaps you'll see us for a day before you come here.

Yrs affly E.W.

Have you read a little book called "The Prison," by one Brewster? He is a friend of Mrs. Winty Chanler's, who sent it to me. I haven't had time to take it seriously, but from the first pages I gather that life—or at least the individual consciousness—is the Prison, & the whole a metaphysical allegory, rather well done. But metaphysics "sortent de ma compétence," as a gardien at the Louvre once said to me, when I asked him where a certain carved ivory had come from—.

Au revoir, dear Sally. Yrs—why, this is a postscript! Never mind, I can't say too often that I am yours affectionately.

Ms:BL

To Sara Norton

Lenox, Mass.
August 29 [1902]

Dearest Sally

You & those dear dogs! You must have wondered why I left you so long unacknowledged; but the parcel arrived just after we left for Newport last week, & Anna[1] did not forward it, so that I didn't know what awaited me till our return last night.—It is a charming picture, with all the grace & spontaneity of a chance photograph that has not been "sat for," & I am so glad you sent it.

I had a very pleasant week at Newport. Dry, brilliant weather (not a fog), magnificent tennis (I am a devout spectator of that game) & the sight & conversation of some old friends—if I mentioned the President among them, would Ashfield shudder at the name?[2] Well, I do delight in him, & the two hours I spent in his society at the Chanler christening gave me great satisfaction.[3] I saw a great deal of Daisy Chanler, who is dear & wonderful, serene & unhurried, among seven children & the turmoil of the Newport season. If you care for tennis I wish you had seen the final match between Larned & Doherty.[4] It gave me a sense of being at a Greek game—the brilliancy of the scene, the festal dresses, the grace & ease of the two players, & the strange intensity of silence to which that chattering crowd was subdued. It seems to me such a beautiful game—without violence, noise, brutality—quick, graceful, rhythmic, with a setting of turf & sky.

We got home last night & the dogs turned somersaults for joy.— This is not a real letter, for I am rather tired & breathless—but you shall have one soon—

I am so delighted that my friends the Jusserands[5] are coming to Washington—

With much love (& I hope you are really better)

Your affte   E.W.

Ms:BL

1. The German-born Anna Bahlmann, in her early thirties at this time. She had been the governess for the children of Lewis Rutherfurd, the distinguished Columbia professor of astronomy, and had given German lessons to the adolescent Edith Jones. She had recently become Edith Wharton's secretary and literary assistant.

2. Theodore Roosevelt had been President since September 1901, when President William McKinley was assassinated by the anarchist Leon Czolgosz.

Charles Eliot Norton was contemptuous of Roosevelt, regarding him as a windbag and cowboy. On September 5, EW was among those who gathered to hear the President give a little speech in Lenox about the Anti-Trust Act. He had just been in a fairly serious accident, in which his carriage collided with a trolley car and he was thrown onto the road. In her report to Sara Norton, Edith wrote: "I think if you could have seen the President here the other day, all bleeding and swollen from that hideous accident, and could have heard the few very quiet and fitting words he said to the crowd gathered to receive him, you would have agreed that he is not all—or nearly all—bronco-buster."

3. The occasion for Roosevelt's visit to Newport was the christening of Theodore Chanler, the newly born son of Margaret and Winthrop Chanler and named for the President.

4. The final match for the American tennis championship, held in the Newport Casino, was between William A. Larned, later said to be the finest American tennis player before Bill Tilden, and the English R. F. Doherty, four-time All-England champion. Larned won in what was described as a long and exciting contest.

5. Jules Jusserand (1855–1932), known by many as a distinguished literary historian, became French Ambassador to the United States in 1902 and served in that role for more than twenty years. Since 1895, he had been married to the American-born Elise Richards, whose sister Marion was a friend of EW's. See letter to Henry James, September 3, 1912.

To Margaret Terry Chanler

Lenox, Mass.
September 7 [1902]

Dear Daisy

I look back on those few hours with you as a kind of oasis in an uncommonly sandy summer. How I wish things didn't so persistently arrange themselves to keep us in different places!

I am returning your two books (The Statuette[1] &c, & the James book[2]) because, in the present tumult of moving I cannot read them with any kind of consecutiveness. In the train they gave me enchanting glimpses—that is, the Brewster book did; I like it immensely, far better than his others, though they interested me. This one is full of charming things—the allegory of the great island, in the 2d letter, for instance. And on almost every page I found a phrase that lingers. I am going to order a copy for myself.

With regard to "Religious Experience," I won't express an opinion because I have read only the first chapters.

I have just heard from England that my poor sister-in-law[3] has been very ill, with a horribly painful thing called arthritis. She & Beatrix[4] expect to sail on Sept 21st, & Beatrix wishes to bring her to us here as soon as they land. She will probably not be with us for more than a week or ten days—till their house in town is ready, & after that I hope you will keep your promise of coming. I don't like to name a date till I know their plans a little more definitely, but I don't think Minnie will stay more than a week.

Affly Yrs   Edith W.

As soon as I got back I looked up my notes for "The Valley," to see how I could have put the feast of the Purification in Nov! I found from my Italian calendar that it was the *Presentation*, & I suppose Purification was a slip of mine—or possibly of the printer's. At any rate, I don't think I have made any "gaffe" quite as colossal as that of Miss Marie Corelli,[5] who, in her last novel (as I see by the papers) makes a Jesuit commit suicide in his haste to reach the kingdom of heaven.

Ms:BL

1. *The Statuette and the Background*, a dialogue about art and reality, by Henry Brewster.

2. William James's *The Varieties of Religious Experience* (1902).

3. Mary Cadwalader Jones, née Rawle (1850–1935), of distinguished Philadelphia lineage. In 1870, she had married EW's brother Fred. The marriage was soon dissolved, but EW and "Minnie" Jones became ever closer friends as the years passed. Mrs. Jones's home on East Eleventh Street in New York was a hospitable meeting place for Henry James and many others.

4. Beatrix Jones (1872–1959), an apprentice landscape gardener, was the daughter of Mary Cadwalader Jones.

5. Marie Corelli (i.e., Mary Mackay, 1855–1924), the author of many best-selling melodramatic romances, was at the peak of her fame in the early 1900s. Her last novel was *Temporal Power*.

To William Crary Brownell

The Mount
Lenox, Mass
September 12, 1902
This is our new address but
we don't move in till the 20th.

Dear Mr. Brownell,

Many thanks for the cheque for $2,191 81/100, which, even to the 81 cents, is welcome to an author in the last throes of house-building—

I am glad to see the new House Decoration[1] has made a good start, but not surprised to find that the G.I. is not being fought for at the railway-stalls— The wonder to me is that the Valley should have reached such heights. I am charmed with the 1 vol. Edition, for which I was just about to write & thank you when your letter came. By the way, I am going to send you a long letter which Mr. James wrote me the other day about the "Valley."[2] You will see there is a personal note in it, so don't circulate it please, beyond Mr. Scribner & Mr. Burlingame. The letter was a great surprise to me, as I never send Mr. James my books, & should not have expected him to be in the least interested in "The Valley."

I rec'd your note of Aug. 14th about Es War,[3] but didn't answer it, as you said you were going off on a holiday (which was a good one, I hope,) & the matter was not urgent. With regard to leave to translate, would it not be better if the request were to come from the Messrs. Scribner? They might mention to Sudermann that the translation will be made under the supervision of the translator of "Es Lebe" (in which character only I am likely to have any identity to him), & that I will write a short introduction to it. Then, as to the play, I am still engaged in trying to find out whether Mrs. Campbell had any right to give me the publishing right. My lawyer has again put the question to hers, & I hope for an answer this week. (It's no use asking her.) The play is ready for you now, but Norman Hapgood,[4] who was here the other day, was so pleased with my translation that he carried it off for a few days in order to write an article on it. If I hear it is all right about the copyright I can send it to you next week. I enclose herewith the "Translator's Note."

Yrs Sincerely
E. Wharton

Don't ask me what I think of the Wings of the Dove[5]—

Ms:FL

1. *The Decoration of Houses*, by Edith Wharton and Ogden Codman, Jr., had been published by Charles Scribner's Sons in 1897. This was one of several reprintings.

2. Henry James's letter of August 17, 1902, praised *The Valley of Decision* fulsomely, the eulogy ending: "In the presence of a book so accomplished, pondered, saturated, so exquisitely studied and so brilliant and interesting from a literary point of view, I feel that just now heartily to congratulate you covers plenty of ground." But he had very serious advice to offer for EW's future work: "Let it suffer the wrong of being crudely hinted as my desire earnestly, tenderly, intelligently to admonish you ... admonish, I say, in favour of the American subject. Don't pass it by—the immediate, the real, the only, the yours, the novelist's that it waits for ... *Do New York!* The 1st-hand account is precious."

3. *Es War*: a novel by the German writer Hermann Sudermann (1857-1928), published in 1897. EW had just completed a translation of Sudermann's new play, *Es Lebe das Leben*, for Mrs. Pat Campbell. EW's proposed English title

was *Long Live Life,* but Mrs. Campbell held out for the inappropriate *The Joy of Living.* The play had only a brief run on Broadway, but the published book that EW mentions did rather well. EW did not go on to translate *Es War.*

4. Norman Hapgood (1868–1937), writer and editor, recently had brought out *The Stage in America.* He was the older brother of the journalist and fiction writer Hutchins Hapgood.

5. Henry James's letter, just quoted from, began by saying that he had asked "the Scribners to send you a rather long-winded (but I hope not hopelessly heavy) novel of mine that they are to issue by the end of this month (a thing called *The Wings of the Dove*)."

To Sara Norton

The Mount
Lenox, Mass.
September 30 [1902]

Finalmente!—a moment in which to thank you for your dear long letter of two weeks ago & more, which has long since been answered mentally, though not (ha! ha!) *pen*tally. The latter weapon has rusted in its scabbard since we began to move (the process has been so prolonged that I can only put it in that way). Zwei Seelen wohnen, ach, in meine Brust,[1] & the Compleat Housekeeper has had the upper hand for the last weeks; but now I am beginning to recover my sense of proportion, & the first good I get therefrom is to find you uppermost in my thoughts.

I had a visit from Grenville Winthrop[2] yesterday, in which he said such pleasant & sympathetic things of his visit to Ashfield that I began to understand the juxtaposition, which had puzzled me. The fact is, I had thought him (with every virtue under heaven) a rather opaque body; & you are all so translucent. But I daresay I did him an injustice. He has nice tastes, certainly (I don't mean only in liking you, though that is a test), but he seems to me to want digging out & airing—Query?—

I hope you are getting those restful days you hoped for at Ashfield. I send you this there, as Mr. Winthrop thought you had not left. Here, on the rare days when it doesn't rain, we have had delicious warm bloomy weather—a "patine" on everything. We have been in the new house ten days, & have enjoyed every minute of it. The views are exquisite, & it is all so still & sylvan. I have never seen the Michaelmas daisies as beautiful as this year—the lanes are purple—

And how about Rome? Don't even let yourself think that it can't be. Say at once that it shall be; because we are going out by the Southern Line about the end of December, & it strikes me as one of the absolutely "indiquées" things that you should go with us—hein? Now, don't raise all sorts of conscientious New England objections, but try to be a pagan, & see how nice this would be, & what an opportunity for you to have a staid elderly travelling companion & a strong manly arm to defend you. We are not going directly to Rome, as the Dr. thinks Teddy should be in a warmer climate through January; but we could drop you at Naples, & then go to Sicily or the Riviera, & about Feb. 1st we mean to reach Rome. We hoped to put off sailing till January, but the Dr. who has just seen Teddy, says *please* to go not later than the end of December—or a week or two earlier. We are told the Maria Theresa is the best ship to go on, & shall be guided by her dates of sailing.—

Ponder these things!

Yr affte
E.W.

Ms:BL

1. Goethe, *Faust*: "Two souls, alas, do dwell within my breast." *Meine* should read *meiner*.

2. Grenville Winthrop (1864–1943), New York lawyer and art collector and the younger son of EW's old friend Egerton Winthrop. See letter to Margaret Terry Chanler, March 8, 1903.

To Richard Watson Gilder[1]

The Mount,
Lenox, Mass.
October 10, 1902

Dear Mr. Gilder

The terms you propose for the garden articles[2] are quite satisfactory, but I always like to make my business arrangements as definite as possible, & I therefore write to ask if you will kindly put me "en rapport" with the publishers, so that I may settle that part of the affair at the same time.—In this respect there is one thing which I must stipulate; & that is that, in the publication of the book, what I consider the rules of English spelling shall be respected.

In the magazine I suppose one must submit to being Websterized; but I can't stand the thought of being made to say clew & theater permanently, & as the Macmillans & Scribners respect these prejudices on the part of their authors, I am sure the Century Co. will show the same consideration. Seriously, I think it a pity that you publishers still cling to those particular forms of spelling, against which, thank goodness, there is now such a general reaction in this country. At any rate, in a book about beautiful gardens, there ought not to be any vulgar orthography!

Pardon my frankness—but I always care very much for the make-up of my books.

Sincerely Yrs Edith Wharton

Ms:BL

1. Richard Watson Gilder (1844–1909) served on the staff of *Scribner's Monthly* (not to be confused with *Scribner's Magazine*, of later origin). When it was succeeded by the *Century*, he became editor of that periodical, and remained there all his life.

2. These articles, written after extensive travel and study in Italy, were collected in the volume of 1904 *Italian Villas and Their Gardens*

To William Crary Brownell

The Mount
Lenox, Mass.
November 6 [1902]

Dear Mr. Brownell

Here is some twaddle from Mrs. Campbell. I have written her that, as she & her solicitor were both informed several months ago that you were to publish my translation of Es Lebe, it would have been perfectly easy for her to notify me or Mr. Scribner that she wished a note about the acting rights inserted. I added that I would send her letter to you & that you would do "whatever was practical" (I mean you collectively) about inserting such a notice now. Cela n'engage à rien— Don't bother to answer—

Re the poems, that was a neat thrust about the implied superiority of the prose. Well—I think it is better. & then there are degrees in prose & in poetry—below a certain point—well, it simply isn't poetry; & I am not sure I've ever reached the "poetry line." But if Mr. Burlingame likes Vesalius[1] (which has made me want to hide under the furniture ever since I've seen it in print), there is no telling how I may rise in my own estimation. One difficulty is that my verse is so "fugitive," that most of it has run quite away; I haven't any copies & I shouldn't know where to find any but the latest things. Still—château qui parle:—you see I'm listening already![2]

Yours sincerely
    Edith Wharton

Have you seen the James review in the Critic? You have disarmed my suspicions & I have signed the contract & return it—

Ms:FL

1. EW's poem "Vesalius in Zante (1564)" is a blank verse monologue of some two hundred lines about the sixteenth-century Italian anatomist and surgeon Vesalius, shortly before his death. EW's explanatory note tells us that Vesalius was given the chair of surgery at the University of Padua, and that while there he composed a work on the structure of the human body that largely refuted the views of the Greek physician Galen. The work caused such a furor that Vesalius quit his post and went to Spain, where he became physician in the court of Emperor Charles V. He grew rich and successful, but increasingly found court life intolerable. In 1563, he set off on a pilgrimage to Jerusalem. A new treatise on the body by Fallopius, who succeeded him at Padua, suggested that Vesalius's theories might now find acceptance. In fact, Padua recalled him; but Vesalius died in 1564, on his way back from Jerusalem.

"Vesalius" was included in *Artemis to Actaeon*, EW's first volume of poetry, in 1909.

2. EW is drawing upon an old French saying: "Château qui parle, femme qui écoute, sont prêts à se rendre." ("A castle which parleys, a woman who listens, are ready to surrender.")

To Alfred Austin[1]

Hotel Royal
San Remo
January 21 [1903]

Dear Mr Austin

Few things have given me greater pleasure than your letter, which has just reached me here after having had to retrace its way from America.

I know what an authority you are in matters Italian, & it has been a great satisfaction to me that my book has received its warmest welcome from those who, like yourself, have lived in & *with* Italy. It was for "voi altri" that I wrote, & I was willing to take the risk of boring the rest of the world (as I appear to have done in England) for the sake of trying to give, to those who love Italy, some impression of that moment of transition which no one, hitherto, seems to have cared to write about.

I am especially gratified by what you say of my treatment of the religious side of the subject, for I tried to hold the balance as evenly as possible in describing the influence of the Church on the various classes of society, & the few Catholics I know who are familiar with the conditions in Italy at that period seem to think, with you, that I have painted them fairly.—

We are in Europe, as you see, & I hope to meet you in England in the spring, & to thank you in person for taking the trouble to send me your impressions of "The Valley of Decision." I am almost forgetting, by the way, to say how much I appreciate your mention of my work in your address to the Dante Society. "The Valley of Decision," by the way, is coming out shortly in the "Nuova Antologia."[2]

We hope to be in London by the end of April if I can find any lawful or unlawful way of taking into your cruel country a very small & dear dog whom I cannot possibly leave to himself on the continent, since he has never yet deserted me in a difficulty!

When is that barbarous law to be repealed?

Believe me
Sincerely Yrs
    Edith Wharton

If by any chance you are to be in Rome in February or March, will you not send me a line to the Bristol?

Ms:FL

1. Alfred Austin (1835–1913) was named Poet Laureate of England by Lord Salisbury, Queen Victoria's Prime Minister, in 1896, to succeed Alfred Lord Tennyson. EW had no better opinion of Austin's verse than most other literary people, but she came to like the man and enjoy his company.

2. A literary periodical published in Rome. *The Valley of Decision* would begin to appear in it in the summer of 1903.

To Margaret Terry Chanler

Rome
March 8 [1903]

Dear Daisy

I meant to send you my "sensations de Rome" before this, but when I am here I am always so busy absorbing life at every pore that there never seems time to squeeze anything out. Nevertheless, you don't need to be told, I am sure, that I have thought of you very often in scenes which are so associated with you. We have been here a month, & we leave, alas, the day after tomorrow, with a sense at once of regret & repleteness. I think sometimes that it is almost a pity to enjoy Italy as much as I do, because the acuteness of my sensations makes them rather exhausting; but when I see the stupid Italians I have met here, completely insensitive to their surroundings, & ignorant of the treasures of art & history among which they have grown up, I begin to think it is better to be an American, & bring to it all a mind & eye unblunted by custom. The only person I have met here who knows *anything* of art & architecture (the only Italian, bien entendu!) is your friend Countess Pasolini,[1] who is like a cultivated English or American woman in her sense of beauty & her knowledge of the past. She has done everything imaginable to add to our enjoyment here, & her house is like a London salon, where people lunch & dine when they want to meet, instead of going thro' the everlasting Roman tea-drinking which consumes so many precious hours. But I will not get on the subject of visiting in Rome, for it arouses my worst language.

Instead, I will tell you how very sympathetic I also find the Brewsters. We have lunched with them twice, & little Miss Brewster,[2] who has completely captivated Teddy, has been most kind about getting per-messi for inaccessible villas, even to forcing the doors of the Villa Albani when everyone else had tried & failed.—Mr. Brewster I like greatly & should like to see often; & the whole milieu is so sympathetic & charming that I leave it with great regret. You see, therefore, dear Daisy, how much your letters have added to my pleasure in Rome; & I must not forget also to mention Mrs. Crawshay,[3] who has been very kind, though her addiction to the Roman habit of asking people to tea instead of lunch or dinner has made it difficult for me to see much of her, as I am generally too tired to go out at that hour.

We have seen a great many other people, of course, but somehow they fade into insignificance beside the place itself, & I look with amazement at the Americans & English who come here for a few weeks, & give all their time & strength to forcing their way into a society not particularly anxious to receive them. We have had perfect weather, which has given us the opportunity for some delightful days in the country, at Frascati, Albano, Tivoli &c; & the other day George Meyer[4] took us in his automobile to Caprarola. I think it is the most beautiful excursion I ever made in Italy. Have you ever done it? The view on the ridge between Ronciglione & Caprarola, looking down on one side of the Lago di Vico, & on the other on the wide plain with Soracte springing up from it in "magnificent isolation," was like one of Turner's Italian visions, which are so much nearer the reality than the work of the modern realists.

On the 10th we go to Viterbo, & thence drive to Orvieto. Then to Siena, to see some villas, to Florence, Venice, &c. We sail from Antwerp on April 25th, so our time is painfully short.

I have heard of you now & then from Egerton,[5] & in his last letter he said you had been staying with him & had been obliged to leave rather suddenly because your governess was ill. I hope it was not serious, & that you have been able to get away again, for you know my sentiments about Newport in winter!

Do write me a little line care Munroe & Co. 7 Rue Scribe to tell me all about yourself—   Affly Yrs   Edith W—

I have also consumed several quarts of tea with Princess Barratinsky.[6]

Ms:BL

1. Countess Maria Pasolini, particularly knowledgeable about seventeenth- and eighteenth-century architecture and the sister of another Italian friend of EW, Countess Rasponi.

2. The sister of Henry Brewster, referred to earlier (letter to Margaret Terry Chanler, May 17, 1902), and whom she now meets.

3. Mary Crawshay, then living in Rome, was the sister of Sir John Leslie, the husband of the former Leonie Jerome of New York. Leonie herself was the sister of Jennie Jerome, Lady Randolph Churchill. EW was here beginning a long friendship with the witty and warmhearted Mary Crawshay.

4. The American Ambassador to Italy. The drive from Rome to Caprarola and back was EW's first ride in an automobile, and she found it incredible that the hundred-mile round trip could be made in an afternoon with still time to inspect the villa and gardens at Caprarola. The car was fast and luxurious, EW would recall in her memoirs, but "without hood or screen, or any protection from the wind. My husband was put behind with the chauffeur, while I had the high seat like a coachman's box beside the Ambassador. . . . Off we tore across the Campagna, over humps and bumps, through ditches and across gutters, wind-swept, dust-enveloped, I clinging to my sailor-hat, and George Meyer (luckily) to the wheel."

5. Egerton Leigh Winthrop (born 1839), EW's longtime New York friend. A descendant of John Winthrop, the first governor of the Massachusetts Bay Colony, Egerton Winthrop had been practicing law in New York City since the 1860s. He was also a discerning collector of paintings and antiques.

6. Probably the actress Princess Barriatinsky.

To Sara Norton

Hotel Bristol
Florence
March 17 [1903]

Dearest Sally

I wept mentally (for I never do physically!) over your poor dear letter, which has just come. How well I know those bitter times, when great trials & small inconveniences pile themselves together on the tired body & strained nerves, & how often have I experienced the fact that when one goes on board ship exhausted & praying for rest, one has a rough voyage & exasperating landing! What you went through, however, surpasses anything I ever heard of, & I hope some of the passengers will say an earnest word to the Dominion Line.

Don't speak of the disappointment of our leaving Rome before you came. There were so many moments when we did the kind of thing that I know you would have enjoyed, & that would have been delicious to talk of afterward. It is part of our friendship that we should never see anything of each other!

I am glad you had sunshine for that heavenly journey from Naples to Rome. It is one of the loveliest bits of Italy— How I wish you had been with us since we left Rome—at Viterbo, Montefiascone, Orvieto, & the delicious villas near Siena! We did not reach here till last night, & Miss Paget (Vernon Lee)[1] has such a prodigious list of villas for me to see near here, & is taking so much trouble to arrange expeditions for us, that I think we shall have to stay here longer than I expected— perhaps ten days.

We had on our little trip as far as Siena a young couple whom I think you will like—the Willie Bucklers.[2] He is Harry White's step-brother, & she English, a niece of Froude & Max Müller. I mention them because they seem to be great friends of your brother's, so you will probably see them, as they have gone back to Rome. Do be careful about colds, by the way, in Rome. Teddy & I went from one to another, in spite of the heavenly weather; & did not recover till we left. The place must be full of influenza germs. Don't go to the villa Borghese (the Museum) without overshoes or cork-soled boots, for the floors are glacial.

When you are a little better, & have leisure to write, will you give me your advice on the following question. Miss Paget (whom you wd like, I know) is very anxious to go to America, for the quaintest of reasons—"to visit the out of the way parts of New England." She cannot afford to go without paying her expenses, which she proposes to do by lecturing—she would lecture on aesthetics, "Art & Life," & that kind of thing, & I think she would do it well, judging from her books. She does not want to "lecture to fashionable women in bonnets," with a list of millionaire patronesses, for which I respect her; but would like a college audience, men or girls—Bryn Mawr, Radcliffe, Harvard & so on. Her idea is to go to America next August, say, & she must be back before Xmas. If she could do her New England in August & Sept, & lecture in Oct & Nov, it would fit very well. In Boston I should say she might give one or two lectures to a general public too. Now I don't want you to do anything about this but tell me from whom I could get *practical* advice for her. Would Barrett Wendell be a good person, & do you know his address in England?—I am sure he would not mind my bothering him—

Miss Paget has been so kind to me that I should like to do what I can, & I believe her lectures wd be decidedly worth hearing—

I can't say how sorry I am that yr father has had the influenza again. Don't write till you feel like it—

Yr affte
　　E.W

Mitou³ sends you his best love—

Ms:BL

1. See letter to Edward L. Burlingame, July 30, 1894.
2. William Hepburn Buckler (1867–1952), archaeologist and foreign service officer. EW knew him as the younger half-brother of Henry White, the American diplomatist who married Margaret Rutherfurd (on White, see letter to Morton Fullerton, June 5, 1908). Buckler was married to Georgie Walrond, the niece, as EW says, of the English historian J. A. Froude and of Max Müller, professor of comparative mythology at Oxford. He was also a friend of the Rome-based Richard Norton.
3. The Whartons' Pekinese.

To Richard Watson Gilder

Florence
March 18, 1903

Dear Mr. Gilder

Since I wrote you the other day from Rome we have been off on a villa hunt at Viterbo & Siena, & are now settled here for the exploration of Tuscan gardens. We have seen the gardens at Caprarola (to which it is *very* difficult to obtain access), & also the wonderful Villa Lante at Bagnaja, the Marchese Chigi's Villa Cetinale in the hill country behind Siena, & three other remarkable gardens near Siena.—In all, I have already seen, photographed, & made notes on, no less than 26 villas, many unknown or almost inaccessible, & I hope to do nearly as many more in the next month.—

My object in writing is to point out that the subject has grown so far beyond what I expected when I first took it up, & has so complicated our plan of travel, that I feel the price I originally agreed on for the six articles is less than I ought to have asked. When you suggested the idea to me, I was so charmed at the prospect of studying a few of the great Italian gardens, that I did not think much of the practical side of the question. You know, of course, that I do not "live by my pen," & did not expect these articles to pay the expenses of our Italian trip; but neither did I realize how much they would increase our expenses!—In Rome, when I was continually on the hunt, I had to make long carriage excursions three or four times a week, & at Viterbo & Siena all the villas were from five to ten miles distant, & meant a carriage for the afternoon or for the day. Here I find I must not only take long drives into the country, but go & stay at several small places in the neighbourhood, & drive from there to villas otherwise inaccessible. In addition, I have taken innumerable photographs, wh. I have developed on the spot in order to classify them, & I have had to buy old books on gardens & villas in order to make sure that I am not missing any important villas still existing. All this has increased our expenses considerably—especially, of course, I mean, the trips to out of the way towns & the long drives—& though you may think such investigations are unnecessary for the magazine articles, you will appreciate, I am sure, how much they will add to the value & importance of the book, & to its selling capacity.

Dining room of the Whartons' home at 884 Park Avenue, New York City.
Beinecke Library, Yale University.

Edward R. (Teddy)
Wharton at Land's
End, Newport,
Rhode Island, 1895.
*Beinecke Library,
Yale University.*

Edith Wharton on
horseback, Land's
End, 1898.
*Beinecke Library,
Yale University.*

Edith Wharton, 1900. *Beinecke Library, Yale University.*

The Mount, Lenox, Massachusetts, 1905. *Courtesy of the Lenox Library Association.*

View from the terrace at The Mount. *Beinecke Library, Yale University.*

The library at The Mount. *Beinecke Library, Yale University.*

Sara Norton and Teddy Wharton at
Ashfield, the Nortons' country home near
Lenox, Massachusetts. *By permission of the
Houghton Library, Harvard University.*

William Crary Brownell,
1903. *Firestone Library,
Princeton University.*

Paul Bourget, Hyères, France, January 1904. The photograph is inscribed on the back in Edith Wharton's handwriting: "Le Plantier, Costebelle. Bourget in front of house." *Beinecke Library, Yale University.*

Paul Bourget at the wheel of the Whartons' new Panhard, with Teddy and Edith Wharton in the rear seat and Charles Cook, their chauffeur, standing in front. *Beinecke Library, Yale University.*

Edith Wharton, 1905. *William Royall Tyler Collection,*
Lily Library, University of Indiana.

The Whartons' residence at 58 Rue de Varenne, Faubourg
St. Germain, Paris. *Collection of R. W. B. Lewis and Nancy Lewis.*

I think Mr. Johnson[1] fully realizes the importance of a careful study of old plans & the inspection of the greatest number possible of gardens, in order to write with some sort of system & comprehensiveness on a subject which, hitherto, has been treated in English only in the most amateurish fashion. Both here & in Rome people have taken such interest in my work that I have had wonderful opportunities for seeing all that I wanted, & here especially "Vernon Lee" is putting me in the way of everything that can be of use.

The price named by you, & accepted by me, was $1500. for the six articles; & I should be quite satisfied if you would raise that to $2000. —I am aware that such a request is unusual after an agreement has been made; & it is for this reason that I have gone into such detail in explaining why I find the terms agreed on inadequate to the work I have to do. You must remember that I have accepted an unusually low royalty on the book, though it is *sure* to have a popular success—& this being the case, I hope you will realize that the price of the articles should be somewhat higher—I receive $500 for a short story, wh. is much less hard work—& does not increase my hotel bills to such a degree!—

I am hoping to get out to see Edith Rucellai[2] between villas if I can make time.—

With kind regards,

Sincerely Yrs
    Edith Wharton.

Our address is
Munroe & Co
7 Rue Scribe Paris
till April 25 when we sail. Then Lenox— Where *is* Mr. Parrish?[3] Not a word from him yet!

Ms:BL

1. Robert Underwood Johnson (1853–1937), associate editor of the *Century*, a highly regarded poet in his time and an influential figure in the world of letters.

2. The former Edith Bronson, the daughter of Katherine De Kay Bronson, much-valued friend and hostess in her Casa Alvisi in Venice of Robert Brown-

ing, Henry James, and many others. (Mrs. Bronson died in 1901.) EW had known Edith Bronson in Newport. The latter was now married to Conte Cosimo Rucellai, of the age-old aristocratic Florentine family. She was also the niece of Helena De Kay Gilder, the wife of Richard Gilder.

3. Maxfield Parrish (1870–1966), popular magazine illustrator—the *Century, Ladies' Home Journal*, and others—in darkly colorful Pre-Raphaelite manner. He would do the illustrations for *Italian Villas and Their Gardens.*

To Sara Norton

The Mount
Lenox, Mass.
June 5 [1903]

Dear Sally

Your letter glowing with the reflection of the National Gallery came yesterday, & made me feel more acutely than ever the contrast between the old & the new, between the stored beauty & tradition & amenity over there, & the crassness here. My first few weeks in America are always miserable, because the tastes I am cursed with are all of a kind that cannot be gratified here, & I am not enough in sympathy with our "gros public" to make up for the lack on the aesthetic side. One's friends are delightful; but *we* are none of us Americans, we don't think or feel as the Americans do, we are the wretched exotics produced in a European glass-house, the most déplacé & useless class on earth! All of which outburst is due to my first sight of American streets, my first hearing of American voices, & the wild, dishevelled backwoods look of everything when one first comes home! You see in my heart of hearts, a heart never unbosomed, I feel in America as you say you do in England—out of sympathy with everything. And in England I like it *all*—institutions, traditions, mannerisms, conservatisms, everything but the women's clothes, & the having to go to church every Sunday.

We arrived safely & comfortably, after a long slow crossing on the best steamer I ever was on, & came at once to Lenox. It is very pleasant to be taking one's ease in one's own house, but out of doors the scene is depressing. There has been an appalling drought of nine weeks or more, & never has this fresh showery country looked so unlike itself. The dust is indescribable, the grass parched & brown, flowers & vegetables stunted, & still no promise of rain! You may fancy how our poor place looks, still in the rough, with all its bald patches emphasized. In addition, our good gardener has failed us, we know not why, whether from drink or some other demoralization, but after spending a great deal of money on the place all winter there are no results, & we have been obliged to get a new man. This has been a great blow, as we can't afford to do much more this year— I try to console myself by writing about Italian gardens instead of looking at my own.

Two days after we landed my niece Beatrix was taken ill with appendicitis. It was a slight attack, & the operation was successfully performed two days ago, but it is a great trial, as she & her mother were going abroad next week, & had rented their house at Bar Harbour, dismissed servants, &c. I expect to have her here as soon as she can be moved, & I doubt if they can sail before August.

Yes, I got your little note about the writing-case, & I am so glad it was right. I am glad also that you are missing this ugly burnt-up June, which wd depress you as it does me. When you write again do tell me how your ear is since the treatment in Paris. I am wonderfully well, & still look on Salsomaggiore[1] as a kind of Lourdes.

The dear dogs were so glad to see us. Miza looks younger than ever, but old Jules is very rheumatic.

Thanks again for your letter, dear Sally—

Affly Yrs   E.W.

I am so delighted that you think the Maison du Péché as remarkable as I do. It is so full of beauty & feeling, so profoundly moving, so unlike the average French novel in every way.

Ms:BL

1. Salsomaggiore—"Salso," as EW would often call it—is a health resort halfway between Parma and Piacenza in north-central Italy. EW went there for treatment of her recurring asthma, and though she described the surroundings as unredeemedly ugly, she admitted that the visits did her much good.

To William Crary Brownell

The Mount
Lenox, Mass.
August 16, 1903

Dear Mr Brownell,

Why shouldn't we publish this autumn my collection of Italian sketches?¹ I had forgotten all about them; but as my first article on Italian villas is coming out in the Century in Nov., it seems to me it might be a happy moment— If "Sanctuary"² appears, as I think you said, in October, why should a volume of so different a character, coming five or six weeks later, be de trop? I believe the book would sell well, for there is such a great rush to Italy every autumn now on the Mediterranean steamers, & people so often ask me where these articles can be found—

I don't think I should attempt illustrations, though of course several *are* illustrated.

If I remember, those published are:

An Alpine Posting Inn

A Tuscan Shrine

Sub Umbra Liliorum (Parma)

Picturesque Milan—

A Midsummer Week's Dream—

Sanctuaries of the Pennine Alps.—

I could add say two more—one (if you decide on pictures) wd be an account of Ct. Visconti's villa at Cernusco, near Milan, of which I have a complete serial of photos, inside & out, a history of the house, etc.— it could be called "A Lombard Country House & its story." It is only mentioned incidentally in my villa articles, as it has no old gardens left, & the most interesting part is the interior—

I was very sorry to learn that things are going badly with you— I understand what it means, for my husband is very poorly & I have had an anxious summer— I can't do consecutive work, but this Italian book would be a pleasure to prepare.

Sincerely Yrs
     E. Wharton—

P.S. If you decide against illustrations, I can do another article in place of "A Lombard Country House"—

Ms:FL

1. *Italian Backgrounds*, of which EW goes on to list the table of contents, was published in March 1905.
2. The short novel *Sanctuary* ran serially in *Scribner's*, beginning in July 1903. It would be published in book form on October 23.

To William Crary Brownell

Costebelle, par Hyères
January 7, 1904

Dear Mr. Brownell,

When I was in Paris last week I read the proofs of a novel by my friend Mr. Howard Sturgis,[1] which is to be brought out in England in the Spring, I forget by whom—I think either Grant Richards or Methuen. Mr. Sturgis has only written two books before—a boys' book called "Tim" which had a great success in England, & a year or two later (some ten years since), a short novel called "All That Was Possible," full of delicate qualities which was never fully appreciated in England, & was refused by American publishers on the ground that the heroine was a lady with a past!—Since then, he has done nothing till this new book, "Belchamber," a novel of English "hig lif" which seems to me so remarkable in donnée & character-drawing that, as soon as I read it, I asked if he had already found a publisher in America— He said he had not, & after the rejection of "All That Was Possible" he seemed to think it peine perdue to offer his book on the other side of the Atlantic—which is really his side, as you probably know, since he is a brother of Julian Sturgis, & a son of old Mr. Russell Sturgis, the London banker—Mr. James, whom I saw in London before I read "Belchamber," thinks the situation very strong & original—but I am sure it will need neither his commendation nor mine to interest you & Mr.

Scribner & I am writing to you quite spontaneously, simply because, when there is a good thing going, I want you to have it.

I have told Mr. Sturgis to send you the ms., & his address, in case you wish to write him about it, is

Queen's Acre

Windsor, Berks.

Mr James came up from Rye & spent the day with us. He looks, without his beard, like a blend of Coquelin & Lord Rosebery,[2] but seems in good spirits, & talks, thank heaven, more lucidly than he writes.

I am still sunk in the state of "abrutissement"[3] which always overcomes me when I first come to Europe, but hope to revive sufficiently to send you the promised story for the Spring volume not later than March 1st. It takes six weeks for me to get over the change of climate. We are here for a while amid palms & roses to be with the Bourgets, then we move to Rome.

My husband has revived completely, as he always does in a warm climate, & is quite happy whenever he reads of a blizzard in New York—I do hope you are well, & that 1904 is going to treat you better than its predecessor— Will you please remember me to Mr. Scribner, & ask him to read "Belchamber"?

Yrs Sincerely
    Edith Wharton

Ms:FL

1. Howard Overing Sturgis, London-born (1854), a son of the eminent Bostonian and banker Russell Sturgis, a partner in the powerful London firm of Baring Brothers. Howard had grown up and still lived in the family home in Windsor, Queen's Acre—Qu'Acre, in later allusions. There Henry James, the young Percy Lubbock, and eventually EW were welcome houseguests. Sturgis's novel *Belchamber*, which EW presses (in vain) upon Brownell, was tormentedly autobiographical on one level, and dealt with an unconsummated marriage, adultery, and the death of an illegitimate child. It was published in America by G. P. Putnam's Sons in 1905, and earned a measure of grudging admiration.

2. The references are to the great French comedian, best remembered for his portrayal of Cyrano de Bergerac; and Queen Victoria's strong-featured Prime Minister.

3. Stupefaction.

To Sara Norton

Hyde Park Hotel
London
May 5. [1904]

Dear Sally,

I have sent you no sign of life for the last few weeks, or rather many weeks—but some beggarly post-cards, which at least, I hope, showed you that if inarticulate I was not unforgetful.

I don't quite know when I last wrote, but it was far back in the dreariest winter I have ever spent. I call it so because the Riviera climate brought back the nervous indigestion & bad headaches which I had managed to shake off after years of misery, & I was so depressed by this return of my old ailment that I found it hard to write. Finally I ended off with influenza & laryngitis, & as soon as I was on my legs again we started on an enchanting motor-trip across France to Pau & down to the borders of Spain, & then up through Périgueux, Limoges, Bourges & Blois to Paris. Every step of the way was a delight, for we had perfect weather & saw unforgettable things, but the long days in the open air, & the rush of new impressions, had a stupefying effect, & I could not keep my eyes open at night when we reached our destination. Finally we reached Paris, & after ten hurried & fatiguing days came over to England. We had to leave behind our funny little "Nicette"—(Mitou's future wife—I think I wrote you about her), & my brother[1] took pity on us & offered her a home, where she is very happy, but I miss her beyond words! We had planned to stay in England till nearly the end of June, but I have just heard that *none* of the servants I had last year are coming back, & to get a household together we shall probably have to sail in about four weeks.

We have decided to sell our dear motor, the most perfect of its kind, for we cannot afford to pay the heavy duties, & so we are snatching as many excursions as we can, & so far, luckily, the weather has been good.

Last Sunday we went down to Tring & lunched with the Whitridges in their dear little house, which you doubtless saw last year. Mrs. Ward,[2] whom I am not destined to meet, is of course in Italy—

We did meet, however, Mrs. Woodhouse,[3] who captivated us both, & with whom we are to dine next week. I don't know when I have met an Englishwoman so alive at all points. We are going to take her down to Eton in the motor to see her boy. We are also going to run down to see Henry James, who has just gone back to Rye. He is never in London when we are.

We have one or two lunches & dinners ahead, but of the few people I know the greater number are ill or away or in affliction, & so we have not been out much.

I wish I knew how you are—your last letter, written in March, spoke of high mounds of snow in the streets, & we hear from Mrs. Wharton that the spring has been very backward, & that Lenox is still wintry— I am rather glad, for I shall not miss so many flowers.

This morning we motored down to Cambridge, & saw the exquisite "Backs" in their glory—limes & beeches in fresh radiant leaf, the turf sown with daisies, the gardens glowing with spring flowers, the old mellow walls bathed in pale sunshine. How much we miss in not having such accumulated beauties to feed on now & then at home! I enjoy them so keenly that the contrast makes me miserable, & I think it almost a pity for an American who loves the country ever to come to England.

With which pessimistic sentiment, & much love, I close—

Yr affte E.W.

Ms:BL

1. Harry Jones.

2. The novelist Mrs. Humphry Ward (1851–1920), the former Mary Augusta Arnold (see letter to Sara Norton, January 24, 1902). Her most widely praised novel to this date was *Robert Elsmere*, in 1888, a narrative of conflicting attitudes set in the Oxford she had come to know after marrying T. Humphry Ward,

then an Oxford don. EW would eventually meet Mrs. Ward and visit the Wards' country home, Stocks, near the village of Tring in Buckinghamshire.

3. The former Eleanor Arnold, a daughter of Matthew Arnold, was married to Armine Woodhouse, Member of Parliament from Essex.

To William Crary Brownell

The Mount
Lenox, Mass.
June 25 [1904]

Dear Mr. Brownell,

I return the reviews¹ with many thanks. I have never before been discouraged by criticism, because when the critics have found fault with me I have usually abounded in their sense, & seen, as I thought, a way of doing better the next time; but the continued cry that I am an echo of Mr. James (whose books of the last ten years I can't read, much as I delight in the man), & the assumption that the people I write about are not "real" because they are not navvies & char-women, makes me feel rather hopeless. I write about what I see, what I happen to be nearest to, which is surely better than doing cowboys de chic.... But this is not business. As to yr. letter of June 23, it fills me with compunction. Of course the understanding was that, on our return to Italy, I should get, or take, photos to complete the Backgrounds. But the bad weather in Italy made it impossible for us to go there, on my husband's account, & I should of course have written you that I couldn't get the photos, since they are not of a kind that one can order from a distance.

I am *very* sorry, & make my excuses to you all— Now what shall we do? I have another article, "March in Italy," which is nearly done, & which will make the book of the requisite length, I think—but if you want photos we are at a stand-still.

It is more than likely that we may go to Italy in the winter, for though my husband is so much better, he seems to be so only because we had no cold weather—still, that will not be decided till his Dr. comes home in September—Meanwhile I must leave it to you to decide whether the book shall be put off on the chance of my being able to get photos on the spot next winter (& also do still another article) or whether you want to give up the pictures—

I might get some photos for Italian Backgrounds (the article) but for Splügen impossible!

I am glad Mrs. Brownell is improving at the Pier, & I still hope for a Sunday from you later on—

My hand is all right, thanks—

Yrs Guiltily
    E. Wharton

Wouldn't it have helped "The Descent" to put in the two new stories?

Ms:FL

1. Of *The Descent of Man*, EW's third collection of short stories, published in April 1904.

To Sara Norton

The Nichewaug
Petersham, Mass.
Friday morning—
[August 19, 1904]

Dearest Sally

I am writing you from this most improbable place, where a breakdown has detained us over-night, because, since I rec'd your letter, it has been impossible for me to write before—I found it on arriving at Groton late on Tuesday night, & on Wed. morning I was obliged to rush into Boston to the oculist's. He put bella-donna in my eyes, & made writing impossible for 24 hours— Yesterday at 9 o'c we started for *Deerfield*, whence I intended to telephone you in the evening; but, alas, the motor broke down & it took all the afternoon to repair it, so we had to spend the night here; & today we are going down to Springfield, where I must take the train, as we have people coming to stay.

All this is to explain my silence, which must have surprised you. I am so grieved about your father's illness. What a nightmare to have people arrive just at that moment! I am in hopes that you are now quite relieved about him. I am so glad you found such a good nurse, & one who is acceptable to the patient. Most American nurses are so manner-less that I should throw things at [them] if subjected to their ministra-tions. But I must avoid the subject of America—for I have been spending my first night in an American "Summer hotel," & I despair of the Re-public! Such dreariness, such whining sallow women, such utter absence of the amenities, such crass food, crass manners, crass landscape!! And, mind you, it is a new & fashionable hotel. What a horror it is for a whole nation to be developing without the sense of beauty, & eating bananas for breakfast.

Dear Sally, I do hope things are well with you again— Give many messages from us both to Mr. Norton & write me when you have time—

Yrs ever   E.W.

Ms:BL

To Charles Eliot Norton

The Mount
Lenox, Mass.
July 1 [1905]

Dear Mr. Norton,

The "bath of beauty" through which, as Mr. James said, we journeyed back to Lenox, rounded off most appropriately our few delightful hours at Ashfield.[1]

We came by Goshen & *all* the Hamptons, to Westfield, Huntington, & Becket, reaching here at 1.30 almost surfeited with the loveliness we had passed through—over good roads, by the way! My one regret was that Sally had not the courage to come with us.

Mr James left this morning, carrying away, I think, a real tenderness for this little corner of his big country, & rejoicing so much that he had been with you just before leaving.

We hope to descend to you—or rather ascend to you—again later,
& meanwhile I am ever

Affectionately Yours
    Edith Wharton

Ms:HL

1. The Norton family's country home in Massachusetts, about forty miles
from EW's Lenox. Henry James, spending a few days with the Whartons at
the end of his long tour of the United States, accompanied them on a visit to
Ashfield.

To William Crary Brownell

The Mount
Lenox, Mass.
August 5, 1905

Dear Mr. Brownell,

Even when I sank to the depth of letting the illustrations be put in
the book[1]—&, oh, I wish I hadn't now!—I never contemplated a text
in the title-page.[2] It was all very well for The Valley, where the verse
simply "constated" a fact, but in this case, where it inculcates a moral,
I might surely be suspected of plagiarizing from Mrs. Margaret Sangster's beautiful volume, "Five Days with God."[3]

Seriously, I think the title explains itself amply as the tale progresses,
& I have taken the liberty of drawing an inexorable blue line through
the text.

I am pushing off to the end any reference to what you say about my
story—I am so surprised & pleased, & altogether taken aback, that I
can't decently compose my countenance about it. I was pleased with
bits, myself; but as I go over the proofs the whole thing strikes me as
so loosely built, with so many dangling threads, & cul-de-sacs, & long
dusty stretches, that I had reached the point of wondering how I had
ever dared to try my hand at a long thing— So your seeing a certain
amount of architecture in it rejoices me above everything—my theory

of what the novel ought to be is so exorbitant, that I am always reminded of Daudet's "Je rêve d'un aigle, j'accouche d'un colibri."—[4]

Well— thanks for taking the trouble to write me what you did, & may Moosehead do you all the good in the world—

Yrs Sincerely E. Wharton

I approve choice of frontpiece.

Ms:FL

1. *The House of Mirth*, to be published on October 14, 1905, in a first edition of forty thousand copies.
2. The original epigraph, which EW now deletes, is from Ecclesiastes 7:4: "The heart of the wise is in the house of mourning; but the heart of fools is in the house of mirth."
3. Margaret Sangster (1838–1912) was an extremely popular American poet, one of whose main themes was the proper performance of religious duties.
4. A characteristic reflection by Alphonse Daudet (1840–1897) about his experience as a novelist: "I dream of an eagle, and I give birth to a hummingbird."

To Charles Scribner

The Mount
Lenox, Mass.
November 11, 1905

Dear Mr. Scribner,

It is a very beautiful thought to me that 80,000 people should want to read "The House of Mirth," & if the number should ascend to 100,000 I fear my pleasure would exceed the bounds of decency.

Seriously, I am of course immensely interested & amused by all these "returns," & very grateful to you for sending them to me.—And by the way, I hope you got that photograph I sent you about ten days ago, with my eyes down, *trying to look modest*?! The photographer swore he would send it off punctually, but I have had my doubts, as he hasn't sent me one yet. It was to go direct to Mr. Chapin.

I shall be in town for one day next week—Friday, the 17th—& if by any chance you should want to see me about anything, will you send a line to 23 E. 33d St?—I am going to see Miss Marbury[1] about dramatizing the H. of M., as I am having so many bids for it.

Thanks again for your letter.

Sincerely Yrs
    Edith Wharton

Ms:FL

1. Elisabeth Marbury (1856–1933), friend and companion of Elsie de Wolfe (see letter to Mary Cadwalader Jones, January 7, 1916) and one of the first successful author's agents. Among her clients at this time was the playwright Clyde Fitch.

To William Roscoe Thayer[1]

The Mount,
Lenox, Mass
November 11 [1905]

Dear Professor Thayer,

By a pleasant coincidence, I was talking of you with Robert Minturn[2] a few weeks ago, saying how much I admired your essay on historical methods in the "Atlantic," & how deeply I was indebted to "The Dawn of Italian Independence" for such light on that intricate & engrossing period as I needed in writing my Italian novel.

Judge then, how pleased & surprised I was to receive your letter the other day, & to learn that I had been able to make ever so slight a return for the great pleasure your admirable book has long given me.

I am particularly & quite inordinately pleased with what you say of my having—to your mind—been able to maintain my readers' interest in a group of persons so intrinsically uninteresting, except as a social manifestation. I knew that my great difficulty lay there, & if you think I have surmounted it, I shall go about with a high head.—But—before we leave the subject—I must protest, & emphatically, against the suggestion that I have "stripped" New York society. New York society is still amply clad, & the little corner of its garment that I lifted was meant to show only that little atrophied organ—the group of idle & dull people—that exists in any big & wealthy social body. If it seems more conspicuous in New York than in an old civilization, it is because the whole social organization with us is so much smaller & less elaborate —& if, as I believe, it is more harmful in its influence, it is because fewer responsibilities attach to money with us than in other societies.—

Forgive this long discourse—but you see I had to come to the defense of my own town, which, I assure you, has many mansions outside of the little House of Mirth.

I hope when I am next in Boston I may have the pleasure of thanking you in person for your letter, which I value more than anything my book has brought me.

Sincerely Yrs
    Edith Wharton

I wish you felt a little more kindly toward poor Lily!

Ms:HL

1. William Roscoe Thayer (1859–1923), Boston writer, biographer, and historian.

2. Minturn, afflicted with chronic ill health, was a linguist and a connoisseur of art; he was a member of a leading New York family, and an old friend of EW.

To Edward L. Burlingame

The Mount
November 23 [1905]

Dear Mr. Burlingame,

There is sweet music in "I told you so," when used as you use it! Thank you very much for writing to remind me of your hopeful prognostications—I have not heard from Mr. Brownell since he wrote, about a month ago, a very kind letter to break to me, with all gentleness, the fact that the H. of M. would probably not go above 40,000.—

I am especially glad to find that you think its large circulation a sign of awakening taste in our fellow-countrymen—at least in 100,000 of them. I was almost afraid that, reversing the experience of Saul the son of Kish, I had gone out to seek a kingdom & found all the asses!![1]

I sent Mr. Scribner only the *serious* letters, but I have a trunkful of funny ones which I will bring to town with me. One lady is so carried away that she writes: "I love, not every word in the book, but every period & comma." I hope she meant to insert an "only" after the "not."—

Well, it's all great fun, & you did it all by accepting the Last Giustiniani[2]—do you remember?

    Sincerely Yrs
        Edith Wharton

Ms:FL

1. The reference is to 1 Samuel 9.
2. EW's poem "The Last Giustiniani" was her first work to see print. It was accepted by Edward L. Burlingame for publication in the October 1889 issue of *Scribner's*. The twelve-stanza poem is a piece of historical romance set in eighteenth-century Italy and tells of the last member of the Giustiniani family, who was released from his monkish vows in order to marry and perpetuate his race. The same theme was dramatized in *Guy Domville* (1895), by Henry James, who may have read EW's poem.

To Dr. Morgan Dix[1]

                                        The Mount
                                        Lenox, Mass.
                                        December 5 [1905]

Dear Dr. Dix,

You would have to write in a very different strain to keep me even twenty-four hours from answering your letter; & I must begin by telling you how touched I am that you would have found time to send it, & how proud—yes, quite inordinately so!—that you should have thought my novel worthy of such careful reading & close analysis.—

Few things could have pleased me more than the special form which your commendation has taken; for, lightly as I think of my own equipment, I could not do anything if I did not think seriously of my trade; & the more I have considered it, the more has it seemed to me valuable & interesting only in so far as it is "a criticism of life."—It almost seems to me that bad & good fiction (using the words in their ethical sense) might be defined as the kind which treats of life trivially & superficially, & that which probes deep enough to get at the relation with the eternal laws; & the novelist who has this feeling is so often discouraged by the comments of readers & critics who think a book "unpleasant" because it deals with unpleasant conditions, that it is a high solace & encouragement to come upon the recognition of one's motive. *No* novel worth anything can be anything but a novel "with a purpose," & if anyone who cared for the moral issue did not see in my work that *I* care for it, I should have no one to blame but myself—or at least my inadequate means of rendering my effects.

Social conditions as they are just now in our new world, where the sudden possession of money has come without inherited obligations, or any traditional sense of solidarity between the classes, is a vast & absorbing field for the novelist, & I wish a great master could arise to deal with it—but perhaps I may have a chance to talk of these things with you, for I do not mean to be again in New York without making a very determined effort to see you & Mrs. Dix.

We never stay there long now, because the cold weather is bad for my husband, but we shall be in our house during January, & perhaps we can persuade you & Mrs. Dix to come & dine some night alone so that we may have an unrestrained talk.

I remember with pride your allusion to my little story, "The Reckoning"[2]—& it has always been a great pleasure to me that, in your busy & beneficent life, you have found time to follow with such sympathy what I have tried to do. Believe me, dear Dr. Dix,

Ever sincerely Yrs,
Edith Wharton

Ms:Archives of Trinity Church Parish.

1. Morgan Dix (1827–1908) was rector of Trinity Church in New York from 1862 onwards. His long letter of December 1, 1905, said in part: "This book places you at the head of the living novelists of our country or of the English-

writing authors of our day. It is a terrible but just arraignment of the social misconduct which begins in folly and ends in moral and spiritual death.... To me the reading of your book has been like a walking the wards of some infirmary set apart for the treatment of pestilential disease: the same ghastly wrecks of humanity, the same mephitic odours, the same miasma of afflorescent corruption."

2. "The Reckoning" was contained in *The Descent of Man* of 1904. It is the sad tale of an emancipated young woman who, after jettisoning her husband on the principle of being faithful to her own desires, is herself set aside by her second husband on the same doctrine.

To Sara Norton

Biltmore House[1]
December 26 [1905]

Dear Sally,

The Greek essays[2] reached me on Christmas Eve, & received a very warm welcome, for I know Mr. Butcher's work through his share in the Lang Odyssey, which was our constant companion in our wanderings through the Aegean years ago. I have not read this book, & shall do so with the more appreciation as I have just been reading Pater's Plato[3] & some of the dialogues, & am in the mood for the Hellenic.—Thank you for it, & also for the Christmas card.

The journey here was frightfully fatiguing, but this divine landscape, "under a roof of blue Ionian weather," makes up for all the hardship, & prolongs for me a little the sweet illusion of autumn, which must soon be lost in the horrors of the thrice-loathsome New York.—Yesterday we had a big Xmas fete for the 350 people on the estate—a tree 30 ft high, Punch & Judy, conjuror, presents & "refreshments." It would have interested you, it was done so well & sympathetically, each person's wants being thought of, from mother to last baby.—In this matchless weather the walks thro' the park are a joy I should like to share with you—great sheets of fruited ivy pouring over terrace walls, yellow stars still shining on the bare branches of the nudiflora, jasmine, & masses of juniper, heath, honeysuckle, rhododendron & laurel making an evergreen covert so different from our denuded New England lanes.—

Alas, that it is so far from everything & that beyond the park, as James said, there is only "a vast niggery wilderness."—I hope you had a good Christmas, all of you, & that your father keeps well.

Affly yrs
     E. W.

We are all so delighted to have the Robinsons[4] in New York.

Ms:BL

1. The enormous mansion erected on an estate of 130,000 acres southwest of Ashville, North Carolina, by George Vanderbilt (1862–1914), the son of William Henry Vanderbilt. The architect Richard Morris Hunt worked with Vanderbilt over the plans for the $3,000,000 building; and the landscape gardening so much admired by EW was designed by Frederick Law Olmsted.

2. *Some Aspects of Greek Genius*, by Samuel Henry Butcher, who had made a prose translation of the *Odyssey* with Andrew Lang.

3. *Plato and Platonism* (1893), a collection of lectures by Walter Pater (1839–1894).

4. Probably Corinne Roosevelt Robinson and her husband Douglas Robinson. See letter to Mrs. Robinson, March 2, 1914.

To Sara Norton

                              Curtis Hotel
                              Lenox, Massachusetts
                              Wednesday
                              [February 21, 1906]

Dear Sally,

Alas, that you should not have come! The weather is bright & mild, & even a tired heart (& I have that kind of an organ too) could not feel any effort in doing its work in this spring-like air. I wish I had insisted a little more! What a pleasure it wd have been to talk over together that admirable Ostwald lecture,[1] which greeted me this morning, & which I have already devoured. Ah, how it lifts one up to hear such a voice as that in the midst of all the psychological-pietistical juggling of which your friend W. James is the source & chief distributor! It has a fine Stoic note—the note of Seneca & Epictetus—with the other-regarding experience of the Christian centuries fortifying, not weakening it.—Thank you for sending me such a book.—It refreshed me all the more because I chanced to get out of the library here last night Paulsen's "Introduction to Philosophy,"[2] with a "foreword" by le-dit James—& at the first page I was in the thick of the familiar jargon: "Religion & atheism stand opposite each other not as theories, but as expressions of the will, & differing practical attitudes toward life"—& "humanity will never be satisfied with scientific knowledge to explain its inward relation to reality."—What other kind of knowledge is it capable of receiving? Oh, dear—oh, how slowly the wheels turn, & how often the chariot slips back!—

It is delightful to be here, & see trees against the sky, & *hear only silence.* Thank heaven I can get away from the world in a few hours, when I have the chance. It takes me very little time to shake off the accretions that town forms on one.—If only our winter climate were humane enough to make life in the country less severe! Well, I must stop now, & go over to the Mount.—Thank you again for Ostwald. I do hope you are feeling better.

Affly Yrs   E.W.

Have you read Kuno Fischer's Geschichte der neueren Philosophie?[3] I am just reading the vol. on Schopenhauer, & it is a perfect delight— so lucid & direct in style—almost as good prose as Schopenhauer's— & so full of ideas. There are 9 fat vols, & I'm [two words missing].

Ms:HL

1. *Individuality and Immortality*, a lecture delivered and published in America in 1906, by the German scholar Wilhelm Ostwald.

2. *Introduction to Philosophy*, by Friedrich Paulsen, published originally in 1855 and translated by F. Milly. William James's brief preface praised Paulsen for his "anti-absolutism."

3. The multivolumed history by Kuno Fischer (1824–1907) appeared between 1897 and 1904.

To Robert Grant

884 Park Avenue

February 26 [1906]

Dear Mr. Grant,

Your letter makes me still more regretful that we have had to give up our plan of going to Mr. Dorr[1] for a few days this month.—We had hoped to manage it, but I have been very much tied down by my play,[2] & also by a thrilling fight with our S.P.C.A., which is in such a bad way that its own members have had to lead the attack against it. I was drawn into this fray by the fact that so few people cared enough about it to do the work, & it has taken lots of time, & is not over yet, so Boston fades from the horizon for this year—to my sorrow!—We expect to sail on March 10th, for two months only, & before that I shall be giving Clyde Fitch all the time I can spare from "our dumb friends." (No one who knew my dogs wd have designated the brute creation in that way.) The play is great fun, & I am learning so much that is useful in my own trade that, even if it fails, I shall not regret the work. Mr. Fitch has made a capital scenario, & I do all the dialogue—he absolutely refuses to write a word.—It would be delightful to talk this all over with you, & range through the whole delectable region of *Shop*, where we sometimes meet for pleasant but too-brief hours.—I love the name for your short stories, & I should hold out, if I were you! All the masterpieces of fiction have been pot-boilers, & I think the name a very honourable one.—

I wish I could hear about the new novel—but that will come to pass at the Mount next summer, I hope.—You know you owe us one 1906[3] visit, as well as those due this year!—

Please thank Mrs. Grant for her hospitable message, & believe me ever yrs sincerely

E. Wharton

Ms:BL

1. George Dorr was an editor of the *Century* magazine and a Lenox neighbor of the Whartons.

2. A contract for the play version of *The House of Mirth* had been signed with

the producer Charles Frohman in January 1906. As EW explains below, the dramatization was a collaborative effort with Clyde Fitch (1865–1909), at this time the most popular living American playwright.

3. EW meant to write 1905.

To Sara Norton

884 Park Avenue.
March 1 [1906]

Dear Sally,

We are sailing on the 10th—for Paris first, & then for six weeks in England. But our plans are not very definite, & I am going chiefly for a rest & the kind of mental refreshment that I can get only là bas. Oh, the curse of having been brought up there, & having it ineradically in one's blood! I enjoyed my three days at Lenox very much, & constantly regretted that you were not there with me.—Since my return I have been reading (for the first time!) Sabatier's Saint Francis,¹ & have come across a sentence which amused me greatly, in view of the amount of nervous tissue I have been giving this winter to the cause of the poor animals here.

He is writing (rather apologetically) of Francis's love for his sisters the swallows, & says: "La sympathie de François pour les animaux n'a rien de la *sensiblerie* qu'étalent bruyamment certaines associations contemporaines"! I suppose Sabatier is a neo-Catholic, & under the curious Catholic dread of falling into the heresy that animals have souls—which was Leo XIII's reason for refusing to support the S.P.C.A. work in Italy!

Well—it is rather a sweet hot house atmosphere (Sabatier's) after the strong mountain air of Ostwald's book. I gave the latter to Egerton Winthrop, by the way, & he was profoundly struck by it—as much as I was. I envy you for knowing such a man.—My last days here must be given to the sensiblerie of my S.P.C.A. fight, & to the numerous "last things" before a departure—but do send a line to tell me how you all are, & write me Care Munroe & Co. 7 Rue Scribe while we are away. We expect to be at the Mount by June 15th.

I have been reading Butcher's Aspects of Greek Genius with great

joy—& am now reading Wilamowitz's translation of the Aeschylus Or-
estes trilogy,[2] which promises well. Do you know his translations? Mrs.
H. Ward told me of them.

Yr affte   E. W.

Could you send me another copy of Piépoudré?[3]

Ms:BL

1. *Vie de Saint François d'Assise*, by Paul Sabatier (1858–1928), had appeared
in 1893. Sabatier was in fact a Protestant theologian, and learned in religious
history; but he shared the doctrinal opposition to the heresy mentioned. The
sentence quoted: "The sympathy of Francis for animals has none of the *sentimentality* noisily displayed by certain contemporary associations."

2. The highly regarded translation into German of the *Oresteia* by the distinguished scholar Ulrich von Wilamowitz-Moellendorff was published in 1896.

3. A recently published essay by Charles Eliot Norton, "The Court of Piépoudré." "The mere name makes me want to write a poem," EW told Sara
Norton. "I love these little by-ways of history."

To Sara Norton

The Mount
Lenox, Mass.
(Tuesday August 7 1906)

! ! ! ! ! ! ! Seven minutes from your door we were in a ditch,
& hiring a local "team" to pull us out ! ! ! ! ! As Cook[1] remarked: "It
never rains but it pours over this way!"

Still, it was not very bad, though I couldn't resist this sensational
beginning. About a mile from Ashfield we met a nervous man & woman
in a buggy. Their horse was as calm as a mill-pond, but as soon as they
saw us they turned him up the bank, thus projecting the buggy at right
angles across the narrow road. We tried to squeeze by in the space they
left, but the whole edge of the road gave way under us, & we sank
seven fathom deep in mud! I wish you could have seen Cook look at
his over-turned car!—Well, the neighbourhood soon assembled, the

"team" pulled us out undamaged, the village philosopher remarked: "Thar's a spring under the ro'd just thar," & 35 minutes later we were skimming along as well as ever, & I was saying: "Thank goodness Sally didn't come!"

I said it louder still when, near Pittsfield, a wild rain-storm descended on us, & we raced home the rest of the way with the fire balls crashing behind.

It was *not* a good day for a beginner at motoring, but we took no harm, & finished off the evening by reading the Symposium.

I only hope the invasion of three did not tire your father, & that you will ask Teddy & me again later.

I was sorry you would not let me re-read your poems while I was with you yesterday. I did not want to write about them because I wanted to show you, in detail, just how & where I think they need to be changed. I don't know that I can sum up my meaning on paper, unless by saying that, when you say that you have tried not to be "poetic"— by which, of course, you mean ornate, rhetorical, imagée—I think you are trying to skip a necessary "étape" on the way to Parnassus.—Such bareness as "she neither feels nor sees"[2] is the result of a great deal of writing, of a long & expert process of elimination, selection, concentration of idea & expression. It is not *being simple* so much as being excessively subtle; & the less-practised simplicity is apt to have too loose a "weave." That is the criticism I wanted—with much more explicitness & illustration—to make on your lines, which I should like to re-read with you some day in that light. Personally, I think a long apprenticeship should be given to form before it is thrown overboard—& I don't see why, with your bent, you don't give it. Here is as much as I can make clear without a talk—but that, I hope, will come soon.

Yrs Ever
    E.W

Ms:BL

1. Charles Cook, a young man in his twenties from the adjoining town of Lee, had been taken on as a chauffeur and a mechanic by the Whartons in the summer of 1904.

2. A misquotation of line 6, "She neither hears nor sees," in Wordsworth's "Lucy" poem "A Slumber Did My Spirit Seal."

To Mrs. Alfred Austin[1]

The Mount
Lenox, Mass.
August 14 [1906]

Dear Mrs. Austin,

I hope you received safely the new "Petit Larousse" which I sent you last May from Versailles. As you did not have my address, I know it was impossible for you to let me know if it reached you, & I meant to write a line at the time to announce its coming; but our motor-flight was carrying us, at that moment, so rapidly from point to point, that the time slipped by without my letter's being written.

Though I am always sorry to leave England, we had no cause to repent our change of plan, for our French "giro" was a wonderful success, with only one day's rain to mar it, & in England we heard that the cold weather continued throughout May. We picked up the car at Boulogne, the day after we left Swinford,[2] & went by Arras to Amiens, thence to Beauvais & Rouen, & down the Seine, by Les Andelys, with its strange ghost of a fortress, to Nantes & then to Versailles. From Versailles we went to Fontainebleau, thence to Orléans & down the Loire to Tours; & from Tours, encouraged by the fine weather, we dashed down into Auvergne, seeing by the way the beautiful Indre country, & George Sand's Nohant—We found Auvergne, in some respects, the most interesting thing we had seen in France, with its strange volcanic landscape, its characteristic churches, the terraced vineyards suggesting Italy, & the castles on every hilltop making one feel one's self in Germany. Our time was too short for more than a bird's-eye view, but we mean to go back & see every inch of it some day.

We returned to Paris just in time to *leap* on the steamer, & here we are sunk into our usual monotonous country life, which would be such a surprise to our European friends, who see us only flying from place to place in our eagerness to crowd all we can into our holiday.—Here I write every morning, & then devote myself to horticulture; while Teddy plays golf & cuts down trees.—At present he is off salmon-fishing in Canada, & I am reading Vernon's "Purgatorio"[3] (thanks to you!) with a friend who is as much delighted with it as I was when I saw it at Swinford.—I have sent for the other volumes, which are rather hard to get, & shall be—temporarily!—an authority on Dante by the end of the summer.

I hope that everything has gone very well with both you & Mr. Austin since we saw you. It is always a regret to us both that we cannot welcome you here, & show you some of our pretty New England scenery, of which I am so often reminded in my drives about Swinford.

I am enclosing a new, but not very good, photograph of our garden, & some post-cards of the surrounding "paysage" to give you an idea of the setting in which our lives are spent.—Please think of us, here as everywhere, as two affectionate & appreciative friends, who keep a warm place in their thoughts for Swinford.

Affly Yours
    Edith Wharton

Ms:FL

1. The former Hester Bellair.
2. The Austins' home, Swinford Old Manor in Ashford, Kent.
3. *Readings on the Purgatorio of Dante* (1897), by William Warren Vernon (1834–1919), who also did "readings" on the *Inferno* and the *Paradiso*.

To Robert Grant

Wolcott Hotel
New York
January 4 [1907]

Dear Mr. Grant,

For the last two months I have been writing you letters in my head, about the play, & other topics of equally general interest—& have been prevented from putting the said letters on paper only by the storm & stress—& the literal physical fatigue, too—of finishing "The Fruit of the Tree."[1]

But here comes your note of Sunday to rouse the sense of how much I want to talk to you—& so, with one foot on the ship, & bits of grey matter scattered everywhere between Pittsfield & Paris, I gather up the fragments as best I can, & proceed to thank you for your good wishes & all the nice things you say.

I wish my in-laws would sometimes ask me to stay in Boston, for I always enjoy a dip into that rarefied atmosphere; but they don't, & the temperature of the American hotel is such a source of cold in the head & heat in the temper to me that I just stay away.

I wanted, especially, to tell you volumes about the play,[2] which most of my friends carefully avoid mentioning in my presence, as though it were a recently-deceased child (& an illegitimate one at that!), while I am thirsting to discuss the oddities of its production, the causes of its failure, & everything connected with its brief & pathetic career. But it would take several sheets of "Authors' Pad" to do justice to the subject, & I will only say that the adventure leaves me without a regret (except for good, kind Fitch & the actors) because I learned so much from it, for my work, & in a general way, that I feel as if I'd robbed Frohman in his sleep!

I'm very sorry about your insomnia, by the way (see how nicely I manage my transitions!)—I had a brief taste of it this autumn, & can picture the horrors of the real thing. I wish you could step on the "Amerika" with us tonight, & take a few weeks off.—I am glad the new book advances, quand même. There is nothing like the fun of it, is there? Ten chapters to the good, & no feeling of discouragement I regard, from my loose N. Y. standpoint, as promise of great things. I find that, with practice, one does get to judge one's self objectively.

Before we leave literature, by the way, I must tell you of the nicest thing that Mr. Scribner did the other day. You may remember my asking you, over a year ago, what price I ought to put on the serial rights of my next novel (which turned out to be the F. of the Tree). You said $8000, & the Scribners agreed; but the other day Mr. Scribner sent for me, & said the success of the H. of M. had been greater than they expected, & had consequently increased the value of the next born; & that they proposed to pay me $10,000 instead of $8,000; & thereupon he handed me the cheque!

Publishers come in for such all round abuse that I feel as if this ought to be proclaimed aloud, for the sake of the act itself, & also of the way in which it was done.

Teddy sends you many messages of regret for having missed you in Boston, but we look forward to seeing you & Mrs. Grant at the Mount next summer.

Thanks for your book suggestions. I send in return "Sex & Charac-ter" by Otto Weininger,[3] & Shaw's new book "Dramatic Opinions."

Yrs sincerely
        E. Wharton

Good luck to you all for 1907!

Ms:BL

1. The novel was published in October 1907.

2. *The House of Mirth* opened in Detroit on September 14, 1906, to a full house and a great deal of applause. The New York opening was at the Savoy Theater on the night of October 22, with Fay Davis as Lily Bart and a cast that included Grant Mitchell and Lumsden Hare. EW thought them all poorly rehearsed. The *New York Times* review called the work "a doleful play," and in the *Herald*'s opinion it was "not a success." The play closed after a few per-formances.

3. *Sex and Character*, by Otto Weininger (1880–1903). This book, by the twenty-three-year-old writer, was an electrifying success in Europe, and was drawn upon for four decades. It maintained that women were by nature (or character) physical and brainless, and the more so, the more feminine. Men became more spiritual as they became more male; and homosexuality was the ideal condition. "Women are matter, which can assume any shape." Woman, in her passion for coupling, was simply expressing the "endless striving of nothing to be something."

To Eunice Maynard[1]

An Bord der "Amerika"
den January 7 [1907]

Dear Eunice,

This being our third consecutive smooth day, I think I had better take advantage of it to thank you for that wonderful basket of "delicatessen," which surprised & enchanted me so much by yielding up olives & their oil, & various other precious essences, instead of the traditional harvest of grape-fruit & mandarins which might well be named "The Fruit of the Sea."

It was really very dear & clever of you to collect all these appetizing things, & if I have a choice among them, I think I thank you most for the olive oil, as the salad on board ship is always drier than the champagne.

We are really having a good rest after those wild N.Y. days (you had a sample!), for this ship is "demoralizingly comfortable," as H. James says of England, & I am rest-curing like a lady, in a Louis XVI boudoir (incidentally converted into T.W.'s bedroom at night), with a writing-desk, a pink shaded lamp, curtains of vieux-rose silk, & a red azalea blooming on the centre table!—After the Wolcott it seems like heaven, or a salon in "The Fighting Chance," & I can hardly bear to think of leaving it so soon. We have a daily paper to keep us in touch with land, but the crowning charm is the presence, at my bedside, of a telephone that *never rings*!!!

Thanks again, dear Eunice, for the good things & the good thoughts—and au revoir to you all in Paris in April.

Affly Yrs
Edith W.

Ms:LA

1. EW had known the former Eunice Ives in Lenox, where she spent summers with her parents. In 1903, Eunice married Walter Maynard (b. 1871), director, by inheritance, of a New York publisher of school books. EW and the Maynards were warm friends over several decades.

To W. Morton Fullerton

58 R. de Varenne
Thursday Evening
[Spring 1907]

Dear Mr. Fullerton,

Many thanks for what you have done about the book—I sent at once for M. Du Bos,[1] who tells me that the ms is now being read by the "Temps"[2]—but, as it is improbable that they will be willing to receive the volume "en feuilleton" without some "coupures,"[3] & as we are unwilling to make them, I should like very much to know if there is any chance of being admitted to the Revue de Paris[4] within the next six or seven months. If there were such a chance, I see no reason why we should not submit the duplicate ms *unofficially* to Mr. Rivoire,[5] with the understanding that we can do nothing definite till we hear the answer of the Temps.

Will you think this over, & we can talk of it when you come tomorrow?

Sincerely Yrs,
  Edith Wharton

Ms:UT

1. Charles Du Bos (1882–1939), a gifted young critic plagued by sometimes imaginary ill health, was a protégé of Paul Bourget, who introduced him to EW as a possible translator of *The House of Mirth*. (On Paul Bourget, see letter to Sara Norton, December 18, 1907, note 1.) EW agreed, took to Du Bos at once and worked with him on the task. This is the "ms" which was being considered for publication.
2. *Le Temps*: the famous French newspaper begun in 1861. It maintained high standards of literature and criticism.
3. "en feuilleton" . . . "coupures": serially, without some cuts.
4. A distinguished monthly literary review, founded in 1894.
5. Probably André Rivoire (1872–1930).

To Sara Norton

58 Rue de Varenne
April 21 [1907]

Dear Sally,

Since last writing I have to thank you for the "Spelling Bee"[1] & for the interesting account of the Longfellow centenary. I am so glad Mr. Thayer recorded it, for he wrote so sympathetically, but it seemed to me that Mr. Higginson, in his estimate of the poet, showed very little of the "moderation" praised by Mr. Thayer![2]—

I am very sorry to hear that your father has had a bad cold since then, & also that you have been worried about your brother Eliot. What a "série noire"! It seems time for your household to sail into calmer waters, & luckily things do alternate in human affairs & peace generally follows turmoil—but often elle se fait attendre!—

I wish indeed you could have been with us at dear Nohant, which I hope H.J. intends to celebrate.³—I thought of you again at Port Royal, where we went last week, when Gaillard Lapsley⁴ was staying with us. He wanted to make a little motor trip near Paris, & we agreed that there was no objective point that appealed more strongly to the imagination, so Mr. James & he & I went out there. It is a touching poetic little valley, with the merest relics, as you know, of the monastery & church, & though, at Grignan, I felt that nothing could be more revolting than the destructive rage of the Revolution, the cold fury which had passed a law decreeing the ruin of Port Royal was ten times more odious when one was face to face with its work.—

Our motor trip ended as brilliantly as it had begun.—We came back through the Morvan, by Avallon, Vézelay & Auxerre. But perhaps I wrote you of this?—I have an idea that I sent you a line when we got back to Paris.—We were deeply impressed by the beauty & the strongly marked *personality* of Burgundy. What a splendid province!

Your friend Fullerton, whom we see frequently, is writing a series of charming articles on the Rhône valley in the Revue de Paris. Do you ever see it? He is very intelligent, but slightly mysterious, I think.

Do you think Owen Wister's book will help on the Cause? I hope so—but I did not think it quite as amusing as you do. And then it irritates me to feel that flippancy is the only tone in which a serious subject of any kind may be made interesting to our public.—Owen Wister wrote me in the autumn that he thought there was no use in writing seriously on the subject, & I suppose he is right. But it is discouraging.

I hope Lily, your father & all the rest of the household are progressing toward complete health, & that the furies have let up on poor Shady Hill "pour de bon."

Ever yrs affly
    E.W.

Ms:BL

1. *How Doth the Simple Spelling Bee?* (1907), by Owen Wister (1860–1938), novelist and short story writer, author of *The Virginian* (1902).

2. A celebration of the hundredth anniversary of the birth of Henry Wadsworth Longfellow had taken place in Cambridge on February 24. (In 1879, Longfellow had passed along several poems by Edith Jones to William Dean Howells at the *Atlantic Monthly*. Howells chose one of them for the magazine.) Among those participating in the event were William Roscoe Thayer and Thomas Wentworth Higginson (1823–1911), the commander of a black regiment in the Civil War, man of letters and editor with Mabel Todd of the poetry of Emily Dickinson.

3. Henry James had come over from England to join EW and Teddy on a whirlwind "motor-flight" south to Nohant, the home of George Sand, and then through Poitiers down to Pau, and north through Avignon to Lyons and Dijon.

4. Gaillard Thomas Lapsley (1871–1949) graduated from Harvard and stayed on to pursue graduate study in medieval English history. He eventually was appointed to teach that field at Trinity College in Cambridge. EW and Lapsley first met in 1904, by which time Lapsley had a solid reputation as a history scholar and had become notably English (he pronounced his name "Gillyard"). Their friendship was one of the closest and longest-lasting in EW's life.

To Charles Eliot Norton

Paris
May 15 [1907]

Dear Mr Norton,

Our modest post-card brought an unexpectedly generous return in the shape of your delightful letter, the enjoyment of which I was able to share with Mr. James before he left us last week.[1]—

The impression of those tormented, sinister capitals in the choir of Chauvigny was so strange & haunting that we felt we must share it with one of those "che sanno"—I only wish we could have shown you the whole church, on its proud fortified cliff. Our whole journey through the Poitou was full of wonder for me, & as for the return by the Morvan, when I saw for the first time Avallon, Vézelay & Auxerre, there was a sense of suffocation from the excess of suggestions received. This France is so rich, so varied, so packed with old "états d'âme" & their visible expressions!

Well—we are returning to a country where the atmosphere is thin enough to permit my over-crowded sensations to "settle"!—

Mr James left us last week, after giving us two months of a companionship unfailingly delightful, wise & kind.—The more one knows him the more one wonders & admires the mixture of wisdom & tolerance, of sensitiveness & sympathy, that makes his heart even more interesting to contemplate than his mind. He has gone on to Italy for a few weeks, & after that he says he returns to England *for life.*

We give up our delightful apartment today, & move to my brother's,[2] to remain with him till we sail at the end of the month; & by June 8th we hope to be at Lenox.

I venture to enclose a short word to Sally, on the subject of a commission she asked me to attend to.—I hope real spring has come to you at last, & that you are all feeling better, & beginning to shake off the bad memories of the winter.

Teddy wishes to be very particularly remembered to you, & I am, dear Mr. Norton,

Affly Yours ever,
  Edith Wharton

I am so glad you liked the little "Motor-flight."[3] I hope to do another on my return. I can't write here!

Ms:HL

1. After their return to Paris, and another briefer excursion, James had stayed on for a month: "One of the most agreeable times I have ever had in Paris," James wrote, "through living in singularly well-appointed privacy in this fine old Rive Gauche quarter."

2. Harry Jones's apartment at 3 Place des Etats-Unis, in the 16th *arrondissement.*

3. The first of the articles to be collected in *A Motor-Flight Through France* in 1908.

To William Crary Brownell

Lenox

July 29 [1907]

Oh, dear   .   .   .   oh, dear   .   .   .   The dots in the page-proofs are as far apart as ever   .   .   .   one could drive a coach & four between them. I have returned proofs with an urgent marginal note & a diagram. *Please* reinforce by a few remarks, & show them *any* French novel!   E.W.

Ms: Postcard, FL

To W. Morton Fullerton

The Mount

Lenox, Mass.

October 15 [1907]

Dear Mr. Fullerton,

We are so pleased that you have not forgotten your promise to look us up—especially as dear H. J. in a letter received last week, sceptically prophesied:—"You won't see Fullerton."

We shall be delighted to see you here when you have pronounced your discours at Bryn Mawr[1] (& do please bring me a copy of it, won't you?), & you will find a good train leaving New York at   , & another in the afternoon at   .[2] I don't know, on second thought, why I call either good, for the train service between here & town has been execrable this last year; but at any rate, they are the best we have, & the morning one is not likely to be more than half an hour late!

We shall hope for you, then, either on Friday evening, or on Saturday morning, & your "few hours" will, I trust, be elastic enough to extend over Sunday, as I want to show you some of our mountain land-scapes, & have time for some good talks too.[3]

I am so glad you are going to talk about dear James at Bryn Mawr.

Yours sincerely

Edith Wharton

I enclose time-table.

Ms:UT

1. A lecture on the literary career of Henry James, occasioned by the ongoing New York Edition of his work. It was expanded into a long, appreciative and penetrating essay on the Edition and James's unique contributions to the art of the novel. The essay appeared in the April 1910 issue of the *Quarterly Review*.

2. EW obviously intended to fill in the train times after consulting the schedule, but forgot to do so.

PART THREE

58 Rue de Varenne
1907–1910

Introduction

❀

IN DECEMBER 1907, Edith Wharton was back in Paris at the 58 Rue de Varenne apartment. The atmosphere, she said, produced a "demoralizing happiness" in her. The state of mind was due not only to the Faubourg surroundings but also to the presence in the city of Morton Fullerton, an American journalist on the staff of the Paris office of the London *Times*. Fullerton, born in Norwich, Connecticut, in 1865, had graduated from Harvard after a brilliant undergraduate career, had served as literary adviser on a Boston newspaper and then gravitated to London, where he found a job on the *Times*. In his London years, he became an ardent disciple of Henry James and a friend of Oscar Wilde; he also enjoyed a liaison with Margaret Brooke, the Ranee of Sarawak. In the early 1890s, Fullerton was transferred to the Paris office of the *Times*, from which, among other events, he covered the two trials of Alfred Dreyfus. He was married briefly in 1903 to a French *chanteuse*; and was otherwise involved erotically with a number of individuals of both sexes. Fullerton's combination of dreamy idealism, literary sophistication, and sexual vitality proved widely appealing.

Edith Wharton met him in the spring of 1907, and thought him intelligent but mysterious; he was of some help in securing a publisher for the French *House of Mirth*. After Fullerton visited The Mount in the autumn, Edith began a journal addressed to him; in it, she confided the progress of the love affair that came fully into being in the first months of 1908, the scene being Paris and its environs. The course of the affair during the years 1908 to 1910, particularly as it was reflected in the letters to Fullerton, has been sketched in the general introduction, and need not be repeated here.

While carrying on the clandestine adventure and working with her

usual zeal on short stories, travel articles, a novel, and several translations, Edith Wharton also kept up a full and varied social life—both in
the literary and aristocratic *salons* like the one in the Rue de Grenelle
conducted by her new friend Comtesse Rosa de Fitz-James, and in the
well-populated American community in Paris. In the latter part of 1908,
after a summer in Lenox, Edith came to England, where, in part through
the kindly offices of Henry James, she was taken into the heart of the
Edwardian world and introduced to its most prominent writers, its political leaders, its titled and warmly hospitable London hostesses, its
garden parties. Perhaps never before in the English-speaking world, and
certainly never since, has there been such an easy and fruitful mingling
of the social, political, literary, and artistic.

Visits to England, indeed, punctuated this period in Edith Wharton's
life, though one tends to think of it as the era of Paris and Morton
Fullerton. In the summer of 1909, she had another memorable social
whirl. "I didn't see very many people," she writes Sara Norton, and
then goes on to mention Sir Ian Hamilton, various Trevelyans, the
Humphry Wards, George and Fanny Prothero, Ruth Draper, Lady
Stanley, and of course Henry James. The social chapter was tucked in
between a night with Fullerton at the Charing Cross Hotel in London,
about which Edith wrote a glowingly candid poetic account, and a month-
long English fling with her lover.

She crossed the channel again in March 1910 for a very different
reason: to bring such comfort as she could to Henry James, who was in
a condition of suicidal melancholia. It was by all odds the darkest hour
in James's life, and the cause of it (as it seems from this distance) was
the silence and indifference that had greeted the New York Edition of
his writings, a venture on which James had lavished enormous amounts
of time, planning, and rhetorical energy. James in fact recovered, and
was able to survive the death of his brother William in June. By the
year's end, he and Edith Wharton were dining together pleasurably—
Walter Berry and Morton Fullerton sharing the table with them—in the
Belmont Hotel in New York City.

The New York visit was for the purpose of seeing Teddy Wharton
off to California and the start of a trip around the world with the family
friend Johnson Morton. The final component in Edith Wharton's life in
this time was the health and the activities of her husband. In the winter

of 1908, Teddy, now fifty-eight years old, began to have fits of nervous depression, accompanied by headaches and irascibility. The development corresponded exactly with the start of Edith Wharton's intimate relations with Morton Fullerton; that affair was even made possible, or made easier, when Teddy betook himself to an American spa for treatment. He spent most of 1909 in Lenox and Boston; when he reappeared in Paris in November, it was evident that he was seriously ill. He suffered from acute pains in almost every part of his body; on the mental side, he alternated between wild exuberance and frozen gloom. Teddy then revealed suddenly that he had embezzled $50,000 from Edith Wharton's trust fund, of which he was a trustee, had bought a house and property in a fashionable section of Boston, and had established his mistress there. He had lost the balance of the money, apparently, in bad investments.

In the spring of 1910, Teddy, under several kinds of pressure, entered the Kuranstalt Bellevue in Kreuzlingen, Switzerland. The stay there did him little good, however, and the next move decided on—by Edith Wharton and her medical advisers—was to send Teddy off on a long trip. With the faithful and watchful Johnny Morton, Teddy left New York on October 18, and Edith sailed for France ten days later.

To Robert Grant

> The Mount,
> Lenox, Mass.
> November 19 [1907]

Dear Mr. Grant,

It is very good of you to take time to write me such an interesting & really helpful analysis of my book[1]—but before thanking you for it, I must throw in a parenthesis to say that I have never yet learned what became of the copy originally meant for you. I rec'd my "advance" copies just before going away on a motor-trip of a week, & they were laid out (but that sounds too mortuary!) with the addresses of the privileged recipients attached, to be sent immediately, but when I got your note on my return the butler (who is the family forwarding agent) said that no volume had been found addressed to Judge Grant! My only solution is that someone staying in the house may have carried it off— but I am very anxious to know how *you* knew it was not lost in the mail? I don't think I can wait till we meet to hear that!!—

I am very much pleased that you like the construction of the book, & I more than agree with you that I haven't been able to keep the characters from being, so to speak, mere *building-material*. The fact is that I am beginning to see exactly where my weakest point is.—I conceive my subjects like a man—that is, rather more architectonically & dramatically than most women—& then execute them like a woman; or rather, I sacrifice, to my desire for construction & breadth, the small incidental effects that women have always excelled in, the episodical characterisation, I mean. The worst of it is that this fault is congenital, & not the result of an ambition to do big things. As soon as I look at a subject from the novel-angle I see it in its relation to a larger whole, in all its remotest connotations; & I can't help trying to take them in, at the cost of the smaller realism that I arrive at, I think, better in my short stories. This is the reason why I have always obscurely felt that I didn't know how to write a novel. I feel it more clearly after each attempt, because it is in such sharp contrast to the sense of authority with which I take hold of a short story.—I think it ought to be a warning to stop; but, alas, I see things more & more from the novel-angle, so that I'm enclosed in a vicious circle from which I suspect silence to be the only escape.

I am very glad, though, that you *do* feel a structural unity in the thing, for some people have criticized the book for the lack of this very thing, & that rather discouraged me. After all, one knows one's weak points so well, that it's rather bewildering to have the critics overlook them & invent others that (one is fairly sure) don't exist—or exist in a less measure.

Your letter is very illuminating, & I am very grateful to you for taking the trouble to write it. It will be a real help to me when I try again.

I am sorry to hear you have reached a "blind alley" in your book. What a hateful trade it is! But suddenly a door will open for you in the blank wall.

I am delighted to hear that your young athlete is safe & sound, & Teddy will rejoice in the New York paper's characterization of him. He (the pronoun refers to Teddy) is off shooting now, & comes back only four or five days before we sail.

Thanks again, dear Mr. Grant. Yrs ever sincerely Edith Wharton

Ms:BL

1. *The Fruit of the Tree*, published on October 19, in a first edition of fifty thousand copies.

To Sara Norton

Paris
December 18 [1907]

Dear Sally— Your letter of farewell reached me on the steamer, & the sun was shining so brightly & balmily when we sailed that your picture of turbid waves lapping sullenly against the prow didn't at all fit—but by night-fall the said turbid waves were upon us, & they shook & harried & hunted us from one continent to the other. We really had a brutal crossing, but it was a very short one, luckily, as we were on a fast boat—& already, in less than a week, the horrors have faded, & I am sunk in the usual demoralizing happiness which this atmosphere produces in me. Dieu que c'est beau after six months of eye-starving! The tranquil majesty of the architectural lines, the wonderful blurred winter lights, the long lines of lamps garlanding the avenues & the quays—je l'ai dans mon sang! We have been lucky, too, in having lots of sunshine to see it by, & last Sunday my brother carried us off in his motor to see an old Louis XIII château down in Normandy, & all the way the fields were so green, with cattle grazing in them, & the lights on the Seine so tender & hazy, that it seemed more like late March than late Dec.—& in the wayside gardens the tea-roses & chrysanthemums were still in bloom!

We shall be with my brother till next week, & so far I have not seen or done much, or looked people up. But tomorrow we go to the Academy to see Bourget[1] receive Maurice Donnay,[2] & in the evening to a dinner which the B.s are giving to Donnay, & where there will be some rather interesting people.

My little translator, Charles Du Bos, is in the seventh heaven because

"Chez les Heureux du Monde"[3] is making itself immensely talked about, & his translation is much praised. The volume is to come out in March, I believe.

I shall have more amusing things to tell you later, when we are in the rue de Varenne & have begun to see people. This is only meant to carry you all—rather tardily, I fear—our best wishes & most affectionate thoughts for Christmas.—

I hope your father is better now, & has quite recovered from his acute attack of birthdayitis.

Affly Yr E. W.

Please give many messages to Mrs. Kuhn[4] when you or Lily see her.

Do you know Mr. Baker, this year's Hyde lecturer at the Sorbonne? He has asked to be brought to see me, & is to come tomorrow, I believe.

Ms:BL

1. Paul Bourget (1852–1935), novelist, essayist, and Academician, was at this time one of the leading men of letters in France. EW had known him since 1893, when Bourget, with his wife, the former Minnie David, visited Newport.

2. Maurice Donnay (1859–1945) was the author of a number of elegant comedies about Parisian life. He was elected to the French Academy in 1907.

3. The French title of *The House of Mirth*.

4. A friend of the Nortons whom EW admired for her courageous bearing during a long and protracted illness.

To Edward L. Burlingame

58 Rue de Varenne
January 27, 1908

Dear Mr. Burlingame,

I shall be sending home next week to my type-writer a story of about 12,000 words (or perhaps a little more) called "The Pretext."

I will tell her to send it directly to you, knowing that you will make allowances for inevitable queer misreadings, & also for the lack of final revision.—Then you can either return the copy to me for revision, or, if you prefer, have it printed, & let me work my will on the galleys.— I suggest this latter alternative because I think you said you were rather badly off for short stories.—

I think of sending you a shorter one—"The Verdict"—in a month or six weeks.—I write in great haste, to catch the post, but with mille amitiés to you all from both of us.

Sincerely Yrs
E Wharton

I am trying to get Mr. Morton Fullerton to finish & send you an admirable article on Henry James which he has been writing, because I thought it would come out in the magazine so opportunely just now. He says just what I have always been wanting to say about the great man.—If the idea "vous va" I will try once more to get him to give the last touches.—I have got a lot of my friends here to subscribe for the "definitive edition," which is an admirable piece of book-making.[1] Everyone likes it.

Ms:FL

1. The twenty-four volumes of *The Novels and Tales of Henry James*—labeled the New York Edition by James himself—had begun to appear in December 1907. The edition was published by Scribners.

To W. Morton Fullerton

58 Rue de Varenne
Sunday
[January 13, 1908]

Dear Mr. Fullerton,

Do you care for the Italian theatre—& if yes, will you go with me on the 13th to see La Figlia di Iorio?[1] I am going to as many of the performances as possible, & as my husband objects to the language, I am obliged to throw myself on the charity of my friends. We should be very glad if you would dine with us first at 7.30.

Sincerely Yrs,
    E. Wharton

Ms:UT

1. A tragic drama by Gabriele d'Annunzio, first performed in 1904.

To William Crary Brownell

58 Rue de Varenne
February 24, 1908

Dear Mr. Brownell,

I never thought that proof-reading could become a pleasure; but it has been made so by your sympathetic & stimulating marginal notes. What a delightful way of corresponding with you!—You have lifted me really out of the depths about my little articles. I had been plunged there by Mr. Fullerton (a past master on questions of Burgundian topography & history) who, after insisting on reading two of the chétif little efforts, genially remarked: "The idea is charming, if you'd only put something into the articles."

Well, it seems I *did*, for those who have eyes to see; for I don't want any other appreciation, cher maître, than yours. As to your critical suggestions, need I say that I concur? Only, by my comparison between the thick-set "prudent" French Romanesque, & the late Gothic, I didn't mean to say—& do I quite say?—that the former was better construction; only that, where it *has* survived, it does give a greater sense of durability. "Pas?"—

I am especially touched that you shd have noticed & liked what I said about the incipient Gothic of Vézelay—I felt that so deeply that I did hope to be given the grace to say it!—

I think I'll omit the preface. It *is* too short, & I can't think of a way of lengthening it.

The "Heureux du Monde" are going crescendo, & the "Fruit" is to be translated by the Comtesse de Galard, who is an experienced translator, & will do it well, I fancy. It is a great surprise to me that there should be a demand for it, but they seem to think so.—

Would you mind telling Mr. Burlingame from me that I will give him a definite answer in another week or so about the serial for next Jany? —I'm afraid it won't be favorable, for my husband has been very poorly again for the last six weeks—much as he was four years ago—& this has upset my working plans, & seems likely to unsettle things for some time to come.

Thanks again for those precious annotations.

Yrs ever sincerely
E. Wharton

Ms:FL

To W. Morton Fullerton

[Late February 1908]

Mon ami, Don't let me drag you out at such an early hour tomorrow! What I want to speak to you about will keep till Saturday . . .

Unless, indeed, I can be of use in carrying you to your Ministère, & we can talk en route? I shall have the motor here at 10,30, at any rate, as I have des courses à faire.

We ought to start for le Bréau[1] at about 10 o'c on Saturday.

Thursday eve'g—I have found in Emerson (from Euripides, I suppose) just the phrase for you—& *me*. "The moment my eyes fell on him I was content."[2]

Ms:UT

1. Le Bréau, on the road to Fontainebleau, was the hospitable home of the expatriate American couple Walter and Matilda Gay. The former was a painter of genuine accomplishment, with a particular talent for architectural watercolors. Matilda Gay was the daughter of William Travers, a leading light in the old New York society Edith Jones had grown up in.

2. From Emerson's "Character," in *Essays* (2d ser.). The remark is part of an imagined dialogue with Iole, the daughter of King Eurytus, with whom the famous Greek hero Hercules fell in love. " 'O Iole! how did you know that Hercules was a god?' 'Because,' answered Iole, 'I was content the moment my eyes fell on him.' " The basis is in fact Sophocles: Iole appears as a captive maiden in *The Trachiniae*.

To Charles Eliot Norton

58 Rue de Varenne
March 2 [1908]

Dear Mr. Norton,

I was delighted to get your charming letter by hand of Sally, but distressed to think that the obligation to write it should all this time have been looming on your horizon.—I was more than thanked by the note you sent me before we sailed, had thanks been needed in return for the expression of affection I was so glad to have an excuse for making!—

Since I last wrote to Sally, Teddy has quite recovered from his attack of neurasthenia, & is in his "assiette ordinaire"; but his troublesome gout still persists, & the Dr. thinks that only baths will really cure it, as the gout medicines have exhausted their efficacy.—There is no good cure here to which one can go at this season, & he thinks of sailing a few weeks before me, & taking the baths at the Hot Springs early in April, as he is most anxious not to be laid up this summer. If he does this, I shall stay on here till the lease of this apartment expires, & then perhaps go to my brother for a short time, & sail about May 20th.— But we shall not decide for another week.—

When Sally last wrote she asked me to ask Mr. Fullerton about the fate of the Times.—Will you tell her from me that he has been almost as much in the dark as the public, but he dined here last week, & met Mr. Frederick Macmillan,[1] fresh from London, who was much better informed than the Times office here, & who fears that Harmsworth[2] (worse than Pearson!) will buy the paper. In that case, Mr. Fullerton & the other correspondents would probably all leave, & they are naturally anxious at present.—Mr. Macmillan seemed to think that something would be decided very shortly.—

Will you please also thank Sally for sending me the various articles on my namesake's play, & also the "Violet Ray" article, which I had already, & which is most interesting.—I wonder if she has seen "Darwinism Today" by Kellogg?[3] I am told it is admirable.—

You will both be amused to hear that my verses on "The Old Pole Star" have called forth a burst of praise from Professor David Todd of Amherst,[4] the astronomer, who invites me to write a sequel on Vega, "the Polaris of the future"—& winds up eloquently, & elegantly:—

"Our cold facts (astronomical, he means) are staggering enough, & poetic too; but it takes a mighty dainty word-juggler to put them in acceptable metre."—

We see very interesting people here, & I like the life more & more. I like especially André Chevrillon,[5] Taine's nephew, whose admirable books on India & the East you probably know, & who is a man of the finest *quality* all through. Mr. Victor Bérard,[6] the author of the big book "Homère et les Phéniciens," is another of the same kind, but so desperately hard-worked that one can hardly see him.—And in society the average of intelligence is certainly higher than elsewhere, & one is less likely to spend a dull evening.

I wonder if you saw Mr. Tardieu,[7] & found him as cheery & companionable as we did?—Mr. Berry[8] wrote me that his prophecies of war between Japan & the U.S. were considered rather ill-advised, & that Jusserand was disturbed.—Did you get that impression in Cambridge?

I was glad to hear from Sally that Lily[9] was quite convalescent again.

This carries a great deal of love to you all, & many messages from Teddy—& for you, dear Mr. Norton, the affectionate thoughts of your friend

 Edith

Ms:HL

 1. Frederick Macmillan (1851–1936) was chairman of Macmillan & Company, the London publishing house. He would be knighted in 1909.

 2. A fierce struggle for ownership and control of the London *Times* was in

progress, the chief contenders being Alfred Charles Harmsworth, Lord North-cliffe (born 1865) and Cyril Arthur Pearson (born 1866), already the proprietor of a number of English newspapers. On March 2, the day of this letter, Harms-worth brought things to a climax with an offer of £320,000; a London court then decided in his favor. C. F. Moberly Bell, who had energetically aided Harmsworth throughout the complex maneuverings, became managing director of the *Times*. The identity of Harmsworth as the new proprietor was officially kept secret, but it is clear from EW's letter that at least some outside the *Times* circle knew of it.

3. *Darwinism Today: A Discussion of Present-Day Scientific Criticism of the Darwin-ian Selection Theories*, by Vernon Lyman Kellogg (1867–1937), published in 1907.

4. David Todd (1855–1939), who had been professor of astronomy at Am-herst College since 1892, was earning worldwide recognition for his astronom-ical studies, particularly his studies of eclipses. In 1879, he had married Mabel Loomis of Washington, D.C. Soon after the couple settled in Amherst in 1881, Mabel Todd entered into a long affair with Austin Dickinson, the older brother of Emily Dickinson. Mabel Todd became the most important editorial figure in the publication of Emily Dickinson's writings.

EW's twenty-line poem meditates on the polestar as a guide to travelers and, by extension, to the aspiring human race.

5. André Chevrillon (1864–1957), the nephew (as EW says) of Hippolyte Taine, the extraordinarily influential historian who had died in 1893, was a man of letters and a critic who introduced Kipling and Meredith, among others, to French readers.

6. A noted Greek scholar and director of the Ecole des Hautes Etudes in Paris.

7. André Tardieu (1876–1945), the author of several brilliant articles on the political scene and about to take part in that scene. He was a close friend of Morton Fullerton.

8. Walter Van Rensselaer Berry was born in 1859, grew up in Albany and graduated from Harvard in 1881. Edith Jones met him in Bar Harbor, Maine, in the summer of 1883, but the friendship did not develop until 1897, when Berry became EW's literary counselor and adviser on style for *The Decoration of Houses* and the early stories and novels. He had been practicing law in Wash-ington since 1884, with a special skill in international law.

9. Sara Norton's sister Elizabeth.

To W. Morton Fullerton

Friday Eve'g
[Early March 1908]

I am so glad, Dear, to have had that little word from you.—Some day I hope you will take the great plunge.[1] There are so many reasons for it in your case—reasons of character as well as of mind. The sense that you are part of a great machine, & not an independent force, will end, after a time, in dulling the finest things in you, & in weakening the strong. It will make you more & more indifferent to values & feelings to which you are naturally sensitive, & by impoverishing you thus will dispose you more & more to accept small passing compensations & satisfactions in place of the long effort & the large achievement for which you were made. Nothing could be more disastrous to a heart & mind like yours than to accept the small change of life in place of one of its big rewards. It is natural enough—in your situation, & in such a dissolvent as this place—that you should gradually resign yourself to such a bargain, & end one day by finding that you can no longer forego the small change, & must therefore give up the hope of the big reward. But you will never be completely satisfied, you will always feel the finer things, & know what you have missed—& hear the echo of the voices that called to you.

Isn't there a little truth in this guess?—

As to our possible trip next week, *that* will help you in a small way, by giving you for a moment a different angle of vision; & if you can make it, you will feel more & more the need of the big plunge.

Don't smile at this letter. I don't know many people who are worth having it written to them—

I'm so glad the article is well started!

Ms:UT

1. I.e., to leave the London *Times*, especially in view of possible changes.

To W. Morton Fullerton

Wed Evening
[58 Rue de Varenne
Early March 1908]

Do you want me to lunch with you tomorrow, cuor mio? Getting home just now, I find myself put-off by Rosa,[1] owing to Henri de L.'s[2] illness.—So I can slip off beautifully—if you have time & are free. Please say *frankly*, won't you, if it's not convenient? I should like it to be somewhere at the end of the earth (rive gauche) where there is bad food, & no chance of meeting aquaintances.—If you tell me where, I'll come—or better, meet you at the Louvre at one o'c, in the shadow of Jean Gougon's Diana.[3]—*Let me know early*. If not, then on Friday, same combinazione.—

No, I won't give up, no, I won't believe it's the end, no, I am going to fight for my life—I know it now!

Keep Friday evening if you can.

Ms:UT

1. Comtesse Rosa de Fitz-James, Vienna-born of Jewish descent, presided over one of the most active *salons* in the Faubourg St. Germain. Aristocrats, diplomats, and men and women of letters from several nations appeared regularly at its gatherings.

2. Prince and Princess Henri de Ligne were frequent attendants at the Fitz-James *salon*.

3. Jean Gougon, or Goujon, was a sixteenth-century French sculptor and architect (he died around 1567).

To W. Morton Fullerton

[58 Rue de Varenne
Early March 1908]

Dear, Remember, please, how impatient & anxious I shall be to know the sequel of the Bell letter[1] ...

————Do you know what I was thinking last night, when you asked me, & I couldn't tell you?—Only that the way you've spent your emotional life, while I've—bien malgré moi—hoarded mine, is what puts the great gulf between us, & sets us not only on opposite shores, but at hopelessly distant points of our respective shores ... Do you see what I mean?

And I'm so afraid that the treasures I long to unpack for you, that have come to me in magic ships from enchanted islands, are only, to you, the old familiar red calico & beads of the clever trader, who has had dealings in every latitude, & knows just what to carry in the hold to please the simple native—I'm so afraid of this, that often & often I stuff my shining treasures back into their box, lest I should see you smiling at them!

Well! And if you do? It's *your* loss, after all! And if you can't come into the room without my feeling all over me a ripple of flame, & if, wherever you touch me, a heart beats under your touch, & if, when you hold me, & I don't speak, it's because all the words in me seem to have become throbbing pulses, & all my thoughts are a great golden blur—why should I be afraid of your smiling at me, when I can turn the beads & calico back into such beauty—?

Ms:UT

1. A reference to the anonymous communication to the London *Observer*, written in fact by Alfred Harmsworth and published on February 23. It was entitled "The Truth about *The Times*," and focused on "the position of Moberly Bell." It was part of the calculated deception involved in the warfare over control of the *Times*. See letter to Charles Eliot Norton, March 2, 1908.

To Sara Norton

58 Rue de Varenne
March 16 [1908]

Dear Sally,

My letter to your father gave you all our news up to date, & since then the only event in our lives has been Teddy's decision to sail next Sat., the 21st, in order to take at once the gout cure at the Hot Springs. His gout is growing steadily worse, & the Dr. here does not wish to give him any more "médicaments," nor yet to let him take baths anywhere in France earlier than the end of May; & as Dr. Kinnicutt[1] writes that he may safely go to the Hot Springs early in April, he has wisely decided to sail at once, & break up the attack without more delay. He is in his usual spirits again, & perfectly relieved about himself since it has become clear that his neurasthenia was due entirely to gout in the head.—I think the baths & the out-door life at the Hot Springs will be the best thing in the world for him, & he is glad to be going, since his gout really makes his life miserable, & is growing so much worse.

I shall stay on quietly in Paris till I join him in Lenox at the end of May, & as I am obliged to give up this ap't on April 15, my brother, who is going to America on business next month has very kindly offered to lend me his house, 3 Place des Etats Unis.—Think how delightful for me!—

Our dear Henry James is bringing out a comedy (to be acted by the Forbes Robertsons)[2] in Edinburgh on March 26, & if it succeeds there it is to go to London in May. Between the two trials he promised me a visit, so I shall not be quite solitary.—

I enjoy Paris more & more, as I get hold of more agreeable & interesting people—& the climate seems just what I need. No throats, no hoarseness, no asthma—because there is no dust, & no change of temperature of 40 degrees in a night.—

I have been reading—am still reading, in fact—a very interesting but rather painful book by Prof. Aulard, called "Taine, historien,"[3] in which he demolishes Taine's methods as a scientific historian, & shows him to have been rather a brilliant fantaisiste, absolutely "de bonne foi," but constitutionally incapable of objective representation of facts.—As Taine was one of the formative influences of my youth—the greatest after Darwin, Spencer & Lecky—I feel as if things were falling in ruins; but I am told that historians of the class of Seignobos[4] have for ten years or more said what Aulard now publishes.—At any rate the book is worth reading.—André Chevrillon, whom I see a good deal, & who is much distressed at this very disastrous attack on his uncle, told me the other night that the book has been well answered in the last Mercure de France[5]—but I have not yet seen the article.

Did I tell you my great joy over the fact that Mr. Chevrillon, who is certainly now the first literary critic in France, is to write an "appreciation" of my dear Brownell in the Revue de Paris, & that an old friend of mine, Jane d'Oilliamson,[6] is to translate with me two chapters of "French Traits," to be published with the article?

She has already translated admirably 3 stories of mine for the Revue des 2 Mondes,[7] so I know the work will be well done; & it will mean honour & recognition for Brownell, such as he has never had in his own country.—I wish you could know my friend Jane d'O. She was the Princesse Jane de Polignac, & she & I were girls together in Cannes 23 years ago, & have taken things up just where we left them. (She was not in Paris last year, so I found her this winter for the first time.) She is a delightful, admirable creature, & you & she would understand & appreciate each other.

I can't agree with you about the James prefaces,[8]—I think the one to "The Portrait of a Lady" the best definition of the novelist's art ever written—& there are masterly things in the Casamassima one. Read them with detachment & tell me if I am not right!—

I hope that Lily goes on well, & your father also, & that you get good news of Margaret[9] on her travels.—

Did you ever see the joyous Tardieu? He seems to have delighted the friends to whom I sent him in Washington. My love to your father & to you.

> Yr affte E.W.

Ms:BL

1. Dr. Francis Kinnicutt (1846–1913) was professor of clinical medicine at the College of Physicians and Surgeons in New York, and on the staff of several city hospitals. He had been Teddy Wharton's personal physician for several years, offering a series of diagnoses of his patient's ailments, and determining gradually that the root trouble was "mental."

2. James's play *The High Bid* (from his short story "Covering End") had its tryout in Edinburgh in March 1908, produced by Johnston Forbes-Robertson, who played the lead male role of Captain Yule. His wife, Gertrude Elliott, played the part of the American Mrs. Gracedew. The play was fairly well received, but no real London run followed.

3. *Taine, historien de la Révolution française* (1908), by Alphonse Aulard.

4. Charles Seignobos (1854–1942). Historians of his "class" were bringing scientific methods to bear on the study of history.

5. The monthly literary and artistic review, founded in 1890, was at the height of its fame in the 1900s.

6. Jane d'Oilliamson, here described by EW, translated "The Reckoning," "Souls Belated" and "The Confessional" into French. *French Traits* is the volume of criticism by Brownell mentioned earlier.

7. *Le Revue des Deux Mondes*, founded in 1829, was by this time one of the foremost periodicals in Europe. Balzac, Hugo, George Sand, and Sainte-Beuve were among the writers whose work appeared in it.

8. To the volumes in the New York Edition.

9. Another of Charles Eliot Norton's daughters.

To W. Morton Fullerton

Sunday morning
[Early April 1908]

Cher aimé, Of the extent to which I have been tiresome & "impossible," & not-worth-giving-another-thought-to, I am perfectly, & oh so penitently aware—n'en doutez pas! I "walk dreadfully illumined," believe me.

On the practical side, as to yr particular suggestion, I'm not as stupid as you think. In my case it would not be "the least risk," but possibly the greatest, to follow your plan, even if I could—as assuredly I should—finally overcome my reluctance.[1]

At least believe that I am unhappy, more than I can say, about it all. At first—yes—I hesitated, because I thought it, for you, not very real; & I'm so proud! And then, when I *did* believe it was real for you, that letter you wrote a few weeks ago paralyzed me—then, when everything would have been easy! I mean when you said "réfléchissez," to me whose curse it has always been to do so too much & too long! It drove me straight back into my numb dumb former self, the self that never believed in its chance of having any warm personal life, like other, luckier people. There you have the whole story— And now when you "make a sign" I'll answer—whenever you make it. Only arrange somehow beforehand—

I'm not worthy to write to or to think about; my only merit is that I'm unsparingly honest. But that's not a charm, alas!—

I'll let you know the moment I am free. It might be Monday or

Wed.—(If your sister² comes on Tuesday). Could you, on your side, tell me when *you* are likely to be? Next Friday, Sat, Sunday, are absolutely mine, en tout cas.

I beg instant cremation for this—

Would you send me that letter you spoke of today, & hadn't with you? When you tell me about yourself, & your situation, & your difficulties—only then do I feel a tenderness in your liking, a something that may go on living a quiet life in you long after the glory has departed from your poor

E

Ms:UT

1. The reference is to a much-discussed plan for the two of them to go away together, as EW once put it, "for twenty-four hours to a little inn in the country in the depths of a green wood."

2. Katherine Fullerton (born 1879) was in fact Morton Fullerton's first cousin, but she had been brought up in the Fullerton household believing she was his sister. It was only during her graduate years at Bryn Mawr College, around 1903, that she learned she was an adopted child, the daughter of a younger brother of Morton's father. The information served to liberate the deep, passionate love Katherine had felt for Morton from an early age. In the fall of 1907, Fullerton, on his visit to America, called on Katherine at Bryn Mawr, and to her understanding they became engaged to be married.

To Sara Norton

58 Rue de Varenne
April 12 [1908]

Dear Sally— I am too sorry to hear such a wretched report of Lily as you send in your last letter. Of all discouraging things, few are more so than to be made worse instead of better by a "cure" deliberately sought, & confidently relied on. It is too bad that Lily should have seen that painful accident, & been hurt by the exertion it led to. What a detestable year you have all had, you poor dear Shady Hillers, & how I wish I could wave a wand & lift all the clouds!—Tell Lily, if it's any comfort, that for *twelve* years I seldom knew what it was to be, for more than an hour or two of the twenty four, without an intense feeling of nausea, & such unutterable fatigue that when I got up I was always more tired than when I lay down. This form of neurasthenia consumed the best years of my youth, & left, in some sort, an irreparable shade on my life. Mais quoi! I worked through it, & came out on the other side, & so will she, in a much shorter time, I hope.

I daresay you have seen Teddy by this time, & he has told you all the latest news of the rue de Varenne. The chronicle closes tomorrow, when I move to my brother's, 3 Place des Etats Unis, to remain till I sail. Mr. James's play had a complete success at Edinburgh on the first night, so I suppose it will be brought out in London early next month. Meanwhile, he vows he is coming to me soon after Easter—but seeing is believing! He is still at work on his Scribner edition, & it ties him down very much.

Yes—I've read Julia Bride, & found it living & vivid, & all the things *you* don't. "Non ragionam,"[1] for we shall never agree on the last H. J. manner. At any rate, we're "d'accord" about the author of The Portrait of a Lady.—Please read, & like as much as you can, two stories of mine that ought to be coming out soon in Scribners: "The Pretext" & "The Verdict." The only things I've done this idle winter!—

No, I haven't read Mallock's Socialism,[2] but I am going to. Pearsall Smith[3] *is* a brother of Mrs. Berenson's, & is—or was—a great friend of Sally Fairchild's. How is dear Sally? Give her my love if she is still at Cambridge. She never writes me a line, but my fidelity is unshaken.

Mrs. Humphry Ward's progress through the "States" is very amusing. She seems to like all the things that would most appal me—I mean the publicity, reportering &c. But I fancy she'll have more than enough before she bids goodbye to Liberty enlightening the world. I do hope your father is well enough to permit of your having Dorothy Ward to stay. I thought she seemed so nice when we once briefly met.

Goodbye—my love to Shady Hill. Je t'embrasse de tout coeur, chère.

Yrs E. W.

Ms:BL

1. "Let us not speak of it": from Virgil's words to Dante in *Inferno* III, as, crossing the gateway into hell, they come upon the "trimmers": "Non ragionam di lor, ma guarda e passa."

2. *A Critical Examination of Socialism* (1907), by William Hurrell Mallock.

3. Logan Pearsall Smith (1865–1946), originally of a Quaker family in Philadelphia, now permanently residing in England. He was one of the most felicitous writers of prose in his time; *Trivia*, the first of his still readable volumes of aphorisms about life and literature, came out in 1902. As EW says, he was the brother of Mary Pearsall Smith, who had married Bernard Berenson a few years earlier. EW and Logan would become firm friends.

To W. Morton Fullerton

Wednesday
[Late April 1908]

Voisin, Durand,[1] etc!—No—but if you could get away in time from your tiresome shop, why might one not take the train to Versailles & dine there, on such a good evening as this promises to be?—Is this uncomfortable & impracticable?

If there were a good train at about 7 o'c, I might meet you at the Invalides Station—only, again, I *might* be late, because of the people coming to tea.

If we do this, don't wait for me outside, but let me come in & *find you*—à cause de Cook!

If this "combinazione" is not possible, telephone me at any time between 1.30 & 2.30— Or send me a petit bleu as soon as possible. I am thirsty for green trees even after dark!—But you'll have to let me know about trains.

No—I've found an indicateur, & there seems to be a good one at 7. & one at 7.18, & I should try for the first, & certainly get the second.

But *please* tell me frankly if you think it's a stupid idea. Si nous allons, ne le dites pas à H.J.—Je lui dirai que j'ai été invité à dîner avec des amis.

Ms:UT

1. Two of the most elegant Paris restaurants.

To W. Morton Fullerton

Wednesday evening
[April 29, 1908]

About tomorrow—I'm afraid I can't go to the Salon after all. What with my grippe, & the rush that dear James's presence causes (& from which I have to defend him as best I can)—what with it all, & that *awful* translating besides, I'm tired—tired—*tired*!—But if you are free after luncheon tomorrow, & could come as early as may be convenient, we might go for a quiet turn in the Bois instead.—I have to send H.J. to Blanche's[1] in the motor at 2:15, & after that I'll *borrow it* for myself.

Howells & a lot of people have just been here for tea, et je me demande how I am going to drag myself now to the rue de Grenelle.[2] I wish I were deep, deep in the country!

Are you coming to dine with *me* next Tuesday*? Perhaps you haven't yet decided? Ayez un bon mouvement! H.J. is dining with some of his idolaters that evening—

You're to be asked to lunch with the Gays on Sunday "to meet" H.J.—& his satellite.

*or Wednesday, if you prefer

Ms:UT

1. Henry James, during a fortnight's stay with EW at the Rue de Varenne, had agreed to sit for his portrait by Jacques-Emile Blanche in the latter's home at Passy. Blanche (1861–1942) was a much admired portrait painter who had already done portraits of such literary figures as Hardy, George Moore, and the as yet unknown Marcel Proust. He was also a discriminating collector of modern painting.

2. Rosa de Fitz-James's *salon*, EW writes in her memoir, "looked out on a mossy turf and trees of an eighteenth century *hôtel* standing between court and garden in the rue de Grenelle."

To W. Morton Fullerton

Sunday
[May 3, 1908]

Will you meet Henry & me at Durand's at *one* o'c tomorrow, & lunch with us there, instead of Pl. des E. Unis?—Then, if he goes on to his portrait, we might perhaps go for a little to the Salon?—

I am so glad you liked our excursion yesterday—I wish you would tell me that your cold is really no worse for it.

Isn't this Beauvais choir[1] (as you made me see it—I hadn't before):—

Si distende in circular figura

In tanto, che la sua circonferenza

Sarebbe al sol troppo larga cintura?

I was thinking all the while of the wheeling rose, as we stood in your little street, but couldn't remember the lines.

& then again:—

La vista mia nell'ampio e nell'altezza

Non si smarriva, ma tutto prendeva

Il quanto e il quale di *quella allegrezza* . . .[2]

Beauvais really seems built out of Par. XXX . . . but I pause, remembering that I address the traveller who says: " 'We' can see, but 'we' can't feel"—

A demain. E.

Ms:UT

1. EW describes Beauvais cathedral and her reactions to it in the second chapter of *A Motor-Flight Through France*: "the great mad dream of Beauvais choir—the cathedral without a nave—the Kubla Khan of architecture."

2. The lines from *Paradiso* XXX (103–105, 118–120), in the prose translation of John D. Sinclair: "[The light that makes the Creator visible to every creature] spreads to so wide a circle that the circumference would be too great a girdle for the sun. . . . My sight did not lose itself in the breadth and height, but took in all the extent and quality of that rejoicing."

To W. Morton Fullerton

Sunday
[May 1908]

Oh, mon cher aimé, I don't think you can know what that little word of yours means to me today.

No, Dear, I don't mistake your silence. I am never so sure of you, I mean of your being happy with me, as when you don't feel it necessary to speak, because then I know that my nearness is no obstacle, no *interruption* to you; that I am part of the air you breathe.

I understand that, & I understand also what prompted you to write that little message just when you did. You knew I was sad at saying goodbye to you. You knew why sometimes I draw back from your least touch. I am so afraid—*so* afraid—of seeming to expect more than you can give, & of thus making my love for you less helpful to you, less what I wish it to be. And sometimes mon corps ne peut pas oublier ton corps. & then I am miserable.

I shouldn't say this if you hadn't shown me that you understood. I don't want to have any plan of conduct with you—to behave in this way or that way—but just to be natural, to be completely myself. And the completest expression of that self is in the desire to help you, to give you the chance to develop what is in you, & to live the best life you can. Nothing else counts for me now, Dear, except the wish to do some good work, & to have you see in it the reflection of all the beauty you have shown me.

Ton amie—E.

Believe me, a man of your intellectual value *has* a "market value" when he brings such volonté to his task as you are capable of. This I never have doubted.

Ms:UT

To W. Morton Fullerton

Tuesday
[May 17, 1908]

Alas, Dear—if you had felt as I felt, or a fraction of what I feel, you would not have "wondered if I had a friend with me," or if I should have been *surprised* at being surprised—you wouldn't have cared, because you wd have wanted so much to see me that nothing else would have counted. . . .

Sometimes I feel that I *can't* go on like this: from moments of such nearness, when the last shadow of separateness melts, back into a complete néant of silence, of not hearing, not knowing—being left to feel that I have been like a "course" served & cleared away! . .

Voilà ma dernière nouvelle. El je me remets au travail—

Ms:UT

To W. Morton Fullerton

[c. May 20, 1908]

I am mad about you Dear Heart and sick at the thought of our parting and the days of separation and longing that are to follow. It is a wonderful world that you have created for me, Morton dear, but how I am to adjust it to the *other* world is difficult to conceive. Perhaps when I am once more on land my mental vision may be clearer—at present, in the whole universe I see but one thing, am conscious of but one thing, you, and our love for each other.

Ms:UT

To Sara Norton

Friday—in a fog off S. Hook
May 29 [1908]

Dear Sally,

I had no time to thank you for your long letter before sailing; or rather, strictly speaking, when I say "no time" I mean no courage to hold the pen. Now that I have something of a foothold in Paris & various publishing & other entanglements (funny word!) I find that the letters to-be-answered "foisonnent" just as they do at home, & without Anna's ready hand to relieve me of the impersonal ones. (Interruption while I discard the ship-pen & fetch my own.)—

I think I wrote you just before dear Henry James came to me. He gave me a beautiful fortnight of his dear incomparable self, but I saw, after all, very little of him, because in a laudable but ill-advised moment of self-sacrifice I persuaded him to sit to Jacques Blanche for his portrait—& while the result is distinctly *good* I'm not sure it was worth the price!—At any rate we had one glorious day at Beauvais, to which we motored, which he had never seen, & which made on him the same impression of singing, *choiring* glory that it always does on me.—As I write, I suddenly feel that I've told you all this before. But no! I am sure I haven't written you as lately as that.—My last weeks in Paris were delicious. I made some beautiful excursions, to Provins, Montfort-l'Amaury, Montmorency, & back to exquisite Senlis—& then Paris itself was so radiant! I hated to leave it.

On board ship I've been deep in Kellogg's Darwinism Today, which is admirably done (do you know it?) & am following it with Lock's Heredity & Variation.[1] In the interval I read Paul Mariéton's Histoire d'Amour[2] (*George* & Alfred) which he gave me before I sailed, & which is well-done & interesting—as when are they *not*, the darlings?

I have also written one entire short story,[3] & taken up again my sadly neglected great American Novel—so you see the influence of American activity extends at least as far as the Banks!—We hoped to land this eve'g at 7 o'c, but we are enveloped in fog & shall probably have to sleep on board, & par conséquent not reach the Mount till tomorrow night—such a bore!—Do send me a line there soon to tell me your plans, & how you all are.—Best love to yr. father & Lily, & thank the latter, please, for her letter. It was so nice of her to write.

Affly yrs—
    E.W.

Ms:BL

1. *The Recent Progress in the Study of Variation, Heredity and Evolution* (1906), by Robert Heath Lock.

2. *Une Histoire d'amour*, by Paul Mariéton, about George Sand and Alfred de Musset, was published in 1897.

3. "The Choice."

To W. Morton Fullerton

[The Mount
Lenox, Mass.]
Friday June 5 [1908]

This is one of the days when it is more than I can bear.—

I suppose I ought to qualify that *more* by an "almost," since I am here & the lake is là-bas—& I *am* bearing it. But just now, when I heard that the motor, en route for Hâvre, had run into a tree & been smashed (bursting tire), I felt the wish that I had been in it, & smashed with it, & nothing left of all this disquiet but a "coeur arrêté." ... So the total result seems to be that I, who always took life on its own terms, now want it only on mine!—& yet I do my *best*. I grind steadily at the novel every morning, I steep myself in my books, I stupefy myself with long walks, & all seems going well, till suddenly I stop & say:— "Tomorrow is *Saturday*———" or: "The last time I wore this dress it was at Meudon. . . ." & there's all the work to do over again, the stone to roll up hill once more!—

You used to ask me so often to tell you again "il quanto e il quale." Well—take the measure of them once for all in this first complete dé-faillance, & in my confessing it to you!

. . . .

No! I will write no more like that. Instead, I will think of the things you are doing & seeing. *What* a day at the Panthéon yesterday! Did you see it all happen? How I like Harry White's being there,[1] when all the other Ambassadors sent excuses! Write me all about it, if you have time; & at any rate, send me your Times article. And then tell me about the mysterious Steinheil murder—& above all about the "Ogresse":[2] you know I adore horrors & mysteries., & your friend Aidé[3] never had a more impassioned reader of his "creepy stories" than I was in my youth. . . .

I have just had a long letter from Carl Snyder,[4] who has been ill, poor man, & has given up his "New Revelation" book (I think because I told him it sounded like a Drummond title!)⁵ for one on the origin of life. I should say it was a good moment for a popular summing up on that subject, for the English & Am. books I've read so far—Kellogg included—barely glance at it. Snyder expects to spend part of the summer here, or near here, & I am glad, for I shall have some one to talk to.—I don't mind the solitude—what I can't *endure*, just yet, is the things one has to talk about!

I'm still writing you on this horrid transparent paper, because what I've ordered hasn't come. Make my excuses to your eyes, won't you?

June 6th, Saturday.

Happy season, that sends the ships quickly across smooth seas, & brings me your letters sooner than I had hoped! The second has just come—the one dated in the Ambervalia—& I read it in just such "firm weather of the early summer-time" as Marius walked through at the head of the procession.⁶ And I write the answer on a Saturday, when one might have gone out & breathed the scent of the bean-fields & of "the young leaves that were almost as fragrant as flowers"...

It was *dear* of you to write again so soon. Know that every letter gives me a pleasure you can hardly imagine—& yet that I shall *so* understand if there comes a break—so that, in the same breath, I am moved to say: "Write," & "Don't write"—which means, write always when you want to, & never—not once!—when you are busy, or in the least feel it as a thing-to-be-done. I don't want to put any more of those into your life!—

It is curious—& fatal—que vous trouvez toujours moyen to say the thing that *comes nearest*. In this letter you tell me you have been looking over "the documents in the case"—& only yesterday, I had done the same thing!—It is curious, too that the note you wrote last Oct. asking if you might come for a day or two was tossed down on my writing table among a lot of rubbish, lay there, miraculously surviving destruction, all the autumn, & appeared to me just as I was sailing—preserved, no doubt, by its predestined significance. Que tout cela est bête—& dear!— But what I like best in your letter (I mean this last one) is the word "camaraderie." I was never sure that you cared for it, or felt it . . . that you thought I *gave* it . . .

It is irony, though, that I should read your praise of my "adjusting myself to the facts" just at the moment when—for the first time almost—I completely fail to do so! "Wear the mask—" heavens! I ought to know how! I have had time to learn. But I'm tired—tired—life is too long as well as too short—& then the fatality that it should be just you & me—

You chained at one end of the world, & I at the other. . . . My strength used to be that I could say, like the Monsieur in the Arnold poem: "They, believe me, who await no gifts from chance, have conquered fate—"[7]

Goodbye, goodbye.—Write or don't write, as you feel the impulse— but hold me long & close in your thoughts. I shall take up so little room, & it's only there that I'm happy!—

If I don't write next week, it will be because I can't throw off this black mood, & don't want to indulge it—at your expense!—

Ms:UT

1. Henry White (1850–1927) was the American Ambassador to France during EW's first years in Paris, 1907 to 1909. He had previously served as Secretary of the Embassy in London and as Ambassador to Italy; he has been called "the first professional American diplomat." EW had known him since 1879, when he married Margaret Rutherfurd, the oldest of the children of Lewis Rutherfurd, with whom Edith Jones was friendly in the Newport summers.

On June 4, 1908, the ashes of Emile Zola were transferred to the Pantheon in Paris, to join the other illustrious dead. The event aroused the fury of the anti-Dreyfus contingent, because of Zola's effective intercession in the case (*J'accuse*). During the ceremony, with Ambassador White and others in attendance and Dreyfus (whose conviction had been overturned in 1906) conspicuously present, a possibly crazed journalist named Gregori shot and wounded Dreyfus.

2. On May 30, 1908, four supposed burglars strangled a painter named Adolphe-Charles Steinheil and his mother-in-law in Steinheil's villa in the Vaugirard section of Paris. The event caused an uproar in the press, and the excitement would increase when, in November 1908, Mme. Steinheil, the painter's wife, was charged with complicity in the deaths, the theory being that she drugged or poisoned the victims before they were murdered. Mme. Steinheil was acquitted in 1909 after a sensational trial, but the public remained convinced of her guilt. (Note supplied by Alan Gribben. See Sources and Acknowledgments.)

3. Hamilton Aïdé (1826–1907), a long-standing friend of Henry James and a London companion of Morton Fullerton, was the author of *Morals and Mysteries* (the tales of 1872 enjoyed by the youthful EW) and several novels.

4. A young oceanologist whom EW was just coming to know.

5. The Scottish writer Henry Drummond (1851–1897) was among those seeking to reconcile biblical Christianity and the theory of evolution.

6. Walter Pater, *Marius the Epicurean* (1885).

7. Lines 247–248 of Matthew Arnold's "Resignation: to Fausta" (in the volume of 1853): "Yet they, believe me, who await/ No gifts from Chance, have conquered Fate."

To W. Morton Fullerton

[The Mount]

Monday, June 8 [1908]

Just now, as the last course of luncheon was being served with due solemnity, I had a sudden vision of our first luncheon at Duval's, with the kindly prognathous lady-in-waiting, & the moist hippopotamus American with his cucumber-faced female—do you remember? And then the second day, when the old gentleman in the corner kept us so long in suspense, & finally softened just as we despaired?

And how kind people were wherever we went—our friends in the train at Creil, our waiter at Montmorency, that dearest of concierges in the jardin de Mme Turquet—*yes*, even the Sneezing Man in the dining-room of the Grand Cerf, who drove us out under the lilacs in the court!

—Admire the ingenuity of woman! I vowed I wouldn't write you again until I had overcome my black mood—& thereupon set to work to overcome it, *in order to write you.* Can you match that outside of Liguori?[1]—I really am better today, but yesterday, in my despair, I very nearly cabled you the one word: *Inconsolable.* Luckily I bethought me in time that you might feel impelled to answer, & as our telegrams are all telephoned from the village—si figuri!!

I am ashamed to write so often, because, with this life I lead here, there's absolutely nothing to tell. I have finished three more chapters of my novel (this reminds me of: "J'ai tué six loups"),² & I've read Lock's "Heredity & Variation," & begun Dépéret's "Transformations du Monde Animal,"³ which seems to be another of the admirable "popular exposition" books in the red series.—That reminds me—do you know "L'Hérédité" by Delage,⁴ which Kellogg constantly speaks of as the best on the subject? And if you do, could I understand it, even in bits? I must confess to being always a little ahurie when I meet with biophors & determinants—though they seem like old friends after the allelomorphs & heterozygotes in Lock's "simple" exposition of Mendelism.⁵—My biological reading is always embarrassed by the fact that I can't help seeing all these funny creatures with faces & gestures—the biophors, for instance, small & anxious to please, the determinants loud & domineering, with eye-glasses; so that I am burdened with a hideous new fauna, to which that monstrous animal the heterozygote, has just added another & peculiarly complicated silhouette—

Oh, dear—what nonsense to send three thousand miles!

—Shall we talk of you instead? Do you want to know some of the things I like you for? (you've never told *me*!)—Well—one is that kind of time-keeping, comparing mind you have—that led you, for instance, in your last letter, to speak of "the camaraderie we invented, *or, it being predestined, we discovered*"— How I laughed over that revision, I who revise, who "edit" every sentence as I utter it, & to whom, in the most rushing moments, words keep their sharp edges of difference!

Et puis—I like the way in which you instantly discriminate between the essential & the superfluous, in people & things—& your feeling as I do about the "green worms" of life—caring about the waitress's losing her tip if we moved our table, & being worried lest the taxi-man you sent back to me at the R. des Deux Mondes should have waited & missed a fare—if you knew how every little thing like that *sank in*!

And then—most of all, perhaps—for the quality I least know how to define—unless one calls it a "radiant reasonableness." Because you & I (I think I have it too, you see!) are almost the only people I know who feel the "natural magic," au-delà, dream-side of things, & yet need the netteté, the line—in thinking, in conduct—yes! in feeling too!— And I've always felt about that poor dear maligned Goddess of Reason as somebody in Comus does about Philosophy—

> "How charming is divine philosophy!
> Not harsh and crabbèd, as dull fools suppose,
> But musical as is Apollo's lute . . ."⁶

June 10th. I said:—"This letter shall not be as long as the last—I shall keep it over till the next steamer. One must make one's self wanted, waited for, &c, &c—" & then everything in me cried out—

No! The basest thing about the state of "caring" is the tendency to bargain and calculate, as if it were a game of skill played between antagonistics. (We know it is—soit! Just as we know—or were supposed to till lately—that we hadn't any "free-will"; nevertheless:—) Pascal's terrible "il faut de l'adresse pour aimer"⁷ has a noble side if it means the exercise of tact, insight, sympathy, self-effacement; but it is the most sordid of counsels if it appeals to the instinct to dole out, dissemble, keep in suspense, in order to prolong a little a feeling that hasn't enough vitality to survive without such aids.—There would have been the making of an accomplished flirt in me, because my lucidity shows me each move of the game—but that, in the same instant, a reaction of contempt makes me sweep all the counters off the board & cry out:—"Take them all—I don't want to win—I want to lose everything to you!"—But I pause, remembering you once told me that, on this topic, I serve up the stalest of platitudes with an air of triumphant discovery!—

June 11th Such a happy thing has happened.—Two or three days ago, in the garden, I heard a cuckoo-call from the woods.—I never heard it before in America, & actually believed we had no American cuckoo—at least no New England variety. I set it down to a cuckoo clock somewhere in the servants' quarters; but this morning it came again, sweeter, more insistent, the very voice of Montmorency.—This time I knew it was no clock, & my bird books informed me that there is a cuckoo who "ranges" as far north as this; but he must be rare, for our coachman, who is a savant ornithologist, told me he *thought* he had heard the note once, in his seven years here, but was not even sure of that!—

I said I would write only to *answer* you; but the papers tell me that the Kronprinz is due this morning & so I am answering the letter that she (or he?) may be bringing—*is* bringing, I am going to believe!—If you knew how I long for the moment when it will be *your* turn to answer, when I shall no longer feel that my letters are being cast into the void. But that will not be for another week. . . .

I meant to tell you in Paris how glad I should be of a chance to see your sister. Is there any possibility of her coming our way before she goes to Europe? If yes, I wish you would give her my message, & ask her to let me know—in spite of the cruel things I suspect her of saying—so justly—as to my inability to do justice to the tender sentiment in fiction! She should remember that mine is the low & photographic order of talent qui a besoin de se documenter—& consequently. . . .

How I hate to stop talking to you! Goodbye—

Ms:UT

1. Liguori: the eighteenth-century Italian bishop familiarly known as Saint Alphonsus Liguori. In his writings, Liguori often employed a kind of casuistry similar to that which EW here attributes to herself. The saint's tactic is referred to as "equiprobabilism."

2. Phrase in an offhand note from the King of Spain, absent on a hunt, to the Queen, in Victor Hugo's *Ruy Blas* (1838), act 3, scene 3: "Madame, il fait grand vent et j'ai tué six loups. Carlos."

3. *Les Transformations du monde animal,* by Charles Jean Julien Déperet (1854–1929), published in 1907, was a study of ancient forms of life and evolution, and formed part of a series called Bibliothèque de Philosophie Scientifique.

4. *L'Hérédité et les grands problèmes de la biologie générale,* by Yves Delage (1854–1920), published in 1903.

5. I.e., the theories of heredity propounded by Gregor Johann Mendel, the nineteenth-century Austrian naturalist.

6. Lines 476–48 of John Milton's *Comus* (1637).

7. From *Discours sur les passions d'amour,* a thirty-two-page text first discovered and published in 1843 and republished in 1900. This relatively obscure treatise, or sequence of aphorisms and *aperçus,* was long attributed to Blaise Pascal (1623–1662), and thought to come from his "worldly period," 1652–1653. EW believed it to be by Pascal, whom she revered above all French writers. Recent scholarship, however, suggests that the little work was compiled after Pascal's death, possibly incorporating some of his maxims.

The passage in question: "L'amour donne de l'esprit; il se soutient par l'esprit. Il faut de l'adresse pour aimer" ("Love gives one spirit; it sustains itself by spirit. One needs skill in order to love").

To W. Morton Fullerton

[The Mount]
June 19 [1908]

When I sent you, eight days ago, that desperate word: "Don't write me again!" I didn't guess that you were already acting on it! Not a line from you in nine days—since your letter of June 2d. Eleven days at least must have passed without your feeling the impulse to write . . .

You know I never wanted you to write unless *you* wanted to! And I always understood it would not go on for long. But this is so sudden that I almost fear you are ill, or that something has happened to trouble you.

Think! You have not even answered *my first letter*, my letter from the steamer, which must have reached you on the 10th; & five steamers have come in, that might have brought an answer to it.—Don't think I didn't mean what I said when I last wrote, or what I reiterated to you so often before we said goodbye: that I don't want from you a sign, a gesture, that is not voluntary, spontaneous—irrepressible!—

No—I am still of that mind. Only, as I said, this is so unbelievably sudden. My reason, even—my reason much more than my *feeling*—tells me it must be some accident that has kept you silent; & then my anxiety begins its conjectures.

Send a word, dear, to reassure me. And if it's not *that*, but the other alternative, surely you're not afraid to say so?—My last letter will have shown you how I have foreseen, how I have accepted, such a contingency. Do you suppose I have ever, for a moment, ceased to see the thousand reasons *why* it was inevitable, & likely to be not far distant?

Allons donc! You shall see what I am made of—only don't be afraid to trust me to the utmost of my lucidity and my philosophy!

—But no! I don't ask you to say anything that might be painful to you. Simply write: "Chère camarade, I am well—things are well with me"; & I shall understand, & accept—& think of you as you would like a friend to think.—Above all, don't see any hidden reproach in this. There is nothing in it but tenderness and understanding.

I am well, and the week since I wrote last has managed to get itself lived. And the novel goes on. And people come and go.—I can't tell you more now, but another time, perhaps—

And now & always I am yr so affectionate E.

Ms:UT

To Charles Eliot Norton

[The Mount]
June 30 [1908]

Dear Mr. Norton,

When Teddy & I heard yesterday from Lily of Taffy's sad taking-off we both really felt a personal regret in addition to our profound sympathy for his master.

His artless but engaging ways, his candid enjoyment of his dinner, his judicious habit of exercising by means of those daily rushes up & down the road, had for so many years interested & attracted us that he occupies a very special place in our crowded dog-memories.

As for *your* feelings, I can picture them with intensity, since to do so I have only to relive my poor Jules' last hours & farewell looks, about a year ago!—

Somebody says "l'espoir est le plus fidèle des amants"—but I really think it should be put in the plural & applied to dogs. Staunch & faithful little lovers that they are, they give back a hundred fold every sign of love one ever gives them—& it mitigates the pang of losing them to know how very happy a little affection has made them.

Teddy joins me in condolences, & we both send our love to Sally.

Ever affly yours
Edith W.

Ms:HL

To W. Morton Fullerton

[The Mount]
July 1 [1908]

At last, my dearest, your letter of the 21st ... Que voulez vous que je vous dise? Your silence of nineteen days seems to me a very conclusive, anticipated answer to my miserable cry! You didn't wait to be *asked* what was "best"!

But don't read a hint of reproach in this. I have spent three weeks of horrible sadness, because I feared from your silence that within ten days of our goodbye the very meaning of me had become a weariness. And I suffered—no matter how much; but I said to myself: "I chose the risk, I accept the consequences." And that is what I shall always say—

Only, cher, one must be a little blind—or else a little relieved at the "reasonableness" of my attitude—to read in my note of the 11th anything but an appeal for frankness—a desperate desire to know, *at once*, and have the thing over. Don't be afraid! I can only reiterate it. Anything on earth wd be better (I've learned that in these last three weeks) than to sit here and wonder: *What was I to him, then?* I assure you I've practised my "Non dolet!"[1]

If "joyousness" is the quality que vous exigez in those who feel an affection for you, I can understand how this tone must bore you—& it was because I understood it, instinctively, that I piled up all my news about my novel, my garden, any stuff I could think of. But to whom do I say it? You know that well enough!—

Let us for once speak out. "Mme de Clèves has never really lived."[2] Only she had a glimpse of what it was like, once, for two months, & shut down into her black box again, she struggles with tragic futility, to push the lid back a little & breathe. And you want her to be "joyous"?—Eh bien, sachez that she very nearly jumped on a steamer this very week & went back to be joyous. I don't honestly think that any consideration on earth would have kept her from doing it, except the fact that her joyousness would have been acquired at the price of the present inconvenience & lasting & hideous discomfort of the wretched author of the said joyousness!—Et voilà ... Only don't tell me again that you understand "it would be better for the novel" if I had no thought of you. That's cruel.—

As for you—happy being!—you count on being able to tell me by the autumn that your own problems have solved themselves, & that you are "no longer worrying."—This is vague, but I suppose it means that things look better at the office—I hope so with all my heart!—

I don't know where "my" next year will be. Just now it looks more like Rome than Paris. I am so weary that I think I'd rather stay here in the snow.... I don't suppose there ever was such a ridiculous fate as mine! When people say to me, as they do nowadays: "How well you look—you haven't looked like this in years!" I feel like cursing my stupid buoyancy and health as I used to curse my long dreary years of illness. All à rebours—all upside down! And when I think of all the things I have that other people want—& that I've never cared a fig for!—no, no, I won't go on ... not *now*. For I had for a moment the one thing on earth, the dear, the unforgettable hour—only the heart *is* insatiable, isn't it, & when you write me: "Every second of that hour was for me but the promise of dearer moments to come," I begin to hope again tout bêtement—*how* bêtement!

Thank you for Bérard's petit bleu. I am sorry Jane has been bothering you about these things. Needless to say it was without my knowledge, & I'll tell her to stop. It is absurd to keep you rushing about Paris with her manuscripts. Thank you also for Delage. Vous me comblez!—who is the journalist who describes so sympathetically the "Englander" with the "sanften blauen Augen"?[3]—(je les croyais gris?)—I see you can read German after all!—

You must have had a delicious moment seeing Mme de Clèves at the Théâtre des Arts. I wish I'd been there ... The words run from my pen, & the pen turns back & stabs me. *Been there!*—I see Simone[4] again, & Polyphème[5] ... The aching distinctness with which I relive & relive & relive every moment, every phrase, every look of it all, is one of the worst pains now. Oh, the curse of an imagination! Enfin—

Oh, I must stop—I dread so to bore you with long letters!—Excuse me, won't you, for the cable?—Your silence puzzled me a little, after those three dear letters you wrote me the first week, & knowing the confusion that sometimes arises here between the two houses of the same name, I feared a letter might have gone astray ... I ought to have remembered that such things happen only in novels.

It would be a great joy if you could send me a line once a week— only never, *never* under compulsion!—And, when your plans are settled,—about coming to America,—it you were to tell me it would be kind. Even if you're *not* coming, I should be rid of the ache of wondering. . . .

Dearest, I love you so deeply that you owe me just one thing—the truth. Never be afraid to say: "Ma pauvre amie, c'est fini."—That is what I meant when I said I couldn't bear to watch the dwindling & fading.—When the time comes, just put my notes & letters in a bundle, & send them back, & I shall understand. . . . I am like one who went out seeking for friendship, & found a kingdom. Don't you suppose I know that the blessedness *is all* on my side?—

Que je vous aime, que je vous aime! Tell me you haven't yet forgotten—

Ms:UT

1. *Non dolet*: "It does not hurt." These were the words of Pompeia Paulina, the wife of the Roman philosopher and playwright Seneca, after her husband had slashed her wrists in a suicide pact.

2. Probably a line from the play version of the novel *La Princesse de Clèves* (1678), by Mme. de La Fayette. It was currently running in Paris, as EW mentions later. In the story, Mme. de Clèves, trapped in a loveless marriage, falls in love with the Duc de Nemours and he with her. She remains faithful, however, and even discloses the situation to her husband. The latter dies of a broken heart, and Mme. de Clèves retires to a convent.

3. "The 'Englishman' with the 'soft blue eyes.' "

4. Mme. Simone (born Pauline Benda in 1877) was one of the most celebrated *comédiennes* of the period. She appeared in works by Rostand and Henri Bernstein, and performed with Sarah Bernhardt; and was said to have known every one of consequence in Paris during *La Belle Epoque*. Mme. Simone lived on well into the post–World War II era.

5. *Polyphème*, a verse play in two acts by Albert Samain (1858–1900), a leading *symboliste* poet and co-founder in 1891 of the literary periodical *Mercur de France*. *Polyphème* is drawn from a theme treated by Theocritus and Ovid: the aging giant who falls in love with the young maiden Galatée and who blinds himself to avoid being stricken by her beauty. It had evidently been produced in the previous theatrical season in Paris.

To Sara Norton

The Mount
July 7 [1908]

Dear Sally,

How are you bearing this lowest round of the Inferno? Here it has not been above 84°, & yet the last two days are the worst I have ever known for oppressiveness. I suppose my hay-fever makes me feel the want of air more than if I were breathing normally. Frequent thunder showers bring no relief as yet, & I can think of no place where I should like so much to be as on the deck of an oceansteamer—turned eastward! If my hay-fever doesn't mend soon there is just a chance that I *may* sail on the 16th, to see if the voyage will break it up, & possibly take some inhalations at Aix or Salso. Teddy will be away fishing for about 3 weeks in Aug., & I might take advantage of that to run off, getting back about Sept. 1st. But I hesitate to interrupt my work, so I shan't do it unless I am really worse these next days.—I am tempted by the fact that the motor is there, & won't be back till about Aug. 15.

I see Mrs. Kuhn often, & her vitality grows more amazing as she becomes more death-like to look at. She even laughed at a joke the other day! But, oh, if I had morphia in reach, as she has, how quickly I'd cut the knot!

Please give your father my love, & tell him how much touched we both were by his letter. I remember his reading me the charming little poem he speaks of, one evening at Ashfield two years ago.—

I am deep in my novel, & am reading, as a diversion between times, "Jenseits von Gut und Böse."[1] I never read any Nietzsche before, except a glance at Zarathustra, which didn't tempt me but this is *great* fun—full of wit & originality & poetry—dashes of Meredith & even Whitman. He has no system, & not much logic, but wonderful flashes of insight, & a power of breaking through conventions that is most exhilarating, & clears the air as our thunderstorms just now do—not! I think it salutary, now & then, to be made to realize what he calls "die Unwerthung aller Werthe,"[2] & really get back to a wholesome basis of naked instinct.

There are times when I *hate* what Christianity has left in our blood —or rather, one might say, taken out of it—by its cursed assumption of the split between body & soul.

Do read him if you haven't!—

No news here except inside my head, & that is all melted grey matter today!—

Yr affte
　　E.W.

Ms:BL

1. Nietzsche's text of 1887, translated into English as *Beyond Good and Evil*, was a vehement attack on traditional and Christian morality.

2. "The re-evaluation of all values."

To W. Morton Fullerton

[The Mount]
August 26 [1908]

Dear, won't you tell me soon the meaning of this silence?

At first I thought it might mean that your sentimental mood had cooled, & that you feared to let me see the change; & I wrote, nearly a month ago, to tell you how natural I should think such a change on your part, & how I hoped that our friendship—so dear to me!—might survive it.—It would have been easy, after that letter, to send a friendly: "Yes, chère amie—" surely, having known me so well all those months, you could have trusted to my understanding it?

But the silence continues! It was not *that* you wanted? For a time I fancied you were too busy & happy to think of writing—perhaps even to glance at my letters when they came. But even so—there are degrees in the lapse from such intimacy as ours into complete silence & oblivion; & if the inclination to write had died out, must not you, who are so sensitive & imaginative, have asked yourself to what conjectures you were leaving me, & how I should suffer at being so abruptly & inexplicably cut off from all news of you?

I re-read your letters the other day, & I will not believe that the man who wrote them did not feel them, & did not know enough of the woman to whom they were written to trust to her love & courage, rather than leave her to this aching uncertainty.

What has brought about such a change? Oh, no matter what it is—
only tell me!

I could take my life up again courageously if I only understood; for
whatever those months were to you, to me they were a great gift, a
wonderful enrichment; & still I rejoice & give thanks for them! You
woke me from a long lethargy, a dull acquiescence in conventional re-
strictions, a needless self-effacement. If I was awkward & inarticulate it
was because, literally, all one side of me was asleep.

I remember, that night we went to the "Figlia di Iorio," that in the
scene in the cave, where the Figlia sends him back to his mother (I
forget all their names), & as he goes he turns & kisses her, & *then she
can't let him go*—I remember you turned to me & said laughing: "That's
something you don't know anything about."

Well! I *did* know, soon afterward; & if I still remained inexpressive,
unwilling, "always drawing away," as you said, it was because I discovered in myself such possibilities of feeling on that side that I feared,
if I let you love me too much, I might lose courage when the time came
to go away!—Surely you saw this, & understood how I dreaded to be
to you, *even for an instant*, the "donna non più giovane" who clings &
encumbers—how, situated as I was, I thought I could best show my
love by refraining—& abstaining? You saw it was all because I loved
you?

And when you spoke of your uncertain future, your longing to break
away & do the work you really like, didn't you see how my heart *broke*
with the thought that, if I had been younger & prettier, everything
might have been different—that we might have had together, at least
for a short time, a life of exquisite collaborations—a life in which your
gifts would have had full scope, & you would have been able to do the
distinguished & beautiful things that you ought to do?—Now, I hope,
your future has after all arranged itself happily, just as you despaired,
—but remember that *those were my thoughts* when you were calling me
"conventional" . . .

I never expected to tell you this; but under the weight of this silence
I don't know what to say or leave unsaid. After nearly a month my
frank tender of friendship remains unanswered. If that was not what
you wished, what *is* then your feeling for me? My reason rejects the
idea that a man like you, who has felt a warm sympathy for a woman

like me, can suddenly, from one day to another, without any act or word on her part, lose even a friendly regard for her, & discard the mere outward signs of consideration by which friendship speaks. And so I am almost driven to conclude that your silence has another meaning, which I have not guessed. If any feeling subsists under it, may these words reach it, & tell you what I felt in silence when we were together!

Yes, dear, I loved you then, & I love you now, as you then wished me to; only I have learned that one must put all the happiness one can into each moment, & I will never again love you "sadly," since that displeases you.

You see I am once more assuming that you *do* care what I feel, in spite of this mystery! How can it be that the sympathy between two people like ourselves, so many-sided, so steeped in imagination, should end from one day to another like a mere "passade"—end by my passing, within a few weeks, utterly out of your memory? By all that I know you are, by all I am myself conscious of being, I declare that I am unable to believe it!

You told me once I should write better for this experience of loving. I felt it to be so, & I came home so fired by the desire that my work should please you! But this incomprehensible silence, the sense of your utter indifference to everything that concerns me, has stunned me. It has come so suddenly . . .

This is the last time I shall write you, dear, unless the strange spell is broken. And my last word is one of tenderness for the friend I love —for the lover I worshipped.

Goodbye, dear.

Oh, I don't want my letters back, dearest! I said that in my other letter only to make it easier for you if you were seeking a transition—

Do you suppose I care what becomes of them if you don't care?

Is it really to my dear friend—*to Henry's friend*—to "dearest Morton"—that I have written this?

Ms:UT

To Sara Norton

The Mount
Lenox, Mass.
Saturday
[October 17, 1908]

Dear Sally,

I am touched to the depths by your letter of yesterday. Your last note gave no impression of such an impending change.[1]

How I grieve with you, ache for you, poor child, the more perhaps as what you speak of is only partly intelligible, or is not so at all. But if it is a retrospect of wasted, wasteful pain, oh then how my own joins itself to yours!

Don't give the French story another thought—above all, don't bother to return it. I will call you up this evening.

If by "could I have done differently," you mean where your father was concerned—no one who knows you could dream of thinking so. If you mean where you were concerned—alas, I should like to get up on the house-top & cry to all who come after us: "Take your own life, every one of you!"

Well, I think of you with deep sympathy, knowing all the while it can't help you.

Yrs Ever, E.W.

Ms:BL

1. Charles Eliot Norton was dying.

To Charles Eliot Norton

The Mount
Lenox, Mass.
Sunday [Fall 1908]

Dear Mr Norton,

Do you know, I wanted two days ago to write & ask you to cast a glance at my little "Motor-flight" book; & then I refrained because I thought I might, by so doing, put you to the trouble of dictating an answer.—Now your dear note has come of its own accord, & given me a quite peculiar pleasure.

I am so glad you cared to look at the book & have Sally read you a little of it.—I always remembered with so much pride the message you once sent me about one of the articles in it.

Teddy & I both send you our love & most affectionate greetings. There is much more that I should like to say, but fear to weary you with; but I can sum it up in this—that I hope you will think of me as one of the many who have been stimulated & delighted by your interest & sympathy, & helped by your affection.

> Ever yours
> Edith

Ms:HL

To Sara Norton

> Queen's Acre
> Windsor
> November 18 [1908]

Dear Sally— I think I wrote you just after getting to London; but I had three such crowded days there that I am not sure about dates. Did I tell you that Gaillard Lapsley came up to lunch with me, & that I found him in good spirits, & looking *much* better than when he stayed with us at Lenox two years ago?

Dear Mr. James very nobly stayed on in London, so that he might go to Rye with me in the motor; & Howard Sturgis also stayed on, so that he & I, H.J. & Mr. Berry lunched & dined & saw pictures together. One day I motored down to Cassiobury to see Lady Essex,¹ & we took in St. Albans by the way. Cassiobury is full of beautiful Grinling Gibbons carvings, room after room garlanded & festooned with masses of fruit & flowers.

The next day H.J., W.B. & I motored to Rye. It was a perfect summer day, & we took in the Dulwich gallery on the way, & then, when we reached Maidstone, decided to dash across to Canterbury, where we had a delicious half hour at sunset, & then crossed the marshes in the dark to Rye. The next day was again glorious, & we motored Walter over to Dover, & saw him off for Egypt;[2] then returned to Rye by Lympne Castle, on the high ridge above the marshes. The next day I motored over to Ashford & lunched with the Alfred Austins, & the day after that H.J. took me to see the Morton Frewens at Brede,[3] a strange ghostly old house of pre-Henry VIII architecture, extraordinarily picturesque; then to Brickwall, another Frewen place, a beautiful half-timbered house wh. I knew well from photos.—The day before yesterday H.J. & I motored over here, to Howard Sturgis's, another beautiful run, by Bodiam Castle, Reigate, Dorking & Leatherhead. At Box Hill, H.J. suddenly decided that he wanted me to see Meredith, & I was taken in protesting, for I think such visits rather an intrusion; but great was my surprise to be received with outstretched hands & the exclamation: "My dear child, I've read every word you've written, & I've always wanted to see you! I'm flying through France in your motor at this moment."[4]

He was a wonderful thing to see himself, radiating light & life from every feature & every tone of his voice—so different from the ruined man I had had described to me!—It was a fine impression.

Yesterday dear H.J. went back to Rye to my sorrow. I shall never forget his welcome & his kindness.—Here I am also in the atmosphere of kindness, but there is no one *quite* like him.

Yesterday Howard took me to a most interesting ceremony at Eton, when the King & Queen opened the new Memorial Hall built in memory of the Eton men who fell in S. Africa. Our seats were just under the Royal dais, so we saw & heard to perfection, & it was very pretty, picturesque & well-done. Next week I am going up to Lady St. Helier's,[5] where a long string of engagements awaits me. London is full, on account of Parliament, & everybody is so friendly. Last week the Duchess of Manchester[6] asked me to dine to meet Asquith & Balfour,[7] & I was sorry to have missed that. Barrie[8] has asked me to go with him to see his new play, which is the success of the season, & I am very glad, as seats are impossible to get.

I rec'd your letter while I was at Rye, & how well I know, dear Sally, the *ebb-tide* time that you are going through! It is the worst of all. I hope your cold is better, & that things are at least going quietly & not disturbingly. I shall not give up the hope of seeing you later in Paris.

I still think you should publish your father's letters, with an intro-duction, & a slight thread of narrative to string them on, & H.J. thinks so too, & agrees that *you* are the person to do it. The regular "biography" has been over-done, but the letters wd. certainly be appreciated.—

I am sleeping better, & am very glad I came away, for the change & movement carry me along, help to form an *outer surface*. But the mortal desolation is there, will always be there.

Thank you for Prof. Thayer's article. It was *pleasant*, & "respectable," but I thought it much less well done than the leading article you sent me from the Boston paper—was it the Globe or Herald? I have always wondered who did that.

Goodbye, dear Sally.
     Yr affte E.W.

Ms:BL

1. Adèle Grant of New York was now married to the seventh Earl of Essex.

2. Berry had been appointed judge on the International Tribunal in Cairo, Egypt.

3. Morton Frewen, sportsman and traveler, married to Clara Jerome, the sister of Jennie Jerome Churchill. Brede was a fourteenth-century manor house with a vast hall and magnificent fireplaces. Some years earlier, Frewen had rented Brede to Stephen and Cora Crane.

4. George Meredith, the novelist and poet, was eighty years old in 1908. In *A Backward Glance*, EW gives a fuller account of this meeting. After she had withdrawn a little to talk with two other visitors, she kept "watching from my corner the nobly confronted profiles of the two old friends. . . . As they sat there, James benignly listening, Meredith eloquently discoursing, and their old deep regard for each other burning steadily through the surface eloquence and the surface attentiveness, I felt I was in great company and I was glad."

5. The former Mary Mackenzie of Scotland; married to Colonel Stanley of the Coldstream Guards; after his death, she married Francis Jeune, who became the first Baron St. Helier. Lady St. Helier was one of the great literary hostesses of the Edwardian era.

6. The Duchess of Manchester had been the socially prominent Consuelo Yznaga of New York, where Edith Jones had known her as a young girl.

7. Herbert Asquith, the liberal politician, recently had become Prime Minister and would remain in office until 1916.

Arthur James Balfour, the Tory leader, had been Prime Minister from 1902 to 1905.

8. James Barrie (1860–1937, knighted in 1913) was the author of *The Admirable Crichton* in 1902 and *Peter Pan* in 1904. His new play was *What Every Woman Knows.*

To Sara Norton

52 Portland Place W.

December 3 [1908]

Dear Sally,

Thank you for the interesting account of your father's books, & for the Lee-Hamilton[1] article, wh. gave me nothing new, as I knew his history fairly well. It is a pity there hasn't been a more intelligent review of his work.

I think I wrote last from Windsor—or had I already come here? Well, here have I been for ten very crowded days, overwhelmed by Lady St. Helier's kindness, & as much struck as ever by the incessant English hospitality. There are so many people in town that to my ignorant eye it seems just like "the season," & everybody in London passes through this house. We have had beautiful weather till two days ago, so that I was able to give my mornings to pleasant sight-seeing prowls, and there has been something to do all day—& that for the present is my chief need.

I went to Cliveden[2] last Saturday, to the young Waldorf Astors, & met there a large & very charming party—Mr. Balfour, Sir Frank Lascelles,[3] Ld Ribblesdale,[4] Ld & Lady Elcho,[5] Dcess of Manchester, Lady Essex, Howard Sturgis, &c &c. It was easy & pleasant, & we all got on well with each other. As for Cliveden, even in the white November fog it was exquisite, & I left with regret. Dear Henry J. came up from Rye for two days this week, & stayed here with Lady St. H., breaking through his inveterate rule of always going to his club. He was dear & devoted & there is no one like him. He is coming again on Sat. next, & we are motoring down to Windsor to spend Sunday with Howard Sturgis. I am then coming back here for three days, to keep various engagements, & after that I shall start at a leisurely pace for the continent, perhaps stopping a day or two at Rye.—I am still vague about this.—Next week I am going with Mr. Barrie to see his play & lunching with Mr. Gosse[6] at the House of Lords. Today I was to have gone to tea with Miss May Sinclair,[7] whom I met here one evening, but I could find no other time to go to the Duchess of Sutherland,[8] whom I like, & who is in London only for two days or so; so I shall try to see Miss S. another time.—Tonight George Alexander has sent me stalls for his new play, by Sutro;[9] but I fear it is not thrilling. Tomorrow I lunch with Lady Bective,[10] next day with your friend Lady Pollock,[11] today we have a lot of people, rather amusing, at luncheon—& so on, & so on! Among other things, I am going down to spend a day at Limpsfield with Ld & Lady Burghclere.[12] I wonder if you know her? She is charming, & was very kind to me when we were last here.—

J. Morton[13] is here, staying with Sir P. Burne-Jones,[14] & he & I devoted a morning to the Abbey the other day. He sails soon, I believe.

I hope you are feeling better, & there is less over-whelming work to be dealt with. You must not give up the idea of coming abroad. Only give me as much notice as you can, since I ask people to stay from time to time, & I want to keep your room free for you whenever you can come.

I sleep much better since I came to London, & I wish you the same solace, for you must need it as much.

Yrs affly
   E.W.

After Jan. 1st
   58 rue de Varenne.
I spent all the afternoon in the H. of Commons yesterday, hoping to hear Balfour on the Education Bill, but only dull people spoke.

1. Eugene Lee-Hamilton, the half-brother of EW's friend Vernon Lee. He had recovered miraculously from a long period of invalidism, and was playing something of a role in the world of letters.

2. The three-hundred-acre estate above the Thames of the expatriate American William Waldorf Astor and his brilliant authoritarian wife, the former Nancy Langhorne.

3. The British Ambassador to Russia since 1895.

4. Lord Ribblesdale: brother-in-law of Prime Minister Asquith, former Lord-in-Waiting to Queen Victoria, a Master of Buck Hounds, and a patron of French racing.

5. Lord Hugo Elcho, Member of Parliament and the eldest son of the tenth Earl of Wemyss and Lady Mary Elcho. EW would soon go to Stanway, their home at the foot of the Cotswold hills in Gloucestershire, for a weekend party in her honor. Stanway was one of the main gathering places for Edwardian life. Lady Elcho, later Lady Wemyss, was to be a cherished friend of EW for almost thirty years.

6. Edmund Gosse (1849–1928), "the official British man of Letters," in H. G. Wells's phrase; librarian for the House of Lords; author of several literary biographies, and in 1907 of the superb memoir *Father and Son*.

7. The novelist May Sinclair (1863–1946), author of *The Divine Fire* in 1904, was active in feminist causes and a thoughtful student of writings on psychoanalysis. Her work has been revived in the 1980s.

8. Lady Millicent Fanny St. Clair Erskine, a daughter of the Earl of Roslyn, was married to the fourth Duke of Sutherland. Henry James once described her as "amiable and 'literary.' " She was the author of several novels.

9. George Alexander (1858–1918), manager of the St. James's Theatre in London. He had produced Henry James's ill-fated *Guy Domville* in 1895. The new play by the English dramatist Alfred Sutro (1863–1933) was *The Building of Bridges*.

10. The name of this gracious and attractive person would soon become a point of reference in EW's English circle. Howard Sturgis was so charmed by Lady Bective that he proposed the word "bective" as a synonym for charming. Elaborating on the notion at a Queen's Acre lunch table, he would hold that there were some who were "bective"; others were "abective"; and finally those who were *"absolument imbectes."*

11. Lord Frederick Pollock, the distinguished jurist, and Lady Pollock were particular friends of Henry James.

12. Lady Winifred Burghclere was a writer on English historical subjects and a public figure of some note. Her husband, Lord Burghclere, was president of the Board of Agriculture.

13. Johnson Morton, about the same age as EW, was a frequent visitor at The Mount. He enjoyed a modest career as a writer, and worked hard for the poor of Boston.

14. Sir Philip Burne-Jones (1861–1926), painter and son of the Pre-Raphaelite painter Sir Edward Burne-Jones.

To W. Morton Fullerton

52, Portland Place,
(London) W.
December 19 [1908]

Dear Mr. Fullerton,

You have—if they still survive—a few notes & letters of no value to your archives, but which happen to fill a deplorable lacuna in those of their writer.

I shall be in Paris on Monday next—the 21st—for a day only, & I write to ask if you would be kind enough to send them to me that day at my brother's.

Perhaps the best way of making sure that they come straight into my own hands would be to register them.

Yrs sincerely
E. Wharton

Ms:UT

To John Hugh Smith[1]

Avignon
December 26 [1908]

Merry Christmas!

Dear Mr. Smith,

Was I—or were *you*—all the complicated things you say? It seemed to me so much simpler! I'm afraid I always go with outstretched hands toward any opportunity for a free & frank exchange of ideas, & am too much given to omitting the preliminary forms where I find a fundamental likeness of mind!

It was a great pleasure to wander over the cosmos with you in that easy fashion, & if you liked it too, for whom are you concerned, & why do you plan better things for our next meeting? Beware of gilding the lily!

The elopement,[2] though not without its vicissitudes (of which I will give you the details when we meet) has worked as well, I suppose, as elopements can, or any other human institution. We had an adorable day of sunshine & beauty at Dijon, which dear Howard really enjoyed; & we met there some old friends of mine, the Comte & Ctesse Arthur de Vogüé, who are great folk in the Dijonnais, & have a beautiful old place at Commarin, about 25 miles from Dijon. They insisted on our lunching with them en route for Lyons, & we had a delightful two hours in the old house of wh. I send you the portrait, which passed untouched through the Revolution, & is packed with old tapestries (*such* Gobelins!), old furniture & family portraits. There we met another friend of mine, Ctesse Robert de Fitz James, who was immensely "struck" by "ce charmant Enès-Smith,"[3] & insisted on his going to dine & the opera with her on our return to Paris, asking Howard & me to come too, rather as an after-thought!!! Babe's moustache has an extra spiral in it since this incident.

Unfortunately Commarin took us out of our way, & we didn't leave there as early as we ought—& we had two tyre punctures after dark, & reached Lyons at one a.m.! It was at this point that the strain of the elopement rather told on Howard, & he began to wonder why he had "passed across the glimmering seas" instead of Christmassing peacefully at Quaker. But he behaved with heroism, & continued the journey yesterday without a murmur. Now we are taking a rest here before our next flight, & luckily there is sunshine for this beautiful place.

I shall look for you, then, toward the end of Jan., & will try to "corser" the programme as much as possible, & provide all the Faubourgian emotions that I can—but remember that, where the ladies are concerned, the Babe will have been before you!

> Yrs sincerely
> Edith Wharton

Thanks for trying to find the Hardy poem for me.
Ionica has become a livre de chevet.[4]

Ms:BL

1. A. John Hugh Smith (born 1881) came from an influential family of English landed gentry that had produced bankers, admirals, and merchants. At age twenty-seven, he was beginning a career in banking, with a special competence in Anglo-Russian financial affairs. On meeting John Hugh Smith a few weeks

before at Stanway, EW was immensely struck with him. After passing further time in her company at Cirencester and Queen's Acre, Hugh Smith wrote EW: "I want to say something that I find rather difficult to express. When I see you again our friendship will have one quality which was not altogether present here in London. The fact of such an obviously brilliant person such as you being so exceptionally kind to me has at times made me a little self-conscious —even when I was alone with you. And the simplicity I sought was not helped by Howard Sturgis's and Mr. James's amused though perfectly kind remarks. . . . In Paris we shall be able to go ahead and eliminate this Jacobean element in our relation."

2. EW and Howard Sturgis had crossed over to France just before Christmas, and had made the trip to the Dijonnais here described.

3. The travelers had been joined by Sturgis's companion William Haynes Smith, affectionately known as "the Babe"; EW gives a phonetic spelling to Rosa de Fitz-James's pronunciation of his name.

4. *Ionica*: poems of 1891 by William Johnson (1823–1892), who signed his prose writings with the additional surname Cory. His poetry mingled the Hellenic with the modern. He is best known for his famous line: "They told me, Heraclitus, they told me you were dead."

Livre de chevet: a book kept by the bedside.

To John Hugh Smith

58 Rue de Varenne
February 2 [1909]

My dear Mr. John,

You may imagine that no ordinary fatality has kept me all these days from thanking you for that beautiful, that admirable cigarette-case—& that too at a moment when it needed all the robustness of the self-conceit which Howard deprecates in me to convince me that you wouldn't, after all, think better of your intention! But somehow, I felt sure that the Impulsive Idiot would have his way, in spite of the counsels of the Prudent Prodigy[1] (who will, I hope, get hopelessly left behind in the race of life!); and as I too forgot the box at the moment of leave-taking it was really in my possession before I could "doubt my happiness."

All the more reason, then, to tell you sooner how I am enjoying it, & how I flourish it in the faces of envious friends (female especially)!

And the restraining cause has been, not one big tragic obstacle—like the "floo," or a declaration from George Moore[2]—but simply a ravening pack of things-to-be-done, assailing me at once from all sides, into whose ravening maws I have had to cast one pleasant thing after another, to get away with my life. Never did I know such a storm of letters, notes, books to be thanked for, & small domestic riddles to be solved—with a sad background of "grippe-d" & gouty husband to be excused from dinners & cheered at the family fire-side! These are indeed the moments, dear Mr. John, when one has the nostalgia of the idle, the "wasted" hours; the hours when one was neither useful, altruistic nor industrious, & no one on earth was "the better" for one's being anywhere!

Et voilà—

No, I don't remember about Flaubert's first love, mais je me renseignerai— And I'm so glad you like the wonderful letters. They were long a chevet book of mine. Adolphe[3] I knew you'd like, you who have a scent for the rare & fine. And don't forget to get G. Sand's equally wonderful answers to Flaubert—equal not, of course, in "brilliancy," but in wisdom & serenity as fine as anything I know.

I'm working at my "Tales of Men,"[4] but life is so jerky & incoherent now that the ink doesn't flow very fast. And yet "alles Entschiedende ensteht trotzdem,"[5] as the Prudent Prodigy might point out—confound him!

Oh—I must tell you the last phase of the Blanche story. We lunched there last Sunday, & just before luncheon B. took me aside & said confidentially: "Mrs Wharton, in a day or two you will receive—" (I listen with conscious cast-down lids & straining ears) "the first number of a new literary review to which I hope you will subscribe—*to please me!*"—

G Moore was there, & revealed himself so monstrous, incredible & repulsive a bounder that I had to annihilate him; which I did to my satisfaction, so completely that there were no recognizable fragments to gather up. I don't excel at such moments, normally, but in this case the greatness of the opportunity inspired me, & when he began to talk to me about the "ladies he had written about in his memoirs, & who, funnily enough, were rather flattered," I said: "I should think *you* would have been flattered at their even having heard of your book"; & having tasted blood I proceeded to wade in it . . .

The silver pen handle was sent to Charles St yesterday, not having been found immediately after you left. The Scribner order for the Jameses has also been despatched—

Send me now & then some record of that fine registering-instrument of yours. I shall be cheered & interested by the spectacle, & simply glad, as a friend, to have news of you.

Yrs ever sincerely E.W.

Alas, I don't know when, or if, we shall go to England—or anywhere—ever!

Ms:BL

1. The Impulsive Idiot and the Prudent Prodigy: the two sides of his nature, as John Hugh Smith himself defined them.

2. George Moore (1852–1933), prolific Anglo-Irish novelist and a leader in the literary movement that led away from Victorian mores. He also collaborated in the planning of the Irish National Theatre. Further on in this letter, EW recounts a set-to with Moore.

3. *Adolphe*, the novel by Benjamin Constant published in 1816; the tale of a seducer pursued by his victim.

4. *Tales of Men and Ghosts* (ten stories, including "The Legend," "The Eyes," and "Afterward") would be published in 1910.

5. "All decisive matters are coming to pass *even so*." EW meant to write "Entscheidende."

To John Hugh Smith

58 Rue de Varenne
February 12 [1909]

It's not an unguent, my dear John Hugh—but a wonderful "Rose Dentrifice" (or some such floral name) that I want from the flower-garden of Floris,¹ if you'll kindly tell him so. I know it's called "Rose," at any rate; & that ought to guide you to the right flacon. Will you ask him to send me one, & will you pay him, & let me know how much I owe you?—

Dear me! What *jeunes féroces* you & Percy[2] are—I shuddered at your reasons for repudiating "Olive Latimer"[3] so scornfully. If what you said had been addressed to Mrs. Campbell's acting, I shd have understood; but no, it's the subject you scorn. My first impulse, *of course*, was to truckle—but, as I cast my eye backward over literature, I seemed to remember a few other neurotic women who were discontented with their husbands & relations—one Clytemnestra, e.g., & Phaedra, & Iseult, & Anna Karenine & Pia Tolomei,[4] too Francesca da Rimini— who still live in the imagination, & will, I fancy, outlast Shaw—not to speak of Barrie! And I wonder, among all the tangles of this mortal coil, which one contains tighter knots to undo, & consequently suggests more tugging, & pain, & diversified elements of misery, than the marriage tie—& which, consequently, is more "made to the hand" of the psychologist & the dramatist? Allez! It's all in the point of view. We love Shaw because he's knocked over a few tottering conventions; but his satires won't outlast the special weaknesses he satirizes, because they're too specialized & don't deal with the general human fate. It's only the imagination that "sees things whole" that can keep its visions alive—& so far those imaginations haven't been afraid to deal with the common, inevitable mortal problems . . .

Now I wait for you—

Yes, the Chamberlain poem was good— Thanks for sending it. We are detained here by the dentist—I mean my husband is—& I don't expect to leave till the 19th or 20th.

Ever yrs sincerely
E. W.

I use Rose Tooth Wash, Floris, Jermyn St, sole manufacturer—

Ms:BL

1. The well-known shop on Jermyn Street in London: see postscript to letter.

2. Percy Lubbock (1879–1965), an ardent disciple of Henry James, a younger friend of Howard Sturgis, and a Cambridge classmate of John Hugh Smith. EW met Lubbock (then twenty-seven years old) at Queen's Acre in 1906; his first book, a fictionalized biography of Elizabeth Barrett Browning, had just appeared.

3. A play by Rudolf Besier, featuring Mrs. Pat Campbell.

4. The spirit, among the late repentants in *Purgatorio* v, who introduces her-self to the travelers as "*la Pia,*" and says that "*Siena mi fê; disfecemi Maremma*" —"Siena made me: Maremma unmade me." She is thought to have belonged to a leading family of Siena—originally identified as the Tolomei clan, but this has been proven impossible—who was imprisoned by her husband in a castle in the Maremma and murdered by his orders.

To W. Morton Fullerton

[February 1909[1]]
Tuesday

Are you coming to dine tonight? And am I not wrong in asking you, when I know how stupid, disappointing, altogether "impossible" you found me yesterday?—Alas, the long isolation has made me inarticulate, & yet I wasn't meant to be! But that doesn't help now, I suppose ... And then yesterday morning I was *paralyzed* by not getting your note till 11, knowing it must have been written, & having the conviction that it must have got into the wrong hands, yet being unable to find out ...

"But why didn't you forget all that?" ...

Tant pis! Only don't let us *pretend*. Think of me, Dear, in the old way, the only way in which I may be a little worth while—& don't, above all, feel obliged to try to make *me* think what isn't! Please!—

So, if you come & dine, let it be with the old friend of last year, who knits & reads—qui t'aime, qui t'aime, mais qui sait qu'elle ne sait pas te le dire, et qui se taira désormais ...

Ms:UT

1. Fullerton added at top of letter: "Feb. 23 After!!!"

To John Hugh Smith

Hotel de Crillon
Place de la Concorde
April 30 [1909]

My dear John Hugh,

Vanity came to my rescue, & assured me that your long silence could only be due to the fact that the things you wanted to say were not of a kind to be committed to paper by a cautious hand! If it hadn't been for this soothing reflection I should have felt rather badly—but as it was I have gone about puffed up by a sense of importance which I trust you will be too generous to take from me!—My own delay in replying to your letter was caused by an odious attack of influenza, which fell upon me the very week I migrated from the rue de V.—I actually had to crawl out of bed to get here, & the result was that I dragged along, half well, for another week.—During this time I "enjoyed an agreeable gloom," like the good little boy in Berquin's "Mirror of the Mind"[1] & despaired of the republic to an extent unusual in one of my light nature.

So you see your cry of boredom "struck an answering chord," as the novelist says, & far from reproving it I secretly echoed it! I do perfectly understand your impatience to get hold of some more engrossing work in the line you have chosen, & your feeling that your other interests are irrelevant— The answer is that one can't always tell, & that to *have* the interests is such an immense, ineffable pull over the people who haven't, that the rest hardly counts. To have as few numb tracts in one's consciousness as possible—that seems to me, so far, the most desirable thing in life, even though the Furies do dance in hob-nailed shoes on the sensitive tracts at a rate that sometimes makes one wish for any form of anaesthesia.

I'm starting in on Man Tales V (no royalties for you on this one!), which is such a tremendous subject that I'm sure it is going to crush me. I have been reading a very interesting article by Ernest Seillière[2] on a correspondence between Taine & Nietzsche. I long to send it to you, but it came out in a tiresome report of some Ecole des Sciences Politiques, & he has asked to have his copy back; so I must wait & tell you at Whitsuntide— Aren't you coming before? We are—or should be— such near neighbors now, & we could have some good talks together & do some theatres. And in a week I get my new motor, & we can go farther afield than Montfort. Apropos of Montfort—I told my friend Madame d'Oilliamson about your epitaph, "tué à la chasse par Mgr le Dauphin," & she got the Duc de Luynes to motor her over to M. last week from Dampierre, & found that the défunt (whose name I again forget) was her husband's great uncle; & stranger still, that the pension accorded to the family by Louis XVI (6000 fcs) to atone for the Dauphin's bad aim, *is still being paid* to her aunt, Comtesse d'Oilliamson!!

Next week you will probably receive "Artemis to Actaeon & Other Verses" by E.W.[3]—I'll put an illegible inscription in the vol. when we meet. I see that Mr. Hewlett[4] has been before me in addressing himself metrically to the lady, but I don't think his Artemis & mine live in the same street.

Do write me soon, & tell me lots of things—

Yr affte friend
    E.W.

Ms:BL

1. Arnaud Berquin (1747–1791) was the author of numerous stories for children. His artlessly didactic little tales were the source of the word "*berquinade*." *The Looking-Glass for the Mind* (in one version of the title) was a collection of his stories for English readers, taken from his ongoing volumes, *L'Ami des Enfants*.

2. Ernest-Antoine-Aimé-Léon Seillière (born 1866), moral and political philosopher, author of a four-volume work (1903 ff.) on "the philosophy of imperialism," one volume of which was devoted to Nietzsche and the theme of the Romantic revolt against reason.

3. *Artemis to Actaeon*, the first of EW's two collections of poems, had just been published by Scribners.

4. Maurice Hewlett (1861–1923), novelist, poet, and essayist, with a taste for the historically romantic.

To W. Morton Fullerton

Wed Evng
[May 10, 1909]

Pauvre *Cher*!

The tiresome woman is *buried*, once for all, I promise, & only the novelist survives!

Viens déjeuner avec elle sans crainte demain.

I am in such a veine de travail that you are yet going to find your prophecy come true about my work.—It's going to be *"better than before."*

My heart ached to see you so tired today, & to think that I was part of the tire.

Cela ne sera plus ainsi ... I love you even better than I knew.

Ms:UT

To W. Morton Fullerton

Wednesday Night
[May 1909]

I am so happy at what you told me about "Ogrin"!¹—you'd understand why, if you knew how often & often I've said to myself (like the Jongleur de N. Dame): "Oh, if once I could *make* something for him that people—indifferent strangers—might talk about & find good; & if he might hear them praising it, while he sat silent & said to himself: 'Good people, it's not *hers*, it's mine!' "

Et voilà—cela m'est arrivé, et je suis heureuse ...

It's just because everything in our whole story counts so much for me that I wrote you as I did last Saturday, & tried to say what I did just now.

Don't think me sentimental or "petite fille"—still less, the woman who tries to make herself more interesting. It's just this—the situation *is* changed, & I, who like to *walk up to things*, recognize it, & am ready to accept it—only it must be nettement!

I recognize, also, perfect freedom in loving and in un-loving; but only on condition that it is associated with equal sincerity.

Since things are as they are now, I look on you as free to carry your soucis cardiaques where you please; *but* on condition that you & I become again, in our talk & our gestes, the good comrades we were two years ago. If I thought that you could continue to talk to me & to *be* with me as you were this afternoon, while you had, at the same time, even transiently, even à fleur d'épiderme, the same attitude to any one else, I should think you had failed in the loyalty due to a love like mine, as freely & unconditionally given as mine has been.

That I may not be tempted to think this—that you may be spared, perhaps, the thought of hurting me (it would make you unhappy, I know!)—let us go back gaily & goodhumouredly to our former state ... that is the form my fierté takes!

You see I've been so happy, Dear, that nothing could make me quite sad except the feeling that you had had less sense of freedom in loving me than I wanted you to have.

Vale!

Ms:UT

1. "Ogrin the Hermit," a long narrative poem EW had written in recent days. It is based upon a retelling of the Tristan and Iseult legend (by the literary historian Joseph Bédier), according to which the lovers, fleeing Iseult's husband King Mark, are given shelter by the hermit Ogrin. The narrative theme is the conflict between piety and sensuality, between Christian teachings and the influences of "the old gods" of an earlier time. It is profoundly autobiographical. EW's handwritten copy was inscribed to Fullerton: "*Per Te, Sempre Per Te.*"

To Frederick Macmillan

Crillon—
May 29, 1909

Dear Mr. Macmillan

Please excuse my delay in answering your letter of the 17th. I have not been well, or should not have kept you waiting so long.

It is most kind of you to offer me the opportunity to do the book on

Paris which our poor friend had planned but, even if I had not my hands full for months ahead, I should not feel either the ability or the inclination to do such a piece of work. A book on Paris, in addition to special qualifications in the author, requires an intimate & varied acquaintance with the most complex of cities, in all its aspects, historical, architectural & sociological.

Have you ever thought of my friend Mr. Morton Fullerton of the Times as combining an unusual number of these qualities? If there were a short time limit I should not suggest his name, but if you are willing to wait, as you say, I know no one half as well qualified to do the work charmingly as well as thoroughly. You have probably read lately his interesting article on "The Crisis of the State in France," in the National Review for May, which has been spoken of throughout the whole continental press; but I don't know if you have seen the volume he published in French a few years ago, "Terres Françaises," which was crowned by the French Academy, & which I have frequently heard men of letters here speak of as the best "appreciation" of French scenery & history ever written by a foreigner.

I think if you will ask Mr. Henry James, who knows Mr. Fullerton intimately, he will confirm what I say as to his ability to do the kind of book you want.—I make this suggestion entirely on my own authority, & without knowing whether he would feel able to undertake the task in addition to his regular work; but I hope you will be able to persuade him to, for the sake of all lovers of Paris.[1]

I shall be in London in about ten days, & meanwhile my address, after June 3d, will be care of Howard Sturgis Esqre, Windsor.

I am leaving to the last my thanks for the volume of my poems, & also of the cheap ed. of the House of Mirth. The latter is a marvel, & I am delighted with it.—I also like very much the binding of "Artemis," but I don't quite understand why the paper is so much less good in quality than that which Mr. Scribner used for his own edition.

With kindest regards to Mrs. Macmillan, & in the hope of soon seeing you,

Sincerely yrs
　　Edith Wharton

Ms:British Museum

1. Macmillan did invite Fullerton to write the book about Paris. EW and James, meanwhile, hatched a little conspiracy whereby EW would forward £100 to James who would then send it on—as from himself—to Macmillan, to serve as an advance on the book. Fullerton was entirely privy to this scheme. In fact, Macmillan put up the hundred pounds, with James standing as surety in case Fullerton failed to produce. Fullerton never did write the book, but Macmillan made no effort to recoup the advance.

To W. Morton Fullerton

[Hotel Crillon]
Thursday Evn'g
[May 1909]

Your letter has just come.

Have I ever advised you to do the *easy* thing?—No—you know it! —Then listen to me, dear, when I say don't go on Saturday.

Why should you be ordered about in that way? She[1] knows where you are to be found, & that she can see you when she appoints a time to meet you—or rather when *you* appoint a time convenient to meet *her*—in the rue F.

Meanwhile there is no reason why you should go to Rueil to see— under heaven knows what conditions—a person whom you believe to be half-mad, or at any rate dangerous.—Consider this well, & don't say you will go until you see me tomorrow.—

When the interview does take place, why should it not take place before witnesses? Have you not a friend who would go with you? Or could you not take an homme d'affaires, if there are business matters to be settled? Such scenes as you were exposed to before leaving Paris more than justify your dealing with the whole matter now on a business footing. You will answer that she will be "furious." Let her be! Was she not "furious" when she saw you alone, & you gave her all she demanded, before you left?—Don't commit the folly of risking any unnecessary danger in contact with an irresponsible person.

One last word of advice— Have the whole matter out in one interview. Don't leave anything to a sequel; & oh, *hang* your furniture, or

whatever else you may wish back! Anything, of course, but papers; &
I understand you have all of these that you actually know of.

Won't you let me know about what time you'll come tomorrow a.m.?
Come to lunch at one if you prefer. I'm alone— Forgive this long
lecture!

Is there no man you can consult?

Ms:UT

1. Mme. Henrietta Mirecourt, an older woman who at one time lived at the
same address as Fullerton—2 Rue de la Chaussée d'Antin—and may have been
the owner of the building. Fullerton had been carrying on an affair with her
for a number of years, perhaps since the late 1890s. During one of Fullerton's
absences from Paris, Mme. Mirecourt seems to have made off with some of
Fullerton's furniture and a batch of his private papers. The latter revealed an
adulterous affair with Margaret Brooke, the Ranee of Sarawak, and a homosex-
ual relation with the sculptor Ronald Gower. Mme. Mirecourt had been using
the letters as a way of forcing Fullerton to return to her. Judging from the
present letter, he had regained most of the papers. The sum of money made
available to Fullerton—see the preceding letter to Macmillan—was nonetheless
to be deployed by Fullerton to settle his accounts with Henrietta Mirecourt.

To W. Morton Fullerton

34 Brook St.
Friday
[July 1909]

Cher, I wrote you to Plymouth yesterday, as they told me at the steamer
office that a letter would reach you there.

But in case it doesn't, here is my address: *today till Monday*.

Care Alfred Austin Esqr

Swinford Old Manor

   Ashford, Kent—

or, in telegraphing, leave out Swinford Old Manor.

After Monday, Métropole, Folkestone.

I wrote in such haste yesterday that I may have given you the impression of a somewhat alarming determination to take possession of your time. Let me correct it! I only wanted to make my plans clear, or rather to show that I have none, to speak of, for the early part of next week; not in the least to say "you are to do this or that."

I also forgot to tell you about Macmillan. I saw him the other day, & he told me he had written you rue Fabert to say that he wanted you to do the Paris book, & seemed surprised that you had not answered. I told Henry about it, & he said you ought to get a good price, as the Macmillans expect the books of this series to sell very well. Henry is to have a good royalty (so, I suppose) & £1000[1] advance, & he seemed to think they would do about the same for you. I mention this in case you see Macmillan before going to Rye.

I send you the Times of yesterday & today. You will be gladder to see that than anything, n'est ce pas, cher?

Do let me hear at the earliest moment—

Ms:UT

1. EW most likely meant to write £100.

To Sara Norton

Queen's Acre, Windsor.
July 7, 1909

Dear Sally,

Your letter has just come, & confirmed all my fears. I knew things had been going wrong with you, & piling up on you, & that you had probably yourself been ill under the storm & stress of them. And when, each time that I saw Dorothy Ward, she also reported not having heard from you, I became still more sure. I am *so* sorry that you have had such a succession of worries & fatigues & contretemps—& how that ruthless heat must have aggravated them all! I am especially sorry about Denis, who cd. have relieved you of so many practical details. Have you at least found a good substitute? It isn't easy!

I wish you didn't have to go back so soon to Shady Hill; but perhaps after the abnormal heat there will come a cool August. Here it has been steadily wet & cold ever since I arrived, & I have not yet had on a summer dress!—I have spent the greater part of the month at Windsor, having found London rather oppressive after a week. I was more tired than I imagined, & I never feel very well in England; so that when, par-dessus le marché, I developed a furious case of hay-fever, I was glad to creep away here & be quiet. In London I didn't see very many people, for at the height of the Season everyone is engaged weeks ahead, & one must be there for a certain length of time to get into the current. But I dined & lunched out two or three times & went to one or two music-halls (the theatres are not worth it, except the Irish plays at the Court, which dear Henry took me to). I have seen the Wards several times. I lunched there in town, meeting the Protheros,¹ Sir Ian Hamil-ton,² etc., & then, one Sunday, Henry & I motored over to Stocks³ & lunched. That day they had Lady Stanley of Alderley,⁴ various Trevel-yans,⁵ & a clever little American, Miss Draper,⁶ who did some mono-logues which delighted Henry.

Then last Sunday, Dorothy Ward & Beatrix came here to tea, so we have had several meetings, as you see.

In the way of pictures there is nothing very interesting, except some Holbeins at the Burlington—& I don't care for Holbein! However, I have made a bid for a divine little Bonnington⁷ wh. is to be sold at Christies' the day after to-morrow, & wh. of course I shan't get! I have been to Oxford & to Cambridge, have spent two days with Mrs. Sheridan⁸ at Frampton Court, have lunched at Cliveden (& backed out of a big house-party there), have lunched & dined several times with the Duch-ess of Manchester, have declined a house-party at Cassiobury, & tea-ed there instead with all the mightiest in the land—& have enjoyed chiefly my moments of quiet here. Hay-fever depresses me frightfully, & then I care less & less for "general society," & more & more for just a few friends.

To-morrow I am going up to town for a night, & the day after to the Alfred Austins' for Sunday; & next week I go back to Paris.—I have heard of an attractive apartment there, & think it may suit us. Mean-while I continue to get the most cheerful reports of Teddy, who is in great spirits, & is now fishing in Canada. His mother has been rather seriously ill, but is better again, astounding woman that she is! I was afraid the heat would exhaust her, but her powers of resistance are boundless.—

Dear little Anna Bahlmann is coming out to join me in two or three weeks, & Teddy will either come with her or a fortnight later. The Drs. wish to give him another fortnight or so of the serum treatment wh. has worked so well with his teeth, & so he returns to Boston after his fishing, & then they will decide how long he must stay.

I have seen several beautiful old houses—Athelhampton, Montacute & Wolfeton, near Dorchester.

How sad the return to Ashfield must have been to you. I always "evoke" your dear father in his library there, or in the basket chair outside, under the trees. I am glad the garden is pretty & satisfactory. I was afraid the heat wd. ravage it.

Do you remember the day we sat on the verandah, & your father read Donne to us? And that evening, in the sitting room, he read Matthew Arnold. I think it was once when Walter Berry was with me, & I have always kept a specially charming memory of that afternoon & evening. But best of all I like to picture him as I saw him that last time at Shady Hill, last summer, coming so gallantly down the steps to tell Cook what road to take to go to Beverly! It was such a pleasant last vision of him, in full alertness & activity. You have beautiful memories to live with, at any rate, & a light shining down the past.

Write me soon again, care Munroe, 7 rue Scribe—& don't talk *bosh* about my not wanting to hear from you!

Yrs. affly.
   E.W.

There is a curious exhibition of Ford Madox Brown's[9] pictures in London. What a strange unnatural phase of art!

Ms:BL

1. George Walter Prothero (1848–1922), Cambridge historian and editor of the long-established literary periodical the *Quarterly Review*, and his wife, Fanny. The latter was a particular friend of Henry James.

2. Sir Ian Hamilton (1853–1947), one of the ablest military figures of his

generation, though his career would eventually be darkened by his role in the disastrous Dardanelles campaign in 1915. He was a cultivated and courtly person, and EW would enjoy his company, intermittently, for many years.

3. The country home of the Humphry Wards, near the village of Tring in Buckinghamshire.

4. The wife of Baron (Arthur) Stanley of Alderley. The latter's younger brother had been the first husband of EW's London friend and hostess, Lady St. Helier.

5. In 1904, Mrs. Ward's younger daughter, Janet Penrose, married George Macaulay Trevelyan (1876?–1962), one of the great historians of the period; he had just completed the second of his remarkable studies of Garibaldi.

6. Ruth Draper (1884–1956) would become the most brilliant stage monologuist in American theater history. EW refers to her rather condescendingly, but James was immensely taken with Miss Draper and even wrote a sketch for her (see *Complete Plays*, 1949).

7. Richard Parkes Bonington (EW added an "n") (1802–1828), a link between the English watercolorists and the Barbizon school in France.

8. Clare Frewen, a gifted sculptress (1885–1970), was married to Wilfred Sheridan.

9. Ford Madox Brown (1821–1893) was associated with the Pre-Raphaelite painters, most closely with Dante Gabriel Rossetti. His grandson was the novelist Ford Madox Ford.

To John Hugh Smith

Hotel Crillon
July 21 [1909]

Dear John Hugh,

Thank you a thousand times for sending me the Nation review, which I should not have seen otherwise as Macmillan seems to have given up his usual practice of sending me the notices of my books.

I won't pretend that I'm not most awfully pleased! Vague praise is well enough, but to have one's critic dot his *i*s like this is a rare & exquisite experience.

Here I am again, in a very nice apartment up in the sky, overlooking the whole of Paris, & consequently very cool; & here I am likely to stay for some time, as I think I've found just what we need in the way of permanent quarters—not an hôtel, alas, but *such* a good apartment! It is nearly opposite 58 rue de V., & looks south over the Cité de Varenne & the Doudeauville gardens. I don't think Teddy will need to keep his boots in the library, but the absence of such picturesque touches will be partly atoned for by the vulgar convenience of his being able to leave his room without going through the drawing-room. Also we shall be able to offer you a bachelor suite with its own latch-key, so that next winter you can combine Woollett-ing with the high thinking of the Faubourg St. Germain.

I didn't leave England till the 17th, for just as I was tearing myself from the Laureate's arms the Master of Rye, doubtless inflamed by jealousy, telegraphed me that he wanted to be taken on a little motor trip, & with my usual docility I countermanded Paris plans & turned Hortense's prow westward. We had three delightful days (with *real* weather, too!), & then I bade goodbye to the Master at Canterbury & dashed across the channel.—Howard's mingled admiration & disapproval of this last "coup" has called forth one of his best letters, & I've come to the conclusion that it's much more fun to worry one's friends than to "charm" them—though I've never tried the latter.

Henry was delighted with his water-colour, & it has an honourable place on the wall of his dear little panelled drawing-room. Mr. Leggatt didn't make a very clever guess about the price of the Bonnington, did he?—I was in despair at first, but now I'm very glad I didn't pay £360 for it, as I've got such lots of buying to do for the new apartment, if we get it. How I wish you were here to prowl for furniture with me! It's just the season for bargains.

Do let me know when you are coming, for I think I shall stay on for several weeks. Teddy intended to sail on Aug 1st but his mother is seriously ill, & he is not likely to get away as soon as that; & I shall probably await him here, unless the heat becomes excessive(!).

Well—I say to you, as Howard says to me in his last: "Keep it up —run your race—fly your flight—live your romances—drain the cup of pleasure to the dregs"—but when exhaustion sets in, think of your affte friend, the Hermitess of the Crillon.

Ms:BL

To W. Morton Fullerton

Thursday night—
August 12 [1909]

Mon aimé, It is just a month today since I came down to dinner at Rye, & found you standing by the hearth in the drawing-room talking to Henry. (Your back was turned to the door, & you didn't *feel me come in*, but went on talking. . . .)

During that month I have been completely happy. I have had everything in life that I ever longed for, & more than I ever imagined! Et je tenais à te le dire before the anniversary is over . . .

Ms:UT

To W. Morton Fullerton

In an old painted room of Le Fayel-Oise
Saturday Night [Late summer 1909]

My Dearest Love,

I am writing you this because, this afternoon, I passed by the dear old crooked church of Creil, where I spent such a happy hour with you a year & a half ago . . .

Before that, I had no personal life: since then you have given me all imaginable joy.

Nothing can take it from me now, or diminish it in my eyes, save the discovery that what has set my whole being free may gradually, imperceptibly, have become a kind of irksome bondage to you.

That is my besetting fear, & to spare you such a possibility is my constant thought.

It is impossible, in the nature of things, that our lives should run parallel much longer. I have faced the fact, & accepted it, & I am not afraid, except when I think of the pain & pity you may feel for *me*.

That I long to spare you; & so I want to tell you now, Dear, that I know how unequal the exchange is between us, how little I have to give that a man like you can care for, & how ready I am, when the transition comes, to be again the good comrade you once found me.

My only dread is lest my love should blind me, & my heart whisper "Tomorrow" when my reason says "Today" ... To escape that possibility, can't we make a pact that you shall give the signal, & one day simply call me "mon ami" instead of "mon amie"? If I felt sure of your doing that, I should be content!

I can't say this to you, because when I do you take me in your arms; et alors, je n'ai plus de volonté.

But it is *true*, & needs to be said: et je suis convaincue qu'il ne faut, des deux côtés, qu'un peu de bonne volonté et de franchise pour traverser l'étape difficile sans ébranler ce fonds de camaraderie qui subsistera toujours entre nous. Je tenais à te le dire.—

Please let me know on Monday as early as possible if you are coming to dine.—

Ms:UT

To Bernard Berenson[1]

H. de Crillon
Sunday
[Late September 1909]

Dear Mr. Berenson, I saw Mr. Fullerton last evening, & he is very eager to make a part of Mr. Adams's[2] happy "combination." He thinks he can surely free himself for one of the three evenings you named— most probably for tomorrow, Monday; but he must ask his chief first, & is not likely to see him till one o'c today.—He will send me a positive answer this afternoon, & meanwhile I write to ask if you will—or if you can—keep yourself free till I have it.

Yrs sincerely,
    E. Wharton

Ms:VT

1. See introduction to Part IV.
2. Henry Adams, seventy-one at this date, was in Paris with some frequency, usually staying in an apartment on the Avenue du Bois de Boulogne (renamed

the Avenue Foch in 1929), near that of his friend Elizabeth Cameron. (See letter to Mrs. Cameron, November 26, 1915.) EW and Adams had known one another for many years, though their friendship properly speaking had begun only in the spring of 1908.

To Sara Norton

> Offranville
> Seine-Inférieure
> October 20 [1909]

Dear Sally,

Thank you for Jack Chapman's[1] article on Harvard. It seems to me terribly true, doesn't it to you? But Bayard Cutting Jr.[2] who has been in Paris for two or three days, & who is passionately interested in Harvard, & in the whole University question in America, thinks J.C. much too destructive, & doesn't, moreover, agree with his view of what Harvard's "Mission" should be. And still I'm unconvinced!

I have been having a touch of grippe, which pulled me down, as it always does, out of all proportion to its severity; so I fled for two or three days chez les Jacques Blanches, who have a charming old Louis XIV "manoir" in this wooded corner of Normandy, a few miles from Dieppe. Yesterday we wandered about all day in the motor, & I was struck by the immense richness & variety of appeal to the eye & the imagination in every corner of the "terres françaises." Such exquisite things we saw at every turn—& this is a mere chance patch of the beautiful thickly-woven fabric. And then they wonder that, là bas, we have no temperament & no poetry!—

Dieppe is an extraordinarily handsome & "sobre" old city—do you know it?—with rows of solid bürgerliche Louis XIV houses, and fine Italian arcades along the port; & the church is exquisitely light & lofty ... To-day I motor back to Paris, in the rain, alas! But we've had fine weather hitherto.

And what do you think happened to me last Monday? I was getting out of the motor at the door of the H. de Crillon, when I saw two or three people looking into the air. I looked also, & there was an aeroplane, high up against the sky, just above the "Chevaux de Marly," &

emerging on the Place de la Concorde. It sailed obliquely across the Place, incredibly high above the obelisk, against a golden sunset, with a new moon between flitting clouds, & crossing the Seine in the direction of the Panthéon, lost itself in a flight of birds that was just crossing the sky, reappeared far off, a speck against the clouds, & disappeared at last into the twilight. And it was the Comte de Lambert[3] in a Wright biplane, who had just flown across from Juvisy—& it was the *first time* that an aeroplane has ever crossed a great city!! Think "what soul was mine" —& what a setting in which to see one's first aeroplane flight!—How I wish you had been there.—

I must stop now, for the motor snorts. Write me soon, & tell me you've finally decided to join Lily, & that we shall see you some time this winter in the rue de V.—under more cheerful conditions, I hope!

Yrs ever affly
E.W.

I saw a great deal of Berenson when he was in Paris a week or two ago, & we talked about you. I had never met him before, beyond an introduction once in Florence, years ago.

Ms:HL

1. John Jay Chapman (1862–1933), essayist, critic, and translator, and a strikingly original writer and personality. His wife, Elizabeth Chanler, was the sister of Winthrop Chanler.

2. Bayard Cutting, Jr., was the son of a cultivated railroad tycoon; EW had come to know the family soon after her marriage. Young Bayard (born 1880) was a person of immense promise, greatly admired by his teacher George Santayana at Harvard. He had served as private secretary to the American Ambassador in London, Joseph Choate, and, while doing so, met and married Lady Sybil Cuffe, the daughter of an Irish peer. EW had spent time with the couple during her visit to Florence in 1903, by which time Cutting was already suffering from lung trouble. He died in 1910.

3. The Russian-born Comte Charles de Lambert had been a pupil of Wilbur Wright, and in fact the American aviator was in the seat behind him.

To W. Morton Fullerton

Sat.
November 27, 1909

Cher ami—Can you arrange, some day next week—before Wednesday—to bring, or send, me such fragments of correspondence as still exist? I have asked you this once or twice, as you know, & you have given the talk a turn which has made it impossible for me to insist without all sorts of tragic implications that I wished above all to avoid.

Therefore I write instead.

In one sense, as I told you, I am indifferent to the fate of this literature. In another sense, my love of order makes me resent the way in which inanimate things survive their uses! Et voilà tout—

Do me—please!—the great & friendly favour of seeing nothing like an "ultimatum"—nothing solemn or final or in any way important—in this simple request.

To treat it as naturally as I do will really be the friendliest geste you can make.

I have good news from James, who is coming to stay with us when we are installés.

Ms:UT

To Sara Norton

Hotel Vier Jahreszeiten
München
December 2 [1909]

Dear Sally— Yes, München actually, though I can hardly believe it! When Teddy arrived a month ago with his sister, I hoped he would take me off on a motor-dash, for I was really stale from over-Paris. But he was so indisposed to move that we lingered on until Nannie¹ finally decided to go to Pau, & after numerous plans, & variations of plans, & modifications of the variations, & deviations from the modifications, it was settled that Teddy should "run" her down to Pau in the motor, while I came here for a week's holiday with Anna, who, as I probably told you, is Nannie's Gesellschäfterin[2] for the winter.—I was glad to get away anywhere, but my real goal was Berlin, where I have never been, & where I wanted to see the pictures & the theatres—not to speak of the Wax Bust! Strange to say, however, no sleeping for Berlin could be had for several days, & as it is necessary for me to be in Paris next week, on account of work at the apt. I thought of Munich instead, & here we are, enjoying it hugely!—I was unlucky enough to start by a visit to the Glyptothek, which is colder than anything Cook or Peary ever felt, & drips with sepulchral damp; so I promptly caught cold, which rather restricts my excursioning. But we had a splendid evening yesterday at the Schauspielhaus, where we saw Kabale und Liebe[3] delightfully played in stage setting & costumes reproduced from Chodowiecki's prints. Tonight we go again, & we have also spent delightful hours at the splendid National Museum, which is luckily Gehitzt. The Pinakothek is closed for repairs, worse luck, so we go tomorrow to Ausbach, thence to Würzburg, to see the longed-for Tiepolos at the Prince Bishop's Palace, then to Bruchsal, Karlsruhe, & back to Paris. You see the trip is very "rococo." I am very fond of German 18th century things (chiefly on Goethe's account, I think) & I've always wanted to see some of these funny little palaces & Lustschlösser; though Dec. isn't the best moment!—

It was a great regret to find you had decided to go straight to Naples, though I don't wonder you did. I hope you've had a fairly good crossing, & a chance to rest. Write me as soon as you can about Rome, & your plans. Perhaps when you get back to the Riviera we may motor down to see you—though it is quite impossible to foresee what we shall do, as Teddy is not well at all. I thought him much *too* well when he arrived—too excited especially about "business" & "investments"— & now the reaction has come, alas, & the whole thing is complicated by Nannie's incredible blindness & stupidity, & determination not to recognize *any* nervous disorder. It is too long & complicated to write, but the break-down has come exactly *as* & *when* Dr. Kinnicutt told me it would last March. So I can make no plans, but only live again from hand to mouth, as before.—We expect to get into the apt about Xmas.

Till then, address H. de Crillon. The apt is 53. rue de Varenne.

Teddy gets back to Paris to meet me, next week, & then I send Anna down to join Nannie at Pau.

Best love, & better luck than of late!—

Yr Affte   E.W.

Ms:BL

1. Nancy Wharton, the younger sister of Teddy Wharton. Following the death of their mother in 1909, Nannie devoted all her energies to her brother.

2. Female companion.

3. The play, first performed in 1874, by Johann Christoph Friedrich von Schiller (1759–1805).

To W. Morton Fullerton

[53 Rue de Varenne]
Friday 9 P.M.
[Early January 1910]

My Dearest— My number is 53. & the tel. 706-13.

I am sorry to have put you to the trouble of writing that hurried note.

Just before it came I sent you to the Hotel some verses I had written as a goodbye to 403! With them was a note. Seeing you so busy & harassed, I want you to think no more of it. We will leave the solution of my problem—which I put to you in all sincerity—till a quieter time comes for you. Meanwhile, I want to love you in any way that gives you peace, & not more bother!

I am in such a state of exasperated sensitiveness just now that I lie awake & cry all night, with the despair of the future before me—but I can be anything, do anything, to help *you!*—

If Northcliffe[1] fails, & you want to come at the last moment, you'll find us taking our first melancholy repast at 8 o'c at 53.

You understand, don't you, that I wanted you to be *the first* there?

Do, at least, let me know if anything new happens.

Ms:UT

1. Lord Northcliffe, the proprietor of the London *Times* (Alfred Harmsworth acquired the title in 1905). See letter to Charles Eliot Norton, March 2, 1908, note 2.

To W. Morton Fullerton

[53 Rue de Varenne]

Tuesday [Winter 1910]

When I received your note of last night I was really alarmed, & sent a line to your hotel at 9 o'c this morning, to beg you to rest for a day or two, & to ask if there was anything I could do to help you *in any way*,—but you were not there!

What am I to think?—

When I don't write you for two or three days (purposely) you write & telephone to know what is the matter. When I *do* write, & ask if I can help you, or see you for a moment, you tell me that you are too ill—and when I send to your hotel at 9 a.m. *you are not there*!

You know what I must think—what I have thought during these last mysterious three months, when again & again, seeing how things were, I gave you every chance for an easy transition to amitié!—

I don't know why you refused; but since you did, I must ask you now—*implore you*—not to build up any more of these elaborate écha-faudages of pretexts, like last Saturday's St. Germain!—Mon pauvre ami, comprends donc que je comprends, que je t'aime, que je suis tou-jours la tendre amie que tu retrouvera quand tu en aura besoin—but spare me these little hurts. They are so unneeded—and every time an incident like this happens, I am sick again with all the accumulated sickness of these last unintelligible months—

I hear you say: "What! I haven't the right to be absent from my hotel at 9 in the morning, or any other hour?"—You have *every* right, Dear, over every moment of your time, & every feeling.—Only don't tell me the night before: "I am too ill to see you."

Don't you understand that what hurts me is not *the fact* of the change, which I find myself able to accept with a kind of cheerful stoicism that reassures me?—It's not that, Dear, but the pain, the unutterable pain, of thinking you incapable of understanding my frankness & my honest desire to let you lead your own life.—You say: "I will be all you have the right to expect."—If I have any rights, I renounce them.—Don't write me in that way again ... The one thing I can't bear is the thought that I represent to you *the woman who has to be lied to* ... And if I think this, it is your own conduct that has brought it about.—Vous l'avez voulu—

Don't answer. It's useless.—I am your camarade—

Ms:UT

To W. Morton Fullerton

[53 Rue de Varenne]
Sunday night—
[Winter 1910]

Mon ami, I sent you just now—in haste, with people waiting for me—a word which may have seemed impatient & irritated.—That is the last note I wish to sound.

Three or four times I have given you the opportunity to make, gaily & good-humouredly, the transition which seems to me inevitable; & you have not chosen to do it. Therefore I will give you my "motives," though they could hardly, I think, be "unrevealed," even to perceptions much less fine than yours.—What you wish, apparently, is to take of my life the inmost & uttermost that a woman—a woman like me—can give, for an hour, now & then, when it suits you; & when the hour is over, to leave me out of your mind & out of your life as a man leaves the companion who has accorded him a transient distraction. I think I am worth more than that, or worth, perhaps I had better say, something quite different.... Don't imagine that I expect to see you often, or even to hear from you regularly. I know that a relation like ours has its inevitable stages, & that *that* stage is past. I know you haven't time to come, often haven't time to write; but I know also that sometimes you have a moment, & that when one loves one never fails to use such a moment. Poor human nature has only a limited number of signs by which to express itself—& these signs, in cases like ours, are always much the same!—You hoped to find me last Thursday, in order to ask if I were free for Saturday. But I was out—& no other possibility of reaching me occurred to you!—Non, mon ami, ne me dites pas de ces choses-là. . . . Don't you see that, if you accepted the solution I offer, you would not have to rack your brains to find such explanations? My friends are free to see me or not see me, think of me or not think of me, as they please! They find me when they choose to, & when they are otherwise preoccupied they don't have to assure me that they still feel an affection for me.

But I do ask something more of the man who asks to be more than my friend; & so must any woman who is proud enough to be worth loving . . . No, Dear, I know you haven't time to write; but one word would suffice me— You haven't time to seal & stamp an envelope; but a post-card addressed by you would be a message in itself!

And if a woman asks these signs, it is not necessarily because she is "sentimental," or jealous, or wishes to dominate a man, or restrict his freedom; but because these are the ways in which the heart speaks, & because, when two people are separated, there are no other ways available.

There are my "motives," Dear, once for all; & the request prompted by them springs from the fear—I really believe—that even the letters in question should constitute a kind of silent importunity!

I wanted to spare you this explanation, & for that reason, left every door open; & a week ago last Saturday, when you came to luncheon, I quite sincerely thought we were in accord on the subject, & that "the reign of the spirit" was to begin!—You wished otherwise, apparently —yet, after we said goodbye, you could let nine days pass—living at my very door—without concerning yourself to know if I were well or ill, happy or unhappy, here or away.—

Don't see the least hint of a reproach in what I have written. It is a frank explanation of the *reason why*—that's all!—

8 p.m.—Your telephone message has just come & I see that, as I feared, my hurried petit bleu must have seemed impatient.

I am therefore sending you just what I had written, to show how earnestly I wish that you should feel no unkindness in what I ask.—It is unreasonable for me to expect you to arrange the matter for me tomorrow, however; & if I don't leave till Tuesday night, Tuesday will do as well. Or we can wait till I come back, if it is more convenient.

I will let you know if I can lunch tomorrow, but probably not.

In case it's *not*, please remember that, for me, there is much, much left between us. It is less so for you, I know; but there are women of whom I have heard you speak affectionately, & with regard. Let me be one of them, won't you?

Ms: UT

To W. Morton Fullerton

The Berkeley Hotel
Piccadilly W. [London]
Friday
[March 18, 1910]

I can't tell you, Dear, "what heart was mine" yesterday afternoon, when I drove out of Charing Cross for the first time since I issued forth from that seuil sacré last June! I tried to catch a glimpse of The Window, but fate had of course placed it on the off-side of the building ...[1]

When I reached the hotel I was met by a note from Nephew-James[2] saying that Henry had had a very bad 24 hours, & wouldn't be able to see me—then, at any rate. This, naturally, set me wondering to what purpose Providence had let me get up at 6.30 a.m., & take my toilsome way across the sea; but as I was forlornly dressing, in walked (into the sitting-room, bien entendu!) a very handsome & deep voiced young man—no other than le dit nephew—who had flown "round" to announce a sudden "up," & to beg me to rush at once to Garlants.[3] He told me, in a few words, Osler's opinion: that H. J. had destroyed his stomach by years of Fletcherizing, & having reduced it to almost complete inaction, had been starved for the last few months. This—& the solitude of Rye—had brought on nervous depression, with "almost hysterical" ups & downs; but Osler found *all* the organs sound, including the heart, & believes the condition can be entirely remedied by gradually accustoming the poor atrophied one to do its natural work.[4] Et voilà—

I flew to Garlants after this explanation—& there he was, & we fell on each other's necks & stood tranced in long embraces; & he was *so* glad to see me that I understood quite well why I had got up at 6.30 a.m. to come to him!—Wonderfully enough, he *looked* better than when we left him at Canterbury—less red, congested & tired. And I never saw him more sweet, affectionate, responsive & *happy*! I had been told not to stay more than half an hour, but he wouldn't let me go, walked down two long flights to the door with me, & I think at a sign would have gone hatless to Pall Mall to put me in a cab! He plans to go to the National Gallery with me today, & to take me to a matinée tomorrow —but all this is at the mercy of the next swing of the pendulum, & I am prepared to hear that he was over-excited yesterday, & is "down" again this morning. He told me that, when he was in one of his "states," he had to take bromide to keep from "shaking all over"; & Harry James, who seems un esprit pondéré, & judicious in the choice of words, used "hysterical" in its exact sense, I imagine.

So here I am, hanging on the telephone, & awaiting orders from Garlants'—Osler, by the way, has put him off till Tuesday (wh., I suspect vaguely, may have been arranged by Henry on my account), so I shall be with him here all these next days, & shall feel there was a good reason for my coming.—The day before I left, I hadn't, from 8 a.m. till midnight—*exactly*—one minute of rest, & I am feeling the effect now. You are chronically in the same state, & have learned to bear it with silent stoicism—but I still grumble!

Henry asked for you with such tenderness that you wd write him a little word of congratulation & souhaite if you could hear the inflexion of his voice as he said:—"Down there, alone at Rye, I used to lie & think of Morton, & *ache* over him."

How little I believe in Howard Sturgis's theory, that he is self-sufficient, & just lets us love him out of god-like benevolence! I never saw anyone who needed *warmth* more than he does—he's dying for want of it.

Et toi, ami? Tu n'abuse pas des dragées du Congo?—Beware of Mrs. Paine![5]—Excuse this ribald joke, & don't let it, as they say of children, "put ideas in your head."—Goodbye, soigne-toi, sois heureux et aime moi un peu—quand tu as le temps, et que le coeur t'en dit . . .

Ms:UT

1. EW is recalling the occasion on June 4, 1909, when she and Fullerton spent the night together in Suite 92 at the Charing Cross Hotel, perhaps the most passionate and fulfilling moment in her relationship with Fullerton. In the immediate wake of it, she wrote the poem "Terminus," with its direct beginning: "Wonderful was the long secret night you gave me, my Lover . . ."

2. Henry James—"Harry" in the family, and Henry III for the biographers —born in 1879, was the oldest son of William James. He had always been a favorite of his uncle Henry. At the moment, Harry was practicing law in New York City.

3. Garland's (spelled with a "d") Hotel on Suffolk Street.

4. For half a dozen years, James had been "Fletcherizing": that is, following the regimen of the American author and lecturer Horace Fletcher (1849–1919), who in books like *Glutton or Epicure* and *The A.B.-Z of Nutrition* had advocated the slow and lengthy mastication of food. But after the noted physician Sir William Osler (who had previously treated William James) gave the novelist a thorough physical examination on March 14, he reported that James had done no real damage to his digestive system by his chewing habits, and that he was "splendid for his age," which was not quite sixty-seven. See Leon Edel, *Henry James: The Master*, p. 441. It was William James, meanwhile, writing from America, who diagnosed his brother's condition as "melancholia." See following letter.

5. A character involved in some sort of scandal in Paris. See letter to Fullerton, April 26, 1910.

To W. Morton Fullerton

The Berkeley Hotel
Piccadilly, W. [London]
Saturday March 19 [1910]

What joy, Dear, to find your letter on coming in last night, & how "beautiful" of *you* to find time to write it at the end of that long Duez day![1]

I won't say that I needed it desperately, because that is my chronic state; but if ever I wanted to feel you near me, & to know that you were thinking of those dear days last summer, it was yesterday, after being again with James.—I was told to come after luncheon; & when I entered, there lay a prone motionless James, with a stony stricken face, who just turned his tragic eyes toward me—the eyes of a man who has looked on the Medusa! The good nephew slipped out, & I sat down beside the sofa, & for a terrible hour looked into the black depths over which he is hanging—the superimposed "abysses" of all his fiction. I, who have always seen him so serene, so completely the master of his wonderful emotional instrument—who thought of him when I described the man in "The Legend"[2] as so sensitive to human contacts & yet so *secure* from them; I could hardly believe it was the same James who cried out to me his fear, his despair, his craving for the "cessation of consciousness," & all his unspeakable loneliness & need of comfort, & inability to be comforted! "Not to wake—not to wake—" that was his refrain; "& then one *does* wake, & one looks again into the blackness of life, & everything ministers to it—all one reads & sees & hears." And London is a torture—& the thought of the return to Rye intolerable; his hotel uninhabitable; any other hotel not to be considered; life without a nurse too difficult; the nurse at Rye insufferable; another strange nurse impossible; solitude suicidal; & companionship excruciating. Don't think I am exaggerating: it was all this & more—with cries, with tears, & a sudden effondrement at the end, when, after pleading with me to stay—"Don't go, my child, don't go—think of my awful loneliness!" —he wanted me no more, & could hardly wait for me to be out of the door!—In all this darkness there are two perfectly palpable blackest points: first, that he can't write a line (or even read), & second, that his nephew is obliged to sail next Friday, & Prof. Wm. James,[3] who is coming out, does not arrive till April 5th; so he will have a fortnight quite alone. Then Osler's desertion (which I thought, in my fatuity, James had planned!) has helped to demoralize him, & he says: "Of what use to me is a specialist whom I can't even count on seeing if I stay in town?" When I left him yesterday he had almost decided to return to Rye today; & I am waiting now to hear from Harry James what has been decided.—I had a talk with the latter last evening, & told him I thought his uncle's case one much more for a neurologist than a man like Osler. He begins to think so too, but is afraid of the bad effect if Henry suspects he is neurotic, & is being treated by a neurologist. My impression is that he knows more about himself than any of us, & that what his nephew fears for him might be rather a relief—for he said to me yesterday: "I need a Dr. I can talk to, can send for at any moment —a Dr. who is almost a nurse." And that is just the sort of rôle that a neurologist plays.

The situation is grave, & Osler, like all specialists, seems to me not to have seen anything outside his special organ. The worst part of it is his being alone just now, at what almost seems the decisive moment in his illness.

I am so haunted by this that I have written over to ask Dr. Magun if he thinks it possible for Teddy (with White)[4] to come over to Folkestone for a fortnight (since James will certainly return to Lamb House in a few days); & then I could faire la navette between Folkestone & Rye till Wm James arrives.

I suppose this sounds mad to you—but then all the conditions of my life are mad at this moment! I believe it could be done, & perhaps even do Teddy a little good; but probably the Dr. will not dare advise it, & I shall have to go back on Tuesday. I can't well leave my post for longer.

Et toi, Cher? You tell me all about [Dr.] Isch Wall, & nothing about yourself. How like you! I wished for you yesterday when I stood before the divine little Bonnington in the Salting collection, which makes the magnificent Constables close by look like "literature," it has such a kind of "Grecian urn" completeness. Surely he was the Keats of painting.—

Last night Willie Haynes-Smith (my Hugh-Smith being grippé & en deuil) took me to the Palace, where we saw Lady Constance Stewart Richardson[5] (even to the most intimate interstices of her person) caper amateurishly through a country-house imitation of Isadora,[6] & Polaire[7] drearily contort herself in attitudes whose "suggestivity" was so restricted by the fear of the Censor that it would have taken an eye much more, or less, innocent than mine to be suggestioned. But, as my companion said, "It was from Paris, & so they knew they oughtn't to be looking at it," & that helped. I was glad to see, however, that two lively & cheerful young men who threw bottles, hats & other missiles with superhuman grace & dexterity, received much more applause than the two females who permitted themselves (as James wrote) to be "nudely examined."—

Dieu, quelle lettre! But it's two weeks since I talked with you—so forgive!

Un mot, n'est-ce pas, mon aimé?—

Qu'on est loin de 92!

Later. He leaves for Rye today.[8]

Ms: UT

1. Earlier in the month, a French government agent named F. Duez had confessed to embezzling $1 million of funds derived from the sale of church property. It was suspected that he might have made away with twice that amount. The financial scandal threatened to have grave political repercussions, with the opponents of Premier Briand exploiting it to bring him down. Deputies and senators rallied to Briand's support, and he weathered the crisis.

2. One of the stories in *Tales of Men and Ghosts.* It tells of a writer, a philosopher of some kind, named John Pellerin, who grows so despondent at the failure of his "message" to have the slightest attention paid to it that he drops out of sight and allows it to be believed that he is dead. He turns up again as John Winterman, rejoins society briefly only to discover that others are making immense profits by popularizing his message, and disappears again. It is on several counts one of EW's most remarkable tales; and it suggests that her imagination, at least, had grasped the truth about Henry James's suicidal despair—that it was due fundamentally to literary failure, to the indifference and silence that had greeted the New York Edition of his work.

3. William James and his wife, Alice, had sailed from Boston around March 20. William, as would soon be evident, was in far more serious physical condition than Henry; he would spend some time seeking relief in Bad Nauheim, and would then return with Alice and Henry to his New Hampshire home. He died there on August 26.

4. Arthur White (born about 1860), the Cockney Englishman who had joined the Wharton household in 1888 as butler and general overseer. During these troubled years, the invaluable White regularly accompanied Teddy Wharton on trips to America or to health-cure places.

5. The British dancer who liked to perform in bare feet.

6. Isadora Duncan (1878–1927) was by now heralded as one of the great and original dancers of the time.

7. Mlle. Polaire (1877–1939) was a star of the French stage and music halls in the first two decades of the twentieth century. She claimed to have the smallest waist in the world (fourteen inches) and enjoyed revealing it. (Note supplied by Alan Gribben.)

8. Added on the envelope.

To W. Morton Fullerton

Queen's Acre,
Windsor
Monday March 24, 1910

Dearest— I have just had a telegram from Anna saying that the Dr. "distinctly approves" of my plan of bringing Teddy over to Folkestone, & one from Teddy announcing that he will join me there tomorrow night.

It is an intense relief, for I said goodbye to James la mort dans l'âme, though there was a mieux again on Saturday, & he actually joined me for an hour at the Repertory Theatre matinée, where he had a box. These sudden changes are so unnatural & alarming in such a nature as his, & the ups are so much less up than the downs are down, that I dread the reaction when his nephew leaves on Thursday, & am infinitely glad that I shall be there to help him through that bad moment —as far as one *can* help him! Then he has incessant preoccupations about money—he talked of it constantly to Howard & me, & it was one of his reasons for wishing to leave London—& even if they are unreal, as his rigid nephew maintains, they are no less a serious factor in the case; & after the nephew is gone I hope to induce him to let me arrange that matter for him. Seeing more of the nephew, I have decided that, all his family having been the victims of the neurotic, unreliable Wm James, he has had to harden himself against "nerves," & does not see that the sudden break-down of a solid équilibré character like Henry's is very different, (& must be differently dealt with) from the chronic flares & twitches of the other brother—William o' the wisp James. And for this reason, while he is of great practical help, I don't think he understands how serious the situation is. If he did, he would not leave.

—Luckily Osler turned up unexpectedly in town for an hour on Saturday morning, saw Henry again, & agreed that he had better go back to Rye—doubtless understanding the impossibility of leaving a man in his state alone in a London hotel. But I don't think Rye a solution, & I am full of forebodings, & so is Howard, to whom James spoke openly of suicide.—Enfin, now I shall feel that for the next ten days I can do *my best*, whatever that's worth. But what a strange situation I shall be in, entre mes deux malades!—And what queer uses destiny makes of me! So different from those I fancied I was made for.—All I know is that I seem to have perennial springs of strength to draw on—& that they never flowed so freely as since my love for you has fed them.—

Here is a telegram from Henry, just received.[1] He went back to Rye on Saturday—I forgot to say—after the hour at the theatre. And now I have wired that I am to be at Folkestone, & shall see him soon.

And you, Dear? Shall I find a letter when I go up to town this afternoon? Do, at any rate, write me whenever you can to the Métropole, Folkestone. Do you remember our cold late sea-sick supper there last June, en route pour Terminus?[2]

Mon ami, serre moi un instant sur ton coeur. I didn't think I was to be so long without seeing you!

Ms:UT

1. James's telegram read:
   WHARTON QUEENS ACRE
   DID JOURNEY SUCCESSFULLY BETTER YESTERDAY LESS
   WELL TODAY BUT HOME HOPEFUL. JAMES
2. See letter to Fullerton, March, 18, 1910, note 1.

To W. Morton Fullerton

Thursday
[Mid-April 1910]

Don't think I am "fâchée," as you said yesterday; but I am sad & bewildered beyond words, & with all my other cares & bewilderments, I can't go on like this!

When I went away I thought I shd perhaps hear once from you. But you wrote me every day—you wrote me as you used to *three years ago*! And you provoked me to answer in the same way, because I could not see for what other purpose you were writing. I thought you wanted me to write what was in my heart!

Then I come back, & not a word, not a sign. You know that *here* it is impossible to exchange two words, & you come here, & come without even letting me know, so that it was a mere accident that I was at home. You go away, & again dead silence. I have been back three days, & I seem not to exist for you. I don't understand.

If I could lean on *some feeling* in you—a good & loyal friendship, if there's nothing else!—then I could go on, bear things, write, & arrange my life . . .

Now, ballottée perpetually between one illusion & another by your strange confused conduct of the last six months, I can't any longer find a point de repère. I don't know what you want, or what I am! You write to me like a lover, you treat me like a casual acquaintance!

Which are you—what am I?

Casual acquaintance, no; but a friend, yes. I've always told you I foresaw that solution, & accepted it in advance. But a certain consistency of affection is a fundamental part of friendship. One must know à quoi s'en tenir. And just as I think we have reached that stage, you revert abruptly to the other relation, & assume that I have noticed no change in you, & that I have not suffered or wondered at it, but have carried on my life in serene insensibility until you chose to enter again suddenly into it.

I have borne all these inconsistencies & incoherences as long as I could, because I love you so much, & because I am so sorry for things in your life that are difficult & wearing—but I have never been capricious or exacting, I have never, I think, added to those difficulties, but have tried to lighten them for you by a frank & faithful friendship. Only now a sense of my worth, & a sense also that I can bear no more, makes me write this to you. Write me no more such letters as you sent me in England.

It is a cruel & capricious amusement.—It was not necessary to hurt me thus! I understand something of life, I judged you long ago, & I accepted you as you are, admiring all your gifts & your great charm,

& seeking only to give you the kind of affection that should help you most, & lay the least claim on you in return. But one cannot have all one's passionate tenderness demanded one day, & ignored the next, without reason or explanation, as it has pleased you to do since your *enigmatic change in December*. I have had a difficult year—but the pain within my pain, the last turn of the screw, has been the impossibility of knowing what you wanted of me, & what you felt for me—at a time when it seemed natural that, if you had any sincere feeling for me, you should see my need of an equable friendship—I don't say love because that is not made to order!—but the kind of tried tenderness that old friends seek in each other in difficult moments of life. My life was better before I knew you. That is, for me, the sad conclusion of this sad year. And it is a bitter thing to say to the one being one has ever loved d'amour.[1]

Ms:UT

1. "Aimer d'amour": to love with all self-giving love.

To Bernard Berenson

53 Rue de Varenne
April 22 [1910]

Dear Mr. Berenson,

A thousand thanks for Sassetta,[1] & more for the letter heralding him! I haven't read the book yet, because my life for the last ten days has been incompatible with any kind of peace, recueillement or enjoyment. I've been down in the Drains!! But the volume lies there, holding out a promise of all these things, & reminding me of a charming poem which I read yesterday under a Chinese painting in the Musée Guimet:—

"Personne ne vient heurter la porte.

Les ombres des sapins s'entre-croisent.

Et quand je me lève de la sieste je vais tout droit à la source puiser de l'eau fraîche, et chercher des branches de sapin pour en faire un bon thé amer" . . . [2]

You see from this maladif desire for peace & seclusion that I'm straining a good deal on my nerve-leash—and I *am*! So much so that, if I can arrange for my sister-in-law to come & stay with my husband for two or three weeks, I think seriously of a dash away about April 30th. I may go to Florence for a day or two, then to Siena, to the Bourgets, if they are still there; & as to your Roman proposal, ma foi, je ne dis pas non! Your party doesn't alarm me—au contraire—but your hotel does! Your hotels always do! I suppose they express a natural reaction against the fact that people would expect a person dedicated to Art to stay at the Spada d'Oro or the Cappello d'Argento; & I can understand that the sense of that expectation would drive one *nearly* to the Ritz & the Grand Hotel—but not quite. I'm still a slave to the picturesque, & want a Trasteverina dancing the Tarantella in front of a Locanda to the music of a Pifferaro[3]—for which purpose I usually go to the Bristol.

Dear me! What fun it is to write all this; but is it possible that I may be going to *do* it? I can't believe it, but sometimes "exteriorizing" a plan makes it come off, & so I abandon myself to the joy of these details.

I had a very sad letter just now from St. André,[4] dreadfully blue at learning, as he was leaving Rome, that you were all to arrive there. I'm so sorry, for I knew how much he looked forward to seeing you.

I am sending at once for Meyer's introductory vol., for "origins" of all sorts fascinate my imagination. Thank you for telling me.

I have also transmitted to Mr. Berry[5] your charming invitation, which will come with a sharp edge of irony to a man chained to the Bench at Cairo till the end of June!!

Why are the few, the very few, nice people in the world always at the antipodes—each, that is, at a different one?—I hope, at any rate, yours & mine may some day coincide, or coalesce, or whatever one ought to call it, if not in Italy next month, then certainly in June here.

Please remember me to Mrs Berenson, who will certainly not remember her one brief glimpse of *me*, at La Doccia, years ago—[6]

    & believe me
        Sincerely Yrs
        E. Wharton

Ms:VT

1. *A Sienese Painter of the Franciscan Legend* (1909), by Bernard Berenson. This 74-page book about the Sienese painter Sassetta (c. 1392–1451) originally appeared as a two-part article in the English periodical *Burlington Magazine*.

2. "No one comes to knock at the door.

The shadows of the fir-trees intertwine.

And when I arise from rest I shall go to the spring to draw fresh water, and to look for branches of fir to make good bitter tea."

3. EW's version of some images in a mid-nineteenth-century book about Rome she had come upon in her early years. She recalls the imagery in *A Backward Glance*.

4. Alfred de St. André, a member of EW's French circle. He seems to have had no particular vocation or achievement, but he was always good company, even in periods of gloom, and was a valued guide to little-known parts of Paris.

5. Berry was still serving as a judge on the International Tribune in Cairo. He would resign as of June 20.

6. EW had first met the Berensons in March 1903, during her tour of Italian villa gardens. The encounter took place at Villa La Doccia, the imposing home in Fiesole of Henry Cannon, an old Philadelphia friend of Mary Berenson. Quite unknown to herself, EW made a hateful impression on the Berensons: "intolerable miffiness, rudeness, self-absorption" (Mary); "she sniffed, she sneered, she jeered, she lost no occasion for putting in the wounding word" (Bernard).

To W. Morton Fullerton

53 Rue de Varenne
Tuesday
[April 26, 1910]

"Be sure you bring Morton Fullerton tomorrow evening—I want to ask him exactly what he meant in saying that the Parisians wouldn't have allowed any one else to say to them what I did—" Such were the last words of Theodore the First[1] as we left the Opera amid the acclamations of the populace!

I have only to add: "Be sure you bring your coupe-file[2] with Morton Fullerton," for it will immensely facilitate our departure from the Embassy.

We will dine at any hour you like, if you will give us the pleasure of coming here—preferably 8.30, but the hour is of no importance as we are alone.

I am heart-broken by a letter from James, who has had a bad rechute
& has had to give up the motor.

Affectueusement votre E.

The Prest has asked me to write an article on him for the Figaro.
Don't you think I shd be mad to attempt it?

[Added newspaper clipping]

Interrogé sur ses relations avec Mme Paine, il a fourni certains détails, en
exprimant le regret d'être contraint pour sa défense à dévoiler des choses
sur lesquelles il aurait voulu garder le secret.

Charmant homme, votre ami!

Ms:UT

1. Theodore Roosevelt, who had left the White House in March 1909, was
in the later stages of a year-long tour of Africa and Europe. The former Pres-
ident had written in advance to Robert Bacon, the American Ambassador in
Paris: "On no account fail to arrange my visit with Mrs. Wharton." A tea party
was organized at 53 Rue de Varenne for 5:30 on the afternoon of April 25.
Among those invited were Jules Jusserand, the highly literate and long-time
French Ambassador to Washington, André Tardieu, Victor Bérard, André
Chevrillon, and the Academician Comte Othenin d'Haussonville. "No women,"
EW informed Fullerton, "il redoute les 'mondanités' autant que vous."

Two days before, Roosevelt had given a speech at the Sorbonne, "Citizenship in a Republic," in which he extolled the virtues of manliness and unceasing
effort in the fierce struggle for a better society, while vehemently attacking the
pose of cynicism. "Let the man of learning, the man of lettered leisure beware
of that queer and cheap temptation to pose to himself and to others as the
cynic.... There is no more unhealthy being, no man less worthy of respect,
than he who really holds, or feigns to hold, an attitude of sneering disbelief
toward all that is great and lofty."

At the tea party on the twenty-fifth, Morton Fullerton had ten minutes of
talk with Roosevelt, and during it he made the comment that the President
quoted to EW the next evening as they were leaving the opera. See following
letter.

2. Coupe-file: police pass for vehicles.

To W. Morton Fullerton

53 Rue de Varenne
April 27 [1910]

Cher ami,

My personal inconvenience, which was of the slightest, was nothing compared to my regret at having been importunate in trying to help you. It is one of the saddest accidents of friendship. I thought you really wanted to see Mr. Roosevelt, & the opportunity had been "worked up" admirably.[1] Je n'ai pas à apprécier your reasons for rejecting it, the more so as they still escape me.

Your vision of our ménage as flitting from one fête to another, fills me with amazement. Teddy is not well enough to go anywhere, & has not been out in the evening since he returned. He appeared the other afternoon only because he felt it necessary to make the effort out of regard for Mr. R.

I am not free tomorrow—indeed I cannot ever, without preparation & difficulty, liberate myself before 4 o'c. Therefore, as *you* are no longer free on the only day of the week when you dispose of the afternoon hours, let us regard the Seine as the Atlantic, & ourselves as geographically sundered till some new cataclysm makes things over, & brings us together.

I have sent your notes to Mr. R. with the explanation you asked me to give—

Yrs   E. W.

I sent Cook to the Times with the coupe-file early this a.m.

Don't think it is not a great regret to me not to see you. It is. But your hours seem to be as inexorable as mine, so I try to make the best of it.

Ms:UT

1. Though Roosevelt urged EW to "bring Morton Fullerton tomorrow evening" to a gathering at the American Embassy, Fullerton decided not to go. He explained to himself, in a long note appended to this letter, that in the "Embassy crush," he would have "fumbled with my ideas, and undone the

impression made at the Wharton tea." He wrote a report of his thoughts about the Sorbonne speech, and gave it to EW to pass on to the President, as she duly did. Fullerton perhaps said that the Parisian audience might have interpreted Roosevelt's harsh words about the men of learning and letters as a direct attack upon the French lettered class; and that it was a sign of the French admiration for Roosevelt that the audience did not take offense.

In his note to himself, Fullerton admitted that EW "was disapp. almost indignant" over his failure to go to the Embassy, "n'y comprenait rien, in fact thought me a fool."

To W. Morton Fullerton

Friday 29th
[April 1910]

The Roosevelt letter is yours, of course.[1] I didn't mean you to return it.

You say nothing of having received a sad letter of H. J.'s, which I sent you on Wednesday.—If you *did* receive this, you rec'd with it a line from me, which I can't think you meant to leave unanswered. It was in reply to your note, asking if I could see you yesterday. In it I said that I was not free yesterday, & that I was tied fast, just now, in the early afternoons, & cd see you only after 4 o'c, & consequently only on Saturdays.

As you know, I haven't asked you for a moment of your Saturdays these last months, though I have told you frankly that my complete & sudden exclusion from them made me feel perplexed & unhappy—given the fact that, when we *do* meet, you won't accept the tone of amitié which seems to me the natural footing for this new situation. But your Saturdays *are* free, & therefore are yours, not mine!

Now, however, I am in a situation where my hours are as rigorously portioned off as yours; & not being able to free myself after luncheon, I told you I could suggest only Saturday afternoons—

If you rec'd this, & your silence means that you accept the fact of never seeing me, since it is impossible to spare me even an hour on Saturdays, don't be afraid to tell me so. I don't ask your reasons; & you need not fear my being "hurt." I am ready to accept the *fact*—the suspense & incomprehension are what hurt, & keep me from getting my-self "in hand."

Don't see in this any ruse to regain possession of your time. The simple fact is that things here are growing rapidly & terribly worse, & that only toward tea-time can I be sure of not being "on duty." You, on your side, may be held by necessities as urgent, of which I know nothing.

Let us be frank with each other, & have faith in each other's good sense!

Send me a word today, Dear, to show your faith in *mine*: no matter how short, if it is clear & definite. If you tell me that at present we are not to see each other, I shall understand. My love for you is larger than all the pangs of vanity & jealousy!

The *not understanding* is the one unendurable and needless thing. All the rest, Dear, my heart has turned to beauty—& will one day turn to peace.

Ms:UT

1. The letter mentioned reads:

April 27th 1910
My dear Mrs. Wharton:

Indeed you did not appreciate my coming nearly as much as I did! I thoroughly enjoyed it, and it was delightful to catch a glimpse of you at the Opera, and again at the Embassy.

Will you give my warm regards to Fullerton? What an able fellow he is! I was greatly struck by the paper you enclosed. Give my warm regards to your husband also.

Faithfully yours,
Theodore Roosevelt

To W. Morton Fullerton

53 Rue de Varenne
Thursday eve'g
[May 1910]

Thank you, Dear, for writing. I don't mean to bother you like that often. But send me a line now & then to tell me how things are in the normal world outside this house.

Nietzschean! There would have been a time for such a word—last autumn, when I held absolute freedom in my hand, & didn't take it because I saw that you thought I ought not to. Don't see a shadow of reproach in this. You were right—& probably, in any case, I should not have done it.

But I must always either refrain altogether—make the "gran rifiuto" —or else do what I do with my might. I said I would do this thing, & *I must*. Besides, the situation being what it is, what, *practically*, do you mean by your advice? The Whartons adroitly refuse to recognize the strain I am under, & the impossibility, for a person with nerves strung like mine, to go on leading indefinitely the life I am now leading. They say: "The responsibility rests with his wife—we merely reserve the right to criticize." *He* has only one thought—to be with me all day, every day. If I try to escape, he will follow; if I protest, & say I want to be left alone, they will say that I deserted him when he was ill. The Drs all tell me that as yet compulsory seclusion is impossible, & that practically he may do what he pleases!—And if you knew, if you *knew*, what the days are, what the hours are, what our talks are, interminable repetitions of the same weary round of inanities & puerilities; & all with the knowledge definitely before me, put there by all the Drs, that what is killing me is doing him no good!

What, in these conditions, do you advise? Walter Berry wants me to ask for a separation—but that seems to me to have become impossible *now*.

This delay of the dentist's, which seems really inevitable, means that his sister will only remain with him 5 days at Lausanne, as she means to go off on the 18th on a trip with some friends. She expects me to join him at Lausanne when she leaves, which will give me just *five days* of rest—& if I don't, I'm afraid that, as soon as she leaves, he will start in pursuit of me, wherever I am.

I said once that my life was better before I knew you. That is not so, for it is good to have lived once *in the round*, for ever so short a time. But my life *is* harder now because of those few months last summer, when I had my one glimpse of what a good camaraderie might be—the kind of thing that some women have at least for a few years! Before I knew you I had grown so impersonal, so accustomed to be my own only comrade, that even what I am going through now would have touched me less. When one is a lonely-hearted & remembering creature, as I am, it is a misfortune to love too late, & as completely as I have loved you. Everything else grows so ghostly afterward.

This is only said to excuse these interminable letters! Il faut en prendre votre parti. As soon as I can get a rest, & rebuild, my will to live will come back, & with it my resources. Meanwhile, write me when you can, & tell me what you are doing—& send me word of the Quarante Cinq!

Ms:UT

To Elizabeth Frelinghuysen Davis Lodge[1]

53 Rue de Varenne
June 20 [1910]

Dearest Bessy,

Whenever you write to me it warms my heart, & brings Bay nearer. Not that he is ever far, heaven knows; but it is as if he came into the room with your letter.

I am glad you are to be with your Aunt for part of the summer, for it will make her so happy to have you there. Oh, dear Bessy, our last summer at the Mount, all together—![2]

I shall never, never forget that warm afternoon on the thymy hillside over the little blue lake. Not that I shall ever forget *any of it*, or that his absence will ever leave less of a void in my life; but that particular sun-drenched fragrant hour was so full of him, so like him in its warmth & brightness & abounding sense of life!—

I am waiting eagerly to see what Mr. Adams writes.[3] When is the edition to come out? How I want to have a long talk with you, to hear all these things, & many many more, & to sit with you, & feel he is there with us!—Yes, I say to you again, what you have had was worth paying any price for. You had life in the round, & for most of us it is such a poor lop-sided thing. And you have your children, who are a part of him; & I can imagine what that must be.[4] I know it doesn't make the long hours any shorter, or the empty evenings less empty; & I realize the full force of the contrast between having *him* & having any other companionship; & yet I say that you have been blessed among women.

Poor Walter escapes from his Inferno next week, & I hope to have him here for a fortnight before he sails for America. He has been cruelly over-worked, & is very tired, but his enteritis has been cured, thank goodness.—

Teddy has been now for three weeks at Kreuzlingen on Lake Constance, where there is a very comfortable well-appointed sanatorium, said to be the best on the Continent.[5] He has his own apartment in a villa in the grounds, & the devoted White is with him; but the Dr. would not let me or his sister stay with him, or even in the neighbourhood. He takes douches, massage, & electric baths, & his days are cut out for him, which is a good thing in such cases. He has gained physically, but otherwise there is no improvement so far.

Mr. Adams told me that the children were all radiant when he left Washington. Do you remember when Cabot ate the green mosquito netting, & the fun we had over it?—I think so often of the day when Walter first brought Bay to see me, at the Gordon, in that far-off spring;[6] & the very first words we exchanged made us friends, & we never lost a single precious minute afterward! I wonder if anyone ever had just his gift of reaching to the essential things in his relations with his friends, so that there were no *dead moments* in one's communion with him, but every one counted, & left a trace, & forged a link?—And then I remember the evening when he & Walter were going to the theatre with us, & Walter said: "If you want to make Bay perfectly happy, ask Miss Davis—" & I asked you, & Bay *was* perfectly happy!

I am hard at work on a short novel[7] which I have taken up since Teddy went to Switzerland, & hope to have time to get well started while I am here alone. It has been impossible to work except spasmodically these last months, & more & more I find that Salvation is there, & there only.

I will give Teddy your message, & it will please him very much. We can write to him as often as we wish, & send him books, papers, &c; & he writes me once or twice a week.—

Adieu, Chère. Je t'embrasse bien tendrement.
        Edith

Please give my love to Mrs. Gray.

Copy provided by Ambassador Henry Cabot Lodge

1. George Cabot ("Bay") Lodge, her husband, had died on August 21, 1909, at the age of thirty-six.
2. 1906.
3. *The Life of George Cabot Lodge*, by Henry Adams, would appear in 1911.
4. The children: Henry Cabot, age eight; John Davis, seven; and Helena, five.
5. Kuranstalt Bellevue at Kreuzlingen, on the Swiss side of Lake Constance. The director was the able and humane Dr. Binswanger.
6. In the spring of 1898, the ailing EW, with Teddy, was staying at the Gordon Hotel in Washington, with Walter Berry in attendance.
7. *Ethan Frome.*

To W. Morton Fullerton

June 25 [1910]

Dear, there was never a moment, from the very first, when I did not foresee such a thought on your part as the one we talked of today; there was never a moment, even when we were nearest, that I did not feel it was latent in your mind. And still I took what you gave me, & was glad, & was not afraid.

You are as free as you were before we ever met. If you ever doubted this, doubt it no more.

And now let us think of your future—

Ms:UT

To W. Morton Fullerton

Wednesday eve
[Summer 1910]

Mon cher aimé—tu m'as rendu bien malheureuse—et ce n'est pas un reproche que je te fais!

But I had honestly believed, since our last talk, that you were conscious of the incident of last summer only as lifting something from your mind—only in the "absence of pain" sense which is supposed to be the definition of happiness! Certainly, at least, you had wondrously succeeded in making me feel that this was what you felt—& had thus incalculably increased & deepened my happiness.

Now I find this has all been a delusion—& I take my pen up in the vain hope that some argument may flow from it which I did not find when we were talking.

But none comes to me save the one with which I began—that you have made me very unhappy, & that at this moment I have almost the right to ask to be spared!

Everything ahead of me is so dark, Dear, save what you are to me, & what I might be to you. *That* is little enough, heaven knows, for the reasons we know: the fact of all I lack, of all I perhaps never had! But I could be the helpful comrade who walked beside you for a stretch & helped carry your load. And now suddenly you tell me that no one can help you carry it; et il me semble que je m'enfonce seule dans la nuit—

But the last word of all, Dear, is that, whatever you wish, I shall understand; I shall even understand your *not* understanding—because, as you wrote me once, long ago, in the very beginning: "I love you so much, Dear, that I want only what you want."

Je t'embrasse tendrement.

Ms:UT

To W. Morton Fullerton

Friday Morning
[Late June 1910]

Cher, It rains petits bleus Ch. d'Antin!

Mais voilà—I can't always help telling you when I'm worried, & I have just had a letter from White saying that things have been again *very bad* at Kreuzlingen, that Teddy threatens to leave at once & return here, & that he (White) advises me to be prepared for his immediate arrival, as he "doesn't know what to think" about the situation.

White is so judicious, & so accustomed to these alternations of mood, that the situation must be grave for him to send me such a letter. Judge of the effect on me!

Le moyen de travailler dans une telle situation!

Oh, be kind, Dear, be sorry for me. You don't know what it is to say to myself, as I do, that my work is, must be, my only refuge, my only raison d'être, & then, as soon as I feel my wings, to be struck down again like this! And such has been the history of the last 18 months.— Ah, j'en ai assez, et à quel point!—

Please try to arrange for the Russian ballet next Tuesday. I won't oblige you this time to bring me home in a cab!—

Ms:UT

To W. Morton Fullerton

Divonne les Bains
July 19 [1910]

Cher Ami, your petit bleu woke me out of a sound sleep last Wednesday night at 11.30, & I could not answer it the next morning, as we started early for Nancy.

We had the luck to choose the 14th of July[1] for that particular étape, & all that evening, from the windows of our hotel, in the Place Stanislas, we looked out on a scene that was like a Cochin water-colour of a Louis XV fête. The beautiful buildings were all festooned with garlands of lights, their balustrades & vases & statues relieved against a deep blue night sky, great rockets rushing up into it & showering down in bursts of blue & gold & silver on the crowds below—& quietly overhead a great golden moon, to take possession of it all when the illuminations died out. Think of seeing the fête nationale in such a poetic guise as that!

We went from Nancy to Dijon, & yesterday came over the Col de la Faucille to Divonne, getting a wonderful descent on the lake of Geneva. The spirit of adventure has grown on what has so wonderfully fed it in these few days, & this afternoon we are starting for—Italy! Rien que cela! We are so near, & the weather is so divine, that it's irresistible.—

Things are straightening themselves out for me, & I can go with a quiet mind. The news from Constance is better, & things there likely to remain as they are for the present, & I profit from the lull to take a desperately needed rest. I feel better already, & at peace for the first time in how many dreary months?—

I am amused by your request that I should "let" you see me on my return! I was fairly accessible for three weeks before leaving, & had even fatuously supposed that you would profit by the fact to come & say goodbye; but when you wrote me that you were going to St. Germain instead, I measured the extent of my vanity! Sans rancune, however—& I herewith graciously accord you the privilege of gazing on my countenance when it once more rises on your horizon. I can't say "write," for I don't know quite where we are going—but à bientôt & good luck.

Yrs,   E. W

Ms:UT

1. Bastille Day.

To Bernard Berenson

Belmont Hotel
New York
October 3, 1910

My Dear Friend,

I meant to write you last week, but I have been plunged in dumb despair since our arrival.

I told you, I think, that I came chiefly to see a certain Doctor here—our "family physician"—who has followed Teddy's case since his first attack six or seven years ago, & who has more common sense than any other of the clan that I know, & more influence over Teddy & his family.[1]

En bien, my good friends the Eumenides were not napping, for the day after our arrival they laid low the said M.D. with lumbago & influenza, & here have we been waiting for ten mortal days, in infernal heat, & looking over the brick & iron landscape of this appalling city, from a (fortunately) high-perched apartment, from which it looks exactly like a Mercator's projection of hell[2]—with the river of pitch, & the iron bridges, & the "elevated" marking off the bolgie, & Blackwell's Island opposite for the City of Dis!

Each day we've been told the Dr. might arrive on the next, or the after-next, & so have lingered on, in a dreary désoeuvrement & suspense that I leave you to picture. Today his coming seemed "almost certain"; but there is no word yet, & I fear another delay. All this has been bad for my husband, & has, of course, made all plans impossible for me.

You must be just arriving in Paris! Oh when "that city shall I see"? —I have taken my passage on the St Paul, Oct 15, & I'm praying that (supposing I get off) I may find you still there, & disposed to prolong your stay even *after* Nov 1st. As you said, friends are few, & opportunities fewer, & one must "grapple" when & how one can!—

I wished for you the other day, when, for a brief hour, I had Walter Berry & Fullerton here. The latter rushed off at once to see his people, but Walter has been with us, angelically, ever since we arrived. He goes to Washington tonight, & hopes to sail in two or three weeks.—Send me a line to 53 rue de V.—or rather telephone there, & they'll give you the latest advices as to my whereabouts. At present the chances are in favour of my being able to sail on the 15th.

Yr weary friend
E. W.

Ms:VT

1. EW was waiting for Dr. Kinnicutt to examine Teddy Wharton prior to the latter's departure for a trip around the world with the family friend Johnson Morton. See letter to Sara Norton, December 3, 1908, note 13.

2. Gerardus Mercator (1512–1594) was a geographer, cartographer, and globe-maker.

To W. Morton Fullerton

53 Rue de Varenne
Tuesday
October 25 [1910]

Cher Ami,

Your letter to the steamer was mysteriously égarée, & reached me only after we had started, & consequently—to my regret—after I had posted my line of farewell to you.

I was the more sorry because I think I never had a letter from you that gave me such deep & unmixed pleasure.[1] It made me feel that I had really solved the problem of being of use to you, of making of our friendship something worthwhile to you, & happy & consoling to me. —I am glad you "didn't want me to go," & that you felt désemparé at the thought of remaining in New York without being able to report to me your experiences & experiments. Je fais la part of friendship & affection in this cry, but I know that it contains a residue of reality outside of these sentiments. You are using atrophied muscles, & of course it hurts to walk! It is just because of that fact that I have been wishing for so long to see you out of that engrenage before you were utterly subdued to it & could no longer, as it were, *re-create* yourself, & begin an independent existence.

If you had gone into the Times as a man it wd. have been different; its action on you wd have been different, & you wd have reacted differently. But you were caught as a boy, snatched up into the machinery, & whirled in with it. The result was: a highly intelligent automaton. This happened to you, moreover, in a strange land, where you had no stake in the life of the community & were accountable to no outside consensus of judgement, & for a very young man, no matter how intelligent he is, & how independent of outside approval, such a social criterion is formative & fortifying & wholesome.

The consequences with you were what they are almost certain to be in such a case: that you let yourself drift, put all your will-power into the strict fulfillment of your professional task, & outside of that made no effort to shape your life on any strong clear lines, or to prepare your character, or your "relations" in such a way as to meet such a contingency as now faces you.—

As against these disadvantages, you have the immense "pull" of an extremely adaptable intelligence, varied gifts, & a charming personality. With such advantages, a man of your age holds his fortune in his hand, unless he has ill-health to fight; & here again the trumps are on your side. A few more years of Times slavery, & you wd no longer have had the energy or the flexibility to *make yourself over*; for that, in certain ways, is what you must do. But you have them still, & you have before you—fortunate being!—years enough ahead of full mental & bodily activity to make it well worth while to undertake the reconstruction.

You will have now to do what has never been your task: *to give orders to your-self.* You have been a bureaucrat in a milieu of bureaucracy, & it is a good thing for you to be plunged for a while in an atmosphere of intensely independent effort. Even if the ends struggled for are unsympathetic, the "tone" is stimulating, & I wish that—now you are not obliged to be back at a fixed date—you wd take a longer draught of it.

This letter might sound "priggish" to any one who didn't know me; but you do, & I am not afraid! I want to see your admirable intelligence directing a will as strong as *it* is fine, with a definite plan of life worked out, & a definite goal aimed at; & I *shall* see it, my Dear, & shall rejoice if I have had ever so small a share in the doing!—

Take whatever turns up in the way of provisional work là-bas. You have pot-boiled for years for the Times, & it won't hurt you to pot-boil a while on your own account, especially as you'll have leisure now for real production as well. Don't be unduly anxious if no permanent work offers itself within the next few months, but use your next two years to test & to discipline your power of independent activity, to form habits of systematic daily work, to develop your relations with people worthy to appreciate your character & your intelligence—to *be* Morton Fullerton, at his best & fullest, instead of "a Paris correspondent of the L. T."—

I've had a wonderfully good & quick trip, & I landed at Cherbourg early yesterday, Monday, morning, & I reached the rue de V. for tea! Literally not a human being on board with whom to exchange a word; & for the first time in my life I was too tired not only to write, but to read—so the long hours were rather weary, & I am still very tired, as you see from this slovenly script.

But I wanted to tell you at once how much your letter touched me, & how I thank you for writing it.

In a few days I hope to have a long report of your editorial, & other encounters since I sailed, & also news of Henry, about whom I am still anxious.—

I have seen no one yet, but this blessed pause can't last long.

L'amica tua
   E—

Ms:UT

1. Fullerton was on the verge of taking a long leave of absence from his Paris job with the London *Times*. In New York, EW had arranged for him to see Henry White and others, with a view to possible literary commissions.

PART FOUR

Separations and Sojourns

1911–1914

Introduction

❀

AFTER A HARDWORKING and relatively *un*social winter and spring of 1911 in Paris—the creative involvement was chiefly with the novella *Ethan Frome*—Edith Wharton returned to America and The Mount in July, there to take part in what Henry James called "the last act of your personal drama." Teddy Wharton, in the wake of his world tour, was physically in good trim; but he was woefully unstable, alternating scenes of violent recrimination with collapses into weeping and self-reproach. There were wrangles about money, and on Teddy's part incoherent accusations that presumably conveyed his helpless resentment over Edith's affair with Fullerton. After a painful ten days, Edith wrote her husband (the letter delivered to his room): "As nothing I have done seems to satisfy you for more than a few hours, I now think it is best to accede to your often repeated suggestions that we should live apart."

Before that stormy sequence, Edith had enjoyed the simultaneous presence at The Mount of Henry James, Gaillard Lapsley, and John Hugh Smith, the literate and attractive young English banker whom she had met at the home of Lady Elcho in December 1908. James was in exemplary form, at one moment evoking his Albany cousins, the Emmets, with a rhetorical display that Edith Wharton would perfectly record in *A Backward Glance*. "Were ever such splendours poured out on mortal heads as descended on ours during that fiery week?" Edith asked Lapsley afterward, referring both to James and to the fierce summer heat. It was perhaps Edith Wharton's most memorable experience at The Mount, and it was her last. She arrived back in France to learn that Teddy had sold their Lenox home. Her American life was at an end.

Ethan Frome made its appearance in *Scribner's Magazine* during these same months, and as a book at the end of September. Its author was pleased by the reviews: "They don't know *why* it's good," she said to Fullerton, "but they are right: it *is*." The sales, however, were disappointing, no more than forty-two hundred by mid-November. As before, Mrs. Wharton charged the publisher with poor advertising. Charles Scribner replied with patience and statistics; sales rose to seven thousand before very long; but in May 1912, Edith Wharton announced unexpectedly that she had given her next novel, *The Reef*, to D. Appleton and Company (which published it at the end of the year). Her other novel-in-progress, *The Custom of the Country*, still was contracted for by Scribners; but Edith Wharton was beginning the slow disaffiliation from her publisher of two decades.

It was in the fall of 1911 that Edith, traveling with Walter Berry, paid her first visit to Villa I Tatti, the home of Bernhard and Mary Berenson outside Florence. Berenson (he spelled his first name with an *h* until the First War) was forty-six in 1911. He was of Lithuanian Jewish background, and had come to Boston as a child with his parents. At Harvard, he was an exceptional and conspicuous student; he worked with Morton Fullerton on the collegiate *Monthly*. In 1894, he became the European agent for the immensely energetic art collector Isabella Stewart ("Mrs. Jack") Gardner; and by 1911, he was also the extremely active consultant for the Duveen brothers, and had begun to earn a small fortune as an "expertiser." At the same time, he was recognized as the greatest living commentator on Italian Renaissance painting.

In 1900, Berenson married Mary Costelloe, the former Mary Pearsall Smith, of a Philadelphia Quaker family, and the widow of an Irish barrister. They made their home at the Villa I Tatti (a name of undiscoverable origin) below the village of Settignano. Edith Wharton had been introduced to the Berensons at a nearby residence in 1903, but it had been a decidedly unsuccessful meeting. The friendship with Berenson began in the fall of 1909, and with Mary, more cautiously, a few years later. The visit in 1911 helped to solidify what would be one of the key relationships in Edith Wharton's life and in her letters.

Edith and Walter Berry were in Italy again in the spring of 1912. Berry was now her male companion of choice on these excursions, and her dearest male friend; though according to the available evidence, never her physical lover. (Her former lover, Fullerton, was called upon from time to time for his literary advice, especially about the composition—

facture was Edith's French word—of *The Reef.*) On the 1912 *giro*, the travelers made their way up to the Tuscan monastery at La Verna, where, in 1224, St. Francis of Assisi received the stigmata; the attendant misadventures provided Edith with high comic drama.

Edith Wharton was constantly on the move in these last prewar years; and her productivity—*Ethan Frome* and two very substantial and carefully wrought novels—is the more astonishing. *The Reef*, in fact, was virtually *written* on the move. In July of 1912, Edith was in England, driving down to Rye for a stay with Henry James; the latter expressed enormous alarm at the coming upheaval, but went on to enjoy himself greatly. In the spring of 1913, Edith and Berry toured Sicily together. That same summer, Edith and Berenson drove across Germany together, Edith arriving at the meeting-point in a state of complete exhaustion after the labor of finishing *The Custom of the Country*; she begged the skeptical Berenson to let the trip begin with a few restful days in a quiet inn in the woods. In between these larger jaunts, Edith could be seen hastening to the Italian spa at Salsomaggiore—"Salso"— to take treatment for asthma and other symptoms of restlessness and anxiety. Even here, she worked away at her novel: "fiction in the morning," she told Berenson, "and friction in the pomeriggio."

Despite such occasional jocularity of tone, these were severely trying days for Edith Wharton. The year 1913 saw one crisis after another: an estrangement from her brother Harry because of her alleged rudeness to Harry's mistress and fiancée; a temporary estrangement from Henry James over a perhaps ill-conceived plan to give him a present of money for his seventieth birthday; the indignities of bringing her divorce suit to court (the decree was granted on April 16, 1913).

At the year's end, Edith Wharton crossed to New York to attend the marriage of her niece Beatrix Jones, a landscape architect of renown, and Max Farrand, professor of American history at Yale. It was a crowded visit, the next to last that Edith Wharton would make to her native country. Her appetite for travel unappeased and her taste for the primitive and the non-European suddenly increasing, Edith, in March of 1914, made a little tour of North Africa, stopping at various remote and enchanting places in Algeria and Tunisia, and at Timgad, in the former country, having the most frightening experience of her life when she awoke to find a strange man bending over her bed in the darkness. Four months after that trip, Edith and Berry spent three weeks wandering contentedly through Spain, the peak moment being an exploration of the caves at Altamira with their prehistoric drawings of bisons.

From Pamplona on July 26, 1914, Edith wrote Berenson: "The international news in this morning's paper here is pretty black. I wonder." With Berry, she returned to Paris to hear talk of nothing but war. The French government ordered a general mobilization on August 1. Germany declared war on France two days later. On August 4, the Great War had begun.

To Bernard Berenson

53 Rue de Varenne
January 4 [1911]

Cher Ami,

When your letter of last week came, Barrett Wendell, Walter and Fullerton were dining with me, and I am sure you must have heard at I Tatti the chorus of welcomes it received! It was almost as if you'd joined our little square party in person—and made us the more regret that you *hadn't*.

First let me say that I'm glad you've at least been having a few *giorni su*. I wonder if it isn't the way of all nervous illnesses to oscillate in that clock-like way? I'm always si e no when I am tired—a gray day and then a—well, relatively pink one!—But I wish the affirmative days wd, in your case, join hands and exclude the others. If my coming to Florence in March could further this cause I should ask no better reason! Only long before then the cure will have been affected, I'm sure.

I am driving harder and harder at that ridiculous nouvelle, which has grown into a large long-legged hobbledehoy of a young novel.[1] 20,000 long it is already, and growing. I have to let its frocks down every day, and soon it will be in trousers! However, I see an end, for I'm over the hard explanatory part, and the vitesse acquise is beginning to rush me along. The scene is laid at Starkfield, Mass, and the nearest cosmopolis is called Shadd's Falls. It amuses me to do that décor in the rue de Varenne.

I haven't read Marie Claire, and hadn't heard that Mirbeau[2] was accused of it. I thought rather Charles Louis Philippe?[3]—I've sent for Hauptmann's Emanuel Quint—but I thought it was by Karl, the brother.[4] Enfin, nous verrons—I am seeing hardly any one at present, because I can't when I'm story-telling. The theatres—thank heaven—are beneath contempt, and there is nothing bright on the horizon but Isadora in a fortnight, and the Russian ballet in May. I hear there is to be a Hindu ballet, music by Reynaldo Hahn,[5] scenery and costumes by Bakst,[6] to be given in London for the coronation, and "repeated" first here. And many lesser wonders also.—

I am hoping very much to get down to Florence toward the end of March, and then back to the unescapable Salso. I *must* go there, and I want to get back here before May and the Russians.

Won't you tell Mrs. Berenson again how I grieved at missing my Christmas with you?—

A bientôt trotzdem—and do write me

Ever yrs,
    E. Wharton

Of course you've seen the account of Tolstoi's "last days"[7] in the Times?

Ms:VT

1. *Ethan Frome.*
2. Octave Mirbeau (1850–1917), the author of fictional works that vigorously criticized the restraints imposed by religion and education; *Le Jardin des supplices* was an especially celebrated text. It was Mirbeau who wrote the preface to *Marie-Claire* (1910), an autobiographical novel by Marguerite Audoux (1863–1937).
3. Charles-Louis Philippe (1874–1909) was another novelist helped and encouraged by Mirbeau. His work dealt with the poor and the wretched in city life and the provinces. *Bubu de Montparnasse* in 1901 had served to establish him.
4. *Der Narr in Christo Emanuel Quint* (1910) was a novel by Gerhart Hauptmann (1862–1946), otherwise celebrated as a playwright of exceptional powers who worked in the naturalist idiom. The novel tells of a poor outcast who undergoes visions and is believed by some to be Christ in the Second Coming.

He comes to believe it himself, and the novel closes without shutting off any of the possibilities.

Carl Hauptmann (1858–1921) was the less well-known older brother.

5. Reynaldo Hahn (1874–1947), Venezuela-born composer of operas and chamber music, and the leading dramatic composer in France.

6. The Russian painter Léon Bakst (1866–1924) had come to Paris in 1906, and eventually settled there. He painted scenery for the Russian ballet produced by Diaghilev, as well as the Hindu ballet here mentioned to be given in London at the coronation of King George V.

7. Leo Tolstoy had died on November 8, 1910.

To Barrett Wendell

53 Rue de Varenne
March 5 [1911]

Dear Mr. Wendell,

It was very kind & thoughtful of you to write as you did to Morton Fullerton.¹

He brought me your letter, of course; & I want to tell you at once what a help it has been to me to receive this perfectly fresh & unbiased opinion.

Mr. Morton writes me constantly, but he tries to put things in the best light, though without disguising that there have been difficult moments. I had read between the lines of his letters that he had been under a great strain, & was trying to worry me as little as possible; & what you write of course confirms this impression.

Teddy writes me constantly, but his letters are just what they have been for the last two years—a continuous ebb & flow of nervousness & agitation.

I am sorry that he was not willing to see Mrs. Wendell. It is always a bad sign when he avoids old friends.

I have not had any word about the Nobel Prize from Mr. Rhodes,² & as I knew you had asked him to write to me I finally wrote him about three weeks ago.

I also wrote to Mr. Howells, & Gaillard Lapsley has been at work in England, with encouraging results.

I enclose a copy of part of a letter which Edmund Gosse wrote me the other day. He has a great deal of influence with the English Committee.

I also enclose a memorandum about the Swedish Committee wh. the Swedish Minister here sent me. You will see that you were right in thinking that the American "boom" should be started through the American Academy³—

When I hear from Mr. Howells & Mr. Rhodes I will let you know the result.

I hope you have found your daughter well, & that you will have a prosperous journey homeward.

I am more grateful than I can say for your sympathy.

Please excuse this illegible letter. I have not been well lately, & fatigue, with me, always takes the form of illegibleness & aphasia!

Many kind regards to Mrs. Wendell—

Yours Sincerely
    Edith Wharton

I expect Teddy here in four weeks.

Ms:HL

1. Wendell, on a world tour with his wife and daughter, had encountered Teddy Wharton in Calcutta, on the long trip with Johnson Morton (see letter to Berenson, October 3, 1910). Wendell had written his former student Morton Fullerton about the meeting.

2. The campaign to win the Nobel Prize in Literature for Henry James was led chiefly by EW herself, with Howells in America and Gosse in England acting as lieutenants. EW also enlisted the help of James F. Rhodes, an American historian who had valuable "contacts" in the literary and political world, and William Milligan Sloane, professor of history at Columbia. The campaign was of course unsuccessful; no American would be awarded the Nobel Prize in literature until Sinclair Lewis in 1930.

3. Henry James was elected to the American Academy of Arts and Letters in 1905.

To Bernard Berenson

53 Rue de Varenne
April 27 [1911]

Cher Maître—

How you rejuvenate me by asking if it would be "proper" for you to come and see me alone at Salso!! I can only say: I want so much to see you that I hope you'll come, *even if it is*.—Not a word yet from the mysterious Bonardi![1] I wrote him a full week ago, asking him to fix a date. However, je fais mes malles for May 10th, and I hope you'll do the same—approximately.—My previous cures have lasted only 16 days, so don't procrastinate.

I shall stop a night in Milan—the 10th—to see Bonardi, and then dash for Salso.

Oh, *do* come! et à bientôt, j'espère.

E.W.

W.B. is overworked and under-healthed, voilà tout. I'm so sorry you're not better either.

Ms:VT

1. An Italian physician sometimes consulted by EW.

To W. Morton Fullerton

Gd. H. des Thermes
Salsomaggiore
May 12, 1910 [1911][1]

Cher Ami,

Your letter is a god-send. Thank you for taking pity on my loneliness!—

You see I am using your pen to thank you. I didn't have time to change the "nib," but I am getting used to it & acquiring a new hand.

I am desperately lonely here. If the place had any charm, if it had even *one* green shady walk, I shouldn't mind; but it is literally a wilderness of glare & gravel, with factory chimneys on the sky-line instead of campanili.

The weather is divine, but when the only use one can make of it is to trudge alone along a dusty road past endless trattorie where noisy indigènes are bowling & drinking, one begrudges such waste of such a good thing. As for the full moon soaring above the hills at night, I close my shutters on it & think gloomy thoughts.

Usually at this season the hotel is full, & one finds a few speak-able to people, & generally some acquaintances. This time there are not more than 30 people here, all German or Italian, & none interesting looking but the Duke of the Abruzzi—and alas I am not Miss Elkins! —The worst of it is that I may be kept here longer than usual. The Dr. thinks this strange "dry congestion" inside the head which I have suffered with so much for the last two years is nothing local, or caused by external irritation. He finds my arterial tension abnormal, & thinks the whole trouble may be due to some disturbance of the circulation, which would require special treatment.

He is keeping me under observation till next week, & meanwhile I am taking the inhalations twice a day, as before. But I shan't know my fate till Sunday or Monday. Isn't it a bore?

With the egotism of the invalid I have talked about myself first; but I have been thinking of you all the while. The Saunders scene was very characteristic. I'm so glad you met those men there! What an oaf he is —& what a mean nature too.

I'm sorry that article III doesn't "come." I thought it was liquid lava a week ago. Is it the difficulty of avoiding delicate allusions, or over-abundance of matter, or what?—The Scotland episode *is* funny! And how characteristic of Harrison.

I wish you had definite news of some of your irons-in-the-fire, but the only one I believe in is your own sound brain & your own stout will. And in that sign you'll conquer.

I enclose a nice letter from Gosse, as well as the Nolhac document, which I don't wholly understand. Keep Gosse till we meet.

How I wish you were here! How I should enjoy going with you to Parma & Cremona & some of the places to which I shall soon be making solitary pilgrimage.

So far, Wagner's Life[2] has saved mine—literally! I don't know what

I shall do when it's done. Everything will seem insipid—even Nietzsche. The rest of my library (snatched up at haphazard) consists of Hugo's Post-scriptum,[3] Renan's Averroès,[4] which I've never read, Flaubert's Novembre,[5] Lewes's History of Philosophy,[6] which I love & haven't read for years, Emerson, Reynolds's Discourses on Art[7]—*such* a mixture of drivel & insight, (as when he says of Poussin[8] that he was "naturalized in antiquity")—Dostoievsky's "Idiot," Melville's "Moby Dick" (do you share my taste for Melville? I like him almost as well, & in the same way, as Borrow[9]), Woltmann's "Die Germanen in Frankreich,"[10] —& Bazalgette's translation of "Leaves of Grass,"[11] which Walter sent me à titre de curiosité & which is a tour de force!! "When lilacs last" is unbelievably well done. The book must surely have a great influence on the young Frenchmen of letters. Do find out if the 45 know it. I am going to get his Life of Whitman at once, for a man who can so translate him is sure to have interesting things to say of him.[12]

I have begun my article on Henry,[13] but I have a very tired head & the inhalations are stupefying. So no great results.

Je suis triste à mourir. I wish I had known you when I was twenty-five. We might have had some good days together.

Write me when you have time. It helps me through the days. Merci, cher.

Yrs
    E.W.

Thanks for the Times clippings. I was glad to have the Keats notice. The other is impayable! Only five hundred—I thought there were more fools than that in England.

I am beginning to be worried by Bélogou's[14] long silence. Do go to his house & ask if they have heard from him.

Ms:UT

1. Misdated 1910 by EW.

2. *Mein Leben*, by Richard Wagner (died 1883), was published in Munich in 1911, and appeared as *My Life* the same year in London and New York.

3. *Post-scriptum de ma vie*, a posthumous work of Victor Hugo (died 1885), had been published in 1901.

4. *Averroès et l'Averroïsme: Essai historique,* by Ernest Rénan (1823–1892), reprinted in 1903.

5. *Novembre* (1842) was the last and perhaps the most important of Flaubert's youthful writings. A rendering of adolescent dreams and longings, and the portrait of a farm girl who alternates between the sensual and the mystical and who becomes a prostitute, *Novembre* in many ways prefigured *Madame Bovary* of 1857.

6. George Henry Lewes (1817–1878), probably best known as the "husband" of George Eliot, was also of interest to EW as a philosopher and an historian of philosophy. His *History of Philosophy from Thales to Comte,* originally published in 1845–1846 under a slightly different title, was reissued in 1867.

7. *Discourses on Art,* delivered between 1769 and 1790 by Sir Joshua Reynolds (1723–1792) to his students at the Royal Academy, had been reprinted in 1909.

8. Nicolas Poussin (1594–1665).

9. George Henry Borrow (1803–1881), who made his home in Suffolk, was the author of colorful fictionalized accounts of his travels in Europe and the East; *Lavengro* (1851) is the best known of his writings.

10. This study of Germans in France by Ludwig Woltmann (1871–1907) appeared in 1907.

11. *Feuilles d'Herbes,* the translation of Whitman's *Leaves of Grass* by Léon Bazalgette (1873–1928), came out in 1909.

EW's prediction of the influence of this translation would be amply fulfilled. An entire generation of French writers would draw upon it.

12. Bazalgette's *Walt Whitman: l'homme et son oeuvre* was published in 1908.

13. EW did not complete this proposed article on the New York Edition.

14. Léon Bélogou, a world-traveling mining engineer, was one of EW's favorites in the Paris circle.

To Bernard Berenson

Grand Hôtel des Thermes
Salsomaggiore
May 16 [1911]

Cher Maître,

The persistence with which you refuse to come to Salso makes me feel as though you must have been here before: such repugnance seems so natural to those who know the place!!

But as you say you *don't*, I won't dilate upon it, lest I should by chance check a tardy impulse on your part to come and find out.—My cure progresses punctually and the Dr. has given me my ticket of leave for the 27th. Alas, that I must rush back to Paris in order to launch my household for the U.S., and follow in my turn a fortnight later!

In your letter which awaited me at Milan was a question so flattering that I'm still wondering how it is that I failed to answer it. You asked if you might see the proofs of my short-novel. If I had imagined that it could interest you I should have brought them with me; but I didn't. You know that, literally, c'est le cas de dire that it's not "your size"; only an anecdote in 45,000 words! But it will begin its brief career in August Scribner, and appear later in a volumelet. So you won't have many months of suspense. And I'm at work now on a real magnum opus,[1] whose bulk alone ought to recommend it to you: a vast novel that is piling up the words as if publishers paid by the syllable.

The cure here is not very conducive to literary activity worse luck. Two deep drinks of salt steam per diem put my brain into a state of gentle torpor, and the only thing that rouses me is Wagner's incomparable inexhaustible Life. What a book! What a history! What a novelist he would have been! I dole it out to myself preciously, trying to prolong the feast as long as I can, and get irresistibly drawn back to the large furry volumes whenever my eye lights on them. If he'd written like Nietzsche or Schopenhauer the book wd have been immortal. But "what a jargon," as the late Bishop Bedell said to Egerton Winthrop of the French language! I never read worse—not even in German!

I see that you have thwarted my efforts to lure Mrs. Griswold here;[2] & not content with refusing to come, she sends me post-cards in which she boasts of lunching with you. How cruel women can be to each other.

The solitude here is becoming uncanny. I haven't spoken to a soul but my maid since I left Paris. I shouldn't mind a bit if there were one or two good walks. But the backyards of Jersey City, as seen from the train, are the nearest image of Salso that I can give you.

I paid myself a day to Parma in the motor, but it was so dusty that I had to have both windows shut most of the time (on account of my cure), and so cold in the churches that (again for the same reason) I had to scuttle in and out as if I were doing them between trains.—I

found Correggio's putti as boursouflés as ever, especially those horrid fat
Baby-Show monsters in the trellis of S. Paolo,³ & didn't much care for
anything but the outside of the Duomo and the in-and-outside of the
Baptistery, which I've always thought one of the most impressive things
in Italy. There's a splendid romanesque church at Borgo San Domino,
by the way, with finer lions than at Parma and a beautiful apse. Doesn't
that tempt you?

Send me a line anyhow.

Has Mrs. Berenson come back? If she has, do tell her how deeply I
sympathize with her.

Bien à vous,
    E. Wharton

Have you read Fullerton's article "When England Awakes," in the May
National? But I think I asked you this before. Do at any rate. It is giving
him a big success.

Ms:VT

1. *The Custom of the Country.* On May 15, EW had written Fullerton: "I am
working steadily at 'The Custom,' but am still only revising; & I can't tell any
longer whether I'm really improving it, or only undergoing an attack of scru-
pulosis. However, the scene bet. Undine & Van Degen in Paris doesn't satisfy
me, & I must rewrite it entirely before I can go on. I've introduced a new
character—Indiana Frusk—who interests me very much! But when, at this rate,
will the poor book be done?"

2. On Josephine Griswold, see letter to Berenson, December 12, 1920, note 2.

3. The ceiling decoration of the Camera di San Paolo in Parma drawn by
Correggio in 1519 included the Triumph of Diana, Adonis, and several *putti*
(cupids). EW found the *putti* "puffed up" (boursouflés).

To W. Morton Fullerton

The Mount,
Lenox, Mass.
July 3 [1911]

Mon Cher—

The "mingled emotions" of getting back here yesterday! They are so many and so closely entangled, that I can only extricate myself from them sufficiently to note the queerness of my writing to *you* about them: just as I did three years ago.

Well! On landing I heard that Teddy had gone fishing with his brother. I found a letter from him informing me that his motor would meet me at the station at Lee, and also that he was better and had driven himself in the car last week from here to Groton (140 miles!).

I likewise learned from H. Edgar[1] that, after agreeing to the sale of the place, he had made a sudden volte-face and raised an obstacle, trifling in itself, which had put off the purchaser. Et voilà!

The heat is bad, and so is the drought; but in spite of both the place is really beautiful, and so much leafier & more "fondu" than two years ago that I was amazed at the success of my [efforts]. Decidedly, I'm a better landscape gardener than novelist, and this place, every line of which is my own work, far surpasses the House of Mirth.—The most wonderful incident of my return was the finding here of my devoted and admirable head gardener who had, as you know, given me "warning" months ago & had finally said, as a great favour, that he wd stay till July 1st! Now it turns out that, when it came to the point, he *could not go*: he loved too much the work of our hands, and in the first two minutes of our talk, without a definite word, it was understood between us that he stays as long as I do. I never saw a more mouvant example of devotion to one's calling. He *couldn't* miss the first long walk with me yesterday afternoon, the going over every detail, the instant noting, on my part, of all he had done in my absence, the visit to every individual tree, shrub, creeper, fern, "flower in the crannied wall"—every tiniest little bulb and root that we had planted together! It is the sort of emotion a good gardener very rarely gets in this country where so few people with places care about them intelligently, and really work on them; and he sacrificed for it the prospect of a secure future and unlimited sway over some millionaire's orchids!

Je vous le donne en détail because it *is* such a donnée.

The American papers are announcing at great *length* that you are doing Bourget into English.[2] Your sister's story in Scribner is remarkable: far ahead of the Missionary Lady, & much more original in treatment.[3] I want to write her about it, but feel shy!

And you, my Dear? I put "faire suivre" on my envelope in the hope that you have really carried out my advice, and fled from the beasts at Ephesus. If you *have*, may you be in some dim leafy nook, where the cuckoo calls with the note of Montmorency, and you can get the false voices out of your ears and hear the real ones again!

Forgive this slovenly letter: It will show you how tired I am. It is a gain at any rate to be here alone for the next ten days. I hope to persuade Henry to come before Teddy comes back, though he now (I mean H.) alleges the usual complications and says he can't possibly be here before the 17th. Did you know that Oxford and Harvard—*at last!*— gave him his Hon. Degree last week? He received the latter, of course, in person. His letter was very good in tone.

On glancing back, I see I forgot to finish my anecdote about Teddy's motor. No sign of it when I arrived at Lee!! Luckily White was there, and when I asked about it he said: "Why Mr. Wharton never ordered his motor sent for to meet you. It is put away and he has no chauffeur"!!!

White had provided a chariot, of course, and I give you the anecdote only à titre de document.

Cher ami, is it possible that I shall see you here? I went out on my terrace last night, and took up my interrupted communion with Vega, Arcturus and Altair; but there was no moon on the lake. It will take three weeks for it to get there: hâtez vous, mon ami!—

As for my future, it is impenetrable at present. "Que faire dans une pareille nuit? Attendre le jour."

A vous,
   E.W.

Write me *everything*—

Ms:UT

1. Herman Le Roy Edgar (1865–1938) was a cousin of EW, his mother having been Elizabeth Rhinelander. He was a real estate broker, and acted as executor or trustee of many properties, including those of EW.

2. Fullerton was completing an English translation of Bourget's play *Le Tribun*, which was having a long run in Paris and which EW and others thought might appeal to a London audience. Elisabeth Marbury acted as Fullerton's agent, and EW wrote an English theatrical figure about it; but the enterprise did not succeed.

3. Katherine Fullerton Gerould's first volume of stories, *Vain Oblations*, would appear in 1914.

To Gaillard Lapsley

The Mount
Lenox, Mass.
Tuesday
July 18 [1911]

Dear Gaillard,

It looks by now as though you might come here on Monday—without discomfort to yourself! But I'll wire you on Saturday, definitely.

Things have been all kinds of colours since you left, but we're now in a calm zone. Teddy looks splendidly, and is really much better in every way.

Meanwhile the Only One¹ was packed off safely in a cold rain on Friday, & I'm hoping to hear today of his safe arrival.

Were ever such splendours poured out on mortal heads as descended on ours during that fiery week?—

I had a big talk with him the day after you left,—or the afternoon of that day—of which I'll tell you.

So glad you were able to jump onto the moving train as it left the station!

Affly Yrs,
E.W.

Ms:BL

1. Henry James was at the end of a year in America that had begun with the death of his brother William the previous August. He had come to the Mount on July 8 and had stayed until the fourteenth. Gaillard Lapsley, coming over from the family home in Rhode Island, and John Hugh Smith, on his first visit to the United States, completed the party.

To William Fisher Wharton[1]

The Mount
July 22, 1911

Dear Billy,

Teddy has probably told you that before I sailed for home I received an offer for the Mount, which I referred to him, asking him to decide it as he thought best. My reasons for considering the offer were based, as you no doubt know, on the condition of his health, and also on the fact that when he was in Paris in April he repeatedly told me that he was unwilling to live with me at the Mount unless he resumed the financial management of the place: a condition I thought it unadvisable to accept, for his own sake. In fact, during his stay in Paris the question of money preoccupied him so much that I was finally obliged to say that I would not go back to the Mount this summer unless he promised not to discuss money matters at all; and he gave me his word that he would not.

When I landed I learned that he had not agreed to the sale of the Mount, for reasons which I thought perfectly fair; and though the offer was still open, I felt, as soon as I saw how much better and stronger he was, that it was much better for us to keep the place. We were therefore quite of one mind on that point.

Teddy, however, did not keep to his agreement with regard to the discussion of money matters, and reopened the question at once in a tone which was completely unjustified by any act or word of mine, & which I could not & would not tolerate.

I told him this frankly, & I added that, in the circumstances, I felt it would perhaps be better to sell the Mount after all, since it seemed as difficult for him to live here as elsewhere without raising questions that make reasonable and peaceful relations impossible between us.

After a day or two Teddy understood that my attitude was justified by his conduct, & told me that such incidents would not occur again if I would overlook what he had said.

I am perfectly ready to do this, but I feel the time has now come when it is best for both of us that the understanding we have reached should be definitely set down in writing & known to his family; so here it is in as few words as possible.

I shall keep the Mount, & give Teddy the management of it, depositing a certain sum each month in the bank here for that purpose. I shall stay here with Teddy till the middle of Sept., if he keeps his promise to remain on pleasant terms with me. I shall then return to Europe, to take my second cure at Salsomaggiore, & Teddy will join me in Europe in March, if he wishes to do so, & feels that he is still able to keep to his agreement to avoid useless & disagreeable discussions. While I am away he will continue to manage the place, & we will return here next summer if all goes well.

Teddy furthermore accepts my suggestion that he should resign from his position as my trustee, & thus rid his mind of business preoccupations which have for the last few years been only a source of useless distress to him.—

I shall neglect nothing on my part to make this arrangement satisfactory, but I shall consider it at an end should Teddy again raise any of the questions that may now be regarded as closed between us, or should he, by his tone or his attitude toward me, make it impossible for me to lead a peaceful life with him.

His general improvement is so great that, once this matter is settled, and he is again busying himself with the place, there is every reason for hoping that he will find no difficulty in keeping to his side of the bargain.

I have asked him to add a line to tell you that he has read what I have written & has agreed to the conditions as I have stated them.

Affly Yours
    Edith Wharton[2]

Ms:BL

1. William Fisher Wharton (1847–1919), the older brother of Teddy Wharton, graduated from Harvard College and the Harvard Law School. For a pe-

riod, he was in public service, as a member of the Massachusetts House of Representatives, and then (1889–1893) as Assistant Secretary of State under Benjamin Harrison. He practiced law from his office on State Street in Boston, and made his home in Groton, Massachusetts.

He was first married to Fanny Pickman; after her death, he married Susan Carberry Lane, in 1891.

2. This letter and the two following ones exist in the handwritten copy by EW's secretary, Anna Bahlmann.

To William Fisher Wharton

The Mount
Sunday
July 23, 1911

Dear Billy,

When I wrote you the enclosed letter yesterday I thought that Teddy had reached a normal state of mind, & that I had at last succeeded in disposing of the numerous difficulties which he is in the habit of raising whenever I attempt to arrive at some kind of definite plan of life with him.

At 8 o'clock yesterday evening he came into my room, thanked me for what I had done, said that the arrangement made him very happy, & that the care of the place & management of the household accounts would be a great interest to him, & agreed that I should write you a short statement of the agreement we had come to, with a line from him corroborating it.

Feeling for the first time that his greatly improved physical condition warranted my giving him complete control of the household expenses & the management of the place, as he had had it heretofore, I told him that I would have a monthly sum deposited in the bank in his name for that purpose, & give him full authority over its expenditure. This is the thing he has dwelt on so persistently for the last two years, & which I have hitherto had to refuse because I saw that he was incapable of assuming any responsibility with regard to money matters.

These points having been explicitly stated & agreed upon, I thought that a peaceful solution had at last been reached, & that he saw for the first time how he had been spoiling all his chances of health and happiness by brooding over chimerical worries which existed only in his own imagination.

Two hours later I showed him the enclosed letter to you, & told him that if he thought any of the statements therein were inaccurate I should be glad to have him point them out. He became extremely angry, & replied that the whole substance of the letter was untrue, since it would give you the impression that I was "behaving well" to him, whereas I had inflicted a most cruel and unnecessary humiliation on him in asking him to resign his trusteeship, that he had never agreed to this, & that if I still made it a condition it was useless for us to try to live together either here or elsewhere, & that for his part he thought there had better be a final break between us at once, as he should take no interest in managing the Mount & running the household if I turned him out of the trust.

Teddy has spoken to me frequently in this way in the last two years, & the vehemence of his tone & the bitterness of his charges of cruelty, meanness and vindictiveness on my part have increased so much since his return from India that in Paris, where scenes of the kind were of daily occurrence, I nearly made up my mind to take him at his word & agree to a separation.

I wished, however, to let him try a return to his old life at the Mount, & his wonderful physical improvement made me hope so earnestly for a corresponding mental change, that I tolerated these scenes as long as there seemed any chance of amelioration. Unfortunately, however, in spite of his general improvement, my presence still seems associated in his mind solely with the idea of money, & his unceasing irritability, & the tone he now takes in speaking to me, have made the continuance of a reasonable life between us impossible, & the last ten days have shown me that the fact of my meeting all his wishes, even to giving him the control of a large part of my income, is not enough to satisfy him.

After each of these scenes there is a reaction of tears & self-accusation, when he sees he has gone too far & is frightened at the result; but this is always again followed by a fresh outburst of irritability, with complete oblivion of all apologies & promises; & I need not say that such relations are as exhausting to me as they must be injurious to him. I have therefore reluctantly decided that, since being with me still excites in him the same money-preoccupations, it is best that I should take him at his word & put an end to this last unsuccessful experiment.

I think the enclosed letter will show you that I was ready to do all that I could; but I wish to add, with respect to the Trust, that my reason for asking for his resignation was that I had attempted *all other means* of putting a stop to money discussions between us, & hoped that, once this purely formal responsibility was off his shoulders, he might put the subject out of his mind. I put this to him fully when I first wrote him on the subject three months ago.

Now that Teddy is so well, & able to lead a life of so much greater activity, I trust that, once he is removed from the associations which my presence seems to suggest, he will be able to find for himself a mode of life that will make him happier than anything I am able to do for him.

I shall have $500 a month deposited at his banker's, & this, in addition to his own income, ought to relieve him of all material cares.

You and Susy have always made me feel that you understood the difficulties of my situation, & the fact that I was doing my best to help Teddy; & I want to thank you for this now.[1]

Affly. Yours
Edith Wharton

Ms:BL

1. Billy Wharton's reply to these letters said in part—and in EW's paraphrasing—that he and Susan felt sure that Teddy's troubles were caused largely "by the realization that he and I were not so happy together as we used to be, and that we were getting estranged from each other more and more each year." EW's answer to this exists only in incomplete draft. After reviewing recent events and paraphrasing Billy's contention, she went on: "I absolutely deny that there has been any change of behaviour on my part, or any cause of 'estrangement,' save that produced within the last three or four months by his own disregard of all courtesy and self-control in his behaviour to me."

To Edward R. Wharton

The Mount
Monday
July 24, 1911.

Dear Teddy,

I am much obliged to you for writing to H. Edgar that you will resign the trust; & I wish to repeat here that I asked you to do so, after having tried every other expedient to distract you from your endless worrying about money, in the hope that, once you were relieved of a duty you were not well enough to discharge, you would cease to worry about it.

I wish you had taken my request in the spirit in which I made it to you three months ago, giving you the reasons I have just named. Instead of this, on your arrival here, you met me with a scene of such violent and unjustified abuse that, as you know, my first impulse was to leave you at once.

You implored me not to do this, & I agreed to stay on here for the next few weeks, provided such scenes were not repeated, & to join you here again next summer. You then asked to come to Paris in March & stay with me there till our return. I agreed to this also, & I furthermore offered, of my own accord, to give you back the full management of this place & of the household, & to deposit a sum of money in the bank here in your name for that purpose.

As this was what you have always attached more importance to than anything else, I hoped you would be satisfied, & that I should be spared the recurrence of scenes which made a peaceful & dignified life impossible between us; & you gave me your promise to that effect.

Regardless of this, the scenes have been renewed more than once in the last week.—Finally, the day before yesterday, you came to me, asked me to forgive you, said that you were perfectly happy in the arrangement proposed, & renewed your promise to control your nerves & your temper.—

Within two hours from this you had reopened the question of the trust, accusing me of seeking to humiliate & wound you by my request, abusing me for my treatment of you during the last few years, & saying that, rather than live with me here or elsewhere after you had resigned the trust, you preferred an immediate break.

You had said this many times before, & I had disregarded it, hoping that on your return here, & with the resumption of your old interests & occupations, you would regain a normal view of life.

But your behaviour since your return has done nothing to encourage this hope, & as nothing I have done seems to satisfy you for more than a few hours, I now think it is best to accede to your often repeated suggestion that we should live apart.

I am sorry indeed, but I have done all I can to help your recovery & make you contented, & I am tired out, & unwilling to go through any more scenes like those of the last fortnight.

I have written this to Billy, as I wish him to know that I have done all I could.

> Yrs.
> E.W.

H. Edgar will deposit $500 a month in your Boston bank, beginning with this month.

Ms:BL

To Bernard Berenson

> The Mount
> August 6 [1911]

Dear Friend,—

How wonderful of you all, là bas, with Harry Custs¹ to talk to & Persian miniatures to look at, to remember me & want to know what is happening!

I am overcome with gratitude whenever I get one of the beneficent letters that "La Bande" bestow on me.

This beginning sounds as if I were very sorry for myself; but, as far as my actual geographical situation goes, I am *not*. This place of ours is really beautiful; & the stillness, the greenness, the exuberance of my flowers, the perfume of my hemlock woods, & above all the moonlight nights on my big terrace, overlooking the lake, are a very satisfying change from six months of Paris. Really, the amenities, the sylvan sweetnesses, of the Mount (which you would have to see to believe) reconcile me to America. *But* my particular difficulty is not much helped by such mitigations. My husband is much better physically. He drives his motor, plays golf, has been salmon-fishing, etc. But his nervous excitability is very great, & the uncertainty, the ups-&-downs of the days, are inexpressibly wearing & unsettling to me.

I have only one fixed point ahead; & that is, the determination to get back to Salso by Sept 20th. My hay fever is so much better that I am determined to take the second cure. So I shall probably sail about Sept 7th. I should like to turn toward Florence in Oct (after Salso) if you are likely to be there.

I had dear Henry James here for a week before he sailed. Apart from his suffering from the inhuman heat he was wonderfully well & in such a high strain of discursiveness that one wanted never to have one's tablets out of one's hands.

W.B. came home about three weeks ago to recueillir son héritage,[2] which he still hopes may be done without litigation. He came to us for two days, & is now in the Venusberg—Newport!!

As for the Big Novel—well, you may fancy that the conditions for work have not been the most propitious. Still, I'm digging away at it with dogged obstinacy. It remains to be seen how far this will replace freedom & inspiration.

You know I'm really pleased that you missed me at the Russian ballet. It's the sensation of all others that must be sympathetically shared for completeness. I wish I could have shared Shaw's play with *you!*— but *not* R.U. Johnson!!—

Please give many messages from me to Mrs. Berenson, & tell her that I now hope for a meeting in October.

St. Moritz next, I suppose? Gather ye roses while ye may! but don't quite forget

The Hermit of Western Massachussets,
   Edith Wharton

Ms:VT

1. Harry Cust (EW uses the plural form to include Mrs. Cust) was the cultivated and attractive editor of the widely read evening paper *Pall Mall Gazette*. EW had met him at Stanway in December 1908, and they exchanged examples of great kisses in literature (*Troilus and Cressida, The Red and the Black*, etc.).

2. Walter Berry was at the start of a long-drawn-out negotiation about his inheritance.

To John Hugh Smith

The Mount
August 6 [1911]

Dear John,

Many thanks for your beautiful answer to my beautiful letter.

I am so glad you left America feeling that it is a problem not to be solved in three weeks. May I hope that you were generous enough to suspend your judgement of our weather also?

Because really it was almost as unnatural as some of our other recent phenomena!

I do wish you hadn't had such a bad first impression; but I'm glad you are coming back so soon, & at the best time of the year, to correct it. My only regret is that there is so little chance of my still being here. My hay fever is really so much better that I have almost decided to sail on Sept 7th & take the second cure which is so strongly advised. But if by chance I stay I'll let you know before you sail.

Things here were rather bad after my husband got back. He is much better physically, but very nervous & excitable. I have decided not to sell the Mount for the present, on the chance that he may improve & really benefit by the life here—& needless to say, our purchaser, as soon as he found me indifferent, expressed a readiness to wait!

America can't be quite so summarily treated & so lightly dismissed as our great Henry thinks; but at the present stage of its strange unfolding it isn't exactly a propitious "ambiance" for the arts, & I can understand his feeling as he does. Balzac would not have!

I am so glad you saw Mr. James as you did. I never knew him more completely & lavishly himself; and that *greatness* in him is just the all-enclosing fact. Let me have a word soon—even if it's hacked out of the rock. I wish I had Moses—his wand though!

Yr aff. friend,
    E. Wharton

Ms:BL

To Sara Norton

The Mount
Saturday
August 26 [1911]

Dear Sally,

We were so disappointed!

We meant to "propose" ourselves for luncheon to-day, but the rain makes the Ashfield roads quite impossible (Teddy never got back till 7.30 the other day!) & so we gave it up.

We *might* come next Monday or Tuesday, if you would not mind our bringing Morton Fullerton, who is probably coming to-morrow, to stay till Wednesday with us. I can't quite say now wh. day it wd. be, but I think Monday. Will you wire or tel. if either day is possible to you?

We have had a *very* large offer for the Mount since I last wrote you, & have very suddenly decided to sell it. The reasons are partly economic, & partly based on Teddy's condition. The place is *very* expensive, so much so that it requires constant care & adjustment to keep it from being *too* much so; & with a big country place you know how hard it is to maintain that balance!—Still, I was prepared to do it if Teddy had felt disposed to manage the place, as he was eager to do at one time. When it came to the point, however, he said that, with Reynolds' gone, he felt he was not well enough & dreaded the constant responsibility. He is so much better mentally & morally that we were able to survey the whole field quietly & impartially & I left the decision entirely to him except that I was rather on the side of keeping the place *if possible*.

I think, however, we may find a better solution in a small place on the seashore, where he can sail & swim, & where there are not 150 acres to look after! Perhaps somewhere near Boston.

I tell you this so that, if we come next week, you may not *bewail* the Mount in his presence. I *do* bewail it in many ways, but I rather think it was best to sell. At any rate, Teddy is better than he has been in three years, & that lifts loads & loads from me.

I have had a terrible two years.

Yrs ever affly
    E.

Excuse this slovenly scrawl.

Ms:BL

1. The head gardener extolled by EW in her letter to Fullerton of July 3, 1911.

To W. Morton Fullerton

Salsomaggiore
September 22 [1911]

Cher Ami—

Your long journal letter came today, & contained everything that the heart of the recipient could ask, except two "vital" facts (as the American press wd say): namely, the date of your sailing, & the address to which I am to send this.—You say: "There'll be just time for a letter" —but that's all. A tout hasard, therefore, knowing your cat-like attachment to the familiar spot, I write to the Murray Hill, whither I have already sent a short note from Paris, & some newspapers.—

Yes—he *promised* not to sell the Mount to any one, at any price, till after I had reached Paris & he had communicated with me; & to remind him, I sent back a line to the same effect by the pilot. Moreover, Egerton W. & I spent the whole evening before, till you came in, in urging on him the advisability of keeping the place & looking after it himself. I was to put aside for him $8000. a year for the purpose, & he was to keep his whole income for his own amusement. What more did he want?

Yet when I landed I found his cable saying he had sold! And today comes a letter; he is apparently much pleased with what he has done, & makes *no* allusion to the agreement made when we parted! Je suis toute bouleversée et triste. I don't know what I'm to do with him when next summer comes. I believe the sale is a *great* mistake (even though it was a "magnificent one.") Can't you understand how such incoherences wear me out, even when he is amiable, as he has been lately?

Oh, je suis lasse, *lasse*. And I have honestly tried to do what seemed right. No more of this weary subject.

You are quite right about the reporters. I felt it as soon as I had time to think. If Anna had not behaved like such a fool, with her mysterious signals & antics, & if I had not been so tired & nervous, I should have talked to them—or, if possible, got you to do so.

I am glad you found your sister well, & in possession of such a fine son & such a satisfactory husband[1]—not to speak of the "career" I know she has before her.—

I approve every word of what you said to Sears.[2] You are getting to be terribly astute! I hope for some definite news next week,—Have you seen Scribner, & the Century people?

That was a good letter from Leyret.[3] Of course one lives by such things, & not by bread alone. The disaster of my life was that for too long I was utterly starved of all that—& could not console myself with anything else. Apropos—I have just had a very good letter from H.J., who is staying in Scotland with my sister-in-law Minnie Jones, or rather with her cousin Mr. Cadwalader, for whom she plays hostess on his moor. Henry is in radiant good humour & spirits, & tells me that he has got hold of Ethan Frome in Scribner's, & that "it is going to be a triumph." I think it's the first unqualified praise I ever had from him, & it does me good, as Leyret's did you.—I wish though, he'd read the little story first "en volume."

Please don't talk of the books at 53 rue de V. as *mine*. They are the property of my dear friend M.F. to which I rejoice to give shelter till they find their way back to his own shelves, as they will some day. Meanwhile I am glad to learn that some of them have become so valuable.

I spent a few feverish days in Paris, where I saw an incredible number of people: Gays, Jusserands, St André, Bélogou, Berenson, etc. etc. Bélogou, by the way, abandoned the American trip because he was caught in 3 successive typhoons, & reached Japan a month late. He is blooming & prosperous, & brought me a charming old god of longevity from Tokio.

I lunched with him, & was waited on by a *butler* (the concierge!) in token of his grandeur, but insisted on seeing Zoé[4] afterward—for which I think she was grateful.

Berenson I saw constantly, & have received from him, since I arrived here, two delightful books, of which you must make the acquaintance if you haven't already. They are both by Coulton: "From St Francis to Dante," & "A Mediaeval Garner."[5] The former is a translation of the main part of Fra Salimbeni's chronicle, strung on a thread of vivid vigorous narrative; the other an admirable recueil of mediaeval literature, beginning with some of the earliest chronicles—well chosen & well annotated. On the steamer I read (but have not yet finished) "The Mediaeval Mind,"[6] which I greatly like.

Althanassiades had already given me the glad tidings of Miss Marbury's acceptance—& had likewise sent me a "bunch" of poems. Such stuff! I also found a drivelling novel, the last-born (!) of R. d'Humières,[7] avec dédicace, & a rather good book of E. Seillière's, "Les Mystiques du Néo-romantisme," wh. he had also sent me. In this, the chapter on the Pan-German idea, built up on Gobineau[8] & Vacher de Laponge (whom I used to talk to you about) would interest you, I know. But it's a good deal easier to buy books than to have to thank the authors for them—generally!

I have been for three days in this Purgatory—worse than ever now, for the Italian season beats its full, & shrieking squalling Princesses, Duchesses & prostitutes encumber the ground at every step. Not a soul to speak to but Lady Ripon,[9] who is amiable but not interesting. The Dr. is *amazed* at my "well-ness." He seemed to think last spring there was so little chance of curing such an obstinate case. I have twelve more deadly days here—& then I fly to Florence, to the Berensons, & afterward, I hope, to Rome.

I suppose you are sailing the first week in October, & I have doubts about this precious document ever reaching you.

Well, bon voyage et bonne chance, cher ami! In Paris, when you have time to write, the concierge at 53 rue de V. will give you my address.

Yrs

    E.W.

Ms:UT

1. In June 1910, Katherine Fullerton married Gordon Gerould, an instructor in English at Princeton who was at the start of a distinguished career as a Chaucer scholar.

2. J. H. Sears, an editor at Appleton and Company who also served as a writer's agent.

3. Henri Leyret (born 1864), author of a book about the Dreyfus case and other works on politics and governments.

4. Presumably, Bélogou's housekeeper.

5. Two texts translated and edited by the English historian G. G. Coulton (1858–1947). "Fra Salimbeni's chronicle" is the thirteenth-century monk's story of the period from 1168 to 1287.

6. This magisterial two-volume study by Henry Osborn Taylor (1856–1941) was published in London in 1911.

7. Vicomte Robert d'Humières, EW's Faubourg St. Germain neighbor and friend, was primarily a translator of English fiction. He had translated Kipling and Hardy, and had done about a third of EW's *The Custom of the Country* at the time of his death in action in 1915. Despite the acerbity in the present allusion, EW was very fond of d'Humières.

8. Joseph-Arthur de Gobineau (1816–1882) was a diplomat, novelist, and historian who spoke forthrightly about "the inequality of the races" and the need for "racial aristocracy," chiefly Teutonic. *Gobinisme*, so-called, was favored by Pan-Germanics. Its theories coincided to some extent with those of Georges Vacher Laponge (1854–1936), a French anthropologist and student of the Aryan race.

9. Gladys, Marchioness of Ripon (formerly Countess de Grey), was the hostess at Coombe Court in Surrey, where some of the most lavish of the Edwardian garden parties took place. She was a beautiful and imperious woman who engaged in a large number of love affairs; and she was also a leading patroness of the arts and brought together writers, musicians, and art critics at these gatherings.

To Mary Cadwalader Jones[1]

Grand Hôtel des Thermes
Salsomaggiore
September 23, 1911

Dear Minnie,

Just after I wrote you the other day your dear kind letter came back from the Mount, & I must tell you before you sail how it touched me. The first weeks (after Henry was with us) were about as bad as they could be, & finally I struck, packed my trunk & departed for Newport, saying I'd had enough of it.—After two weeks of prayers & entreaties (in which Billy Wharton took an energetic part) I said I would "give another trial," & this time Teddy seemed at last to realize that he must pull himself together—*and did so.* In short, this episode seems to have done more than all the doctors put together toward restoring his nervous equilibrium. From that time till I sailed he was perfectly good-tempered, reasonable & "nice," and I want every one to know that, as far as I can judge, he is now quite well again.

Of course this business of selling the Mount while I was at sea, after promising me *not to do so*, is proof that his purposes are still vague & vacillating, & that he forgets, or re-arranges in his memory, the most definite & emphatic agreement, half an hour after it is over. But, for all ordinary "rapports" of life he is now possible for the first time in nearly three years—& that's a good deal to be thankful for!—

I had such a good letter from H.J. from Millden. & I hear encouraging reports of his "boom" for the Nobel prize. James Rhodes (completely converted), Prof. Sloane et al. seem to have been working hard, & unanimously, under Mr. Howells's influence, & at any rate we'll have a big appeal to present to the mysterious Swedish Committee. Unluckily everybody was scattered when I was in the U.S., so I couldn't see any of the above-named. But you'll be able to in the early winter.

I'm so pleased that you like Ethan! He was written in the only quiet time I've had in the last distracted two years.

But I laughed "fit to bust" at your lending him to dear sweet Mrs. Winthrop! What a bewildered hour she must have had, digesting him.

Berenson has just sent me a book so altogether delightful that I've written Bumpus to send it to you at Symonds for sea-reading. It is Coulton's "St. Francis to Dante"—but don't be put off by the wishy-washy title. It's really an almost-whole translation of Fra Salimbeni's chronicle, & simply the most delicious bit of mediaeval gossip I ever came across. You won't have a bored minute with it!—

And now goodbye & good voyage & good winter. It's a real disappointment not to have had a few days with you in Paris.

Affly yrs,
    E.W.

Please thank Trix again for her offer to help Reynolds, and tell her I have just heard from him that he does not expect to be able to get back to America till Dec.—

I think I told you I was going on from here to the Berensons, & (if she's in Florence) to Sybil Cutting²—

Morton Fullerton is in America, but sails early next month. I think I told you this in my other letter, though. His National Review articles continue to attract a great deal of attention in the political world.

Ms:BL

1. EW's sister-in-law. On "Minnie" Jones and her daughter Beatrix (the "Trix" mentioned in a postscript), see letter to Margaret Terry Chanler, September 7, 1902, fns. 3 and 4.

2. Her husband, Bayard Cutting, Jr., had died of consumption in 1910.

To W. Morton Fullerton

Villa "I Tatti"
Settignano, Florence
October 16 [1911]

Cher Ami,

We arrived yesterday, after two wondrous days across the mountains from Rimini.

I was *so* glad to find your two letters here (among many others that I could have spared!) & to know that you had really been able to get off on the Savoie. But I thought I shd have had a line from you after your arrival in Paris, if only a post card.

I am infinitely pleased at what you say in your letter from Brockton:

that if you get the chance you feel sure now you'll "be able to prove your raison d'être." Of course you will! And I don't believe the Sears work will interfere as much as you think after you've got into the routine.

You speak of one letter from me at the Murray Hill. I wrote you twice there, & also sent you some newspapers.

Thank you for the clipping about Ethan.—I have had another already, in the same strain, from a New York paper. They don't know *why* it's good, but they are right: it *is*. Vous verrez que je ferai encore mieux!

My "home news" (!) is ghastly. The legend has now crystallized. Teddy has told everyone that I "insisted" on selling the Mount, & thus have deprived him in his old age of a home & of his one hope of getting well.

I *try* to stiffen myself against this, but I can't.

If I didn't feel the irresistible "call" to write I should give up the last struggle for an individual existence, & turn into a nurse & dame de compagnie for Teddy, because, after all my experiments & efforts, I have found no solution to the problem between doing this & breaking altogether. The present makeshift existence is utterly destructive to any sustained imaginative work, which *must* be à l'abri of nagging & fault-finding, & of great unexpected shocks, such as I am perpetually getting. Yet I see no hope of anything better—none, none!

Do forgive me—you who have material problems to deal with, & must really fight with the beasts at Ephesus. Oh, can it be that some day we shall be free & quiet, & able to do our work?—*you* will, I feel sure.

I may get back to Paris by Nov. 7th. I will let you know as soon as my plans are settled. If so, I shall stay there a week or ten days, & perhaps then go over to England. In that case I cd joyfully help you with the play, if you wish me to, while I'm in Paris. Yes, I think of you often—& much.

E.W.

He is coming to Paris in Dec.

Ms:UT

To Henry James

[Villa I Tatti
Settignano
October 17, 1911]

Climbing hills and fording torrents,
Here we are at last in Florence,
Or rather perching on the piano
Nobile, at Settignano.
Doing picture galleries? No, sir!
Motoring to Vallombrosa,
Pienza, Siena, tutte quante,
High above the dome of Dante;
Then (compelled by the busy lawyer),
Back to France by a scorciatoia.[1]

E.W.—W.B. [2]—

Ms:Postcard, BL

1. Shortcut.
2. The verse was written by EW, but the card was also initialed by Walter
Berry, the "busy lawyer" in question.

To Charles Scribner

53 Rue de Varenne
November 27 [1911]

Dear Mr. Scribner,

Many thanks for your letter of Nov. 16th, telling me that you have
deposited $1000. additional advance on "Ethan Frome."

I am somewhat puzzled by the figures you give regarding the number
of copies sold. You say that at the date of writing 4200 copies have
sold. I must have had a dozen letters from friends in New York &
Boston, dated about Nov. 1st, & saying that the first edition was then
sold out & the book absolutely unobtainable, & as I supposed you must
certainly have printed 5000, your figures are naturally a surprise. What

did the first edition consist of?—As far as it is possible to judge from reviews & from the personal letters constantly pouring in, "Ethan" is having a more immediate & general success than "The House of Mirth," & this impression was corroborated for me the other day, by a friend who sailed about Nov 1st, & who told me that when she tried to get it at Brentano's they told her it was out of print & that they had more demand for it than for any novel published this autumn.—So you can understand my being surprised at the figures you give, & your making no mention of a second edition.[1]

Thank you for enquiring about the title of "The Custom of the Country."—It is unfortunate, indeed; but, as Mrs. Fraser's book came out at least ten years ago, & was of so entirely different a character, I am wondering if there would be any confusion or any harm done to the sale if I keep the title? Of course I have a perfect right to, as it is "in the public domain," & Beaumont & Fletcher (weren't they the originators?—No. I think it was a later dramatist)[2] can't be disturbed by our pilferings!—In any event, thank you for announcing "The Wake," on the chance that I may have to use that title as a substitute.

With regard to the serial publication of "The Custom," I see you must have misunderstood a phrase in my letter. I definitely told Mr. Burlingame, when I found he was unprepared to make room for it at the date I suggested, that I would *not* publish it serially in Scribner's. What I probably meant to say to you was that, if Mr. Burlingame had accepted my date, the book wd have been ready for him, but that, as he had not, & I had not had the useful stimulus of a fixed time for delivery, I had put "The Custom" temporarily aside for something else which I now intend to finish first.—[3]

Thanks very much for your good wishes for the winter. I am wonderfully well since my cure at Salsomaggiore, and trying to make the most of my quiet days here. It is a splendid place for work.

Yrs sincerely,
   E. Wharton

Ms:FL

1. In reply, Charles Scribner wrote: "Nothing is more difficult to meet than the statement of an author's friends who report that a book is selling tremen-

dously or cannot be had at the best bookstores. Retail clerks are very apt to say whatever they think a customer wishes to hear." He gave EW a week-by-week breakdown of sales in four Boston stores (300 copies in all), and in Brentano's, New York (283). By late February 1912, sales from *Ethan Frome* had reached nearly 7,000; but it would not be a true commercial success until the 1940s.

2. *The Custom of the Country* was the title of a singularly bawdy play by John Fletcher and Philip Massinger, written around 1620.

3. *The Reef.*

To Sara Norton

53 Rue de Varenne
December 30 [1911]

You could really not have thought of anything, dear Sally, that would have interested me more than the Goethe-Carlyle correspondence.¹ As you surmised, I had never seen the book; & I am touched at your taking the trouble to hunt it down for me, & happy "de le tenir de votre amitié."

It came this morning & I have already flown through it & got many curious glimpses. How simple & discursive they were—& how extraordinarily fatuous of Mrs. C. to send a lock of her "peerless hair" to Weimar! It makes one feel that the sense of humour must be a comparatively modern invention.

I was in London for ten days just before Xmas, & ran into Lily in the National Gallery—but I suddenly remember telling you this on a flying post-card. (I am absorbed in a new novel, & occasionally lose the sense of time & place & repeat myself inanely.) She also came to tea with H. James, G. Lapsley & Percy Lubbock, & looked extremely well in a becoming hat with a red feather!—

Christmas here was very quiet, but I am immensely cheered this winter by the presence here of Daisy Chanler who is one of the people I am fondest of. My musical fervour is waxing more & more, & we go to concerts together whenever we can. But the important ones don't begin till later. My object is still to hear Beethoven, & more Beethoven, in whatever way & of whatever kind I can.

By the way, I wonder if you have seen Vincent d'Indy's life of Bee-thoven?[2] It is a short volume, in which he demolishes practically the *whole* of the Beethoven legend, including the identity of the Unsterbliche Geliebte & describes his life as a series of artistic & financial triumphs! True to French principles of book-making he gives no authority what-ever for these statements.

I am glad your work goes on well. I always wondered why you did not do it alone, but I hope Mr. Howe's collaboration does not extend beyond arranging the letters with you. Your name alone ought to be associated with the book.[3]

Teddy sails this week, I suppose. I sent White out ten days ago to come back with him, & they will probably take the first good steamer going. I rather think we shall go to the Riviera soon after he arrives— by February, at any rate—for I have urged him to bring his small motor with him, & motoring in a good climate will be the best thing for him. Meanwhile I am trying to do as much work as I can.

I sent you Romain Rolland's Michael Angelo the other day because his Beethoven & Tolstoy biographies were so remarkable,[4] but I haven't read this, & can't answer for its being as good.

This carries you, dear Sally, my ever affectionate thoughts.

E.W.

Ms:BL

1. *Correspondence Between Goethe and Carlyle*, edited by Charles Eliot Norton (1887).

2. *Beethoven, biographie critique* (1911), by Vincent d'Indy.

3. Sara Norton was editing the letters of her father, in collaboration with the New England scholar Mark De Wolfe Howe. The two volumes would appear in 1913.

4. Romain Rolland (1866–1944), who had achieved literary fame with his long *"roman-fleuve" Jean-Christophe* (1904–1912), was the author of biographies of Beethoven (1903) and Tolstoy (1911), as well as Michelangelo in 1905.

To Bernard Berenson

53 Rue de Varenne
January 7, 1912

My dear Friend,

I have left unanswered for a long time a letter in which there were many things to answer. Why were you not in talking reach when it came! I have been unusually tired & surmenée since I came back from England, & a little parenthesis of grippe has also intervened. Likewise I have been trying to finish the laborious & discouraging revision of a singularly bad translation of "Ethan Frome" & also to snatch some mornings of work on Ethan's successor. Net result: inability to enjoy a talk with a friend, unless he *is* within speaking distance.

This morning, however, I must, tant bien que mal, thank you for your letter, & tell you how grieved I was at the news it brought of your decision not to come our way till later. I had "kinder" counted on you for a day or two about this time. Your plans always seem to be modified in the sense of seeing less of you, never more, than one had hoped.

Your New Year "vous,"[1] in the shape of the Oxforder Buch Deutscher Poesie, came without a sign of its origin—I knew it was from you, though, & wrote to Bain to verify—which he did. Thank you so much! It always interests me to see on what theory the anthologist works, & this Herr Doktor's ways are as mysterious as the Almighty's. He gives pages of Goethe & leaves out Prometheus & the great poem to Frau von Stein, he gives Hofmannsthal (& *not* George) & leaves out the Terzinen, & in fact all the best things but "Manche, freilich,"—& he expurgates Walther von der Vogelweide, & makes the lovers in the delicious little Tandaradei lyric nebeneinander sitzen instead of— He evidently feels about that godless Minnesinger as the Spectator feels about me: "The author [of Ethan Frome] is apparently without moral sense."[2]

N'empêche pas, luckily, that there are lots of good things in the book, & that I am delighted de le tenir de votre amitié.

Blanche (though I see him frequently) had not imparted to me the tale of your projected dis-union & I wonder if the Sanguinary One did not lay the responsibility on him as lightly as she charges me with unspeakable calumnies *re* the landscape gardening of the Gamberaja? I hear she is still uttering Harpy-cries for me, & on the first occasion I am to furnish a Mithra bath for her. So far, I've eluded my fate.[3]

I have just had disturbing news of my husband's condition. He cabled before Xmas that he wished to join me here, & I immediately sent out our devoted butler to bring him back. Now the latter cables that Teddy is not as well, & does not wish to come, & I may very possibly have to sail next Wednesday.

Walter's case is not yet over, but he expects it to end this week. The prospects are favourable, so far.

I suppose he will come back some time in January. Perhaps I may cross him at sea!—

I will send you a line as soon as I have a definite plan. Meanwhile this brings you all my wishes for good books to read—I don't know, for you & me, ce que l'on pourrait souhaiter de mieux!—except health enough to read them.

I do hope I shall see you before many more ages.

Yr affte friend
    E. W.

Henry Adams is reported from New York, well & frivolous.

Ms:VT

1. In acknowledging or sending New Year's greetings to close friends, EW sometimes used the English word "vows," sometimes the French word for "vows" (i.e., "voeux"), and sometimes, as here, the playful made-up word "vous."

2. In addition to Goethe and the poems of his that EW wished had been included in this collection, she mentions: Hugo von Hofmannsthal (1874–1929) and some of the finest of his poetry, written before his operatic collaborations with Richard Strauss; Stefan George (1868–1933); and Walther von der Vogelweide (c. 1170–1230), the greatest Middle High German lyric poet, and the author of a series of love poems (*Minnelieder*), in the best of which, courtly conventions being set aside, the lovers (as EW remarks) do more than "sit near each other."

3. A spot of private joking with Berenson. Villa Gamberaia (so spelled to-day) lies on the Settignano slopes; it was given lengthy treatment by EW in *Italian Villas*. "The Sanguinary One" may be Contessa Serristori, who lived in the neighborhood. See following letter.

To Bernard Berenson

53 Rue de Varenne
March 14 [1912]

Dear Friend,

Do forgive me for not answering your letter. It is always such a comprehensive kind of joy to hear from you that my impulse is to burst into ink within the twenty four hours; but for the last month I've had:

1. My husband to "go round" with (he won't leave the house without me)

2. The translation of "Ethan Frome" to reprendre d'un bout à l'autre with the dear, devoted but not—precisely—hustling Charlie Du Bos

3. My new "op.," at its mid-crisis, wailing for me every morning like an infant for the bottle—

4. Bills, business, notes, telephone, & the usual endless petrifying drip of Little Things . . .

Et voilà pourquoi—

I'm so glad you noted my silence, though! You wrote me once that you'd had a "good letter" from me (from England, in Dec.) & as my epistolary art had never before been commended, I'm always (perhaps too consciously) vowing that I'll re-capture that first fine careless rapture; so that beginning a letter to you has the excitement of a literary adventure as well as the joy of communing with a friend. Unluckily for Literature, I always forget the former, & remember only the latter pleasure when I'm once under way!—

But now about *you*. What of this mysterious accident? Were you motoring, scaling walls into jardins secrets, or ski-ing over into the Casentino? Do tell me what you were doing *this time*!—I'm very sorry for the result, en tout cas,—But not a bit sorry for you for having to go to Naples. Ça non! St André started off the other day in high feather, expecting to cull you en route, & I followed him enviously on the map.

We're having such a divine Italian spring here that the "bourgeotte" is worse in me than usual, & I'm praying *hard* that I may get off by mid-April. But I can't the least bit tell. Teddy's state of mind is just the same. He won't budge without me. He left his little open motor in America, so that he *never* goes out, never, literally, unless I take him. He is well physically, but au moral just the same. I'm beginning to feel the dead weight of it, as I always do after a few weeks. And I can naturally make no plans.

Walter (who has won his case) is not any too well, & I wish he cd get away, but his partner is in America & he has to stick to the ship till l'autre gets back, when I hope he'll "quit" for good. Madame Serristori[1] dined here a week or two ago, & I also dined "avec" her at St André's. She was radiating both times, & it's a joy to watch her hands talking. How I wish I belonged to a plastic race & drew beautiful hieroglyphs with my person, instead of having to depend on dull old words!

Forgive this particularly dingy assortment, & send me a big bundle in return soon—won't you?—Need I say that when I start it will be for Italy? So don't tell me you're coming to Paris about that time. Many affectionate remembrances to Mrs. Berenson, et bien à vous

E.W.

Ms:VT

1. Spanish-born Contessa Hortense Serristori, Berenson's exceedingly attractive friend and neighbor. She and EW would never like each other.

To Bernard Berenson

[Salsomaggiore]
May 27 [1912]

Here I am, blissfully steeped in ink & iodine—fiction in the morning & friction in the pomeriggio.

Do come & join the dance!—The weather's perfect, & man isn't vile because he's absent.

How & where are you?

E.W

Ms:Postcard, VT

To W. Morton Fullerton

Palace Hotel
Rome
June 19 [1912]

Cher Ami— I found your letter late yesterday eve'g, on returning from Benedict's cave in the heights above Subiaco, where I thought of you (with a more special thought) when the monk who showed us about the monastery of St Scholastica showed us the Lactantius wh. was the second book printed in Italy, & printed in that very place, as you doubtless knew, O Bibliophile.

I am glad you are off to Luxembourg, & hope you will find your solitude there as deep & well-defended as Benedict's must have been in that dark cliff above the gorge of the Anio.—

You see I am not at the ends of the Earth yet, but I seem to be tending thither, for we start for Naples tomorrow whence, after saluting the Rodds at Posillipo, we expect to cross to Sicily for a few days. After that, I don't know, but it will probably be our southern most étape, for Walter is not well, & I disapprove even of the Sicilian expedition, much as it tempts me! The good hotels there are all closed at this season, & the frittura mista (& even mystica) is precarious diet for an invalid.— Otherwise all goes well.

Rome is cool, delightful & beautiful—or would be, but for the horrible, pervasive, unescapable, blinding, glaring Victor Emanuel monument, which obliterates the Capitol, crushes St Peter's, & is visible in every direction as far off as Soracte.[1] I had no idea it was such a National Disaster.

I wish I cd tell you of half the wonders & beauties that I've seen— but you wd howl for mercy if I began!—

You got my p.c. I hope, saying that I'd decided not to send you the Reef chapters for the present?—

Savourez your holiday to the utmost, & *finish the book*.

Yrs Ever   E.W

I haven't *any* photo. Appleton may reproduce any of the published ones if he can find one. Give him yours!—

P.S

I reopen to say that your letter of the 17th has just come, & that I am grinning broadly at your summing up of yourself as a "coeur simple." Ah, Dieu, non!—

I'm glad you're really off. The concierge will have nothing heavier than this to forward to you (from me, at least!) as I am decidedly *not* sending you the last chapters yet.

Send me a line rue de V. when you have time. Since writing this morning I've decided to turn north at once, as it's rather too hot for more southern explorations, & I shall drop my companion at Plombières for the cure in a few days & then go off somewhere to a solitude with Anna to finish the Reef.

Ms:UT

1. The Victor Emmanuel monument, begun in 1885, was unveiled in 1911.

To W. Morton Fullerton

Hôtel Cavour
Milan
June 25 [1912]

Cher Ami,

I am turning back across the Alps to tackle the Reef. For a day or two I shall be at Vevey, after that I mean to try some quiet place in Germany, I think. I must be where I can hire a "Remington" for Anna, so the solitudes I long for are out of the question.

Are you at Luxembourg? I doubt it!—Enfin, wherever you are, I hope the work goes.—Do you think you could perhaps come & see me somewhere for a day or two next month, so that I cd go over the Reef with you? I don't think I've ever been so worried & uncertain about the "facture" of a book—I've no doubts about the stuff! If it were possible for you to do this, I'd transport myself to some point not too remote. For instance, if you're still at Luxembourg I could go to a place in the Vosges or near Strasbourg somewhere, next week. If you've gone back to Paris we could choose some other point. My course from Vevey will be north eastward. If you would come to pay Anna & me a little visit of three or four days, & read the whole book, it would help immensely.

Write rue de V.—Letters are forwarded every three or four days. How are things going with you?

I hope for a letter from you in the batch that I ought to receive this p.m. here. Bien à vous

E W.

Suggest any meeting point you like. There is nothing fixed about my route.

Ms:UT

To Bernard Berenson

Grand Hôtel de Vevey
& Palace Hotel
Saturday
June 29, 1912

My dear Friend,

You will probably have seen Walter by this time, & learned the abrupt end of our unlucky "giro." As you foresaw, the long hours of motoring, the changes of temperature & the queer food, were all, as it were, fuel for his enteritis, & it began to rage furiously after the *desultory* days I sketched for you on my post-card! I finally declined to go to Sicily, & we started back by supposedly "easy" stages to Venice, where he agreed to rest for a few days. The first day (Rome-Spoleto) he insisted on motoring up to San Oreste, & wasn't pleased when I refused to climb Soracte in a blazing sun at 3.30 p.m.!! But I wouldn't, so that day was fairly quiet. The next, he studied the map, & decided on going to Camaldoli, via Pieve San Stefano & La Verna.[1] We started at about 10 o'c, & were to "do" La Verna & dine at Camaldoli. Ye gods! At 11 p.m. we were hanging over dizzy precipices in the Apennines, unable to turn back & almost unable (but for Cook's wonderful coolness & skill) to go on. Our luggage was all taken off & hauled behind us on a cart by a wild peasant, others escorted us with big stones to put behind the wheels at the worst ascents, & thus, at 11.30, *fourbus*, we reached the gates of La Verna, where it took us a good half hour to rouse the Frati, & Walter, under their relentless eyes, had to sup on oil soup & anchovies & cheese before they'd let him go to bed!!—(The road we took was given plain as day in Tarridi, but, as the friars said, is a mere mulepath!)—

That seemed almost enough, but wasn't—the Furies had only just taken their apéritif! The next day the car had to be *let down by ropes* to a point about ¾ of a mile below the monastery, Cook steering down the vertical descent, & twenty men hanging on to a funa [rope] that, thank the Lord, *didn't break*. Meanwhile Walter had developed an agony of inflammation in a tooth, & we had to speed ventre à terre from Bibbiena to Florence, where the dentist told him it wd take at least ten days to mend; so he decided to go straight to Paris. As he preferred motoring, on account of the heat, we started for Milan, where he was to take the night train. We went over the Abetone, & just after we left Modena a crazy coachman drove full tilt out of a side road (Cook "horning" hard at the time), lost his head when he saw the car, & smashed straight into us. A pile of stones saved us from pitching into the deep stream by the roadside, but my poor maid was thrown out & nearly drowned. All the glass was smashed in front, & when we finally got patched up again I had to sit till 11.30 p.m. holding my umbrella open (inside the car) to keep the night wind off my maid's drippy head & Walter's tortured tooth! We reached the station *3 minutes* before his train left & I crawled back to the Cavour for a two days' rest. Et voilà—

Do you wonder that I'm going back to Paris to sit down in the rue de Varenne for a while?—Unluckily I had disbanded the servants, so must wait a few days while they reassemble, & I shan't arrive till Thursday; when I do so hope to find you still!

Please, if you are there, keep a minute free from the aigrettes.

I almost cried when you described your emotions at the descent from the Passo d'Aprica to the Valtellina. It is the most beautiful scene in Italy to me—perhaps partly because I was so happy when I saw it.[2] But no—it didn't need that! I know every foot of that Edolo route, & before the Val Camonica was spoilt by the steam tram there was no more riante valley south of the Alps. But oh *ain't* it hot lying at Lovere?—

Please let me hear you in Paris when I reach no. 53.—

Yr Aff
   E. W

Has your pseudo-grandfatherhood arrived?—

Did you read the opening of the defense of Paterno's lawyer? "Quel uomo, che aveva un *boudoir di cocotte*, voi volete farmi credere che era un uomo brutale, violente e senza coltura?" Textuel!

Important p.s.

Do please be a real friend & find out for me whether la Marbury would let me her villa³ for the next two or three months, or even six weeks? I *must* finish my book, & I see I've got to settle down somewhere to do it. I shd so like that!

Ms:VT

1. The monastery of La Verna, which squats imposingly at the edge of steep chalk cliffs, was the site in 1224 on which Francis of Assisi received the stigmata. The monastery of Camaldoli, lying to the north of La Verna in the Apennines of the Casentino section of Tuscany and reached by an equally narrow and curving mountain road, was built in the twelfth century; above it is the silent and gracious hermitage, established in 1012.

2. EW and Teddy Wharton had crossed the Passo d'Aprica into the Valtellina and then Val Camonica in the summer of 1899.

3. Villa Trianon in Versailles, which Elisabeth Marbury and Elsie de Wolfe had bought in 1904 and restored over the next few years. They began to occupy it in 1907. (On Elsie de Wolfe, see letter to Mary Cadwalader Jones, January 7, 1916, note 4.)

Edith Wharton, 1907.
Beinecke Library, Yale University.

Edith Wharton: publicity photo, 1908.
William Royall Tyler Collection, Lily Library, University of Indiana.

Morton Fullerton, around 1908. *Collection of R. W. B. Lewis and Nancy Lewis (originally from Marian Mainwaring).*

Edith Wharton, 1911.
Beinecke Library, Yale University.

Portrait of Henry James, by Jacques-Emile
Blanche, Paris, 1908. *Bequest of Mrs. Katharine
Dexter McCormick, The National Portrait
Gallery, Smithsonian Institution.*

Howard Sturgis with a friend (probably William Haynes Smith) on
the front steps at Queen's Acre, Windsor, England, 1909.
Beinecke Library, Yale University.

Monday, June 8th

Just now, as the last course of luncheon was being served with due solemnity, I had a sudden vision of our first luncheon at Duval's, with the kindly prognathous lady-in-waiting, & the moist hippopotamus Américain with his cucumber-faced female—do you remember? And then the second day, when the old gentleman in the corner kept us so long in suspense, & finally softened just as we despaired?

And how kind people were wherever he went — our friends in the train at Creil, our waiter at Montmorency, that dearest of concierges in le Jardin de Mme Furquet — yes, even the Sleeping Man in the dining-room of the Grand Cerf, who drove us out under the lilacs in the court!

Letter from Edith Wharton, The Mount, June 8, 1908, to Morton Fullerton.
Harry Ransom Humanities Research Center, The University of Texas at Austin.

View of
Salsomaggiore,
Italy, from a
postcard written
by Edith
Wharton to
Morton
Fullerton,
May 21, 1911.
*Beinecke Library,
Yale University.*

Walter Berry at The Mount,
1911. *Beinecke Library, Yale
University.*

Charles Cook, the chauffeur, with unidentified friend, standing by the Whartons' Mercedes. *Beinecke Library, Yale University.*

Walter Berry, Edith Wharton, and a French officer in the forward area at Verdun, 1915. *Beinecke Library, Yale University.*

GRAND HÔTEL DU COQ HARDI
& CAFÉ DU COMMERCE
VERDUN
MEUSE

ÉMILE CLÉMENT
PROPRIÉTAIRE

Téléphone 68

VERDUN, le 28th February 1915

Dearest Cher Master,

After nearly six months at the same job I felt a yearning to get away for a few days, & also a great desire to find out what was really wanted in some of the hospitals near the front, from which such lamentable tales have reached us. It took a good deal of demarching & countermarching to get a laissez-passer, for it has always been a great deal more difficult to go east than north, & especially so, these last weeks, on account of the "spies & espions" (as White calls them), & also of the movements of troops, more recently. However, thanks to Paul & to Mr. Cambon (the Berlin one) I did, a day or two ago, get a splendid permesso, & immediately loaded up the motor with clothes & medicaments & dashed off from Paris with Walter yesterday morning. We went first to Châlons s/ Marne, & it was extraordinary, not more than 4 hours from Paris, to find ourselves to all appearance completely in the war-zone. It is the big base of the eastern army, & the streets swarm with soldiers & with military motors & ambulances. We went to see a hospital with 900 cases of typhoid, where

---

Letter from Edith Wharton, Verdun, February 28, 1915, to Henry James.
Beinecke Library, Yale University.

Edith Wharton and Walter Berry (*at right*) with two French officers in the battle
area, Verdun, February 1915. *Beinecke Library, Yale University.*

Margaret Terry Chanler, around 1918, from
the frontispiece of her memoirs, *Roman Spring*
(Boston: Little, Brown & Co., 1934). *Courtesy
of her grandson, David Pickman.*

Elisina Royall Tyler, 1918. *William Royall Tyler
Collection, Lily Library, University of Indiana.*

Charles Scribner II
(1854–1930).
*Firestone Library,
Princeton University.*

A class of Belgian children,
1918, wards of the Children of
Flanders Rescue Committee,
of which Edith Wharton was
chairman. *Beinecke Library,
Yale University.*

The villa Jean-
Marie at St. Brice,
near Paris, "in
1918" (Edith
Wharton's
handwriting).
*Beinecke Library,
Yale University.*

Le Barbier, éditeur   St-BRICE-sous-FORÊT (S.-et-Oise). - Jean-Marie   *in 1918*

To W. Morton Fullerton

Offranville
Seine-Inférieure
Monday
[August 12, 1912]

Cher Ami,

I went to a Beauty Show at Folkestone with Claude Phillips¹ (where we tied for the first prize) & picked up a microbe which is increasing & multiplying in my throat & nose today! I am consequently obliged to put off leaving here till tomorrow. I count on you for dinner tomorrow nevertheless, & this is merely to ask if you will drop a line in the morning to Appleton, to say that the end of "The Reef" will go to them *positively* this week. I shd greatly like to revise the last 6 chapters after an interval of a fortnight—say about Sept 1st. Will you ask them if they will let me do this on the proofs, or if they prefer to hold back the printing of this last portion till they receive my revised copy? Please explain that I mean only *verbal revision*, not re-writing of the chapters: the kind of thing that Scribner always lets me do to my proofs.—I shan't send the chapters till I've read them to you, & this will help me to make one revision, but I want time for another, after an interval, for it's essential that these last chapters should be especially ripe & homogeneous (what a combination of adjectives!)—

More of this tomorrow—

Mille amitiés—
     E.W

Ms:UT

1. Claude Phillips (1846–1924), keeper of the Wallace Collection in London. EW had met him at Lamb House.

To Gaillard Lapsley

53 Rue de Varenne
August 19 [1912]

Dear Gaillard,

It was sad to be in England the other day & not see you. I should have written sooner to tell you so, & also to thank you for your letter from the steamer; but for the last two months my book has really held me tight. Now it's out of—no, I'm out of *its* clutches, I mean, & I'm taking a holiday of a dim kind before tackling the next one (for Scribner's "sirrial" next winter.)

I'm so glad you started off for là bas in such good form after your hard winter. I suppose your Etretat holiday did you good in spite of the sea-fuzz. Why is it you are always doomed to the seaside, as I used to be? I'm delighted you had your sister with you. How wise of her to break away!

I had three good weeks in England with Henry & Howard, but much regretted not seeing Percy (whom Henry calls "the only *man of letters* in England"!). He was notified (at my request) of my presence at Quaker, but curtly declined to come & see me.

Henry seems pretty well—not more. He has violent ups & downs, & is evidently extremely worried about himself. He was with me nearly all the time I was in England, & I even took him to Cliveden for three or four days. He was captivated by Nancy Astor, & completely ravished by Cliveden itself, which—oddly enough—he didn't know, & which was in its deepest stillest summer beauty; but unluckily he had one of his heart-attacks the last day, & got a panic, & I had to rush him back to Rye in the motor. I stopped at Lamb House for a night before leaving England, & found him better, & reassured, but he had another attack the next day.¹ The Drs tell him it's digestive, but I can see he doesn't believe them; & anyhow, the pain frightens him.

His Browning is out in the Quarterly.² Do read it.

Teddy, after extensive dental operations, which seem to have given him considerable relief, is off fishing with his brother till Sept. 15. After that he says he means to come abroad.

I felt I could never again face another winter here like the last, & I wrote him some six weeks ago proposing that I shd take a house in N. Y. for the winter, & that we shd then look about for some small place in the country wh. would not be such a burden to me as the Mount, but where he might "keep chickens," as he expresses it. I told him I thought I had a chance of getting rid of the lease of this apartment, & that I wd rather settle down quietly for the rest of my days in some place that he was satisfied with, & where I could write steadily, than undergo longer the endless "tiraillements" & ever-recurring uncertainties of the present situation.

Result: frantic cables, "Don't come—don't sublet apartment—entirely disapprove plan—" & thereafter 20 pages bitterly reproaching me for "worrying" him with such an absurd suggestion at a time when his nerves ought to be spared!

Finally, a calmer letter came the other day, emphatically & altogether refusing to consider the possibility of living in America! So there we are. More ink wasted & nothing done.

If by chance you see Florence La Farge,[3] do give her my best love. I never hear from her, but think of her very often.

Write me soon, dear Gaillard. But don't tell me anything about the Mount, for there's a great ache there still. Yrs Affly E. W.

I wish I could see Mrs. Hoppin some time when she is in Paris.

I'm just off to Pougues to spend a few days with the Bourgets—then I shall go with Anna to a cure in Dauphiné where she has to take the baths for her rheumatism.

Ms:BL

1. During EW's twenty-four-hour visit to Lamb House, Henry James wrote Howard Sturgis that "She has held us ... spell-bound, this pair of hours, by her admirable talk. She never was more wound up and going, or more ready, it would appear, for new worlds to conquer."

2. Henry James had read his essay "The Novel in *The Ring and the Book*" at the ceremony on May 7 to honor the hundredth anniversary of Browning's birth.

3. Florence La Farge, the wife of the architect Grant La Farge (the eldest son of John La Farge, the painter) and a woman of great erudition.

To Henry James

Château de Barante
[Southern France]
September 3 [1912]

Dearest Cher Maître,

How are you & what have you been doing since my vigilant eye has been off you? I am in the château of Prosper de Barante, the friend, lover, cousin, correspondent (or all four) of nearly everybody in the de Staël-Récamier group, & spent all last evening reading Récamier, de Staël, Chateaubriand, & Joubert letters, not to speak of earlier & later ones of equal interest, from Rousseau to Mérimée.¹ How I did want you to be here!—

(Continuation next day, from Vic sur Cère, in the Massif du Cantal) —I had to dash down early yesterday morning to see my host's first editions (in a library of 50,000 volumes!), & look again at the family portraits & the miniatures of the irresistible Prosper's loves, from Cormine to Caroline Murat—& after that it was time to jump into the motor & start; so my plan of telling you all about Barante was broken in two. It is a wonderful place, about 30 miles from Clermont Ferrand, in an immense English-looking park, with big oaks & cattle, &, from the house, incomparable views over the whole Puy de Dôme region, the Mont Dore, & this Massif du Cantal that we're now in. Mr. de Barante is a Paris friend who had always adjured me to come to Barante whenever I was in Auvergne, & who is really worth seeing there, under grandpa Prosper's out-spread glory, every little sparkle of which he zealously polishes up every morning. It's altogether the most interesting glimpse of French "Shatter Life" I've ever had.

Well—to revert.—I left Paris about a fortnight ago, & went for a week to be with the Minnie Pauls² at Pougues les Eaux, a vile place where, in a sinister little mouldy villa, they live (!) as Paul says: "Comme des cloportes sous une pierre."

I "mealed" with them, but enjoyed the relative advantages of a clean room & a bath-room at the neighbouring hotel. We roamed the country in the motor, & I tried to coax them to come off with me for ten days (with their own motor, which they had there). Minnie was very anxious to come, & *he* wanted to, but couldn't make up his mind what day he would start; so after a week I departed without them. My old friend

Marion Richards[3] was villegiaturing with the Jusserands in J's "maison familiale," in the Lyonnais (such a dear old XVIII maison bourgeoise, in a garden full of clipped box, looking over all the plain of the Lyonnais to the mountains); & I picked her up there & spent an hour or two with the J's. It was a refreshing atmosphere after the drug-dreariness in which the M.P.s are sunk to their chins. (Paul's first remark on my arriving at Pougues was: "Ah, je vous ferai voir l'homme qui nous lave les intestins, et qui est en même temps le jardinier de l'évêque hérésiarque qui habite en face de l'hôtel." That really boxed his compass!)

Well—we went from the Jusserands' to Vichy for a day or two, then to Barante, & now we're here in this primitive pleasant mountain place, where we shall "lay" for a day or two more before going on to Vernet & the eastern Pyrenees. The sun is out at last, & we are going to follow it south for another week or ten days, possibly over the edge of Spain. —I shall be back in Paris toward the 20th of September for a few days, & after that I'm uncertain.—Teddy seems to be really better, & quite relieved of the pain in his face, since his teeth are gone. He announces his intention of sailing for England at the end of this month.—Marion is a perfect traveller. Everything interests & amuses her, & as she had never been in Auvergne the Romanesque churches are quite new to her, & she knows enough of architecture to be aware of what they "stand for," as we say in Boston—

Don't write me, but keep well & think of me very often—

Yr devoted Edith

P.S. Walter cabled me last week that he had hopes of a prompt settlement.

Ms:BL

1. Guillaume-Prosper Brugière, Baron de Barante (1782–1866), the grandfather of EW's host, was a literary critic and historian, and a youthful admirer of Mme. de Staël: i.e., the famous writer of letters, Anne-Louise-Germaine Necker (1766–1817). Jeanne-Françoise, Mme. Récamier (1777–1849), the closest and perhaps only woman friend of Mme. de Staël, maintained a *salon* in Paris, of which the literary hero was François-René de Chateaubriand (1768–1848), whose short tale *Atala* in 1801 made him famous. Joseph Joubert (1754

–1824) was a distinguished lecturer on spiritualist philosophy. Prosper Barante, in 1806, married the granddaughter of one of the loves of Jean-Jacques Rousseau. Prosper Mérimée (1803–1870) was a highly admired novelist, author of *Chronique du règne de Charles IX* in 1829.

2. Minnie and Paul Bourget.

3. Marion Richards was the sister of Elise Richards, the wife of Jules Jusserand. See letter to Sara Norton, August 29, 1902, note 5.

To John Jay Chapman

53 Rue de Varenne
October 8, 1912

Dear John Chapman,

Reading your "Wm James,"[1] & talking of you a great deal with Daisy & Bob Minturn these last days, has brought you so close that it seems queer, & all wrong, not to be telling you face to face how much I admire the said opus, instead of scratching these brief words of appreciation with a weary proof revising wrist.

Oh, *how* you do it, when you do do it, & why don't you oftener? These too few pages are so packed with fine & penetrating things that I want you to be looking over my shoulder while my finger points: "Here—& here—& here!" And how you've managed to balance the big heart & the considerably less ponderable brain of your subject, when all the world has been so persistently confusing his two organs for the last fifteen years!

It needed doing, & no one cd have done it so well. I only wish you'd developed it.

Thanks for such a good hour.

Yours ever
E. Wharton

Ms:HL

1. Chapman's essay on his former teacher William James was included in *Memories and Milestones* (1915).

To W. Morton Fullerton

53 Rue de Varenne
Sunday
[October 1912]

Cher Ami,

I have read only about half of this last part, because, in my ignorance of the subject, it is useless for me to go on without having first read the preceding chapters. Nevertheless, I can see that you have an immense number of important things to say, that your documentation is full & effectively used, & that the construction of the book is logical & the presentation—the groupings, rather—of the facts extremely striking.

It is because I see this, I believe, as you do, that you have done something valuable & original, that I am going to risk an outspoken criticism of the thing I'm most competent to speak about: the style in which the book is written.

As it stands, I believe this style will be a serious obstacle to the success the book ought to have. Do, cher ami, in your own words, "adopt a franker idiom"! Such an argument ought to be as bare, as nervous, as manly & energetic as the young Sophocles of your poor sculptor; & you've hung it with all the heavy tin draperies of the Times jargon—that most prolix & pedantic of all the dead languages.—For the last years—I've said it before, I know!—you've read too much French & too much *Times*. I can't too strongly urge you to drop both tongues for a few weeks, & go back to English—to what Arnold called "prose of the centre." Read Emerson, read Tyndall, read Froud[e] even, read Arnold—get away from authors of your own métier, from all the scientific-politico-economic charabia[1] of your own specialists into the clear air of the born writers—& then turn to "Science & Patriotism"[2] (wh. I dipped into again the other day at Rye) & see how capable you are of writing well, & how you've let yourself be smothered in the flabby *tentacularities* of "our own correspondent's" lingo. Drop 30 per cent of your Latinisms ("engendering a divergency" & so on), mow down every old cliché, uproot all the dragging circumlocutions, compress, diversify, clarify, vivify, & you'll make a book that will be read & talked of not only by the experts but by the big "intelligent public" you want to reach.

You can't do this now—you're too tired & too steeped in what you've written. Put the ms aside for a month, go to England, see people, read

English books (not newspapers), & then return to "Internationalities" with a fresh eye & a fresh ear. It's a tired book now, & you must make it a vigorous one. It needs just what you do: fresh air & muscle.

When you come back to it you'll be able to give it the life it lacks. Newer & more vivid images will occur to you, words arrange themselves in less hackneyed groupings, & the originality of your ideas communicate itself to the speech in which you express them.

If I were to "think over" this letter I probably shouldn't send it—so I'm rushing it off to you at once! I shouldn't have said a word of it if I didn't seriously believe the book risks failure as it is, & if I didn't know how much you stake on it. The opinion isn't mine alone, but that—unanimously—of the few worth-while people with whom I've talked of your recent articles—of the last two or three years, I mean. It was the general comment on the American article. It is Henry's view even more emphatically than mine.

And I venture to tell you all this, because you can write the other language, as all your earlier things prove, & need only go back & dip in the reviving spring.

Do what I advise—break away from Paris, & from French, & from work—put off publication till February—not a bad time—& make the book a book that will make *you*!

And now curse me in as good Saxon as you like; but no Latin imprecations please!

Yrs E. W

I've made notes about halfway through these last pages—

Ms:UT

1. Charabia: gibberish.
2. Fullerton's *Patriotism and Science: Some Studies in Historic Psychology* had appeared in Boston in 1893.

To W. Morton Fullerton

53 Rue de Varenne
[November 1912]

Cher Ami,

Thanks for the Whitman—& I will see that Walter gets his book.

I am much distressed by a phrase in your note: "your general report of the *interest* of my matter discourages me" &c &c.

What do you mean? All I said of your *matter* was that it seemed to me extraordinarily rich & interesting, & presented with admirable consecutiveness & clearness.

All my criticisms referred to your *langue*, & if you re-read my letter I am sure you will see that I say so explicitly. If I gave you the impression that the persons who had spoken to me of your articles had criticized the matter or the ideas, that is also a misunderstanding. I heard only admiration of both. The one thing criticized was your language, as being not as light, flexible & *personal* as your ideas.

This book seems to me to be written in the language of fatigue. The immense pressure of what you have to say, & the anxiety lest you should leave out or misplace any fact or idea in your ingeniously close chain, have made you perforce neglect the form a little. You will come back to it with a new eye, & see what I mean, & how to remedy it.

I repeat again: *go to England.* You need it, & you need it now. Give yr last chapters to the National by all means. Seeing them in print will help you too. And do show the ms to some one else.—I shd not have written what I have if I did not *know* that you have written a remarkable book, & desire with all my heart that it should be appreciated at its full worth.

E. W.

Ms:UT

To Bernard Berenson

53 Rue de Varenne
November 23 [1912]

Dear B. B.,

I'm sending you my book,¹ though I don't want to, because I'm sick about it—poor miserable lifeless lump that it is!

But if I didn't send it you'd wonder why; so I "execute myself" (in the English as well as the French sense) herewith. Only *please* don't read it! Put it in the visitors' rooms, or lend it to somebody to read in the train & let it get lost. (It never will—a conscientious stranger will pick it up, employ detectives to find the owner, & send it back!)

Anyhow, remember it's not *me*, though I thought it was when I was writing it—& that *next time* I'm going to do something worthwhile!!

Yrs affly
E. W.

On his way back to Paris Cook came across a motor hopelessly *jammed*. It was that of Mrs. Ripley-Scott, & he brought their chauffeur & luggage back with him ... Die Ewige Wiederkunft—

Ms:VT

1. *The Reef.*

To John Hugh Smith

53 Rue de Varenne
November 25 [1912]

Dear John,

I shall never say again that your letters are inexpressive! This is one of the kindest I ever had from any one. I'm touched at your thinking so much of my worries, & understanding them & me as you do. It's an effort of imagination that people of your age are usually too busy to make.

My brother doesn't get back till this evening & I shan't have a complete view of the situation till I see him; but I think it will take the turn my friends want it to.

If only my work were better it would be all I need! But my kind of half-talent isn't much use as an escape—at least more than temporarily. Still—there are lots & lots of other things, & it's not often that I drop into a stagnant back-water of indifference, such as I'm in now. Come over soon & pull me out into mid-current. I can put you up any time.

Your Affte friend,
    E. W.

I *wish* you'd remind me of the other book I meant to send you.

Ms:BL

To Gaillard Lapsley

53 Rue de Varenne
February 8 [1913]

Dear Gaillard,

I don't—I can't!—flatter myself that you want me to go to England half as much as I want to go there myself! I've been thinking every day for the last two weeks that I should be able to get off—but delays of a hateful & unforeseen kind are perpetually springing up. My cousin H. Edgar came over from N. Y. to spend last week with me & try to put a little order into my chaotic situation; but so far the matter is not concluded, for the simple reason that the other side is never long enough in one place to be parleyed with. In addition, I have had a perfectly horrible & tragic experience with my brother Harry, who is now completely under the rule of the woman he lives with[1]—& apparently this woman, & he, at her instigation, have hated me for two years for *not* asking to make her acquaintance (how could I when he never even spoke to me of her?), & this hatred has suddenly & crazily broken out, just at the moment of all my other worries.—Heaven forbid that anyone I know shd taste the horrors of the fortnight I've just been through.

My cousin shed light on the situation regarding my brother & told me he had had frequent glimpses of this smoldering "rancune"—but there was nothing he cd do to help me.

My dear, I'm coming over to the arms of all of you just as soon as I possibly can.

Your affte   E. W.

I haven't asked about you, or said a word of our beloved Henry. (The present plan is given up.) I'm just an aching mass of egoism at this moment.

Ms:BL

1. A Russian-born Countess, first name Tecla. She and Harry Jones were about to marry.

Private and confidential.

March 1913

Dear ¹

April 15th next is Henry James's 70th birthday.

His English friends and admirers have raised a fund to present him with a portrait. We believe that his American friends will be at least as eager to ask him to accept a gift commemorating this date.

In view of the shortness of time, such commemoration, we think, might most appropriately take the form of a sum of money (not less than $5,000) for the purchase of a gift, the choice of which would be left to him.

The gift will be accompanied by a letter of birthday greeting, signed by all the subscribers.

This circular is addressed to a restricted number of his personal friends and admirers. The success of the plan therefore depends upon their immediate and generous response.

You will no doubt agree with us that this proposal should be kept *strictly confidential* for the present, so that it may not reach Henry James prematurely.

Wm. D Howells²   Edith Wharton

Cheques, drawn to the order of Edith Wharton, should be mailed to her (53 rue de Varenne, Paris) not later than April 2nd.

Persons desirous of contributing, who receive this notice too late, may cable to Mrs. Wharton up to April 12th their intention to subscribe.

Copy:BL

1. This letter was sent to thirty-nine individuals in America, among them: Henry Adams, Sturgis Bigelow, Egerton Winthrop, John Cadwalader, Henry White, Senator Lodge, Barrett Wendell, Walter Maynard, Owen Wister, S. Weir Mitchell, Mrs. Daniel Merriman, Henry Higginson, George Vanderbilt, and Charles Scribner.

2. Howells's name was added in ink by EW.

To Barrett Wendell

53 Rue de Varenne
March 13, 1913

Dear Mr. Wendell,

You will probably wonder why I have delayed all these months to follow up our friend B.B.'s letter written to you at my request last November on the subject of the Harvard Professors' salaries. It is a question I am as much interested in as ever, but I have had so many private preoccupations during the past winter that I have had to put the whole subject aside till I can deal with it more adequately than I could now. As soon as that moment comes you will hear from me again.

Meanwhile I am writing to tell you—or rather to let the enclosed circular tell you—of a plan to celebrate Henry James's 70th birthday. When I learned what his English friends were doing (I enclose their circular also) it seemed to me that his compatriots would always regret not having made a "geste" of the same kind; & I have therefore (with the help of Gaillard Lapsley) hastily improvised the enclosed circular, which I hope Mr. Howells will sign with me.

It wd have been preferable to have eight or ten signatures, but there is no time to obtain them, & it seemed therefore simpler to ask Mr. Howells to sign, as his very old & close friend, & the doyen of American letters, & to add my name so that contributions may be sent to me here—there being no time, either, to organize a committee in America.

For the same reason, gifts in specie are all we can ask—& I am not sorry, for Mr. James is just settling himself in a flat in London, & it seems to me a fortunate pretext to let him get himself just what he wants, & not load him with some costly irrelevance of our choosing.

I hope very much you will approve of this hastily improvised plan, & will give it the immense help of speaking about it to some of Mr. James's old Boston friends. I enclose the list that Gaillard & I have made, but we both feel it is weak in Boston names. We feel that only two categories shd be included—*real* friends & *real* admirers (even if the personal acquaintance is slight.) I think both these groups have an equal right to join in the gift, but the inclusion of any other element might suggest the idea of "raising a fund," & at once alter the whole nature of the gift. So I trust to your tact & judgment to increase the Boston list as you see fit.

I am sending 30 or 40 circulars to Robert Minturn, 116 East 22d St, who is a great friend of Mr. James's, & have asked him if possible to see Mr. Howells & get him to add his signature to mine. If Mr. Howells is out of reach we can think of no alternative but to get three or four people in great haste—would you & Robert Grant sign? Henry Adams could be telegraphed to, & wd consent, of course, & so wd Sturgis Bigelow—& of course R. Minturn himself.

I will ask R. Minturn to communicate with you about this, & to send you some circulars.

I wish there had been more time; but we *must* do it, mustn't we?—
Excuse my hurried letter, & believe me

Yours ever sincerely
    Edith Wharton

I have put on the enclosed list the amount of the subscriptions promised so far. Of course the names alone, *not the individual sums*, will be made known. This is only for private circulation.

G. Lapsley gives to the English fund.—

Ms:HL

To Gaillard Lapsley

53 Rue de Varenne
Easter. March 23 [1913]

Dear Gaillard,

It's all settled![1] But don't say a word to anyone, as the decree can't be pronounced till the courts sit again next week. I feel as if Pelions & Ossas had been lifted off me, & now at last know how tired I am!

I'm starting on the 28th. but *not* for England. I thought I'd rather wait till Howard is out of prison again, poor dear, which won't be for some weeks, I fear, as the second operation doesn't take place for another ten days. And I have rather a longing to see spring come again in Italy, & be all day in the air & the sun.

I shall motor down in your direction, & if we go through Bordighera I'll let you know; but I'm rather longing to jump over from Monte Carlo to Sicily (or at least Naples), if the Cunarders are still going to Egypt.

All is still vague, as things were settled only the day before yesterday, & I'm still pinching myself.

The delay, of course, was due simply to the impossibility of "locating" T.—He suddenly arrived three days ago, & the citation was served, & every-thing settled, in 24 hours.—[2]

I have nearly $1000 for the Henry fund, & an enthusiastic backer in Mrs. Roger Wolcott, who has given me $100, & suggested (& written to) several Boston people. I think we'll pull it off!—I hope you're getting a deep rich rest & lots of sun,

Yr affte friend,
E. W.

Ms:BL

1. The divorce decree.

2. Teddy had come over from America in December 1912, had stopped briefly in Paris (without calling at the Rue de Varenne), moved on to Monte Carlo, and was heard of elsewhere, with a high-powered car and a chauffeur, and various women. He then reappeared in Paris, and a summons was instantly served.

To Gaillard Lapsley

Spezia
April 2 [1913]

Dear Gaillard,

My trip has been completely poisoned by Henry's letter, & the rest I came away to get seems farther from me than ever.[1] There was nothing on earth I valued as much as his affection—I can never get over this.

I have written him what I read you, merely adding—what I momentarily forgot—that I had nothing whatever to do with originating the Birthday plan. The English project was of course started by Gosse, & when I found America cd not join (since we couldn't ask the U.S. to subscribe for a portrait to be given to the N. P. Gallery), I dropped the idea entirely.

When Walter Berry arrived from America I told him about it, & he said at once: "Oh, but we *must* do something of the kind in America." I said: "I'm too tired to undertake anything of the kind," & he insisted & said he would do it, & at once wrote to two or three people. You know what followed, because you were in Paris at the time.

What I should like best is that you should go & see Henry on his birthday, or the day after, & tell him the exact facts—that we all felt, when the English circular was sent out, how *impossible* it was that his American friends should not make the same "geste," how the two cd not be combined, & how we had modeled our circular *exactly* on the English one, & planned to do just what they had done, merely asking him to choose the present he liked best, instead of inflicting some irrelevant horror on him forever. If you will do this—& I know you will —it will be a great kindness to me, for the idea that he pictures me as a meddling philanthropist is too intolerable.

You have no doubt heard that Howard stood the operation well.

It was so nice to see you the other day—or would have been if we hadn't been simultaneously so shattered!!

Your affte friend
Edith

Please show Henry the little letter that was to have been sent with the present, & tell him the idea was that he should choose a fine piece of old furniture or something of the kind. *Above all, please* make him understand that in answering his letter I could not have been more explicit than I was without breaking my promise not to reveal the English plan. I want this to be made as clear as possible.

E.

Ms:BL

1. News of EW's requests for funds to make a seventieth birthday present of at least $5,000 reached the ears of James's nephews Harry, in New York, and Billy, in Boston. It was Billy who cabled word about it to James, who cabled back at once: "Immense thanks for warning taking instant prohibitive action please express to individuals approached my horror money absolutely returned, UNCLE." In a follow-up letter to Billy, James said: "A more reckless and indiscreet undertaking, with no ghost of preliminary leave asked, no hint of a sounding taken, I cannot possibly conceive."
   "Henry's letter" to EW has not survived. Presumably it said something of the same thing in a far more moderate manner.

To Mary Berenson

Rome
Hotel Excelsior
April 10 [1913]

Dearest Mary,

The beneficent influences of I Tatti seemed to extend over the whole of central Italy! They followed us through our whole wonderful run to Montepulciano, causing the heavens to diluviate only while we were devouring our delicious ham sandwiches in blissful disregard of meteorological conditions, & dispelling the clouds in time to give us the full wonder of the run from Monte Sansavino to Monte Oliveto.¹ The sudden burst of it, from the height of Chiusura, is one of the most "saisissant" things in Italy.—We spent a delightful hour among the frescoes, & then went on to Montepulciano, which so enchanted us, under a wild streaming golden sunset, that we captured the only rooms with "stufe" at the Marzocco, & spent the evening roaming among the San Gallo palaces. What an extraordinary little place it is—and how little it gets gushed over!

Yesterday morning we had another glorious run, to Orvieto, where we lunched; there the deluge set in, clouds enveloped all the heights, & we had to give up Todi. On the Ciminian pass the fog was so thick that we had to go half speed & toot like a "liner"!—

Here I have been overtaken by another radiation from I Tatti in the shape of a huge (but not too huge!) box of those blessed peppermints. Panoplied & steeled in this fashion against Sicilian microbes, I shall set forth rejoicing tomorrow for Naples & Palermo! Thank you for that too.

I shd have been quite happy with you if B. B. had been a little better. Do send me a line to the Bertolini, Naples, to say how he is getting on. I hope we didn't tire him too much.

Did the Lost Daughter[2] finally turn up? Please tell her how much I regretted missing her.—

B. B. must have been *furious* that the Pope didn't die in time to stop the Ball!—No sign of the Kimberleys. I'm afraid we passed them in the fog.

With my most affectionate thoughts, dear Mary,

Ever yours
    Edith W.

Tell B. B. it *was* the Wm Jameses[3] who did the whole thing about giving away the Birthday Scheme. H. J. was entirely misled by them, & feels very sorry about it now. I have had the most charming letter from Barrett Wendell about it.[4]

Ms:VT

1. Monte Oliveto Maggiore, a Benedictine abbey lying twenty-two miles southeast of Siena. The "Great Cloisters" are adorned with thirty-six frescoes depicting the life of St. Benedict, by Luca Signorelli (1498) and Il Sodoma (1505–1508).

2. Karin Costelloe, the twenty-four-year-old daughter of Mary Berenson and her first husband, Francis Costelloe, who had died in December 1899.

3. The younger William, or Billy.

4. Wendell said in part that after their talks in Paris, he felt that "what touches you has come to seem more nearly to concern my own life than by any right or reason it should." As to the "birthday matter," he went on, "I cannot a bit regret it. There could never be impulse or sentiment more gentle than that which possessed us all."

To Barrett Wendell

53 Rue de Varenne
April 12, 1913

Dear Mr. Wendell,

Owing to an unfriendly misrepresentation of the nature and intention of the Birthday Gift which Mr. James's friends had planned to offer him, he has made known that he prefers not to accept it.

The committee regret that they have therefore no alternative but to return your cheque, which they enclose with their sincerest thanks.[1]

Ms:HL

1. This formal communication (here unsigned, but presumably accompanied by a personal note from EW) was sent to all those who had contributed to the birthday fund.

To Sara Norton

April 12, 1913
[Naples]

Dearest Sally,

I sent you yesterday an ecstatic post card from Monte Cassino—the goal of many dreams!—& in a moment of aberration addressed it to 83 *Irving* St.!—I don't know where its peregrinations will eventually lead it, but meanwhile I send this supplementary line to your real address, as I want to thank you without delay for your kind & sympathetic note about the poor thwarted Birthday gift (which did not originate with me, by the way). It was apparently Mr Howells who betrayed our confidence, & revealed the plan to Mrs Wm James, who cabled to H. J. that

I was "raising a fund" for his support—apparently giving him the impression that I was collecting money to pay his debts or buy him an annuity! He lost his head completely, & cabled to her to put a stop to the plan at once—& I was thereupon notified by Dr Bigelow.[1] You may imagine my feelings, & those of the other friends who had planned the little demonstration on the lines of the English one—which was started by Mr. Gosse & Mr Barrie.—We purposely stated in the circular that we wished to leave the selection of the gift to H. J., as we couldn't well offer him another portrait, & we all felt it would be so much more satisfactory to let him choose some handsome old piece of furniture, or other object of art, rather than burden him with something he might not like.

The circular was marked "Private & Confidential—" &, as Mr. Wendell remarks, in an indignant letter just received from him, the suggestion of privacy wd have been *implicit* in such a communication to any one of decent feeling, even if it had not been expressly enjoined.—It always interests me to see the sense of honour of such hyperscrupulous persons as Mr. Howells & Mrs Wm James display itself in its full beauty! The spectacle is profoundly edifying. And poor Mr. James has been made really ill, & his friends unhappy—& some of them deeply hurt —for the sake of this display of ultra-righteousness!

Gaillard Lapsley—who was one of the chief promoters of the plan— saw Mr. James in London last week, & told me he was very much upset, & admitted he had been completely misinformed.

I have been staying with the Berensons, & motored down here the day before yesterday on my way to Sicily, where I am going for a few days. Monte Cassino was unimaginably beautiful, & I am hoping for great joys from Sicily, wh. I haven't seen for twenty years or more.

Excuse this very untidy letter—I am writing in bed, after a long delicious day at Pompeii.—

I hear from Anna that you & I are together in the April Scribner— tant mieux! I'm impatient to see your first instalment.

I'll write soon again.

Yr affte
   E. W.

Ms:BL

1. It was Sturgis Bigelow (born 1850), after a lengthy discussion with Barrett Wendell in Cambridge, who had cabled EW that the birthday plan must be given up. Bigelow, after abandoning a medical career and putting in ten years of study in Japan, was now a lecturer on Buddhist doctrine at Harvard. He had been a close friend of Bay Lodge, and had advised EW on Teddy Wharton's mental disorders.

To Gaillard Lapsley

Naples
April 14 [1913]

Dear Gaillard

Your letter enclosing Barrett Wendell's has come just as I am leaving for Sicily, & I can only send a line to say how *very* glad I am to have had the chance of reading it. He & R. Minturn have shown the greatest tact & kindness with respect to the unhappy Birthday enterprise, & I am only sorry that I shd [have] given them so much trouble in vain.

As to what Mr Wendell writes of my own affairs, I am very much touched by it, & wish you would tell him so. Considering the extraordinary attitude of Teddy's family from the outset, I hardly hoped that any one in Boston wd. see the situation as it really is, & that Mr Wendell, whom I see so seldom, & really know so slightly, should take the view he does, is a great comfort to me—for I do sometimes feel a great soreness & indignation at the way in which the Whartons have treated me.

Bless you, my Dear, for your unfailing sympathy & your affectionate words.

It has been raining all day as hard as it did at Monte Carlo—& Vesuvius has a cap of new snow! So you see one must go to H. Sedgwick to find the real Italy!!—

Yr affte friend
E. W

N.B. The 2 sheets stuck together, with odd results

Ms:BL

To Bernard Berenson

Girgenti
April 19 [1913]

Dear B. B.,

At last the luck has changed, & for the last three days we[1] have been having Sicilian, not to say Ionian, weather. We haven't wasted a drop of it, either; for here we are, after drinking up all the wonders of the world en route. We left Palermo two days ago, & went across those wonderful mountains behind Monreale to the Gaggera ford, where we lassoed two mettlesome mules & pranced up the sacred heights to the most inspired solitude on earth. What a place! ("Segeste's worthwhile, isn't it?" I said to an American friend we met in Palermo; who replied impartially: "well, you know it was never finished; but the situation's good" . . .)

Well! That ought to have been enough for one day; but on we went to Trapani, through unfolding beauties; & just before sunset we climbed to the top of Eryx,[2] & pottered about that strange little dream-town of S. Giuliano, with its beautifully patterned pavements, & silent little mouldering palaces & churches, & the great castle piled up on the out-ermost cliff between sea & sky. How does it happen to be so clean & still & beautiful, such a contrast to all the sordid little Sicilian borghi, almost like a mountain-Bruges in its cloistral silence & order? When we got back to the Trapani hotel after this hour of communion with the Erycinian Venus, we were pained to read, in the very shadow of her temple, this notice appended in our rooms: "Le signore sono pregate di ricevere le visite dei signori nel salone pubblico, per riguardo agli usi severi del paese".[3]—What degenerate days—though I may add that in the restaurant, which regorged with commercial gents, le signore seemed to be exercising the traditional privileges of the priestesses; nor do I think that the rites were concluded in the salone pubblico.

That first day has taken so much space that I must foreshorten yesterday—which, as it happened, was considerably longer! We mo-tored back as far as Calatafimi, & than came down to Selinunte, where we lunched under the tumbled temples, & then flew on to Girgenti. To-morrow we start with the lark & go via Castrogiovanni & Nicosia to Taormina—if we can get there! If not, we'll sleep at Nicosia. Then we shall come back along the coast to Catania & Syracuse, & finally motor across from Catania to Palermo. The mountain roads are so much better than those along the shore that we expect, in this way, to get the maximum of comfort as well as of scenery. We met a young Catanian at Palermo who had done Catania to Palermo in a day, & said the roads were "like a billiard."

We pine for you both, & I'm already planning a summer cruise around the island, with an ascent of Etna, & another visit to Mount Eryx *without a night* at the Grand Hotel de Trapani! Voulez vous en être?

I do hope you're feeling better, & ceasing to part with your precious pounds. What fun if you could have been here!—Do send me a line Excelsior, Palermo, if you feel like it.

Your affte friend
E. W.

Please thank Mary for her letter.

And the palaces of Trapani!—how do they happen to be so much finer than any at Palermo? And why was Selinus built on a stretch of coast without harbour? And what song did the sirens sing—&c, &c? Oh, how many things I want to ask you!

Ms:VT

1. EW was traveling with Walter Berry.
2. Monte Erice, above the village of Erice, the Greek and Phoenician Eryx.
3. "Ladies are requested to receive visits from gentlemen in the public salon, out of consideration for the strict customs of the region."

To W. Morton Fullerton

Grand Hotel
Castello a Mare
Taormina
April 22, 1913

"Then on a peak close to the stars they founded the seat of Idalian Venus"[1]—

We sat on that peak of Eryx the other afternoon, looking out over one of the most beautiful landscapes in Sicily, after a morning in the mountains of Segesta,[2] with a distant glimpse of sea shining through the immense columns of the temple. It was such an incredible beginning—that first day's run from Palermo to the west coast & Trapani—that I was afraid that nothing that came after would seem worth while; but then I had only "done" Sicily before from a yacht, & didn't know what the centre of the island could show. From Trapani to Selinunte & Girgenti & from Girgenti straight across the mountains to the central cliff of Enna-Castrogiovanni, & from there on to Nicosia, on another wonderful peak—all the way has been beautiful, with all possible varieties of beauty, & under such a sky, & above such a sea, as the most flagrant coloured post-cards understate!—After the deluges on the way down it is like being in the heart of an immense sapphire.

All this time I've had no news from you but one letter, rec'd in Rome or Naples about ten days ago, explaining why you hadn't taken the Matin offer. If it was necessary to enter into a long contract that naturally changes the conditions—but I wish I had been able to talk things over with you! Meanwhile the book[3] has come out, & I'm so anxious to hear what the reviews are saying, & above all what the Times has said. I hope you'll bear in mind my remoteness from newspapers, & send me such clippings as you can spare.

I fancy Henry's book[4] is also awaiting me at the rue de V.—Have you received a copy, & what do you think of it?—I think I wrote you that Lapsley had seen Henry in London, & found the W. James clan had completely misled him, apparently making him think I was trying to raise an annuity for his old age. I think he regrets very much what he did, & the way in which he did it, & he must have regretted it still more in the act of receiving from "over 250" of his English friends the very same kind of offering he spurned from twenty or thirty compatriots!

I felt very badly about it for a while, but all this sun & air & sweetness are so healing that worries & pains seem far off, at any rate for the present. I love the long days in the motor, & the great adventurous flights over unknown roads, & even (the next morning, when I'm out in the air again) the queer inns to which the roads but too frequently lead! There was one at Nicosia, the night before last, at which my descente de lit[5] seemed to be made of all the tatters of all the beggars in Italy.—

We have still a bit of the S. E. corner to investigate, & then go back across the mountains to Castrogiovanni, & thence to Palermo—& after that even Paestum will seem tame, I'm afraid—not to speak of the rue de V!—

Send me a line to the Hotel Excelsior, Rome, to tell me all the news —yours, I mean.—I have it on my conscience that I didn't let Mr Sears know that the road I recommended from Spezia to Lucca, has been completely défoncée, & is now as bad as the other along the coast. Please apologize to him if he's started—though I inferred from your last letter that he was staying on in Paris.

I do hope you're better than when you wrote. I read of your being at a Sunday party, so I suppose you are—& it must be cheering to see the Book out! I trust it's racing at break-neck speed to a second edition.

Amitiés toujours
   E. W

I can't give Mr Sears an answer yet. I must think the matter over— [On front:] I've almost lost the use of the pen!

Ms:UT

1. Virgil, *Aeneid*, Book V, lines 759–760. EW is no doubt quoting from memory. The original passage may be translated: "Then on the peak of Eryx close to the stars there was founded the seat of Idalian Venus." The narrative voice is that of Virgil.

2. EW varies her spelling of this ancient town, of which only the ruins survive.

3. Fullerton's *Problems of Power: A Study of International Politics from Sadowa to Kirk-Kilissé*, published by Scribners and dedicated to Theodore Roosevelt (who wrote so favorable a review that Fullerton was overwhelmed).

4. *A Small Boy and Others*, the first volume of Henry James's autobiography.

5. Descente de lit: bedside rug.

To Charles Scribner

Naples
April 29 [1913]

Dear Mr. Scribner,

Your letter of April 3d reached me only two or three days ago, as I have been motoring in the remotenesses of Sicily.

It was *very* kind of you to send me Mr. James's letter, & I am delighted at the complete success of the plan,[1] & warmly appreciative of all you have done. It did my heart good to read the letter.

I hear on all sides that "A Small Boy & Others" is delightful, & I hope so much it will have a popular success.—Mr. James seems to be much better, & is reported as talking enthusiastically of the new novel.

With renewed thanks,

Yours ever sincerely
　　Edith Wharton

Ms:FL

1. This plan anteceded the birthday effort by many months. After visiting with James the previous summer in England, EW became convinced that money worries were inhibiting his work. She wrote Charles Scribner asking that the firm offer James an advance of $8,000 on his next novel, half to be paid on signing the contract, with funds provided by her. The transaction was carried out; Scribner's letter of April 3 enclosed a letter from James acknowledging "with lively appreciation" the receipt of $4,000, less the agent's fee, as an advance on *The Ivory Tower*. "Our fell purpose was successfully accomplished," Scribner informed EW. "I feel rather mean and caddish and must continue so to the end of my days. Please never give me away."

To W. Morton Fullerton

Hotel Excelsior
Rome
May 3 [1913]

Cher Ami,

I arrived last night, rather tired by the long run from Naples—but I want to send a line at once to thank you for your letter, & to say that you did *absolutely right* in telling the reporters that you knew nothing of my divorce.—I have told all my friends of it, & that is sufficient. I obtained it on the ground of adultery in Boston, London & France, with documents à l'appui, duly recorded by the court;[1] & you are [at] liberty to say this to any friend of mine who speaks to you about the matter. In case of any other enquiries, please simply say what you have already said: "*I know nothing.*" As you know, the public can't get at the register of the French courts, & the reporters will soon tire of their vain researches. It's a tiresome moment to traverse—but no more.—And thanks for doing just what you did.

Sorrento, La Cava, Paestum, have all been beautiful; but yesterday the incomparable road by Baiae, Gaeta & the Pontine Marshes was suddenly—halfway to Rome—blotted out by a deluge. It was such a disappointment!—

I shall be at the Berensons' again in two or three days, & probably in Paris about the 10th or 15th. Don't tell many people, as I don't want to be overwhelmed just at first. I *must* get back to work!—Undine is already making the press ring—I hope she'll keep it up.

I'm *so* impatient to see the Book! I wish I dared have it forwarded to Florence, but it wd be weeks on the way. Dr. Bigelow has sent me a letter from young Henry James wh. has made me simply speechless with indignation. He says they (the family) had considered it their duty to notify H. J. of the Birthday gift, as I had already twice "tried to relieve" their uncle, & had "been stopped"—by them, I suppose!

I shall not tell Henry of this, but shall write to the young man, & ask him to put an immediate stop to the circulation of this outrageous lie. I shd like to ask, in addition, why they permitted their uncle to accept an equivalent amount from strangers, if they wd not consent to their compatriots' gift?—Certainly, once he had refused ours, he put himself doubly in the wrong by accepting the English present.

Everyone in Boston—Wendell, Sturgis, &c—is as indignant & disgusted as I am.

This is a wretched scrawl, but the long hours of motoring are still in my head.

Mille amitiés
    E. W.

Ms:UT

1. The divorce decree, granted on April 16, 1913, by the Tribunal de Grande Instance de Paris, declared that, on the basis of documents submitted, it was evident (in English translation) "that Mr. Wharton maintained adulterous relations in Boston in 1908 and 1909 . . . [and] attached himself to various women both in London and Monte Carlo, and had relations with them of a character gravely injurious to the petitioner."

To Mary Berenson

53 Rue de Varenne
May 20 [1913]

Dear Mary,

I had no idea that Henri[1] meant to leave, nor had my butler. When the latter spoke to Henri about your letter, he denied having spoken to you, & said he had no idea of leaving me, & was perfectly contented here!—However, after that little episode I think it is as well he should go, & as soon as I can replace him he will be free. He is a very good servant, but needs the discipline of a man like White, who keeps a firm hand over his footmen. I don't know how well he would do without that restraint. He is intelligent, obliging & active, but without much "character" (in the English sense), & rather feebly insincere, as you can see by what has happened. There is no reason why he shouldn't have told me he wanted to take a place as valet—it is natural that a good footman should want to "better himself" in the course of time, & I should have done all I could to help him. But he doesn't even seem to know his own mind, for he allowed White to order a new livery for him last week after his return, & still declares he has no wish to leave!

I was so sorry to hear that B. B. had been poorly again. It's too bad —& I wish he'd try one of the German stomach-restorers.—The Bacchae must have been very fine. It would have been delightful to stay over for it—& still more delightful to be able to fly from Paris now.

I am literally submerged by notes, telephones, compatriots, clothes, & all sorts of futilities, & so tired of it all that I wish a good earthquake would sweep the place clean.—The journey back was beautiful to the last minute, & Mr. Scott[2] is a traveller after my own heart. He probably told you of our last thrilling vision of the Jean Cousin windows at Sens, during a tremendous black thunderstorm, with the lightning illuminating the smoldering reds & blues. Everything since then has been flat prose.

I want to write a real letter, but simply can't, for proofs & work await me, & you must take this as bringing you many more thoughts than my hunted pen can express at present.

Again, all my thanks for those golden days at Tatti, that still send a far-off gleam across the Paris mud.

Yours very affly
Edith W.

Tell B. B. I wish he were dining here tonight with his friend Belle Herbert.

I don't think I can let Henri go before July 15th, unless I happen to find some one to take his place.

Ms:VT

1. A young footman in EW's Paris household, about to transfer to Villa I Tatti.

2. Geoffrey Scott (1883–1929) was on the verge of publishing what would soon be regarded as a classic in its field, *The Architecture of Humanism*. The work owed more than a little to the teachings of Scott's friend and mentor Bernard Berenson.

To Bernard Berenson

53 Rue de Varenne
Saturday
August 2, 1913

Dearest B. B.,

Of course I'm not going to lâcher!¹ But the hot weather & the noise here, & the hard grind at my last chapters,² have rather used me up, & I want to ask d'avance if you would so far modify our itinerary as to give me three or four days in some green woody *walky* place where I can recover my nerves before we attack big towns?—You see I'm essentially a country person, & pine in towns in summer; & when I'm rather overdone, as I am at present, the feeling becomes a phobia.

Our trip interests me so much that I shall get over this feeling as soon as I'm a little rested, & I'm sure Baedeker will suggest some blessed retreat to you.—Don't be hard on me, or think me uncertain or capricious. I'm not—but simply dead tired, from having always, these last months, a little too much to do. Remember that everything the all-beneficent Mary does for you falls on me alone—household, cheque book, publishers, servant questions, business letters, proofs—*and* my book! In addition, I've found a poor ill kitchen-boy since I got back, & have had to sack a heartless chef who's been a beast to him.

How quickly I shall forget this in our first Waldeinsamkeit![3]—I'm rejoicing in the trip, & expect to get by Tuesday night to the Hotel Brasseur, Luxembourg, & on Wednesday to the Hotel Bellevue, Coblentz.

What do you say to joining me there? If you want to go to Bonn, it seems useless for me to go to Cologne, as we shall have to retrace our steps; & the motor run from Coblentz to Bonn ought to be pretty.

Send me a wire or a line to Luxembourg—perhaps a wire is safest.

I hope you're having good hours in Belgium—

Yr Affte friend
    E. W

We can settle our next étape when we meet at Coblentz.

Ms:VT

1. EW and Berenson were planning a tour of Germany together.
2. Of *The Custom of the Country*.
3. Sylvan solitude. "Waldeinsamkeit" was also the title of a poem by Emerson (*May-Day and Other Pieces*).

To Bernard Berenson

53 Rue de Varenne
Tuesday
August 5 [1913]

Dearest B.B.,

Your letter has just come, & I have answered in all sincerity. I *want* to go with you, je m'en réjouis, & as I know you don't want a break-neck pace I'm sure we can reconcile more or less repose with the truest interests not of British commerce but of Italian art.—I was frightfully tired a few days ago, but I am feeling much better now, & no doubt these enforced two days in bed are the best preparation I could have for our giro.—I won't ask you for any more Waldeinsamkeit than you can afford to give, & if after three weeks I am too tired, I'll tell you so perfectly frankly. I can't imagine how a friendship like ours can embarrass itself with pretenses of any sort, or why we should nous entendre less completely if I happened not to be well enough to carry out the whole plan of the trip with you. Can you?—Meanwhile the weather is getting cool & cloudy, & that is de bon augure for the start.—If you have any disinclination to go to Luxembourg, don't do so, but meet me at the Bellevue, Coblentz, on Thursday, or at H. du Nord, Cologne, on Friday.

I don't want you to begin the start by doing something you'd rather not, but I sincerely thought it a pity for you to miss Luxembourg.

Yours affly
    Edith[1]

Ms:VT

1. Note added at the end by Berenson for Mary Berenson's benefit: "Aug. 6. To him who hath understanding this is an inimitable document. What it means is that in 3 wks W. [i.e., Berry] will have finished his cure. Should he however get tired of it before, then she would chuck me to join him.

"And you see how kind, & unselfish & frank she is!!"

To Mary Berenson

Hotel Zum Kurfürsten
Fulda
Aug 14 [1913]

Dearest Mary,

You have no doubt heard from B. B. that he has found himself with a partial invalid on his hands, instead of the active practical person who was to organize an extended tour & spare him all its fatigue & annoyances.

I don't know in what terms he has written of me, but I can only say that, in the circumstances, he has behaved extremely well. I warned him in advance that I was afraid I shouldn't be of much use unless I had a week's holiday in a greenwood, but I think he fancied I was just uncertain & coy, & a little gentle firmness would soon cure me of that idea. It wasn't till I collapsed at Cologne, & reached a point of morbid self-abnegation which impelled me to urge him to go off without me, & take the motor, that he realized I wasn't shamming. He knew that in normal health I wouldn't offer to lend my best friend my motor if there was the least hope of my being able to use it for even an hour a day; & alarmed by this significant symptom he stayed, & privately obtained the address of the best alienists in Cologne.

I hasten to add that 48 hours of rest, & a promise to take me for a week to a place where there were a great many trees & no pictures, did much to advance my convalescence; & the day before yesterday he managed to get me as far as Nauheim (with *such* a charming hour at Wetzlar by the way!). Yesterday we started for Oberhof (where I am credibly assured there is not a single picture), but, after battening at the Frankfort Gallery for an hour or two he got rather unmanageable again, & insisted on conducting the remainder of the trip on principles of his own, which involved reconstructing the solar system with an audacity undreamed by Galileo, & assuring me that we "must be all right because we were going due East" while we were actually plunging into a particularly showy sunset.

The result was that, after grazing Würzburg, & one or two other places as remote from our destination, we wound up at Fulda, a few Kms from Frankfort, after a day that would have sufficed to take us across the Andes— Unluckily Fulda is so charming that he now pretends it's the best thing that could have happened; but I don't think yesterday's lesson will be wholly forgotten.

Anyhow, he is really proving an excellent pupil, a trifle headstrong at times, but lively, intelligent & anxious to learn; & I think you will find when he joins you again that his motor training has made strides. He has already learned (by bitter experience) to give his address when he sends an "answer-paid" telegram for rooms to a crowded hotel; he has found out that to pull up a motor window with a jerk & leave it dangling does *not* constitute shutting it; that keeping one's eyes on the map without looking at the points of the compass, or asking the indigenous where one is, is not an infallible way of reaching one's destination; & that raw fresh herring garnished with onion is *not* a dish he *cares* to eat at 8.30 p.m. though he insisted on my ordering it last night.

In addition to this negative progress, he has learned several useful things that appear to have been omitted from his earlier education, such as going through galleries with a quick firm step instead of gaping & dawdling; letting Nicette sit on his lap when she feels like it; getting out of the motor to ask the way of an intelligent-looking person on the corner, instead of calling out to the village idiot or a deaf octogenarian from one's seat; & abstaining from shallow generalizations such as: "You'll find it's always safe in Germany to follow the telegraph poles," or: "On mountain roads there are never any cross-roads one need bother about," with geological remarks about his companion's "not understanding the conformation of the country."

Such, dear Mary, have been the results of our first eight days of travel; & my pupil's aptitude & eagerness to learn give me every hope of continued progress. I take pleasure in adding that he is good tempered, punctual & polite, & always brushes his hair for dinner, & puts on his muffler when it grows chilly. He takes an intelligent interest in all he sees, reads the guide-book attentively, & is very careful about his money—my attempt to give him 5 pfennigs yesterday instead of ½ a mark having at once called forth a protest.

I will soon send you another report of our trip, & can only hope that yours is proving as agreeable & instructive.

Yours ever affly
    Edith

Ms:VT

To Mary Berenson

Hotel Bellevue
Dresden
August 24 [1913]

Dearest Mary,

We have had three such good days here that, in spite of the pictures & the music Berlin is holding out to us, I am sorry to be just jumping into the motor! Then the sun came out & warmed our backbones for the first time; & it has been so delicious looking out from my windows at the Elbe, over the really Villa d'Estean garden of this romantically situated hotel, where only man & food are vile. Even the glories of the Esplanade won't approach that view!

B. B. has been very busy with the pictures, & seems not to have felt the stupefying effect of our sudden descent from Oberhof. The change of air—or from air to no air—has reduced my brain to pulp, but he has borne with me beautifully, even when I thought Claude & Poussin[1] were all one painter (because their pictures were all in the same room!), & asked him if Parsifal were part of the Ring. You may judge from these samples of my conversation what my mental condition is—but luckily I don't feel tired anymore, except overhead—& that doesn't matter when one is motoring.—Then in the afternoons we have been out to the Bastei, as he has no doubt written you; such a glorious magically combined bit of landscape—do you remember it? And such good tea & honey on the terrace! You will be interested to hear that, the other day out there, when a friendly German stopped to speak to Nicette, & said to B. B. "I suppose your little dog *always* goes about with you?" he answered with genuine pride: "Aber *natürlich*!"—I tell him his biographers will trace throughout northern Germany a legend of his dog-devotion which will cause weeks of controversy in the Times!

Do send me a line to the Esplanade & tell me Mr. Scott's present address in England, & when he will be back there with Mr. Pinsent[2] in Sept.—I'm thinking seriously about going back to buy my Epping house,[3] & if I do go I want to arrange to meet them both there, as Mr Scott suggested.

I'm so sorry our golden journey[4] to Berlin is nearly over, & wish I could continue on; but it would make rather a far flight back to Paris if

I went to Vienna.—I wish also that Brides were on my return route, &
I could come & tell you all about it.

Buon bagno, & much love
    Edith

An aigretteful American lady & sposo stopped yesterday before Rem-
brandt with Saskia on his knee.
She: That's Rembrandt's portrait of himself with his wife.
He: (not a man to be fooled.) Ugh! How on earth could he paint
himself?
She: Well, he *did*—
    (They walk away.)

Ms:VT

1. The French painters Claude Lorrain (1600–1682) and Nicolas Poussin
(1594–1665). From EW's earlier references to Poussin, in letters and in *Italian
Villas*, it is clear that the alleged confusion is a comic invention.
    2. Cecil Pinsent, friend and associate of Geoffrey Scott.
    3. On a recent trip to England, EW had looked at a property called Coop-
ersale, near Mary Hunter's Hill Hall, in the neighborhood of Epping Forest.
For several reasons—including the change in her situation following her
divorce—she thought of buying Coopersale and making her home in England.
Negotiations went forward for some time, but were eventually abandoned.
    4. Berenson drew ironic squiggly lines around this phrase.

To John Hugh Smith

Hotel Römerbad
Badenweiler
September 4 [1913]

Dear John,
    I must send you a line from this remote & trippery little place to
wish you good luck on your long trip. I wish I had seen you again

before you start[ed], & I shall count on having you with me in November.

Yes, the Dresden hotel has suffered just the change you guessed—the food is bad, the service non-existent, & the people cheeky & don't-care; but in spite of all, the situation is so enchanting, the garden so lovely, Dresden itself such a splendid river-city, that I remember now only the delights.—After Dresden I went to Berlin for ten days, & never ceased to marvel at the cleanliness, order, & general perfection. It is the model modern Town! And, oh, the pictures there! How I wish we could have looked at them together. Berenson, interesting as he is in a gallery, is much too purely technical, & reminds me often of the hero of a story I have never written, who killed himself because, as the result of too continuous chemical research, he could see people & things only as aggregated atoms.—I have never looked at pictures with any one who "reacted" so in unison with me as you do, & some time we must have a few days in those two galleries.

I am stopping in this hole for 48 hours to give my old maid¹ a chance to go & see her family, near by; then I go back to Le Touquet (but *not* to the Hermitage!) to see Mrs. Lodge for a few days.

You would give me a scolding if you knew at what a low ebb I am just now—no heart for anything, &, what's considerably worse (since there's no demand for *that* organ) no head for books! I can't read—& I've never got as low as that before. Don't scold, though: wait till you're my age first. Not that I mind the number of my years: not a bit! Only, on the road to them, one goes through some things—at least I have—that turn everything bitter.

When shall I send you my book—*our* book? It will be out about the end of Oct.

Goodbye, my dear. Have all the good days you can, & send me word of them now & then.

    Your affte friend,
        Edith W.

I don't know if I even told you how I enjoyed seeing your splendid mother!

I didn't write you about the Palma Vecchio because it is being cleaned, or something.

So glad you are going to read George Eliot. Skip Silas Marner &
Adam Bede.

Ms:BL

1. Catharine Gross, originally from Alsace, had been EW's maid, housekeeper, and companion for thirty years, and was now in her early sixties. EW
depended upon her absolutely, and had grown fonder of "Gross" or "Grossie"
(as she called her) than almost any one else in her life.

To W. Morton Fullerton

53 Rue de Varenne
September 10 [1913]

Cher Ami,

The 10th of Sept—more than a month since you sailed!—& not a
line or a sign from you! I have post-carded, written & cabled you (congratulations on the Ribbon), to the care of Mr. Lambert, all to no purpose; & the situation is becoming so like our earlier one in our mutual
history that I should be quite romantically rejuvenated by it—if there
were any Eau de Jouvence strong enough to do the trick for me any
more!

Meanwhile I'm sincerely concerned to know how things are going
with you, & distressed lest you should have been met by bad news at
home or some other contretemps.

Today, moreover, I have a letter from Henry (well, & extremely en
train), who says this: "A fortnight ago I was struck by my nephew
Harry's saying, when I had spoken by chance of Morton, his intelligence, experience, &c; 'they would give anything for him at the State
Dept. He's exactly the kind they are looking for & can't get.' And Harry
doesn't talk in the air, & is of the most excellent judgement & observation."

I copy this for you, because it's possible the said Harry (he's Treas.
of the Rockefeller Institute, an important post) *might* be of use—& I
have at once sent your address to Henry, who will no doubt write to
"Harry."—(The latter, of course, is the odious Only Begetter of the

birthday fiasco—but I'll forgive him even that if he can do you a good turn.)

I "saw Germany" with Berenson for three or four weeks, very interestingly & agreeably, though I was too tired & out of tune to get the full benefit of the opportunity. It left me, however, with an increased sense of his genuinely affectionate "niceness" & of his amazingly comprehensive brain. It's the most remarkable (merely critical, as opposed to inventive) mind that I know.—I motored back alone from Berlin, & am going next week to spend a few days with lonely Bessy Lodge at Le Touquet.—After that I shall probably come back here, faute de mieux, though I dread the returning throngs who pass through in Oct.—I shall probably go to England toward the end of October.—

Do let me hear soon—

Bien à vous
    E. W

I am lunching today with M. & Mme. Zoé de Bauville.

Ms:UT

To Bernard Berenson

53 Rue de Varenne
January 30, 1914

Dearest B.B.,

Your calligraphy is always a welcome sight, & never more so than today, for I appreciate—none better!—the magnitude of the effort involved in writing even two lines to a friend from the New-Ritz vortex.

My own communings with the absent were reduced, there,¹ to "half-rates" or "long distances," & I had the appalling sense that this was not due to the shortness of my stay, but was in the inmost nature of things, & just as likely to go on for six months as for a mad fortnight!

Yes, it's very nice to be petted & feasted—but I don't see how you can stand more than two or three weeks of that queer rootless life. I felt my individuality shrivelling a little every day, till I had somehow the sense of being a mere "jeton" in a game, that hurried & purposeless hands were feverishly moving from one little square to another—a kind of nightmare chess without rules or issue.

Well! It was a great show, though my impressions were, of course, of a much more restricted kind than yours. The result of them is that, under all the new ardours & the new attitudes, I found everybody just the same as before, about a millimeter below the service [surface]; with the one difference (not a gain, I think) of a newly developed self-consciousness about "New York" which wove itself in & out of every topic. Boston always has been self-conscious about Boston, but the one distinction of ugly, patchy, scrappy New York was that it didn't get off from itself & measure & generalize: it had that in common with Paris & London. But now it hasn't any longer.

Meanwhile here I am back in the shade of my village clocher, with the same slumbrous routine going on again—The Abbé[2] & the Bourgets & the others coming in to dine occasionally, & between these gentle flurries long book-evenings, or a concert with Bélogou. Et voilà.

It was dear of you to write, & since the miracle has happened once, may it renew itself! And do come back soon.

Your affte   E. W.

Charlie is at last definitely better—recovering rapidly—& has gone to Cannes, with the hope of Florence later.

All my "bande" are *fêting* the little Ctesse Kayserling, who seems a sweet ingenuous little philosopheress, with charming Chinese eyes.

Ms:VT

1. New York City. In December, EW had returned to America to attend the wedding of her niece Beatrix Jones (forty-two years old, and with an international reputation as a landscape gardener) and Max Farrand (forty-four, professor of history at Yale and a leading scholar in constitutional history). EW had been "petted and feasted" in particular by her sister-in-law Minnie Jones, the mother of the bride, and by her old friends Eunice and Walter Maynard.

2. Abbé Arthur Mugnier, about sixty, was vicar of the Church of Ste. Clotilde in the seventh arrondissement, and perhaps the best-loved man in Paris. He was both witty and saintly, and an accomplished converter to Catholicism. EW had known him since 1908.

To Corinne Roosevelt Robinson[1]

53 Rue de Varenne
March 2 [1914]

Dear Mrs. Robinson,

Your precious manuscript is neither lost nor unread, though by this
time both possibilities may have occurred to you—so long have I left
you without a word!

The fact is, my wonderful New York fortnight reduced me to absolute
inarticulateness—of tongue & pen. I could do nothing after I got back
but vegetate & think how delightful it had all been. And moreover I
had acquired a proficiency in telephoning & telegraphing which seemed
to have done away with my ability to express myself in any less lapidary
style.

I read the poems, however, with the stillest & sunniest of oceans as
a setting, & I find them full of feeling & warmth, & of *you*. Their great
sincerity & directness are as striking as in the earlier volume, but it
seems to me you have not quite avoided a certain monotony of rhythm
in the longer ones, & especially that in blank verse. You know I think
criticisms of technique are the only useful ones—the other kind one
must draw out of one's self, one's experience, one's comparisons, one's
"inward ear." But technique can be cultivated, & chiefly, I think, by
reading only the best & rarest things, until one instinctively rejects the
easy, accommodating form, where the sentiment helps the verse to dissemble its deficiencies. The cultivation of the rhythmical sense is all the
more important because there develops with it, undoubtedly, an acuter
sense for the right word, right in sound, significance, colour—& also
in expressiveness. The whole thing—all the complex process—is really
one, & once one begins to wait attentively on the mysteries of sound
in verse, the need of the more expressive word, the more imaginative
image, develops also, & one asks more of one's self, one seeks to extract
more from each sensation & emotion, & to distil that "more" into fewer
& intenser syllables.

Please forgive my slipping into a treatise—but all these things "me
passionnent" so much (& more & more) that I can't help it!

I wish you hadn't been so continuously away from N.Y. while I was
there, & that we could have had more than that one short & interrupted

talk. Is there no chance of your coming abroad this summer? I am going off for the spring to Algeria & then Italy, but I hope to be back in June.

Thanks again for trusting the poems to me, & believe me ever

Affly yrs
    Edith Wharton

Ms:HL

1. Corinne Roosevelt Robinson (born 1861) was the younger sister of Theodore Roosevelt. In 1882, she had married Douglas Robinson, the heir to a real estate fortune; they made their home in New Jersey. The manuscript EW was commenting on would appear shortly, via Scribners, as *One Woman to Another and Other Poems*. EW had also offered detailed technical suggestions on Mrs. Robinson's earlier volume, in 1912, *The Call of Brotherhood and Other Poems*.

To W. Morton Fullerton

Royal Hotel
Algerie¹
April 9 [1914]

After hesitating whether we should start at dawn today for a gazelle hunt in the mountains of Alabaster we decided, instead, to go to the Red Village of the Oasis of El Kantara! Such are the opportunities that strew our path in this magic land.—What most amazes me is that beyond the *so* narrow thread of civilization along the coast, Europe has made no mark. Even in the outskirts of the desert, as well as on the lower slopes of Kabylia, things are much as they must have been 5000 years ago. We have been passing through all the stage properties of the romantics, with the growing conviction that Fromentin, Decamps e tutti quanti understated, & erred on the side of the prosaic.

From Algiers we made a two days' trip to the oasis of Ben Saada, due south. There we saw a sort of epitome of it all—the caravans of camels, the nomads, the wonderful white figures in the silent sun-baked streets, the brilliant violet-&-rose-&-orange women washing in the "oued," the Ouled-Naïls dancing ventriloquently on a white roof-terrace in the moonlight, their hands fluttering like tied birds—& all the rest of it. Then we tried to cross La Grande Kabylie, but there was snow on the passes & we had to turn back to Bougie. From there we motored yesterday across a kind of pre-desert, a high plateau, solemn & bare & caravan-seamed, to the red gorge of El Kantara, the gates of the Sahara. We slept there in an inn in the very neck of the ravine, between the scarlet cliffs & the yellow torrent, with a white moon hanging between the twin peaks, & the Mountains of Alabaster, flushed with sunset, to the south.—Then we came here, across them, this morning, into the real authentic desert heat. Everything quivers with it, & closed shutters & a tiled bath room seem better than love & glory—if one were offered that alternative!

I was anxious to go south, another two days, to Touggourt, but it can't be done en auto, & I'm afraid of the long trip across the desert, so we reluctantly turn north-east to Timgad & Constantine. I hope we may get to Tebessa before going on to Tunis.

Poor Lapsley reached Algiers grippé & miserable, & after struggling on as far as Bougie, decided to turn back to Europe. I'm very sorry, but relieved, on the whole, as it was an evident effort to him to keep on.

The letter from Meredith pleased Anna very much, & she asks me to thank you. I equally enjoyed the article in the Catholic World, & Percy Lubbock is enchanted to learn that Hall Caine & I do not think deeply. After being bracketed in Henry's article with Galsworthy & Hichens (wasn't it?) I feel that my niche in the Hall of Fame is in the most fashionable of its many mansions.[2]

I don't see how I can ever go back to Europe & look at ugly monkeys in comic clothes after such perpetual manifestations of human beauty as surround one here. *How* I understand Lady Hester Stanhope![3] As the lady said:—Why wasn't I told?—

Is this the kind of letter you like to get from me? It would do very well in a memoir, wouldn't it?

Only I don't know how to sign it—

Ms:UT

1. On March 29, EW had sailed from Marseilles to Algiers on the S.S. *Timgad*. She was accompanied by Percy Lubbock (temporarily her houseguest),

Anna Bahlmann, Charles Cook (in charge of the Mercedes, also on board), and a new young personal maid, Elise Duvlenck, who was quickly proving herself indispensable. Lapsley began with the party, but as EW explains, he fell prey to dysentery and went back to Europe.

2. Hall Caine (1853–1931), a prolific and popular novelist, would be knighted for his achievements. EW had met John Galsworthy (1867–1933) in London in December 1908, when the English novelist was being hailed as the author of *The Man of Property*, the first volume in the Forsyte series. Robert Hichens (1864–1950) was the author of the widely selling *The Garden of Allah* in 1904.

3. Lady Hester Stanhope (1776–1839), a niece of the younger Pitt, cut short a brilliant social career in England to establish herself in a remote corner of Lebanon. She became a legendary figure, much admired and visited by European literary figures.

To Bernard Berenson

> Majestic Hotel
> Tunis
> April 16 [1914]

Dearest B. B.,

How can I conceal the fact that I'm glad Paris wasn't quite Paris without the rue de V.?—I'm thinking already how completely Florence will be Settignano to me again next month, since you & Mary are willing!

Of course I'm coming—only asking you, as usual, a few days latitude as to date, & perfect frankness if the one I finally fix on doesn't fit with your plans. My idea is to reach you about May 8th or 9th, & I will let you know various addresses on the way, so that you can check or divert my approach if necessary.—I expect to be at the H. Excelsior, Palermo, on the 23d of this month, & at the ditto, Naples, on the 26th.

I'm not sure I told you that poor Lapsley had a kind of grippe which obliged him to turn back at Bougie. Since then Percy Lubbock & Anna & I have had some wonderful days. Tomorrow we are going to Kairouan, Sfax & Gabès (as far south as it is prudent at this season, for, alas, we are too late for the utmost oases), & then we come back here & cross to Sicily.—We have made the trip a month too late for the oases, & a month too early for Kabylia! It's a bore that the extreme differences in climate make it almost impossible to combine the mountains & the desert.

The latter attracts me much more, but Kabylia is interesting on account of the beautiful & extraordinarily picturesque Berbers.—As for this place, it's a cauldron of "louxoure" (as d'Annunzio says), & one can't take two steps in the native quarter, the amazing, unbelievable bazaars, without feeling one's self in an unexpurgated page of the Arabian Nights! You *must* see & do it all with me soon.

At Algiers the beauty & nobility of the native types makes the whole scene poetic—here, with equal picturesqueness & variety, it's all effeminacy, obesity, obscenity or black savageness. But, oh, the dresses, the types, the ways of walking, sprawling, squatting—& the sun-sprinkled depths of the vaulted bazaars, & the white walls, the blue shadows, the tiled colonnades, the sudden fig-trees, the blacks carrying baskets of rose buds on their heads, & the little solemn pale children in the booths, holding skeins of silk or scraps of leather, & the slippery fig-coloured babies in bangles & rags insinuating themselves into every crack of the crowd!—Well, it's made me so lyrical that I'd almost forgotten to tell you of a horrid adventure I had at Timgad the other day—or rather, the other midnight.—We spent the night in the very lonely inn beside the ruins, so that we might bask in them by moonlight, & I remarked to Percy Lubbock, as we looked out over the wild African campagna: "This is the way my grandparents saw the Forum, in the days when it was dangerous to sleep at Radicofani on account of the brigands."

I went to bed without much noticing where my maid & the others "lay," except that it was down another passage—& in the middle of the night was waked by a noise in my room, put out my hand for the matches (no electric light), & touched a man who was bending over me!—Don't let *anybody* talk to me about being frightened who hasn't known that sensation. I was half-conscious of a very brief struggle in the blackness, & of his being rather small, & I think *not* an Arab—but my shrieks must have frightened him, for I got the door unlocked (it was next to the bed, luckily), & went bellowing out into the deeper blackness of the passage. He must have slipped out after me (he had been hidden under my bed), for when, after a perfectly *awful* interval, people with candles & without trousers began to appear down the dark distances, there was no one in my room—but a suspicious desire on the part of the hotel people to parley, & exclaim that it couldn't have been, & do *everything* but search the house.—The whole atmosphere of the place was indescribably sinister, & I wasn't surprised to hear, at Constantine & again here, that there had been two or three robberies there in the last year, & that "on commençait à en parler."—It was a really horrid moment—but I lost nothing but my voice, which was reduced for several days to a faint squeak!—I would rather have given him my cheque book than gone through that minute when I touched him . . . Brrr!—

I'm surprised you didn't see the Bourgets, for they seemed surprised they hadn't seen you! I'm sure from what Minnie B. wrote me that they didn't get your cards.—

I'm sorry you thought Charlie looking less well. I feel very anxious about him.—His case seems so mysterious.

I have fairly good news of Walter. He has done a tremendous trip through Southern India, & casually says he has "lost pounds". I can't transmit your message, for he is on the way home, & was uncertain as to his route, owing to the immense difficulty of getting a cabin at Bombay.

With much love to Mary, & joyful thoughts of reunion with you both,

Yrs affly
    E. W

I haven't got Coopersale¹ yet, but still hope to get that or something else in England.—

Ms:VT

1. See letter to Mary Berenson, August 24, 1913.

To Gaillard Lapsley

Majestic Hotel
Tunis
April 23 [1914]

Dear Gaillard,

You will have heard from Percy, & will understand why I've so far only sent you a beggarly post-card or two. After my Timgad adventure I was in the unreasonable but not unnatural state of not being able to write to any one without telling the whole story, & yet of dreading to tell it!

Now it has all receded into some remote geological past, crowded out by a series of such beautiful impressions & such delightful hours that we multiply our lamentations at your having missed them.

Carthage, especially, wrung us with the sense of your privation—it is so beautiful, so august & so shadowy. But it's all delicious, & Percy & I have now reached the point of wondering why we *even* go back to Europe to get the Encyclopaedia Britannica before plunging forever into the desert! We are grinning over the fact that the boat we were to have taken yesterday went wrong, thus giving us another week here, & to-morrow we are plunging off again into the desert. Luckily the weather is still cool, & we are cheerfully facing an afternoon's motor run & a night in the train to see two more oasis-Towns!

Percy has probably also told you that I have acquired for you in the bazaars here a precious phial of essence of sandalwood & sycamore, which, diluted with the purest alcohol, is said to—mais ne précisons pas! Vous m'en donnerez des nouvelles—or your victims will. We spent a morning bargaining with a perfumer for jasmine, attar of roses & sandalwood essence, & came away so empoverished that I daren't go back into that "Scrikh"! But that was nothing to our buying a so-called ambergris necklace from a "coloured" prostitute in the bazaars at Sfax!! It appears that to be seen with one of these fragrant baubles in one's hands is to lose one's reputation forever.—When we came back I told Anna of my purchase, & said: "These chaplets are said to make the negresses irresistible to the Arabs."

A. Oh—is it a kind of charm?

Me. No—it's simply that they smell so awfully good.

A. (puzzled, but still seeking.) Oh—I thought it was like something that has been blessed by the Pope. (Percy's hilarity has to be choked off.)

The hermit of Carlyle Mansions hasn't vouchsafed us a sign, in spite of a shower of provocative post-cards, so I'm in hopes we shall find a letter from you at Naples reporting your lunch with him. If he were here his comments would be beyond price!

Percy grows more & more, & his quality keeps pace with his quantity! I never had a more delightful travelling companion, & we *so* like the same things, for the same reasons, & with the same intensity, that every sight & sound seems to reach us through the same golden mist of satisfaction.

Well—I do begrudge your not being enveloped in that luminous haze, & wish I could at least send you a scrap of it in this letter.—I hope you got thoroughly rested at Bordighera & are taking up Cambridge life with unabated energy.

Yours affly
E. W.

It would be delightful to find a line from you at the Hotel Excelsior, Naples, before May 7th.

Ms:BL

To Bernard Berenson

Hotel Excelsior
Naples
May 1 [1914]

Dearest B. B.,

With a tired hand & a tireder hotel pen I must send you a rapid word of thanks for your Palermitan letter which was sent back here to wait for me, & greeted me on my arrival at dawn this morning.—We crossed from Tunis on a craft called the Città di Siracusa, which must have been launched before the victorious Greek galleys ploughed the waves on that classic coast. I had the "lusso," & I wish you could have seen it!

After our spicy days in the desert & the oasis, where everything is fragrant & balmy, it was a sudden plunge back into the good old European grime. With much difficulty we managed to charter two crippled sea-chairs (veterans of the first Trans-Atlantics, probably) for which we paid two lire, & managed to balance ourselves on them with considerable acrobatic skill, & thanks to a perfectly calm sea. Last night, when we went on board again after a few hours off at Palermo, a jabbering rabble was in possession of all the benches, & our chairs were nowhere to be found! After vain appeals to stewards & subordinates, Percy Lubbock demanded them *of the Captain* (who was just then steering us through a channel beset with dangers), & the latter, without any apparent surprise, gave orders that they should be produced—whereupon the cover of one of the boats was unbuttoned, & the chairs were brought out!!! Isn't it just like the hunting of the Snark? The stewards strolled up & down the promenade deck arm in arm, smoking cigarettes & throwing them among the passengers' feet—& the stokers quarrelled so fearfully in the engine room (or whatever the ship's bowels are called) that after vainly imploring to have them silenced we shut down *all* the sky lights on them—after which they began to attend to business, & brought us here in good time!—

I'm so dépayseé & lost in this grimacing European crowd that the only statue I cared for this afternoon in the museum was a newly unpacked one which hadn't yet been unveiled! Seriously, you can't think how depressing it is instinctively to *look away* from people in the streets, instead of gloating on them as we've been doing for this last month. No one knows—yet—what North Africa is, & you *must* come & find out before the Teuton hordes do. They are here in their might now, Ach-gotting over everything, & in the museum I heard a beefy bridegroom point out a Silenus to his Gretchen with the instructive note: "Der Erzieher des Bacchus."[1]

How do your plans & Mary's fit in with my going to you about the 12th? Don't hesitate to say if any earlier or later date suits better.— Well—baci deliranti, as they say in the agony column of the Mattino— & à très bientôt.

Yrs affly
  E. W

Don't I know the chaotic feeling of the first days at home! I hope you've recovered. Walter didn't sail till April 18th, & I fancy he will have to go straight to Paris to meet his sister, as he has been so delayed.—

Ms:VT

1. "The Tutor of Bacchus."

To W. Morton Fullerton

Palace Hotel
Orvieto
May 11 [1914]

Your letter overtakes me here, & I am sorry indeed that this dreadful strain should come on your poor mother just as she was recovering from her accident. It is a terrible situation for her, & she seems to me the only person to be considered. It is always she who has had to pay, isn't it?

Why has your brother not provided a nurse long ago? The description of your mother's nights is horrible. I thought your sister-in-law was now much better off, & that they were prepared to do something to make your parents' life a little easier. Forgive me if I add that I can't think with any sort of patience that the money you ought to be giving them is going to a woman who got it from you only because you were afraid she would blackmail you. I know you think there were other reasons—there were, no doubt, reasons for giving her some compensation, but none whatever for binding yourself for life to pension her, when you had no settled means of support.[1] If I say this it is because I wonder if some clever lawyer like Harper could not get you out of that bondage even now, by proving that you have no fixed income, & can't count on earning enough for your own support. Every penny you can spare belongs to your mother after your father's death, & you ought to make some sort of fight, now you are not afraid of a scandal at the Times, to free yourself from being bled any longer.

As for going to America, it seems to me terrible that your mother should be left alone after your brother leaves. I understand yr difficulty, & I should think the best thing would be to wait until it is fairly certain that your father can't live more than a few weeks, & *then* sail at once, in order to be with her through the worst days—which will be the ones before his death. Afterward, you will have to be there in any case.—

No, my Timgad adventure didn't reduce me to silence, but simply the sense that I haven't anything to say, or rather that nothing I say reaches you.—It *was* a bore, though, for I had been sleeping very badly for the last two or three months, & was just beginning to feel a little better when the hateful thing happened, & of course murdered sleep for a long time to come. It was the inability to get a light, even the gleam of a match, that was so horrible—& it seemed to last *so* long! I should be very glad to die, but it's no fun struggling with you don't know what in the dark—

I am hearing lately on all sides of Teddy's breakdown,[2] but no one has given me any details, & till your letter came I supposed he was in America. It is dreadful to me not to be able to do anything for him—but I suppose Dr. Dupré is right in saying that these cycles will continue indefinitely without increasing in violence, for everything else he predicted five years ago has come true. Therefore probably this phase will pass like the others, & when it does his family will say he has had neuralgia, as they did before. Nothing will enlighten them, because they don't want to be enlightened—but they may get very weary of trying to look after him.

The ed. of the Yale Review wrote & asked me if I wd give them an article on Moreau de St. Méry, & I suggested that you might. I can't tell you his name, for his letter came just after my Timgad shock, & I somehow lost it, & had to ask Max Farrand to transmit my answer.—

I'm going tomorrow to the Berensons', & shall probably be there for some time. Their address is

I Tatti, Settignano, Florence.

Let me hear there what news you receive, & what you decide on doing.

E. W.

I enclose yr letters in another envelope—no, after all, I find they will fit in this.

Ms:UT

1. Since leaving the Paris office of the London *Times,* Fullerton had no regular income, but seems to have felt still obligated to his former mistress Henrietta Mirecourt.

2. Teddy Wharton was reported to be in Paris with his sister, and very ill. He had recovered sufficiently to return to America before EW herself reached Paris.

To Bernard Berenson
Grand Hotel Norte y Londres
Burgos[1]
July 26 [1914]

Dearest B. B.,

The other day Walter insisted on going to the Cinema at Bilbao, & I was so glad he did, for the stupendo dramma di 3 mila metri was called: "Comment on visite une ville au galop." But he only smiled as the panting travellers spun by, & said, when it was over: "Well, we ought to start by 9 sharp tomorrow."

This anecdote explains why I have sent you only a breathless postcard or two. The giro has been wonderful & beautiful, & Spain in July is the most delicious place imaginable; but how tell it in Spanish, or any other language, when one tumbles out of the motor at 7 p.m to leap into it again at 9? However, all the glorious hours of air & scenery have been so soothing & exhilarating that I can't complain of fatigue, but only of not having time to chew each day's nourishment. Decidedly, I'm a ruminant!

Well, after Montserrat, which is by far the most romantically & improbably beautiful thing I know, we motored over the Col de Tosas back to the French Pyrenees, where we lost two or three days trying to see peaks & passes in the rain. Then we turned south, motored down the beautiful coast road from Bayonne to Santander, & from there went to Santillana (a delicious little sort of Spanish Sabbioneta)—& from Santillana walked about a mile across grassy heights & hay-fields to the Altamira cave!!! Yes, we've really seen the big earth-shaking beasts, roaring & butting & galloping over the low-rock-roof—& as we walked there, through the long grass, in the sunshine, Walter kept saying: "I can't believe it—I can't believe it!" & when we came out it seemed more incredible still! There they are, as visible & vivid as in the picture-books, with the dampness "suinting" through the rock in big drops—& why the deuce hasn't it carried the colours with it??? Anyhow, Walter, in standing up (one has to ramp most of the way) bumped his white linen hat against the bison's side (the famous snorting one), & behold, when we came out into the sun, there were red marks, prehistoric stigmata, all over the said hat! Alors—???

But we've *seen them*; which is more, I fancy, than most of the people who have written about them can say.

We had a beautiful run over the mountains from the sea to Burgos, & another, yesterday, wonderfully different, but as fine, to Pampluna, where we now are. The old Navarre towns on their red rocks are splendid—& one, Estella, has two or three half-ruined early Gothic churches one above the other on a hill, as at Toscanella.

Today, alas, we get back to France, & at the end of the week to Paris, where I have a faint hope of catching you on your way I don't know where.

I shall be at the Crillon on the 31st for a night only, probably—then to England. What would be far better would be that I should find you still there, & ready to come to Stocks with me!

Do send me a line to the Crillon, won't you?

The international news in this morning's paper here is pretty black. I wonder? Goodbye or, I hope, aurevoir somewhere.

Yours affly
E. W.

Ms:VT

1. EW and Walter Berry had come to Spain on July 10, and had spent a fortnight wandering across the country.

PART FIVE

The Writer in Wartime
1914–1918

Introduction

❀

EDITH WHARTON lost little time in finding herself a useful wartime occupation. Within a fortnight of the outbreak of hostilities, she opened an *ouvroir*, a workroom, for Parisian seamstresses who had been deprived of work when the fashionable ladies in the Faubourg took to sewing garments for the troops. The *ouvroir* eventually gave employment to as many as one hundred women at a time, with Mme. Wharton procuring work orders through her connections in France and America.

Like most of her friends, Edith Wharton was sure that the war would be over, with a French triumph, in a matter of months, and saw no reason to cancel her plan of renting the Humphry Wards' summer home, Stocks, in Buckinghamshire for a season. Near the end of August, she managed to get herself and staff across the Channel; and it was while she was in residence at Stocks that the Battle of the Marne took place, the military event that put an end to any expectation of a swift and crushing victory by either side. Edith struggled back to Paris in late September. The frightful British casualties in and around the town of Ypres in Flanders was a further portent that the horror would be long-drawn-out. "*My* sense," Edith wrote Lapsley in November, "is completely of living again in the year 1000, with the last trump imminent."

She now began what would grow into an enormous effort to provide care for the civilian refugees who were pouring into the city from the ravaged battle areas. The American Hostels for Refugees, opened in November 1914 with $500 and a few bits of furniture, were soon operating in half a dozen houses and apartments in Paris, with a big lunchroom, a grocery-distribution point, a clothing depot, a free clinic, a coal-delivery service, a day nursery, classrooms, and an employment agency: these in addition to the lodgings that took in 9,300 refugees in the first year. The hostels were supported by donations, some of them large, collected by a network of interlocking committees in Paris, New York, Philadelphia, and Boston.

The *sine qua non* for the running of the hostels was Elisina Tyler, a young woman of authentic beauty who had been born in Florence as Elisina Palamadessi di Castelvecchio and was a descendant of Louis Napoleon. Edith and Elisina had "clicked" (in Edith's word) from the moment they met in 1912. Elisina's talents—they included great stamina, an enjoyment and mastery of committee work, fluidity in three languages, and an ability to subdue her own potent and even aggressive personality to Edith Wharton's sufficiently for the tasks in hand—were exactly what the situation called for. Elisina had been married since 1910 (after separating from her first husband, the noted English publisher Grant Richards) to Royall Tyler, an art historian specializing in Spanish studies. He was in a direct line from the Royall Tyler who was the first significant American playwright; and in Berenson's praise of him, "perfectly genuine and very lovable, a real scholar and a man of taste."

With the hostels and the *ouvroir* going along healthily, Edith Wharton, during the first six months of 1915, made a series of motor tours of the front lines, to observe conditions, to deliver medical supplies, and to inquire into needs. The first two visits to the Verdun area, east of Paris, in February, were described by Edith to Henry James in letters that the Master not inaccurately called "inexpressibly splendid bounties." A tour of Belgium in early summer and the spectacle of untold numbers of Flemish children picked up in the cellars of wrecked homes and in burned-out villages led (at the request of the Belgian government) to yet another "war charity": the Children of Flanders Rescue Committee. Before 1915 was out, six homes were being run for this committee in Paris and the outskirts and as far away as the Normandy coast. Seven hundred fifty children and 150 elderly persons and nuns had been taken in— "my prettiest and showiest and altogether most appealing charity," Edith called it in a brochure.

For this organization, Edith Wharton was chairman, with Elisina and Royall Tyler vice-president and secretary-treasurer. "I can't tell thee how many committees [Edith] is chairman of," Mary Berenson wrote her husband, "and where she is chairman she does all." For the fourth and last of her war charities, Edith found time only to serve as vice-president (the president was Mrs. Edward Tuck, the wife of a wealthy American philanthropist resident in Paris). This was a cure program for the *tuberculeux de guerre*: French soldiers who had contracted tuberculosis in the evil conditions of the forward trenches.

Mary Berenson, warming visibly to Edith Wharton, said of her what other friends and onlookers were saying: that she spoke less of her "good works" than anyone similarly occupied on the Paris scene, and indeed turned them off laughingly. After Mme. Wharton was made a Chevalier of the Legion of Honor by the President of France in April 1916, the *Figaro* concluded its article on the award by remarking that "this energy, this apostle's faith, are hidden beneath an air . . . of deceptive nonchalance, of smiling grace." The only work of fiction to come (belatedly) out of her wartime activities, "The Refugees," makes gentle mockery of the whole rescue enterprise by having an American professor mistaken for a French refugee, on his arrival in England, and swept off for lavish treatment to a baronial country home.

Edith Wharton's fiction-writing career came to a standstill during the first two years of the war. Her considerable journalistic skills were exercised in a number of articles, mostly in *Scribner's*, about her visits to the front; they were published by Scribner later in 1915 as *Fighting France, from Dunkerque to Belfort*. When *Xingu and Other Stories* came out in October 1916, Edith explained to Lapsley that all the stories in it except "Coming Home" (itself a trifle) were written before the war. But in the same letter, she confided that she was at last back at work, and that a short novel of hers was about to appear in *McClure's Magazine*.

The new work was *Summer*, a companion piece to *Ethan Frome*—its author referred to it as "the hot Ethan"—and set in the same rural Berkshires region as its predecessor. *McClure's* paid $7,000 for the serial, which ran in the periodical from February through August 1917: Edith Wharton's first taste of the large sums of money that could be made from popular American magazines. The novella itself, one of the most compelling of all her fictional writings, signaled Edith Wharton's committed return to her métier. *The Marne*, a mildly engaging novel, followed in 1918, and *The Age of Innocence* two years after that.

It was a time for old friends to draw together, as Edith told Lapsley; and it was a time of desolating loss. Mme. Wharton's social and literary friend Robert d'Humières was killed in action, as was her former footman Henri; she heard daily, as it seemed, of the loss of the husbands, brothers, sons of her French women friends. Death struck in other ways. Anna Bahlmann died of cancer; and in New York, Edith's friend and mentor from her early adulthood, Egerton Winthrop, died of age and accompanying illness. Worst of all was the stroke suffered by Henry James in December 1915 and his death three months later. James's friendship, Edith wrote, "was the pride and honour of my life"; and about James and Winthrop, she said to Sara Norton that "between them, they made up the sum of the best I have known in human nature."

Edith Wharton's spirits sank to their lowest in the icy winter of 1917, as the war entered its fourth calendar year. But they rose quickly when America declared war on Germany in April 1 of that year; and when the first American regiment arrived in Paris in time for a Fourth of July parade, the outlook seemed to her to have brightened enough for a change of pace and environment. In September, with Walter Berry, she crossed to North Africa and made a tour, by military car, of Morocco, as the guest of the Resident General of the French protectorate, her friend General Hubert Lyautey. Her inspection of the annual fair at Rabat, her witnessing of ritual dances, her visits to the Casbah and the Sultan's harem—all profoundly and illuminatingly different experiences than she was accustomed to in Europe—were eloquently narrated in her volume of 1920, *In Morocco*.

The spectacular parade on Independence Day in 1918 filled Edith Wharton's heart with patriotic joy, and she exulted to Minnie Jones about "our wonderful incredible troops ... marching with long rhythmical musical stride that filled the French with admiration and wonder." Victory was intoxicatingly in the air. Looking beyond the war's end to a life of tranquillity and literary dedication, Edith set about purchasing a villa, Jean-Marie, at a discreet distance from Paris.

To Bernard Berenson

53 Rue de Varenne
August 11 [1914]

Dearest B. B.,

Your card to Stocks has just come. Walter & I didn't get back from Spain till the night of July 29, & I was tranquilly preparing to cross on the 1st when I was blocked here.¹ I didn't write you because I had no letters from England, & mine were apparently not received.

After a day or two at the Crillon I moved to the apartment with my maid & Gross, & we got a bonne à tout faire. My sister-in-law Minnie Jones was also caught here, so I have taken her in. It is all thrillingly interesting, but very sad to see one's friends going to the slaughter.

There is so much to say that I won't begin now—but, oh, *think* of this time last year! Hasn't it shaken all the foundations of reality for you?

English letters are just beginning to come, & we are being told by kind friends that we can *easily* cross, as boats are running daily! Of course they are—trains on this side are the difficulty. In a few days it will be possible to go in relative comfort, & with a little luggage. I am staying on in the hope that in another week I may prevail on the authorities to let me take my motor, a vital necessity at Stocks—

All well, & every one cheerful & calm. Walter had some money, & is acting as banker for all the stranded beauties²—including your affte

E. W

If you are in London, do be really kind & go to see, at 9 Half Moon St., poor heart-broken Bessy Lodge, en pouvoir des beaux-parents.

Ms:VT

1. EW had rented Stocks, the country home of the Humphry Wards, for the summer. On August 1, a "general mobilization" was declared in France, and civilian travel was at once severely limited.

2. Berry was now president of the American Chamber of Commerce in Paris.

To Bernard Berenson

53 Rue de Varenne
August 22 [1914]

Dearest B. B.,

So glad to get your letter by the belliqueux Henri,¹ who arrived breathing fire the day before yesterday, & is carrying in the coal for us till his country calls him.

The Red Cross is "chock-full," & I doubt if they will take him, but I'm going to "faire des démarches."

It is impossible, here, to arrive at the detachment necessary to admire the scenery—though Paris never looked so appealingly humanly beautiful as now—poor Andromeda!—with the monster careering up to her.

I have plunged into work. Finding that no one had thought of coming to the help of the unemployed work-girls, I have opened a work-room where I feed them & pay them 1fc a day. My compatriots (mostly unknown to me) have come to my aid, & we have 20 women working already, & I long to enlarge it & take in many more. The silly idiot women who have turned their drawing-rooms into hospitals (at great expense), & are now making shirts for the wounded, are robbing the poor stranded ouvrières of their only means of living, & the Red Cross is beginning to be severely criticized by the Syndicat du Travail for its immense work-rooms where femmes du monde do the work the others ought to have—so my "ouvroir" has excited a good deal of interest, & I hope we may get help to carry it on. So far we have about 2,800 fcs, which enables us to keep 30 women for about 2 months, perhaps more—*

I'm coming over next week, next Thursday probably, & shall count on you *much* and *long* at Stocks.—Did Sybil ever get to America, & if not, what is her address?—

Much love to Mary—

Yours affly
  E.W.

Walter is busier & busier with stranded beauties & having the time of his life!

* Excuse all this—I can't see or think of anything but the looming horror, & its cruel effects here already.

Ms:VT

1. EW's former footman, who had transferred to the Berensons at I Tatti.

To Sara Norton

Stocks, Tring
September 2 [1914]

Dear Sally,

I hardly know with what feelings I sit down & write to you in this still & lonely place where I had dreamed of being so happy with my friends, & of seeing you among them!

I am all alone here, & without the heart to ask any one to join me. I feel as if this immense burden of horror could best be borne alone for the present.—I left Paris only six days ago, having stayed on there a month to organize & raise funds for a paying work-room for the poor unemployed women in our quarter. It was the first one to be opened in Paris (except some "soupes populaires"), & the consequence was that people were very generous, & after I had collected enough money to carry it on for three or four months, & seen orders pouring in from all sides, I decided to leave it in the very capable hands of the young woman who founded it with me, & come over here for a few weeks' rest. My servants & luggage were all here, & I had been picnicking in the rue de V. with a bonne à tout faire & a maid; & I thought it seemed foolish not to enjoy Stocks for a while. I left, therefore, on the 27th, & the very next day came the dreadful news of the German advance & the probable siege of Paris,[1] & I felt like a deserter! It was a perfect thunderbolt. I was seeing every day people in touch with the different ministries, & everyone thought the war would be fought out in Belgium & on the northern border. You can understand how I feel—as if my co-workers must think I had planned my flight when I said I was going off for three or four weeks.

My first idea was to try to go back at once, but I hear that General Joffre may order all "bouches inutiles" out of Paris, & as foreigners would certainly come under that head I am waiting for the next developments. Today is intolerable—the anniversary of Sedan, & the Germans within 68 miles of Paris!—

The "atrocities" one hears of *are true*. I know of many, alas, too well authenticated. Spread it abroad as much as you can. It should be known that it is to America's interest to help stem this hideous flood of savagery by opinion if it may not be by action. No civilized race can remain neutral in feeling now.

All this time I am not asking about you—but you know I want to hear, & that I hope that your homecoming was peaceful, & that you have been able to help your poor sister-in-law.

How are you? Has Ashfield done you good? Send me all your news here, for this address is safest.

Yours affly
E. W.

I stopped at Rye to see H.J., & found him momentarily unwell—a digestive "crise"—but looking far better than when I last saw him nearly a year ago. The gain is immense.

Ms:BL

1. By the end of August, a million German soldiers had passed through Belgium into France. The armies of General von Kluck were pushing to within an hour's drive of Paris; on September 2, the day this letter was written, the French government left the city to set itself up in Bordeaux.

To Bernard Berenson

Stocks, Tring
[c. September 3, 1914]

Dearest B. B.,

I've simply been too sad to write! But one mustn't confess such things even to one's self, & in the dark.

Well—I got over all right, as I believe I wrote you from Rye. Walter went back to Paris in the motor, & shipped his sister off in it to Dieppe, & I have just heard of her arrival.—Walter means to stay in Paris, & I quite understand his staying as long as he possibly can. He will probably get Herrick[1] to keep him as part of the Embassy staff.

I am simply sick & heart-broken at having left my work-room there at a time when I might have been of real use. I thought I could go back easily in two or three weeks—so little did one dream, in Paris, eight days ago, of what has happened since!

Alas, alas, it's too late now. I've tried, through the French Embassy, to get sent back, but, though they will give me every possible paper, they can't guarantee my getting there, & it would be fifty times worse to be caught in some small French town where I should be utterly useless than to stay here, where I may be of some help— Mrs. Ward has just got to London, & I have written to ask if she objects to my turning part of this house into a convalescent home, as they were asking yesterday for 8000 more beds for convalescents—

Meanwhile, why won't you & Mary come "right away?"—Why not tomorrow?—No one here but Percy Lubbock. *Do* come!—Where is Geoffrey Scott? I want so much to see him—

Yours affly
  Edith

Ms:VT

1. Myron T. Herrick, the American Ambassador to France.

To Bernard Berenson

Stocks, Tring
Monday
[Early September 1914]

Dearest B. B.,

I'm sorry you & Mary couldn't come yesterday, for it is divinely lovely here—& I'm leaving it! Not, alas, to go back to Paris, however, as I long to, but only to London, where I shall inhabit the Wards' *other* house instead of this. They came up from Scotland the other day, & proposed what I had been rather longing to suggest to them—namely that I should take their house at 25 Grosvenor Place, & let them come here. I accepted at once, for this loneliness in which I sit inactive seems to make things worse—if the worst can be made worse! In town I shall be a little nearer Paris & news, & shall see people, which helps, now that I can't read or scribble.—Could we perhaps meet & lunch or tea in town on Wed.? I am going to move that day, & I thought of spending the night with H. Sturgis at Windsor, to give the servants a chance to settle down in Grosvenor Place.

Let me know if we can make a combinazione. Cook & the motor got through from Havre night before last. Walter is in Paris & means to stay. I had from him yesterday a short line, evidently a postscript to a letter I've lost—Cook says Paris is perfectly calm, & *the Russians are in France.* An Indian contingent has also arrived. Kitchener was in Havre for a day while he, Cook, was waiting for his boat, & presumably went to the front.

Yours affly
E. W.

One wonders what that poor wisp of a Henri is doing! I could do nothing for him at the Red X.

Ms:VT

To Sara Norton

53 Rue de Varenne
September 27 [1914]

Dear Sally,

Just as I was leaving England I heard of the death of your uncle Mr. William Darwin[1]—What a sad year it has been for you, apart from the great general tragedy in which we are all involved!—I am glad you were with him all the spring—that must be pleasant to look back to now.

I am back in Paris much sooner than I had expected, as the philanthropic lady in whose settlement I had established my work-room, fled before the German approach & put her 50 compatriots into the streets! The situation was complicated by the fact that her manageress (& confidential friend) carried off *all* the funds (nearly $2000!), & that we got them back only through the intervention of the Red Cross, under whom I am working—

It was a nasty & a very mysterious experience, & if I had not asked one or two friends here to keep an eye on the work in my absence[,] I should have known nothing, as they never notified me they were leaving.—As it was, I was immediately told by telegraph, & came back as soon as I could.

Meanwhile the Petit St Thomas had very handsomely put at our disposal an apt. in their new building, & we now have 50 women working there, & shall take more soon.—

I am very busy, of course, as I now manage the place myself—nominally, at least, for the real work of cutting-out, organizing & supervising the work is done by a charming young girl, the niece of the musical critic Jean Landormy, who was working at the Foyer "par dévouement," & who, indignant at what happened there, at once took charge of the new work-room for me.

Of course I have to relieve her for a few hours every day, & to shop, scrape up more contributions, &c. And all this keeps me busy & interested, so that I feel the oppression of the war much less than I did in England.

The general impression is now that the awful business will go on all winter, so every one is beginning to "confection" knitted things, & I think of starting a knitting-room later. We make supplies for the various hospitals, giving a certain percentage to the Croix Rouge, & we also take orders from private hospitals & various other charities—we even dress-make on a modest scale, as we have several skilled lingères & couturières!

I regret very much not having been in Paris during the week of panic.² It must have been a strange sight— Most people expected that the Germans wd. be here within 48 hours— Now there is a general sense of reassurance, though, as Victor Bérard said to me yesterday, "C'est encore l'angoisse"—& *will* be, till the beast is dug out of his present lair.—Still, Paris is taking heart, people are coming back in thousands, there is more light in the streets, & I suppose soon a few more shops will open.

Have you read "The Anglo-German Problem" by Prof. Sarolea? It is so far ahead of any other book I have seen on the subject that it ought to be known everywhere. He is head of the dept. of French at Edinburgh University—

The excitement here now is seeing the German prisoners pass through.

The people behave admirably—there is not a sound from them as the beasts go by. Every one has been out on the battlefields, & a friend brought me back an éclat d'obus yesterday. But helmets are almost unattainable—they say the Germans sell them at a high price as soon as they are taken prisoners!

The American Ambulance is doing good work, & lots of Americans are working in other private hospitals.—As to the horrors & outrages, I'm afraid they are too often true.—Lady Gladstone, head of the Belgian refugee committee in London, told a friend of mine she had seen a Belgian woman with her ears cut off. And of course the deliberate slaughter of "hostages" in defenceless towns is proved over & over again.

Well—it seems strange to be sending such tales to peaceful Ashfield. I can see the lovely blue September distances, the golden trees, the autumn glitter on the meadows— I can smell it & touch it!—

I'm glad your father went without seeing what we are seeing now. Let me hear soon how things are with you.

Your affte E W.

Ms:BL

1. Sara Norton's aunt, Sarah Sedgwick (the sister of Charles Eliot Norton's first wife, Susan), had married William Darwin, a son of Charles Darwin, and one of the most engaging members of the clan.

2. The Battle of the Marne, the first crucial turning point in the war, was waged between September 6 and 12 (while EW was at Stocks). General Joffre was the French commander in chief; but it was the military governor of Paris, General Gallieni, who seized the popular imagination by sending six thousand troops in six hundred Parisian taxicabs racing to the front. The German armies finally fell back to a static position on the Aisne River, and the possibility of a swift defeat of the Allies in France was over.

To Bernard Berenson

53 Rue de Varenne
September 30 [1914]

Dearest B. B.,

I'm so glad to get your letter—but you must forgive if I send in return a scrawl traced by a hand shaking with fatigue, & guided by a brain wobbling with imbecility—

I'm not used to philanthropy, & since I got back & took over my work-room from Walter's heroic shoulders I've been at it every day from 8 a.m. till dinner. As soon as peace is declared I shall renounce good works forever!

My journey over was 22 hours long, but perfectly comfortable, & Paris is extremely interesting, not because there's more news than in London—there's ever so much less!—but because most of the fluffy fuzzy people have gone, & the ones left are working hard & seeing each other quietly.—Last night Fullerton, Victor Bérard & W. dined here, & we laughed till 11.30. Bérard was wonderful—of endless good stories he told, the best was this, said to him lately by a Montenegrin volunteer:

"Vous savez, entre nous, les Serbes, c'est peu de chose—mais nous, *avec les Russes*, nous sommes deux cents millions!"[1]

I'm so glad to hear of Miss Costelloe's engagement.[2] Please give her all my "vous," & many many messages. I loved your description of the pre-Bayeux fiancé!—I met Desmond MacCarthy[3] a few years ago, & share your sentiments—& oh, how well he writes! I remember some things in the extinct New Quarterly that thrilled me with quiet satisfaction. Fullerton has started his lecture-plan, & expects to sail in 3 weeks—St André is still grinding bravely at the Croix Rouge. He says meeting the wounded at the stations is the worst.

No—I'm too tired. I can't go on—except to send you tender thoughts, & to beg for another letter.

Sarolea is A1!

Yours affly
E. W.

Ms:VT

1. "You know, just between ourselves, the Serbs don't amount to much—but *with the Russians* we are two hundred million!"

2. Karin Costelloe had just become engaged to Adrian Stephen, the brother of Virginia Woolf.

3. Desmond MacCarthy, drama critic and then literary editor of the *New Statesman*; he was a fine literary essayist. EW had admired an article by MacCarthy in praise of John Donne some years before.

To Gaillard Lapsley

53 Rue de Varenne
November 8 [1914]

Dearest Gaillard,

I literally don't know whether I've written you yet in ink, or only with such a feeble trickle of grey matter as leaks away, at odd moments, from my immediate & prosaic shop-keeping concerns.

I know I've sent you many letters of this latter kind, spun out into the air like cobwebs flung across distances, but though I hope they *do* produce a dim vague sense of communion, they don't (to my taste, anyhow) replace a good paper-&-pen interview. So here goes, with all my excuses for the long silence, which I'm sure Percy's & Henry's explanations will have made you understand.

I *did* yearn, here alone over my knitting, when I heard of that orgy at Qua'cre! Lord, how good it must have been. Don't you think the martial truculent Henry is by far the best we've seen yet? The "Lieutenant Colonel to the Earl of Mar"[1] was nothing to him! I hope to beguile him over here later, for Paris is well worth seeing; & he *would* see it. It's all so quiet, & yet one has so completely the impression of having one's ear at the receiver. You must come to me for part of your vacation.

Your Cambridge impressions must be very curious & interesting. I hope you're well enough to get their full value. *My* sense is completely of living again in the year 1000, with the last trump imminent. And at times I don't feel à la hauteur! There are so many people who seem nowadays like left-overs—dead flies shaken down out of a summer hotel window curtain! We shall never lodge in *that* summer hotel again.

I must stop now, with a fond embrace, & an appeal for a quick answer.

Your affte
E. W.

You should see Charlie Du Bos, working from 8 a.m. to 8 p.m. over a Refugee Hostel, & doing it admirably!
*She*² works all day at my shop, equally admirably.

Ms:BL

1. A literary reference, apparently, to one of the Scottish Earls of Mar, perhaps the sixth Earl (1675–1732), who made himself head of the followers of James Edward, the Old Pretender to the English throne, and whose forces were defeated by a rival chieftain in November 1715.
2. EW's forty-horsepower Mercedes, baptized Hortense.

To Mary Berenson

53 Rue de Varenne
December 20 [1914]

Dearest Mary,
Even if I had not made you that more-than-paper promise about the Berlin chronicle, I should have written long ago, if only to applaud & give thanks for *B.*B.'s magnificent portrait en pied of *P.B.*—a work which ought certainly to find its place in some national French portrait gallery of the future! And again I ought to have told you how I rejoiced in the incredible fairy tale of your getting back your bag & all that in it was. Be sure I have been palpitating over all your péripéties since you left me to my loneliness, & if I haven't told you so it is still for the same weary reason—because I'm too busy all day & too tired at night. One of the things which proves me to be not made for philanthropy (indeed Percy L. says he can forgive me only because I so visibly hate what I am doing)—one of the proofs of my inadequacy is that in the evening, instead of being able to sit down for a pen-prattle with my friends, I am mentally embrouillée, & can only drowze over La France Contem-

poraine or such-like. By the way, I've been reading lately a *very* good book for beginners (which is what I always am when it's a question of history), "Europe since 1815," by one Hazen, who, of all things, is a prof. of history at Smith College, Northampton! It's so clear & architectural, & well mapped & bibliographed, that I have really got a picture of things out of it.

And now for Walter—who ought long ago to have written you his own story. Well, he saw everything, went everywhere, says he had a very interesting time—& so far has totally failed to do for me what Mr. Hazen has: give me a picture. I can't *see* anything he has seen. And so I've been far less interested than I expected. Somehow, his imagination seems much less sensitive than it used to be, & what I call (in novel-writing) "the illuminating incident" doesn't seem to have caught his attention. Solid facts in plenty, of course: la noce à tout casser at Berlin, living (as he lived) no more expensive than usual, streets & shops jammed, &c. What struck him most was the mass of fresh unused soldiers in every town he went to, & the streams & streams of military trains carrying them *westward* at the very moment when Russia was announcing that German army corps were being transferred to the Eastern front. He was depressed, also, by the undoubted fact that the whole of Germany believes, as one man, the war to have been forced upon it by English ambitions. He thinks it a universally popular war, & is convinced that, whatever happens to the Hohenzollerns, the Germans will defend every inch of their territory—He visited several prisoners' camps, & found them fairly decent—about like ordinary barracks.—His account of Belgium was harrowing. He brought back all that remains of the library of Louvain—a tiny iron dragon which some children picked up in the ruins. They have no doubt there that all the books are safe in Berlin! The town was burnt systematically, *after* looting.

He also brought one of the tiny silvery lozenges which they threw into the burning houses to make them blow up—& as he always has it in his pocket, & has had a very bad cough ever since he returned, I never see him slip a tablet into his mouth without expecting him to go through the ceiling.

Since Bordeaux returned, Paris has assumed its normal look to a certain extent, & now seems more like a dowdy capital than some great dedicated city. You saw it at its best. I made 10,000 fcs at my little ouvroir sale, to everybody's amazement, & thanks to that, & to various subscriptions, the refugees are being cared for in increasing numbers, & we are giving a Xmas party of 800 at our rue Taitbout house!—My beloved Charlie, haggard, valiant & indefatigable, still gives all his time to the work, & we now have a big vestiaire in Pardi's ex-shop, where your friend Mrs. Scott grimly receives parcels & Mrs. Frank Laurance & others more amiably & tactfully distribute them to the poor things in weary waiting rows.

Did I tell you, by the way, that I had a delightful letter some time ago from Mr. Cannon, sending me $100 for the ouvroir, & asking me to let him know if I wanted more? Je n'y manquerai pas!—

What you tell me about the Italian situation is deeply interesting, & I'm glad the sacro egoismo is not their only motive power.

I send you both my fondest love, & shall try to get off & see you later. I love yr refugee story.

> Your affte
>   Edith

My best love to the Ingegnere.[1]

Ms:VT

1. A playful reference to Geoffrey Scott.

To Mary Berenson

> Ouvroir de Mme Wharton
> Au Petit St Thomas
> 25 Rue de l'Université
> January 12 [1915]

Dearest Mary,

I have left your letter unanswered much longer than I meant to, but Sybil will tell you how one thing treads on another's heels in these rushing days.—The Hostels are getting along well, but they take a lot of nursing, & reams of letter writing; & then, about a month ago, Satan

(who finds *much* more mischief for busy than idle hands—stupid Watts!)
put in my way the offer of Vincent d'Indy, Capet & one or two other
musicians to come & give a little series of concerts at my apartment, à
titre gracieux, for the poor musicians who are starving. It sounded too
good to miss, & the one bright prospect of the winter; & I vaguely
thought one had only to "throw open one's doors," as aristocratic hostesses do in fiction. Oh my! I'd rather write a three volume novel than
do it again! They were a *great* success, & we made a lot of money (I
gave two); but for ten days I was never at peace a quarter of a second,
& even now that Mildred Bliss[1] has taken over the next two I have to
be calling on the artists, having the programmes printed, reconciling
jealous performers, & picking up lots of loose threads. However, it's
the only chance of hearing any really good music this winter, & we *are*
hearing it. There are to be four more, & then I shall found a rest-home
for myself—but *where?*—Evidently not in Italy, judging from the latest
advices!

I was so glad to hear from your letter that there was a chance of
seeing Mr. Thorold[2] here. I should have been, also, so glad to ask him
to stay; but Anna arrived from America just before Xmas, & as I have
Percy also, & he has started in, at my suggestion, on some Red Cross
research work in the hospitals here, & will stay for some time, I shan't
have a room to offer Mr. Thorold. I'm too sorry, for it wd have been a
great pleasure; but I shall write a line & ask him to stop over & lunch
& dine if he can.

Last Sunday I motored down to Chartres again, & the cathedral, in
a glow of winter sun, seemed more magically beautiful & appealing
than ever. To go from there to Isch-Wall's[3] hospital, & look at the rows
of young white stricken faces, with the vision of the horror in their fixed
eyes, shattered me for the rest of the day. I don't know anything ghast-
lier & more idiotic than "doing" hospitals en touriste, like museums!

I do hope Sybil wasn't quite Kaput when she arrived. But as she
walked through the whole length & breadth of the American ambulance,
& survived to tell the tale, I take the rosiest view of her health. By the
way, here's a story for the egregio ingegnere. Mrs. Cutting[4] sent me out
some wool by an American trained nurse who had been despatched to
Paris by a philanthropic millionaire to nurse the wounded. Mrs. Cutting

thought she had not found a job, & asked me to see about it; so I wrote her, & rec'd the following reply.

"Glad you got the wool alright. Don't know what Mrs. Cutting means, as am at Am. Amb." If she amputates limbs as ruthlessly as language, what a treasure for the Am. Amb.!

Last night I dined at the Ritz with Adele Essex & Mrs. Astor. There were four other tables occupied, & after dinner we all had to sit on the same sofa to keep warm, & a ghost of a waiter in a long apron shuffled up & down the endless empty vista of the hall, obviously revisiting the scene of his earthly activities. I never saw anything so spectral. Of course we gave him an obole.

Please embrace B. B. & tell him I've a long letter for him up my sleeve.

Your affte
Edith.

Fond things to the Egregio.
I got such a sad letter from Mme Hubert the other day.

Ms:VT

1. The former Mildred Barnes (born 1879), the daughter of Demas Barnes, U.S. Congressman from Ohio, was married in 1908 to Robert Woods Bliss, who had been Secretary of the American Embassy in Paris after serving in St. Petersburg and elsewhere. Mrs. Bliss, who had gone to a private school in Paris and knew the city very well, was at this time working with a committee for the housing of French children from the war zone. Later, she would be associated with the American Red Cross. Her wartime activities brought her innumerable honors.

2. Algar Thorold, an English Catholic writer and biographer, and occasional visitor at Villa I Tatti.

3. Dr. Isch Wall was a nerve specialist by training, one of the most skillful practitioners in France. He had advised EW about her husband's condition, and also had given medical advice to Fullerton.

4. Mrs. Olivia Cutting, widow of the railroad tycoon Bayard Cutting, Sr., and mother of the younger Bayard.

To Henry James

Grand Hôtel du Coq Hardi
Verdun
February 28, 1915

Dearest Cher Maître,

After nearly six months at the same job I felt a yearning to get away for a few days, & also a great desire to find out what was really wanted in some of the hospitals near the front, from which such lamentable tales have reached us.

It took a good deal of démarching & counter marching to get a laissez-passer, for it has always been a great deal more difficult to go East than North, & especially so, these last weeks, on account of the "spies & espions" (as White calls them), & also of the movements of troops, more recently. However, thanks to Paul & to Mr. Cambon[1] (the Berlin one) I did, a day or two ago, get a splendid permesso, & immediately loaded up the motor with clothes & medicaments & dashed off from Paris with Walter yesterday morning. We went first to Châlons s/ Marne, & it was extraordinary, not more than 4 hours from Paris, to find ourselves to all appearance completely in the war-zone. It is the big base of the Eastern army, & the streets swarm with soldiers & with military motors & ambulances. We went to see a hospital with 900 cases of typhoid, where *everything* was lacking—a depressing beginning, for even if I had emptied my motor-load into their laps it would have been a goutte d'eau in a desert. But I promised to report, & try to come back with more supplies next week.

This morning we left Châlons & headed for Verdun. At Ste Menehould we had to get permission to go farther, as the Grand Quartier Général can't give it unless the local staff consents. First they said it was impossible—but the Captain had read one of my books, so he told the Colonel it was all right, & the Colonel said: "Very well—mais filez vite, for there is big fighting going on nearby, & this afternoon the wounded are to be evacuated from the front, & we want no motors on the road."

About 15 kms farther we came to Clermont-en-Argonne, of which you have read—one of the most utterly ravaged places in this region. It looks exactly like Pompeii—I felt as if I must be going to lunch at the Hotel Diomède!

Instead we ate filet & fried potatoes in the kitchen of the Hospice where Soeur Rosnet, the wonderful sister who stuck to her wounded when the Germans came, gave us a welcome proportioned to the things she needed for the new batch of wounded that she is expecting tonight.—Suddenly we heard the cannon roaring close by, & a woman rushed in to say that we could see the fighting from the back of a house across the street. We tore over, & there, from a garden we looked across the valley to a height about 5 miles away, where white puffs & scarlet flashes kept springing up all over the dark hillside. It was the hill above Vauquois, where there has been desperate fighting for two days. The Germans were firing from the top at the French trenches below (hidden from us by an intervening rise of the ground); & the French were assaulting, & *their* puffs & flashes were half way up the hill. And so we saw the reason why there are to be so many wounded at Clermont tonight!

We went to Verdun after lunch, stopping at Blercourt to see a touching little ambulance where the sick & the nervously shattered are sent till they can be moved. Most of them are in the village church, four rows of beds down the nave, & when we went in the curé was just ringing the bell for vespers. Then he went & put on his vestments, & reappeared at the lighted altar with his acolyte, & incense began to float over the pale heads on the pillows, & the villagers came into the church, &, standing between the beds, sang a strange wailing thing that repeats at the end of every verse:

"*Sauvez, sauvez la France,*
   Ne l'abandonnez pas!"—*It was poignant.*

To complete our sensations—I forgot to put the incident in its right place—we saw a column of soldiers marching along the road this morning, coming toward us, between a handful of cavalry. Walter said: "Look at their coats! They're covered with mud." And when they came nearer, we saw the coats were pale grey, & they were a hundred or so German prisoners, fresh picked from that dark wood where we were to see the red flashes later in the day.

We got here about 4, & presented ourselves at the Citadel, where the officer who took our papers had read me too—wasn't it funny?—& turned out to be Henri de Jouvenel, the husband of Colette Willy!!![2] —He was very nice, but much amazed at my having succeeded in getting here. He said: "Vous êtes la première femme qui soit venue à Verdun"—& at the Hospital they told me the same thing. The town is dead—nearly all the civil population evacuated, & the garrison, I suppose, in the trenches. The cannon booms continuously about 10 miles away.—Tomorrow we go to Bar le Duc & then back to Châlons & home. I shall come again in a few days with lots of things, now that I know what is needed.

This reads like one of Mme. Waddington's letters to Henrietta,[3] but I'm so awed by all I've seen that I can only prattle.

I shall have to take this to Paris to post—it takes 8 days for letters to go from here.

I thought my sensations de guerre might interest you even in this artless shape.

Your devoted Edith

9 p.m. & the cannon still booming.

Ms:BL

1. Jules Cambon (1845–1935) was the French Ambassador to Berlin from 1907 to the outbreak of the war; he was currently Secretary General in the Ministry of Foreign Affairs. His brother Paul Cambon, no less gifted, was Ambassador to London. The "Paul" here mentioned is Paul Bourget.

2. Sidonie-Gabrielle Colette (1873–1954), one of the outstanding French writers of her time, began by collaborating with her first husband, Henri Gauthier-Villars, in the series of "Claudine" novels, which were signed by his pen name "Willy." From 1904 to 1916, Colette wrote under the name Colette Willy; thereafter, she signed herself Colette. Her second husband, Henri de Jouvenel, was a journalist.

3. *Italian Letters of a Diplomat's Wife* (1905), by Mary King Waddington; letters over two periods—1880 and 1904—to the author's mother, Mrs. Charles King, and to her sister Henrietta.

To Henry James

53 Rue de Varenne
March 11 [1915]

Cherest Maître,

Your letter of the 5th, which I found here on my return last night, demands such moving incidents that the chronicle I have to send this time is not à la hauteur. The second trip was like all sequels—except that it certainly wasn't a mistake! But it *was* less high in colour than the first adventure, & resulted in several disappointments, as well as in some interesting moments—indeed, once within the military zone *every* moment is interesting.

We left 5 days ago & went straight to Verdun in a bitter rain, dropping bundles of shirts & boxes of fresh eggs & bags of oranges at the various ambulances I told you of. At Verdun we looked up our médecin en chef, who had promised to take us to see an ambulance on the first line, in the Hauts de Meuse; but, alas, it has been moved nearer to Les Eparges where there was such hard fighting that we couldn't be allowed to go. However, thanks to a lucky laissez passer, we *did* get, with him & the Director of the Service de Santé of that region, to an ambulance on the Meuse, within about 7 Kms of Les Eparges—a hamlet plunged to the eaves in mud, where beds had been rigged up in two or three little houses, a primitive operating-room installed, &c. Picture this all under a white winter sky, driving great flurries of snow across the mud-&-cinder-coloured landscape, with the steel-cold Meuse winding between beaten poplars—Cook standing with Her in a knot of mud-coated military motors & artillery horses, soldiers coming & going, cavalrymen riding up with messages, poor bandaged creatures in rag-bag clothes leaning in doorways, & always, over & above us, the boom, boom, boom of the guns on the grey heights to the east. It was Winter War to the fullest, just in that little insignificant corner of the immense affair!—And those big summing-up impressions meet one at every turn. I shall never forget the 15 mile run from Verdun to that particular ambulance, across a snow-covered rolling country sweeping up to the white sky, with no one in sight but now & then a cavalry patrol with a blown cloak struggling along against the wind.—

Then we went to another village on the west bank of the Meuse, where there is a colony of *1500* "éclopés" waiting to pick up strength enough to be shipped on to the next dépôt d'éclopés in the rear. Here also the church—a big dreary disaffected one—is full to the doors, but it is not a hospital but a human stable. The poor devils sleep on straw, in queer little compartments made of plaited straw screens, in each of which compartments a dozen or so are crammed, in their trench clothes (no undressing possible)—with nothing that I could see to be thankful for but the fact that they were out of the mud, & in a sort of fetid stable-heat. It was *awful*—& the Directeur du Service de Santé was so complacent!

In other places, of course, we saw things better done—but for a Horror-of-War picture, that one won't soon be superseded. At least I hope not!

I had everywhere le meilleur accueil from the Drs & Service de Santé, & came back with a long list of wants. We had hoped to get back to Nancy & Gerbéviller, but at Ligny en Barrois we came across a sulky commandant who kept us waiting 4 hours & then refused the permit—so we had to turn back to Châlons! We got there at about 7 p. m., on the coldest day imaginable, "only to learn" that *every* hotel, even to the lowest of the "garnis," was absolutely full. We applied for a permit to go on to Epernay (20 Kms), but were politely éconduits, as motors can't circulate in the war zone après la tombée de la nuit. We went back to the hotel where we were known, & the land-lady told us she had two rooms, requisitioned by the Grand Quartier Général, which had not been called for that night, & which we might get. In the restaurant, where we went to dine before making our appeal to the Quartier Gén-éral, we met our friend Jean Louis Vaudoyer,[1] who is attached to the Q. G.—He gave us little hope, but said we could go & try! So after dinner we got into the motor again & went through the pitch black icy streets to the Hôtel de Ville, where I sent in my papers & my appeal. A polite officer came out & was désolé—but it was against the rules! I tried to harrow him, but in vain. Finally he suggested giving us a permit to go back to Paris—a 7 hours' run on a dark night, with the strong probability of being turned back at the first railway crossing, as experience had convinced us that hardly any of the sentinels can read!!—We went back to the motor, & Vaudoyer very kindly suggested that we might camp for the night in a little flat he has in a maison bourgeoise, which he uses only in the day time—*if* we found the landlady still up, or could wake her! He couldn't go with us, as he was on duty, & it was past the hour (9.30) when one is allowed to be in the streets. And as we stood in the pitch blackness of the deserted street, & he whispered: "C'est au no. 9, rue de l'Arquebuse—si l'on vous arrête, le mot est 'Jéna,'" I suddenly refused to believe that *any* of it was true, or happening to *me*, or that a nice boy who dines with me & sends me chocolates for Nouvel An, was whispering a *pass-word* to me, & adding: "Quand vous le dites au chauffeur, prenez garde qu'une sentinelle ne vous entende pas"— It was no use trying to keep up the pretense of reality any longer!

Luckily his rooms *were* real, & the landlady was awake, & made fires—but Cook slept in the motor, wrapped in Red Cross dressing-gowns & pillowed on gauze pads!—And so we got through the night —& yesterday morning, when we left for Paris, we understood why Châlons was so crowded, for the cannon was crashing uninterruptedly, & seemingly much nearer than usual, & troops were streaming through the town in the direction of Suippes in a long unbroken train—the biggest lot of them we had yet seen.

We lunched at Meaux, & went to see the Bishop, who took us over his hospital, & a splendid dépôt d'éclopés he has organized with library, games, douches, & all kinds of blessings—& here I am again & must go back to work instead of telling you more adventures. I hope to get off again in 10 days—but one can't be sure of permits nowadays.

> Your devoted
> Edith

No, no, you must keep the £6 for English needs—bless you!

Ms:BL

1. Jean-Louis Vaudoyer (1883–1963), a gifted young French writer; a friend of Marcel Proust, and a frequent visitor at the Rue de Varenne.

To Elisina Tyler[1]

53 Rue de Varenne
[April 1915]

Dear Good Fairy,

I really can't wait till tomorrow afternoon to tell you how I thank you & bless you & admire you for all you've done!

And now do stay quiet & nurse that poor foot.

Yrs gratefully
E Wharton

Thursday evg

Ms:WRT

1. See introduction to this section.

To Henry James

Grand Hôtel
Nancy
May 14, 1915

Dearest cher Maître,

I don't dare write you except when I'm scaling heights or exploring trenches, & as I'm yearning for news of you I've asked—& obtained —a permit for the front in Lorraine & the Vosges.—Walter & I started out three days ago, going first to Châlons, & then through the ravaged & wiped-out towns of Sermaize-les-Bains, Poquy, & several others, to Commercy, where the cannon was thundering but life seemed fairly normal. Then we came on here the day before yesterday, armed with a letter for General Humbert, in command of the army of Lorraine. As luck would have it, I found out just as I was leaving Paris that a great friend of mine, Raymond Recouly,[1] is one of his aides-de-camp, so we were received with the greatest kindness, & have almost been allowed to play in the Boche trenches. Yesterday we went to see the incredibly destroyed Gerbéviller, where we spent a very interesting hour with Mr.

Liégeay, who acted as mayor during the German invasion, & who took us over the lamentable ruins of what must have been his once charming old house, with a terraced garden overhanging the valley, & told us the tale of his three days in the cellar, with wife & other womenkind, their house blazing above their heads, & the Germans shooting & torturing people all through the town. The details are fantastic—but I must hurry on to our trip today. We lunched at the Quartier Général with Genl Humbert & his staff, & then started in an army motor with Recouly to make the tour of the Grande Couronne de Nancy, ending up at Mousson & Pont à Mousson, within about a mile of the German trenches, which were in full view. Very few people have been allowed to go to Pont à Mousson, as it is bombarded almost daily, & only last Friday a number of people were killed there. Luckily today they didn't happen to be firing, so we got there. We went to the Military Hospital, which lies on the Moselle, directly under the Bois le Prêtre, where there has been very violent fighting these last few days, & from which the Germans were driven (to the next ridge) only the night before last.

We could see from the garden of the Hospital (which is all ploughed up with shells) the deadly slope they have left, & all the other ridges from which they still rake the town. But far more interesting is Mousson, a ruined castle & hamlet on a sharp cone (like an Italian hill town) high above the river. We could only motor up about a third of the way, for beyond that the motor wd have been seen, & the slope is swept by German batteries. From there we walked to the top, & Recouly would not even let us stop to look at the view lest we shd be repérés. Once on top we were safe in the lee of the castle, & creeping around it we climbed through a series of wattled trenches to the chapel on the summit, which is an artillery observation post. The view is magnificent, & in clear weather Metz is clearly visible, about 18 miles off.—Today was cloudy, & we could just make it out in the blur. Near by, just across the valley, was the hill called "Le Yon," trenched to the top & facing the hills held by the enemy. Below the Yon, & between it & Pont à Mousson, the whole river valley up to the gates of Pont à Mousson, almost, is held by the Germans also. We looked across with glasses at the farm of Belair, which is hardly a mile from where we were, & where they are strongly planted. In trying to show me something, Walter put his hand (not his arm, only *his hand*) through the window of the chapel,

& instantly one of the artillery officers pulled him back & said: "Prenez garde, Monsieur. On pourrait vous voir!" & you may imagine the sense it gave us of almost feeling their breath in our faces. Walter, who has fewer thrills than course through my ardent old bones, pretends he didn't feel them as near as at Vauquois, where we saw the flame of their guns in that Dantean wood; but the fact of having to *hide* from their invisible eyes gave me an even acuter sense of being in the very gates of Hell.

May 15—Today Recouly is taking us off again to see other military scenes inaccessible to the civilian. When Barrès[2] was here about 10 days ago Recouly took him over the same ground, but they were unable to get to Pt. à Mousson, as it was being bombarded; so we were in luck yesterday.—And now I must break off to go about some Red Cross business in Nancy.

I'm going to see you next month if I can possibly get away.

Your devotedest Edith

We go from here all through the Vosges to Belfort, then home.

Ms:BL

1. Raymond Recouly (born 1876), journalist and world traveler, had written books on Indo-China and Manchuria, and a study of English life and manners.
2. Maurice Barrès (1862–1923) was a novelist of strong political interests. He espoused a kind of mystical nationalism and had been a vehement anti-Dreyfusard.

To Charles Scribner

53 Rue de Varenne
June 28, 1915

Dear Mr. Scribner,

I have just received your cable, saying that you would like an article about my trip to the North.

I am back after eight days of wonderful adventures, and hope to go off again next month to see the little corner of reconquered Alsace, which no one has been allowed to visit as yet.

I have been given such unexpected opportunities for seeing things at the front that you might perhaps care to collect the articles (I suppose there will be five) in a small volume to be published in the autumn.[1] I am in hopes of being able to give you some interesting photographs for the Lorraine article. Those taken by the soldier who was with us are too small to be satisfactory, but I have sent for the films and think I can have them successfully enlarged. I am sorry there has been a delay about getting them, but I hope they will go to you, with the article, in about ten days. I shall have some good photos of the last trip also.

We were in Cassel last week when it was bombarded, and I was allowed to see Ypres, which no one is allowed to go to, as the road between Poperinge and Ypres is continually under fire. I was also in Dunkerque a few hours after the last bombardment, and at Nieuport, the road to which is also under fire.

Some months ago I told you that you could count on the completion of my novel by the spring of 1916;[2] but I thought then that the war would be over by August. Now we are looking forward to a winter campaign and the whole situation is so overwhelming and unescapable that I feel less and less able to turn my mind from it. May I suggest, during the next six months, giving you instead four or five short stories, not precisely war stories, but on subjects suggested by the war? So many extraordinary and dramatic situations are springing out of the huge conflict that the temptation to use a few of them is irresistible. I have three in mind already and shall get to work on them as soon as I can finish my articles.[3]

I am sorry to fail you in regard to the novel, in which I still take a deep interest, and which I hope to do after the war; but if I attempted it now it would be a failure.

Yours sincerely,
    Edith Wharton

It was by my advice that Mr. Recouly held back his article on General Joffre. I wanted him to bring out some strategic points not before known, and it was necessary to have some diagrams drawn for it by a military draughtsman.

I am sending you a photograph of some of the "Children of Flanders" whom the Belgian government has asked me to look after here.⁴ We have nearly seven hundred in all, and I think this little account of the work will interest you.

Ms:FL

1. *Fighting France, from Dunkerque to Belfort*, published in the autumn of 1915.

2. The novel in question was *Literature*, originally intended as a portrait of the American artist circa 1913, when EW set to work on it. It was based in part on the poet and playwright William Vaughn Moody, and in part on EW's own personal, family, and literary experience. It was never completed.

3. In fact, the only short story related to the war that EW wrote was "Coming Home"; see letter to Gaillard Lapsley, December 21, 1916.

4. The Children of Flanders Rescue Committee was organized by EW in April 1915 at the request of the Belgian Ministry of the Interior. Its aim was to take care of as many as possible of the untold numbers of children picked up amid the ruins—in city, village, country—of war-ravaged Belgium.

*To Royal Cortissoz*¹

53 Rue de Varenne
August 11, 1915

Dear Mr. Cortissoz,

I have suggested to Mr. Vollard, the friend and biographer of Cézanne, to send you a copy of his extraordinary book on Cézanne,² of which you have doubtless seen a review in the London Times.

This book was of course prepared before the war, and as such literature is at present somewhat under an eclipse here, it would be a real service to Mr. Vollard to make the work known in America, and an equal service to the American public to be told of its value. No one can do this with more authority than you, & I have told Mr. Vollard that I was entrusting his book to the hands most capable of celebrating it. It is really a remarkable production, and if you have not already seen and reviewed it, you will be grateful to me.

Yours very sincerely
    Edith Wharton

Ms:BL

1. Royal Cortissoz (1869–1948) had been the art critic of the *New York Herald Tribune* since 1891 and would continue to be for another thirty-three years. His views were notably conservative and eventually antimodernist.

2. *Paul Cézanne*, by Ambroise Vollard (1865–1939), was published in 1914 by Vollard's own press.

To Henry James

53 Rue de Varenne
August 11 [1915]

Dearest Rédacteur,

Thank you again & again, & de tout coeur, for everything—including the jolly Hardy malediction, just come by the same post as your letters. What a splendid script, & *how* good of him!—And yesterday Joffre sent me word that he would give me "une page" too.—[1]

As for your blessed self, of course you'd much better send your contribution direct to Scribner, *registered*. I will announce its arrival in the letter I am sending him today.

Thank you also for your pamphlet, which I had not yet seen, & with which I shall delect myself the day after tomorrow, en route to Alsace.

I will hand it on later to Morton, who has quite completely abandoned me. All through Anna's severe operation & illness he never even telephoned to ask for news of her—or of me—& it must be six weeks since I have seen him. He will turn up again when I can be of use to him.—Enfin!—

Your ever grateful
Edith

Ms:BL

1. James, Hardy, and Joffre contributed to the volume being compiled and edited by EW, *The Book of the Homeless* (*Le Livre des sans foyer*), published by Scribners and Macmillan at the end of 1915. The proceeds went to EW's American Hostels and the Children of Flanders Rescue Committee.

There were nearly seventy contributors. Marshal Joffre, Commander in Chief of the French Armies, wrote a tribute, and Theodore Roosevelt an introduction. Among the poets represented were Hardy (a three-stanza work addressed to Germany as "Instigator of the Ruin"), Rupert Brooke, Claudel, Cocteau, Anna de Noailles, Santayana, and Yeats ("A Reason for Keeping Silent": "I think it better that at times like these/ We poets keep our mouths shut"). Prose offerings came from James (a tribute to the British soldier), Conrad, Bourget, Gosse, Maeterlinck. Paintings and sketches were supplied by Monet (an early pastel landscape), Bakst, Sargent, Max Beerbohm, Rodin, Renoir, and Charles Dana Gibson, among others; and d'Indy and Stravinsky contributed musical scores.

All told, about $15,000 went to EW's charities from the sale of the book and an auction of some of its contents.

To W. Morton Fullerton

53 Rue de Varenne
Sunday
September 5, 1915

My dear Mr. Fullerton,

Mrs. Wharton begs you to excuse her not writing herself, as she is up to her eyes in work & has Mrs. Jones staying here besides.

She asks me to ask you if you could conveniently send for your books, as she has to find room for a lot of furniture. Of course she has been delighted to keep the books for you, but now she is herself pressed for room. If it were not for that she wouldn't think of asking you to take them away. They have been carefully packed in 25 or 30 boxes. Could you make it convenient to send for them on Wednesday morning? That would solve her problem nicely, though she regrets having to give you the trouble.

Mrs. Wharton sends you her kindest regards, & hopes you will come in soon to see her; Mrs. Jones wishes to be remembered to you, & I remain

Always yours sincerely & cordially
   Anna Bahlmann

Ms:UT

To Bernard Berenson

53 Rue de Varenne
October 15, 1915

Dearest B.B.,

Just a line to tell you that our poor little Henri was killed on the 30th. One of his friends has just brought us the news, & all my servants are crying their eyes out. Oh, this long horror! It comes home with a special pang when an obscure soldier drops out of the lines, & one happens to know what an eager spirit beat in him. I can never forget that Henri was *not* brave physically, & that he was réformé, & had a struggle to get himself sent to the front. Poor boy! Gross asks me to tell Mary that she has 88 fcs left of the money she was to send him. She wishes to know if she is to return it to Mary or to send it to Henri's family.

I'll write you a real letter soon. This is just to tell you about Henri. My love, & *such* a wish to see you.

Edith

Ms:VT

To Elizabeth Cameron[1]

The Costebelle Hotels
Hyères
November 26, 1915

Dearest Lizzie,

Hurrah for making other people do one's work! It adds a peculiar zest to my laziness to see a big bundle of registered stuff carried into my sunny flowery sitting room, & know that you & Miss Herbert[2] have robbed it of all its terrors.—The first batch arrived today, & I am basking in the thought of the work it has given you.

In the future, by the way, please tell Miss. H. *not* to forward books, newspapers or pamphlets, or simple notes of thanks like two or three you sent. The rest is enough without this added burden!

It is heavenly here, & I marvel at the thought that I used to be *bored* on the Riviera! I didn't realize how tired I was till I began to rest. It is delicious just to dawdle about in the sun, & smell the eucalyptus & pines, & arrange bushels of flowers bought for 50 centimes under a yellow awning in a market smelling of tunny-fish & olives—

My two companions & I went to Toulon yesterday & had an enchanting afternoon on the picturesque quays, which I didn't know before. Bélogou has gone back to Paris, but Gide[3] stays a day or two longer, & Robert Norton[4] has just wired me that he will join me here on the 4th. I am so glad he is taking a rest at last, & it will be delightful to have him here.

The Bourgets are well, & I shall potter about with them when Gide leaves me. I am glad I didn't go to them for their villino is just as I remembered it: charming to look at, but without *one ray* of sun; whereas here I soak in it all day.

My love & gratitude, dearest Lizzie. I long to send you some flowers, but I'm afraid it's no use in war time.

> Your gratefullest
> Edith

In putting the notice in Tuesday's Herald I see they left out the important last phrase: "Donations should be sent to Mrs. Wharton, 53 Rue de V."!!

Ms:National Gallery, Washington, D.C.; copy supplied by Jerome Edelstein, Librarian

1. Elizabeth Sherman Cameron (1857–1944), the estranged wife of Senator James Donald Cameron of Pennsylvania (himself in his early eighties). Her personal life had centered on Henry Adams, and his on her, for many years. Mrs. Cameron's daughter Martha was married to Ronald Lindsay, a talented younger member of the British Foreign Office. Now back in Paris for a long stay, Elizabeth Cameron worked efficiently with EW in several of the refugee organizations, and on this occasion took over for EW when the latter was on her Riviera rest cure.

2. EW's new English secretary, L. C. ("Dolly") Herbert.

3. EW came to know André Gide (1869–1951), the most esteemed writer and editor in the younger French generation, when he joined the Franco-American General Committee for the Hostels.

4. Robert Norton, about forty-seven years old in 1915 and a man of striking

dark good looks, had been a clerk in the English Foreign Office and had served in Stockholm and Paris. Around the turn of the century, he became private secretary to Lord Salisbury, the Conservative Prime Minister. In 1903, he went into private business in "the City," and did so well that he was soon able to retire and devote himself to his real interest, which was landscape painting. EW met him at the same December 1908 house party at Stanway, the Elchos' home in Gloucestershire, where she was introduced to John Hugh Smith. Norton provided EW with a steady and disinterested friendship for nearly thirty years, and gave her perhaps the most relaxing company she ever knew. During the war, he worked in the Admiralty in London.

To Theodora Bosanquet[1]

Costebelle Hotels
Hyères
December 4, 1915

Dear Miss Bosanquet,

I was sent down here ten days ago for a rest of two or three weeks, & your telegram has just been forwarded to me.

I can't tell you how I feel—I am in despair at being so far off. I am telegraphing you today to ask if you think I had better come; but I am almost sure you will say no, for the present at any rate, for it probably would not be well to have Mr. James think I had rushed over on account of his illness, & every one knows that people don't come & go nowadays between England & France without a special reason. If this dreadful thing had to happen, how I wish I could have been in England at the time! I am also writing Mrs. Charles Hunter[2] to let me know what she thinks. I shall wait here, at any rate, till I hear more, so please write & wire me *here*—I am thankful Burgess[3] was with Mr. James, & above all that he was not at Rye. It is all so unforeseen—I had expected a sudden heart-attack at any time, but never had thought of this far worse thing.[4]

Of course in some cases of partial paralysis, even at Mr. James's age, complete recovery takes place. I have known such instances. But with his weak heart that seems improbable.

I shall be so thankful when you have time to write the details.—I suppose you have cabled his people? Surely some one will come from America.

Thank you again, dear Miss Bosanquet, for always remembering to let me hear when there is any cause for anxiety.

Above all, tell me quite frankly what you think I had better do.

Yours very sincerely
E. Wharton

If you think I had better not come for the present, please let me know when I can write to him—if it is advisable to write—& how much I can appear to know.

Ms:HL

1. Theodora Bosanquet became James's amanuensis in 1907, during the work on the New York Edition; her employer described her as young and "boyish" and worth all the other secretaries put together.

2. Mary (Mrs. Charles) Hunter was the mistress of Hill Hall, a stately Elizabethan mansion near Epping, the site of many Georgian gatherings of the sociable and the artistic. EW had encountered her at Salsomaggiore.

3. Burgess Noakes had been taken on as houseboy by Henry James in the 1880s, and had since risen to a key position in his household.

4. James had suffered a stroke on December 2, in his Chelsea lodgings.

To Gaillard Lapsley

53 Rue de Varenne
December 17 [1915]

Dearest Gaillard, No, I didn't send the beautiful thing—I wish I had!—I have been placidly stagnating in divine sunshine at Costebelle for nearly a month—& it was there the blow came.

I thought of you so much, from the first minute, & said to you, mentally, all the things you have just written me, & especially that cry of the heart: "Thank god, *we never wasted him!*" No, not a fraction of a second of him.

I very nearly went to England last week, as Miss Bosanquet told me he had asked for me. Luckily she was able to say that I had wired at once saying I wanted to come; & this, it appears, pleased him.—In the end, I didn't go, because I was sure it would agitate him.—

I said goodbye to him eight days ago, after a wire from Mrs. Hunter saying the end was coming; then there began to arrive the dreadful news—I can call it nothing else!—that he was "getting better." Today, however, on arriving here just now, I find another letter from Miss Bosanquet saying that neither she nor the nurses believe he will live. Yes—all my "blue distances" will be shut out forever when he goes. His friendship has been the pride & honour of my life. Plus ne m'est rien after such a gift as that—except the memory of it.

Dearest Gaillard, thank you for writing. No, luckily I was not alone at Costebelle, but had the Bourgets, who loved him dearly, & Robert Norton, whom I am very fond of, & who revered him (how one puts it in the past!) So I was able to talk of him to people who understood.

Can't you come & see me for a little while, later? Please do.

Your affte
　　Edith

Yes, I'm so glad about Percy. I had a delightful letter from Walter Maynard the other day—

I may still go to London any day.

I hadn't heard what Mrs. Prothero told you. How like him![1]

Ms:BL

1. In her memoirs, EW wrote that James "is said to have told his old friend Lady Prothero, when she saw him after the first stroke, that in the very act of falling (he was dressing at the time) he heard in the room a voice which was distinctly, it seemed, not his own, saying: 'So here it is at last, the distinguished thing!'" Lady Prothero reported this to Gaillard Lapsley.

To Mary Cadwalader Jones

53 Rue de Varenne
January 7, 1916

Dear Minnie— I asked Miss Herbert to send you a hasty letter with the list of donations rec'd here in answer to my Times article. I enclose herewith a letter to be inserted in the Times[1] when you have added the donations rec'd in N.Y.—Of course add yr address to mine at the end of the letter.

Olivia Cutting (Jr) sent me 5000 fcs, & asked to be entered as "anonymous." If I forgot to tell Miss Herbert this, please see that Olivia's name is not mentioned in the list. I don't know how to thank you for all you are doing, or to excuse myself for my delay in answering yr letters, & for the incompleteness of my replies. The fact is, I am on the brink of a complete break-down. My rest at Costebelle was shattered by the terrible shock about Henry, & I came back here to a "surcroît de besogne" & a mountain of letters wh. I have not yet been able to deal with. Then the demand of Miss Robinson Smith for official recognition by the War Office gave me a good deal of trouble & involved great fatigue. People in America don't seem to understand that at the most critical period of a terrible war it is hard to get the attention of the War Office for any matter outside the real business of the nation. I hope Mr. Justin Godart's letter was satisfactory, & that it arrived in time.

Yesterday the first convoy given by the War Relief Committee was ready to be shown, & I took our Ambassador to see it, & also Emile Berr of the Figaro—I am enclosing the newspaper notices to Miss Robinson Smith.

You cabled me some time ago asking what I wanted bought with a gift of $50. It seemed foolish to waste money on cabling a reply, & I meant to write at once asking for dark blue serge, to be sent through the Clearing House as usual. Please express my warmest gratitude to the donor, & also my excuses for this long delay.

And now another important point. The Russian Ballet (in the person of Dhiagilew)[2] is disposed to give a matinée de bienfaisance at the Opera, of wh. half the receipts are to go to a Russian war charity, & the other half to the American Hostels & Foyer Franco Belge. Dhiagilew is very ready to do this for us. He is a great friend of Blanche's, & he knows Alice Garrett, who has been very kind to him, & given him lots of letters to fashionable operatic people in N.Y. The obstacle may be Mr. Otto Kahn,[3] who, as I understand it, more or less finances the ballet & who will have to be won over to this scheme. Alice has written Eunice Maynard about it, & I think you had better see her as soon as you receive this, & also perhaps ask Josephine Griswold to interest herself in the project. I am sure she will if she is in N.Y. I am writing to Elsie de Wolfe,[4] & you had better see her too. The thing, of course, is for some of the opera ladies who have hitherto cold-shouldered Mr. Kahn to "jolly" him enough to obtain his consent to this benefit, & then make it as fashionable as possible. They gave one here just before sailing, at the opera, which cleared about 20,000 fcs for the British Red Cross; but in N.Y, half the receipts ought to be a good deal more than this.

I have had ten days of dreadful bother moving my ouvroir. But the government, realizing they had made a "gaffe," have ordered me an "amende honorable" by hiring & putting at my disposal "pour la durée de la guerre" a whole floor in a big building of the Boulevard St. Germain, in wh. I hope to be installed at the end of next week. I will cable you as soon as I am *sure*; there are still details to settle.

I am so dreadfully overdone that I must ask you to forgive me if I don't answer all your questions. The photos were done while I was away, & were not what I expected; but I have not found anyone with imagination enough to get the right groups, & it is quite impossible to find time to do it myself— I will acknowledge gradually all the donations rec'd here, & will try to write to the principal donors who have given through you. I have not even written yet to thank Walter Maynard for his delightful letter & his readiness to help. When you see him, give him my love, & tell him how grateful I am. Miss Herbert is a broken reed as a secretary. She is ill half the time, & has not yet learned stenography, so I am not much better off, except that she must not get things so inextricably muddled. It seems impossible to find any one here, except Elisina, who is efficient, & I can't load her with my whole job besides her own!

The small lingerie orders are very worrying. I think hereafter it wd be better to refuse any of less than $20, on the ground that the price of materials is going up so much. We certainly can't make chemises for less than 15–20 fcs, & night-gowns for less than 20–25 fcs— In future, if any one wants to order lingerie at the ouvroir, it will be best to address directly to Mlle. L. C. Herbert, 31 rue St Dominique, & she will translate & explain to Mlle. Landormy,⁵ & will acknowledge the order. I feel I shall have to go away in February for a month or two, & this will relieve me of one fussy thing, & she can do it perfectly.

All my love. I send the letter to the Times in another envelope, also duplicate list of subscriptions. Olivia *is* "anonymous."

yours E.W.

Ms:BL

1. EW's letter appeared in the *Times* on March 18, 1916, under the heading "Mrs. Wharton's Charity." It reported that the American Hostels for Refugees in Paris were at present caring permanently for three thousand refugees, and had found work for four thousand more. Additional funds were urgently needed, however, to prepare a great many more rooms in newly acquired houses for occupancy by incoming refugees. The letter concluded with grateful acknowledgement of those who had responded to a similar plea in a letter to the *Times* the previous autumn.

On September 19, 1916, the *Times* printed a third letter from Mrs. Wharton, this one requesting financial aid to help establish sanataria for French soldiers who had contracted tuberculosis in the trenches. See letter to Berenson, February 17, 1917.

2. The Russian impresario, Sergei Pavlovich Diaghilev (1872–1929), had been producing operas and then ballets and concerts in Paris since 1908. His companies had also performed in London, Berlin, and America.

3. Otto Kahn (1867–1934), German-born banker and philanthropist, chairman of the board of the Metropolitan Opera and generous supporter of musical events.

4. Elsie de Wolfe (1865–1950), actress, businesswoman, highly influential interior decorator, legendary hostess. EW had had some dealings with her a good many years before, when she (EW) was attempting to write for the stage. Elsie de Wolfe's French home, which she shared with Elisabeth Marbury, was the Villa Trianon in Versailles.

5. Renée Landormy, the niece of a French music critic, had been one of the first to join EW in her wartime work.

To Gaillard Lapsley

53 Rue de Varenne
January 10, 1916

Dearest Gaillard,

In defiance of the Stern Daughter of the Voice of God, who is waiting to dictate business letters to me, I must immediately send you hug for hug.

Bless you for your good letter, disappointing though it is. I wish you hadn't told me you so nearly decided to come to me this month only to dash the cup from my lips. I do so yearn for my friends these days—& now, especially, the longing to be with one of our little Qua'cre group is acute. Certainly, we "had him first," didn't we, in the sense of having the finest, rarest & fullest of him whenever he was with us? And so, now, after suffering dreadfully at the thought of being so far away, & of not even having had a real goodbye from him before leaving England, I have reached a mood of acceptance, & quite realize the uselessness of going to England, even if I were allowed to see him—I don't suppose he suffers as much as one's imagination suffers for him; & I feel that the poor dear being who is carried every day to the drawing-room window to look at the boats on the river is just a shadowy substitute he has left with us for a little while—to take in kind enquirers!

Our Henry was gone when I was in London in October.

I do feel, you know, that your reasons for *not* coming to see me are a little like those which prevent the elderly married couple in a Howells novel of 450 pages from telling the young girl in their charge that they have heard that the young man who is "attentive" to her once drove another girl to a quilting party. Hang Mrs. Hoppin, & her marriage, & the things one can't say to ladies the week before they marry (wh. opens vistas!). I'm not going to be married, & I wish to goodness you had come, & I miss you, & resent the lost chance. Do make a dash over *now*, just for a few days, *please*. I shall probably be at Costebelle in March.—yours ever affly Edith.

Ms:BL

To Theodora Bosanquet

53 Rue de Varenne
March 1 [1916]

Dear Miss Bosanquet,

It was very kind of you to telegraph, & I need not say what relief your news brought ... I was so glad to know the end was quiet & unconscious.[1]

You will be feeling a great void now; but you will have happy & dear memories of the long years of your collaboration with one of the wisest & noblest men that ever lived. We who knew him well know how great he would have been if he had never written a line.

I send you my deepest sympathy, & I hope you will now go off quietly to the country to rest & think of your own work—

Thank you again for your kindness in always remembering my longing for news.

Yours very sincerely
Edith Wharton

I hope you will let me hear from you sometimes.

Ms:HL

1. Henry James had died on February 28.

To Gaillard Lapsley

53 Rue de Varenne
March 1, [1916]

Dearest Gaillard,

Let us keep together all the closer now, we few who had him at his best. Send my love to Percy, please.

Your affte   Edith

Ms:BL

To André Gide

53 Rue de Varenne
5 mars 1916

Cher Monsieur Gide—

Votre lettre m'a profondément touchée, car ce sentiment dont vous parlez, de l'obscurité autour de soi, toujours plus froid et plus épais, me hante depuis longtemps aussi, et l'extinction de ce grand rayonnement que fut l'âme de Henry James en devient doublement tragique.

Il est mort sans souffrir, en dormant. Je suis heureuse de penser que la fin est venue, si paisiblement, et plus tôt qu'on ne pouvait l'espérer; mais ma vie est tellement amoindrie par cette mort, par cette *immense absence*, que je n'ose pas penser à l'avenir . . .

Quelle affreuse aventure vous avez eue! Et quel miracle de vous en être échappés sains et saufs, avec votre gentille ménagerie!

Nous avons vécu ici des jours bien angoissants. Aujourd'hui les nouvelles sont meilleures. Mais à quel prix!—

Merci encore de votre bonne lettre. Rappelez moi, je vous en prie, au souvenir de Madame Gide, et croyez à mes sentiments les meilleurs.

Edith Wharton

J'oubliais sottement de vous remercier de ce que vous me dites de votre conversation avec M. Proust— Plus je réfléchis, plus la question de la publication de ces quelques chapitres me paraît problématique.

Songez donc que *30* seraient d'une autre main, 16 seulement de celle de d'Humières! Et que d'Ungeon [?] et Mme d'H. voudraient que *chaque correction* faite au texte des 16 fut désignée dans une note. C'est absurde et impossible. Mon avis est, en résumé, de ne pas publier la traduction. Dois-je l'écrire à M. Proust? Voulez-vous me le faire savoir?

Transcribed by Professor Jacques Cotnam from ms. in the Bibliothèque Jacques Doucet of the University of Paris.

53 Rue de Varenne
March 5, 1916

Dear Monsieur Gide—

Your letter touched me deeply, for the feeling you speak of, of the darkness around one that grows ever colder and thicker, has also haunted me for a long time, and with the extinction of the great radiance that was the soul of Henry James it becomes doubly tragic.

He died without suffering, while asleep. I am happy to think that the end came so peacefully, and sooner than one could hope; but my life is so diminished by this death, this *immense absence*, that I dare not think of the future.

What a frightful adventure you have had! And what a miracle that you escaped from it safe and sound with your nice menagerie.

We have lived through some very agonizing days here.[1] Today the news is better. But at what a cost!

Thank you again for your letter. Please remember me to Madame Gide, and believe me to be yours very sincerely,

Edith Wharton

I foolishly forgot to thank you for what you tell me about your conversation with M. Proust.[2] The more I think about it, the more doubtful becomes the question of the publication of these chapters.

Imagine that 30 would be by another hand, only 16 by the hand of d'Humières! And that d'Ungeon [?] and Mme. d'H want *every correction* made in the text of the 16 indicated by a note. It is absurd and impossible. My advice, in short, is not to publish the translation. Should I write to M. Proust? Would you let me know?

1. The heavy German attack on Verdun had been going forward since early February. Before it came to a halt in June, 300,000 French soldiers had lost their lives and nearly as many Germans.

2. EW's friend Robert d'Humières had completed about one-third of his translation of *The Custom of the Country* at the time of his death in action, in the summer of 1915. EW, at least, believed there was some possibility that Marcel Proust might take over the remainder of the text. He never did, of course, and no French translation was ever completed.

To Barrett Wendell

Golf Hôtel
Beauvallon s/Mer
April 17, 1916

Dear Mr. Wendell,

Thank you de tout coeur for sending me your article about Henry James.¹ I like especially the part which begins: "His last months were tragic." It is a true interpretation of his point of view, which I did not share when he took his decision, but on which the subsequent course of things at home has shed a corroborative glare. It is indeed hard for some of us to "accept America as it seems to be today," & his change of citizenship was the revolt of a sensitive conscience bred in the old ideals, & outraged by the divergence between act & utterance which has come to be a matter of course for the new American. I am very glad you put all this in so clear a light for Boston readers, & that the first word spoken of him there should have been one of insight & tenderness.

"The Book of the Homeless" did not reach this side of the world till two or three weeks ago, & it was only then that I saw your beautiful quatrain. Thank you so much for writing it for my book. The whole volume is a credit to us, don't you think so? It is considered by far the best of the war-books, & of course artistically there is no comparison. Berkely Updike has done his part admirably.—The Times had an enthusiastic article about it. If only it could have come out before Xmas we should have made a fortune.

Thank you again, dear Mr. Wendell, &, with kindest remembrances to Mrs. Wendell, please believe me, yours ever sincerely,

Edith Wharton

Ms:HL

1. "Henry James, an Appreciation," *Boston Evening Transcript*, March 1, 1916.

To Mary Cadwalader Jones

Golf Hôtel
Beauvallon s/Mer
April 17, 1916

Dear Minnie,

I was really stunned by the news of Anna's death,[1] coming so suddenly, & so soon after Egerton's.[2] Not that I "wish her back"—heaven forbid! There was only suffering ahead, & she had no illusions about it, & this is the very end she prayed, but dared not hope, for. Only I wish she had stayed here, & I could have been with her to the end. Kansas City could never have seemed as much like home to her as the rue de V., where she was—I won't say "comfortable," for that she resolutely refused to be—but at least used to things, & properly waited on. Poor little unquiet bewildered & tender soul! I wish I could have done more for her this last hard year.

Thank you for cabling me about poor Bob.[3] This is a bad blow to me too. And I was hoping to hear the end had come for *him*; it's so little likely that recovery will mean anything but misery for him.

I rec'd a little note yesterday from Egerton enclosing $250 for my work! It is such a dear goodbye from the friend who never failed me.

My "rest" hasn't been much of a one, as you may imagine, & I'm going back next week to relieve my poor surmenés collaborators.

Much love to you all, & please don't overwork.

Yrs affly
E.W.

I have asked Herman to send you $50 to pay for past cables. Hereafter, do please send him an account of your cabling expenses. If you do, I shall feel so much freer to ask you to cable.—So many thanks for the new Masters.[4] Since I've seen his "mug" in an illustrated paper I have grave misgivings about his talent!

Ms:BL

1. Anna Bahlmann had been operated on for cancer some time previously. She died on a visit to Kansas City.

2. Egerton Winthrop had died in New York, at age seventy-seven. See letter to Sara Norton, June 14, 1916.

3. Robert Minturn. See letter to William Roscoe Thayer, November 11, 1905, note 2.

4. *Spoon River Anthology*, by Edgar Lee Masters (1868?–1950), was published in 1915.

To Gaillard Lapsley

53 Rue de Varenne
June 7, 1916

Dearest Gaillard,

The enclosed letters explain themselves—[1]

Please back me up if the occasion arises. It would be too bad if Percy were not to edit the letters—

Yrs affly Edith

I like Miss James[2] very much, & of course my proposed letter to her begins & ends with all sorts of amenities left out of the copy.

Ms:BL

1. The following two letters.

2. Margaret Mary ("Peggy") James (born 1887), the third surviving child and the only daughter of William James.

Copy of a letter addressed to Mr. Gosse.

June 6, 1916

Dear Mr. Gosse,

I have just received a letter from Miss Peggy James, in which she asks if I will give her copies of Henry James's letters to me, to be used in a volume which she is to prepare and which is apparently to be the definite presentation of his letters. I quote from Miss James's letter:

> "We are collecting Uncle Henry's letters because my brother and I hope to make a selection of them later for publication. I hope you approve of this, and think as we do, that they will be all that is wanted in the way of a Biography and also that it is wise to have the family do it, as we have such wealth of material in the shape of letters to the family, that go back as far as his very first European times."

As you know, I have shared from the first your feeling that Percy Lubbock is the one person fitted for this very delicate task, & I wrote urgently to Howard Sturgis some time ago asking him to use all his influence with Mrs. James[1] and to appeal to you for support. I am not sure if he has done the latter; but I know that such hints as he may have given Mrs. James have not been listened to. I know Mrs. James and Miss James too slightly to have ventured to obtrude my own opinion; but as Miss James seems to ask it I have decided to send her the answer which I enclose. I am sending it to you first because I should like to be able to say that, soon after Henry's death, you wrote me expressing the hope that Percy would be asked to edit his letters; but of course I do not wish to say this without your consent. I shall therefore await your reply before sending my letter to Miss James.

I have talked the matter over with Morton Fullerton who has a large and very interesting collection of letters. He has had the same request from the family, but has not answered it, as he wished to consult me first; and he and I are both unwilling to give our letters if the book is to be edited by the family, for the simple reason that we think it necessary that the work should be done by some one familiar with the atmosphere in which Henry and our small group communed together. The letters are full of allusions and cross-references that could not possibly be intelligible to any one who was not of the group; and when I say "the letters" I mean also those addressed to Howard Sturgis, Gaillard Lapsley, and Percy himself. The same objection would apply to almost all his European correspondence, and you must share this feeling, quite apart from your wish to see the work done by some one whose literary instinct and previous training fit him for the task.

If the family persist in their idea of editing the letters themselves, Morton Fullerton and I have decided not to give ours, but to bring them out in a small volume edited by Percy. I hope this may not be necessary, as it would be much more interesting to group all the letters, together; but if Percy is not chosen as editor, I should hope to induce Howard Sturgis and Mr. Lapsley, and perhaps one or two others, to keep their letters for our volume, which might be called: "Letters to a Group of Friends."

Please tell me exactly what you think, and let us try, by united effort, to "faire valoir" all the beauty and the significance of these precious pages.

> Yours very sincerely
> Edith Wharton.

Typescript ms:BL

1. Alice Gibbens James (born 1849), the widow of William James.

Copy of a letter addressed to Miss Margaret James— not yet sent.

June 1916

Dear Miss James,

I am glad to hear that Mr. James's letters are to be collected for publication and I quite understand your feeling that, in certain respects, the family alone can elucidate the early letters and put them in proper relation to his life. But since you are kind enough to ask my opinion as to the editing of the whole collection, perhaps you will let me tell you frankly what I think, taking my own letters from your uncle as a basis for my argument. These letters are very numerous, and parts of them are so interesting and beautiful that they ought certainly to be published. But they are so full of allusions and cross-references that the task of preparing them will be extremely difficult. This is perhaps especially true of the letters written to me and to the small group of intimate friends—all intimate with each other as well as with your uncle—to whom he wrote in the same mood and about the same things. I mean especially Mr. Sturgis, Mr. Fullerton, Mr. Lapsley and Percy Lubbock. No doubt the same thing is true of other groups of friends; but certainly in our case it would be almost necessary that these letters should be edited by some one familiar with the atmosphere in which they were written.

Shortly after your uncle's death Mr. Gosse wrote me to say how much he hoped that whatever was said about him would be said by Percy Lubbock, as he felt that no one was so well qualified to interpret and express your uncle's mind and character.[1] I share this feeling completely, not only because of Percy Lubbock's extraordinary literary sense and his experience in biographical work, but because he had an almost magical insight into your uncle's point of view. Not an allusion, not an association of ideas, seems to escape him; and his understanding of Mr. James's mind was so complete, that he appreciates the books on America as intensely, and with as complete an understanding of their local colour, as any American reader.

I know you must all wish above everything to make a book that shall represent Mr. James as completely as possible, and while it is certain that no one but the family could supply certain materials and certain suggestions, it seems to me that for the co-ordinating of the whole it would be a pity not to make use of such exceptional qualifications as Percy's. I have written you exactly what I think because I feel sure you would not have asked my opinion if you had not wished me to do so. I know that all of Mr. James's intimate friends who know Percy have long felt that he was peculiarly qualified to do this particular work, and I venture to suggest your considering the point carefully before coming to a decision.

With regard to my own letters from Mr. James, my time just now is so much taken up by war charities that I fear it would be impossible for me to go over them. I have a great number,[2] and they would all have to be re-read and sorted. Moreover, those he wrote me while I lived in America, which are among the most interesting, are in a storage warehouse and out of reach till the war is over. Therefore, in any case, I see no hope of being able to undertake the work at present.

Yours very sincerely
  Edith Wharton.

Ms:BL

1. This sentence was deleted before the letter was sent. See letter to Howard Sturgis, June 17, 1916.

2. In all, 177.

To Sara Norton

53 Rue de Varenne
June 14, 1916

Dear Sally,

I have been very slow in thanking you for your precious box of clothing, because I wanted to write a real letter, & I usually have to wait for a "jour férié" to indulge in that luxury.

But the things came duly, & were joyfully unpacked, & swallowed up by our hungry protégés; & it is only the expression of my gratitude that lags behind.

I have been very much over-worked since I came back from my holiday in the south at the end of April. There are always new tasks to undertake, & it is a joy to do one's utmost. But I am getting very "stale"—or rather I can't put much heart into anything now that the friends I loved best have been taken from me. I can't rally from the double blow of Henry James's death, & then Egerton Winthrop's, one so soon after the other—& followed so quickly by poor little Anna's!

Nothing can console me for the loss of the two wisest & best men I ever knew. Though they seemed the poles apart, & one was a genius & the other simply an "honnête homme" in the fullest sense of the word, they were akin in all their deepest feelings & instincts, & their beauty of character was of the same kind. They both saw things steadily & sincerely, without conventional humbug (though most people thought Egerton the slave of convention), & they were never afraid of what they saw. And both their hearts were as tender as their judgement was wise.

I think of them both so much that I can't help writing about them to you who will understand.—There is not much else to say, for my days are one long dull drudgery, & my heart is heavy with the sorrow of all my friends who are in mourning, or trembling for the lives of sons & husbands.

France continues to be magnificent, & one envies the people who have a real "patrie." I'm glad your father didn't live to see what America has become.

How are you, & how is Lily, & what are your plans for the summer? Do write me soon.

Yours ever affly
E.W.

The Bourgets are in Paris & would send love if they knew I was writing—

Ms:BL

To Howard Sturgis

53 Rue de Varenne
June 17, 1916

Dearest Howard,

Of course I agree with every word you say, & have no idea of "brusking" the Jameses. But since they asked my advice, it was too good an opportunity to be missed!

I modified the letter, leaving out all references to Mr. Gosse, as he wrote me that they had said nothing to him about their plans; I simply said that I knew Henry's friends thought that Percy was tout indiqué for the work.

You say you are "committed"; but wait & see. They don't intend to do anything for five or six years (so they told Gosse), & if my proposal about Percy is not accepted, & they say they are going to do the book themselves, you might very well (supposing the alternative plan of "Letters to a Group of Friends" is realized) say that your letters really belong to that group, & that, as they (the J.s) can do nothing for so long, you prefer to give your letters to Percy.

But all this is in the region of conjecture. What I hope is that they will come to their senses, & accept Percy for the whole job.[1] Of course the great & grim brother[2] will be referred to; & there, I suspect, is the real stumbling block. He hates me (I don't know why, but I fancy simply for the cosmopolitan & bejewelled immorality of which he regards me as a brilliant & baleful example), & he's quite capable of getting his back up because of me. Peggy, par contre, likes me, & I get on with her. We'll see!

I wish I had a "pull" on some of their Cambridge (Mass.) crowd.

Je t'embrasse tendrement.

E.W.

Pass this on to Gaillard & Percy, s.v.p.

Ms:BL

1. Percy Lubbock was, at last, invited by the family to edit the letters of Henry James; the two volumes came out in 1920. The first volume of Leon Edel's immeasurably more complete edition of James's letters appeared in 1974, and opens (pp. xiii–xxx) with a lively account of the transactions, subterfuges, and strategies that lay behind the Lubbock production.

2. The younger Henry James.

To W. Morton Fullerton

Fontainebleau

August 12 [1916]

Cher Ami— I agree with all you say, & entirely approve your suggestion about writing the facts frankly to Mr. Sears.¹ I suggested consulting Walter not because I wanted him to tell me how I ought to feel, or act, but because he is very wily, & it occurred to me that he might help find a pretext that would make it easier for Mr. Sears to release me if possible. But he is at Deauville, & I am not sure what day he is coming back. If he does not turn up by Thursday, write to Sears by all means.

Of course I meant in any case to sign my Appleton contract. I will send it off at once.

You miss one point in my letter. I don't care a fig if people know that the Cosmopolitan belongs to Hearst²—& I agree with you that few *do.* What I hate is taking money from such a hound, & helping "boom" his magazine—as I suppose my novel would; or else, why give me such a price?

I am quite ill enough for Mr. Sears to tell the Cosmopolitan that I am afraid to sign a contract at present, & prefer to drop the negotiation; then he can arrange with McClure for a later date.

The only thing I want to know—if this change of magazine can be managed—is whether McClure is solvent—at least presumably. I want the money! I am sorry to have given you so much trouble.

Thanks for understanding—

Amitiés.
      E.W.

Ms:UT

1. This letter deals with EW's effort, aided by Fullerton and by Sears, the Appleton editor, to stop negotiations with *Cosmopolitan* magazine for the serializing of her novella *Summer.* She wanted the work taken by *McClure's,* as indeed it was.

2. William Randolph Hearst (1863–1951) had, in 1905, added *Cosmopolitan* to his growing list of newspapers and magazines.

To William R. Tyler

> 53 Rue de Varenne
> Sunday
> November 11 [1916]

Dear William,

I have just heard from your mother that you are keeping your birthday today,¹ and I am so sorry that I was not asked to the party!

I can promise you that I should have come without being asked, if only I had known about it before I arranged to go to the country today. As I cannot come, however, I am sending a little pet to replace me, and as he is very handsome and most beautifully dressed I am almost sure he will remind you of me.

As you know, parrots talk, and I have asked this one to give you my love and wish you a great many happy returns of the day.

If he does this prettily and politely you may give him a bit of the cheese I am sending with him; but if he is noisy and vulgar, as I am told parrots sometimes are, you had better have him cooked and give him to Béguin to eat.

I want very much to see you again, and hope you will soon come to lunch with me. If your mother is very good perhaps you might bring her too.

With my best birthday wishes

Your affte friend
    Edith Wharton

Ms:WRT

1. The son of Elisina and Royall Tyler was six.

To W. Morton Fullerton

December 12 [1916]

Dear Mr. Morton Fullerton (vide yr. signature!!)

No economy is unwelcome to me in these days! Here is the cable I want to send, & with which I should not have presumed to trouble you (or use les deniers d'Appleton):

"Wharton would be greatly obliged if Maclure would pay for novel[1] before Christmas. Last chapters sent by hand November thirtieth."!!!!

Come & lunch on Sat.

Mrs. E. Wharton

Chevalier de la Légion d'Honneur.[2]

Ms:HL

1. *Summer.*
2. EW was made a Chevalier of the Legion of Honor by the President of France in April 1916.

To Barrett Wendell

53 Rue de Varenne
December 14, 1916

Dear Mr. Wendell,

Please give a welcome to Monsieur Jacques Copeau, one of the editors of the Nouvelle Revue Française & the manager of the Théâtre du Vieux Colombier, which made such a successful start the year before the war with Shakespearian performances, & also with Claudel[1] & the modern school.

Monsieur Copeau has been sent to America by the French government to give lectures & readings in French literature. He is well known here as a reader, & I have advised him to give readings from Baudelaire, Verlaine, Rimbaud, Mallarmé & their group, & also from the younger French poets.

Anything you can do to further his plans, (especially if you can arrange for a lecture at Harvard) will be one link more between the two countries, since Monsieur Copeau goes officially to speak of French letters.

In any case, I know you will enjoy seeing him & talking with him about France.

With my kindest remembrances to Mrs. Wendell,

Yours ever sincerely
    Edith Wharton

Ms:HL

1. Paul Claudel (1868–1955), poet and dramatist, and a member of the French Foreign Service.

To Gaillard Lapsley

53 Rue de Varenne
December 21, 1916

Dearest Gaillard,

What a joy to see your writing! It is good of you to regard "Xingu"[1] as a substitute for a letter—but it was not meant to be. I wrote you after you got back from America, but evidently my missive went astray. I am so oppressed nowadays by the sense that this fate awaits nearly every letter that I have reduced my correspondence to business necessities.

I'm awfully glad you like the book, & that every one seems to think it shows growth. But I don't deserve any of the coruscating things you say about it. *All* the stories except Coming Home were written before the war! Having made this confession, I'll add that I have written a book in the last six months—a shortish novel, which is coming out shortly in Maclure's. It is known to its author & her familiars as the Hot Ethan, the scene being laid in the neighbourhood of Windsor Mountain, & the time being summer which is also the title of the book. There's a Fourth of July at Pittsfield that few people but you & I are capable of appreciating! I don't know how on earth the thing got itself written in the scramble & scuffle of my present life: but it *did*, & I think you'll like it. Anyhow, the setting will amuse you.

It is a great trial never to see you & Percy & Howard. I get lonelier & lonelier as the weary months go on. The Berensons have been here, & are coming back after a short parenthesis in Spain. They want to take me to Florence for a month, but I don't think I can go so far away, or leave France at all. Probably I shall just go to the Riviera next month for a short rest of two or three weeks.—

I simply pine for Qua'cre, & our happy few; & the great void left by Henry seems the greater & darker because we can't talk of him. How long—how long?

I am sorry you have such a weight of cares of your own, dearest Gaillard. I think of you always so affectionately & wish so much that the burden were less heavy for you. Yes! One can carry one's load without the aid of joy—but it's a long cold road. Do write me from Qua'cre when—& if—you get there.

Your Affte
Edith

Ms:BL

1. *Xingu and Other Stories* had appeared in October.

To John Jay Chapman

53 Rue de Varenne
January 10, 1917

Dear Mr. Chapman,

What a jolly book![1] I shouldn't have seen it if you hadn't sent it, for I am too busy to think of ordering books, & spend my midnight leisure in re-reading the old ones.

This is almost as good as the "Winds of Doctrine," though not quite up to that incomparable work; & whatever Santayana has to say one eternally thanks him for saying it so perfectly.

France is greater than ever in these dark stagnant-feu days, & one is more & more glad to be here, seeing & marvelling.

Many messages to Mrs. Chapman, & thanks again for the book.

Yours sincerely
　　Edith Wharton

Ms:HL

1. *Egotism in German Philosophy* (1916), by George Santayana.

To Charles Scribner

53 Rue de Varenne
January 15, 1917

Dear Mr. Scribner,

I am filled with compunction at the thought that I have not yet acknowledged your letter of Dec. 7th, enclosing the draft of $500 on account of the sale of the Book of the Homeless. There are moments when the daily job here is too much for me; & the interval between Xmas & New Year, when your letter arrived, was one them.

Please excuse the long delay, & accept my thanks for this most welcome payment. I hope there may be another later!

Your letter of Dec. 27th has just come, enquiring about the book publication of "Summer," my short serial appearing in Maclure's.[1] I always prefer, as you know, to publish with you, & always offer you first whatever I write; but when I offered you "Summer," & the other tale I have been writing at the same time, you wrote me you would have no space in the magazine for either of them for a long time to come, & that you preferred to wait till I could finish "Literature" after the war.[2]

In consequence of this answer, I took up again a long standing offer of Messrs Appleton,[3] which combined serial publication in one of several magazines with book publication by them, on terms so advantageous that, in view of your refusal, I should not have felt justified in rejecting the opportunity.

I regret very much that "Summer" should not be appearing in Scribner's, where I always feel more at home than anywhere else.

Thank you for the offer to publish the volume; but, for the reasons I have given, the arrangement would not be possible.

I hope Mr. Recouly's articles on Russia will be interesting. There is certainly a good deal to say on that subject—!

As to our own country, I prefer silence, because I really don't understand any longer.—

Yours very sincerely
E. Wharton

Thank you so much for sending my books to the Chicago bazaar. It was quite by mistake that my sister-in-law asked you for that large number of books for the Boston sale. The fly-leaves were to have been sent direct to Boston where copies had already been bought, & I can't imagine why she made the request!

Ms:FL

1. *McClure's Magazine*, founded in 1893, was in somewhat of a decline since the end of its "muckraking" period. The editor happily paid EW $7,000 for serial rights to *Summer*.

2. This is a slight misstatement about the long and confusing exchange between Charles Scribner and EW dating back to the spring of 1916. In effect, EW was saying that if *Scribner's*, the magazine, was unable to serialize her novels virtually upon request, she preferred to go elsewhere for *book* publication. Summarizing this position, Scribner asked: "Is not this treating us with

less consideration than our previous relations entitled us to expect?" "The other tale" was *The Glimpses of the Moon*, begun in 1916, and published eventually by Appleton in 1922.

3. The New York publishing house was begun in the early 1830s by Daniel Appleton; in 1838, it took the name D. Appleton & Company. The founder's four sons carried on the firm.

To Bernard Berenson

53 Rue de Varenne
January 29, 1917

Just as I finished my letter of yesterday, in came "The Study & Crit. &c, No. 3," and I must dash off a word of gratitude & rejoicing; for on the very first page I find an "execution" of the Last Supper.[1]

Ever since I first saw it (at 17) I've wanted to bash that picture's face, & now, now, at last, the most authorized fist in the world has done the job for me! Hooray!!!

I haven't had time to get any farther, but that tardy act of justice will warm my soul all day & draw me back to your precious pages tonight.—Bless you!—

All the same, I wish it was you who had walked in instead—

Yrs affly E.W.

Later. I've just chucked the refugees & read on—I couldn't help it. Oh, bless you again & again: especially for "What is true of life is true of art: its ultimate aim is ecstasy," & what follows. It coincided so thrillingly with the "aesthetic" of my own métier that I've so long yearned to write that I could hug you—& myself!

When, when, when shall we talk of all these things?

Ms:VT

1. In his essay on Leonardo da Vinci in *The Study and Criticism of Italian Art*, (3d ser., 1916), Berenson wrote: "As a boy I felt a repulsion for Leonardo's 'Last Supper.' The faces were uncanny, their expressions forced, their agitation alarmed me." After trying for years to understand the popularity of the paint-

ing, he still felt that, though the composition was "wonderful," the characters in the scene were "a pack of vehement, gesticulating, noisy foreigners." He went on to speak of the "Mona Lisa" as "the estranging image of a woman beyond the reach of my sympathies ... with a look I could not fathom, watchful, sly, secure"; and of Leonardo's "John the Baptist" as "a well-fleshed epicene creature, with an equivocal leer."

To Bernard Berenson

53 Rue de Varenne
February 4 [1917]

Dearest B.B., "J'ai toujours *sur les bords du coeur* une lettre pour vous; je n'ai qu'à l'incliner vers vous, et la lettre part."

I came across this charming phrase in the Correspondance de Barbey d'Aurevilly[1] at 3 a.m. today; for I've adopted as my motto a variant of Wilson's "Too proud to fight" which runs "Too cold to sleep."—Anyhow, in this case insomnia was rewarded by my discovery; & now that I've found a formula I shall more often tilt my heart toward you.

It's the only thing left of me that's not below zero, after so many days of this inexorable cold. Really, my brains & bones are "marbrifiés" (B. d'Aurevilly again), & only a faint tick at the thought of a friend reminds me that one organ still lives under its marble casing. If you think that Mary's letter describing your cold corridors made me shiver, you & she are mistaken—I'm too hard frozen!—

I do wish, though, you'd stayed at the Ritz, where the millionaires, it seems, are still keeping warm. It must be depressing not to be able to use the library; I'm suffering from the same privation—on a modest scale—as I can't get at the books in my Grand Saloon.—Really, the times *are* portentous, & everything that happens is on a gigantic scale, in space & time both. It's everything bigger, & for longer, than we're used to.

The only cheerful thing that has happened is your Leonardo. Walter & Charlie & Bourget & I are licking our chilly chops over it—& I daresay many others, but they're the only people I've had a word with yet. It's *splendid*, such a glorious "sample" of the big book you promised me to write when we were motoring toward Denmark—that I feel pretty sure the book is more than half done already. How I wish you were here, that I might gloat with you successively over each admirable point, & then again take a general gloat (claquement général) over the whole point of view. The way your mind dominates your erudition, & takes a Righi view of the whole, makes me feel as if I were sitting over a good fire. (Curse that allusion to a snow-mountain!)

Please tell Mary that I laughed loud & long over Geoffrey's picture of McQueen. Personally, I should say he was made for Trano & Casati, & I don't see why he wasn't allowed to fulfill his destiny.

I'm *so* sorry to hear that poor Sybil[2] has been—& still is—so very unwell. What hard luck she has! To live at Medici & hardly ever be able to enjoy it . . .

I had such a nice letter from *feu* Cannon the other day, enclosing a fat cheque. I'm *so* glad he's not the one whose obituary somebody told us of. He writes from a place called "Cocoa"; American town nomenclature never palls, does it?—I have also received from Ed. Robinson a long brief about Mr. Theodore Davis's[3] will, & about a letter probably forged by his promising young nephew. Have you heard of this litigation? Robinson calls it a "grim New England tragedy," but I can't see much thrill in it— The document is too thick to reach you, I fancy; but I'll send it—or try to—if you like.

Will you tell Mary that "La Passion de notre frère le Poilu" is out of print, but as soon as it appears again, I'll send her the dozen she wants. It's worth all the "Jeux" ever written, isn't it?—

Please tilt me-ward by return of post, & meanwhile think of me so fondly that I shall feel it a little through the cold—

yrs affly
      Edith

Ms:VT

1. Jules-Amédée Barbey d'Aurevilly (1808–1889), novelist and critic.

2. Lady Sybil, with her daughter Iris Cutting, was now living in Villa Medici, on the Fiesole slope.

3. Edward Robinson (1858–1931) was director of the Metropolitan Museum of Art in New York from 1910 to 1931, and was one of the world's greatest experts on classical art.

Theodore Davis was an American copper king, and a collector of paintings.

To Bernard Berenson

53 Rue de Varenne
February 9, 1917

Dearest B.B., it's so easy & so delightful to tell you things because you let one see that you like to be told! It would have spoilt half my joy in the Leonardo if I hadn't felt sure that you would welcome my appreciation of it.—I'm so used, these many years, to contracting at a word that expanding, as I do at yours, makes me extraordinarily happy.—

Oh, yes, you ought to be here! Not only because you're so wanted, but because I "kinder feel" that intelligent Americans have a right—since last Sunday—to be in the centre of things.¹ I'm sure a good jerk on your part would break through the technical difficulties. Do try!—I'll try to get you a job here—some sort of an Embassy job—I mean the semblance of one—if you'll only come!

I can't say you'd care to loaf in the Stanzone *here*, though! The cold is still grim, though there is a false glittering sun overhead every day.

Eric Maclagan² is here again, & came to dine last night. Nothing new; I see the same small group, & one says less & less about the situation because the suspense makes comment vainer than ever.

It is a comfort to see Bélogou again. He is evidently still more or less in bondage—but (as I suspect) disgusted by the milieu, & pining for good talks with his own kind.

I turned from Traubel³ to the Goethe-Schiller⁴ correspondence, into which I'd often dipped without ever getting a sense of *a swim.* And I don't get it now. Decidedly not. Goethe always Schillered when he wrote to Schiller, didn't he? That's the reason why, generally, tran-scribed talks are so much more satisfactory than letters. People talk more for themselves, apparently, & write more for their correspondents. Anyhow, this book is not for me.

I'm thirsting for the other Traubel vol.—Does the kind Logan say positively that he can't get it? I'm insatiable, & should like to try every means.—By the way, please tell Mary I skipped the Emerson in the Supp. because I supposed it was by Benson Brock (that's his real name, you know!) Now I'll go back & read it. I ought to add that I ascribed it to le dit grand écrivain only because of its commanding position on the first page!!

I'm so sorry that Mary was still too poorly to enjoy the Stanzone. I hope when this reaches you she will have been lizarding for several days. Oh, how every bone of me yearns for the sun & you!

Yrs affly
Edith

Ms:VT

1. On February 3, President Wilson, in response to the unrestricted submarine warfare being waged by the Germans, broke off diplomatic relations with Germany and ordered American vessels to arm themselves for defense. The declaration of war would follow in two months.

2. Eric Maclagan (1879–1951), the son of the former Archbishop of York, was currently head of the British Ministry of Information in Paris. He had been assistant keeper of architecture and sculpture in the Victoria and Albert Museum, and would later become its director.

3. The third volume of *With Walt Whitman in Camden*, by Horace Traubel (1858–1919), his diary of visits and talks with Whitman, was published in 1914.

4. Presumably *Briefwechsel zwischen Schiller und Goethe in den Jahren 1794 bis 1805*; 3 vols., 1901.

To Bernard Berenson

53 Rue de Varenne
February 17, 1917

Dearest B.B.,

I can't help hoping that my official summons in behalf of the Tuberculeux may bring you back![1]—What a joy if it did. As the hymn says, "I need you every hour." You're the one person who understands everything—*"from the centre all round to the sea."*

Lately I've been exploring fields that I roamed in in my tender youth (at 14!) & hadn't since revisited; the German Chansons de Geste[2] & the Edda.[3]—I have been all on fire, poor old perpetual combustible that I am, with the Göttersagen of the older Edda, especially Wöluspa, & the song of Thrym & Odin's Rune Song, & the splendid ruffianly Harbarslied; & when I looked around my little group there wasn't one to unpack to—not one! Sometimes my heart gets so tight from that sort of loneliness—you don't know it as I do! What I'm telling you sounds puerile at this moment; but those sorrows are as real as one's baby griefs, aren't they? . . . Well, last night I dined with Rosa, & sat next to little Desjoyeaux, who was just as deceptively responsive & comprehending as they all are—up to a certain point; & in my thirst for sympathy I told him about the song of Helga the Hunding's Daughter, & quoted the wonderful *groosley* warning of Sigrun's maid at the end: (see yr Simrock for the real thing):[4]

"Be not so bold, daughter of the Skioldungs, as to fare alone to the huts of the Dead. *More powerful at night are the ghosts of the dead heroes than in the light of day.*" (Only "huts" ought to be "dwellings" in English.)

Well, you ought to have seen poor little Latin Desjoyeaux! He did his very best, not only to please me, but to be à la hauteur; but he could only anxiously stammer: "Oui . . . c'est curieux, en effet . . ."

Oh, dear! Isn't it queer that *we* can understand Racine, & that *they* can't hear the rustle of the Urwald?[5] Sometimes I think there's no loneliness like that of having too many strings to one's harp! I've never forgotten that giro to the forgotten country when we twanged them all—or at least I did! (Though it's a lyre one twangs; I don't remember how one "operates" a harp?)

Dear me—what a flight! Now I must plump down to refugee-land again.—

I'll send you the big Davis document if you don't come. But oh, *do*! —I do hope Mary is better. She ought to be in such sunshine as you describe.

Yrs affly
E.W.

Ms:VT

1. In the spring of 1916, EW had helped inaugurate a cure program for *les tuberculeux de guerre*: French soldiers who had contracted tuberculosis in the awful conditions of the forward trenches. EW herself served as a vice-president of the head committee, and in this capacity she had sent Berenson a formal invitation to come to Paris and join in the work.

2. German Chansons de Geste: EW's way of referring to the thirteenth-

century *Minnelieder* and the poetry of Walther von der Vogelweide. See letter to Berenson, January 7, 1912.

3. The Edda: Old Icelandic works. The older or "poetic" Edda, to which EW refers, is a collection of Scandinavian poetry of the thirteenth century, but some of it dating from much earlier periods. The first of its two parts consists of songs about the gods—"Göttersagen"— and EW names four of the most striking among them: Wöluspa (the Sybil's prophecy), the song of Thrym, Odin's Rune Song, and the Harbar(d)slied, a comical dialogue between the disguised Odin and Thor.

4. The other part of the poetic Edda is made up of songs about heroes. EW slightly misnames the song she quoted to M. Desjoyeaux. The derivative English title is *The Second Lay of Helgi Hunding's Bane* (Helgi the slayer of Hunding). It tells how the heroic young Helgi slew the enemy of his father, King Hunding. Sigrun, a Valkyrie maiden, was smitten with love for Helgi; they married and had children. Then Sigrun's brother Dag killed Helgi.

Sigrun goes to the burial hill and holds converse with the ghost of Helgi. When she proposes to seek him out the following night, her maid speaks the warning—a "groosley" warning, as EW calls it in her version of the German "gruselig" (gruesome)—quoted by EW to her dinner companion.

Simrock: Karl Simrock, whose German translation of the poetic Edda (with that of the Brothers Grimm) had a large influence on nineteenth-century German literature and art. Richard Wagner drew his narrative materials for *The Ring of the Nibelungen* (which EW had attended with Berenson in Berlin in 1913) from the Simrock translation. It was this German version that EW had read as an adolescent, and from an English translation of which she quotes.

5. Urwald: literally, primeval forest.

To General John J. Pershing[1]

53 Rue de Varenne
July 22, 1917

My dear General Pershing,

I am much honoured by your taking the trouble to write me about my war-work in France, and by your commendation of it.

A great part of its success is to be ascribed to my devoted and indefatigable helpers, to whom a proportionately large share of your praise is due, and who will be as much gratified as I have been by your letter.

Believe me,

Yours very sincerely
(signed) Edith Wharton.

[Note to Elisina Tyler appended:]
I have had the letter & my answer translated, & sent to the French members & to the "chefs d'emplois" of the Hostels.

Copy:WRT

1. John Joseph Pershing (1860–1948) had been appointed commander of the American Expeditionary Force in France in May 1917.

To André Gide

10 août [1917]

Cher Monsieur,

J'ai beaucoup tardé à vous remercier de votre lettre, et cependant elle m'a fait un bien grand plaisir. J'ai surtout été très touchée que vous ayiez [*sic*] pris la peine de copier cette jolie page de la lettre de votre neveu que j'ai lue depuis à beaucoup de mes compatriotes. Quel charmant tableau il a tracé de cette rencontre avec "les Américaines"! Parmi tant de visions tristes, celle là est toute rayonnante de jeunesse et de soleil. Acceptons-en l'heureux présage.

Merci d'avoir eu l'aimable pensée de m'envoyer cette belle édition de l'Immoraliste. Je suis heureuse de la tenir de votre amitié, et précisément au moment où je me prépare—du moins je l'espère—pour un voyage au Maroc, et où votre belle évocation de ce désert que j'ai tant aimé, au lieu de réveiller ma nostalgie, me donnera l'avant-goût de ce qui m'attend là-bas.

Que dites-vous de cette idée d'entreprendre un tel voyage à ce moment ci, et me trouvez-vous tout à fait folle? Il paraît que le Gouvernement organise une "tournée officielle" pour visiter la foire de Rabat, et on m'a invitée de m'y joindre. On nous promènera en auto de Tanger à Fez, Meknès, Rabat, et même, paraît-il, jusqu'à Marrakech. L'itinéraire me tente beaucoup et quoique le voyage sera certainement très fatigant j'ai bien envie d'accepter.

En attendant, je me repose ici pendant quelques semaines, et je corrige les épreuves de la traduction de mon petit roman, qui doit paraître le mois prochain dans la Revue de Paris. La traduction est lamentable —mais il ne faut pas que vous le disiez! Attendez, je vous prie, que je vous envoie un exemplaire anglais du livre, et évitez de lire la Revue de P. pendant quelques semaines!—

Après avoir vu Charlie constamment jusqu'au moment de mon départ pour Fleury, vers le 14 juillet, je n'ai plus eu de ses nouvelles! J'ai écrit plusieurs fois à La Celle St Cloud, et j'ai su qu'il était allé avec ses parents visiter la tombe de son frère au front, par conséquent il a dû aller mieux; mais il ne répond pas à mes lettres, et cela me préoccupe, car je crains qu'il ne soit moins bien depuis ce voyage, qui a dû être très fatigant et très éprouvant.

J'ai appris par des amis de New York que M. Copeau avait eu beaucoup de succès, et qu'il allait ouvrir un théâtre là bas. Tant mieux pour nous!

Je vous enverrai très prochainement un exemplaire de "Summer" le plus tôt possible.—Lisez-le avec indulgence, car il a été fait un peu à bâtons rompus, à cause des réfugiés!—

Croyez, je vous prie, cher Monsieur, à mes sentiments très sincères.

Edith Wharton

Transcribed by Professor Jacques Cotnam from ms. in the Bibliothèque Jacques Doucet of the University of Paris.

Dear Monsieur,

I am very late in thanking you for your letter, and yet it gave me a great deal of pleasure. I was especially touched that you took the trouble to copy that nice page from your nephew's letter, which I have since read to many of my compatriots. What a charming picture he has drawn of his encounter with "the American women"! Amid so many sad spectacles, this one is radiant with youth and sunshine. Let us accept it as a happy presage.

Thanks for having had the kind thought of sending me this beautiful edition of *L'Immoraliste*.[1] I am happy to have it as a gesture of your friendship, and exactly at the moment when I am preparing—at least I hope so—for a trip to Morocco, where your beautiful evocation of the desert that I have loved so much, instead of re-awakening my nostalgia, will give me an advance-taste of what is waiting for me there.

What do you say about the idea of undertaking such a trip at this moment, and do you think me altogether crazy? It seems that the government is organizing an "official tour" to visit the fair at Rabat, and I have been invited to join it.[2] We will be conducted by an auto from Tangier to Fez, Meknès, Rabat, and even, it seems, as far as Marrakech. The itinerary tempts me very much, and though the trip will be tiring I am inclined to accept.

While waiting, I am resting here for a few weeks, correcting the proofs of the translation of my short novel,[3] which is to appear next month in the Revue de Paris. The translation is lamentable—but you must not say so! I beg you to wait until I can send you an English copy of the book, and avoid reading the Revue de Paris for several weeks!

After having seen Charlie constantly up to the moment of my departure for Fleury around July 14, I have had no more news of him! I wrote several times to La Celle St. Cloud, and I knew that he had gone with his parents to visit the grave of his brother at the front, so that he must have been better; but he does not answer my letters, and that worries me for I fear that he may be less well after this journey, which must have been very tiring and very taxing.

I have learned from friends in New York that M. Copeau[4] has had a great deal of success, and that he is going to open a theatre over there. So much the better for us!

I will send you very soon a copy of *Summer*, as quickly as possible. —Read it with indulgence, for it was done in fits and starts because of the refugees.

Please believe me, dear Monsieur, yours very sincerely,
    Edith Wharton

1. Gide's novel was published originally in 1902.

2. See letter to Mary Cadwalader Jones, September 26, 1917.

3. *Summer*.

4. See letter to Barrett Wendell, December 14, 1916. Copeau was a friend and literary associate of Gide's.

To Bernard Berenson

Fontainebleau
September 4, 1917

Dearest B.B.,

Oh, do you really, *really* think—or better still—feel all that about "Summer"?—It's such a wonderful sensation to find, when one comes out from behind the "haute lisse" frame of the story-teller, that one's picture lives to other eyes as well as to one's own—the picture so blindly woven from the back of the frame!

I was beginning to think there must be a resemblance to nature from the shy & frightened letters I've been getting from the few old friends in Boston to whom I feel bound, in friendliness, to send a copy. D'autre part, their official organ, the Transcript, has a really understanding & honest article, over a column of close type, saying the book "will have reverberations both loud & long."

I'm so particularly glad you like old man Royall. Of course, *he's* the book!.—And, oh, how it does agreeably titillate the author's vanity to have his pet phrases quoted to him!* Non, c'est trop beau ... Bless you.

Well, we're really off for the Maghreb. I start on the 15th, & Walter picks me up a day later at Madrid. It will be a ventre à terre trip, as he has so many big jobs on his hands in Paris; but never mind, I'll just "poser les jalons" for a good long giro later with you & Mary.

It's so queer to be going to a country that has next to no books about it!—Just a few twaddling "journals" by military explorers, no good at all—& one fairly good vol. by Aubin, wh. takes in only a small bit. I wrote to Chevrillon for a list, & this is the result.—

I'm seeing here a great deal of a very agreeable Cte Gilbert de Voisins (whom I knew before the war) whom you must meet some day. He has just married the divorced (& much maltreated) wife of Pierre Louys, a sister of Mme. H. de Régnier, a nice but not thrilling person.[1] Gilbert de V. is a grandson of Taglioni, & his mother was an English Ralli. It makes the queerest mixture, but a very pleasant one.

I suppose I shall be back in Paris about Oct 25th. When are you coming? By that time I look forward to be—more or less—"living like a lady again," having coalesced most of the "oeuvres" with the Red Cross.—Whereof I send you the accompanying picture—a speaking likeness—from New York!

Much love to you both. I'll write from Mauretania.

Yrs affly
     Edith W

* You see I'm getting a little confused about my sex! A form of megalomania—

Ms:VT

1. Pierre Louÿs (1870–1925), author of elegantly erotic works, including *Chansons de Bilitis* in 1894. He had married a daughter of the Cuban-French poet José-Maria de Heredia; her sister was the wife of the *symboliste* poet Henri de Régnier (1864–1936).

To Mary Cadwalader Jones

Grand Hôtel de la Tour Hassen
Rabat (Maroc)
September 26, 1917

Dear Minnie,

I write from a fairy world, where a motor from the "Résidence" stands always at the door to carry us to new wonders, & where every expedition takes one straight into Harun-al-Raschid land.

When we arrived at Tangier last week an officer of General Lyautey's[1] staff met us at the landing, & after 2 days there we were sent off to Rabat by motor—a wild flight across the desolate bled over the old "piste" which is gradually being turned into a road, but which was impassable to motors a year ago, & still necessitates a strong backbone like mine! —On arriving here in the evening we found rooms ready for us in this hotel, which is two steps from the Résidence. Dear Mr. Koechlin was already here, & is to go on the trip south with us when we leave. I found several young friends on the General's staff, d'Ormesson, Felix de Vogüé & Champion, & altogether there was a friendly coming-home feeling about the arrival that one doesn't often find in strange lands.

Since then, we have simply floated about in Résidence motors, shown the Merimède ruins by the Director of the Beaux Arts, shown the Exhibition by the General himself, & so on. It is impossible to tell you the kindness we have received, or the tact with which, at the same time, we have been allowed to do what we chose.

Yesterday afternoon Mme. Lyautey took me to the Exhibition with her to see the reception of the Sultan, who of course visited her booth (& bought all her lingerie indigène for his harem!). It was very picturesque to see him dashing away afterward preceded by his "garde noire" in scarlet tunics & green & white turbans, all on white horses, & going at a gallop with the royal standard flying ahead of the Sultan's motor, alas!—El Mokri & one or two other dignitaries were with him, & it gave me a good chance to watch their faces while he was choosing things in the stall.—We dine every night either at the Résidence or with one of the officers, & usually take tea with Mme. Lyautey & go out with her afterward.—

The Exhibition, on a great plateau outside the walls, with a beautiful view over the old town & the sea, is very well done. It is arranged in the form of reed-thatched "soukhs" grouped about quadrangles full of flowers, & the booths are all built of cedar wood, so that the air is balmy with it.—There is a great effort to revive Moroccan arts & industries, & the result is already creditable. Mr. Koechlin has done a great deal to direct the effort, & they had a Moroccan show at the Arts Décoratifs last spring.

Certain things, notably the rugs & some of the embroidered curtains, would sell splendidly in America, I am sure.

I spare you the architecture & the landscape because you'll have to read them in Scribner,[2] & give you this worldly chronicle instead, because I thought it more amusing— Tomorrow morning is the "Sacrifice of the Sheep," the great religious ceremony to wh. the Sultan goes in state with all the great feudal chiefs; we are in great luck to see it. The chiefs are here for the Fair, & we are to see some of them chez eux, when we go south.

We shall leave in a few days, I suppose, for Marrakech, Meknès & Fez, & I understand that we are to be lodged in the Resident's palaces, which is a fortifying thought after one or two glimpses of Moroccan inns on the way here! The only drawback is the excessive heat, but I hope to get used to it in time— Meanwhile I must stop & perspire!— I have no letters forwarded, of course, so this can only be an egotistic chronicle of my own doings. But I hope that whatever news of you awaits me in Paris is all good.

Yours affly
        EW   Oh, the relief of having a *real* holiday!

Ms:BL

1. The soldier-statesman General Hubert Lyautey, at sixty-three, was one of the authentic heroes of France. In 1912, he had rescued the Sultan of Morocco from a native uprising, and then seen to the establishment of a French protectorate in the country. He had instituted a vast program of modernization, while protecting the integrity of the old Arab cities and the Moslem religious traditions.

EW had known General and Mme. Lyautey in Paris. On the General's initiative, the French government invited EW and Walter Berry to visit the fair being prepared in the coastal town of Rabat, where new industrial products were to be exhibited alongside ancient artisan skills.

2. EW's articles on this experience, after appearing in *Scribner's*, were collected in her book *In Morocco* (1920).

To Bernard Berenson

Palais du Bon Jelired
Fez
October 2, 1917

Dearest B.B.,

Imagine, after a flight across the bled, passing through battle-mented gate after gate, crossing a dusty open space with mules, camels, story-tellers, & the usual "comparses," & passing through a green doorway into a great court full of flowers. The motor stops before a white palace front, & we enter another court full of more flowers, with orange groves bordered by rushing streams, fountains splashing into tiled tanks, yellow jasmines, pomegranate trees hung with ripe fruit, & beyond a great shady room with a bowing caïd in the step, & an inner court of green & blue & white tiles, with more fountains—for Fez is all fountains! And this is the way we arrived yesterday afternoon at the Residence, which General Lyautey has had opened to receive us, & where I am writing you now from a room looking on an orange grove on one side, & on the other over roofs with overhanging fig trees, & minarets with green tiles under a stone tracery, & beyond the grim wolf-coloured hills with their fortresses commanding each corner of the city. And that is Fez!—

Ever since we got to Rabat it has been fairy tale every minute, but it really culminated in the arrival at the Summer Palace of the Sultan's wives, in cool rooms smelling of matting & cedar wood, with flowers & rushing water everywhere.—

I can't begin to tell you all we've done in the interval since we left Tangier, but every conceivable chance has been given us—seeing the Sacrifice of the Sheep, seeing the Sultan in his harem with his lovely ballet russe concubines, in clothes such as Bakst never dreamed of, lunching at Volubilis with the curator of the ruins in a villa overlooking Moulay Idriss, which is like Castrogiovanni in situation—then going afterward to Moulay Idriss & happening by accident on the ritual dance which takes place only twice a year, which no European was allowed to see till 2 years ago—& we could see now only because we were with French officers!—

Since we have been in Fez we have ridden about in the Soukhs & climbed the hills for views (a splendid military road has just been built all around the city); today we are to see some houses of rich Fasi, & the Medersas, & tomorrow we go to Sefrou. But so far the best thing here has [been] walking around the mosque El Kaironan at the prayer hour, & finding all the doors open, so that we could look in & see the whole perspective, not only of the courts but of the glorious mosque itself. It seems they allow this since last year only, & as we had with us the French government architect, whom they allow to go into the mosque to superintend the repairs, it was possible to linger & gaze as much as we wanted.

All this time I'm not telling you about Meknès, where we spent the night at the charming quarters of the "Subdivision," & sat on a terrace after dinner overlooking the moonlit city.—Meknès is quite apart from everything else, & perhaps with Moulay Idriss, the most extraordinary thing we have seen.—The ruins of Moulay Ismaïl's palaces, gardens, stables, granaries, &c, & the walls surrounding them, are like gigantic South American mysteries—& all built in an adobe that looks like the red tufa of Ronciglione & Caprarola. It is the maddest thing to come on in this land of the infinite detail & the delicate proportion.—But I'm suddenly chilled by the thought that you'll probably see Walter before long, if you're really in Paris, & that he'll tell you all this with more precision if less "flamme."

I do so hope I find your Mary still there when I get back—about the 16th, I suppose—

Yrs affly   Edith

Ms:VT

To Bernard Berenson

Montredon, par Marseille
February 15 [1918]

Dearest B.B.,

The letter I meant to send Mary to welcome her back to the Trocadero shrank to an inarticulate squeak—so overwhelmed was I by Geoffrey's news![1] I wonder, by the way, if she read *his* letter to *me*? I hope he showed it to her, for it really was the perfection of friendly frankness.

Well—if I am reduced to a squeak, she must be dumb—unless, with a sublime heroism of which I believe her wholly capable, she "fixed it up" herself; in which case we are friends no more!—

I have been *practising liking* it for 24 hours now, & am obliged to own that the results are not promising. I hardly ever saw Geoffrey, but some subtle link of understanding on most subjects bound us together with hooks of steel, & never again to see him except encircled by that well-meaning waste of unintelligence; oh, dear—enfin, "c'est la guerre."

I've been wishing for you so much these last three days; I don't know anyone who would be so penetrated by the aching beauty of this place. If you can picture the Villa Borghese (the stone pine & grass amphitheatre part) on the edge of the sea, & leading up by long alleys of plane & pine to a wild & extraordinarily noble bosco of pines, which in turn climbs to the face of a sheer white cliff fantastically cut against a glorious blue sky; & if you set in the axis of the house the château d'Yf, the dazzling harbour, & the white eminence of N. Dame de la Garde, you'll have a hint—no more—of the many strands of Poussin & Claude interwoven into a sort of clear & noble tapestry.

One feels humbled at having missed the chance of being born in such a landscape—until one sees the elderly châtelains in "city clothes" scuttling daily down the divine plane-avenue to catch the train into Marseilles—elle pour "les courses," lui pour "le cercle." And then one is thankful for the Urwald within one . . .

I should be content to bask here for weeks—but Mme. P. is called back to Paris unexpectedly tomorrow to see her son, who has 5 days leave before returning to the front; & as I saw it fretted her to leave me to "stodge" here alone with the good Pastré, I am picking up my tired bones & crawling on to Hyères on Monday.

My address there will be Hôtel Costebelle, Hyères, Var.

Please tell Mary, with my love, that she shall have a real letter soon, & that meanwhile I expect to find on arriving at Costebelle a "clean breast of it" from *her* on the Geoffrey-Sybil affair.

Bless his heart! He says "I'll explain to you how it all happened." Sancta simplicitas!

Well, goodbye, my dear—I suppose some day—in a fortnight or so —I shall have to go back to Paris; but "no one knows how I dread it."

Yrs ever affly   E.W.

Ms:VT

1. Geoffrey Scott and Lady Sybil Cutting had become engaged to be married.

To Elizabeth Cameron

[Paris]

June 22, 1918

Thank you, dearest Lizzie, for your letter of sympathy & understanding about Fred's death.[1]

It is so sad to think that Harry is cut off from me, but then I have known it for a long time & this was just one more proof of what I had long been aware of. Besides the real thing nowadays concerns the real people, & not the poor phantoms who have voluntarily ceased to live so long ago. Minnie & Trix make up to me for my own wretched family, & all my thoughts & interests are with them. I never saw Minnie younger, braver, more gallant & altogether admirable than during the month of really hard work that she spent here with me. She has had a lot of bad knocks lately, but each one seems to make her more resolute to play her part to the full & to the end. I was very anxious about her return voyage, for she landed just as the submarines were making trouble off N.Y., but she simply cabled "Arrived after peaceful voyage"!!—

I am hoping soon to hear from you that you are coming to Paris with Miss Hoyt. I know when it comes to the point you will not let her resign her job. It is *not possible*, after the good record she has made. Especially at this moment it would be cruelly unfair to her. And you must know, dearest Lizzie, that nothing would induce her to leave you alone. You are putting her in a very cruel dilemma, & you must forgive me for saying that I feel sure that no one would have suffered from it more than Martha, who gave herself so heroically & faithfully to the last for the same cause.[2]

Our very old friendship makes me say this to you, dear friend, because Miss Hoyt *can't*, & because I like & admire her so much that I can't bear to think of the distress she is going through now.

I was at Fleury last week, & saw the Gays, who asked tenderly about you. My best love always,

Edith

B.B. has gone to London to join Mary, who is very ill. Do try to see him if you can.

Ms:National Gallery; copy supplied by Jerome Edelstein

1. Frederic Rhinelander Jones, EW's older brother, had died in Paris at the age of seventy-two.

2. Elizabeth Cameron had suffered three successive blows. On March 28, Henry Adams died. Next, her husband, Senator Cameron, succumbed. And, finally, her daughter and only child, Martha (Mrs. Ronald Lindsay), died after a long illness. Mrs. Cameron retreated into her English home, Stepleton House in Dorset, where she clung to her grief and refused to allow anyone to see her. She also proposed dismissing her niece Elizabeth Hoyt, so that she might be entirely alone. See the latter part of the following letter.

To Mary Cadwalader Jones

53 Rue de Varenne
July 7, 1918

Dearest Minnie,

I meant my "very darndest" to get off a letter last Friday telling you about the greatest "Fourth" in history; but the fatigues of that matchless day left me no grey matter with which to describe it on the morrow, & I can only hope that old Mary Waddington[1] isn't one of your regular correspondents, & hasn't intervened *here* too!—

Now comes your letter of the 19th of June, & I'm glad to see the Reef Point at the head of the page, & to know you are in Trix's firm hands, & in for a relative rest.

I am very much better.[2] My three week-ends at Fleury have done me no end of good, & on Aug. 1st I am going to St. Nectaire in Auvergne (the place that cured White, & where he is now), to see if it won't give me back my red corpuscles, or rather keep them from bursting & getting mixed with the others!

I shall have Dr. Isch Wall there to supervise the cure—I shouldn't risk taking it otherwise! But he believes it will give back the hue of life to my grey-green countenance, so it's worth trying.

Now for the Fourth—it was really a great show, only slightly unreal from its sheer beauty, & the extraordinary weight of associations, historic, symbolic, & all the rest, added to the aesthetic perfection of the setting.

I saw it from the Crillon, with an incalculable mass of people—some

say over 50,000—weltering below us, & stacked up solidly on the terrace of the Tuileries.—The great stolid "Villes de France" had their
stone laps full of American & French soldiers with their arms around
each other's necks, & presently down the Champs Elysées trotted the
Garde Nationale, & then our wonderful incredible troops, every man
the same height, & marching with a long rhythmical musical stride that
filled the French with wonder. Two regiments from camps—& then the
infantry & marines from Château Thierry in their trench helmets; then
some poilus from the same sector; then the American Red Cross
nurses—who scored the biggest success of all!!!—Everything & everybody was beflagged, from buildings to cab-horses, every Am. soldier had
flowers in his tunic, & every poilu an Am. flag on his bayonet. The historic
imagination (mine at least) fairly burst in the struggle to deal with all
the associations & analogies the scene evoked.[3] And—wonder of
wonders—the Boches didn't interfere!—

Paris is feeling very confident just now, & I have induced Elisina to
leave for Burgundy this week for a rest. As soon as she gets back I shall
go in my turn. But you had better go on writing to me here, as any
unexpected turn of events may upset all our plans.

I have had a long letter from Coddy about Jean-Marie,[4] of which I
had sent him a p.c. He knows it, & once tried to buy it; thinks its
possibilities endless—& understands it better than any of the French
friends who have seen it. What a queer stick!

Of course I haven't yet begun work there; but I am more & more
hopeful of being able to do so in September. I suppose the absence of
bombardment tends to create optimism.

I am so anxious to know what the financial result of Fred's death will
be for you & Trix.—The "funeral" never took place—or rather was
never announced.—This inky paper, by the way, was intended only for
"foreign use." As I told you, his death having been known here to a
few of my friends, I had to go through the hollow gestures of conventional mourning.

I am so glad you have recovered the films. I wish you had not bothered about my tooth-brushes, bless you! I meant you to send them by
hand, by the next person coming. *Please* don't bother about them, or
anything but resting.

Tell Trix, please, that poor Elizabeth Hoyt is having such a perfectly appalling life at Stepleton with Lizzie that I feel very anxious about her. Ask Trix to write her as often as she can—it is the only way in which her friends can help. She writes me that a nephew of Lizzie's (who?) is going there this week, but she has little hope of the result.

Lizzie is behaving like a mad-woman—sometimes I feel like saying simply, "like a woman"!—I can't understand it, at over 50. I should think the hard drubbing of life wd. by that time have had its effect. But the "enfant malade" prevails to [the] end, with most.

I loved having you when you were here, but I wish your visit were just beginning now instead!—

Little Miss Roosevelt & the Gays are coming to lunch, & Le Roy⁵ is staying with me. Best love to all

Edith

Ms:BL

1. See letter to Henry James, February 28, 1915, note 3.

2. EW had been suffering from anemia.

3. EW was thinking of her great-grandfather, General Ebenezer Stevens, fighting side by side at Yorktown with the Marquis de Lafayette; and of her parents, from the windows of their hotel suite on the Rue de Rivoli, witnessing the scenes of combat and triumph during the revolution of February 1848.

4. "Coddy": Ogden Codman, a New York architect whom EW had known since the early years of her marriage. He had helped her to remodel Land's End, and they had collaborated on *The Decoration of Houses* in 1897. Codman had made his home in a château south of Paris. Jean-Marie was a small estate in the village of St. Brice-sous-Forêt, a dozen miles north of Paris. EW, in search of a home outside the city, had discovered it in 1917, and negotiations were now in progress.

5. Le Roy King, EW's much younger second cousin. He had been a member of EW's American group in Paris since 1908.

To Bernard Berenson

Fontainebleau
August 13, 1918

Dearest B.B.,

Simmons is dead.[1] He died in the Engl. Hospital in Marseilles yesterday morning of double pneumonia. It is all I know as yet.

This breaks me down to the depths. I really loved him dearly—& he had a great sort of younger brotherly affection for me—& we understood each other so completely!

You will feel as I do. He was such a pathetic figure, so surprised & grateful that we all loved & appreciated him as we did, so puzzled to know *why*.

Please thank Mary so much for her letter. I was touched by her making the effort to write, & meant to answer today—but this news has paralyzed me.

He was coming to Paris next week.

He admired you so much—so often he used to ask to be let off an engagement with one or another of us "because Berenson has asked me to dine"; & he was so proud that you liked him.

J'ai le coeur meurtri.

Yrs ever
Edith

Ms:VT

1. Ronald Simmons, a young Yale graduate, had come to Paris to study painting. In 1917, EW signed him on as secretary to the committee for the tubercular military; but the moment America entered the war, Simmons presented himself at the Paris recruiting office, and was commissioned a captain in intelligence, with assignment to the Marseilles area. In the wake of his unexpected death, EW wrote an obituary poem "for R.S.," which was published in *Scribner's*, and dedicated both *The Marne* (1918) and *A Son at the Front* (1923) to him.

To Gaillard Lapsley

53 Rue de Varenne
October 18, 1918

Thank you so much, dearest Gaillard, for sending me the beautifully presented address, which I am taking with me to the country tomorrow for a quiet week-end perusal.

I had you dead—& I won't add buried—last week, for I'd got it into my head that you were on the Lenister, & nothing wouldn't do me but to write to poor driven & pen-weary Percy, & beg him to put on a p.c. "Gaillard is safe"—which, bless him, he mercifully did!

So I am now engaged in combing the sea-weed out of your ambrosial curls, & sitting you up again before a nice coal fire in your nice brown study.—Somehow, one lives in perpetual terror for every body one cares about.

Oh, my dear, to think that in a few months you & Percy & I may be talking ourselves blind together somewhere in the sun!

Yrs affly
E.W.

Did I answer your letter about poor dear Gide? If not, let me tell you now not to worry. He is a mass of quivering "susceptibilities," & invents grievances when he can't find them ready made. Luckily he is so charming that one ends by not minding.

Ms:BL

To Victor Solberg[1]

[October 19, 1918]

Dear Mr. Solberg,

I have received some time ago your letter of September 17th, enclosing several of your poems & asking advice about them. I should have answered before, if I had not been ill & somewhat overworked.

I am very glad to hear that the landscape of France, & especially of the Côte d'Or, has moved your heart & your imagination; it is good to know that some of our soldiers are feeling the beauty of France as well as the bitterness of the ordeal she has undergone.

You ask me frankly what I think of your verses; & I will tell you in reply that I never give an opinion on literary questions unless I can give a frank one. You wish me to tell you 'whether these songs are simply the old songs of Wordsworth, Shelley, Moore, Tennyson, etc, resinging themselves because I have lived with them so much'; & you seem to think that the risk of being subject to the influence of great poets is one that young writers should fear.

There cannot be a greater mistake than this, or one more destructive to any real poetic culture. Every dawning talent has to go through a phase of imitation & subjection to influences, & the great object of the young writer should be, not to fear these influences, but to seek only the greatest, & to assimilate them so that they become part of his stock-in-trade.

I must tell you sincerely that in your own case I do not find the influences you suggest, but rather those of the poet's corner of a daily newspaper. You have evidently felt the beauty of pastoral France very deeply, but to feel it is not enough; poetry is an art as exact & arduous as playing the violin, or sculpture or painting. It presupposes long training & wide reading, & a saturation in the best that the past has to give. I will not express any opinion on your talent because if it is in you to write better poetry, as it may well be, you must prepare yourself for so noble a mission by reading the best, & only the best, & by studying the grammar & etymology of your language as well as the history of its rhythms. It takes a great deal of the deepest kind of culture to write one little poem, & if you will read the lives & letters of some of the poets you mention, you will see that they all had it, even Keats, the greatest of all, though he wrote so young, & died so young.

I am grateful to you for writing to me, for I am interested in any one who cares for English letters.

Yours sincerely

Typescript copy:BL

1. Victor Solberg was a private in the American Expeditionary Force. From Mirebeau, Côte d'Or, he sent Mrs. Wharton some of his verses.

To Thomas N. Rhinelander[1]

53 Rue de Varenne
October 31, 1918

Dearest Tom,

Your letter of Oct. 11th has just come, & when you wrote it you had only my first cable.

Long before this you will have received my first letter, explaining why the form of the cable was so vague & allusive. Had it been otherwise, you would never have received it.

I did at once all the things you tell me that you did: appealed to the Ambassador, to Mr. Drexel, to the Red Cross, to the authorities at Newbold's camp, &c.—; & meanwhile Fred[2] & Le Roy were doing as much on their side—or rather, telling me what to do, since, as a civilian, I can act more rapidly than they.

It is hard to have to write again without giving you even a clue to go on. But, as I have already written & cabled, Tommy Hitchcock was at least six weeks without being able to give a sign to his family, & in many cases it is much longer. When one considers the disarray behind the German lines at this moment it is only natural to allow for a still longer delay without allowing one's self to be discouraged.

We are all on the alert, thinking constantly of Newbold & of you, & allowing no chance of getting news to escape us. So I hope before long we may get a word of some sort.

Please give all my love & sympathy to Kit, & when I cable try to read between the lines!

Yrs ever affly
E.W.

Ms:LA

1. EW's first cousin. His son Newbold—"Bo"—had joined the American Ambulance Corps in France in 1916, and a year later had enlisted in the Army

Air Corps. During several leaves, he paid visits to Cousin Edith in the Rue de Varenne. On September 26, 1918, Bo Rhinelander had taken off with his squadron on a raid deep inside German territory. When the party returned to base, Bo's plane was not among them. EW would later learn that Bo had been shot down and killed, and she arranged a funeral in the village where he crashed.

2. Frederick King, EW's second cousin and the brother of Le Roy King.

PART SIX

The Costs of Energy
1919–1927

Introduction

※

EARLY IN 1919, Edith Wharton fled Paris, where the peace conference had filled the city to bulging with intrusive compatriots, and came down to the Hôtel du Parc in Hyères, on the Mediterranean coast, for a four months' stay. Her companion was Robert Norton, recently released from the British Admiralty, a watercolorist of some talent but relatively little ambition, and a man of striking good looks. The two had known each other for some years, but their mutually nourishing friendship was now just beginning. With Norton, Edith explored the area—Hyères lay a few miles to the east of Toulon—and in the course of their wanderings came upon a curious property in the old part of Hyères, high above the modern town. It resembled a ruined fortress, but in fact had been a convent for "Clarisses," nuns in the order of Ste. Claire, built within the walls of an old château. Its proper name was Ste. Claire du Vieux Château; and Edith Wharton determined to take it on a long lease. An enormous amount of repair was necessary, but Edith fell to with zest: "I am thrilled to the spine," she wrote Royall Tyler, "... and I feel as if I were going to get married—to the right man at last!"

Comparable refurbishing was going forward at the villa outside Paris. Mme. Wharton, with her servants and staff, was able to move into Jean-Marie by mid-summer, and held a ritual opening on August 7. Within months of the armistice, Edith Wharton was organizing a life divided between southern France from December to June, and the quiet village of St. Brice for the rest of the year. Different groups of "regulars" enjoyed the hospitality of the two places. Paris residents and visitors came out in steady numbers to Pavillon Colombe (its original name was restored), a matter of ten miles or so: the Bourgets, the Du Bos, St. André, Rosa de Fitz-James, the witty and erudite art curator Eric

Maclagan. The annual Christmas gathering at Ste. Claire normally included Lapsley, Norton, and Berenson. Edith also made a few ties within the thin Riviera society; and of these the person she quickly came to treasure the most was Philomène de Lévis-Mirepoix, a glowingly lovely young woman in her early thirties from one of the leading ducal families in France. Philomène, having passed through a difficult personal time, was living in Hyères with her five-year-old daughter and her widowed mother.

The costs of restoring and running the two homes were huge, and the large advances Edith Wharton was now receiving were decidedly welcome. Before she came north from Hyères in 1919, she had been paid $18,000 by the *Pictorial Review* for her next serial—after a change of name it would be called *The Age of Innocence*—and to this Appleton added an advance of $15,000 against royalties. Edith Wharton had entered the literary world of the big money; but at the same time, her sheer creative energy in these postwar years seemed boundless.

During the period 1920–1927, from her fifty-eighth through her sixty-fifth year, Edith Wharton produced no less than fourteen volumes: five novels, four novellas (*Old New York*, sold separately and in boxed sets), one collection of short stories, two "travel books," one series of essays on the writing of fiction, one slender volume called *Twelve Poems*. She was writing so much and so variously that she sometimes lost track; the letters between Edith Wharton and Rutger Jewett, her editor at Appleton, became systematically divided into different categories, a dozen or more per letter, most of them carrying the titles of works-in-progress. "You are a wonder," Jewett told her. "Do you marvel that I bow low before such energy?" To give some sense of her earnings: during the five years of 1920 through 1924, as best one can calculate, Edith Wharton's work brought in about $250,000, not much less than $3,000,000 before taxes today.

As one novel followed another, the critical reception almost inevitably grew mixed and even a trifle impatient. *The Age of Innocence* was widely acclaimed, though one critic (Vernon L. Parrington) thought it irrelevant to the political and social issues of the day. *The Glimpses of the Moon*, a light-fingered work at best, aroused hostility in high critical places; *A Son at the Front* was deemed extraordinarily powerful by one reviewer, and the most distasteful war story that another reviewer had ever read.

A Mother's Recompense (1925) was clearly misread by some commentators, and unintelligently praised by others. "As my work reaches its close," Edith said to Minnie Jones after contemplating these responses, "I feel so sure that it is either nothing, or far more than they know. And I wonder, a little desolately, which?" Edmund Wilson, who had had admiring words for Edith Wharton's previous novels, found *Twilight Sleep* an acute piece of social criticism; Dorothy Gilman judged it a disaster. At the present moment, it is fair to say, the last two novels mentioned are being upwardly reappraised.

Within her own literary time, meanwhile, Edith Wharton's acquaintanceship was enlarging. In 1921, the Pulitzer Prize jury for fiction voted for Sinclair Lewis's *Main Street*, only to have their choice rejected by higher authorities and the prize given to *The Age of Innocence*. Lewis wrote a sportsmanlike letter of congratulations to Mrs. Wharton; and the latter—touched to begin with by this first sign that younger American writers even read her work—went on to express the disgust she felt on learning that "the prize shd really have been yours." Sinclair and Grace Hegger Lewis came out to the Pavillon soon after that; Lewis dedicated *Babbitt* to Edith Wharton; and the two novelists saw each other intermittently in the next years.

In the summer of 1925, Edith Wharton replied to a friendly message from F. Scott Fitzgerald, inscribed in a copy of his novel *The Great Gatsby*, by writing a letter of judicious praise for the book and inviting the author to call. Fitzgerald arrived with Teddy Chanler, the youngest of Daisy Chanler's offspring. There followed one of the better-known failed encounters in the American literary annals, with Fitzgerald, a bit drunk, launching confusedly into an off-color story and Mrs. Wharton observing austerely that his narrative lacked data. There was a different comic modality to the visit in 1924, to Ste. Claire, of the gifted and gnomelike English writer William Gerhardi, whose novel about Anglo-Russian life, *Futility*, Edith Wharton had seized upon and had written about handsomely.

Edith Wharton's existence in the 1920s thus alternated in rhythmic contentment between Ste. Claire, with its long-stretching view of the Mediterranean, the dotted Isles of Gold (the Porquerolles) and the far-off Maritime Alps; and the Pavillon Colombe, with its gardens and box hedges and goldfish pond hidden peacefully behind the blank encircling wall. Within these two superb domestic creations, Edith Wharton worked and wrote, prodigiously; and housekept and gardened and entertained, lavishly. But she continued to make the periodic excursion to other lands.

Most years, she put in a fortnight in England, usually staying with friends and hobnobbing enjoyably with the literary folk of the Georgian era and the veterans of the Edwardian epoch. In June 1923, she journeyed to America to receive the honorary degree of doctor of letters at Yale, the first woman so honored by that university. The recipient— "she holds a universally recognized place in the front ranks of the world's living novelists," said the citation—was immensely gratified, despite some disclaimers. The eleven-day visit was the last she would pay to her native country. In the spring of 1926, after months of planning and negotiating, she rented a 360-ton steam yacht, the *Osprey*, and took Daisy Chanler, Norton, and Logan Pearsall Smith (the graceful essayist, and Mary Berenson's brother) on a ten-week cruise through the Aegean. It was, undoubtedly, one of the most exhilarating experiences of her entire life.

A few months after that, Edith and Walter Berry drove across northern Italy, through the picturesque old city of Bergamo and on to Venice, then back through the south Tyrol. It was only weeks later that Berry underwent an emergency operation for appendicitis, and, while still recovering, suffered a stroke. He came down to Hyères for a grumpy convalescence; but in October 1927, he had a second stroke. Edith was able to be with him for the last three days, holding him and murmuring about old days together. Berry died on October 12. "No words can tell of my desolation," Edith wrote Lapsley. "He had been to me in turn all that one being can be to another, in love, in friendship, in understanding."

To Bernard Berenson

Hôtel du Parc
Hyères
January 27, 1919

Dearest B.B.,

I read your letter "stretched on a bank of amaranth & moly," with the blue sea sending little silver splashes up to my toes, & roses & narcissus & mimosa outdoing Coty's best from the centre all round to the sea. In front of us lay two or three Odyssean isles, & the boat with a Lotean sail which is always in the right place was on duty as usual— & this is the way all my days are spent! Seven hours of blue-&-gold & thyme & rosemary & hyacinth & roses every day that the Lord makes; & in the evenings, dozing over a good book!

I read Norton a few extracts from your letter, especially those in which you deplored my absence from the Peace Conference,[1] & we shook our heads & wondered, having lost the key to the cipher!

Bless you, my dear, I was dying of just the kind of thing that brings you to life—& I very nearly *did* die of it. It has taken days & days of healing silence, & warm sun & long walks, to get the poison out of my bones. But now I'm getting as lively as a cricket, & go bustling up & down mountains like an English old maid.

Seriously, you can't think what Provence has been this last month. Never have I seen it so warm, so golden, so windless & full of flowers. I should wish you here a hundred times a day if I were not afraid that a strong will like mine might cause the wish to become a reality! & land you suddenly in this unpolitical arcadia—with disastrous results to our friendship!—

You poor dear B.B., "it's *your* 'obby," as the Yorkshire farmer said to the priest who was reproaching him for not making sufficient sacrifices for his Saviour, who had sacrificed all for him. "It's *is* 'obby, sir," —only I don't think they drop h's in Yorkshire, do they?

No one here that we know, thank God, but the Bourgets, & Bourget, when I can coax him away from politics to books, is of course delightful. Norton is much better, & as happy as a king. We like the same things, & potter all day blissfully.

I had a touching letter from Mary the other day, describing her 4 days' visit to Lizzie C.— My old "fish, cut bait or get out of the boat"

rule of life makes me a little impatient of these self-conscious lamentations (I mean Lizzie's), & I have none of Mary's indulgence, having had
one or two such knocks on the head as neither of those dear things ever
dreamed of, & being still able to sit up & find life—as we've often
agreed—well worth the trouble of getting born.

Goodbye, Dearest Delegate. Write soon. Yrs affly
EW

Ms:VT

1. Berenson was acting as an observer at the Versailles Peace Conference.

To Corinne Roosevelt Robinson

53 Rue de Varenne
June 11, 1919

Dear Mrs. Robinson,

Your book[1] has just come. Thank you so much for it, & for the words
of dedication.

My lines on your brother[2] were written in a rush, out of a heart
wrung with sorrow, sorrow for the lost friend & for the great leader
gone when he was most needed. I am glad you cared for them.

Your own dedicatory lines are very beautiful, & so, indeed, are all
those that your brother has inspired in your little volume.

I like also immensely "Soldier of Pain" & "Thanksgiving 1917."—
Thank you so much for giving me the book.

When I write of your brother my heart chokes in my throat & I can't
go on. No one will ever know what his example & his influence were
to me.

Yours ever affly
E. Wharton

Ms:HL

1. *Service and Sacrifice: Poems*; dedicated "To the memory of my brother Theodore Roosevelt whose watchwords were courage and service, whose life was a trumpet call to loyalty to America."

2. Shortly after Roosevelt's death in 1919, EW wrote a sixty-line blank-verse poem called "Within the Tide." It drew upon a tribal legend she had read of in *The Golden Bough*, which declared that when a man dies his friends come at twilight to the shore and escort him by boat to the lands of the blessed.

To Barrett Wendell

53 Rue de Varenne
July 19, 1919

Dear Mr. Wendell,

I have asked Appleton to send you a copy of my disjointed little articles called "French Ways & their Meaning,"[1] which were written, alas, not soberly & advisedly, as such a theme demands, but in the brief & agitated intervals between refugee committee meetings, air-raids & bombardments. Be indulgent, therefore, & reconstruct out of the fragments the little monument to the glory of France that my scattered bricks were meant to build—if you can! I have been talking a great deal of you lately, for B.B. & Mary are just back from their wonderful Spanish giro, & we dined together last night under the horse chestnuts in the Champs Elysées, & stirred up the old memories & affections that we have in common—& when we do that your name is always one of the first to come up!

I was wishing that you had been with me on the 14th. No one who did not see the Great Procession will know what such a ceremony can be when weather & background, & the behaviour of the crowd, & the attitude & the appearance of every one concerned, & the great thoughts & emotions from which it takes its meaning, all manage to concur in a perfect whole. We seemed really to be looking at a poet's Vision of Victory, so simple, so solemn, so really august (& so miraculously free from little awkward contretemps) was the whole proceeding from beginning to end. I was in a sixth floor of the Champs Elysées, & I saw the great "défilé" from the Arch to the Obelisk, so perfectly ordered & moving so slowly & majestically, that one had time to take in each individual feature, to see the expression on the Generals' faces, to enjoy the glorious beauty of the massed English flags, the strange mediaeval Bayeux tapestry effect of the tanks, the little cluster of glorious aviators with Fouck carrying their flag, the Spahis, the Indians, the splendid Senegalese, the wonderful rhythmic march of our men, the long light British stride—& all the while that our hearts were choking & bursting with the too-muchness of what it all meant!—Like everything else in the war this image of its end was almost audessus des forces humaines, & most of the people I know confessed to being literally "broken" by it for the rest of the day.

I wonder if you have seen "The America of Today," the volume of lectures on the U.S. given at Cambridge last year, which Gaillard Lapsley has edited & written an excellent introduction to? But of course he will have sent it to you. It has some very good things—the Santayana is delicious, & Prof. Canby[2] has some good things—or nearly good— to say on modern American literature. But his tiresome distinction between aristocratic & democratic forms (as if democratic were the necessary synonym of illiteracy) rather blurs & befogs his incidentally just comments. How much longer are we going to think it necessary to be "American" before (or in contradistinction to) being cultivated, being enlightened, being humane, & having the same intellectual discipline as other civilized countries? It is really too easy a disguise for our shortcomings to dress them up as a form of patriotism!

I have enjoyed this talk so much that I have monologued on unduly. Forgive me, & let me have a word some day to prove that you're not afraid of another answer!

With kindest regards to Mrs. Wendell,

Yours ever sincerely
Edith Wharton

Gaillard is coming to stop with me on Aug. 7 at a tiny little place that I have bought near Paris. It is called Jean-Marie, & at St Brice sous Forêt, Seine-et-Oise.

Ms:HL

1. A collection of articles written in the latter months of the war and published in various magazines.

2. Henry Seidel Canby (1878–1961), longtime editor of the *Saturday Review of Literature*, and the author of many books on American writing.

To Charles Scribner

St. Brice
France
September 12, 1919

Dear Mr. Scribner,

I have to thank you, somewhat belatedly, for your letter of August 19th in which you tell me, what I had already heard from Mr. Berry, that the moment does not seem to you a good one for publishing a translation of Mr. Blanche's book. I told Mr. Blanche at the time that some difficulty of this sort might arise, so he was probably not unprepared for your answer.

You remind me that I have not yet replied to your enquiry in a previous letter as to "Literature." The letter in question was, if I remember rightly, in answer to one from me saying that I thought I should be able to take up the book again before long. In the first relief from war anxieties I thought it might be possible to shake off the question which is tormenting all novelists at present: "Did the adventures related in this book happen before the war or did they happen since?" with the resulting difficulty that, if they happened before the war, I seem to have forgotten how people felt and what their point of view was. I should feel ashamed of these hesitations if I did not find that all novelists I know are in much the same predicament. Perhaps it will not last much longer & we shall be able to get back some sort of perspective; but at present, between the objection of the public to so called war-stories and the difficulty of the author to send his imagination backward, the situation is a bewildering one. As you know, I several times during the war, offered to replace "Literature" by other novels, which did not involve the study of such complex social conditions and dealt with people less affected by the war. As you preferred to wait for "Literature" these two tales, "Summer" and "The Marne,"[1] were given to other magazines, and

I continued to hope that I should see my way to going on with "Literature." At present, I can only suggest waiting a few more weeks and then writing to you definitely.

I have just written to tell Mr. Bridges how much I appreciate his careful corrections of the proofs of "In Morocco" which was a difficult book to revise.

Believe me

Yours very sincerely
Edith Wharton

Ms:FL

1. This short novel was published by Appleton earlier in 1919.

To Comte Arthur de Vogüé[1]

[October 1919]

Monsieur,

Madame Arthur de Vogüé m'a dit que vous voudriez quelques lettres pour les milieux littéraires et scientifiques de mon pays. J'ai prié mon ami Mr. Walter Berry de vous donner un mot pour quelques hommes de sciences; mais la nouvelle Amérique est si peu littéraire que je ne sais à qui vous adresser, sauf à mon ami Mr. John Chapman, lettré très fin et écrivain remarquable, qui sera certainement heureux de vous servir de guide.[2]

Ms:HL

Translation:

Dear Sir: Madame Arthur de Vogüé tells me that you would like some letters [of introduction] to the literary and scientific milieus of my country. I have asked my friend Mr. Walter Berry to give you a note to present to several men of science; but the new America is so little literary that I do not know to whom I should direct you, except to my friend Mr. John Chapman, a very fine man of letters and a remarkable writer, who will certainly be happy to act as your guide.

1. The present Comte Arthur de Vogüé was the son of Vicomte Melchior de Vogüé (1848–1910), novelist and author of several studies of the Russian novel. The grandfather, Vicomte Melchior de Vogüé, was the author of *Eglises de la Terre-Sainte* in 1860. See following letter to John Jay Chapman.

2. This letter was written on two sides of EW's calling card, with her name on it, and hence not signed.

To John Jay Chapman

Jean-Marie
St. Brice
October 8, 1919

Dear Mr. Chapman,

This letter will be brought to you by the young Comte de Vogüé, son of the Marquis de Vogüé, & grandson of the Marquis who wrote the great book on the Christian churches of Syria, & who was one of the most admirable & eminent Frenchmen of his day.

Monsieur de Vogüé, who shares in the love of literature & ideas which characterizes his family, is going on a visit to America, partly, I believe, to study financial questions. He wishes to be introduced into "des milieux littéraires et scientifiques," & I have had blushingly to explain that if there can be said to be the remains of a milieu littéraire in the U.S., you & I are its only valid survivors—since Mr. Howells, Mr. Brownell & their contemporaries can hardly be prodded out of their lairs! But I hope I exaggerate, & that you will be able to produce many younger specimens unknown to me, so I commit Monsieur de Vogüé to your hands, trusting you to do the best you can for our trade. He represents such a long & fine literary tradition that I should like him to see such faint traces of ours as survive.—It was a real regret not to see you all again before you started for home.

Yrs ever sincerely
Edith Wharton

Many messages to Mr. Brownell & Mr. Colby.[1]

Ms:HL

1. Probably Frank Moore Colby (1865–1925), professor of history (at Amherst and elsewhere) and an elegant essayist.

To Rutger B. Jewett[1]

Paris
January 5, 1920

Dear Mr. Jewett,

I am sending you by hand by tomorrow's steamer another 25,000 words of "The Age of Innocence," and also the final revision of Book 1. Two or three details important for the holding together of the story have been inserted in this revision and I have written my sister-in-law that you will be kind enough to send it to her at once so that she can make the necessary changes in the proofs. They are all slight but nevertheless important.

I was very much surprised to hear from my sister-in-law the other day that when she called at the Pictorial Review Office for proofs the lady representing Mr. Vance[2] told her that the book was evidently to be a long one and that the editor would evidently have to cut out some passages.

As you know, it was stipulated that the novel furnished to the Pictorial Review should not be less than 100.000 words long. I see no reason to expect that it will exceed this length and it may even fall short by 3 or 4.000 words. In any case as I am prepared to keep my part of the agreement I shall expect the Magazine to do the same and not to tamper with the text of my novel.

I have done really a super-human piece of work in writing, within a year, the best part of two long novels, entirely different in subject and treatment, simply to suit the convenience of the Editor of the Pictorial, and I cannot consent to have my work treated as if it were prose-by-the-yard.

I am sorry to trouble you with these details but I understand from my sister-in-law that you prefer to have my communications with the Review pass through your hands, and it is certainly much more satisfactory for me that they should do so, because I know that you will understand my point of view.

I am sorry to hear that Mrs. Bliss still looks so poorly. She cabled me at Christmas that Mr. Bliss was convalescent, so I hope they have both been able to leave for California.

With kindest wishes for the New Year, believe me,
    Yours sincerely[3]

Copy:BL

1. Rutger Bleecker Jewett, of old New York lineage, the very capable editor at D. Appleton and Co. He also acted as EW's agent in the securing of serial contracts.

2. Arthur Vance, the editor of the New York monthly *Pictorial Review*. The *Review* paid EW $18,000 for serial rights to *The Age of Innocence*, which began to appear in its pages in July 1920.

3. Here as elsewhere the carbon copy does not carry a signature.

To Bernard Berenson

                                        Le Bocage
                                        Hyères
                                        February 21, 1920

Dearest B.B.,

Of course I should have rejoiced in meeting the Raleighs, or any other of the Tatti visitors; but, alas, I see more & more the impossibility of getting away, at least of leaving France, this spring.—The work on Ste. Claire hasn't begun yet, & I must be here to superintend the clearing out of those "Paradon" gardens, planning next September's planting, & so on; then I must get back to Paris to look into the "travaux" at Jean-Marie, clear out 53 rue de V., & see about shipping (in the figurative U.S. sense) its contents to Hyères.

I talk, I know, as if I were moving into Caprarola, & putting, at the same time, the finishing touches to Chatsworth; & really, I believe those two feats might have been accomplished in 1913 more easily, & at no more expense, than getting settled in my two bicoques of Var & S. & O.[1] today.

Every domestic detail has become a kind of Matterhorn, over which one has to be roped & hooked & hoisted, with every chance of perishing in an avalanche or down a precipice on the way; & I see myself, for the next year, with a perpetual rope around my waist, & perpetual spikes in my soles.

Meanwhile, we have been stodging & basking here until a week ago, when the weather "spoilt itself," luckily for the country, which was parched, but regrettably for us, who begrudge every day without its déjeuner sur l'herbe.

Next week, a tribe of Parisians, Ganays, Ferromays, et al, announce themselves at the Golf Hôtel, & after that, for a while, we shall be "en tribu"; but it won't last long. R. Norton still hopes to get to Italy in April, but he is rather afraid that he may have to go back to London instead, for unforeseen board-meetings. He sends you many messages, & says that I am to tell you that he will write as soon as he sees any definite chance of going to see you. Anyhow, after March I expect to be here alone, unless one or two friends take pity on me.—I had hoped to lure you & Mary here next month, but have had no response to the eloquent appeal I addressed to her some time ago on that subject.

This garden is really enchanting, even viewed from the Tatti angle— I wish you'd come & see!—I hope Mary is less tired than when you last wrote. Being an uninterrupted grandmother for so long must be rather wearing.

Yrs ever affly EW

Yes, wasn't it French of Bonnard[2] not to write you himself about the Tiepolos? Walter is deep in the mystery, he writes.

Ms:VT

1. Var and Seine-et-Oise: the two provinces (the Maritime Alps and the section north of Paris where the Seine and the Oise rivers conjoin) where EW was establishing her two new "bicoques" (shacks).

2. Abel Bonnard (born 1883), French poet and novelist.

To Bernard Berenson

53 Rue de Varenne
May 23, 1920

Dearest B.B.,

Having finally arrived here, I had just taken my "most beautiful feather" in hand to send you my belated news when Charlie informed me with firmness that you were expected the next day at the Ritz!!—I dropped my pen, transmitted the glad tidings to the "Unsers"—& was told yesterday by le dit Du Bos (after a protracted dive into the depths of his abysmal serviette) that he had made a mistake, & Mary had written "in a month" & not "tomorrow"!

Well—I can't say it's a disappointment. Age has taught me that the *time* is almost as important as the place in encounters with the loved one; & to deal with any one worth while with my lungs still full of the first plunge into Paris would be a painful task. I had been so drawn back into the Urwald by my quiet summer & quietest winter that I still splutter & gurgle, & wish I could drown & have it over. Whereas in a month I shall be safe at Jean Marie (looking, oh, so sweet this spring!), & can steal in & meet you under the Laurent tree, or in one of your other antres. So you see—

Meanwhile I have to tell you that after I had been torn shrieking from my beloved Hyères I motored north with the faithful St. André through divine weather & via enchanting places. Our étapes were: Montpellier, St Guilhem le Désert & St Martin de Londres, Nîmes, Issoire, Le Puy, St Paulien, Clermont, Mozac, Riom, La Charité, St. Benoît s/ Loire & Germigny-les-Près. I don't mean to say that these were our "stopping" places in the hotel sense, but rather our spiritual stages. You see it was a Romanesque pilgrimage, chiefly planned for St A.'s benefit; but I had been struggling for years to get to St Guilhem le Désert, & that & St Martin (both of the best), & Mozac & St Benoît & Germigny were new to me. As for the spring scenery in Auvergne, I dare boast of it even to Tuscans!—

By the way, R. Norton turned up again at Hyères a week before I left, full of the joys of his sojourn at the Tatti, & of your kindness & Mary's. He has now gone back to England, but promises to reappear in July, when we are planning a pilgrimage to St Benoît & Germigny. Shall you be here then?

Paris is simply awful—a kind of continuous earthquake of motor busses, trams, lorries, taxis & other howling & swooping & colliding engines, with hundreds of thousands of U.S. citizens rushing about in them & tumbling out of them at one's door—&, through it all, the same people placidly telephoning one to come to tea.—I am "sensée être" on the move to Jean-Marie—as indeed I shall be in a week, I hope—& have so far seen only Walter, the Tylers, Charlie, & John Hugh. The fact that Rosa is in Austria makes it easy to lie low, as she is almost my only remaining "Social Welfare Centre."

The country—the banlieue even—is divine, & my humble potager gushes with nightingales. The heaps of rubble & various kitchen-midden have been cleared away, & the little place looks really welcoming. May I see you there soon!—

Charlie tells me that you were not well when Mary wrote. I hope you have recovered, but do let me have a line from one or the other. And will you please thank Mary, to whom no doubt I owe Mr. Pearsall Smith's little book,[1] just arrived?—Give her my fond love, & aurevoir to you both before long.

Yrs ever affly
EW

I have also seen the returning W. Gays, whose picture of New York fairly kept me awake with terror.

Ms:VT

1. *More Trivia*.

To Bernard Berenson

Château Ste Claire
Hyères
December 12, 1920

Glowing indeed, dearest B.B., & fragrant as incense, are the coals you have heaped on my unworthy head! I had sworn to have a letter on its way the week after you sailed; & here have I sat, mute & unresponsive, while you were storing up kind thoughts of me, & finding time to put them on paper.

The reason is the natural one: my tiresome heart (pump, not affective organ) "flanched" again, as it does now whenever I over-exert, & I got down here really dead-beat. My little secretary[1] was taking a holiday, & business letters kept piling up on me at such a rate, after I arrived, that I cd. only deal with them by abandoning my friends—which I did!

All this time, I was yearning over you both, & longing for news of you, & knowing that I didn't deserve it; & getting it, luckily, from Minnie & from Josephine G.,[2] who both told me of your hideous voyage, & of your looking & seeming so well, quand même.

And then came your dear letter, & nearly drew tears from these flinty eyes! I *did* so want "The Age" to be taken not as a "costume piece" but as a "simple & grave" story of two people trying to live up to something that was still "felt in the blood" at that time; & you, & the few other people whose opinion I care about, have made me feel that perhaps I have. Thank you so much for taking the trouble to tell me your impressions of the book.

It's paralyzing to try to tell you of my life here, so other-dimensional is it to what you are plunged in. I found Robert N. waiting for me, with half a dozen water-colours, chiefly done at Aix, that I think you would greatly approve of. We are still at the hotel, though I hope the address I have given will be a reality in another week. I spend my mornings at Ste Claire, watching how "alles grünt und blüht" in a garden hardly six months old. R.N. goes off with his sketching things, we meet at lunch, & in the p.m. usually take one of the tramps in the maquis that you know. The evenings are devoted to tramps in another maquis: "exploring," as Mr. Collins would put it, a heap of new books that keep pouring in from Bain & Affolter, with Gilchrist's Blake[3] (we'd neither of us read it) as a background.—Those are the hours when, again & again, we cry: "Oh, for B.B.!"—And we absolutely *ache* to know if you've read Max's "No. 2, The Pines," his perfectly exquisite reminiscence of the old Swinburne & the old Watts-Dunton at Putney.[4] I don't send it, because you probably saw it when it came out in the Fortnightly, & if not, it's in his new vol. of essays, which you can get là bas more quickly than I can send it.—Then I'm having a private gloat (before we turn to it together) over Santayana's new book.[5] I'd read the James & the Royce (where?), but the other chaps are new to me. "The Moral Background" is precious—& oh, what a tone, what standards!—What else? A really striking, brilliant yet impartial book on Mme de Maintenon, by my friend (Taine's grand-niece) Mme St René Taillandier.

A dull & laboured Seillière on George Sand, whom he doesn't begin to be equal to— And now comes Barrett Wendell's fat book,[6] which he has kindly sent me. I haven't had time to take more than a glance (at the bibliography—they tell so much in such books!), and am saddened to see that, in addressing Harvard students and the general reader in the U.S., he gives only books that have been translated into English, & that La Cité Antique[7] figures as "The Ancient City." All this seems to me terribly pre-masticated & primaire, & so odd as coming from *him*. But I suppose he's subdued to what he works in.

Of course when we get "up to the villa" our literary excursions will be much enlarged, for some 2000 faithful friends await us there. The work has been delayed—of course—but the "best is yet to be," as you so beautifully say of my efforts in fiction: that is, the heat, light & water are "on," & the cleaning & arranging begin next week.—Hyères, as usual, is a delicious desert. Our only playmates are Sir George & Lady Prothero, at a nearby hotel, here for health (his), & obviously pining for London; & my former friend, Philomène de Lévis-Mirepoix[8] (the duke's sister), who ran away with Jean de Subersac before the war. She has bought a little villa here, where she means to live quietly with her little girl & her mother, the dowager Duchess; & she will be a great addition to our little group.—Codman is to look in next week on his way to Cannes, & Gaillard Lapsley comes to Ste Claire for his Xmas vacation—& Adele Essex announces that she's coming to take a look at us in February!

Meanwhile the heavenly beauty & the heavenly quiet enfold me, & I feel that this really is the Cielo della Quieta to which the soul aspires after its stormy voyage. Please look toward it steadfastly through the social uproar, & come & bask in it in March.

Give my best love to Mary, & tell her that I count on her too, after grandchild-land.—I can hardly stop writing, now I've started, so much is still to say—but most of all how affly & faithfully I am yr

EW

When you see Barrett Wendell do tell him how pleased I was at his sending me his book. I'll write to him as soon as I've read it.

Did you read the remarkably good article on Goethe (his new life)⁹ in the Lit. Supp?—Sir G.P. doesn't know who this new hand is. Fancy Lord Haldane's translating dunkles Drang as dark pressure.

Oh, Lord, I was almost forgetting to tell you that, last week, the Académie Française gave me the Prix Montyon (gold medal) for Virtue!!—*Textuel*. Well, it's not a bad thing to have—at 58. It was for oeuvres de guerre—not private ones.

Ms:VT

1. Mlle. Jeanne Duprat.

2. Josephine Griswold, née Houghteling; the mother of Cass Canfield, the publisher, by her first marriage to Augustus Canfield. Her second husband, Frank Gray Griswold, was a merchant and sportsman, the author of many books about sports on land and water.

3. *The Life of William Blake* (1907), by Alexander Gilchrist.

4. Max Beerbohm's essay "No. 2, The Pines" was contained in his volume of essays *And Even Now* in 1920. It is a reminiscence of Beerbohm's visit in the spring of 1899 to the house in Putney where Algernon Charles Swinburne lived for his last thirty years (he died in 1909). The property belonged to Theodore Watts-Dunton (1832–1914), the lawyer turned writer who brought Swinburne there to rescue him from seriously ill health.

5. *Character and Opinion in the United States* (1920), by George Santayana. It contains reminiscences of Santayana's former Harvard colleagues, William James and Josiah Royce, and describes "the moral background" of the American cultural scene as compounded of New England Calvinism and the conditions of the frontier.

6. Barrett Wendell's book, *The Traditions of European Literature from Homer to Dante* (1920), was in fact taken from his lectures in a popular comparative literature course at Harvard.

7. *La Cité Antique*: a seminal work (1864) by French historian Fustel de Coulanges (1830–1899) on the evolution of cities in Greece and under the Roman Empire.

8. Philomène de Lévis-Mirepoix had lived with her ducal family next door to EW on the Rue de Varenne before the war. Now in her early thirties, the shyly charming Philomène had been the author, in 1912, of a delicate work of autobiographical fiction, *Cité des Lampes*.

9. *Goethe* (1920, 2 vols.), by P. Hume Brown. It carried a preface by Richard Burdon Haldane, who also revised portions of the work. "Dark pressure" seems an acceptable translation for "dunkles Drang."

To Mary Cadwalader Jones

Sainte-Claire

December 26, 1920

Dearest Minnie— Thanks a lot for the joint Xmas cable, & for your last good letter, of Dec. 10th, which came a day or two before Xmas.

I'm sorry to hear that things are again not quite smooth in your double household; but I hadn't much hope that my letter would have a permanent effect. You *must* be alone in your own house after this; there is no other solution & it ought to be possible, if our financial affairs continue to improve.—I had a nice letter from Trix, & I think she's really sorry not to come, & I'm really disappointed. But people must work out their own plans as they think best, & from the health point of view I do believe it would have been unwise to come out in Jany, & go back to the rigours of a New York March.

We moved in *at last* two days before Xmas ("we" being Robert N., Gaillard Lapsley, & the faithful household), & yesterday was the happiest Xmas I have spent in many a long year.

I can wish no old woman of my age a better one!

The little house is delicious, so friendly & comfortable, & full of sun & air; but what overwhelms us all—though we thought we knew it— is the endless beauty of the view, or rather the views, for we look south, east & west, "miles & miles," & our quiet-coloured end of evening presents us with a full moon standing over the tower of the great Romanesque church just below the house, & a sunset silhouetting the "Iles d'Or" in black on a sea of silver.

It is good to grow old—as well as to die—"in beauty"; & the beauty of this little place is inexhaustible.

Yesterday we had the divinest Riviera weather, & as we sat on the terrace in the sun taking our coffee after luncheon a joint groan of deliverance escaped us at the thought of London, New York & Paris!

I had a blow last week with which Trix will deeply sympathize. There was a cold mistral, followed by two nights of severe frost (20 Fahrenheit), & *all* the gardens from Marseilles to Mentone were wiped out. My terraces were just beginning to be full of bursting sprouting things, & it was really sickening to see the black crapy rags which, a few hours before, were heliotropes, "anthémises," tradescantia, plumbago, arums, geraniums—all the stock-in-trade of a Riviera garden—dangling woefully from the denuded terraces. The orange trees were severely frozen, & some of the old ones may be lost; & even my splendid old caroube trees, which had put on their glorious dense shining foliage in October, are all frizzled & brown. Eucalyptus & pepper-trees are shrivelled up, & the huge prickly pears that were the pride of the place are falling apart like paper flowers the day after a procession. Even the native wildflowers, acanthus, fennel and valerian, hung limp from their roots, & are only just picking up.

The poor peasants have lost acres of artichokes & early potatoes— almost all that the floods had spared—& the gardens are a sickening sight.

I had a magnificent climbing buddleya which covered one of my highest terrace walls, & was just preparing to hang out its hundreds of yellow plumes—it is as bare as a ship's rigging in a gale! And so the story goes—& the only consolation people can find is that "it hasn't been known since 1870."

Meanwhile normal weather has come back, & my bulbs are all sprouting, & this prodigal nature will repair things in a year—except that some trees may be lost.

I have left hardly any space in which to thank you for sending flowers for poor Harry Munroe's funeral.[1] *How much* do I owe you please?—I have cabled & written to Alice, who must be heart broken.

Poor George M. is pretty ill too, & has gone to Pau for the whole winter.—

I'm so glad to hear that Elizabeth Hoyt is coming so soon, and bringing me a wonderful Island scrap-basket. How dear of you!—I enclose my island Mission gift, with much love to you all.

EW.

Ms:BL

1. Harry Munroe, of Munroe and Co., the bank in Place Vendôme, Paris, where EW had made her financial transactions, and which she used as a mailing address for many years.

To Dr. Beverley Robinson

Sainte Claire

January 21, 1921

Dear Dr. Robinson,

The news of Anna's death[1] comes as a great shock to me, for I had not heard of her illness. Since I have given up Paris, & live entirely in the country, I sometimes miss a letter or a newspaper containing news of friends at home, & thus remain for weeks in ignorance of what has happened to them.

As you know, Anna's presence is bound up with my earliest memories. My father & mother were always devoted to her, & her sweet face is a vivid part of my little-girl picture of our life in New York— But I think everybody who knew her loved her, & she will leave as sweet an image in many hearts. It is a great comfort in sorrow to know that one's friends understand one's loss & share it, & this comfort you will have more than most. I hope it will help you a little through the cruel days of loneliness that come after such a parting at the end of so long a companionship.

My sympathy goes to you all—

Yours ever affly
    Edith Wharton

Ms:BL

1. The former Anna Foster. Her engagement to Dr. Robinson in the summer of 1874 was the occasion for EW's first surviving letter.

To Mary Cadwalader Jones

Sainte Claire
February 17, 1921

Dearest Minnie,

Your letter announcing the signature of the contract with Shubert[1] has just come, & I must give you an immediate hug.—Did ever any lucky author have such a business-manager before, I wonder? As you know, I had no hopes of anything of the kind coming my way; & your news was a real surprise.

I am particularly pleased that Miss Akins[2] intends to dramatize the book. I hope you will tell her so; & also that she will send me "Déclassée" if it has been published.

I am very anxious about the staging & dressing. I could do every stick of furniture & every rag of clothing myself, for every detail of that far-off scene was indelibly stamped on my infant brain. I am so much afraid that the young actors will be "Summit Collar" athletes, with stern jaws & shaven lips, instead of gentlemen. Of course they ought all to have moustaches, & not tooth brush ones, but curved & slightly twisted at the ends. They should wear dark grey frock-coats & tall hats, & always buttonhole-violets by day, a gardenia in evening dress. White waistcoats with their evening clothes, & pumps, *I think*. But you will remember all this as well as I do.—As for their "façons" & their language, since you say that Miss Akins knows European society, please tell her that a N.Y. drawing-room of my childhood was far more like a London one—a du Maurier one of old-fashioned gentlefolk—than anything that modern N.Y. can give her. Above all, beg her to avoid slang & Americanisms, & tell her that English was then the language spoken by American ladies & gentlemen—since she is too young, I'm sure, to have known those happy days herself. Few people nowadays know that many of the young men of our day (in N.Y.) were educated in English Universities, & that English tutors & governesses were frequent & that *no* girl went to a school!* If she does not know this—& does not (equally) keep away from that grotesque stage invention of "Southern chivalry" —she will never get the right atmosphere.

How thrilling if Doris Keane[3] should do Ellen! How I wish I had seen her act. Have you any idea when they mean to bring it out? And, oh, how odd that no one should know that there is a play in "The Reef" all ready to be pulled out!—

Thanks for the revised copy of "The Age." I have written to Jewett suggesting that I should write a preface for the next edition, explaining under what difficulties the book was written, as regards revising & proof-correcting, & also stating my theory as to the writing of "historical" novels, & the small importance of anachronisms.—

I am glad that the book gave Mr. Pollen so much pleasure. It is a small return for the thrill that his naval articles used to give me in the dark years.[4]

I send you a little group on the terrace.

Best love, & all gratitude again.
    E.W.

I've written to ask Walter to arrange about the power of attorney, & will send it as soon as possible.

*And that older women did not wear pince-nez & white false fronts—

Ms:BL

1. For the production of a stage version of *The Age of Innocence*.

2. Zoë Akins (1886–1958), a talented playwright (*The Greeks Had a Word for It* in 1930), did not in fact dramatize *The Age of Innocence*, but would adapt EW's *The Old Maid* at a later date.

3. Doris Keane (1881–1945), an American actress known primarily for her performance as the heroine (an Italian opera singer) in Edward Sheldon's *Romance*, which ran uninterruptedly for five years (1913–1918).

4. Arthur J. H. Pollen (1886–1937), an expert in naval warfare, collected these articles in *The Navy in Battle* in 1918.

To Bernard Berenson

Pavillon Colombe
St Brice-Sous-Forêt
June 7 [1921]

At last the time & the place for writing to you, Dearest B.B.—the first quiet minute I have had since my arrival, without being too utterly tired to make use of it.

Oh, this banlieue! I thought it would be my salvation, but in some respects it is more fatiguing than Paris, for when people come to luncheon (the French, that is) they stay to tea, when an American contingent usually arrives, & the bean-feast is prolonged till 7.30.—Sometimes, when they are congenial (to me & to each other) I actually like it; but even then it leaves me pounded to a jelly. And the other times—when, for instance, poor St A. explains for the 100th time why he can't have a telephone, & how all his friends try to avoid seeing him—then, oh then, the thread that holds me to life seems so tenuous that I rather expect to wake up the next morning among the Blessed.—You have been going through much the same thing, no doubt; but dealt with à deux it's *much less* than half as bad; & if I had a fond husband or admiring daughter to act as buffer—well, all I can say is, I pity 'em!—

Thank you so much for the German & Italian book-addresses, & also, & most particularly, for the beautiful book-presents—the last of which has not yet arrived; happily, I could almost say, since it might tear me from Schraube, who is absorbing.—By the way, have you read Mâle's[1] delightful article on the symbolism of Romanesque sculpture, in the June 1st Revue de Paris? How he does pull off that kind of thing—& his books are so chaotic.

The last Proust[2] is really amazing; but I think he has fourvoyé himself in a subject that can't lead anywhere in art, & belongs only to pathology. What a pity he didn't devote himself to the abnormalities of the normal, which offer a wide enough & untilled enough field, heaven knows.

Apparently every self-respecting American magazine has refused "The Old Maid" on the ground of immorality![3] I suppose one of the periodical (in both sense) waves of pruriency has set in.—But meanwhile Columbia has awarded me the—Pulitzer!!—$1000—prize for the best novel of the year.⁴ The which tainted money will come in particularly handy to polish off the gardens at Ste Claire.

Do you know what has become of, or happened to, Geoffrey? He wrote me a month ago, asking if he could come to see me for a few days on his way to England, on or about June 8th. I said, yes, of course, & as he was afraid of not being able to fix a date long in advance, I asked him to wire me later.—Then people began to ask to be invited; & hearing nothing from Geoffrey, I wrote again, about ten days ago, asking him to wire a date if he could. Still no answer; & the 8th is tomorrow, & Mary Hunter descends upon me on the 13th, as I couldn't leave her in doubt any longer!

G. said nothing about Sybil's coming, & so, as Rodier would say, "neither I."—But as he seems to have vanished, it's not of much consequence either way.

I suppose your visitors' tide is beginning to recede, & I hope Mary is getting a rest, & more chance to enjoy her garden. Here the tribe increaseth like Abou Ben Ahmed's, or a good deal more so, & it looks like an all-summer season.

R. N. writes mopingly from England, where he has hardly had a ray of sun since his return, while here we have hardly had a drop of rain. He returns in a fortnight, to see—Hipwell!

Well, my Dears, goodbye till the next letter.—I languish & pine for you & the library, & the Tatti in general. But the Dr. is not much pleased with my heart, & wants an enormous more period of resting before I do much travelling. And I know he's right.

Sur ce, je vous embrasse tendrement.

    EW.

Do you think Mary cd collect the 1500 lire (wasn't it) for the armoire Geoffrey & Mr. Pinsent made—& sold—for me? It would help to pay Italian books. *I* paid them as soon as it was finished—I think Mary said it adorned "Mr. Strong's" spare-room.

Ms:VT

1. Emile Mâle (1862–1956), the distinguished French art historian. The article probably became part of his book of 1922 on the religious art of twelfth-century France, and the origins of medieval iconography.

2. *Sodome et Gomorrhe I* (1921).

3. The editor of the *Ladies' Home Journal* said of *The Old Maid*: "It's a bit too vigorous for us." The spokesman for the *Metropolitan Magazine* declared it to be powerful but too unpleasant. Referring to this, in a letter to Rutger Jewett of May 23, EW said: "Have the readers of the Metropolitan never read 'The Scarlet Letter' or 'Adam Bede' to mention only the two first classics that come to my mind? And how about my own 'Summer'?"

4. The jury at Columbia University, which sponsored the award, consisted of Robert Morss Lovett, Stuart Sherman, and Hamlin Garland. The Pulitzer Prize in fiction was given annually "for the American novel which shall best present the wholesome atmosphere of American life and the highest standard of American manners and manhood." See letter of August 6, 1921, to Sinclair Lewis.

To W. Morton Fullerton

Sainte-Claire

[June 12, 1921]

Cher ami—yes, "Fumée"[1] had quite vanished. Thanks for restoring it: such a tribute was worth salvaging—though I was *not* the lady you read the book with "years ago."

Ste Claire is no mere parterre of heaven; it is the very "cielo della quieta" that Dante (whom we did read together) found above the Seventh Heaven.[2] You must come & see it when you do the second volume of "Terres Françaises." For rapturous details I refer you to Mr. Brunhes, who was here the other day, & who talked of you. He will tell you that I've found the Great Good Place.

Amitiés
    EW

Ms:HL

1. Turgenev's novel *Smoke*.
2. *Paradiso*, XXX, 52.

To Gaillard Lapsley

Pavillon Colombe
St. Brice-Sous-Forêt
July 5, 1921

Dearest Gaillard,

Deep calleth unto deep—& my "aboutissement" is as unplumbed as yours (though, thank goodness, they're not mentally estranging!)

But I must tell you the joy it is to have you "name the day"— Open arms will receive you here on Sept 1st—Percy hasn't "taken a date" (Mr. Wilson Jr.[1] would say that my English is growing more & more corrupt), but he held out the hope, some time since, that he would be arriving about that time—the which would indeed be luscious!

If Eunice gave you half the messages I charged her with, she will have done a good deal of talking the day she lunched with you. You'll find her, I'm sure, looking remarkably well, & in great spirits. I wish Walter had been with her.

Mr. Ed. Wilson Jr. speaks words that are as balm to me, for it has dawned upon him that perhaps satire *is* my weapon— But I wonder if he's not right when he says I can't write English any more?—I shall take up my pen with a distrustful hand tomorrow at 8 a.m.— Dear Gaillard, but I *shall* be glad to see you! Yrs ever, EW.

I continue, at intervals, to transmit your homages to the Duchess & Mme de Lévis, who, de leur côté, continue to reciprocate.

I've had Sally & Lily N. staying with me. They're in great form, & going to England in 2 or 3 weeks.

Ms:BL

1. Edmund Wilson (1895–1972), who at this early stage in his literary career had "Junior" affixed to his name. In his review of *The Age of Innocence*, Wilson expressed much admiration, but said that the style seemed awkward in some places.

To Sinclair Lewis[1]

Pavillon Colombe
August 6, 1921

My dear Mr. Lewis,

Your letter touched me very deeply; & I should have told you so sooner if it hadn't gone to America (where I have not been since the war), & then travelled back to me here.

What you say is so kind, so generous & so unexpected, that I don't know where to begin to answer. It is the first sign I have ever had— literally—that "les jeunes" at home had ever read a word of me. I had long since resigned myself to the idea that I was regarded by you all as the --- say the Mrs. Humphry Ward of the Western Hemisphere; though at times I wondered why. Your book & Susan Lenox[2] (unexpurgated) have been the only things out of America that have made me cease to despair of the republic—of letters; so you can imagine what a pleasure it is to know that you have read *me*, & cared, & understood. It gives me a "Nunc Dimittis" feeling—or would, if I hadn't still about a hundred subjects to deal with!

As for the Columbia Prize, the kind Appletons have smothered me in newspaper commentary; & when I discovered that I was being rewarded—by one of our leading Universities—for uplifting American morals,[3] I confess I *did* despair.

Subsequently, when I found the prize shd really have been yours, but was withdrawn because your book (I quote from memory) had "offended a number of prominent persons in the Middle West,"[4] disgust was added to despair.—Hope returns to me, however, with your letter, & with the enclosed article, just received.—Some sort of standard *is* emerging from the welter of cant & sentimentality, & if two or three of us are gathered together, I believe we can still save fiction in America.

I wish I could talk to you of all this. Is there no chance of your coming to Paris? I'm only half an hour away— If not, let me at least tell you again how many hopes your book & your letter have waked in me. Believe me, Yrs very sincerely

E. Wharton

Ms:BL

1. Sinclair Lewis (1885–1951) had recently published *Main Street*.

2. *Susan Lenox: Her Fall and Rise*, by David Graham Phillips (1867–1911), published posthumously in 1917; the story of a young small-town woman who passes through various erotic misadventures, including two stints as a prostitute, and survives the murder of her patron and friend before becoming a successful actress on Broadway.

3. See letter to Berenson, June 7, 1921.

4. The jury had in fact chosen *Main Street* for the prize, but the trustees of Columbia rejected the choice on the grounds that the novel gave offense in certain quarters, and awarded the prize instead to *The Age of Innocence*.

To Bernard Berenson

Pavillon Colombe
August 20, 1921

Dearest B.B.— Your letter has just come (only 6 days from Vallombrosa to St Brice!), & I must send an answer flying back, if only for the pleasure of distracting my pen from its dreary "secretarial" jobs.

My little secretary is away, I have found it impossible to replace her, & needless to say every lame duck in my barn-yard has been having "complications," & all the morning, day after day, is taken up with weary weary correspondence. So, just for a change, I fly to Saltino.

Divine place! My two visits there have left in my memory a vision of majestic trees & springy turf for which I've pined ever since. Some day we must all be there together.—And, oh, the "explorations"! How I long to join them!—Soon I shall have a free foot (I mean, shall be book-free), & I swear I won't put myself in chains again till I've been back to the Tatti, & you've been to Spain & Morocco with me—

The book isn't new—dear, no!—I interrupted it last winter to write "The Old Maid," but, as a matter of fact, I began it two years ago, or more, & have been hard at it for a year. It's called "The Glimpses of the Moon," & tries to picture the adventures of a young couple who believe themselves to be completely affranchis & up-to-date, but are continually tripped up by obsolete sensibilities, & discarded ideals.—A difficult subject, which of course seemed the easiest in the world when I began it.

Percy is here now, exquisitely humane, human, calm, luminous—so more & more satisfactory that I bless him for being my friend & wanting to be with me. Next week we pick up G. Lapsley at Rouen, & motor down with him to spend two days at Etretat with Bessy L. (to whom I will give your message), taking in as many monuments as possible on the way.—Yesterday Percy & I went out to St Cloud to see Charlie, who is much better, & who is coming to spend a day here soon.

Percy & G. L. will be with me for several weeks, I hope, & then go to England to stay with Norts, John Hugh & Mary Hunter—toward the 20th of Sept.—Oh, that our paths might somehow cross before Egypt! Aren't you coming to Paris first?—

My fond love to you both

Edith—

Ms:VT

To Elisina Tyler

Pavillon Colombe
September 14, 1921

Dearest Elisina,

As you have so kindly acted as intermediary between Georges Charlot & me, I venture to send you this letter before posting it to him.

When I engaged him, the agreement was that he was to accept whatever work in house or garden he was called on to do when not needed by Franklin.[1] I told him when he was here that I would think over what work he would be given, & let him know. I wished first to talk over the matter with White, who is here at present. He & Franklin have decided that a daily job at fixed hours will be best, as it will avoid possible tiraillements between house & garage, & so I have written, as you see, that I will give him the charge of the chauffage central in the house & dépendances.

I hope this will be all right, but I tremble with fear nowadays when

I engage a new servant, so I thought I shd like you to be au courant, in case he comes to you, & tells you that the *only* thing he won't do is to manage the chauffage!—Thank you d'avance, & excuse my bothering you with this. I engaged "en extra" for 2 months a young maid (bonne) who had been for 6 years with Mme Jean de Pange, to take my 2d housemaid's place. She arrived in a sleeveless dress, to her knees, & when Louisa[2] handed her her cap & apron, said: "Moi—mettre cela? J'aime mieux m'en aller!"—which she did, by the next train, though she had changed her mind by that time, & begged to be kept!—I want to avoid similar surprises with Charlot.

Eric writes that he is just off, & will meet Peter at Buda—[3]

I hug myself when I think you're coming back to Paris.

Yrs ever   Edith—

Ms:WRT

1. Franklin, taken on before the war, was acting as chauffeur and handyman.

2. Louisa Butler, a young Englishwoman, personal maid to EW under Elise's supervision.

3. Royall Tyler—"Peter" to his intimates—was serving as Deputy Commissioner of the American Finance Commission in Budapest.

To Sinclair Lewis

Hôtel de Crillon
Paris
November 28, 1921

Dear Mr. Lewis,

I am a little dizzy!

No one has ever wanted to dedicate a book to me before[1]—& I'm so particularly glad that, now it's happened, the suggestion comes from the author of Main Street.

Yes—of course!

I'm glad, too, to have your address, for, in the throes of leaving St. Brice, I mislaid your letter, & couldn't remember where to send my friend Percy Lubbock's book, "The Craft of Fiction,"[2] which is full of interesting & suggestive things for people of our trade.

I've written to Bain to send it to you at the Hôtel de Russie.

With kind remembrances to Mrs. Lewis,

Yrs sincerely
     E. Wharton

I'm off to Hyères next week.

Ms:BL

1. Lewis proposed dedicating his new novel, *Babbitt*, to EW.
2. *The Craft of Fiction* (1921) examines and honors the narrative methods of Henry James, Flaubert, and Tolstoy, among others.

To Gaillard Lapsley

Hôtel de Crillon
Paris
November 29, 1921

Dearest Gaillard,

I'm glad those reservations to the coast are booked, though I wish it had been sooner!

I'm off on the 5th, thank the Lord—for the lingering summer, here too, has turned into something so grey & glacial & Stygian that I marvel more & more that human beings can live in it.

I've been here for a fortnight, & it hasn't been a gay one. A week ago, Cook had a slight—very *very* slight—stroke! He has recovered wonderfully, & the Drs say he may not have another for 20 years—or ever. But—he must never drive a motor again!

No one, more than you, will feel the tragedy this is to me, & will be to my poor Cook when he knows. At present, he knows he must take a rest of 4 or 5 months, but gradually he must be prepared for the final Entsagung[1]— To put the crowning touch of irony to this all-too-human event, he had just ordered a new Panhard for me, after years of second-hand cars—a new Panhard with *all* the last tips & dodges & wrinkles, which he was to drive down to Hyères on Dec. 15.

I'm in a state of such sadness, a sadness so full of the remembrance of our epic randonnées, that I can't say more.

One thing has touched him greatly. All the "pals" whom he has driven have been in to see him & cheer him up.—

On top of this calamity, I've had a small grievance in the form of a flu which has kept me shut up in my ultra-expensive rooms here, much as I was in London, at the Ritz, when I read the Cambridge Mediaeval through, & fed on gruel—but when Henry & Howard were there to cheer me!

Well—I rejoice that I shall soon see the sun, & see you, dear friend —& that, "materially," I can look after my poor Cook for all his days.

But, oh, the "last rides together"!

I'm glad you're bearing up. For goodness' sake, snuff up eucalyptus, & keep your fire going hard.

Yrs ever so,
   E

MS:BL

1. Renunciation.

To Bernard Berenson

Sainte-Claire
February 21, 1922

Dearest B.B., I sent Mary a line just now by Philomène, but I entrust this to the post in order to say a word about that delightful being of the kind not usually put in hand-carried letters.

The more you see of her, the more you will both like her; & both you & Mary can do so much to carry on the kind of mental training which you saw her need of last year, that I want to give you a reminder. The pity is that, as you saw, her charming eager helpless intelligence has not been left empty, but filled with third-rate flashy rubbish, of the kind that most enervates the mental muscles—"occultism," the Sar Peladan, mediums ("after all, there *is* something in it"), vital fluids, & all the lyre—or the lie! When R. Norton suggested her reading something about Egypt, she refused, on the ground that she wished to keep herself "uninfluenced," which means, that she's too lazy to fix her attention. In short, there is hardly a vicious sentimentalism, or a specious pretext for mental laziness, that doesn't run off her tongue. But something *can* be done—& is still, I'm sure, worth doing!—Above all, please ask Mary not to befuddle her with Freudianism & all its jargon. She'd take to it like a duck to—sewerage. And what she wants is to develop the *conscious*, & not grub after the sub-conscious. She wants to be taught first to see, to attend, to reflect.

All this, you had already observed, & will remark again in the first 24 hours; but I write more particularly to ask you to warn Mary, for another push toward the occult will topple her over once for all into the real Lotus Land, which is the boundless Land of Tosh.

How I wish I were coming! Instead, I'm trying to get up a Hyères season for Walter, who arrives shortly.

Percy is here, & better than ever.

Yrs ever so   EW.

Ms:VT

To Gaillard Lapsley

Sainte-Claire
May 13, 1922

Dearest Gaillard— Our habit of taking each other for granted for long intervals of time is not without its advantages for two "busy people" (as they say chez nous); but I now find that the privation, on *my* side, has lasted too long, & that I want to see your beautiful if unintelligible script again.

The interval this time has been unusually long—so much so that I've taken my smallest note-paper, in despair at the impossibility of crowding into the biggest a quarter of what I want to say—what with crimes

& scandals—& the new Prousts![1] Speaking of the latter, by the way, the day before the 3 vols. appeared I had a letter from an unknown American admirer (apparently possessed of a photograph of me) who finds "my face *irasistable*," & wants to "kiss my eyes into smiles, & draw some of the sadness from my mouth." As the writer is a lady it seemed to me singularly fitting that this frank expression of good will shd coincide with the new gomorrhas. It shows that, once more, our country is unsurpassed in efficiency.

I think one of the reasons why I didn't want to write was Percy. Has he said anything to you about his sojourn here? It was one of the most trying experiences I have ever undergone. His gloom was unrelieved, & as he has simplified social life to the point of totally eliminating the feelings of others from his mind, he treated me & my other guests to some six weeks of a morose & unbroken silence. Really, & seriously, it was alarming—besides being very fatiguing. When he & I were alone it was no better, & so often, when one came into the room suddenly, and he lifted that terrible *some-one else's* face of which you once spoke, the sight of it gave me a cold chill. He never spoke to me of his state of mind, or made any allusion to it in writing afterward, & I have wondered since whether he was in the least aware of what he contributed to my winter in the way of gloom—I only hope it was the remainder of a neglected jaundice, & not the result of being too much with Arthur Benson!—

And you? How are you? Where did you go for Easter? What are your summer plans? You *must* write soon! Everyone has left here but Philomène & her mother, who are off to Salsomaggiore for the cure next month. Minnie Jones has been with me since the middle of March, but has been away for 10 days "doing" Provence. She gets back tonight, & we shall motor slowly northward in about 10 days.

R. Norton is in Paris, where he has been having a small water-colour show. He returns to Rye in a fortnight, & I may possibly go to stay with him in August or September. Meanwhile I'm hard at work finishing "A Son at the Front," & doing last gardening things here—

I suppose you have heard that Sally Norton has had a very severe operation for tumour. Apparently there is no fear of cancer, but very bad & deep "adhesions," & I shd say she was not yet out of danger, though she is at home again.[2] Her illness seems to have had the happy effect of smoothing things out between her & Liz, who has been devoted to her, every one tells me, & to whom she used to be rather relentless at times. Have you tackled Proust? I'm *greatly* disappointed—Alas! Alas!

Do write soon. Yrs ever affly
　　EW

Ms:BL

1. *Sodome et Gomorrhe II.*
2. Sara Norton would die before the end of 1922.

To Bernard Berenson

Pavillon Colombe
St Brice
August 23, 1922

Dearest B.B.— I meant to thank you long ago for your delightful last letter, & your good words about my book[1]—but I have been tangled up in endless things, as usual. It's only at Hyères that I own myself.

My poor brother Harry died ten days ago. It is no present loss, since he had not been allowed by his wife to see me for nearly 10 years, & the only two occasions on which I succeeded in breaking through the barriers produced only a tragic impression of some one enslaved & silenced.

But he was the dearest of brothers to all my youth, & as our separation was produced by no quarrel, & no ill-will of any sort on my part, but only by a kind of mute subterranean determination (apparently) to separate him from all his family, my feeling is one of sadness at the years of lost affection & companionship, & all the reawakened memories of youth.

I am glad you liked my tale, which is a very slight thing, of course; & especially that you like the Clarissa talk. I have just finished "A Son at the Front," as to which you gave me such helpful encouragement—& I think you will like the end. It begins in Scribner's next January.

I have G. Lapsley here now, with a nice young English don, a friend of his, Kenneth Pickthorn, who cares much about books, & especially about French literature—a sort of incipient John-Hugh, but without his many-sidedness—

This afternoon my old friend Robert Grant (Judge Grant) of Boston arrives, & Walter is coming out to dine with him.

On Sept 2d I go to England to spend a week with R. Norton, & then to wander about variously— I am inconsolable at not seeing you. *When* are you coming to Ste Claire, since the Ile de France is erased from your map?

Yrs ever affly   EW.

Phil. is now absorbed in Coué-ism & spiritualism, & I find our talks rather boring, as she is forever challenging a debate. She has gone to La Bourboule with Florence.²

MS:VT

1. *The Glimpses of the Moon.*
2. Philomène's daughter.

To Sinclair Lewis

Pavillon Colombe
August 27, 1922

Dear Mr. Lewis,

There is so much to say about Babbitt that I don't know where to begin—unless at the dedication, which gives me an even warmer glow of satisfaction, now that I've read what follows, than when you first announced it to me!—If I've waited as long as this to have a book dedicated to me, Providence was evidently waiting to find just the Right Book. All my thanks for it.

And what next? Oh, do jump on a steamer, & come over & have a talk about it! It kept me reading till one a.m. the other night, & started me again at 5—& at every page I found something to delight in, & something to talk about.—The prevailing impression, when one has finished, is of an extraordinary vitality & vivacity, an ever-bubbling spring of visual & moral sensibility—& this kind of "liveness" is one of the most important qualities in any work of fiction—or of any other art.

I don't think "Babbitt" as good a novel, in the all round sense, as "Main Street," because in the latter you produced a sense of unity & of depth by reflecting Main Street in the consciousness of a woman who suffered from it because she had points of comparison, & was detached enough to situate it in the universe—whereas Babbitt is in & of Zenith up to his chin & over, & Sinclair Lewis is obliged to do the seeing & comparing for him. But then there is much more life & glow & abundance in the new book; you must have felt a stronger hold on it, & a richer flow. I wonder how much of it the American public, to whom irony seems to have become as unintelligible as Chinese, will even remotely feel? To do anything worth while, one must resolutely close one's ears & eyes to their conception of the novel, and I admire nothing more in your work than your steady balancing on your tight-rope over the sloppy abyss of sentimentality.

I've only begun to say what I wanted, but the rest must be talked— except for one suggestion, which I venture to make now, & that is, that in your next book, you should use slang in dialogue more sparingly. I believe the real art in this respect is to use just enough to *colour* your dialogue, not so much that in a few years it will be almost incomprehensible. It gives more relief to your characters, I'm sure, than to take down their jargon word for word.—

Thank you again for associating my name with a book I so warmly admire & applaud, & believe me, with kindest remembrances to Mrs. Lewis,

 Yours ever sincerely
 E. Wharton

I sent you a copy of my new novel when it came out, but heard afterward that Appleton had forgotten to put "Author's Comps" in any of the copies he sent for me—I hope you guessed it was from me.— Oh, & still another word. Weeks ago I cut the enclosed out of an English paper—I supposed you wd see it & contradict it—but as I have seen no allusion to your doing so, I venture to send you the cutting, which, I am convinced, doesn't represent what you feel, or would wish to say, on the subject.

The way to prove what we are is not to complain of lack of recognition, but to go on doing Babbitts—& Super-Babbitts! But, as I said, I'm sure this idiotic interview doesn't represent you, & I admire your talent so much that I hope very much you will write a line to the Times denying it in substance—or to me, if you prefer, authorizing me to do so in your name—

Final p.s.

Diligent search fails to reveal the said article—but you've surely seen or heard of it—

Ms:BL

To William Gerhardie[1]

> Pavillon Colombe
> October 3, 1922

Dear Sir, Your novel seems to me so much the best thing that I've read about Russia since "Oblomoff"[2]—& I read that long ago—that I hope you will let me tell you how greatly I admire it, & how sure I am that it is the forerunner of many others which are going to give me the same peculiar pleasure.

I should not venture to thrust this praise upon you if I admired your work only as an interpretation of Russia— It is because I feel in it so many of the qualities of the novelist born that I want to cheer you on to the next, in whatever field you mean to place it— And meanwhile, it is a joy to turn back to Kniaz the incomparable, to the "inénarrable" Sir Hugo, to the bedraggled but dauntless Nikolai, to Eisenstein (who is *my* dentist!), & above all to that amorphous agglutinated mass of helpless humanity that trails back & forth across your pages in poor Nikolai's haggard wake!—You not only make your people live, but move & grow—& that's the very devil to achieve.

Do, for all our sakes, keep it up! is the prayer of

Your grateful reader
Edith Wharton

Are you going to be translated into French? It ought to be done *at once*.

Ms:UT

1. William Gerhardie (1895–1977)—spelled Gerhardi during most of his lifetime, and spelled yet differently by EW and others—was born in Russia of English parents. After the war, he came to England and studied at Oxford. It was here that he wrote his first novel, *Futility*.

EW was mainly responsible for the novel's publication in America (by Duffield and Company) in 1922. She contributed a preface, in which, among other things, she found "the most striking quality in Mr. Gerhardi's book" his ability "to focus the two so utterly alien races to which he belongs almost equally by birth and bringing-up—the English and Russian; to sympathise with both, and to depict them for us *as they see each other*."

2. *Oblomov*, the novel by Ivan Alexandrovitch Goncharov; first published in 1859. The first English translation, by C. J. Hogarth, appeared in 1915.

To William Gerhardie

Pavillon Colombe
October 7, 1922

Dear Mr. Gherardi—

It is I who am "confused" (in the French sense) by the flattering epithets you bestow on me. I am so accustomed nowadays to being regarded as a deplorable example of what people used to read in the Dark Ages before the "tranche de vie" had been rediscovered, that my very letter-paper blushes as I thank a novelist of your generation for his praise. But you shall have the last Awful Warning I have produced in that line, though it's not the one I think most likely to plead in my favour.

If you would like to have "Futility" translated into French, will you let me speak about it to some editors & publishers? I have lived in France for some years, & know a good many of them; & there might be a result. It won't be my fault if there is *not*, for my admiration of your book goes a good deal farther than I ventured to express it.

I'm glad there's to be another ready so soon, for I have a horrid uncertain appetite in novels, & the kind I like are so seldom in season. —I know Tchekov, yes, & am delighted that you're to write about him too.¹—I haven't read him from end to end, because I can't bear more than a few pages at a time of that English-of-all-work in which the hapless foreigner is always offered to us, & I'm hoping for a better German translation. Is there one?

What I've read I've admired (some of it) greatly; but I won't qualify or discriminate because that wd lead me into a long talk on the art of the short story.

I'd much rather wait confidently for what you have to say.

Yrs sincerely
    E Wharton

(Oh, I'm a *Mrs Wharton* of long standing!)

It's my dentist's conversation (luckily) rather than his professional ways, that reminded me of Eisenstein—

Do you know a possible translator for Futility?

Ms:UT

1. Gerhardie's *Anton Chehov*, in 1923, was the first published book in English on the Russian fiction writer.

To Gaillard Lapsley

Pavillon Colombe
October 22, 1922

Dearest Gaillard— Bless you for sending me the little volume,¹ which I would rather "tenir de votre amitié" than receive coldly through Bain, to whom I was just writing for it.

I gulped it down in my coarse carnivorous way; & then returned & lingered with slow delight. I'm *sure* it's far above the Shropshire Lad; not only in sudden lifts, but continuously. Nothing in the other book, to my mind, equals VII, X, XII, XXI, XXIX, XXXII—& the *perfect*

"Mercenaries." There's all the difference of all the years in it; that great gift of Experience, the only one we can count on between the cradle & the grave (& that only if we're capable of receiving it); the gift that modern art affects to spurn but will have to go back to, to get effects like these. The famous "continuous excitement" may have vanished; but that far rarer & greater thing, "the depth & not the tumult of the soul," has come instead; & the gods & I approve. Please tell Mr. Housman so, in terms more respectful than this first burst comports.*

Thank you a lot for a precious present.

Yr E. W.

Mrs. George D. Hope, of Kansas City, who has been passing the last few weeks in Paris at the Hotel Plaza Athénée, is leaving by aeroplane for London prior to sailing on November 1 for America. Mrs. Hope is a writer. Her "Quotations and Comments" and "Hopeful Thoughts" have had a wide circulation. Last year she wrote an ode to Mrs. Warren G. Harding, which was set to music and played at several functions given in Mrs. Harding's honor in Washington D.C., where Mrs. Hope is well known socially. Mrs. Hope has been travelling in Belgium, Holland, Germany, Spain and Italy.[2]

Oh, the large unconscious scenery of our native land!

* And "Tell me not—" what music!

Ms:BL

1. *Last Poems*, by A. E. Housman. The little volume consisting of forty-one numbered poems included one entitled "Epitaph on an Army of Mercenaries," and another—cited below by EW—that begins: "Tell me not here, it needs not saying,/ What tune the enchantress plays/ In aftermaths of soft September/ or under blanching Mays . . ."

2. Newspaper item affixed to the page.

To Beatrix Farrand

Sainte-Claire
Hyères
December 12, 1922

Beatrix dear, the tale of the arrival of the motor has just come, in one of your mother's vivid letters, & that first moment was alone worth the price of admission![1] How I wish you'd been there!

I've already written to thank Elizabeth, angel that she is, & now I want to thank you too, for planning & accomplishing the little joke so successfully. The account of the first joy-ride enchanted me, it was so *exactly* what you had predicted!

I'm plunged in distress by the definite & unconcealable discovery that my poor Bérard, who grows stone walls like chick-weed, kills flowers much more successfully & effectually than he does their enemies, such as caterpillars & green fly. He has managed to blast my garden from garret to cellar this year—but luckily his antagonism doesn't include shrubs or creepers, or sea & sky & sunshine—so there's a good deal left. However, I've got the hard task of gardener-hunting ahead of me, & with all my "littery" work waiting & champing to be done, it's rather a bore— Next year I hope you'll see successful results.

Said littery continues to bring in good returns, & I beg you to accept, with my Xmas vous, the enclosed chip from the work-shop.

Best love to you & Max.

Edith

Nettie[2] is coming to stay on Thursday. What fun if you were here at the same time!

Ms:IO

1. EW was initiating the practice of providing her sister-in-law Minnie Jones with $500 a month, wherewith to hire a car and driver at need.

2. Nettie Johnstone, the sister of Gifford Pinchot, one-time chief of the Bureau of Forestry of the United States; she was the wife of Sir Alan Johnstone, a British diplomat. EW had known Lady Johnstone since early in the war.

To Bernard Berenson

Sainte-Claire

January 6, 1923

Dearest B.B.— Thanks for your "vows," & please regard them as a thousand fold reciprocated. We talk of you very often on our long daily wanderings under this perpetual blue Ionian roof, & wish, oh so much, that you had let yourself be torn from your library for the sake of the sea & the hot sunshine here.

Mac[1] must have dined with John-Hugh when I was staying with him last Sept; but if I remember rightly, I had already tackled Ulysses[2] & cast it from me, & *he*, Mack, carried it off with him that very evening. —It's a turgid welter of pornography (the rudest schoolboy kind) & unformed & unimportant drivel; & until the raw ingredients of a pudding *make* a pudding, I shall never believe that the raw material of sensation & thought can make a work of art without the cook's intervening. The same applies to Eliot.[3]

I *know* it's not because I'm getting old that I'm unresponsive. The trouble with all this new stuff is that it's à thèse: the theory comes first, & dominates it. And it will go the way of "unanimisme" & all the other isms.—Grau ist alle Theorie.

But I'm prélassing myself in the new vol. of Mâle,[4] the first really clear business-like statement I've seen of the theory of Graeco-Syrian origins for French Romanesque sculpture. It *is* well done! There are very good things, too, in Gillet's Romanesque Gothic chapters (all I've read.) But, oh, those insulting, those *be-sliming* Piot drawings of Moissac, Vézelay & the rest—ugh!

Phil. is looking forward to going to you soon; but *I* want to come wenn alles grünet und blühet at Pfingsten, das liebliche fest,[5] for example. Only you're never there any more at my times, worse luck!

Gaillard, Norts & I pursue our happy triangular existence. Work in the morning, a joint picnic, & generally a long walk over hill & dale till tea-time. Cela me va, & I am content & well—I wish you gave a better report of yourself. Come here & be cured!—Best love to you & Mary, & fond vous.

Edith

Ms:VT

1. Eric Maclagan.

2. EW read a copy of James Joyce's novel that had been published in Paris in 1922.

3. T. S. Eliot's *The Waste Land* had appeared in the *Criterion*, the quarterly he founded in 1922.

4. Emile Mâle's *L'Art religieux de XIIe siècle en France* (1922).

5. "Whitsuntide the lovely feast."

To William Gerhardie

Sainte-Claire
Hyères
January 14, 1923

Dear Mr. Gerhardi,

I know that Katherine Mansfield was a friend of yours, & that her death[1] must be a great blow, & I want to send you a word of sympathy.

What stupid waste Nature seems to revel in! I ache with misery whenever I see a sensitive plate smashed—there are so few, alas, & the insensitive many are so tough & lasting. It's a pity.

Do tell me, some day, a little about her.

Yrs ever sincerely
E Wharton

Ms:UT

1. Katherine Mansfield, the New Zealand–born author (*The Garden Party and Other Stories*, in 1922), died early in 1923 at the age of thirty-five. Gerhardie dedicated *Futility* to her.

To Robert Bridges[1]

Sainte-Claire
February 11, 1923

Dear Mr. Bridges,

Many thanks for your letter of Jan. 25th. I am very much obliged to Dr. van Dyke for pointing out my mistake in thinking there was a Peace

Congress in Holland in the summer of 1914, and I hope you will be kind enough to tell him so.

I am naturally very sorry to have made this mistake. In the first week of the war I remember being told by Mr. Morton Fullerton that he had met an American on his way to an assemblage of some sort in Holland just before the war broke out, and that he advised him, in view of the menacing situation, to travel by way of Luxembourg. The war broke out, I think, the very next day, and we were naturally amused at the advice which Mr. Fullerton had given.

The episode remained in my memory and I connected it with the Peace Congress, as there had been so much talk of such congresses before the war, and the air was so full of Norman Angell.[2] I ought of course to have verified my recollection by asking Mr. Fullerton, but it never occurred to me that I was wrong, and the episode is so interwoven with my tale that, after twenty-four hours of anxious thought, I see no way of changing it. As a matter of fact, though I naturally dislike to be inaccurate, I am not much troubled, for I have not been writing history but fiction, and all I wanted to do was to render as vividly as possible the state of mind of various types of people (principally neutrals) when the war suddenly exploded all their preconceived ideas and their prearranged way of life. The believer in Norman Angell was a prominent figure at that time, and an element I needed in my picture. If it were not too late I should of course introduce him in a different character; but I see no possibility of doing this now. If I may compare so small a thing as my novel to many great ones, I venture to think that inaccuracies of this kind may be found in most of the great historical novels without detracting from the effect of truth which they produce —provided always the incidents in question threw additional light on the state of mind of the people concerned.

I am enclosing an extra copy of this letter because I should be obliged if you would send it to Dr. van Dyke so that he may know why I have decided not to attempt to change.

Numbers VI-VII-VIII were posted together last week. They are the last I have received, though you speak as if No 9 had already been sent. If so, it will probably be here in a day or two, and I will return it immediately.

I wish I could send you a list of people to whom you might send advance notices about the book, but unfortunately I seldom keep the letters I receive from unknown readers, as they are fairly numerous and take up so much room.

I am glad the comments on the novel continue to be favourable. With many thanks for your letter,

Yours sincerely
E. Wharton

Ms:FL

1. A member of Scribner's editorial staff.

2. Norman Angell (1872–1967), English author and editor, expert in international affairs and finance, and tireless worker for peace. He would be knighted in 1931 and two years later be awarded the Nobel Peace Prize for his efforts.

To Rutger B. Jewett

February 21, 1923

Dear Mr. Jewett,

Many thanks for sending me "The Tree of the Garden." There are very good things in it, and in fact all the first part, in the Yorkshire farm-house, is so delicious that I wished for more. But when the love making begins it becomes too much like Hall Caine in "The Manxman"—which was an uncommonly good book, but does not need to be re-done nowadays. I hope Mr. Booth will do a novel of farm-yard comedy for it seems to me his real originality lies there.

I finished "The Temperate Zone"[1] so hurriedly that I have had some slight changes to make and I send you three revised pages to be passed on to the editor who takes the tale.

Yours sincerely

P.S. to letter of 21st February 1923.

I have just received a letter from Mr. Paul Reynolds proposing to me to write for McCall's Magazine six articles on my recollections of New York Society, at $2.500 an article. New York Society in my youth was a small affair, and I shall have exhausted it fully by the time my "Old New York Stories"[2] are done. But the proposal reminds me of a plan which has been vaguely floating through my mind for some time: namely, the writing of my own early memories, from 1865 to 1885 or 1890, in which I should like to interweave the recollections of my childhood and the beginnings of my literary life.

One of my objects in doing this would be to avoid having it inaccurately done by some one else after my death, should it turn out that my books survive me long enough to make it worth while to write my biography. My original idea was to jot down these remembrances, and put them away for use after my death; but as they would be concerned only with the picture of my family life as a child and young girl, and with my literary development, I see no particular reason for keeping them back. The whole plan is still vague in my mind, but I mention it to you in connection with this offer of McCall's Magazine, because I might possibly jot the articles down in the intervals of my novel writing, and I should like your opinion on the whole question. Meanwhile, perhaps you will be kind enough to write to Mr. Reynolds, or to McCall, and tell him that the New York Society articles are not at all in my line. I prefer to leave it to you as I have an idea that it was Mr. Reynolds who complicated affairs for us before with regard to "Glimpses of the Moon." I enclose his letter to which I shall not reply directly.

Copy:BL

1. EW's story "The Temperate Zone" would be part of her volume *Here and Beyond* in 1926.
2. The four novellas collectively called *Old New York*, which would appear in four volumes, boxed, by Appleton in May 1924. Their subtitles located them in time: *False Dawn* (*The 'Forties*); *The Old Maid* (*The 'Fifties*); *The Spark* (*The 'Sixties*); *New Year's Day* (*The 'Seventies*).

To Corinne Roosevelt Robinson

Sainte-Claire
April 29, 1923

Dear Corinne (may I?)

Thank you so much for sending me the volume of poems[1]— I wish your brother had inspired poetry more nearly on a level with the love

& admiration in the hearts of his versifiers! But there is no Whitman singing in this generation—nor a Lowell, even.—

I was so very glad to see that Lord Charnwood is to write his life.[2] That is all to the good, & no wiser choice could have been made. I look forward impatiently to the appearance of the book— More & more, as time passes, does the shadow of your brother's loss spread across the world. The waste of it—the waste!

Thank you also for the words of dedication, which touched me greatly—

Yours ever affly
    Edith Wharton

Ms:HL

1. A collection of poetical tributes to Theodore Roosevelt.
2. *Theodore Roosevelt*, a biography by Godfrey Rathbone Benson, Lord Charnwood (the author of *Abraham Lincoln* in 1917), appeared in 1923.

To Bernard Berenson

Salsomaggiore
May 19, 1923

Dearest B.B.— To be writing from Italy to you in Greece—at this season, of old so dedicated to the Tatti—seems part of the general post-war topsy-turvyness. And to think that a day's motor-dash might take me to you at the end of my cure, and that I'm turning in the other direction instead, puts the final touch to the muddle. But so it is!—A series of attacks of grippe, of which the last, at Cannes in March, tired my heart a good deal, made me decide to come back to these wonder-waters, & I had the luck to persuade Philomène to come with me. As soon as I took this momentous decision I attached to it the further one of going to you on your return; but not long afterward I was invited by Yale to go out next month & receive a degree of D. Litt.—I declined; though regretfully, I own, for it's the one sort of honour I have ever imagined that cd please me, because I have so loved Letters all my days.

But I wanted to go to Tatti, & *didn't* want, suddenly & inopinément, to cross the Atlantic.

Thereafter, however, came urgent letters, saying that a "Doctorat" had never before been conferred on a woman by any big University in America, that Yale had created a precedent for me, that I couldn't *not* go, &c; so I decided that it would be stupid, & also ungracious to refuse, since the mere voyage has no terrors for me (save that of paying for my stateroom.)—

This decision obliges me to rush back from here on June 2d (to St Brice) & jump on board the Mauretania on the 9th. I shall be "gowned" on June 20, & back in the dark & sanguinary land to which you so appreciatively allude on July 2d—& thereafter shall keep the perspective free until I know definitely about August. But meanwhile I mean to take it for granted that I *do* know, & that Auvergne it is. Hurrah!!

And now, having begun this letter (as I believe one always shd, between friends) by telling you my own history up to date, I have no proper space in which to vibrate about *yours*. Why did fate will that I should take a good part of that incomparable journey as a gaping baby of 28, instead of waiting to do it with you as a sensible & teachable lady of middle age?

Why shouldn't we do it again in a yacht, next summer (June & July 1924), & see what *I* saw & you've missed—all the islands?? If "A Son at the Front" rises to the occasion, I'm game!—

Oh, dear, what rich days you must have been having—& how I understand the peculiar richness of the intervals in bed, with a cold & books! I owe my small amount of literacy to such parentheses.—My fondest love to Mary & you—& bon voyage! For I hope this letter will catch you as you set sail—

Yrs. ever affly
   E.W.

Ms:VT

To Bernard Berenson

S.S. Berengaria.
July 1, 1923

Dearest B.B.— Here I am, drawing hourly nearer to I Tatti, & so full of tales of my adventure that I literally don't know where to begin!— Just 22 days today since I "boarded" the Mauretania, & I haven't lost a minute of the time, except the last afternoon in N.Y., when the unbroken "heat-wave," which began the day I landed, suddenly laid me low & sent me to bed with cold compresses on my head!—Really, I saw & did a lot—& have come back with my stock-in-trade considerably replenished.

As for Yale, the ceremony was really impressive;[1] the last thing I expected it to be! It was a sort of mediaeval pageant, but a real, not a got-up one; & it remains a mystery that the straw-hatted pot-bellied "homme moyen" of the modern U.S. should demand such a show, & know how to create it. I'll tell you all about it—next month!

Then I motored a lot, saw a good many people, stayed with various friends, saw publishers, trustees, &c—& altogether shook off (I hope) the physical apathy which had been creeping over me since the war. But I wish all this cd have been combined with a June visit to I Tatti!—

I hope to be at Pavillon Colombe tomorrow night. Do send me a line there soon, to say how you & Mary are faring, & what's the date of your arrival.

I dread to think what news I shall hear of poor Rosa.[2] I sent her your message before sailing, as she was too ill then for me to see her.

Love to you both.
EW.

Ms:VT

1. The Yale graduation ceremonies were held on the morning of June 20. With the other "honoraries," EW, in cap and gown, walked in the slow procession around the campus and back to Woodbridge Hall, where the degree candidates were waiting.

The citation for EW's doctor of letters degree read: "She holds a universally recognized place in the front ranks of the world's living novelists. She has elevated the level of American literature. We are proud that she is an American, and especially proud to enroll her among the daughters of Yale."

2. Rosa de Fitz-James died soon after this.

To André Gide

Pavillon Colombe
St Brice
23 juillet 1923

Cher Monsieur— En rentrant d'Amérique il y a quinze jours j'ai trouvé ici votre livre avec sa charmante dédicace. Merci d'avoir pensé à moi, et laissez-moi vous dire avec quel intérêt et avec combien d'admiration j'ai lu, d'un bout à l'autre, ce passionnant volume.

C'est la première fois que j'ai vraiment retrouvé Dostoievski sous l'amas de livres que l'on a fait sur lui; vous avez éclairé le labyrinthe et on a le sentiment d'arriver enfin jusqu'à l'homme mystérieux, terrible et troublant que ses autres interprètes avaient enveloppé d'un brouillard de plus en plus épais. Comme on voit que vous êtes né sous un ciel clair!

Merci encore de l'envoi, et croyez à mes sentiments les plus sincères.

E. Wharton

Transcribed by Professor Jacques Cotnam from ms. in the Bibliothèque Jacques Doucet of the University of Paris.

Pavillon Colombe
St Brice
July 23, 1923

Dear Monsieur— On returning from America a fortnight ago, I found here your book with its charming dedication.[1] Thank you for your thought of me, and let me tell you with what interest and with how much admiration I have read this fascinating volume from one end to the other.

This is the first time that I have been able to discover Dostoievski beneath the heap of books that have been written about him; you have illuminated the labyrinth, and one has the feeling of arriving at last at this mysterious, terrible and troubling man that his other interpreters had enveloped in an ever thicker fog. How one sees that you were born under a clear sky!

Thank you for sending it, and believe me to be yours sincerely,

Edith Wharton

1. *Dostoïevsky* (1923), based on a series of lectures Gide gave in 1922.

To Margaret Terry Chanler

Pavillon Colombe
August 5, 1923

Dearest Daisy— It was a great regret not to see you when I was in America, but my friends were so scattered that it was useless (especially with the thermometer at 95) to try to reach them, & I could only vow to go back at a more seasonable time.

I enjoyed my 12 days to the full, & managed to see everybody who was still in reach, & get a lot of interesting impressions of the new America. But I wish you had been there to talk it over with!

I've never even thanked you yet for Valéry's Platonic dialogue.[1] I like him so much that I wish I liked his literature better, but to me it's so cold, so meticulous, & so full of laboured "concetti" that I can't feel a stir of real life in it. And yet goodness knows I don't want everybody to write Babbitts! But adopting the Platonic dialogue, with all its archaeological formulae, seems to me enough to petrify or ossify any drop of new blood or morsel of live flesh & bone the subject might have contained. The best of those reconstitutions seem to me like schoolboy exercises (I wish the modern schoolboy had them to do, by the way!)

Having thus brutally discharged my views at you, I proceed to mention that I am asking Mr. Scribner to send you Percy Lubbock's "Roman Pictures"[2]—I need hardly add that I accord you equal freedom in the expression of your opinion thereon. But I think that as an old Roman you will enjoy its fun— He will also (Scrib, I mean) send you next month "A Son at the Front," as to which, also, I hope you will express your opinion with an equal candour, since most of the help I've had in my writing has come from the plain truths administered by friends.— Do let me hear soon all about you & yours, & especially about your plans for next winter, which tend this way, I trust.

Yrs ever devotedly   Edith

Ms:BL

1. The reference is to one of two recently published dialogues by the cultivated and elegantly cerebral French writer Paul Valéry (1871–1945): *L'Ame et la danse* and *Eupalinos, ou l'Architecte*. Valéry was a Riviera neighbor of EW.

2. *Roman Pictures* (1923), fictive reminiscences of a dilettantish English visitor in Rome, and particularly of the aimless tribe of English-speaking tourists.

To Margaret Terry Chanler

Pavillon Colombe
October 1, 1923

Dearest Daisy— What a good letter! And first let me congratulate you with all my heart on the good news in it. I have heard so much of Beatrice's[1] sweetness & courage & charm that I don't wonder at her being adored. The great luck is that she shd reciprocate, & that her fiancé should be a man you really like, & of your own faith too— Though I don't know her—through a series of untoward circumstances—I want to send her a little wedding present, which I will ask Minnie to transmit—

Your plans for the winter *must* include a good quiet fortnight *at least* at Hyères. The mere description of N.Y. life as practised by the "youngs" makes me long for my lazy terraces, with a jug of Evian, a book, & "thou" under a caroubier bough!—

I'm glad I'm absolved through the intercession of Crashaw, Vaughan & Donne (& I must add Marvell).[2] They must have high powers on the heights of Parnassus.—Alas, my Latin is too imperfect to permit any enjoyment of Lucretius, even with a crib. But such of him as I've got through translations has delighted me. He was a great poet—& that includes most greatnesses.

I'm just back from three delightful holiday weeks in England, & a little breathless (having only arrived last night) with piled-up "courrier," so this isn't half an answer to your delightful letter—but I must thank you for finding time, amid your multifarious whirlings, to read, & have an opinion on, my long book![3]—I'm glad you like it—it's a sort of "lest we forget," & I'm glad I've done it. Of course, from the novelist's point of view, the thing that interested me was the love of the ill-assorted quartette for their boy, & the gradual understanding between the two men.—No, I'm afraid my young Americans don't talk the language as spoken by the Scott Fitzgerald & Sinclair Lewis jeunesse; but I saw dozens of young Americans from all parts of America during the war, & none of them talked it, any more than your sons-in-law do! I believe it's a colossal literary convention, invented by the delightful Sinclair Lewis, & adopted by the throng of lesser ones.—I may add that I have only one young American of *American up-bringing* in the book, & he talks (for about 2 pages, his only appearance) in the language of Pick & Larry White.[4] I mean young "Benny Upsher," who volunteers early in the tale, & disappears. The other young men, George & his friends, have been educated in Europe—except "Boylston," & *he* talks in exactly the English of my poor friend Ronald Simmons, who lived in Providence till he was 24 or 25, but who never used a word that wasn't real English. So I've really been faithful according to my lights.

By the way, if you want the most brilliant & fatiguing "jazz" book I've yet come across, read "the Poor Man" by Stella Benson,⁵ a young English novelist whom all the "youngs" in England consider their best. It makes me want to crawl away & die.

And I said this wasn't to be a long letter. But you're too beguiling, dearest Daisy—

> Yrs ever
> Edith

Ms:BL

1. Mrs. Chanler's daughter, about to be married.

2. In a letter to Margaret Chanler of September 9, EW had defended herself against "the startling charge"—based on her deprecation of Paul Valéry as a poet—of an inability to "feel the ineffable." "C'est un peu fort," she wrote, "to a passionate lover of seventeenth century English poetry, who puts Vaughan & Crashaw higher, in certain quintessential qualities, than any later English poet, & Donne very close to them."

3. *A Son at the Front* was published by Charles Scribner's Sons in September.

4. Margaret Chanler's sons-in-law: Edward Pickman, married to Hester Chanler; and Lawrence White (son of the architect Stanford White) to Laura Chanler.

5. *The Poor Man* was the most recent work of fiction by Stella Benson (1892–1933).

To Beatrix Farrand

> Pavillon Colombe
> October 2, 1923

Dearest Beatry— I hope your arm is really better, & feel almost sure it is, as your mother wrote some time ago that you & Max had left. I won't go again into my feelings of rage & despair when I think of your summer—it leaves me inarticulate!

I'm just back from the laziest three weeks I ever spent in England. I started with vast motor plans, & the determination to visit several nurseries & gardens, but what with a long stretch of "littery work" & a fortnight's hard motoring in France, I found myself so inert, after a day or two in that feather-bed climate, that I just lolled for 8 days at Rye, five or six at Hill & a few in London—all in weather of the balmiest, such as I always find in England at this season. Still, I managed to see Miss Wilmot's garden (& the lady herself!) while I was at Hill. Mrs. Hunter took me over with two or three people that Miss Wilmot knew (or knew about), so she paid not the slightest attention to *me*, & I was glad she didn't, as I felt half asleep, & couldn't remember the name of a single plant! However, it all interested me *afterward*— you know how one sometimes wakes out of these trances, & finds that one has mopped up something with one's spongy brain? The little enclosed gardens must have been lovely when they were less jungly, but the wild garden that happens suddenly in the lawn in front of the house I thought appalling. The plants, of course, were most interesting, & all in glowing health— & considering she has reduced her staff almost to the vanishing point it's a marvel to see such vigour of vegetation. I wish I could go back there some day with a clear brain, & a note-book.

At Hurstmonceux Castle I saw a very beautiful all-purple border, or rather two, facing each other on each side of a long grass walk. There were columbines, stocks, salpiglossis, & I forget what else—but, curiously enough, no Drummond or Venosa verbenas, no ageratums or glorious purple petunias. But it gave one an idea of what might be done.

There has been summer weather all through Sept. & I came back to find my garden really lovely—long borders full of asters, lemon African marigolds, verbenas, dahlias, & all the coreopsis & helenium tribes. What a delicious respite to have summer linger on into October!

Among other joys I found a new bloom of the lovely dwarf coreopses you sent me last spring, & which had been all burnt up in the August heat. I can't remember where the seed came from, nor yet the names of the varieties, so I enclose the flowers of the prettiest, & shd be so grateful for some more seed. This time I shan't let them out of my hands without taking their names & addresses!

The corn failed, alas, owing to the really continuous rain & lack of sun in the early summer. We made three sowings, & only the last succeeded, & that wasn't sweet. But I'm going to try again!

My under-gardener, Emile, has turned out to be a very intelligent man as head gardener, & my garden is really improving immensely. How I wish you could come & see it next summer!

Don't bother to write, for I know this is your busiest season—& your mother keeps me faithfully informed of the family doings—

Love to you & Max.
    Edith

Ms:IO

To Bernard Berenson

Sainte-Claire
January 15, 1924

Dearest B.B.,— I will begin this often planned & long deferred letter to you by telling you that young Cabot Lodge, Bessy's eldest boy, who is staying with me, will be in Florence in a few days. He is such an attractive & intelligent youth, & will be so fully alive to the privilege of seeing you both, & the Tatti, that I feel it's not indiscreet of me to send him; & as he is to be in Florence for a very short time, I have told him that he may telephone on arrival & ask when you can conveniently see him. Above all, make *no* "frais." A cup of tea & an hour by the library fire will be something for him to remember for a long time.

He has been "oriented" toward politics by grand 'pa, & I think his natural bent is toward that, & history, but he has an eager respect for letters, has read a good deal, speaks French & German, & is on the staff of the Boston Transcript (having to earn his living). I know you will like him, or I shouldn't send him.

I've been wanting to write to you ever since I got back, but I wanted to do it soberly & advisedly, & not parenthetically, between "literary output" & drawing cheques for the butcher & baker! But life has submerged me, as it always does before, during & after the holidays, & for the last week my excellent little secretary has been ill with a bad grippe, which has added a good deal to the dullest part of my task. However, I must just give you a hug for 1924, & also tell you—though belatedly —what pleasure you gave me by that good letter you wrote me last autumn about "A Son at the Front." It was a great joy to me to know that you still felt the vitality of the people after a lapse of nearly two years, & that they hadn't "gone bad" in the interval.

The beloved Norts is here, painting from dawn to midnight, & Gaillard Lapsley has just left after spending his Xmas holiday here as usual. Young Cabot leaves today, & poor little Gerhardi* (who was to have come to Florence & couldn't get his passport in time) has arrived for 10 days, such a wistful little Russianized English boy, with only the war & Oxford of England in him, & all the rest pure Russian. He is agonizingly shy, & obviously unused to even as much of "society" as Ste. Claire represents; but intensely eager, curious, full of muddled London-Mercury-&-Adelphi theories(!!) of his art, too poor to buy books, & too ignorant to know what to buy, if he could. You'd like him & I wish you wd let me send him to you with a letter on his way back to Innsbruck, in ten days or so, as he proposes to stop a day or two in Florence. He is *so* shy that when I came down to dinner the first night he didn't recognize me, & thought I was "another lady" in evening dress, & wondered why we went in to dinner without our hostess!!!

Philomène continues her little train-train, & we are trying to get her to read, in the hope that we may thus guide her toward writing. But I don't think she will ever do either!

Walter sails tomorrow—to introduce Sert[1] to an expectant America! *Why?* Non ragionam . . .

Please give my fondest to Mary, & tell her how sorry I was to hear, through Norts, that she had been going through a series of bronchitises—you'll have to come & spend your winters in a mild climate, like the Var, for instance!—

I "have to laugh" at the dogs having to be kept on a low diet on account of the tropic heat of Florence. My Chineses hold their tough little sides at the idea.

Now you know why I don't eat meat in the evenings! It's so that I may not bite your dinner-guests. That second royal evening, by 11.30, I should certainly have given the crown Princess[2] a nip if I hadn't refused veal & soup!!—Well, bless you, dearest B.B. Forgive my long silence, set me a good example by answering this very soon—

Edith

* author of Futility

Ms:VT

1. José María Sert y Badia, a Spanish painter; he had settled in Paris and was coming into a certain prominence in the mid-1920s.
2. Probably a reference to Crown Princess Louise of Sweden, the former Lady Louise Mountbatten and now the wife of Crown Prince Gustav of Sweden (he would be king in 1950). EW met the young royal couple, friends of the Berensons, at I Tatti.

To Margaret Terry Chanler

Pavillon Colombe
July 3, 1924

Dearest Daisy— For weeks I've been waiting for a quiet moment in which to write to you, & here I am now on the eve of Bebo's wedding, & only just sitting down to begin. But perhaps it's just as well, for after the christenings & the wedding you may have a feeling of désoeuvrement, & my letter will have more chance!

I wanted long ago to send you all my sympathy concerning the various family events, all of so happy a kind, & to thank you for your delightful letter; & now comes letter no. II, telling me of Hester's daughter. How shall I ever catch up? And why am I, without a family to keep me busy, so perpetually breathless & behind time? Certainly I have never been more so than since my return here. My cure at Salso was a blessed respite, & so was the week's after-cure at I Tatti, though the continuous scirocco was rather lowering to both hosts & guests. We (Minnie & I) left the BB's about three weeks ago, & came straight here; & on arriving I found 65 letters (three days' mail)!—Among them, needless to say, were many from friends "de passage"; & this, & the necessity of rushing in to Paris for mean utilitarian reasons, & the fact of having friends continually *here*, à demeure—all this has so "robbed me of my rest" that I feel my holidays are too dearly paid for at such a rate.

No doubt I shall shake down soon, however; & meanwhile I am taking advantage of a slight grippe to lie up & write to you—

I'm so glad you like "St François de Sales"[1] on a re-reading; & this reminds me that I've never properly thanked you for the Traité de l'Amour de Dieu.[2]—I started well on it, & found some exquisite things in the first chapters; then the slowness & the repetitions began to discourage me. Yet it's not that I'm not charmed by St François, whatever he says or writes. His letters are a pure delight; I've known them nearly by heart for 40 years. But in the "Traité" I feel the same rather tedious verbosity as in some of the passages of Bérulle & Condreu which the Abbé Bremond quotes with such gusto.[3] The other day I was toiling through one of these long passages, with its crowded lines of pious ejaculation, when suddenly I opened Vaughan & my eye lit on:

"I saw Eternity the other night—" & *there it all was.*[4] Those XVII English mystics spoil one for nearly all the others. But there are enchanting bits all through the Abbé's great book, & I'm now deep in vol. V, having inadvertently read VI first! Alas, I haven't seen the belov'd author, who is in his Pyrenees, or even read his Académie address. But Bourget has promised it to me.

I have read with immense admiration Bainville's Histoire de France,[5] & D. Halévy's "Vauban"[6]—both masterpieces. And I've been much entertained by Paléologue's book on Talleyrand, Metternich, & Chateaubriand.[7]

Since I got back my house has been full. Minnie was here till she went to Aix. Louis Mallet[8] came for several days, then G. Lapsley, who is here till toward the end of July. Mrs. Charlie Hunter comes the day after tomorrow, & Percy Lubbock the day after that—& so it goes. I haven't seen Charlie yet, but he comes to dine tomorrow. St André has been out several times, & he & the Serrnys came to dine a few days ago, & we all talked much & fondly of you.

The idea that you may decide on a winter pied-à-terre here fills us with unmitigated joy. Rome won't do—Royall is right. Italy is an "entremets"—France one's daily bread. You *must* do it—though it will be a blow to Royall that you shd begin your sojourn in his absence. Was it after you left that he was named Deputy Commissioner on the

Finance Commission for Hungary? He & Elisina are already installed at Budapest, & finding themselves rather exiled, though Royall says the work is intensely interesting. It's for 2 years, I believe.

Thank you so much for all the good things you say about the 4 stories— Their chief interest is in showing how many "totems" one may see disappear in one life-time!

Dearest Daisy, how I have enjoyed this good talk with you. Let us have another soon.

Yr devoted
Edith

P.S.—
I'm sorry to hear that Nellie Pickman is so poorly. Your description of Dudley's activities & of his wild garden is charming.⁹ I wish I cd have seen it with you.

Ms:BL

1. Of the several lives of St. François de Sales, Bishop of Geneva (1567–1622), this was perhaps the recently reprinted volume by M. Hamon (first published in 1856).

2. Treatise by St. François (1626), published posthumously.

3. The monumental study by Abbé Henri Bremond (1865–1933), *Histoire littéraire du sentiment religieux en France depuis la fin des guerres de religion jusqu'à nos jours*, had by 1924 reached the sixth of what would be eleven volumes. Volumes 3 to 6 were called *La Conquête mystique*. Abbé Bremond was a much treasured acquaintance of EW.

4. "The World," by Henry Vaughan (1622–1695).

5. *Histoire de France* (1924), by Jacques Bainville (1879–1936).

6. *Vauban* (1923), by Daniel Halévy (1872–1962).

7. *Romantisme et diplomatie* (1924), by the diplomat and historian Maurice Paléologue (1859–1944).

8. Sir Louis Mallet, former Ambassador to Turkey, now living in retirement in southern France.

9. The parents of Mrs. Chanler's son-in-law.

To Rutger B. Jewett

February 25, 1925

Dear Mr. Jewett,

I received a letter the other day from a young woman asking me, in the usual terms, for full particulars of my private life and literary career. This is of daily occurrence, and my only reason for mentioning it is that she said she had first applied to you and Messrs. Scribner's Sons for information. Her letter was addressed not, as usual, in your care, but to Sainte-Claire du Château, so I assume that my address was given to her by Messrs. Appleton or Scribner, and I write this line to ask if you will give orders that my address shall *not* be given to people applying for it. My friends all know where I live, and that is all I care about.[1]

Please excuse my bothering you with this, and believe me,

Yours very sincerely

Copy:BL

1. Jewett replied on March 13: "Don't shoot the organist. He is doing his best. The lady who wrote you got no information from us. Your address is kept a deep secret; instructions have been given that no information shall be issued from this office." In response to inquiries, Jewett said, he always replied that Mrs. Wharton was "travelling in Europe," but that letters addressed to her at Appleton would be forwarded.

To John Hugh Smith

Luchon

May 25, 1925

My dear John, Lots of thanks for your letter. The rue Ventadour had already advised me of the arrival of the £30, for which thanks also.

My St Brice household have wired me that they can be ready for me on the 30th, (Saturday), so I shall arrive that night, & shall hope to see you after all on Whitsunday or Monday. Let me know a little in advance—that is, let me find a wire on arriving on Sat. evening, if possible, to say when you can come. I shall be giving my chauffeur Sunday & Monday to go over the two motors, get the garage in order, &c, & shall have to order a local chariot to fetch you from the station —not obtainable at the last moment on the feasts of the Church!

Bring St A (or *not*) as the inclination moves you.

I'm glad you like "The Mother."[1] I felt, in writing it, all the force of what you say about the incest-element, & its importance in justifying her anguish—but I felt it wd be hardly visible in its exact sense to *her*, & wanted to try to represent the business as it seemed to her, culminating in the incest-vision when she sees the man holding Anne in his arms. It *is*, of course, what an English reviewer (I forget in what paper) reviewing it jointly with Mrs. Woolf's latest,[2] calls it: an old-fashioned novel. I was not trying to follow the new methods, as May Sinclair[3] so pantingly & anxiously does; & my heroine belongs to the day when scruples existed. One reviewer, by the way, explains the title (incidentally remarking that I am always a moralist!) by saying that Kate's reward for sparing her daughter useless pain is "the love of a good man"![4]

I'm delighted that you like my old Fred Landers— *No* other kind of man is as hard to do—at least for me, & I particularly wanted to bring him off because my other man is, necessarily, almost always behind the scenes.—Percy thinks the book is not really one of "my own," & that I betray the fact here & there in its pages. But I am buoyed up by the fact that he has said much the same of all the others—

Robert & I, eating trout on a terrace yesterday above the rushing Garonne, shouted with amusement & appreciation over your Oedipus-complex in a rabbit-warren.—We were on our way to Spain (for the day), to the beautiful valley of Aran, full of strange ancient villages, & incredibly rude & paleolithic churches, with heavy Egyptian columns in the dark interiors, strange Catalan frescoes, & a good deal of negroid sculpture about apses & portals.—I never was in a lovelier or a remoter region. But everything here is enchanting, & all the valleys about Luchon abound in curious & beautiful little churches. Each tiny village has one of its own—I'll bring you photos, to make you still sorrier you didn't come. Aurevoir next week, I hope,

Yrs ever
    EW

Have you read Cte Fleury's "Société du Second Empire," in 4 fat vols?[5] It's full of plums, an inexhaustible mine. And I told you, didn't I, to read Bn Beyem's "Second Empire"?[6] *First rate—*

Ms:BL

1. *The Mother's Recompense* was published in April 1925.
2. *Mrs. Dalloway* by Virginia Woolf (1882–1941).
3. See letter to Sara Norton, December 3, 1908.
4. The denouement of *A Mother's Recompense* turns on the refusal of the mother, Kate Clephane, of the kindly Fred Landers's offer of marriage and her return to self-exile in France.
5. This work of Comte Maurice Fleury (1856–1921) was just appearing.
6. *Le Second Empire*, by the former Belgian diplomat Baron Napoléon Beyem, appeared in two volumes from 1924 to 1926.

To F. Scott Fitzgerald

> Pavillon Colombe
> St. Brice-sous-Forêt
> June 8, 1925

Dear Mr. Fitzgerald,

I have been wandering for the last weeks and found your novel[1]— with its friendly dedication—awaiting me on my arrival here a few days ago.

I am touched at your sending me a copy, for I feel that to your generation, which has taken such a flying leap into the future, I must represent the literary equivalent of tufted furniture and gas chandeliers. So you will understand that it is in a spirit of sincere deprecation that I shall venture, in a few days, to offer you in return the last product of my manufactory.

Meanwhile, let me say at once how much I like Gatsby, or rather His Book, & how great a leap I think you have taken this time—in advance upon your previous work. My present quarrel with you is only this: that to make Gatsby really Great, you ought to have given us his early career (not from the cradle—but from his first visit to the yacht, if not before) instead of a short résumé of it. That would have *situated* him & made his final tragedy a tragedy instead of a "fait divers" for the morning papers.

But you'll tell me that's the old way, & consequently not *your* way; and meanwhile, it's enough to make this reader happy to have met your *perfect* Jew, & the limp Wilson, & assisted at the seedy orgy in the Buchanan flat, with the dazed puppy looking on. Every bit of that is masterly—but the lunch with Hildesheim [Wolfsheim] and his every appearance afterward, make me augur still greater things!

> Thank you again
> Yours sincerely
> Edith Wharton

I have left hardly space to ask if you and Mrs. F.— won't come to lunch or tea some day this week. Do call me.[2]

Ms:FL

1. *The Great Gatsby*, by F. Scott Fitzgerald (1896–1940), was published in the spring of 1925 by Scribners.
2. Fitzgerald came out to the Pavillon Colombe a few days later, accompanied by Theodore Chanler and fortifying himself with several drinks on the way. During an awkward pause in the conversation, Fitzgerald proposed telling "a couple of—er—rather rough stories." EW smiled her approval, and Fitzgerald then got entangled in an anecdote about an American couple who by mistake spent several nights in a Paris bordello. EW, after listening carefully, remarked that Mr. Fitzgerald's story lacked "data." In her diary that evening, EW noted: "To tea, Teddy Chanler and Scott Fitzgerald, the novelist (awful)."

To Margaret Terry Chanler

Pavillon Colombe
June 9, 1925

Dearest Daisy— Your delightful ship-letter has reached me in an hour of peace & recueillement which gives me a chance to enjoy it fully & to answer it at leisure. I got back about a week ago, & have hardly, as yet, taken up any of the social threads. Paris is too busy to be aware of

me (how egregious that sounds—I mean my little handful of Paris!) &
I am really turning into a green shade as I sit undisturbed under my
elms—

Thank you ever so fondly for taking the trouble to tell me *why* you
like my book. Your liking it would be a great joy, but to know why is
a subtle consolation for densities of incomprehension which were really
beginning to discourage me. No one else has noticed "desolation is a
delicate thing,"[1] or understood that the key is there. The title causes
great perplexity, but several reviewers think it means that the mother
was "recompensed" by "the love of an honest man." One enthusiast
thinks it has lifted me to the same height as Galsworthy & another that
I am now equal to Scott Fitzgerald. And the Saturday Review (American) critic says I have missed my chance, because the book "ought to
have ended tragically"—*ought to!*—You will wonder that the priestess
of the Life of Reason shd take such things to heart; & I wonder too. I
never have minded before; but as my work reaches its close, I feel so
sure that it is either nothing, or far more than they know. . . . And I
wonder, a little desolately, which?

Yes—isn't that Shelley line poignant? And, do you know, it's *not*
from the Cenci, as it seems as if it should be, but Prometheus Unbound,
that inexhaustible mine of beauty.

Well—now to other fields: fields of wild flowers in the Pyrenees, so
inconceivably beautiful & rare that they still fill my inward eye. I had
ten days of wonderful motoring with Robert, & vaguely remember sending
you a p.c. We saw Agde (very fine—I didn't know it), the great Cis-
tercian Abbey of Fontfroide, the splendid brick church of Panniers, the
exquisite cloister of St Lizier (close by), & then we plunged into the
Pyrenees at Luchon, & wandered among flowers & Romanesque
churches—little "frustes" inarticulate churchlets among the hills; & even
dipped for one long dazzled day into Spain, motoring to the very end
of the Val d'Aran, which, in its singular spring purity, all narcissus &
gentian & golden poplars & flowering fruit-trees & cold rushing rivulets,
was so like Keats's Eve of St Mark that my heart trembled. "So lasset
uns Hütten bauen," as the disciples say in the delicious German New
Testament—but instead we had to come back to business. Robert went
off to Albi & alentours for painting, & I motored to St Brice by beautiful
stages.

Like all honest letter-writers, I have begun by talking about myself, & having vidé mon sac have now time to turn my attention to yours, which was a real horn of plenty— I'm so glad that London was such a success, & that you got hold of the right people & saw the perfect things. I expect Eric Maclagan to stay some time this summer, & shall then hear all about you & the worries.

I'm glad of your good—relatively—report of Wintie. The augury [three words illegible] but I rather think there has been much quackery & more incompetence. I do hope this time the job will be done seriously.

Didn't you like Bainville's Histoire de France? It's a brilliant thing. There was a good review of Oliver Lodge's ether book[2] in the "Supp." when it came out:—"Sir O.L. talks of ether as if it were as familiar to him as the atmosphere." I don't think men of science have taken him seriously for many a year, though he did good work in his day, I believe.

I'm plunged at this moment in a masterpiece 20 years old, which I had never read: The Life of Pasteur.[3] What a man—& what a book! He *did* feel life to be a vale of soul-making! I wonder who does in the day we live in?

Yes—I got your splendid tulip-list, for which all gratitude, & am ordering from Van Tubergen. My new rose-garden is promising, & I find this soil so decidedly made for rose-growing that I mean to plant hundreds more this autumn, & to root up nearly all the old varieties. The new ones are so much more worth while, & one can now get varieties of every kind to which mildew is unknown.

I wish this were talked instead of written, & I could hear your delightful & stimulating answers. One of my oases ahead is the thought of weeks together next winter at St Claire.—

Please arrange your programs to include that, won't you? And let me know if I can do anything about your apartment or hotel for the winter. I await with impatience news of your arrival, of Hester particularly, & of all your flock.

Yr devoted
Edith

Ms:BL

1. Shelley, *Prometheus Unbound*, line 772. It served as the epigraph for *The Mother's Recompense*.

2. *Ether and Reality* (1925) by Sir Oliver Lodge (1851–1940).

3. Perhaps the biography by Emily Ducloux (1870–1904).

To Mary Cadwalader Jones

Pavillon Colombe
June 12, 1925

Dearest Minnie— Thank you very much for cabling me the news of Mrs. Winthrop's death; but *why?* She was a kindly & pathetic old lady, so helplessly crushed under her wealth, but though I was on very friendly terms with her, I had not seen or heard from her for years, & I never was intimate with Grenville[1]—the very word is a contradiction!

Really, it's useless to cable about any but intimate friends or intimate relatives, like dear Ethel King[2]—& please don't send flowers except on occasions such as Ethel's death. The surviving intimate friends I have là bas—so few now, alas!—are Henrietta Haven,[3] Olivia Cutting & her tribe, Bessy Lodge (& those who concern *her, not* on the Lodge side), dear Bob Grant, Billy Richardson,[4] Berkeley Updike, Lily Norton— If there are others left, I don't recall them. So many have died since 1914!—

I mention this, because it is really a waste of money & trouble to keep announcing by cable deaths of old acquaintances, or friends not communicated with for years—

I do hope you were at Reef Point before the frizzling began— This June seems to have behaved worse than my Yale one did! Here it is hot in the sun, but the nights are cool enough for a light blanket, & a wrap when one sits out of doors, & I don't see how people manage to die of congestion in Paris.

I have just had a perfectly wonderful review of my last "Fiction" article in the N.Y. Herald. Who *can* have written it?[5] I can't believe my eyes. It's educated & intelligent!

Yrs ever affly
Edith

Walter sees no way of sending Robinet's liseuses[6] but by the "American Express." They are really lovely. What shall I do?

P.S. I am under the impression that, in the revised type-copy of "Fiction" which Mr. Scribner has sent you, I neglected to change "article" into "chapter" in my two or three references from one section to another. Would you please in each case make this change? I am very sorry to have overlooked it.

Ms:BL

1. See letter to Sara Norton, September 30, 1902.
2. The mother of Frederick and Le Roy King.
3. Henrietta Cram Haven, the wife of J. Woodward Haven of Stockbridge and New York City. Mrs. Haven was the sister of the Ethel Cram whose fatal riding accident in Lenox in 1905 was one of the seeds of EW's novel *The Fruit of the Tree.*
4. William King (Billy) Richardson, a Boston lawyer who had specialized in patents; a friend of EW since the early days at The Mount.
5. As EW discovered after inquiring of Charles Scribner, the review in question had been written by Royal Cortissoz, the *Herald Tribune* critic. It was the third article by Cortissoz on the series on fiction by EW that had been running in *Scribner's* and would appear as *The Writing of Fiction* later in the year. On August 9, EW wrote Cortissoz to say that his review had at a stroke "consoled me for all the years of random praise & blame, both equally à côté."
6. Bookmarks.

To Gaillard Lapsley

Pavillon Colombe
October 30, 1925

Dearest Gaillard— So many thanks for yr letter of Sept. 6, just recovered from the clutches of the Vigo P.O. It is so full of "actuality," & I am so glad to get at last your sensations de Salso, that I must send a line at once in reply.—I'm glad you got on with Gioia[1] from the first, & I do so hope the treatment will turn out to have been the right thing. But we must go back some time together!

Poor Mrs. Griswold was taken ill again suddenly, just as I was to see her at the Ritz, & rushed off on the next day's steamer. It is such a strange modern habit—one of the many—to hurl suffering people on a train or steamer, & haul them from one hemisphere to another as a cure!

Percy's book is indeed a strange product in the light of his private affairs.[2] I was told yesterday (via London): "Oh, yes, Lady S. is divorcing Scott to marry Percy Lubbock." It all makes me rather sick—for him.

This is the 3d of my friends she has annexed, & I see you & Robert going next, & then B.B., & finally even Walter—kicking & screaming!!! Isn't it queer? When you think of the unintelligible "glapissements," & all the elderly archery— Apparently, with Percy, the fainting did it.[3] He is still much impressed, early Victorianism probably never having come his way before.

Oh, dear, come as quickly as you can to Ste Claire, let's talk & talk & talk.

Yrs affly
E.

I'm so glad you saw Chalmesbury. It's matchless.

Ms:BL

1. Gioia Grant Richards: Elisina Tyler's daughter by her former marriage.
2. Percy's book: *The Region Cloud*, Lubbock's only full-length work of fiction. It describes the relationship, delicately homoerotic and eventually disillusioned, between an aspiring young writer and a prodigiously successful painter, a much older man.
3. From Lady Sybil, EW had heard several times of the occasion when Percy Lubbock had fished his burning cigarette from the back of her dress, whereupon she had fainted into his arms.

To Royal Cortissoz

Sainte-Claire
Hyères
January 15, 1926

Dear Mr. Cortissoz— The book has just come with its so kind & friendly inscription, & I've already read two-thirds of it, with ever-growing interest & appreciation.[1] What you say of Inness especially appeals to me, for I remember seeing some of his landscapes over 20 years ago (& none since), & thinking that there was in them something "greater than *we* knew" at the time—but which made itself felt even to my untrained eyes. I am sure you are right to place him where you do.

As regards La Farge, d'autre part, I can only return a big ?—I shall never forget the sharp drop I felt when I saw his collection of water colours years ago in some French exhibition.

Why do the illustrations suddenly cease when you come to the modern men? It seems such a pity! And do you include in your condemnation of Cézanne all the Provençal landscapes? And did you ever see that great frieze of Gauguin's, with the ridiculous name: "Que sommes nous? Où allons nous?" or something of that sort—which was exhibited in Paris during the war, & then swallowed up by Germany? Lastly—in speaking of Odilon Redon, whom I detest when he is allegorical, ought you to have left out the flower pieces, almost the most exquisite I know?—Mind you, I care only *exceptionally* for these men; but some of the work of each (especially Cézanne & Gauguin) seems to me finer than you seem willing to admit. But as to Prudhon, I must pick a real quarrel. What! Put those bonbonnière Loves & Venuses, & all his mushy mythologies, above the two or three great great portraits in the Louvre—the profoundly "creole" Josephine, & that exquisite boy playing the spinet, supposed to be the young Mozart? ? ? And the lovely black-haired three quarter lady?? Oh, dear Mr. Cortissoz, come back & look *again*!

There—you see how much you have interested me, & can guess how much I should like to talk over this & much more with you.—When Mr. Berry & I made our wonderful pilgrimage to Compostela last September we were always grumbling at your not being with us. When are you coming?

Meanwhile, aurevoir & thanks again.

Yrs ever sincerely
  Edith Wharton

I didn't send you my "Writing of Fiction" out of discretion—because I suppose that, with regard to Scribner publications, you have only to reach out your hand & choose; & also because, after you had written to me so delightfully about the little book, I didn't want to oblige you to write again. But if I was wrong, & you haven't a copy, I should greatly like to send you one—I am sure, however, that Mr. Scribner has anticipated me.

Ms:BL

1. *Art and Common Sense* (1926). Among the painters discussed in the volume and mentioned here by EW are: George Inness (1825–1894), American land-scape painter; John La Farge (1835–1910), painter and stained-glass designer; Paul Cézanne (1839–1906); Paul Gauguin (1848–1903); Odilon Redon (1840–1916), French painter and graphic artist, whose work after 1890 had been chiefly a series of flower studies; and Pierre-Paul Prud'hon (1758–1823), French painter whose portrait of Empress Josephine (1805) was made while he was serving as her drawing teacher.

To Gaillard Lapsley

S. Y. Osprey
Gulf of Corinth
April 11 [1926]

Dearest Gaillard— We have been gone nearly a fortnight now, & have gone from glory to glory, till, as the hymn says, (or wd, had it been addressed to Apollo) yesterday at Delphi we "at his feet adoring fell."[1]

No words can express Delphi, nor tell you the beauty of the approach by the bay of Itea, with the snowy Acrocoraunian mountains in our rear, across the gulf, & ahead of us, over frowning Delphi, Parnassus all white with snow.—The day there was one long loveliness—including, embracing, the veal-&-ham pie which our very accomplished cook packed in the luncheon-basket, & we consumed under hoar olives just below the Castalian Fount—whenas the 200 or so members of the Hellenic Association, who had arrived by steamer at the same time, were feeding in the hotel. Luckily we had been warned of their coming, & so carried provend & hid ourselves among the olives. But the veil that Athene threw over us was not so thick but that Mr. & Mrs. Herbert Fisher, who were of the party, found us out, & came for a chat. They told us that the boat left Venice 10 days ago, & that they had done Athens, Crete, Rhodes, Nauplia, Argos, I *think* Sparta, Aegina, Olympia, Eleusis, &c &c, as well as Spalato, Traü, & Ragusa, & were now on the way back!!!—I told them that Americans were the only people left who understood the meaning of Leisure, & invited them to dine on the Osprey—but their boat carried them off inexorably. We always lie where we have excursioned, so that we may miss no beauties by voyaging at night.—So far the trip has been a perfect success, weather, yacht, company (& cook!) all as one wd wish if one were dreaming of such a tour—but, oh, I do miss you, & you wd add the gilding to the lily!—

We're bound for Acro-Corinth today, & Athens tomorrow. The hotels are all crammed, so we shall stay on the yacht at New Phalerum. After 8 days there, we go to Sunium, Marathon, Chalcis, then Nauplia, Argos, Epidaurus, Mycenae Tyrins, & perhaps Sparta—then through the islands to Rhodes, Cyprus, Crete & back.—

Robert keeps all my accounts for me, & in the rare intervals between these labours makes lovely water colours of Greek ports. Our route, by the way, has been via Palermo, Cephalonia, Zante, Olympia, Delphi— a rapturous day for each, with long lazy intervals of sea between.

Everyone seems permanently happy,[2] except Robert, who, when he saw the 150 ladies of the Hellenic Association grouped about the Castalian Fount in daring costumes evidently ordered with great care at Hampstead, Birmingham & Manchester for the occasion, declared that he would forswear his nationality & take out Greek (or American, I forget which) naturalization papers.

At dinner he was still brooding over these brawny nymphs in grass-green "Mother Hubbards" & Cubist sweaters—& nothing cd distract him from the thought that he might have been married to one of them,

& on that tour. But he isn't.—Well, my dear, bless you. We'll do this again some year when you're free.

> Yrs ever
> 　Edith

Write to me care of Ionian Bank, Athens
In the evening we read aloud "The Odyssey"—or "Blondes."[3]

Ms:BL

1. EW had chartered the *Osprey*, a 360-ton steam yacht from England, carrying five "master cabins" and two cabins for servants. The party boarded the yacht near Hyères, and set out on a ten-week Aegean cruise.

2. In a letter to Mildred Bliss written the same day as this one, EW said: "The party is very pleasant—Daisy Chanler, always a perfect companion, Robert Norton, who makes us lovely sketches of Greek harbours on the way, & acts as interpreter, Pearsall Smith, who had done the trip before with the Berensons, & is most helpful about knowing all the ropes—& a very pleasant Englishman, a Mr. Lawrence, who is at the head of the Medici Society."

3. *Gentlemen Prefer Blondes* (1925), by Anita Loos. In a letter to John Hugh Smith earlier in the year, EW said of this vivacious novel—the diary musings of the cheerfully amoral Lorelei Lee as she moves from Kansas to various Ritz Hotels in Europe—that "the literary committee of Ste. Claire (R. Norton, G. Lapsley, and EW) unhesitatingly pronounce [it] the greatest novel since *Manon Lescaut*." She allowed herself to be quoted as calling it "*the* great American novel."

To Margaret Terry Chanler

Pavillon Colombe
August 11, 1926

Dearest Daisy— Your dear letter came just after I had written to you, & of course I chuck a long list of duty-correspondents to thank you for the uplift.

I'm sorry poor Laura has been feeling tired & out of sorts; your visit must have been a great comfort to her. And now you are in your garden, & I suppose enjoying a much better show of flowers than we've had here, for the cold rainy summer has made everything look mouldy.

The va-et-vient continues at St Brice. I am rather like Paris, & no longer have a morte saison!—The John Garretts[1] turned up the other day, & asked me to lunch with Anita Loos,[2] who is such a sensible & sagacious little creature that I hope you'll run across her some day.— Minnie is here, as I told you, & last week Geoffrey Scott came for a fortnight—a really pitiful figure, dazed at what has happened to him, & thoroughly unhappy, but very dignified & even generous in his way of speaking of Sibyl, who told him he *must* let her divorce him because she wanted to marry Percy! Oh, these lubie grandmothers! They make me sick.

Dearest Daisy, you mustn't lecture me for not appreciating America on the score that I don't know Ethel Derby,[3] for I've known her for years & years, & like her very much, & always take the opportunity of seeing her when I can! Of course there are green isles in that sea of misery—but they're so far apart, & they don't encircle one dancingly, like some islands we know. Alas, there are not enough to go round.

I'm digging away at "Twilight Sleep,"[4] & must end this to take up my task.

> Best love from your devoted
> Edith

Nico had a glorious afternoon yesterday at Senlis. He is dearer than ever.—I'd almost forgotten to tell you how thrilled we all are by the home life of the old Cutting uncle on the yacht! It's truly horrible—& so it is that they have become still richer by his death—when they already have too much—& don't even know what life is.

Ms:BL

1. John Work Garrett (1872–1942), after extensive diplomatic service (including several years as a special assistant during the war to the American Ambassador to France) was appointed Ambassador to Italy in 1929 and served as such until 1933. He was married to the former Alice Warder.

2. See letter to Lapsley, April 11, 1926. The lunch in honor of Anita Loos

and her husband, John Emerson, president of Actors' Equity, took place at the Ritz in Paris.

3. Ethel Derby, born in 1891, was the third child and only daughter of Theodore Roosevelt and Edith Carow Roosevelt. In 1913, she married Richard Derby (1881–1963), a well-to-do New Yorker who was at the start of a very successful career as a surgeon and hospital director. During the war, Mrs. Derby served as chairman of the New York committee for EW's refugee hostels.

Mrs. Chanler's "lecture" was provoked by EW's comments in an earlier letter about *The Pilgrimage of Henry James* (1925) by Van Wyck Brooks. EW thought the book "delightfully written" with an unusually broad range of reference; but it went astray because "the author is determined to assume that human relations in America are intrinsically as interesting as in the old centres of civilization & social life. He clings to Howells's silly 'the whole of human life is left' "—i.e., Howells's rejoinder to Henry James's critique of American society—"& as no one could possibly write as good English as he does, & *really* believe that, I conclude that, like the rest of his wistful minority, he is whistling to keep his courage up."

4. *Twilight Sleep* was published in June 1927 by Appleton.

To Gaillard Lapsley

Annecy

September 28, 1926

Dearest Gaillard— I know how inexorable you are, & was afraid there was no chance of my persuading you to wait; but all the same, it's a great disappointment!—

The Crillon is a severe discipline, & I endure it only by living on my roof-top & thanking heaven I'm not at the Ritz!—I'm sorry that Salso didn't suit your sister. Was it the cure, or just the climate, or the ineffable place?? I hope you haven't lost faith—or how shall I ever have the courage to go back there?

If she liked Venice better, I marvel at her! We fled there from the nauseating heat & dust of the Lombard plain, & spent five days of horror among the human wreckage of the brilliant Lido season!!! No words can tell you what it was. The hero of the year was Cole Porter, the jazz-composer.[1] He had hired the Rezzonico Palace (what of soul was left, I wonder?), where he had given a Venetian festival, & having discovered from "the old books" (sic) that rope-dancing was part of these entertainments, had treated his guests to a rope-dance across the Rezzonico cortile. As the Princess San Faustino said to me with genuine emotion: "It was really magnificent. He revived all the ancient glories of Venice."

From this shallow abyss we fled to the Dolomites—such glorious summits! The chief object of our trip (after we gave up Spain) had been the dead towns between Venice & Trieste—Aquileia, Pomposa, Grado, &c—& then a dash down to Spalato & Ragusa.—But heat & dust made this impossible for me, so we shortened our trip, & came down to Lake Garda, & across to Bergamo. Berenson came from Genoa to meet us at Aosta, & there we had a delightful day with him. Then he went back to Turin to meet Mrs. B., & we crossed yesterday to Annecy, & are now turned homeward.

I am sending you this long history for the mere pleasure of monologuing to you, for I know an answer is not to be hoped for— But then there's December ahead!

So glad the frame was a success, & the birthday.—I'm afraid Josephine Griswold is very ill. I had a courageous but sad letter from her a few days ago—but Len Sands, whom we ran across at Cortina, had heard from some one who had seen the surgeon that he said she would be perfectly well!—?—

Yours ever affly
    E—

Nicky Mariano,[2] who was with B.B., is convinced that Percy will *not* marry S. She underrates S.!

Ms:BL

1. Cole Porter (1891–1964) had settled in Paris in 1917, and married the internationally famous beauty Linda Thomas, whom EW had come to know through Bernard Berenson. Porter's music was popular with the social elite, but he would not have his first real success until *50 Million Frenchmen* in 1929.

2. Nicky Mariano (her first name, never used, was Elisabetta), of aristocratic background, half Baltic and half Neapolitan, joined the staff at Berenson's I Tatti in 1919 as librarian, and had gradually been induced to take general

charge of Berenson's affairs. She remained with Berenson, as chief aid and companion, for forty years. She and EW had not gotten on well at first, but a friendship had begun in the fall of 1923.

To Gaillard Lapsley

Sainte-Claire
Hyères
November 28, 1926

Dearest Gaillard,

Do make haste! Since I got here 10 days ago the weather has been so incredibly benign & beautiful that I am trembling lest the supply should be exhausted before your Blue train gets you here. I read of cataclysms of all sorts at the other end of the Riviera, but here it is hushed & warm & radiant every day, & the garden is in a state of exuberance.

I had a strenuous fortnight in Paris, for Walter Berry chose the second week of my sojourn to be seized with acute appendicitis, necessitating an operation "à chaud"—not particularly pleasant when the patient is over 60— There was no one else to decide things, & I had a good deal of anxiety, & of rushing about, & was glad at last when I cd come down here, leaving him with a good English nurse & no "complications."

The peacefulness of this blessed terrace seemed all the more soothing, & when, two days ago, I finished "Twilight Sleep," I said: "Ouf," as Napoleon said that Europe wd when he died. I had a three days' visit from Lawrence Johnston last week, & now have to depend for social sustenance on dear Philomène—& Gerhardi! Robert is happily painting in Spain, & says firmly that he won't come till the weather spoils—but reassure yourself as to my lack of companionship, for the Duchess is due in a few days.

John Hugh, whom I saw in Paris (& who was most kind & helpful about Walter) tells me that he is much pleased with Percy's book. Incidentally, he also writes that he hears Sybil is going to jilt him for another! I have heard this several times, & am praying it may be true.

In order to bring your arrival nearer in imagination I am sending my usual cheque—(If the Cabinet Noir reads this, the conclusion will be that gentlemen don't take the Train Bleu without being helped!)*

Thank you in advance, & best love— Hurrah for the 21st!

Yrs

    E

* Bring it in 5 & 10 notes, will you?

Did I tell you that Lily Norton gave up a winter abroad, & rushed home to Chestnut St, because Gilbert Murray is going to lecture on poetry at Harvard (the chair founded by her father),[1] & though she apparently doesn't like the Murrays, she felt she ought to be there to provide them with vegetarian food & rooms facing south—which no one else would. After all, what fun it must be to be a Bostonian! It's the only surviving habitat of the Moral Imperative.

Ms:BL

1. Gilbert Murray (1866–1957), currently giving the Charles Eliot Norton lectures at Harvard, was the most brilliant and influential Greek scholar of his time, and professor of Greek at Oxford from 1908 to 1936.

To Robert Woods Bliss

Sainte-Claire

January 2, 1927

My dear Robert,

Your kind & copious wire came yesterday, & I have dashed off orders to London, hoping to scrape together there nearly all my books.

"The Decoration of Houses," written with Ogden Codman, & "Italian Villas," are not available, & "The Touchstone" & "Mme de Treymes" & "The Greater Inclination" & "The Valley of Decision" will probably have to come from America.

I don't stop to thank you, but simply enclose my list, & dash this off,

& reserve the expressions of my gratitude & appreciation for a moment of greater leisure.[1]

My fondest wishes for the best of New Years to you & Mildred—who has got rid of her grippe poison by this time, I hope.

Yrs ever affly
Edith

Walter went back yesterday, greatly fortified by his fortnight of air-cure.

I have ordered the early books mentioned above from New York. The "Twelve Poems"[2] are unobtainable.

Ms:BL

1. Robert Bliss, then American Ambassador to Sweden, and Mildred Bliss organized a move to win the Nobel Prize in literature for Edith Wharton, enlisting the support of Chief Justice Taft, Lord Balfour, and Jules Cambon. EW supplied such books of hers as were on hand for the effort.

Two awards in fact were given in 1927: one to Henri Bergson, the French philosopher, and the second to Grazia Deledda, the novelist of Sardinian life. Writing to Mildred Bliss on January 15, 1928, and saying that she had never had "the least expectation" of receiving the prize, EW questioned the choice of Grazia Deledda when such Italian writers as the novelist Matilde Serao and Federico di Roberto "went to the grave without it" (both had died in 1927), and Gabriele d'Annunzio had yet to be honored.

2. *Twelve Poems*, by Edith Wharton, published by the Medici Society, London (1926).

To Mary Cadwalader Jones

Hôtel de Crillon
January 25, 1927

Dearest Minnie,

Royal Cortissoz, who is here, & who sails tomorrow, will give you the tragic history of the last 10 days. Walter, on his return from Hyères on Jan. 1st, felt so well that he rashly took up his usual very active life—business, charities, legal affairs, & society—with the result that on Jan. 12th he was suddenly seized with aphasia, produced by slight congestion of the brain. There was no paralysis of the body, but the reading & writing "areas" were affected. They have gradually healed, so that he is now able to read with perfect facility, & write a few lines at a time. But the speech remains very much impaired, & as his brain, from the first, has been perfectly lucid, I ask you to imagine the torture he is undergoing! He is like a great powerful bird caught in a net.

They sent for me at once, & I have done what I could—so little! But I have guarded the door, explained to his friends, & consulted with the Drs. who are all hopeful of complete recovery within a few months. They cite many cases of people much older than Walter who have been more "gravement atteints," & have got back to perfectly normal conditions.

If he continues to get on better, the Dr. says I can return to Hyères at the end of this week, & Walter, I hope, will follow next week, under White's escort.

Yesterday Cortissoz lunched with him. Call him up, & he will tell you his impressions. I can't write more today, but thank you for your letters, & do tell Lucy Whitridge that it was in my mind to cable my affte wishes for Joan's wedding, & then this disaster put all dates out of my head—

Yrs ever   E

I am almost forgetting to tell you that I've *at last* bought Ste. Claire, "from the centre all round to the sea."

Walter did it for me when he was at Hyères last month!

Ms:BL

Pavillon Colombe (the villa Jean-Marie at St. Brice), with Edith Wharton at the corner, 1924. *Beinecke Library, Yale University.*

The gardens at Pavillon Colombe. *Beinecke Library, Yale University.*

Edith Wharton, 1925. *Beinecke Library, Yale University.*

Bernard Berenson at Montalcino, 1925. *Berenson Archives, Villa I Tatti, Florence, Italy.*

Sainte-Claire le Château, Hyères, France: the approach.
Beinecke Library, Yale University.

The terrace of Sainte-Claire. *Beinecke Library, Yale University.*

The salon at Sainte-Claire. *Beinecke Library, Yale University.*

Philomène de Lévis-
Mirepoix, around 1925.
*Berenson Archives, Villa
I Tatti, Florence, Italy.*

Lady Sybil Cutting at Villa Medici, mid-1920s. *Berenson Archives, Villa
I Tatti, Florence, Italy.*

The *Osprey*, a steam yacht rented by Edith Wharton for a ten-week cruise through the Aegean, spring 1926. *Beinecke Library, Yale University.*

Catharine Gross, Edith Wharton's lifelong friend and housekeeper, 1930. *Beinecke Library, Yale University.*

Edith Wharton, 1930. *Beinecke Library, Yale University.*

Edith Wharton with Lady Wemyss, H. G. Wells (*foreground, right*), and an unidentified man. *Beinecke Library, Yale University.*

Robert Norton and Edith Wharton on a picnic near Hyères, early 1930s. *Beinecke Library, Yale University.*

Beatrix Farrand at Sainte-Claire, 1934. *Beinecke Library, Yale University.*

Kenneth Clark at Saltwood Castle, around 1950. *Berenson Archives, Villa I Tatti, Florence, Italy.*

Gaillard Lapsley in his study, 1937. *Berenson Archives, Villa I Tatti, Florence, Italy.*

Edith Wharton's last letter, to Matilda Gay, August 4, 1937.
William Royall Tyler Collection, Lily Library, University of Indiana.

To Mary Cadwalader Jones

Sainte-Claire
Hyères
April 11, 1927

Dearest Minnie— Just a line to say that yr letter of April 1, enclosing the "Old Maid" scenario, has just come.[1]

The scenario seems to me excellent. I noted not only the kitchen, which is *perhaps* wrong—though the good housekeeper of those days did go into the kitchen, especially on the eve of festivities. At any rate, Charlotte wd certainly go to interview the cook somewhere—she does in my story.—What is radically wrong is afternoon tea! They would have a light port & cookies, or a dry sherry, wouldn't they?—These little touches are important in a "costume" play.

I am cabling that I like the scenario, as it may hasten matters.

Never mind about the extra chandail[2]—I can't keep all the orders straight, & neither can Mlle D., apparently! Give it to any one you like; I'm too glad to give the extra help to Mme Gondevitch.[3]

What is the news of Lily Norton? I wrote to her some weeks ago, & having had no answer I fear she may be less well.

Will you also find out for me if an article on the "Great American Novel," which I sent to Professor Cross, of the Yale Review, ever reached them?[4] They clamoured for it for two or three months, wrote, cabled, &c, & I finally posted it on *March* 10th, registered, & cabled them to that effect—since when, dead silence! However, I wrote Prof. Cross last week to ask what had happened, & my object now is chiefly to request that you will ask for the proofs for correction—unless there is still time to send them out to me. I forgot to mention this in writing to him.

You see, I continue to take for granted yr willingness to deal with my proofs—& am proportionately grateful!—If there is time to send them, however, I prefer it, because I sometimes make slight changes.

All well here, & weather celestial. A year ago we were at Delphi!—

Yrs ever
E.W.

What has happened to "The Age of Innocence"? It seems to be dead— My best remembrances to Sheldon—[5]

Ms:BL

1. *The Old Maid* was being dramatized by Zoë Akins. It would finally open to a successful run on Broadway in 1935, and win a Pulitzer Prize for Miss Akins.

2. Sweater.

3. The Russian-born Mme. Gondevitch and her husband, a former Russian nobleman, were living in precarious circumstances near Hyères. EW solicited clothes-making orders from America for Mme. Gondevitch, and translating jobs for her spouse.

4. EW's article "The Great American Novel" appeared in the July 1927 issue of the *Yale Review*. The periodical was edited by Wilbur Cross, professor of English at Yale and the author of books on Laurence Sterne and Henry Fielding. He would later serve two terms (1931–1939) as Governor of Connecticut.

5. EW had met the playwright Edward Sheldon (1886–1946) in 1923, on her visit to New York and New Haven. Sheldon had had a series of stage successes, beginning with *Salvation Nell* in 1908. Though completely paralyzed with a form of arthritis since 1923, he continued to work and produce and to entertain friends—among them, in particular, Mary Cadwalader Jones. He interested himself effectively in the matter of transferring EW's writings to stage and screen.

To Upton Sinclair[1]

August 19, 1927

Dear Mr. Sinclair,

I received your novel "Oil"[2] a few months ago, and read it (from the point of view of your skill as a novelist) with great enjoyment and admiration.

It seems to me an excellent story until the moment, all too soon, when it becomes a political pamphlet. I make this criticism without regard to the views which you teach, and which are detestable to me. Had you written in favour of those in which I believe, my judgment would have been exactly the same. I have never known a novel that was good enough to be good in spite of its being adapted to the author's political views.

Having said this, I hasten to add that the charge of obscenity is absurd, & I am glad to join in protesting against it, from the moment that it is clearly understood that my protest applies to that charge only.

I shall be glad if my name is of any use to you in freeing the novel from this unjust and ignorant aspersion.

I should like to add, that while I can understand that the sight of such a life as you describe as being led by your oil millionaires is enough to justify any thoughtful man in the desire to make some radical change in the organization of society, I believe that a wider experience would have shown you that the evils you rightly satirize will be replaced by others more harmful to any sort of civilized living when your hero and his friends have had their way.

Yours sincerely
Edith Wharton

Copy:WRT

1. The enormously prolific writer (1878–1968) was the author at this time of *The Jungle* (1906), *The Metropolis* (1908), and *Jimmie Higgins* (1919), among many other novels.
2. *Oil!* (1927) drew upon the Teapot Dome scandal in the Harding administration. The main character, Bunny Ross, the son of an oil operator, comes to realize the varieties of corruption that seem inseparable from private ownership of the oil industry, and (like Sinclair himself many years before) is converted to socialism.

To John Hugh Smith

Grand Hôtel des Thermes
Salsomaggiore
September 6, 1927

My dear John,

Your letter came two or three days ago, & should have been answered at once if I had not been sunk in the torpor resulting from the inhaling, twice a day, of these beneficent iodine fumes.

I'm glad you are going to see poor Gerhardi. I was afraid you could do nothing for him, but at any rate he will be grateful for your thought, & I'm sure you will think him a worthwhile document—I won't say human being, for there's something too elfish & troll-ish about him.

Do let me know the result of the meeting. If you are due in Paris before long, perhaps you may give it to me de vive voix, for I shall be back on the 16th at the latest, perhaps on the 15th. We leave here the day after tomorrow for Modane, where the motor is to meet us, & if it is not too hellishly hot on the Riviera we shall go down to Hyères by the "route des Alpes" for 24 hours, so that I may see how the work on the house is getting on; & then motor back to St Brice. We are to call at Antigny, by the way, & shall see Peter, back from the Acropolis. That will be fun.

Meanwhile, I hear from Gross that the Abbé Terret's books[1] have arrived at St Brice, & I send you any number of renewed thanks for this monumental reminder of our tour.

I am not worrying about you & Sybil *as yet*, for I know she is in Switzerland, where Gaillard saw her & P. at Lausanne. But if I hear of her in London I shall leap on the first Airways plane as it passes over my garden, & descend on you within the hour. *This kind of thing has got to stop.*

Gaillard, I think, is safe. Sybil made the mistake of calling (after he left Lausanne) on his sister, with Percy, whom the latter likes, & wanted to have a talk with. She wrote to G. that she hadn't been able to exchange a word with Percy, & that Sybil talked so much that her voice became higher & higher, "till I couldn't hear a word she said, & it was just like the whizzing of an electric fan." This has chastened G. a good deal.

I always heard that Crétineau[2] hadn't stolen his name. I'll try to find out from the Abbé Bremond where the supposed book on the Dissolution of the Jesuits can be found. And, by the way, I'm reading an enchanting little sketch of St Francis Xavier, by André Bellesort.[3] I'm sure you'd like it. The description of that incredible Goa in the 16th century, & all the Portuguese settlements along the coast of southern India, is a marvel of picturesqueness.—I love the Jesuit missionaries, & want to know more about one he alludes to, the Père de Nobilis, who made himself a Brahmin to convert the Brahmins.

By the way, he speaks of a very remarkable book (he calls it délicieux), the Histoire de la Cie de Jésus en France, by H. Fourqueray, S.J./ Picard, 1910.—This might fall in with yr present reading.

I shall be glad of a good talk with you, for topics have a way of piling up.

Yrs affly
   E.

Write to St Brice, it will be forwarded.

Did I recommend Halphen, "Les Barbares,"[4] Félix Alcan? Very good.

[Printed advertisement at bottom of hotel stationery: "P.S. lo bevo a tavola il Chianti Brolio e lo raccomando perchè veramente delizioso." In EW's hand:] Pity I can't confirm this from personal experience!

Ms:BL

1. Victor Terret (1856–?), *La sculpture bourguignonne aux XIIe et XIII siècles* (2 vols., 1925).

2. Jacques Crétineau-Joly (1803–1875), author of *Histoire religieuse, politique et littéraire de la Compagnie de Jésus* (3d ed., 1859).

3. André Bellesort (1866–1924), *L'Apôtre des Indes et du Japon, saint François Xavier* (1917).

4. Louis Halphen (1880–1950), *Les Barbares des grands-invasions aux conquêtes turques du XIe siècle* (1926), published by F. Alcan.

To John Hugh Smith

Hôtel de Crillon
October 12, 1927

My dear John,

Walter died this morning.

It was much better— Yesterday afternoon I held him in my arms, & talked to him of old times, & he pressed my hand & remembered.

I'm going back to St Brice.

Edith

Ms:BL

To Gaillard Lapsley

Hôtel de Crillon
October 12, 1927

Dearest Gaillard,

Walter had another stroke ten days ago, & died this morning. All my life goes with him. He knew me all through, & wd see no one else but me.

Edith

I go back to St Brice today.

Ms:BL

To John Hugh Smith

Pavillon Colombe
St Brice
October 15, 1927

My dearest John— All my friends have sent me words of sympathy, but only you have said just what I wanted, what I needed. Thank you, dear.

Yes, I am glad indeed that it is over, but I perceive now that I, who thought I loved solitude, was never for one moment alone—& a great desert lies ahead of me.

The sense of desolation (though of thankfulness too, of course) is unspeakably increased by those last days together, when he wanted me so close, & held me so fast, that all the old flame & glory came back, in the cold shadow of death & parting. Oh, my dear, I sometimes feel I am too old to live through such hours, & take up the daily round again.

But I remember what you say, & I am proud of having kept such a perfect friendship after the great days were over, & always to have felt that, through all the coming & going of things in his eager ambitious life, I was there, in the place he put me in so many years ago, the place of perfect understanding.

I don't think I ever bothered him but once—& when he felt that the busy brilliant days were over, he liked to have me with him, because he knew I wouldn't fuss & sentimentalize, or try to divert his eyes from the end we both knew they were fixed on. He hated humbug—so do I.—And now I'm so grateful to all my friends for understanding what I feel—& you most, dear John.

Edith

Robert is staying with me, & won't leave till after the funeral. He has been kindness itself.

Ms:BL

To Bernard Berenson

Pavillon Colombe
October 25, 1927

Dearest B.B.,
What friends you are—what friends! Since your telegram came yesterday I have felt alive again.[1]
My dears, thank you both with all my heart.

Yrs ever
Edith

Oct 25. 27
A très bientôt—

Ms:VT

1. Berenson had cabled that he and Nicky Mariano would come at once to Paris to be with EW.

PART SEVEN

A World of Difference
1928–1937

Introduction

❀

THE PEAK OF Edith Wharton's success as a widely read and highly paid novelist was reached with *The Children*, a Book-of-the-Month Club selection in September 1928. In two months' time, it had earned its author $95,000 from all sources (including film rights), more than any novel she had ever written. But though she was pleased by the money accruing, Edith was depressed by the banality of the reviews: "uncomprehending drivel (laudatory or not)," as she told her friend the art critic Royal Cortissoz. All thoughts of literary activity, however, were driven away the following winter when some of the stormiest and iciest weather in Riviera history virtually destroyed the gardens at Ste. Claire, over which Edith Wharton had labored so devotedly and imaginatively. While trying to recover from this shock to her system, Edith was stricken with pneumonia and nearly died. A trip to America to accept an honorary degree from Columbia was canceled, and work was impossible. It was mid-summer, 1929, before she was able to pick up her ongoing novel *Hudson River Bracketed*, itself already running in serial form ahead of the schedule she had agreed to.

These disasters might, in fanciful retrospect, be seen as foreshadowings of the economic disaster that befell America and then Europe in the fall of 1929. As it happened, Edith Wharton was slow to feel the effects of the Great Depression. It was not until early in 1932 that the state of things began to come home to her, and she could write Berenson, himself alarmed at the financial news, that "we are all . . . nervously sitting on the thin crust of some volcano." Her novel *The Gods Arrive*, the sequel to *Hudson River Bracketed*, was turned down by several periodicals, ostensibly because of its subject matter (Halo Tarrant's out-of-wedlock pregnancy), but also, as it seems, because of a reluctance to pay Mrs. Wharton's large fees. Her fine, bitter tale "Joy in the House" was rejected by a series of editors on the grounds that its theme (the vindictive cruelty of a betrayed husband) was not suitable for readers who now preferred cheerful and escapist fiction. For the same reason, the story "Duration," after being accepted by *Woman's Home Companion*, was withheld from publication. On being informed of this, Edith Wharton wrote Jewett: "When I think of my position as a writer, I am really staggered by the insolence of the letter."

She was further outraged when the editor at *Ladies' Home Journal* proposed that she cut her memoirs, *A Backward Glance*, by forty thousand words with a proportionate cut in her fee. "Absolutely decline reducing price," Edith cabled Jewett, "and will sue him unless agreement kept." Her rancor lasted through the book publication by Appleton. Indignant at what she regarded as irresponsibly poor advertising, Mrs. Wharton asked to be released from the contract for her next novel. The chairman at Appleton wrote a lengthy and reasoned reply, pointing out that the firm had paid Mrs. Wharton some $578,905 since 1918, and had acted as her agent for serial and film rights. Mrs. Wharton remained with the company.

As the 1930s went forward, she grew ever more conscious as well of the political changes and dangers in the world around her. She saw communism taking over in Spain, and the threat of it in her village of St. Brice. Mussolini and fascism (Berenson was her tutor here) were ruining Italy for her; and Hitler's angry radio speeches horrified her. The bloody and prolonged rioting in Paris in February 1934 had apocalyptic overtones for her; her always lively historical sense was stirred by the event as it had been in the late terrible months of 1914. And it may be that her notably heightened responsiveness in this time to the Church of Rome, its rituals and teachings, arose in part from a feeling of estrangement from the earthly scene, and of doubt about any rational explanation of human affairs.

Her own personal human society was never healthier. Old friends— American, British, French—were continuously on hand, in the Pavillon Colombe summers and the Ste. Claire winters. Several new Riviera friends were of special pleasure to her: Aldous and Maria Huxley (Edith thought that Huxley's *Brave New World* was a masterpiece); and the learned and sympathetic Polish-born anthropologist Bronislaw Malinowski. The affable and rumpled Steven Runciman, emerging as the most distinguished Byzantine historian of his generation, was a prized addition. In 1930, and for a time thereafter, Edith and Morton Fullerton were back in touch, with Edith sounding fondly ironic in messages to her former lover.

The greatest and most enduring new friendship in the last decade of Edith Wharton's life was with Kenneth and Jane Clark. Edith met Clark while touring in Italy in 1930; the Clarks paid their first visit to Ste. Claire in March 1931. Kenneth Clark's extraordinary career as curator and historian of art was already under way with his appointment as keeper of the Ashmolean in Oxford. No one was prouder or happier than Edith Wharton when Clark, at age thirty, was made director of the National Gallery in London, in 1933. She was no less proud when asked to become godmother to the Clarks' infant son, Colin. Between the American woman entering into her seventies and the Englishman entering his thirties there developed the most thoughtful and helpful of friendships.

Edith Wharton's community was not without its troubles. Her vexation with Percy Lubbock, at one time the choicest of her young English literary friends, grew apace, after Sybil Cutting divorced Geoffrey Scott (whom, in Edith's view, she should never have married to begin with) to marry Lubbock. Some unlucky encounters at the Salzburg Festival in 1934 led to an irreparable rupture. Edith Wharton's household staff was breaking asunder. A French cook was killed in a motorcycle crash, his successor had a cerebral hemorrhage on the kitchen floor and died, an Italian servant was murdered by his wife. Even more grievous for Edith Wharton was the death from anemia of Elise, her French personal maid since the Paris days; and not long after (1933), Catharine Gross, who had been Edith's friend and housekeeper since 1884, descended into suicidal mania, drifted into mindlessness and died.

Edith Wharton's literary vigor and inventiveness were far from flagging. In the 1930s, she brought out three volumes of short stories; and the third, *The World Over* in 1936, contained such narrative gems as "Roman Fever," "Pomegranate Seed," and "Duration." She was making admirable progress, at intervals, on a novel called *The Buccaneers*, a story set in the America of Saratoga and New York, and then the England of great country houses in the 1870s. It showed every promise of being one of her most accomplished works of fiction; but it was left incomplete at her death, and was published in 1938 with an outline of the plot by the author and an appreciative note by Gaillard Lapsley. Edith Wharton's financial well-being, meanwhile, was fully restored by the considerable runs on Broadway and on the road of the dramatic versions of *The Old Maid* and *Ethan Frome*. Between 1935 and 1937, the several companies earned her about $130,000.

She was to the last, as she said to Mary Berenson, "an incorrigible life-lover, life-wonderer and adventurer." Intermittent illness or fatigue did nothing to impair her serenity of spirit in these final years, nor her response to the genuinely beautiful. "How thankful I am," she wrote Berenson in April 1937, "to remember that, whether as to people or to places & occasions, I've *always* known the gods the moment I met them." It was a far-echoing remark, and one that connected up half a lifetime: reevoking the passage from Emerson she had first drawn upon, in late February 1908, to tell Morton Fullerton of the nature of her love for him.

Seven weeks after that, Edith Wharton, journeying north from Hyères to St. Brice, suffered a stroke. She was transported by ambulance to Pavillon Colombe, where she lingered on for two more months. On August 4, she wrote a line to Matilda Gay. It showed a flash of her old vitality—she had wanted to visit Matilda that afternoon, she said, "but Elisina & my maid behaved so awfully about it that I had no alternative but to go on dozing on the sofa"—but the handwriting was shaky.

Edith Wharton died on August 11. She had meticulously set down instructions for her funeral and burial in a document of May 1936; and in accordance with them, after a brief service in the Cimetière des Gonards in Versailles, her body was lowered into the double plot she had bought near the grave of Walter Berry.

To Mildred Bliss

Sainte-Claire
Hyères
February 10, 1928

Dearest Mildred,

I have decided to bequeath my property in France partly for the foundation of a home of refuge for hopeless cases of tuberculosis, and partly for the relief of stationary cases (curable) from the sanatoria of Taverny and Groslay,[1] who need to be looked after and cared for longer than the regulation time provided for by the rules of a government sanatorium.

In order to prepare the way for the immediate application of this bequest after my death, I have been advised to reconstitute under its old name, but with certain modifications, the original Committee of the "American Convalescent Homes," founded by me during the war. The immediate object of this revived Committee would be to take care of such cases requiring assistance as are brought to its notice, and to alleviate as much as possible, indirectly, and by means of existing institutions, the class of patients which it hopes later on to receive under its own roof.

In view of the legacy which I intend to make, I have been definitely assured that this Committee, even though it would exercise a very restricted activity until my death, would be granted without delay the "Reconnaissance d'Utilité Publique" of the French Government.

If the Committee can be constituted at once my intention is to dispose of my property in France as follows:

1st—My property at Hyères to be sold, and the capital to constitute the endowment for the sanatorium to be founded.

2d—My property at Saint-Brice-sous-Forêt to be divided into two parts as follows:

The actual Pavillon Colombe and the pleasure-grounds to remain as they are at present. (The upkeep of this house and the grounds would not be a matter of heavy expense.)

A part of the present kitchen-garden to be used for building the two sanatoria. A separate entrance leading to these buildings would be made from the outer road.

The buildings of the actual Pavillon Colombe would serve to lodge the nurses and the "personnel" of the sanatoria.

I hope that, after my death, many of the American friends who were associated with my work during the war, and especially those who live in France and know how much such an organization as that above described is needed, will be disposed to help now, and afterwards to carry out the complete plan as outlined in the accompanying paper.[2]

Yours very affly,
     Edith

Ms:LA

1. The two sanatoria, small private estates just north of Paris, had been established by EW in the spring of 1916.

2. The Committee for the American Convalescent Homes was revived, with Elisina Tyler mostly in charge; but EW's property was eventually bequeathed privately.

To Gaillard Lapsley

Sainte-Claire
February 11, 1928

Dearest Gaillard— Mrs. Billy Wharton cabled to me yesterday that Teddy died on Feb. 7th.[1]—It is a happy release, for the real Teddy went years ago, & these survivals of the body are ghastly beyond expression.—I wanted you to know because you are so dear a friend; but Robert agrees with me that it is useless to make any sort of general announcement, since, technically, it is so long now since our ways parted for good & all.

I hope you are holding your own—

Yrs ever affly
     E.

Ms:BL

1. Teddy Wharton was seventy-nine at the time of his death. To Robert Grant, EW wrote: "I am thankful to think of him at peace after all the weary agitated years." Teddy had been "the kindest of companions till that dreadful blighting illness came upon him." He left an estate of about $56,000 to Pearl Barrett, the trained nurse who took care of him after his sister Nancy's death.

To Rutger B. Jewett

August 10, 1928

Dear Mr. Jewett, Your letter of July 27th has just come, and though I am always sorry to say no when you ask me to do anything which you feel may be of use to Messrs. Appleton, I fear I must put my veto on the cinema plan.[1]

Apart from the fatigue that it would involve I must confess that I should not be greatly flattered at being associated with some of the ladies named in the list who are to figure in this same series; and all I can do to make up for my refusal is to try to find, as soon as possible, a good photographer to take me here in the garden.

Thanks very much for the announcements of the book. I hope the forecast will be realised, and the success of "The Age of Innocence" surpassed. Do send me a few advance copies, if you can, as I am impatient to see the book.

I enclose herewith the cards you have asked me to sign.

Yours very sincerely

P.S.—Do please excuse my long delay in returning the enclosed letter; it came to me a few days before I left for England and I am ashamed to say that I put it aside and forgot it. I hope the delay has not inconvenienced you.

Copy:BL

1. The Will Hays motion picture organization had proposed a special film to be called *Woman Marches On*, to portray the accomplishments of American women in various fields since 1900. There were to be reels on such "notable

women" as Gertrude Vanderbilt Whitney, sculptress and patron of the arts; Dr. Florence Sabin, professor at the Johns Hopkins Medical School who had made major discoveries in lymphatics; Mary Pickford, the film actress; and Kathleen Norris, the popular novelist.

Jewett passed along the proposal to EW, with the notation that there was "an insistent demand" that she be part of the picture, and asking if she would let the producers take films of her in her home in France.

To Gaillard Lapsley

Pavillon Colombe
August 13, 1928

Dearest Gaillard— How have you fared on the way over, I wonder? It was dear of you to write in that final rush, of which only you & I know (I am persuaded) the full horror.—I hope the voyage was comfortable enough to repair the damage.

I was much interested in yr report of a worn but gallant Percy— especially as Philomène, who lunched here last Sunday, told me that Nicky had told her that Sybil gave Geoffrey, as a reason for divorcing him (& marrying P.), that "mawwiage is constwuctive."—I should add that Phil. & her husband[1] have been spending a happy fortnight at I Tatti, where they met Sybil, & found her portentous.

Did I tell you, by the way, that I saw Victoria Cholmondeley in London, & that, ever so gently, discreetly & confidentially she confessed her slight disappointment in Percy's book,[2] & said that "friends of Mary's" thought it odd that Henry, Rhoda[3] & Howard should have been given the centre front? Isn't that charming?

Things are jogging along here. John & Royall spent the week-end with me, & before Royall came John & I motored to Laon & back, making a loop to see the "carrefour de l'Armistice"[4] & the train in which it was signed. I was moved to the marrow, as it was the first time I had been in that part of the world since 1917.—Minnie is going strong, & announced to me the other day: "I am going to order several dinner dresses for this winter.—The fact is, I've made up my mind to *come out of my shell again*. I've kept myself *too much shut up* the last two winters." Oh, how I envy that Berserk fire!—

"The Children"⁵ shd reach you soon after this—I commend most particularly a new book, "The American Band Wagon," by Charles Merz.⁶ It's the best thing of the kind I've seen yet—& by a German Yid, I suppose! I hope you have found all your family flourishing—your coming will make them so, at any rate.

Yrs ever affly
      Edith

I was very sorry not to see Steven Runciman⁷ in London, but I was in a crazy rush.

Ms:BL

1. In the summer of 1926, the marriage was announced of Philomène de Lévis-Mirepoix and Comte Jules de la Forest-Divonne, a young naval officer.

2. Percy Lubbock's new book was *Mary Cholmondeley, a Sketch from Memory*. Mary Cholmondeley (1850–1925) was the author of a number of novels once well regarded, of which the best known was *Red Pottage* in 1899. Among her literary and social friends were Henry James and Howard Sturgis; she and EW had corresponded a little in the 1900s. Victoria Cholmondeley, here cited, was one of her sisters.

3. Rhoda Broughton (1840–1920), whose witty novels of manners were, for their time, somewhat audacious. She had been a long-standing friend of Henry James.

4. Marshal Foch's railway carriage in the forest of Compiègne, where the terms of the armistice ending the Great War had been signed in November 1918.

5. *The Children*, published in September 1928, was a Book-of-the-Month selection.

6. *The Great American Bandwagon*, by Charles Merz (1893–?), dealt in free-wheeling fashion with current American movies, prizefights, sensational murders, men's clothing (plus fours), the state of young people, and allied topics.

7. Steven Runciman (born 1903), a young Scotsman who would become the most accomplished Byzantine historian of the epoch, and would be knighted for his achievements.

To Royal Cortissoz

Pavillon Colombe
October 11, 1928

Dear Mr. Cortissoz— Oh, what a life-giving letter—& how I needed it! I had become passionately attached to my seven children,[1] & the uncomprehending drivel (laudatory or other) that I have so far read about them had really plunged me in the deepest literary discouragement I have ever known.—I kept thinking: "To have had such a vision, & be able to convey only *that* of it!" I know nothing more depressing than to see a book selling & selling, & feel that nobody knows what they're buying. (That sounds like fatuity, but is really the reverse, for I often tell myself: "If they think my book is like that, then I haven't been able to express myself.")

And now your letter comes, & I don't care a fig about any other opinions—because you've understood. The B.B.s did, of course, & the two or three other friends who were with me when I was finishing it. But now it seemed turned into a mere novel—till you came & "did only breathe" on the dead bones. Thank you for the resurrection!

I can't tell you how I appreciate your taking the trouble to go into all the folds & recesses of my little (& big) people's souls—& especially for raising the question of Martin's stoicism on that one occasion,[2] for I had raised it too. But you must remember that daily contact with Judy had shown him how utterly a child she was, under the patches of sophistication, & also how unconscious of *him* except as a guardian & guide, somebody immeasurably wiser—& also older!— I was by many years the youngest in our family, & much thrown, at Judy's age, with men who were my brothers' friends, men 15 or 20 years older than I was, who were the most delightful of comrades & play-fellows. Looking back now, I see there were Boynes among them, but I was all unconscious then. . . . Of course I understood about Walter. And, after all, what was rarest & dearest in him was so indefinable, something to be felt, not written about.—Do you know, "The Children" is the first book I have ever written that he did not read before it was published? And he died a year ago tomorrow.

Thank you again, dear Mr. Cortissoz—I wish fate brought us oftener together.

Yrs ever
  Edith Wharton

I spent 10 good days with the Goyas last May. You ought to have been there. All Renoir & Manet was in him.[3]

Ms:BL

1. The seven children—stepbrothers and stepsisters, the offspring of the same number of frequently marrying parents—in the novel named for them.

2. The chief male figure in the story, the forty-six-year-old bachelor Martin Boyne, has a fleeting vision of an enduring relation with the oldest of the children, fifteen-year-old Judith, but quickly abandons it.

3. After visits to the Prado the previous May, EW had written Berenson about the Goyas. One work was "exactly like a Vermeer painted by Ingres"; the Maja was "a Renoir," and another portrait was "a Manet."

To Gaillard Lapsley

Sainte-Claire
February 25, 1929.
Ultra Confidential

Dearest Gaillard,

I have just taken the momentous decision to sail on the Minnewaska, May 25, with Daisy Chanler, for a 10 days sojourn in Skyscraperville.

Columbia (this is the confidential part) has invited me to receive the Litt. D. on June 4, & as I can combine with this seeing Minnie, who is not coming abroad this summer, & also, I hope, the play, which is still going strong,[1] I have decided to make the jump! How I wish you could come too.—You know how they love silly mysteries in our Universities, so of course you will say nothing as to the first object of the trip.

I must own that I shouldn't have gone (I'm afraid) but for the utter destruction of my garden, which has hit me so hard that I've got to change ideas & scene pretty completely, or lose my usual cheerful "poise."—Don't you think I'm right to go?—[2]

The enclosed is such a jewel that I feel I must pass it on.

Yrs ever   E.

By the way, I wrote about 10 days ago asking Mr. Runciman if he wouldn't come & stay before March 15, & I have had no answer. The post is so disorganized by frost & flu that I daresay my letter or his answer has fallen by the way. Will you ask him?

Have you read Smith's Life of Nollekens?[3] I have always meant to, & now *have*, & it is simply priceless.

A Brighter P.S. (For you & Steven*)

I

A group of movie-kings in N.Y. the other day were deploring that a film (unsuccessful) had been made several years ago out of "The Age of Innocence."

One said: "Don't understand how it failed, with that title. God, what a title! 'The Age of Innocence.' (Differs in different states, you know)."

II

Somebody went to see the play the other day (it is booming) with Minnie, & said afterward: "Mrs. Jones knows the name of every usher!"—Trust *her*.

* & Mr. Housman, of course.

Ms:BL

1. The play version of *The Age of Innocence* opened in New York in December 1928. The dramatization was by Margaret Ayer Barnes (1886–1967), novelist and playwright who would win a Pulitzer Prize in 1930 for *Years of Grace*. With Katharine Cornell in the role of Ellen Olenska, *The Age of Innocence* ran until mid-June 1929, and then was taken on a four months' road tour.

2. A week after writing this letter, EW caught a severe chill, which led to a high fever and heart palpitations. The physical collapse was due in part to the devastation in her gardens. All work was forbidden her for a long period, and the trip to America to receive the honorary degree was canceled.

3. *Nollekens and His Times*, by John Thomas Smith (1766–1833), reprinted in 1929. Joseph Nollekens (1737–1832) was an extremely fashionable portrait sculptor; Laurence Sterne, David Garrick, and William Pitt were among those who sat for him.

To Rutger B. Jewett

July 15, 1929

Dear Mr. Jewett,

I have your letter of July 3rd, enclosing a copy of a letter from the Delineator. I confess that it is somewhat discouraging, after the tremendous effort I have made to finish "Hudson River Bracketed" much more rapidly than I originally intended, to have Mr. Graeve's representative say that "with so much that is already unsatisfactory, a special ending to lop it off short would be indeed the last straw." When I consider what the Delineator is, and what the poorest of my work is in comparison, I confess that I feel indignant at such a tone, and I will never again willingly give a line of mine to the Delineator.[1]

With regard to the end, I cannot possibly fix a date for the closing chapters; as soon as I am able to do it, you may be sure that I will do so. It is going on at a good pace now, but after the chapter which I am sending with this, there will be a delay, as I am going away from home for a month, and cannot send you any more work till I come back, not because I shall not be writing, but because I shall not be able to have my work typed.

With any sort of luck, the book ought to be finished by the end of November, or possibly before; but I have been so harassed by the Delineator that the more I am asked when I shall finish the longer the delay is likely to be.

Yours sincerely

Copy: BL

1. Oscar Graeve, editor of the *Delineator*, without warning or permission had begun to serialize *Hudson River Bracketed* six months ahead of the agreed schedule. "I cannot tell you the harm that Mr. Graeve's inexcusable action has done to me and, I fear, to my novel," EW had written Jewett in February 1929. Her breakdown soon after that put a stop to her work for some months. After returning to her novel, she suggested the possibility of cutting the narrative short, since it was already clear to her that there would be a sequel. In this letter, she quotes the answer to this proposal.

To Gaillard Lapsley

Lamb House
Rye
August 15, 1929

Dearest Gaillard,

Your good letter reached me here, & I was glad to know that you were safely & comfortably on your way to Lemming Land.

I arrived here at 8.30 last Sunday night, having left Hidcote at 10.30 a.m., dropped Emile[1] at Newhaven after his thrilling 2 days & a half at Hidcote, & braved all the Sunday Kippses[2] in motors, charabancs & motor-cycles. I was groaning with fatigue, & expected to figure in the Times & Paris Herald on the 2d day after—"of heart failure." Instead of which I woke after a good sleep, resembling in appearance & morale the rosy-fingered morn, & set to work writing the Big Love Scene in my novel! So talk to me no more about having overdone things on our quiet little ramble. It did me worlds of good, & I am planning next year's tour already.

I have had a very peaceful week here, with divine weather.

Yesterday we went to Bodian, wh. Henry first showed me 20 years ago, & where now Mr. Polloi (as Wells ought to have called his hero) scatters papers & orange peel, & his weedy females sprawl & shout.

Oh, how I hate to see beauty thrown to the beasts, as it is now all over the world!

Well, I'm off home the day after tomorrow, after an uncommonly rich month "due to" your beloved companionship. (Even used correctly, as above, I feel that the phrase must now be quotationed.)

Thank you for all the good camaraderie, & let us vow to row together many times more to the islands of the Blest.

Yrs ever affly
    Edith

My best love to Eunice, when you see her, & many messages to the Bells,[3] Henrietta Haven, &c.

That poem was *not* a parody—I'm sure of that. Try again!

P.S. Five minutes later.—

Robert has just brought in the Times, with the news of Geoffrey's death.[4]

Oh, Gaillard, what a mockery it all is! He had got on his feet, he had pulled himself out of all the sloughs, he was happy, ambitious, hard at work, full of courage & enthusiasm. The Furies had been letting him simmer . . .

I'm glad I had that good day with him. How I wish I'd wired to the steamer! I meant to, & then the thought got crowded out.

His death must have been terribly lonely. Even his few friends in N.Y. were probably all scattered. I don't know to whom to write—but do please get me all the particulars you can.

I hope Percy will be ashamed now of having cut him the other day in London. It wounded him so bitterly.

Only a little while ago you & I were saying: "Why do our friends die one after the other?"

Ms:BL

1. EW's head gardener.
2. The reference is to H. G. Wells's novel *Kipps*, of 1905.
3. Marion and Gordon Bell, friends of EW since the early days at The Mount.
4. Geoffrey Scott died suddenly, of pneumonia, in a hotel in New York City. In September 1927, Scott had been commissioned to edit the mass of papers by or relating to James Boswell that had been discovered in Malahide Castle, in Ireland. He had completed six volumes of the material at the time of his death.

To Grace Hegger Lewis[1]

Pavillon Colombe
August 20, 1929

Dear Mrs. Lewis,

I am so glad to hear from you again after such a long silence! Mr. Lewis wrote to me last winter to tell me of the divorce, but I have not had the heart to answer him, for I kept so pleasant a memory of seeing you both together, here & at Hyères, that I was very much saddened to think that your partnership had ceased to exist. For his case, especially, I wish it had been otherwise.

I am glad you have been off on such an interesting expedition with your boy,[2] and that you have literary plans of your own in view. I was very ill indeed last winter (an infectious grippe which affected my heart), and the Delineator people, who started without my authorization to publish my novel before it was finished, got into a great fright at the interruption in my work. But I have survived, and I am trying to make up for lost time.

Do let me know next time you come abroad, and come out here to see me if you can.

Yours with much sympathy
    Edith Wharton

Ms:UT

1. The former Grace Hegger had been married to Sinclair Lewis since 1913. She gave a fictional account of their marriage in her novel of 1921, *Half a Loaf*.
2. Wells Lewis, born in 1917 and named for H. G. Wells.

To Elisina Tyler

Pavillon Colombe
October 25, 1929

Dearest Elisina,

It is such a delight to have Bill here that I wonder you ever let him go! He arrived yesterday in very good form, & seemingly not tired by his journey.—He caught me in a guilty honeymoon with a gramophone, & we listened to Mozart, Weber & the Rosenkavalier till 9.30, when I sent him to bed!

Today was radiant, & he wisely did his chaise longue in the morning.[1] St André came to lunch, & afterward we motored to Chantilly & back. After tea we had ½ an hour of Brahms, & then I made him go & rest. And now Peter has arrived for dinner, & I hear them shouting with laughter next door.

Before I join them, I must say a word about Nov. 5 & our committee.

Conner[2] has moved to 5 Ave. de l'Opéra, & says we may have our meeting there that afternoon at 6. Bill thinks you are not leaving Antigny till the 4th, so we must arrange plans by letter. Please tell me if

Mlle. Lopez is to send out the notices? I take it for granted that she is to write the secretary's report.—

We must prepare our little circular, projected in the spring, & I will see her about it & draw it up with her advice.

Let me know any further suggestions, please—

I move to the Crillon on the 4th.

Yrs ever affly
    Edith

Ms:WRT

1. The young William Tyler had taken leave from Harrow (where he was preparing for Oxford) after a spot was discovered on his lung. It turned out not to be a serious affliction, but one that needed rest, fresh air, and abundant food.

2. Conner and Mlle. Lopez (mentioned later) were working with the Committee for the American Convalescent Homes.

To Elisina Tyler

Sainte-Claire
January 1, 1930

Dearest Elisina,

I am overwhelmed by what you say of "Hudson Riv." After allowing for all the indulgence of affection, there seems so much more praise than the book deserves—yet I wd rather hear it of this than of any other I have written. It is a theme that I have carried in my mind for years, & that Walter was always urging me to use; indeed I had begun it before the war, but in our own milieu, & the setting of my own youth. After the war it took me long to re-think it & transpose it into the crude terms of modern America; & I am happy to find that my readers think I have succeeded.—John is an excellent critic, & was so patient in reading the early part in type, that I wanted to thank him by my dedication.[1]

The last day of the year was divinely lovely here, & Robert, Lapsley, B.B. & I picnicked under the castle walls of Solliès-Ville, & took a long mountain walk through the pines & olives. When I come back to my room here after one of these long scrambles I think of the weeks during which I had to be carried fr. my bed to the bed next door, & I bless your kind & helpful friendship, wh. spared me every sort of fatigue during those weary days, & gave me the possibility of getting back to normal life so quickly & completely. I can never forget what you did, & want to repeat in 1930 what I have said so often in the year foregoing.

Bill writes that the Goethe finally turned up—& you will have rec'd my letter, wh. crossed yours, telling you how much I admire the lovely painted silk.

You don't speak of your health, so I hope yr. neuritis is cured. I'm so glad that Peter & John had that good day at Provins & Jouarre. Please thank Peter for the p.c. they sent me. With all my most affectionate New Year wishes,

Yrs ever
   Edith

I am sending Jean Stern[2] the cheque for the two beds at Passy.

Did I tell you that Daisy arrives here on the 18th, & that we are going to Spain in March?

Ms:WRT

1. The book was dedicated "To A.J.H.S."
2. A Frenchman associated with the American Convalescent Homes.

To Gaillard Lapsley

Pavillon Colombe
July 15, 1930.

Dearest Gaillard,

Just a line to say goodbye & wish you the best of voyages—also to ask you a favour, which you can render me, "à tête reposée," on board ship.

It is this. When you read the opening chapters of the new "Hudson"[1] you suggested that I shd preface the book with a few lines that shd *not* be a magazine summary of the story, but—something very much better! Only: *What?* I find that the horrible death of poor Roger[2] gave me a sort of brain-blur for the moment, & I can't remember what you proposed.

If *you* can (& knowing your memory, I'm sure the "if" is irrelevant), do jot the idea down on a p.c. & shoot it off to me. I have written 1 ½ more chaps., & am getting interested. What fun it is to make people walk about—or fancy one is doing it!

I saw the other day somewhere (I think in "Life & Letters") that Tolstoy was "overwhelmed by the genius of—Trollope"! I'm re-reading "Framley Parsonage," after the "Last Chronicle of Barset," & I'm also overwhelmed. I want to write an article called "Jane & Anthony." They deserve to be coupled.

Trust me to fix up Salso details.

Yrs ever
  Edith

Do you remember poor crazy sympathetic Romano, the Italian footman? His wife murdered him at Hyères the day of Roger's death! Poor fellow—she was a prostitute, & he did the Nekludoff[3] act in vain.

Doris Charmand died last week.

Ms:BL

1. *The Gods Arrive*, a sequel to *Hudson River Bracketed*, was published in 1932.

2. Roger, who had been taken on as a kitchen worker at age seventeen, had served with EW for eighteen years, most of them as her cook. He died on July 1, following a motorcycle accident.

3. The upper-class character in Tolstoy's novel *Resurrection* (1899) who, having seduced a servant girl and started her on the downward path, encounters her ten years later being convicted of robbery and murder. During her time of imprisonment, he succeeds in effecting a profound change both in her and in himself.

To Gaillard Lapsley

Pavillon Colombe
August 8, 1930

Dearest Gaillard— I ought to be using my morning freshness to add a fraction of a chapter to "The Gods Arrive"—instead of which I lay it at your feet in all its dewiness, as Verlaine wd say (if I had the vol. in reach.)

The truth is, I need the détente of a good talk with you, even across all the unplumbed miles! Imagine that, just a month after poor Roger's death, the house being full, & a long line of guests in the offing, I was suddenly told that the new cook had been found lying in the kitchen covered with blood!!! Most of the local doctors were of course away, but we got a little young "Ersatz" from Sarcelles, who turned out to be very clever. He said at once it was a hemorrhage caused by an abscess on the liver, & that he (the cook) would probably die in the night!¹ Luckily his wife & daughter had come out to spend the day with the poor man, & when they were quieted down the servants again improvised a dinner (W. Gay & Charlie being in the house, & Mary Berenson & Minnie arriving the next day!)— The poor cook survived the night, & was carried off in an ambulance next morning—& the weary cook-hunt began again. What is doubly strange is that W. Gay nearly died in exactly the same way several years ago, & was in fact afterward at death's door for months!

We have now (at least for the time) shaken down again; but I can't tell you how unequal I find myself to such shattering experiences.— Minnie & Mary B. are here, but Charlie has taken himself away, bored, I think, by having to take part in general talk, instead of discoursing to his satellites. I find him hopelessly petite-chapelle-ized, poor darling, & quite unable to talk unless he can pontificate.

Between all these convulsions I had 10 peaceful & harmonious days with John, who certainly ripens beautifully, & is now a thoroughly civilized human being, without oddities & prejudices, & with a delightfully wise & kindly view of life & the cosmos. We saw many unknown (to us) & beautiful monuments in the Indre, Poitou & Anjou, & came back with our eyes full of the glories of Mantes, which are even greater than I had remembered.—

I bear in mind our rendez-vous on Sept. 11, & will take the necessary "dispositions" for the Cavour & the motor. How glad I shall be to see you again!

I hope the American adventure is as happy as the last—& you must certainly be getting all the sun you wanted. Here it has rained every day since you left. Aurevoir next month, & best love always.

Edith

Ms:BL

1. "Cook No. 2," in EW's phrase, died in the last part of August.

To Bernard Berenson

Pavillon Colombe
September 6, 1930

Dearest B.B.

Gli Indifferenti¹ & your note came together two days ago. Mary spoke of Signor Moravia's talent when she was here, & I was waiting to arrive in Italy to get the book. But I am so glad you have sent it to me, because I always try to limber up my tongue by reading a little Italian before I start, & it is much more fun doing it on this than re-reading some old friend.

I have already consumed chap. 1, with amazement at the masterly way in which the family group is situated in time, space & the desert of moral mediocrity. The most interesting thing to look for in the first work of a new novelist is the degree to which the instinct of narrative appears. The character drawing is likely to be immature; the influence of other writers is inevitably visible, but if the writer is *going to be a novelist* his first page inspires the same confidence as the first page of "Werther," which still seems to me the best touchstone for adolescent fiction. And so thank you, dear B.B.—& the rest when I've read the book!

I hope Mary is feeling better since she got back to the mountain air of your Poggio. I respected her incog. while she was in Paris, but sent her a note to the Hôtel de l'Université. I hope she got it? (Not that it required an answer—it was just an Ave—Vale.)—

And now à bientôt. I hail you all fondly across the major desert of Salso!

Yrs affly
  Edith

Ms: VT

1. *Gli Indifferenti* (translated into English as *The Time of Indifference*), the first novel by Alberto Moravia. The novel was completed by Moravia before he was eighteen (he was born in Rome in 1907), but not published until 1929.

To W. Morton Fullerton

Hôtel de Crillon
November 16, 1930

Cher ami,

A thousand thanks for taking the trouble to tell me so many kind things about "Hudson River."

Grateful as I am, it is a shock to find that your avoidance of my presence has for so many years extended to my books! I had flattered myself that though you felt only indifference for the old friend, you still followed her through her books— Why have you robbed me of my few remaining illusions?

I can only hope that "Hudson River" may make you feel that you have lost an—infinitesimal—something by this total rejection of

Yr E

Ms: HL

To W. Morton Fullerton

Sainte Claire
January 11, 1931

Thank you so much, my dear. Like all good deeds, yours entails another—for I know that my only hope of getting my lost letter printed is to enclose a copy of it, with the covering letter which I sent to Mr. Hills, & to implore you to transmit these documents to the Herald.[1] Coming from you, they will feel obliged to print the appeal—whereas if I send it, it will rejoin its fore-runners in the scrap-basket. Merci d'avance!

How odd that I should have so misunderstood what you wrote about the French lady's letter to her unrequited suitor.[2] As a family document it is extremely interesting. So also is your sister's comment on it. But— does she speak from experience? Certainly mine would not carry me as far! I have had many dear friends—& only two in whose case I wanted the friendship to be total.

You see how I lean on one of them, now that the age of good works has come!

Yr   Edith

Ms: HL

1. EW's letter, transmitted by Fullerton to Mr. Hills, an editor of the Paris *Herald*, was eventually published. See following item, dated December 10, 1930.

2. The letter in question was a document belonging to the family of a French woman friend of Fullerton. On first reading it, EW had assumed it was a piece of fiction.

To the Editor of The Paris Herald:

December 10 [1930]

You were kind enough, last year, to publish an appeal from me in behalf of the lotissement of Lutèce, near Garges-lès-Gonesse. This settlement of over 2,000 inhabitants, about 20 kilomètres to the north of Paris, belongs to the group of the so-called Zone Rouge, whose unhappy inhabitants planted their houses in the mud, without school, church, doctors, light, water or drainage, a few years after the war.

A group of heroic curés, often leaving comfortable parishes, have undertaken to give back hope and courage to these sad communities. At Lutèce Abbé Comptour has already created a growing parish, put up a portable church from the devastated regions, and built the Parish House to which your readers so generously contributed last year. Since his work began there have been 30 christenings, 12 marriages and 50 children inscribed for the catechism; and several groups of women, young girls and boy-scouts have been organized. So large is the attendance of patients at the Dispensary founded by the Charité Maternelle that it has been found necessary to double its size; and in short everything is prospering at Lutèce and will continue to prosper if your readers will continue to help.

The Parish House, with a cinema and stage, will be inaugurated at Christmas, but 12,000 francs are needed to pay for furniture, lighting and the installation of the cinema, and for enlarging the dispensary.

Will some of your readers, who are spending a happy Christmas in France, come to our help as they did last year?

Donations may be addressed to me, and each will be personally acknowledged.

Edith Wharton

To Rutger B. Jewett

January 31, 1931

Dear Mr. Jewett,

I have your letter of Jan. 17th, and return herewith a modified ending to "Pomegranate Seed,"[1] which ending will, I hope, be considered sufficiently explicit. I could hardly make it more so without turning a ghost story into a treatise on the sources of the supernatural. Oddly enough, when I wrote this story, last month, I read it aloud to five friends who were staying with me for Christmas. They all liked it, but all remarked with one accord: "Of course it's obvious from the first paragraph that the dead wife wrote the letters"; but they all agreed that the end was perfect.

As for the title, Mr. Schuyler[2] must refresh his classical mythology. When Persephone left the under-world to re-visit her mother, Demeter, her husband, Hades, lord of the infernal regions, gave her a pomegranate seed to eat, because he knew that if he did so she would never be able to remain among the living, but would be drawn back to the company of the dead.

I am so glad you like the last chapters of "The Gods Arrive," and I am sending you the two concluding chapters of Book II.

Yours sincerely

Ms: BL

1. The ghost story was contained in *The World Over* (1936).
2. Loring Schuyler, editor of the *Ladies' Home Journal*.

To W. Morton Fullerton

Sainte-Claire
February 8, 1931.

I'm so sorry to hear that you're still so tired—but it seems to me a poor reason for not coming down here for a ten days' rest. On reflection, however, I perceive that you don't know what staying with me is like —& therefore I understand your reluctance.

Let me explain that: *1st*—Hyères is a social desert, an Ultima Thule of the most ultimate sort.

2d. My cook is used to régimes, & will carry yours out most scrupulously.

3d. I work (or garden) all the morning, & never appear to my guests till lunch.

4th. That there won't be any guests but you!

5th. That the house is surrounded by big terraces that catch all the sun there is.

6th. That curfew tolls at 10.30 every evening.

& *7th*. That you would give me very great pleasure by proving to me that, even short of a South African oasis (alas, if I'd only known sooner!) my company would not be unpleasant to you in such conditions—

Do come.

Yrs   Edith

The little Gioconda article was very prettily done; but G. Moore's secretary is a good deal more exciting. Don't you think so?

Ms:HL

To Bernard Berenson

Sainte-Claire
February 18, 1931

Dearest B.B.,

Please excuse this dictated letter. Walter's sister, Mrs. Alden,[1] has just sent me a letter addressed to Mrs. Harry Crosby[2] (widow of the murderer) of which I enclose a copy. Mrs. Alden leaves the matter altogether to me; but I gather from her bewildered little note that the idea horrifies her as it does me. I have written to her to do nothing further till she hears from me again, and meanwhile I am consulting you and Gaillard Lapsley as to the best means of preventing publication of such a book. (My object in writing to Gaillard is that I think he told me that the said Leon Edel[3] had come to see him, a year or two ago, on the subject of a proposed book about Henry James.)

You will see from the letter to Mrs. Crosby that the latter appears to be in favour of the book. (Probably she hopes to make a little money out of it.) As to the letters which Mr. Edel hopes to get, I have written to Mrs. Alden that Henry kept no letters; and that moreover I know that he and Walter very seldom wrote to each other. My impression is that Walter destroyed all his private correspondence, and for my part I have kept no letters from him except some early ones connected with my literary work. As you know I am trying to get together material for some reminiscences, and I am perfectly willing, in order to try to block Mr. Edel, to say that I *may* write a life of Walter myself. Of course there is no material for a "Life," but a vulgar gossipy book could be manufactured by Edel and Mrs. Crosby, and this, naturally, I want to prevent at all costs.

If you will give me your ideas on this question, I shd be most grateful, for I have no experience to go on.

Weather heavenly here, & *at last*, yesterday evening, a much-needed deluge. Robert has gone to Mme du B.'s, & I am arranging my books with Mme Charpentier. After she goes I shall probably be alone for some time—& that will be good for my work (I hope) if otherwise a little wistful.

I know there is something particularly interesting in your last letter wh. I left unanswered—but it must wait till next time, as the letter is upstairs!

Love to you all,
Edith

Ms:VT

1. Nathalie Alden, the married sister of Walter Berry.
2. Caresse Crosby, literary entrepreneur and the widow of Harry Crosby, the wealthy New York art collector who had died in December 1929 in what was conjectured to be a suicide pact with a young woman. He was a younger cousin of Walter Berry.
3. The youthful Leon Edel, then working at the Sorbonne on a dissertation about Henry James, had written Caresse Crosby with a view—so he said—to writing a life of Walter Berry, and asking permission to see EW's letters to Berry. In fact, Edel was acting for a friend, and in any event EW had recovered and burned all her letters to Berry. In June 1931, Edel called on EW at St. Brice to explain the mild deception, entirely to EW's satisfaction and amusement.

To Elisina Tyler

Sainte Claire
March 9, 1931.

Dearest Elisina,

You are several saints rolled into one, & I am confounded by your inexhaustible goodness to those poor derelict women.[1] I still feel that I ought not to have passed such a load onto you—yet I don't know what wd have become of them if I hadn't.

I had another letter fr. Miss Lever, evidently much exasperated by this last insanity of Dolly's about refusing to leave the rue St. D.—In reply I thought it right to tell Miss L. that I would do my part in seeing the Herberts through this calamity, but that I had now poured out money on them (I really have) for over 15 years, not to speak of time & trouble, & that after their cure I should be obliged to reduce my contribution to the small monthly remittance of 100 fcs which I have always given in addition to everything else.—I thought it only right to let Miss L. know as long as possible in advance, & I also thought that this fact might be used as an argument to decide the H.s to move. They *must* give warning next month, for even if I continued the help I have been giving them, the cousins Fraguier & Co certainly wd not.—My own impression is that they will both be in a "mental home" before many months; but meanwhile I want to do all I can to give Dolly any possible chance to recover. That she will do so I don't for a minute believe; & if there is a permanent break down, then the British authorities will have to deal with the case, I should think. My own income is much reduced, I have to help Minnie out to the tune of $5000 a year, & moreover I have on my shoulders so many poor protégés who are far more to be pitied, that I feel I can no longer devote thousands annually to the Herberts.—Meanwhile, let us hope that Versailles will get them over the worst of their plight—for a time, at any rate.

I wonder if the 2 little boxes of flowers that I posted to you last *Friday* morning from Toulon, reached you on Saturday, as they shd have, & in fairly good condition?

Please don't think of writing on purpose to tell me; but when you next have to write, let me know quite sincerely if they came promptly, so that I may "repeat" if it's worthwhile.

My love & gratitude, as always—
    Edith

Ms:WRT

1 . The tribulations of EW's former English secretary Dolly Herbert and her mother would be of concern and exasperation to EW over a long period. Both

women were ailing and penurious, but refused stubbornly to leave their rooms on Rue St. Dominique and seek less expensive quarters. The Miss Lever mentioned is Dolly's cousin. Later, when Dolly was given a gift of 10,000 francs from EW and others, she spent it on a gravestone in a local cemetery. EW nonetheless continued to help out.

To Gaillard Lapsley

Sainte Claire
April 3, 1931

Dearest Gaillard— I have purposely refrained from writing because I didn't want to make one more straw on your desk; but the silence weighed on me, & I was glad to get your letter & know that all was well with you, & your Ramsgate week had been benignant.

The account of the Duchess's funeral[1] was so sublimely complete that I felt it would be profanation to add a word to *that*—but I felt also that it would "déclencher" an answer if you had the strength to drive a pen!—It (I mean the demise) must be a blessed relief to her long-suffering progeny, & especially to Phil. who of course had to bear all the brunt of her long & dreadful illness. Requiescat!

I have had the really delightful Kenneth Clarks[2] for a short visit since I wrote. They are really rewarding, both of them, & I think they liked it very much, & want to come again. My dear Rex Nicholsons[3] have been here for over a month, & are seriously considering taking the crazy woman's house (which, by the way, is *called* St Pierre, though that may not be its name!) During their stay I had an impromptu week-end composed of Lady Desborough,[4] Ld Stanmore & Louis Mallet, so that the house was once more full to cracking. They all liked each other, & it was a great success.—I do want you to know the Nicholsons—it must be arranged some day soon.

Oh, what fun that you're going to be able to tell me about the Barretts![5] But what a thousand pities we didn't both see it before the incest was extirpated. However, I dare say the actor has found a way of keeping it in quand même.

The Noailles[6] have been *completely* white-washed, the whole Faubourg has been to stay at St B., & the mot d'ordre now is: "Ces Pauvres enfants, il faut les entourer, et les empêcher de retomber sous l'influence de ces vilains gens."—O Sacred Gold!—

The other day some friends of the Metmans, Cte et Ctesse de la Laurencie, came to tea with an éphèbe son, who told Molly Nicholson that he loved to be with people older than himself, & that "in marriage it is never the physics that counts, but only the *sowl* & the mind."

Tell me about St. Runciman's book.[7] What is it about? I don't remember seeing any notice of it. I've enjoyed this nice long crack, & venture to hope that you have.

Yrs ever,
  Edith

I'm going to Rome about May 15 to stay with the Garretts—I've had a very decent note from Edel, who will wait on me in June.

Ms:BL

1. The ornately engraved announcement of the death on March 10, 1931, of Henriette Cathérine Marie de Chabannes la Palice Duchesse Douairière de Lévis-Mirepoix contained more than a hundred of the most ancient aristocratic and royal names in the land.

2. See letter to Mildred Bliss, August 8, 1931.

3. Reginald Popham ("Rex") Nicholson (1874–1950), English colonial official whom EW had come to know and appreciate during the Aegean cruise of 1926. His wife, Molly Nicholson, was said by Nicky Mariano to be like the heroine of an EW novel.

4. Lady (Ettie) and Lord Desborough were prominent in the Edwardian era; EW had probably met them at the Elchos on a visit to Stanway.

5. *The Barretts of Wimpole Street*, the play by Rudolf Besier (the author of *Olive Latimer*, which had incensed Hugh Smith and Lubbock years before), with Katharine Cornell as Elizabeth Barrett Browning. It opened in New York in February 1931.

6. Vicomte Charles de Noailles, a passionate gardener, and his wife, the former Marie-Laure Bischoffsheim, were EW's neighbors in Hyères, occupying the Villa St. Bérnard.

7. *A History of the First Bulgarian Empire* (1930).

To Mildred Bliss

Pavillon Colombe
St Brice
August 8, 1931

Dearest Mildred,

I was so glad to hear from you at last, after so many months of silence. I wonder if you ever received the long letter that I wrote you last winter, giving you the news of our little group? I was hoping to hear from you in return, but I suppose that, as usual, you have been over-worked, and over-burdened with correspondence.

Your friend Señor Danvila is coming to lunch tomorrow, and I only hope that for once we shall have a ray of sun and a little warmth. No words can say what the weather has been this summer—so dark and cold and wet that my poor garden is utterly discouraged.

I did not make my usual spring tour this year, as Daisy Chanler, my usual travelling companion, remained in America; I simply spent a fort-night at Versailles while this house was being prepared, and then came here early in June.

Last month I spent in England, seeing lots of people and amusing myself greatly, as I had not been in London in the season for over twenty years. I saw lots of old friends, such as Barrie and Wells, and made a number of new ones, including the Sitwells,[1] who are really delightful, and so different from what one would suppose from their blatant self-advertising. Among the most charming new friends that I have made in the last year are the Kenneth Clarks,[2] whom I met last autumn at I Tatti. Kenneth Clark is a young friend of B.B.'s, who worked with him for a time at I Tatti, but now plays an important part in the artistic world of London. He has just been appointed Keeper of the Ashmolean, an important post for a young man in the twenties, and as his wife is also exceptionally nice their house is a very pleasant one to go to.

You will have heard so much about the Byzantine Exhibition, and its overwhelming success, that there is little left for me to tell you. Royall has received all the credit which he so richly deserves, for Metman[3] and the other members of the Arts Décoratifs have outdone each other in saying that the whole thing was due to his initiative and his energy. The objects were most beautifully arranged by Jacques Guérin, and your vitrine with the lovely jewels attracted a great deal of attention. The whole thing was really a triumph for every one concerned.

Royall has at last been able to go away to Antigny and work on his book.[4] According to the circular, as you have doubtless seen, the first volume is to appear in October, but I suppose we may have to wait a little longer. With all the terrible business anxieties of the last months, I marvel that he should have been able to keep his mind sufficiently detached to go on with the work whenever he has a moment to spare. He came out to dine with me the other night, before leaving for Antigny, and though of course he was very tired and preoccupied, I thought he looked well.

I do not expect to leave here again until I go to the Berensons' in November. I have a great many people coming to stay, as usual, and the weather is so bad that one is not tempted to travel.

Do let me have a line when you can spare the time. Excuse this dictated letter, and do likewise if you find it less tiring, as I do.

My best love to you & Robert.

Yrs ever affly
Edith

Ms:LA

1. Dame Edith Sitwell (1887–1964), author of *Façade* (1923); Osbert Sitwell (1892–1969), novelist and autobiographer; Sacheverell Sitwell (born 1897), poet and writer on art and travel.

2. Kenneth Clark (1903–1983), art historian, was already known as the author of *The Gothic Revival* in 1928. His remarkable career as a public figure was now under way with his appointment as keeper of the Ashmolean Museum in Oxford. His wife, Jane Clark, had been a student of art history at Oxford when the two met.

3. Louis Metman, head of the Musée des Arts Décoratifs in Paris.

4. Presumably *L'Art byzantine*, written with Hayford Pierce, the basis of the exhibition mentioned by EW, and published in 1932.

To Margaret Terry Chanler

Albergo Palazzo
Roma
November 18, 1931

Dearest Daisy— It seems peculiarly suitable to answer your letter from this incomparable place, on the Feast of S.S. Peter & Paul, & after Pontifical High Mass at S. Paolo f. le Mura! I could hardly find a happier moment, & so I begin this scribble while I wait for Nicky Mariano to go on our afternoon giro.

She & I have stolen a week from time & duty (she from the hard-labour of I Tatti, I from that of my novel) & every moment has been filled with beauty & delight. The weather is very warm & spring-like (spring showers included) & in spite of man's havoc Rome has never seemed to me so beautiful, so matchless. Besides, contrary to my ex-pectations (I had not been here since 1914) man has *not* been wholly vile, & nothing that has been done lately has the criminal horror of the Victor Em. monument, wh. of course I knew. On the contrary, the uncovering of the Republican Temples of the Largo Argentina has been beautifully done, & the fairy loggia & gothic windows of the Palace of the Knights of St John, just being disengaged from rubble, were surely worth seeing again.

We have had the good fortune, also, to have a very beautiful vesper service at St Peter's yesterday, with the exhibition of the relics, wh. I had never seen—& altogether I think between us we have extracted some quintessential Roman honey from the inexhaustible comb—

I must begin (at the end) by explaining that I skipped my Paris fort-night this year, & went straight from St Brice to I Tatti about 3 weeks ago. Mary has been in a nursing home, after a somewhat troublesome bladder operation, & as she was to return at the end of this week (& as Nicky was very tired) I persuaded B.B. with *great* difficulty to let me carry her, Nicky, off for a brief rest & change before the arduous day of Mary's return—for she is a most difficult invalid.—It has done Nicky a lot of good, I think, & me quite as much, & I am starting for Hyères next week (after another short stay at I Tatti) much refreshed by this beautiful interlude. If only you had been with us! When are you & I ever to start on our wanderings again? For Spain I fear it's too late. We shall have to come back to Italy. You will be sorry to hear that Koechlin[1] died a few days ago. It is a terrible blow to Metman, the more so at this time, when he, Metman, is deep in organizing the great French exhibition which takes place in London in January. No one will be mourned by more devoted friends—but they are thankful that he did not linger, as he was paralysed & speechless.

Almost sadder perhaps is the total blindness of the Abbé Mugnier.[2] I knew that he was threatened with it, but now it has come rather suddenly, I imagine. His friends are eking out his poor little income, & Mme. de Castries is asking for subscriptions to provide him with some means of getting about—I suppose a taxi by the day. Of course he has had to resign as Aumônier of the convent. He came to dine in Oct. & I found him very much aged, mentally as well as physically, so I daresay it will not be long before the end for him too.

Every one asks after you, talks of you, longs for you to come back —not least (you may imagine)

your devoted
Edith

Norts—did you know—has given up Lamb House, & taken an enchanting flat in the Ile St Louis—53 Quai Bourbon.

Poor Royall has been sent back to Budapest by the League of Nations, & Elisina has joined him there. They are not any too enchanted!

Ms:BL

1. Raymond Koechlin, French museum curator whom EW had known for many years.
2. See letter to Berenson, January 30, 1914.

To Bernard Berenson

Sainte Claire
January 17, 1932

Dearest B.B.— Thank you for writing from Genoa & sending me Mary's letter, which I return herewith. Certainly the news was excellent at that moment—how I hope you found it even better on arriving!

I'm sorry you missed your Lerici visit, partly for your sake, partly because I wanted an up-to-date "sensation" of that divine spot, which struck me, when I was there over 20 years ago, as more like the "Death of Procris"[1] landscape—in *Mediterraneanism*, not specific outline—than anything else on this dolphinesque coast. I have never forgotten the impression it made on me.—

I hope the burden of home-coming has not been as heavy as you feared, both in regard to Mary & to the general inevitable weight of things that descends on one as if, in opening the front door, one trod on a spring that "released" them.

Here the super-celestial weather pursues its even way. We motored to Marseilles the day before yesterday for Landowska's concert,[2] & I went out to lunch at the Mantes' (Mme de Margérie's[3] sister) who have a beautiful place with really noble trees & a great splendid view. There I saw the Roland de Margéries, who were full of Berlin gossip, & Roland gave me a long list of must-be-read books, to which, however, I attached no overwhelming importance as he is (though clever & competent) the victim of the "dernier bateau" in literature.—Landowska's concert was exquisite, & we brought her back yesterday. She told us that two years running, when she was giving concerts in Russia, she sent down her harpsichord to Yasnaya Poliana (I forget where the *i*.s & *y*.s ought to go) & revealed 17th century music to the old Tolstoy, who knew nothing farther back than Mozart. Her account is very interesting. She will be in Florence about March 5th, & if you see her, turn on Tolstoy.—She is very intimate with the Aurics,[4] so they are coming to lunch today.

And now I must go back to Vance,[5] whose fate hangs on a thread! I think my two days away from him have put him in better perspective.

Best love to Mary, to you & to the Perfect Nick—

Yrs ever
    Edith

Landowska wished to be particularly remembered to you & Mary.

P.S. Was it after you left that I had a letter from Metman saying that the first week of the Exhibition had been a dazzling pecuniary success?

Ms:VT

1. "The Death of Procris": a painting by Peiro di Cosimo (1462–1521) that EW had perhaps seen in the National Gallery in London.

2. Wanda Landowska (1879–1959), Polish-born musical artist, was an effective champion of seventeenth- and eighteenth-century music, and chiefly responsible for the revival of the harpsichord in the twentieth century. She had made her home in Paris since the war.

3. Jeanne de Margéries was the sister of the playwright Edmond Rostand, and the wife of Roland de Margéries, an eminent diplomat.

4. The Aurics: the French composer Georges Auric (1899–1983) and his wife Nora. Auric wrote many ballets and film scores, among the latter the music for Cocteau's *La Belle et la Bête*.

5. Vance Weston, the hero of *The Gods Arrive* and of its predecessor.

To Bernard Berenson

Sainte Claire
January 23, 1932

Dearest B.B.— Robert & I are this moment back from three days of (comparatively) riotous living at Nice, where we went after Landowska's departure, alléchés by a Mozart festival in the shape of several of M.'s operas with Lotte Schoene & a Viennese troupe. On arriving I found your letter from I Tatti, & am distressed beyond measure by what you say of Mary's relapse. Do please write just a p.c. soon to tell me whether the Dr. thinks it just an accidental thing, or a real menace of a new abscess. I do hope not!

I am worried, too, by what you say of your New York cabling & writing. Evidently we are all—I won't say dancing, but nervously sitting, on the thin crust of the same volcano. I hope you refer only to this, & not to some private seismus of your own. Let me know about this too when you have time.

We had two delicious evenings with Die Entführung & Figaro, the latter simply *ravishing*. The troupe was good, the conductor, Hoesslin, remarkable, & Lotte Schoene enchanting. Altogether it was delightful; & so was a wonderful trip we made yesterday, up the valley of the Var to Aspremont, & then, after a precipitous descent, across the river to Gattières—with glorious snow-Alps closing in the North in unbroken white, & orange trees along the road side.—And yet Hyères is best, & I was childishly glad to get back! I'm glad Gaillard wrote to you about your book,[1] for his heart was full of it—as was his last letter to me.—

I mustn't close without mentioning that I FINISHED Vance on Jan. 18th (the Nice romp was in the nature of a self-reward!), & the last chapters will be sent to you as soon as I can decently ask Mme. F.[2] to make another copy of them! She is still doddering from the effect of having re-typed them about 40 times, but will no doubt soon revive.

Please give Mary my fondest love & deepest sympathy. How I wish I cd drop in on you all!

A special embrace for Nick, many messages for Alda,[3] & the affection that you know for you.

Edith

I am very sorry that Lytton Strachey[4] is dead. He was, with Aldous Huxley, the only light left in that particular quarter of the heavens.

Ms:VT

1. *The Italian Painters of the Renaissance* (1930).
2. EW's secretary Jeanne Duprat had married a certain M. Féderich in the 1920s, and was now widowed.
3. Alda Mariano, Nicky Mariano's sister; the wife of Baron Egbert von Anrep and librarian of I Tatti.
4. Lytton Strachey (1880–1932), the author of *Eminent Victorians* (1918). EW had met him a few times, and regarded him as the embodiment of "the old English culture." Strachey's brother Oliver was married to Rae Costelloe, Mary Berenson's daughter.

To Rutger B. Jewett

January 30, 1932

Dear Mr. Jewett,

Your cable announcing that $8.000, on account of "The Gods," had been placed to my credit at the Fifth Avenue Branch of the Chase National Bank, came the day before yesterday, and I must thank you again for your kindness in arranging this matter for me. I am assured by my friends that it is part of the banking business to lend money on interest, but on the rare occasions when I have had to borrow from my bank I have always secretly felt as if the sheriff was at the door, and his hand might fall on my shoulder at any moment; so you may imagine what a burden has been lifted by your cable.

I am now waiting to hear of the arrival of the last chapters.

With renewed thanks,
　　Yours ever sincerely

Copy:BL

To Margaret Terry Chanler

Sainte Claire
March 25, 1932

Dearest Daisy— I have put off answering your letter, with the good tidings that we are really to see you again this year, because, while I was finishing the last chapters of my novel, the correspondence piled up at such a rate that I haven't yet quite tunnelled my way through it —& in such cases, the only way is to write the duty letters first!

But if I haven't written, I have talked of you long & often, with dear Gillet,[1] who was here last month, & is returning after Easter; with B.B., of course, with Robert, & all the come-&-go friends who always cry out: "Et votre amie Daisy? Qu'en avez vous fait, depuis si longtemps?" as though I had you sequestrated in the crypt here under the court!— Instead, I have had you tucked away in my warmest heart-valve, whence every now & then I pull you out to share a good book or a new delightful friend. Of the latter, the winter has brought several, & especially Prof. Malinowski,[2] an ethnologist who has written some remarkable books on tribal life in Melanesia, & whom I met at the Huxleys'. He is lecturer at the School of Economics in London, but is at Tamaris for the winter, with a very intelligent invalid wife & three delightful little girls, & he is himself a charming & highly civilized example of Anglo-Polish culture. The Huxleys[3] are a great joy, but alas they live far away & have no telephone, so our meetings are not as frequent as I could wish. I suppose you have read his "Brave New World," which is a masterpiece of tragic indictment of our ghastly age of Fordian culture. Get it at once, if you haven't. He wrote to me that I had "put the case" already in "Twilight Sleep," & I own I was much set up by his recognition of the fact! I have also been revelling in Ludwig's "Schliemann,"⁴ wh. is unbelievably good, & exciting & interesting. There have been some other good finds, but I put these highest.

B.B. & Nicky are arriving today, returning here for a rest, after the endless & exhausting (to everybody) ups & downs of Mary's illness. She seems to have had one of the mysterious "infections" that are befalling people nowadays, & even now, after nearly 5 months, has not yet been out, or even downstairs. B.B. & Nicky are shattered, & have decided to recuperate here, as her daughters are going to I Tatti for Easter.

I am also expecting the dear Nicholsons, & Kenneth Clark & his wife—& when my visitors scatter I shall probably dip down into Italy for a month.—The idea of returning there with you in the autumn appeals to me greatly—but "color che sanno" all say, *not* Sicily; it is burnt up like a door-mat, & all sodden with scirocco. Why not then range between the Adriatic & Rome, where October is such a perfect month? There's time to talk it over!

We have had—& are still having—a dour & windy spring after our incredibly lovely early winter, & the garden is sulky & cold-bound.

Do let me know when you are coming. I'm impatient for details!

Larry writes to announce Laura's imminent 8th, & I'm so glad that there are going to be such a saving group of nice people in this wilderness of a world.—I hear that Matilda & W.G. are rather shaky (I think it was Berthe de Ganay, here for Easter, who had seen them), & the Abbé Mugnier is said to be very gay & patient in his blindness, with a lecture,⁵ a telephone & a taxi, all supplied by devoted friends.—

Robert is well, & departing, alas, soon to his perfect little flat in the Ile St Louis.

Now send me back *your* budget of news as soon as the hustle of life permits.

Yrs ever affly
    Edith

I've got another charming new friend, Mgr. Chaptal. He came here to see me when he passed through Hyères last month, & we made great friends. I suppose you know him. He sent me a book that I greatly commend to you, "Vol de Nuit," by St Exupéry,[6] & loved my story of Elise's audience at the Vatican when she said: "Sa Sainteté est arrivée entourée de ses Bayadères"—(Swiss guard's striped breeches.)

Ms:BL

1. Louis Gillet (1876–1943), art historian and literary critic; eventually elected to the Academy. When EW met him in the mid-1920s, Gillet was curator of a museum at Chaalis, near Senlis. Gillet translated two of EW's novels: *The Mother's Recompense* (*Le Bilan* [The Balance Sheet]) and *The Children* (*Leurs Enfants*); and four of Berenson's early essays. He was one of EW's most devoted friends in the later years.

2. Bronislaw Malinowski (1884–1942), the anthropologist whose most recent work was *The Sexual Life of Savages in North-Western Melanesia*, about courtship, marriage, and family life among the natives of the Trobriand Islands (1929).

3. Aldous Huxley (1894–1963) and his wife, Maria, had taken a villa at Sanary, some distance from Hyères, for several winters. Huxley's novel *Brave New World* in 1932 followed such earlier ones as *Chrome Yellow, Antic Hay, and Those Barren Leaves*. He was the grandson of T. H. Huxley, whose biological writings EW much admired, and the son of Mrs. Humphry Ward's younger sister Julia.

4. The recently published book on Heinrich Schliemann and his excavations in Greece and Asia Minor, by Emil Ludwig (1881–1948).

5. Lecture: the French word for a reading machine.

6. *Vol de Nuit* (1931; translated into English as *Night Flight*), by Antoine de Saint-Exupéry, aviator and author (1900–1944).

To John Hugh Smith

Hotel de la Ville
Rome
May 23, 1932

My dear John— Did you know that the 7th floor of this hotel has a corner room with 5 windows, of which 3 are glass doors opening on a terrace compared to which our Crillon "altana" looks down on a barnyard? I owe the discovery to B.B., & I had not heretofore imagined that the words "hotel" & "romantic" could be so absolutely synonymous.

We are all but next door to the Trinità dei Monti, & one terrace looks on that, & all s. western Rome, the other over the gardens of the Villa Medici & the Villa Malta. When you throw in a full moon, "dahin, dahin, möcht Ich mit Dir, O mein Geliebter, gehn!"[1]

I left Hyères on the 8th, & motored to I Tatti, to spend two days, & see Mary B. The first day I thought her much better, but my final impression was less favourable. Luckily she decided not to attempt Rome, but to go to Switzerland for a sort of after-cure. I came on here, & B.B. & Nicky joined me about a week ago. Every minute has been rich in enjoyment. I didn't know Rome in its late spring volupté of roses, orange blossoms & nightingales, & really all die Romantiker seem to come to life & walk its streets between the sun-gold & the indigo shadows. Oh, what a place of places!—Every afternoon we go off on a long giro, in the hills or by the sea. An afternoon at Ostia was particularly dreamy & Browningesque. Every now & then Nicky & I escape & hear some fine church music, but I let B.B. wallow alone in the museums—of which he doesn't do much, by the way.

Meanwhile where are you, & how, & when shall I see you? Do send me some news of yourself, & of the troublous times, also. B.B. met yesterday at yr. Embassy a Secretary fresh from Washington who made his hair stand on end with prophecies of ruin & revolution là bas! What of the dollar, & prospects in general? The price of serial fiction (my main support) has dropped *three fourths*, & I tremble at my temerity in having undertaken this motor trip at such a moment! However, mieux vaut mourir en beauté . . .

I hope to be back at St Brice about June 7th; but poor Elise fell & hurt her back on the way down here, & after a week here in a clinic has come back not able to do much, & I've no idea yet when she'll be able to travel— I may have to go straight back by train.—Drop me a line here.—

Yrs ever affly
    E.

I have been re-reading Die Italienische Reise[2] on the spot, & take back what I said of it. You will find it well worth while.

Ms:BL

1. One of the songs sung by the mysterious child Mignon in Goethe's *Wilhelm Meisters Lehrjahre* (1795–1796). Like "Kennst du das Land" in that novel, it expresses a yearning for Italy.

2. *Italienische Reise* (1816–1817), Goethe's account of his travels in Italy.

To Bernard Berenson

Assisi
May 30, 1932

Dearest B.B.— Even to write to you I can hardly turn my eyes from the divinely temperate landscape veiled in tender mists below my window—but I'm gravid with rentré raptures, & a postcard wd never hold them!

We had a glorious run—loitering, as usual; with delicious halts at Spoleto (where we lunched), & at Spello, where the old lady couldn't turn the key in the padlock of the Pinturicchio chapel, & I filled her with mingled dismay & admiration by vaulting lightly (from a chair) over the barrier, & turning on the electric lights myself!! Half way on to Assisi I thought: "Oh, dear, I forgot to turn off the electric lights, & she can't get at them, & she'll be sacked by the Bishop!" *What* a donnée—! Would *you* have gone back?

In spite of these interludes we got here at 3.45; but, alas, in a deluge. The lower church was as dark as a pit; but the monks were singing vespers or some "Hour" or other in the dark depths of the apse, with a faint glimmer on the altar, so I listened instead of looking. It's lucky, by the way, that I phoned for rooms, for 2 big "tours" arrived before me, & unhappy motorists who neglected the same precaution are wandering mournfully from hotel to hotel as I write. Please share this letter with Nicky, & tell her that I shall never forget her angelic kindness to me during the happy Roman days. I feel like an orphan child tonight, & am longing to know *what* (not whom) you've been seeing today, & what joys I've missed.

Saluti to Steinmann, Mrs. Strong, & Morra[1] when he comes.

I hope you've had better news from Mary.

Yrs ever affly
Edith

Elise stood the journey well.

Ms:VT

1. Ernest Steinmann (1866–1934), art historian and head of the Hertziana Library in Rome; longtime friend of Berenson.

Eugénie Sellars Strong (1860–1943), English archaeologist and art historian; frequent visitor to I Tatti, where EW met her.

Count Umberto Morra (born 1900), writer and valued friend to writers and scholars. With Berenson and Nicky Mariano, EW visited Morra at his home in Cortona.

To Nicky Mariano

Loreto. Albergo dei Pellegrini
Tuesday
May 31, 1932

Best beloved Nicky— Today it is your turn—though on the express condition that you *don't answer*!

Last eve'g 89 Olandesi of all sexes arrived at the H. Subasio,[1] & when I went into the upper church this morning I heard a deep distant murmur, & thought: "What luck! Another High Mass!" But it was only their guides megaphoning to them, & the responses were the tramp of their hurrying feet. Luckily they *did* hurry, & in less than no time I had both churches to myself. But, alas, having tried now both evening & morning light, I have to recognize that I *can't* see the 4 great vault frescoes of the Lower Church any more—I had to be satisfied with the rest.

Elise was full of admiration, but as we were leaving I found her principal hope had been to visit the tomb of Sta Chiara, "parce que c'est à Ste Claire que Mme habite—" so we turned back to see it, & when she found a modern statue behind a gilded grating it almost equalled the Bayadères!!

The run today was indescribably beautiful, with changing skies & such endless plays of mountain forms—

We left Assisi at about 11, & with much loitering, & a long parenthesis at Recanati, we were here at 4, sole tenants of the charming "Pellegrini." When I tell you that, this being the last day of the mois de Marie, the high altar of the Basilica flamed with lights, & canons in glorious reds & purples intoned without ceasing, while in the Casa Santa two nuns remained in adoration, & a young Franciscan knelt on the doorstep in pallid ecstasy, you will know how I wished for you! It has been a beautiful day, & I always do wish for you when they happen to me.

I do so hope that you will have better news of your brother-in-law, & that Alda will be able to join you.—Do ask B.B. to send me some news at the Hotel Cavour, Milan, to reach me there on Saturday. What is the latest of Mary?

My best love, & all the thanks imaginable for your dear delightful companionship during Die Zweite Römische Reise—

Yrs ever devotedly
    Edith

Tell B.B. I thought Ojetti's[2] article so very good that I sent it to Norts—

I was very glad I went to Recanati.[3] It is a splendidly perched & proud little town & the *desertness* of that great brick palace impressed me & the shawl he wore "around his arms & knees" quando faceva freddo, as it must have, & bitterly. But I couldn't see *his* room, because "il Conte Eltone era partito in viaggio, e aveva preso la chiave."

Did you know that 2 pale great-nephews still live there, & each has his door-plate on one side of the great portal? *There's* a subject!
"Il Conte Eltone."
"Il Conte Monalduccio."
                    (or "dugio"?)
And the Gates of Glory in between those two invisible names!

Ms:VT

1. I.e., in Assisi.
2. Ugo Ojetti (1871–1946), Italian journalist and critic, conspicuous figure on the Italian cultural scene, founder and editor of the art review *Dedalo*, which published many of Berenson's articles in translation.
3. The home of the great Italian Romantic poet Giacomo Leopardi (1798–1837), the "he" referred to in the next sentence.

To Mary Berenson

Grand Hôtel des Thermes
Salsomaggiore
June 4, 1932

Dearest Mary—

Only a day or two ago did it occur to me that, during my brief stay at I Tatti, I had never said a word to you about the "Life" of B.B.!¹

Considering that you had taken the trouble to send it to me by the "sumjeck's" own hand, such conduct seems at the least ungracious—& I can only hope you didn't set it down as such! The truth is that during my few hours with you there was such a coming & going of people, & so many things came up to be discussed, that the "Life" escaped my mind until I was far away from you. I hope you will forgive this stupid oversight, & above all not think it proved a lack of interest. I was much interested & full of suggestions; but it would have needed a quiet hour with you to bring them to the surface.

First, however, I must explain that when B.B. gave me the manuscript he did not tell me it was not to be published now; had he done so, I shd not have made the verbal suggestions & corrections with which I disfigured your ms. This is a small matter, but I wanted to explain it, as you might have thought my commentaries irrelevant.

As to the chapters, they are of course full of interest, but I think you cd make them much more so by giving more details about B.B.'s boyhood, & his little childhood in Russia, as he has often described it to me; also about his Harvard days, when he was "stupor mundi" to undergraduates & professors. I think the transition to Florence is too abrupt, & also that, once there, you could "situate" the story better by brushing in a more vivid & fuller sketch of the group of students & dilettanti of that vanished Florence—it is all so picturesque, & so far away already! What do you think?

And now, *please* send me "by return" some advice as to how to write my own "Life," for I'm hopelessly stuck, & feel how much easier it wd have been if I'd lived in Florence with picturesque people instead of stodging in New York!

I tore myself, oh, so reluctantly, from my glorious prophet's chamber at the H. de la Ville, & still more so from the inhabitants of the floor above. I don't know who was butchered to make my Roman holiday

(unless it was poor Elise) but I know it was a first-class one, & must
have cost somebody a good deal!

My trip northward was delicious too—Assisi, Loreto, Recanati, Rimini, Ravenna, Ferrara—I hadn't seen any of them in years, & flying from
one to the other over painless perfect roads makes it all so different fr.
the old creaking travel days. Still, perhaps it exasperates the emotional
enjoyment—for I suddenly felt so tired that I decided to "stop off" here
for two nights before taking the train to Paris tomorrow. I shall stop at
the Crillon for 2 days, & I hope there is a letter from you, or about
you, awaiting me at the Cavour, where I pick up my sleeping tickets
tomorrow. I'm sure B.B. or Nicky will have sent a report about you to
meet me there.

Do *please* go warily about teeth! Sometimes it helps—sometimes it
doesn't. I know that American dentists are increasingly opposed to it;
so please don't go too far!

My best rememberances to Logan, & an aurevoir to you both, I hope,
at St Brice.

Yrs ever affly
   Edith

Ms:VT

1. This work was never published.

To Jane Clark

19, Seymour Street
[London]
July 19, 1932

Dearest Jane— How I *did* enjoy my snatch of a visit![1] It was so delicious
to have that good talk with you both, & I do so like to *situate* my friends,
& evoke their setting when I think of them. I didn't find yours as easy
to visualize in advance as the dear Bucklers',[2] & am so glad now to be
able to frame you in those wide quiet rooms, with the blue-green distances & the stream for background. (Being a true friend, I tactfully

exclude the cock-eyed lily-pool!!)—Greatly also did I like my hour in the Museum with Kenneth, & the seeing of those incomparable Guardis, the Canaletto of the Brenta with the lovely peach-coloured lady in the left foreground, the dazzling Uccello, the rosy St Vincent Ferrer, one or two lovely little Wilsons, the quiet green spaces of the 82 yr. old Claude landscape—oh, the description of the verre églomisé in the Tradescant collection!! Thank him for all that, & both of you for your delightful welcome—& *please* send me Kenneth soon to see the Manets—

Yrs ever affly
Edith

Don't fail to run over to Hidcote before Aug. 1st. It is a sight not to be missed. Hidcote Manor, Campden.[3]

Ms:KC

1. To the Clarks' home on Shotover Hill, a few miles outside Oxford.
2. See letter to Sara Norton, March 17, 1903.
3. The English home of EW's friend and fellow gardener Lawrence Johnston.

To Kenneth Clark

Pavillon Colombe
October 12, 1932

My dear Kenneth,

Your letter came just after I had posted mine, & I am covered with vain-glory at the idea that Colin David[1] wants me to be his godmother—but do you suppose he really *does?* It is an age since anything has made me so cocky, & the idea that Nicky is to godmother Colin's other half[2] makes me feel that, whatever Colin's own short-comings turn out to be, his sister, formed by Nicky's guiding hand, will act as a ministering angel to him, & undo all the harm I might create!

But when is the christening to take place? I should hate to have to mother my boy by proxy, & yet how can either Nicky or I be on the spot before next summer?? Have you thought of this in planning for the future welfare of your infants? Whatever you & they decide will be best, & I am practicing godmotherly attitudes, in the hope that things can be tided over without too much risk to their souls.

As for their dear little bodies, I am delighted to hear how handsome & healthy they are, & also that Jane is so blooming.—Please give her my love, & believe, both of you, that I am really very deeply touched at your wanting your old friend to be associated with such a happy beginning.

Yours affly
    Edith

Ms:KC

1. Colin Clark, one of twins born to Jane and Kenneth Clark on April 9, 1932.
2. Colette Clark, Colin's twin sister.

To Kenneth Clark

Sainte-Claire
November 25, 1932

My dear Kenneth,

My letter to Jane must have crossed yours to me, just sent back from I Tatti, where, as you see, I didn't go after all, being held up by the "suites de la grippe" in the shape of such a misery of fatigue that I had to stay in Paris & be given piqûres! I finally got away yesterday, out of a mud-bath into Lapis-&-gold! I've never seen the landscape here look lovelier, & I wish you & Jane & Alan[1] & the hardy twins were all here to enjoy it with me.

How very unlike the exact & methodical Mrs. Tyler to forget the card that went with the cup![2] My mother was born in 1824, & her name was Lucretia Stevens Rhinelander—nothing like as good as her mother, who was Mary Lucille Lucy Anne Stevens, & the daughter of Genl Stevens, who was on Washington's staff, commanded the artillery in the Revolutionary army, & figures twice in the big Trumbull paintings in the Capitol at Washington, once in the surrender of Burgoyne, & once in the ditto of Ld Cornwallis! Are these facts sufficient to satisfy Colin's legitimate curiosity? The cup is obviously American, & I thought might amuse you & Jane for that reason. I don't know anything about American hall-marks, but perhaps at the Ashmolean you may find a book wh. will "situate" this artless object.

I'm so glad you & Jane like it.

Yrs affly
    Edith

I can't see *why* you should pay for the screen, but you are now five against one!!

Ms:KC

1. Alan Clark, born in 1928.
2. The card that was to accompany the baptismal present (and later sent on) read: "I want Colin to have this little silver mug which was my mother's."

To Gaillard Lapsley

Sainte-Claire
March 2, 1933

Dearest Gaillard,

I hate to bother you again—& yet I do! My "Apologia" is on its last lap, & I must be "fixed" on two points. I can't remember when Howard died, except that it was before the end of the war;[1] & I feel sure you can give me this date.

I want to record Henry's great apostrophe to Death—after his stroke—as I don't remember its ever having been mentioned in any article about him. My recollection of it is: "So it's you at last, august stranger!" But am I right? And who heard him say it?[2] Now *don't* feel obliged to write a letter, but just scribble your two answers on a bit of paper.

I hope to finish the confounded thing this week, & I already have offers for a series of articles in the Atlantic, a short story & a novel!

Does this mean that no one can afford to do anything but read?
How about Steven's op.?[3]
I see it is due very soon.

Yrs ever so
       E

I hope I thanked you as you deserve for the exordia,[4] but I'm in a
blur about everything but the weather, which continues to madden me
to crime. It is *still* pouring!!!

Ms:BL

1. Howard Sturgis died in January 1920.
2. See letter to Gaillard Lapsley, December 17, 1915, note 1.
3. Runciman's new opus was *Byzantine Civilization* (1933).
4. Lapsley evidently reminded EW of the occasion, as she described it in *A
Backward Glance*, when a friend of theirs chided James for his insufficient interest
in D. H. Lawrence and asked if he had *really* read any of Lawrence's novels.
To this James replied: "I—I have trifled with the exordia."

To Rutger B. Jewett

April 29, 1933

Dear Mr. Jewett,
"*Retrospect*."[1]—Your letter of April 21st has just come, and I enclose
a copy of the cable I have just sent you in reply.
I was beginning to wonder why I had not heard from you, as the last
chapters of my memoirs were posted from here on March 15th, but I
suppose your letter to I Tatti has been lost. In future, please always
send my correspondence to my own address, unless I ask you to do
otherwise, as my letters are always forwarded regularly and without
delay.
I am not in the least surprised that the editor of the Ladies' Home
Journal finds my reminiscences too long and parts of them "dull." I
always wondered how they could interest such a public as the American

illustrated magazines are addressed to, and he is at liberty to cut out anything he wishes, but not of course to back out of his price.[2] I have the whole of our correspondence on that subject, and will neither take back the manuscript nor accept a lower price for it. No date was ever fixed for delivery, and as I suppose you have transmitted the chapters to the editor as they were received, he has had ample time to form an appreciation of the book. All the literary people to whom I have shown it have told me that I ought to have asked a much higher price, and I am certainly not going to reduce it by a dollar. I assume you went into this question in the letter which you addressed to me in Florence, as you say nothing about it in yours of April 21st, just received.

Desmond MacCarthy, who has read a great part of my reminiscences, is enthusiastic about them, and I am sure the book will have a very large sale, for I have had many letters about the chapter which appeared in The Atlantic.

The Old Maid. I note that Miss Kauser wishes to make use of Zoë Akins's dramatization of "The Old Maid." I did not know this dramatization had ever been finished; but I understand that Zoë Akins is absolutely unreliable, and therefore if any arrangement is made about the play it must be a [sentence incomplete].

Yours very sincerely

May 2nd, 1933.
P.S.—I was just about to post my letter when yours was forwarded from Florence, and at the same time your cable in answer to mine has come.

I have very little to change in respect to what I have already said regarding the attitude of the Ladies' Home Journal. It is of course absurd to say that the arrangement was made five years ago. To the best of my recollection (my literary correspondence being filed and kept at St-Brice) it was about three years ago that the L.H.J. offered me $25.000 for my Reminiscences. I accepted on condition that no date was fixed for the delivery of the manuscript, and since then they have been receiving the manuscript from you as it was written, and no comment has been offered on it and no conditions fixed as to its length. I have been working very hard over this book, and cannot consent to have one-fifth of the price offered suddenly cut off. No doubt the L.H.J. is hard up, but so am I, and I imagine that they have larger funds to draw upon than I have. At any rate it is no advantage to me to have them say that they want only half of the book I have written as I do not know who would take the other half.

The only change I could agree to would be something like the following:

1. To agree that the L.H.J. should cut out all but 60.000 words on condition that everything about Henry James is in the portion rejected by them. This might enable me to place elsewhere this study of Henry James which "Life and Letters" is already anxious to get.

2. For the balance kept by the L.H.J. I would accept $21.000 instead of $25.000, on condition that they agreed to take a short story from me at the price recently offered by the Woman's Home Companion.

I should probably still be a loser on this arrangement, but I would naturally rather avoid taking legal proceedings though I am convinced that if I did so the L.H.J. would be held by the courts to their original agreement.

I am detained here by the serious illness of two members of my household, my old housekeeper and my maid, so all the letters and cables should be addressed to me here till notice to the contrary.

Copy:BL

1. The provisional title of *A Backward Glance.*
2. A fee of $25,000 had been agreed upon for the serialization of EW's memoirs in the *Ladies' Home Journal.* The editor, Loring Schuyler, now proposed that EW cut the manuscript by forty thousand words, with the magazine paying a reduced fee of $20,000. The cable EW sent Jewett (mentioned in the letter's first sentence) read: "Absolutely decline reducing price and will sue him unless agreement kept."

To Mary Berenson

Sainte-Claire
May 26, 1933

Dearest Mary,

Where are you all likely to be in June? My poor Elise is failing slowly¹—everything has been done, but that terrible disease is without mercy. My old Gross is now quite mindless, but gentle & quiet,² so I can settle her at the convent with the faithful sisters; & as soon as Elise's sufferings are over I want to get away as quickly as I can from this House of Usher, & wd go to you if I still felt strong enough by that time. The strain on my heart-strings (I mean the metaphorical ones) is severe, for since Walter's death I've been incurably lonely *inside*, & these two faithful women kept the hearth-fire going.

Don't mind my talking like this; you know I've got lots of "ressort," but this long vigil, alone with all my past, wears the nerves thin. If I come to I Tatti I think I can promise to tighten them up—

My best love to you all.

Edith

Don't on any account let me interfere with any plans, for at the last moment I might not be able to come— I might have to go straight to Paris, as I am getting another butler, & have not found one yet.

Ms:VT

1. Elise was stricken with what was diagnosed as pernicious anemia. She died on May 29.

2. On April 14, the eighty-year-old Gross was seized, in EW's words (to Elisina Tyler), with "senile dementia and suicidal mania." She was transformed into "a wild, frightened and obstinate stranger." She had grown quiet with the passage of days, but EW thought it best to have her taken to the convent at Espérance.

To Bernard Berenson

Stanway, Cheltenham
July 10, 1933

Dearest B.B.,

It is weeks since we have exchanged any signals more direct than a wig-wag through other correspondents, & suddenly I feel an irrepressible need to talk to you directly, though from so far.—I came to England nearly 3 weeks ago, & the complete change of scene & society has done me lots of good. I was so dog-tired, body & mind, that I was very glad of a long rest at Lawrence Johnston's, in the green peace of a garden incredibly different from the one at Menton, but equally perfect. My visit there was broken by a five days' trip to Wales with G. Lapsley, & that also delighted me. We had never either of us been to Wales before, & we dealt with most of the out of the way corners, including Llanthony Abbey, which is really an elfin place, in a lost green valley with the real Kilmeny-feeling about it.—After Wales I went back to Johnnie's, then for 24 hours to my old friend Mrs. Allhusen,[1] (taking on the way the Saxon church at Bradford on Avon, which is a wonder) & then here for a pleasant week-end; the party, Lady (*not* Ld) Wemyss, the Plymouths, Ld Hugo Cecil, & the delightful younger son, Guy Charteris, who is the botanist & bird-lorist, & lastly Robert, whom I first met here 25 years ago! We found ourselves in the Visitors' Book at that distant date, & kissed again with tears!—

I meant to leave for St Brice today, but dear White, who is putting my new household on its legs again, has begged for 3 days more, so I am going up to London to put in the time at Nettie Johnstone's.

I am pining for my own garden, in spite of all the beauties & the friendliness about me—but it can't be helped, & I feel about my lost roses & lilies of 1933 what Santayana wrote:

"O all you beauties I shall never see,
What a great lover you have lost in me."[2]

I hear from Nicky that Mary has wisely decided not to go to England this year, but that you may both join her at Abano for a little tour.

I do hope we are going to see each other before many more months. Have you no mind for Paris in the autumn? Gaillard wants me to go to

Salso with him in early Sept., but that wd give me only 2 months of St Brice, or not even that, & though I know I ought to I shrink from the uprooting— However, we'll see.

Meanwhile, do please write, *long & soon.*—Have you read Pierre Gaxotte's "Siècle de Louis XV"?[3] He was unknown to me—but it's a remarkable book.

If Nick is with you please thank her for her good letter.

Ms:VT

1. The former Dorothy Stanley, the daughter of EW's London friend and hostess Lady St. Helier and her first husband, Colonel J. C. Stanley; married (in 1896) to Henry Allhusen.

2. The last lines (slightly emended by EW) of Sonnet XXI in *Poems* (1923) by George Santayana: "But, O ye beauties I must never see,/ How great a lover you have lost in me!"

3. Published in 1933.

To Bernard Berenson

Pavillon Colombe
July 25, 1933

Dearest B.B.— I must begin by thanking you for your two most precious batches of stamps, lest, swept away by all the rest that is to be said, I should omit the expression of my gratitude, though the sentiment is lively.

With regard to the Abbé Mugnier, I think his letter is a simple expression of joy at his partly recovered sight. He wrote me one also, very simple & affectionate, & I imagine he is doing the same to all his intimate friends. But I will "tâter le terrain" & let you know. Mme de Castries is quite rich enough to bear the expenses of the operation, & in fact in any other country but this thrifty one she would doubtless have assumed the charge of the Abbé's household without beating up subscriptions from all his friends. But the stocking under the mattress speaks louder than blood or friendship here.

I am going to see the Abbé tomorrow, & will let you know about my visit.

Poor Kingsley Porter[1]—how strange that he shd have had a sort of pre-Saxon death in the search (figuratively speaking) of a mysterious Western isle. There is something very Thule-an & St Brendan-ish about it. Eric Mac was very much grieved for his poor wife, & deeply perplexed (as I was, & am) over the silence of all the papers. Have you seen any allusion to his death except the first little notice mentioning that he had gone off alone in his boat?—

I had a very pleasant but brief visit from the Clarks, who took their "baptême de l'air" & came & went by Le Bourget. We prélassed ourselves at the Renoir show, & I, who am a confirmed anti-Renoiriste, had to own that before the fatal period of the Michelin women bathed in currant jelly he did some wonderful things.

The other day, as you doubtless know, Gillet married his tall & pretty daughter at Chaalis, & we had a charming example of a simple, rustic French family gathering, the guests seated on kitchen chairs, the knives & forks brought back unwashed on each plate, &c—& all gay, friendly, full of discours & accolades. Valéry & H. de Régnier were Louisette's witnesses, & Valéry read aloud a singularly artless poem by Mme H. de Régnier, wh. M. de Monzie took for an effusion of Valéry's, no doubt to the latter's unbounded surprise!!

I'm so sorry that Cagnola[2] is "under the knife," but hope he will emerge restored.

I spent last Sat. to Monday at Courance where, among others, were the Polovtsoffs.[3] He read me a really delightful article (which he had given somewhere as a lecture) on the Empress Elizabeth & her court, & I suggested his writing a book on Russian court & society life in the XVIII century, the fashions, architecture, ceremonial, principal personages, &c. Don't you think it wd be a good idea?

I hear frequent praise of Mary's book,[4] & am so glad she has had such an appreciative reception.

I must stop now to do stupid things. Best love to you all, my dear.

Yrs ever
  Edith

Ms:VT

1. Arthur Kingsley Porter (1883–1933), author of studies of medieval architecture and sculpture, and professor of art at Harvard. He apparently drowned

in a storm off the coast of Ireland; but many people refused to believe it, and legends of his being alive persisted for decades.

2. Don Guido Cagnola (1862–1954), art collector.

3. Alexander Polovtsoff, Russian-born art collector.

4. *A Modern Pilgrimage*, Mary Berenson's account (published by Constable, London, in 1932) of a trip to Palestine taken by the Berensons and Nicky Mariano.

To William R. Tyler

Pavillon Colombe
August 4, 1933

Dearest Bill,

Thank you for your good letter. I didn't suppose your engagement[1] was so generally known, or that anything so solemn and early-Victorian as "settlements" (I haven't heard of them since my infancy) were being negotiated.

In the circumstances my suggestions would be irrelevant, and so I will pocket them, and await with impatience the opportunity of welcoming the young lady when she finally approaches Antigny. Meanwhile, please tell her that she is the luckiest damsel on our planet, and that if I were half a century younger she wouldn't have a look-in!

Saluti to the Antignotes.

Yours ever affectionately,
Edoo.

When I saw your mother at the Crillon on my way to England she very kindly took charge for me of a packet of about 6000 Lire, drawn for an unrealized trip to Italy. I think she said she would lock them up in her box at Morgans.

I *may* go to Salso early in Sept. Would you be kind enough to ask her if, le cas échéant, there is any way of getting at them??

Ms:WRT

1. William Tyler was engaged to marry Bettine Fisher-Rowe, the daughter of a British naval officer, and the descendant of a well-established Dorset family.

To Gaillard Lapsley

Grand Hotel de l'Europe
Salzburg
[August 28, 1933]

Dearest Gaillard,

The above address can't surprise you more than it does me! Jeanne Homberg[1] was staying with me about three weeks ago, & she offered, if I wd come to Salzburg, to smooth my way in advance, providing room, bath, seats for every performance &c. And so I suddenly jumped into the train & came for 6 days—& don't regret it!—

The place is packed to the Plimsoll Line, & at every turn one runs into an acquaintance. Almost the first I met, at this hotel, was Percy!! & his first remark was: "Sybil has had a bad night."

I will hasten to reassure you by adding that the following day they were off on an all-day motor trip, & yesterday I saw her sitting on the hard board benches at "Everyman," in the Cathedral Square, at the chill hour of sunset. What humbugs!! I did the proper thing, & asked Percy when she was visible; but an audience has not yet been fixed, & I hope none will be granted, for I can't say that I hanker to see her. I told Percy you had wrecked my autumn by arranging to go to them just when I cd have gone to Salso, & said: "Now, tell me honestly, aren't you going to put him off?" to which he solemnly replied: "I can never tell from day to day."

I may add that I never saw him look better. Ten years younger, & considerably thinner.

But my principal boon companion, feeder & motor charioteer, has been—who do you think?? Your friend Mr. Edwin Morgan! He is at this hotel, & thanks to you combles me with motor lifts, champagne suppers & joy-rides, while we tearfully wish we cd cure you of your morbid taste for going to America!

I'm going back tomorrow night, to join, (at Colombe) poor Nettie Johnstone, whom I have asked to stay for several weeks, as there seemed literally no other place for her to go to. (I need not point out that my week in Salzburg was partly inspired by—the desire for a more life-giving society.)

Musically (& sennically, as your compatriots say) I have taken in: Mozart Mass in St Peter's (divine)—

Everyman ⎫
Faust ⎭ out of door shows, fit for a public abruti by cinema

Mozart Symphony Concert *supremely* conducted by Bruno Walter,[2] an evening of Lieder by Lotte Lehmann,[3] Bruno Walter at the piano—& tonight Oberon at the opera. Not bad?

Well, do send me a line from Salso, for I know I can't hope for one before—

Bon arrivée, & good luck at the Springs.

Yrs ever E

I have had such happy letters from Minnie over your visit. It was a real kindness to go, & I'm so glad you saw Trix.

Kenneth Clark has been appointed Director of the National Gallery.

Ms:BL

1. A friend of EW in Paris and southern France.

2. Bruno Walter (1876–1962), the distinguished German conductor, began his association with the Salzburg summer music festival in 1925.

3. Lotte Lehmann (1888–1976), the German soprano just now reaching the height of her fame.

To Kenneth Clark

Grand Hotel de l'Europe
Salzburg
August 28, 1933

My dear Kenneth,

I am very very glad, & I'm sure you're right to have accepted.[1] I don't agree with B.B. that a regular job is "abrutissant." Real vocations survive such contrarieties, & anything is better than to dangle an uncertain foot & not jump in.

Last week Royall Tyler was staying with me. He told me he had heard in London of yr appointment, & was most enthusiastic & approving—I told him what you had said to me of your doubts, & he entirely shares my view. So I hope the approbation of an Ancient & a Sage will fortify you in your conviction that you were a thousand times right not to make Il Gran Rifiuto.

It was dear of you to write to me as soon as the matter was settled, & I am much touched by your finding the time. When I think of the tidal wave of congratulations that must be surging over you, I hesitate to add this letter; but I had to tell you how I rejoice in your appointment on wh. I believe you & the N.G. are equally to be congratulated—& also to say without delay how greatly I look forward to seeing you both at St Brice toward the end of Sept., for as long as you can make it possible.

I'm glad your mother is settled, & hope that Jane will have a moment in which to rest fr. her labours—though I don't see how or when.

There is so much to say about Salzburg that it must be postponed; but I've had four glorious days of perfect weather & gushing fountains of music. The human part has been very funny—& need I say that Sybil Colfax[2] turned up in the middle of it? The last I heard (3 days earlier) she was on her way to the Huxleys, at Bandol. Unluckily I didn't see her, as she left the morning after I heard of her being here.

Fondest thoughts, & many messages to Jane & the Colins—

Yrs ever affly
    Edith

What does Alan say? And how goes his holiday?—
I go home tomorrow— Taking Oberon in tonight.

Ms:KC

1. In June, Clark had been offered the directorship of the National Gallery by Prime Minister Ramsay MacDonald. In his memoir, *Another Part of the Wood*, (1974), Clark wrote: "I temporised and wrote for advice to a few trusted friends, including Edith Wharton. They all advised me to accept; but, of course, they did not know the situation any more than I did. Finally, I accepted."

2. Lady (Sybil) Colefax, indefatigable London hostess and collector of celebrities; EW, like Clark and Berenson, was warily fond of her.

To Gaillard Lapsley

Pavillon Colombe
September 13, 1933

Dearest Gaillard— The vision of your pathetic figure alone on the threshold of a Salso cure sends me straight to my desk! Who can enter as I can into the endless crannies & convolutions of that eternity of 16 days? Enfin—vous l'avez voulu, Perdican! So I will dry my tears.

Yes, by all means come here if Percy chucks you. I saw him every day that I was at Salzburg, always rushing about with rugs, camp-seats & little parcels; but though we exchanged affabilities, & though Sybil was very continually up & about, no audience was granted me; in view of which, as we were there a week together, I think the enclosed might better have remained unwritten. (Don't return.)

To lighten your gloom I add a second enclosure, almost worthy, this one, to be passed on to Prof. Housman. (Also for keeps.)

My visitation (N.J.) leaves tomorrow, after a month, & I am thinking of going off. I really don't know where; perhaps to Holland for a week. The sound of Time's wingèd chariot is always with me since Elise's death, & there are so many places I want to see & store up! Wales, by the way, is one, & I'm so glad you feel in the same way about it. I so fired Kenneth Clark that he & she dashed off in our tracks, & came back lyrical, especially about Kilpeck. Kenneth says: "Of course there's no doubt that Strygowski built it to prove his wildest theories."

But we must do the Skelligs & that white monastery first! My mouth waters at the picture. And how magical to see Snowdonia the invisible from the deck of yr steamer! Could you see the Llenberis food?? (I might have decided to join you at Salso, if I'd known about the new chef.)

I have had a long letter from Steven R., from the Isle of Eigg, comme quoi he wants to come to Ste Claire for Xmas! Well, he may—I told him I'd put his name down, but couldn't give him much hope—

Yrs ever
E

I suppose you know Kenneth Clark has been appointed Director of the National Gallery—at 30. (His youngest predecessor was 48.)

Ms:BL

To Margaret Terry Chanler

Hotel des Indes
The Hague
October 20, 1933

Dearest Daisy—your good letter has overtaken me here, & I am so glad to have news of you at last, & to know that there is a chance of seeing you at Ste Claire this winter, & even of our carrying out the Egyptian tour. What fun if we could! My situation is the same as yours, financially. Let us, therefore, say: We'll go if we can afford it! And perhaps we shall be able to. I see the boats (all lines) from Marseilles are advertising much reduced rates to Alexandria; & that was the great expense. I admire & applaud you for hunting, & hope you will reciprocate these sentiments when I tell you that since writing last I have made two very fruitful archaeological tours with John Hugh-Smith, one in Normandy, the other & longer one in the Vendée, Charente Infre & Corrèze. Besides that I put in a wild & crowded week at Salzburg, where I saw Laura White suddenly emerge from the mob of 2000 spectators at Faust, gasped a greeting, & lost her again!—& now I'm doing Holland, if you please, "seule avec ma femme de chambre—" & oh how I wish it was Elise!—Still, I've had a thrilling week, & seen oh such things. I spent a week-end with the Duc & Duchesse d'Ursel at their château near Brussels, & "took off" from there; but the season is too late for touring, & I've devoted myself strictly to Amsterdam (which enchanted me), Haarlem & the Hague. If it's not too cold I'm going to Delft tomorrow, & home to St Brice the day after. I shall be there (& in Paris) till about Nov. 10, when I go to I Tatti for a fortnight; & then Ste Claire.

My dear old Gross died peacefully at Hyères about a fortnight ago,[1] & though I wd not have had her live longer her loss makes my life seem emptier than ever, & I had to go away for a while.—I do sympathize with you in having to part from yr devoted household, & you are very brave over it. I'm so glad the Ersatzes are not too bad!

Did you ever see anything as awful as this paper? The hotel is à l'avenant, & full of noisy Americans. But, oh, the pictures!

Did Royall write you that Master Bill Tyler is in New York doing an 8 months' apprenticeship at the Guaranty Trust's school for International banking? He is all alone in America, & it would be very kind of you to recommend him to some of our friends, & to write him a line soon to the Harvard Club. He seems very much interested in his job, & says every one at the bank is awfully kind; but he has met very few people yet, as N.Y. is so empty. He is staying at the Algonquin.

When I was at Amsterdam I saw that Sam Dushkin[2] was playing the Stravinsky concerto at the Concertgebouw next Sunday, & I should like to go back & hear him if only the weather were less wintry, & my engagements fewer at home. I have written to tell him how sorry I am to miss him.

I can't pretend that I shall ever like "living simply" in the sense of economizing; but there's nothing to be done about it, & I only hope we'll get to Egypt trotzdem. (Think what stupid things the people must have done with their money who say they're "happier without"!)

It makes me sick to think of any of my friends reading these choppy fragments of my reminiscences in the Ladies' H.J. They give no idea of the book, & I wish you'd tell everyone to wait & read that.

Please don't make it quite so long between letters again—

Yrs ever affly
    Edith

Ms:BL

1. Two weeks before, EW recorded in her diary: "Darling Gross died peacefully this morning. With me 1884–1933."

2. Samuel Dushkin (1891–1976), Polish-born violinist whom EW came to know through Blair Fairchild, whose protégé he had been. Dushkin was a strong advocate and performer of contemporary music.

To Rutger B. Jewett

October 26, 1933

Dear Mr. Jewett,

I have delayed for some time to answer your letter of Sept. 29th, because I was so much taken aback by Miss Lane's communication that I did not know what to say.[1] When I think of my position as a writer I am really staggered at the insolence of her letter, and if it were possible to make any one of that kind understand what she had done, I should not be sorry to do so. My first impulse is to do nothing about selling "Duration" to another magazine, although I imagine that Ellery Sedgwick would be glad to have it for The Atlantic. I will think the matter over and let you know.

The fact is I am afraid that I cannot write down to the present standard of the American picture magazines. I am in as much need of money as everybody else at this moment and if I could turn out a series of potboilers for magazine consumption I should be only too glad to do so; but I really have difficulty in imagining what they want. I never supposed that their readers took much interest in my work, but I thought the magazine editors required a few well known names. If what they want is that I should write stories like those I see in their pages, I am afraid it is beyond my capacity.

I have just had a letter from Miss Giles, who asks to see me on behalf of the new editor of the Cosmopolitan. As you know I have held out firmly till now against the wiles of Mr. Hearst, but I have been the only one to do so. Many of my friends, for instance, Aldous Huxley and Louis Bromfield,[2] appear to have succumbed at once, and I think you told me some time ago that in the case of the Cosmopolitan Hearst did not intervene personally. I have therefore decided to see Miss Giles and to ask point-blank what the situation is, and if I can reconcile it to my conscience I shall have to give them one of the stories you have in hand.

Many thanks for your letter of Oct. 6th, telling me that you have sent "Kouradjine Limited" to Miss Lane.[3] I confess I should not have done it if you had consulted me; I see no reason for taking her orders in that way and would much rather simply keep "Duration" for my next volume.

I am sorry you are troubled by such a deluge of letters for me. Why should not the Saturday Evening Post re-address them directly to me here? Of course they are all about my memoirs and seem to point to the fact that the book will have some success.

Yours ever sincerely

Copy:BL

1. Gertrude Lane, editor of the *Woman's Home Companion*, had informed Jewett that the magazine would not be able to run EW's story "Duration." "We ordered it, we have bought and paid for it," Miss Lane wrote, "but we cannot publish it." She asked if the story might be taken by the *Atlantic*, so that the *Woman's Home Companion* might get some of its money back. The story apeared in EW's volume *The World Over*.

2. The novelist Louis Bromfield (1896–1956) achieved quick recognition with *The Green Bay Tree* in 1924, the first volume of a tetralogy. Bromfield, who made his home in nearby Senlis, had known EW for several years.

3. "Kouradjine Limited" was sold to Hearst's *Cosmopolitan* magazine for a good figure, and published as "Bread Upon the Waters."

To Royall Tyler

Ste-Claire
February 11, 1934

My dear Royall,

It is good to see your script again; and I am much obliged to you for passing on Bill's enclosure. How he has acclimatized himself! The other day Louis Bromfield, who is in New York, wrote me: "There was a terrible scandal in Connecticut last week. A white girl married a banker."

There is too much sour grapes for my taste in the present American attitude. The time to denounce the bankers was when we were all feeding off their gold plate; not now! At present they have not only my sympathy but my preference. They are the last representatives of our native industries.

I have been here alone for the last 10 days, and badly in need of some one more responsive than the wireless with whom to follow the course of affairs. Boc writes me that the number of deaths published is very much below the known figures.[1]

I am glad that John is well and cheerful, and wish I could see him oftener—Et vous donc.

Why weren't you delegated to administer the finances of Monaco?

My best love to you both—and herewith I return Billy Sunday.

Yours ever affectionately,
Edith

Boc has been allowed to go home, but will have to remain in bed some time longer, as they apparently fear a phlebitis. It's too bad.

Ms:WRT

1. André Boccon-Gibod, a Paris lawyer, had represented EW in her divorce proceedings and had served on the hostels committee during the war.

The "course of affairs" referred to had reached a climax on February 6, when a massive demonstration against the government took place in and around the Place de la Concorde, Paris, and was eventually dispersed by heavy police action with many casualties. The drama began in January with the so-called Stavisky scandal: the revelations of large-scale financial wrongdoings on the part of Serge Stavisky, gambler, crook, and socialite, which seemed to implicate left-wing French politicians and members of the government. Stavisky either shot himself or was gunned down by the police, which led to right-wing charges of cover-up and a call for demonstrations. Rioting occurred intermittently through January, and on February 6 the royalist *Action Française*, with others, urged "the people" to rise against a government that let criminals go unpunished and encouraged socialism.

At least fifteen persons were killed during the action, and a good many seriously injured. The next week follow-up riots resulted in more deaths and many more injuries. This series of events would have a continuing impact on French political activities for many years.

To Bernard Berenson

Sainte-Claire
February 12, 1934

Dearest B.B. I like you to like getting my letters, & my hand having regained its flexibility since I gave up knitting, I hasten to send you my news.

It is "mine" & not ours, for Robert is still prélassing himself at the other end of the Riviera, & as the Huxleys are decidedly too far off for daily use, I have been mostly alone for the last ten days.—Ordinarily I shouldn't have minded, though the weather has been so enchanting that I'm suffering from extases rentrées, but I do find it rather depressing to sit alone in the evenings & wonder what's happening in Paris. The wireless, to which I resorted feverishly during the first days, is evidently so carefully edited that all one gets, between explosions & cork-poppings, is the news of the morning papers—i.e. nothing.

The results of the two days' fighting were much more serious than is generally known, & my solicitor wrote me that in one hospital alone there were ten dead, & it is known that there are many still alive who can't recover.

Between listenings in I've been digging hard at "The Buccaneers,"[1] & about 26,000 words are now done. How I wish I could pop over to I Tatti & try it on you all!

I'm grieved by your news about the old cypresses as only a gardener can be, & one who has suffered such disasters. It's no use being upliftical about it, as people were with me over my caroubes. The Furies know their job, & generally do it thoroughly; but I do hope that in your case the old trees can be persuaded to take root again. So far, we have escaped the cyclones, but poor Johnston's garden was ravaged the day after he & R. & Mrs Lindsay got there. He evidently had the tail of the Corsican blizzard.

I've begun to read Sorel's "L'Europe et la révolution française,"[2] & its evidence of the Ewige Wiederkunft makes it about the most depressing book one cd be engaged on at such a time. For lighter hours, I've gone back to "Can you forgive her?" & "The Prime Minister"—& oh, how good they are! Somehow, Trollope seems to have got nearer the eternal verities than Thackeray. He's more grown-up, & belongs rather with Tolstoy & Balzac. I'm trying now to think out his case in relation to his contemporaries, & a strange & interesting one it is. To them he was simply a good story-teller, whose books one could "leave about." Cela donne à penser.

How I wish I Tatti & Ste Claire had only a mitten-wall between them! Wouldn't I pop in through the communicating door for a long talk tonight?

I do hope Mary is up & about again. When I remember how valiant she was here I feel as if a little warmth & sunshine must soon give her another lift forward.

My best love to her, to Nick & to you.

Yrs ever affly
    Edith

I shall tell Bain, if he can rake up another "Macdermotts,"[3] to send it to you as a next-Xmas present!

Oh—& the beautiful Leonardo & Lorenzo[4] book has just come! Bless you for remembering to send it. I've already had a glimpse of some splendid draped figures, & shall have more to say tonight.

What *is* that beautiful "Annunciation" (two sculptured figures) from Westminster Abbey, in the exhibition? The catalogue doesn't even say what they're made of—

Ms:VT

1. EW completed about three-fifths of this, her last novel, by the time of her death. In book form, as published in 1938, it ran to 355 pages, with EW's outline of the entire story. The volume was edited by Gaillard Lapsley, who provided a judicious afterword.

2. Albert Sorel (1842–1906), *L'Europe et la Révolution francaise*, 8 volumes (1885–1904).

3. *The Macdermotts of Ballycloran* (1847), the first novel by Anthony Trollope (1815–1882).

4. *Leonardo e Credi* (i.e., Lorenzo di Credi, Florentine painter, 1456?–1537), published in *Bollettino d'Arte*, 1933.

To Mary Cadwalader Jones

Sainte-Claire
April 10, 1934

Dearest Minnie— I waited about 10 days before answering about Columbia,[1] & was sorry to cable *No* today. I had made up my mind to go, more to please you than myself, for I am too old to care for Academic honours; but the truth is, the political situation here is too unsettled for me to wish to leave next month. Don't spread this abroad, for of course nothing may happen; but public opinion is unsettled, dissatisfied & disgusted, & many people think some form of civil war inevitable, especially if the Stavisky & Prince gangs[2] (or *gang*, probably) are not soon brought to justice.

Of course, if there *were* any trouble, foreigners would not be disturbed; but their property might be, if there were no one to look after it, & of course if I am on the spot I can count on every kind of protection—

In the circumstances, therefore, I wd rather be in France, as I feel about my houses as a crab must about its carapace. I sometimes envy those who don't, in these days!

I think Jewett is partly right about the "réclame" wh. my taking the degree wd. give; but not as right as he thinks— The Western morons to whom he wishes to sell the book wd not be much affected by my Academic distinction, & the rest of the public—the small rest!—will, I think, be interested in the "costume" side, the pictures, the Old New York stories, & so on. And about 100 will want to read about H. James.

Thank you so much for acting as my substitute in the film contract for "Bread Upon the Waters."³ I wish the sum had more nearly approached the prices I used to get!—And now tell me why you are giving up Aix? If it is from motives of economy, please don't, for I am hugging a little nugget against your arrival.—And couldn't you sail early in June, & come straight to St Brice, for a change? As you know, most of my travelling is done in summer, & as I said to Trix the other day, if only you wd come to Ste Claire instead of St Brice, you wd find me always a fixture here from Dec. to April, whereas in summer I come & go; & this year I am pledged to a long-promised visit to Lady Wemyss, in Scotland, & am also, I hope, going to the Runcimans' in Northumberland, & on two or three other visits—& I may go in August or Sept. to stay near Salzburg, where I enjoyed my musical week intensely last summer. Edwin Morgan intended to take a country house near by for the "musical month," & asked me to stay; & if this comes off I think I will go to him for a few days, then to Vienna, where I've never yet been!

So do sail early, if you can, & enjoy St Brice when the roses & lilies are going strong & people are still in Paris.

I had a dear cable fr. Ned⁴ for Easter, & am writing to him this week. I have had a houseful for the last 3 weeks, but every one is scattered now, & I shall be alone, I suppose, till I leave about April 25 for I Tatti, & then, if things are quiet in France, for Rome. If things seem more unsettled I will come back here, & "wait & see."

I'm so sorry that Trix had such a hideous crossing. I so much hoped that the week at sea wd give her the rest she needed so badly.

Yrs ever affly
  E

You had better continue to address me here—or direct to I Tatti till the end of the month, as they will forward if I get to Rome.

Louisa puts in a request for the enclosed list of bottles—if not too much trouble?

Ms:BL

1. Columbia University, in the person of President Butler, had renewed its invitation to EW to accept a degree of doctor of letters.

2. On Stavisky, see letter to Royall Tyler, February 11, 1934. Counselor Albert Prince was a local judge who had been found dead, tied to a railroad track near Dijon, after having been drugged. He had apparently been associated with Stavisky and was at the point of making some revelations about the whole case. Antigovernment elements again charged a left-wing cover-up.

3. The story "Bread Upon the Waters" was retitled "Charm Incorporated" for its inclusion in *The World Over* (1936).

4. Edward Sheldon.

To John L. B. Williams[1]

June 26, 1934

Dear Mr. Williams,

I have received your letter of June 14th, and am extremely sorry to hear that Mr. Jewett is ill. I hope very much that after taking the rest which he must have needed for so long a time he will regain his usual health. Please tell him how sorry I am to hear of his illness.

1. *Corrections for "A Backward Glance"*.—page 261 is evidently the wrong number, and I shall have to go through the book before I can rectify this mistake.

2. *"The Buccaneers." Serialization.*—I am surprised at your request to keep the manuscript and the synopsis, for when Mr. Jewett last wrote

me he said that it would be preferable to add another 20.000 words (I think) to the book, and to develop the synopsis. The latter point I cannot comply with, but I should like to go on with the work, and to have the duplicate copy here for that purpose.

If the Curtis Company do not come to a decision soon, will you please return the manuscript and synopsis to me?

3. *Advertising "A Backward Glance".*—It seems almost useless to continue this discussion. My opinion is formed on the fact that I see every week the Times Literary Supplement, the Times itself (which has one day in the week for book advertising), the Sunday Times, in which every book that appears is advertised often for weeks at a time, that I often see also, the New Statesman, Time and Tide, the London Mercury, and in fact nearly all the London literary reviews. In not one of them have I seen an advertisement of my book, except in the Literary Times a week after the book came out. I have looked hard and hopefully, but there was not a trace of any kind of advertisement, and I know from previous experience that my readers in England are often put off from buying my books from the fact that they may not remember the title of a particular book, and that they never see my name included in the advertisements of any English literary review.

Nothing can alter this fact, and no advertising of the kind that you speak of can replace the publicity in the press & the literary reviews. Every other publisher, English and American, seems to advertise continuously, and I never see the name of Appleton among them.[2]

As you tell me that Mr. Jewett is anxious to continue placing my work, I am sending you a short story which I have just written, and should be greatly obliged if you would try to place it. I may add that I have definitely decided to give nothing more, in any circumstances whatever, to any of the Hearst publications.

Yours very truly

Copy:BL

1. John Williams was replacing Rutger Jewett—temporarily, it was thought —on the Appleton editorial staff. Jewett was said to be at home, recovering from an illness.

2. To these charges, Williams answered on July 11 that *A Backward Glance*

had been reviewed in fourteen English papers, including the *Times*, the *Times Literary Supplement*, the *New Statesman*, the *Manchester Guardian*, *Punch*, and the *Spectator*. It had been advertised by Appleton in twelve papers, including some of those listed.

To John L. B. Williams

July 11, 1934

Dear Mr. Williams,

Since I wrote you a new batch of reviews and weeklies have come in, and I have looked with curiosity in all of them, American and English, for the smallest advertisement of my book—but in vain!

I will mention among them, The Atlantic Monthly, The Yale Review, Life and Letters, The Saturday Review of Literature, The London Times, the English Sunday Times and the Times Literary Supplement. I am aware that this principle of non-advertising is applied to every one whose books you publish, for not only do I never see my own name, but I never see that of the firm, so that I know that it is not because you think my books unworthy of being advertised that you maintain such silence. As every other publisher old and new, American and English, seems to be advertising more than ever, this policy surprises me; but of course you are entitled to your own views, and authors who disagree with them can only change their publishers. I may as well tell you frankly that I intend to do this for the simple reason that I cannot afford to neglect any chance of selling my books.

As I wrote to Mr. Jewett some time ago, I signed the contract for "The Buccaneers" in great haste, and at a moment when I was unwell and tired, and did not realize till afterward that the English rights were included. It is not only the English rights which I wish to annul; I feel that the time has come for me to make a change, and try my luck elsewhere. No one could appreciate more sincerely than I do the kindness shown me for many years by your firm and the many services they have rendered me; but I feel that I ought to have an equal chance with other authors, and I am far from getting it.

I must throw myself on your generosity in respect to cancelling the contract for the book publication of "The Buccaneers," and I should be very sorry if my request seemed an expression of ingratitude. It is not that by any means but simply the recognition that our views as to promoting the sale of the book are opposed, and that having protested for a number of years against your lack of advertising, I now feel that I am entitled to make a trial elsewhere.

I hope sincerely that Mr. Jewett is improving in the quiet of the country, and that he will soon be able to take up his work again. Please remember me to him most kindly, and believe me,

Yours very truly

P.S. I should be glad to know if another printing of my book is likely. I hear it is selling very well both in England and in America, and there are several more mistakes which I am anxious to correct.[1]

Copy:BL

1. This letter was answered at length, on July 25, by J. W. Hiltman, chairman of the board at Appleton. He began by saying that Mrs. Wharton's letter of July 11 was "so manifestly unfair and unjust that I believe you should have a resumé of our business relations with you covering a period of twenty years." He then noted that for the first three books by EW that Appleton published, she had been paid some $10,689—in advances—beyond what the books had earned.

Hiltman listed the twelve books published by Appleton since *The Marne*, with royalty figures attached to each; the whole amounted to about $200,000. "In addition," he wrote, "we have negotiated for you the sales of serial rights, short stories, motion pictures and dramatic rights amounting to $378,754.50. . . . Altogether we have paid you $578,905.04, which if handled through an agent would have cost you $57,890."

He spoke of the pride the house had taken in the long association with EW, adding: "We had supposed that you were equally pleased with the manner in which your work has been handled. . . . It would be tragic to sever the relations we have enjoyed for so many years, and I hope that your calm judgment will make you wish to recall your letter of July 11."

Hiltman reported that Mr. Jewett had in fact suffered "a severe nervous breakdown, due largely to the depression and general uncertainty that have affected so many of us." They expected Jewett back in October.

As things developed, Jewett seemed to be recovering; but he had a relapse later in the year and died in December.

EW took offense at being reminded of the unearned advances. But she remained with Appleton, who published *The World Over* in 1936, and *The Buccaneers* posthumously in 1938.

To Jane Clark

Pavillon Colombe
October 21, 1934

Dearest Jane,

This is just to thank you for your letter, & to say that Louisa has unearthed a lovely mother-of-pearl penknife, which should, I fear, have gone with you to London. I'm so sorry, but when John brings the red damask I'll give him this for the return journey.

I too am still thinking of Beauvais. I never saw those St Etienne windows so vividly as through your new eyes, & shan't be happy till I have taken you to Troyes & Conches.—Kenneth's idea that the French painting of the Renaissance must be sought on glass & not on canvas has opened a new world to me; & oh, if the old plutocratic times would only return, how thrilling it wd be to subvention some scholarly young man to do a book on Renaissance glass, with French as the central panel, & the other countries enclosing it!

I laughed for an hour at the idea of you spending one week-end at St Brice, & the next at Chatsworth. What a jolly antithesis!

I took a sad & lonely walk with my dogs on the edge of the "Forêt de Montmorency" yesterday, & thought of all the things I wanted to show you both.

So glad the three infants are flourishing. Love to them, & to you both.

Yrs ever affly
    Edith

I found the big book on St Etienne after you had left, but it's sad stuff—except that it gives the dates, & presumed painters, of those magic windows. The one with the death of the abbot, & the queer minotaur devil below, is the Légende de St Claude.

Ms:KC

To Mary Cadwalader Jones

Hôtel de Crillon
November 17, 1934

Dearest Minnie,

Your letter enclosing "Mad" & the court-plaster caught me here yesterday, on the eve of my flight to Italy, & I am still marvelling at the miraculous promptness of your reply.—

I am thrilled by the theatrical news,[1] in spite of its numerous uncertainties, & wish indeed I could have a good crack over it all, with you & Ned. Meanwhile I can only scribble a word of thanks for everything, & enclose the motor cheque, for my last day here is always a hurricane, & I'm off tonight.

I had two good talks last week with that thoroughly delightful person Walter Lippmann,[2] & had him to lunch to meet Vladimir d'Ormesson, who is rapidly becoming the first political leader writer in France, & has resuscitated the moribund Figaro, & given it back its former prestige.

This isn't a letter, but a greeting.

Yrs ever affly
E.

Ms:BL

1. About *The Old Maid*, which was scheduled to open in New York in January 1935.
2. Walter Lippmann (1889–1974) was political commentator for the *Herald Tribune*. His seventh book, *A Preface to Morals*, had appeared in 1929.

To Mary Cadwalader Jones

Sainte-Claire
March 9, 1935

Dearest Minnie,

Many thanks for the charming photograph of the two cousins' going upstairs. It is extraordinarily pretty, and I wish I could see their midnight procession.

I have just had one of Ned's kind cables. When I sent him the other day the story "Confession," suggested by the Lizzie Borden case, I wrote him that I was contemplating a play on the same subject,[2] but I felt that it was more than likely that it had already been used. He has just cabled me that I was right, and suggests my taking the Praslin murder instead. When you see him will you thank him for the suggestion and tell him that I began a novel on the Praslin case two or three years ago, which alas I did not finish;[3] and last year I saw that some one else had used the subject,[4] though probably quite differently, as I had intended the story to begin only after the governess arrives in Stockbridge?

I became so absorbed in writing the first act of the Lizzie Borden play that I am not sorry to have done it, as it was good practice, and Ned will be able to tell me (quite apart from the fact that the subject is not available) what he thinks of my dialogue and construction.

I do not think the story will suffer much from its Borden origin, as you will have seen by this time that it is of no importance in my fable, and my young woman could quite as well have murdered an intolerable husband. As I have heard nothing yet from Mr. Williams about "The Looking Glass,"[5] I have almost decided to ask you to send "Confession" to Pinker.[6] If I do so I will write at the same time to Mr. Williams to explain that I am bound to try my chance wherever I can find an opening, and that, as he knows, I should have done so before if it had not been for Mr. Jewett's illness.

I have not had a word from Mildred for over two years, though I have written her several long letters, and last year and this year she has sent us no money for the Maisons Américaines de Convalescence, and has not even acknowledged my letter on the subject. You may therefore imagine that it is a matter of perfect indifference to me whether the late Mrs. Bliss received a floral offering in my name or not. I hope that she finally decided to leave her millions to Mildred, and that the latter may be inspired to interest herself again in our work.

There are two or three misprints in the first pages of the typed copy of the act I sent to Ned, but I mention this only in case you should want, after all, to show it to any one, as they alter the sense.

I note that you have booked your passage for June 7th. I shall certainly be at St Brice in June, but I cannot tell you when I shall go away on my annual trip. This will have to be left in suspense for the present, as it depends on my work and on various other matters. But I think we can settle that question easily when you arrive. I am delighted that your two doctors have given you such encouragement, and it is confirmed by every one who has seen you within the last few months. I am afraid your quiet summer at Bar Harbour suited you in spite of the quietness.

Yrs ever affly
    E.

Ms:BL

1. The picture was of Delia Lovell (played by Judith Anderson) and Charlotte Lovell (Helen Menken) ascending the stairs, candles in hand, at a moment in *The Old Maid*. The photograph served as a cover for the published version of the play.

2. EW wrote a little more than one act of a play called *Kate Spain*, drawn from her story "Confession" (in *The World Over*). Upon hearing from Sheldon that the subject had already been used, she gave it up.

3. Soon after the war, EW had begun a novel to be called *The Keys of Heaven*. It was the real-life story of Henriette Desportes, who became governess to the children of the Duc and Duchesse de Praslin in the Paris of the 1840s. Falling passionately in love with her, the Duc murdered his insanely jealous wife. While under house arrest, the Duc committed suicide. Henriette thereafter went to America, married the minister Henry Field, and lived with him for a time in the Berkshires.

4. *All This, and Heaven Too*, by Rachel Field (a descendant of Henriette Desportes).

5. "The Looking Glass" was part of *The World Over*.

6. The previous year, EW had become a client of the literary agent James Pinker, the son of Henry James's former agent.

To Kenneth Clark

Sainte-Claire
May 28, 1935

Dearest Kenneth,

I don't know how to thank you and Jane for your wonderful kindness. A day or two ago came her letter telling me of your days in Paris and Venice, and filling me at once with delight and envy; and now here is the splendid "Leonardo"[1] of which I had not expected the appearance so soon. The fact is I have lost my usual rather pedantic and precise relation to Time, and never know exactly when the next thing is going to happen; so that life is full of un-birthday surprises. This is the most beautiful I have had for years, and as soon as Elisina Tyler, who has gone to Cannes for the day, comes back this evening, she will read me your introduction while I gloat over the pictures.

My eyes are growing slowly better, but I am warned not to fatigue them; in fact "no fatigue" is the mot d'ordre at present from morning till night.[2] However, I am now able to motor for over two hours *without* fatigue, and I run up and down the garden paths almost as lightly as I did before the fatal day six weeks ago. The doctor has decided that I am to motor to Paris next week by slow stages, and I am delighted as it will be a heavenly trip, and I shall not feel shaken and banged and bewildered as I always do on long railway journeys. The angelic Elisina Tyler is staying with me till we reach Paris, where I am going to spend two or three days in order to see my doctor and my oculist; then I hope to get installed at St-Brice.

I am still clinging to the Glyndebourne dream, and I really think it may come off, but I prefer not to rouse the attention of the Furies by talking about it above a whisper. Please thank Jane for her delightful letter, and for telling me that I can decide later about Glyndebourne. My trip to Paris will be a good test of what I am able to stand.

We have had lovely cool weather here for the last month, and delicious flowers, of course; for once the storms in the North have not ended up here. I was much disturbed yesterday by a letter from Lawrence Johnston's butler, telling me that he (Johnnie) had been taken ill with bronchial pneumonia the day of his arrival at Sir Philip Sassoon's, and was rather seriously ill. I telegraphed at once and had a telegram from Johnnie saying: "Distinctly better," so I hope that he is out of the woods; but he has so little power of resistance that I am still anxious.

I suppose you continue to see John often. Please tell him that a line from him would be welcome, but do not feel obliged to write yourself, for I shall communicate with you through Leonardo.

Embraces to you all, from

Yrs ever affly
Edith

P.S. I have begun to look at your illustrations. Oh, the eloquence of those hands & arms!

Ms:KC

1. This was perhaps an early portion of what became Kenneth Clark's book on Leonardo da Vinci in 1939, based on lectures given at Yale University in 1936.

2. EW suffered a mild stroke on April 11, 1935, and for a time lost the sight in her left eye. On May 16, EW's secretary, Mme. Fréderich, wrote Morton Fullerton (in French): "Madame Wharton asks me to tell you that she has been very seriously ill for five weeks, and that her convalescence will be long.... She cannot write you herself, because her vision is fatigued, and her doctors forbid her to make use of it for some time."

To John Hugh Smith

Pavillion Colombe
July 25, 1935

My dear John— That Italian dictionary is a perfect wonder, & I can't think how it escaped my vigilant eye. Thank you so much for sending it.

I strongly recommend "Paxton & the Bachelor Duke," by Violet Markham.[1] It is remarkably well done, & every page is interesting. I wonder it hasn't been more talked about, but one can trust the Lit. Supp. to miss anything worthwhile.

I have had a glorious treat since you left. I had appealed in vain to 3 French members of the Italian Exhibition committee—Metman, Jacques Guérin & Carl Dreyfus, to get me in for an hour the morning after the show closed; but they all hm'd & haw'd, & said it couldn't be done. Then I heard by chance that Ugo Ojetti[2] was here, & in a second the trick was done! Elisina & I went in at 11, & had the glorious company all to ourselves, with the exception of a few photographers, & a few officials, among them Carl Dreyfus, who looked smaller than life when he saw me there with Ojetti!!!

It was a divine hour, but so thrilling that before it was over I was shattered, & had to go sit on the terrace until Ojetti was ready to come out to St Brice to lunch. The shock of that great tidal wave of beauty, after nearly 4 months of isolation, was almost more than I could bear; but I did manage to see (really *see*) the divine little Hermitage Leonardo, the Caravaggio Bacchus, the Tintoret Susannah (what a glory!), the Conetisane Antea, the wonderful Lotto portrait from Budapest, the Allori Judith, *cleaned* & radiant—& all my dear old friends from Florence, Rome, Tours &c &c; indeed I marvel, in looking back, at what I did manage to take in, & keep.

I wish I could talk to you about it all before it fades. When am I going to see you again?

Thanks again for the Dictionary.

Yrs ever
E.

Elisina leaves today, & my poor old sister-in-law arrives this afternoon for a fortnight. I shall be glad when that fortnight is over!

Ojetti, who is an "Accademico," told me he recommended "Sorelle Materassi"³ for an Academy prize, but the book was turned down because the author's moeurs are not up to Mussolini's standards. Doesn't it sound like a south-western state in the U.S.?

Ms:BL

1. Violet Markham's book had just been published.
2. Ugo Ojetti: see letter to Nicky Mariano, May 31, 1932, note 2.
3. *Sorelle Materassi* (1934) is generally thought to be the masterwork of the Italian novelist Aldo Palazzeschi (1885–1974).

To Bernard Berenson

Pavillon Colombe
August 14, 1935

Dearest B.B.— I must thank you without delay for your delightful letter. I was much amused at your saying that Ojetti was impressed by the rhythm & ritual of my modest folly! What must he think of the *R.*

& *R.* of I Tatti, where the scale is so much greater, & the R. & R. proportionately more impressive? ? ?—anyhow, he was his most delightful self that day, & I can never thank him enough for giving me that dip of the tip of one toe into Beauty!

It was a good deal better than hearing dear Morra read aloud Moravia, as to whom I remain unconverted & incorrigible—because Faulkner & Céline did it *first*, & did it *nastier*.[1] (I've got an incest donnée up my sleeve that wd make them all look like nursery-rhymes[2]—but business is too bad to sell such Berquinades nowadays.)

I'm so glad that Nick's Sorrento holiday has been a success, though an all too short one. *I* know your way of "urging" her *not* to come back—you fraud! But if I had a Nick, oh, wouldn't I do the same?—I'm distressed at the news from Mary. But I don't suppose you expected the Viennese glamour to last very long, did you? I daresay coming home again may be a temporary uplift—but I hope she won't come too soon. If only she would get on her feet & go about! I'm sure that bed-wallowing ought not to be allowed by the doctors.

I'm hugging the idea that I may get to Italy toward the end of Oct., but don't want to ask the Dr. *too soon*. I'm certainly much stronger, & can stand a great deal more daily wear & tear than a month ago, even—

My best love to you & to Nick, if she's back, & friendliest greetings to Morra.

Yrs ever affly
Edith—

Ms:VT

1. Incest was of course a motif in Faulkner's *The Sound and the Fury* (1929); it is also present in the dark world of *Voyage au bout de la nuit* (1932), by Louis-Ferdinand Céline (1894–1961).

2. "Beatrice Palmato," the story of a long-ongoing incestuous relationship between a wealthy Londoner and his daughter Beatrice. In 1935 or a little earlier, EW wrote an outline of the narrative, and a single father-daughter scene of vivid erotic detail. Both appear as Appendix C in *Edith Wharton: A Biography* (R. W. B. Lewis, Harper & Row, 1975).

To Bernard Berenson

Pavillon Colombe
September 30, 1935

Dearest B.B.,

Your word of sympathy went to my heart, for I know you loved Minnie and appreciated her rare qualities.[1]

I have had an exhausting week in London, but now she is quietly at rest in the lovely little churchyard of Aldbury, where we buried her among her old friends, the Wards and Arnolds.

I got back the day before yesterday, so tired that I can make no plans at present. The doctor says I am no worse, except for this fatigue, but I feel as if I had lost two months of progress toward health. I had no idea that "la mort de quelqu'un" could produce such a series of complications and such endless correspondence & cablings.

I have had a most cheerful letter from Mary (I mean as to her health), and I do so hope that this Viennese experiment will do lasting good.

Oh, to be in Rimini with you!

My fondest love to Nick.

Yrs devotedly
Edith

Ms:VT

1. Mary Cadwalader Jones, age eighty-five, had died suddenly in a London hotel.

To Gaillard Lapsley

Sainte-Claire
February 19, 1936.

Dearest Gaillard— Alas, no, it is not the Buccaneers (as it should have been) who have kept me from writing. I have not done a stroke of work, except one or two little prefaces or introductions (for the English translation of Phil.'s book,[1] for the "Ethan Frome" play,[2] &c), but am now engaged (for the Revue des Deux Mondes) on some reminiscences of Bourget,[3] as I knew him—written after reading the numerous "articles nécrologiques" written by various young or middle-aged "parties" who knew only the old stuffy Academician.

I suggested this to Doumic[4] in a moment of exasperation at the inadequacy of all these official portraits, & as Doumic jumped at the idea I'm in for it!

If I had felt a real "call" to go on with the Bucs I sh'd doubtless have dropped everything else—but I haven't, chiefly I think because my correspondence continues to be almost as crushing as at Xmas. "Ethan" has made a successful appearance in N.Y.,[5] & "The Old Maid" is fighting its way westward through the blizzards, & is coming out in England, in the provinces, next month, & in London (produced by Cochran[6]) in April. All this has brought down on me masses of letters, newspaper notices, offers of translation, &c &c, & I have been rather swamped. So you see you'll soon have to desert Ibsen to hail the arrival of E.W. in London! (Meanwhile, I envy you Rösmersholm which I've always thought *better* than Ghosts—in fact the best.)

It has been very mild here almost all the time, but it rains every day, & blows a gale whenever the rain stops. Mme de Béhague[7] arrived only two days ago, so I had a nice long visit from Robert. Johnnie has been over twice to consult Valmyre,[8] who seems to have done him a great deal of good, & has persuaded him to eat normally; & Norah Lindsay also came for a few days.—But my spate of visits begins this week: B.B. & Nicky (at *last*, poor dears!) arrive the day after tomorrow, & the Nicholsons the following day. (The neat little Furies love to telescope visits in this way.) Then come (later) the Blisses, the Clarks & Lady Wemyss [and] the Boccon-Gibods—so I am not likely to be alone until I leave.

I am getting on well, though I still can't do much; but I spent two days at Cannes last week, & had a "spot" of dentistry, returning none the worse.

I suppose I shall stay here till the middle of May. I had thought of an after-Easter dash to Spain—but I see Spain has gone red!—What a world.

I close hurriedly for the post.

Yrs affly
   E.

Ms:BL

1. *Bénédiction*, a prizewinning novel by Philomène de la Forest-Divonne, writing under the name Claude Silve, was translated into English by Robert Norton, and published in the United States with an introduction by Edith Wharton.

2. *Ethan Frome*, the dramatization of EW's novella by Owen Davis and Donald Davis, was published by Scribner Library in 1939 as a "special student edition" with an introduction by Edith Wharton.

3. "Souvenirs de Bourget d'outre-mer," written in French by EW, was published in the *Revue Hebdomadaire* in June 1936. Paul Bourget had died in 1935.

4. René Doumic (1860–1937), for long a conspicuous figure in Paris literary circles, was director of *Revue des Deux Mondes* from 1916 to 1937, and a member of the Academy since 1910.

5. *Ethan Frome* opened in Philadelphia in January 1936, with Raymond Massey as Ethan, Pauline Lord as Zeena, and Ruth Gordon as Mattie Silver. The play moved on to a run of four months at the National Theater in New York, and later for a very successful career on the road.

6. Charles Blake Cochran (1872–1951), English impresario, later much associated with the plays of Noël Coward.

7. EW had known Martine de Béhague—also known by her married name, Comtesse René de Béarn—since the French woman's valuable support in the charitable organizations of the war years.

8. A local specialist, often consulted by EW's friends.

To Gaillard Lapsley

Sainte-Claire
April 2, 1936

Dearest Gaillard— Do you remember Geoffrey Scott's story of the mutilatissimo warrior? Well, my correspondence has of late been accablantississima; & though no doubt I should be the first to yammer if it stopped totalissimo a ralenti would be welcome—a few cracks into which I cd insert letters to friends, instead of perpetually pushing them aside for business, theatrical, literary or other!

I have been worrying through it all as best I could, sustained by finding in Carrel's wonderful book[1] (have you read it? It's a gold mine) "qu'il ne faut pas ménager de loisirs aux vieillards," & by the regular click of coin in my savings-box as the *three* plays (2 Old Maids & one Ethan) continue their fruitful rounds. I suppose the English Old M., now touring the provinces, will be in London soon, & I hope you will turn your experienced theatrical eye upon it, but only in the way of kindness! I imagine I shd feel as R. Draper does about Ethan—but luckily it just suits the average theatre-goer. It comes out in London this summer, I believe, put on by Cochran.

Lady Wemyss is here with Wilky, & I gave her your message about Elcho. If a faint glimmer reached her as to Elcho's identity, I can hardly say as much about yours; though she did, suddenly, & long afterward, tie you with fluttering fingers to the Navarros—but the knot, I imagine, was soon untied. The poor inner room seems emptier than ever, & if anything were ever needed to teach me to value the precious gift of the vie intérieure, it is the old age of some of my English great lady friends, with minds unfurnished by anything less concrete than the Grand National!—I find Lady W., alas, much more frail than last year, & I shall be glad when she is safe back in England; but after leaving me she goes to Polynésie, & then to Johnnie's. The latter, by the way, appears to be a Valmyre achievement—& B.B. is another! Both have continued to progress steadily under his treatment since they left here, & I have just had a jolly telephone from Johnnie, to whom I expect to pay a visit after Easter.

Meanwhile I have in prospect the Robert Blisses, & the Clarks (for Easter)—& I suppose Johnnie, before long.

I'm secretly hoping that I may get to England in June, if I improve very much in the next two months. I want to see my poor Vivienne Goschen,[2] & it would be good to have a quiet little romp with all the Unser-Einers again. Who knows?—But B.B. hopes to be in London in Sept for a month, & perhaps I shall go then.—My great nostalgia is for Scotland—but these are wild dreams.

I'm glad you've seen Reculver. It's a haunting place, isn't it? How I wish I could see again all the places that have enriched my inner eye! Kein Genuss ist vorübergehend,[3] luckily.

What are your plans?

Yrs affly,
    E

I recommend strongly:
"L'homme, cet inconnu." Carrel.

"The Way of a Transgressor." Negley Farson.[4]

(It's a real name, & Molly N. knows him!)

Santayana is reaching his 100,000th in America![5] It makes me more hopeful about my country.

Steven has sent me a p.c. from Madrid. He is lyrical about the upholstery of the Royal Palace!!!

Ms:BL

1. *L'Homme, cet inconnu* (1935), by Alexis Carrel (1873–1944). Translated into English and widely read as *Man the Unknown*.

2. Vivienne Goschen wrote under the name of Vivienne de Watteville. *Speak to the Earth*, "wanderings and reflections" about Kenya, appeared in 1935 with a preface by Edith Wharton.

3. "No pleasure is transitory." This line from Goethe's *Wilhelm Meister* served as one of the two epigraphs on the title page of EW's autobiography, *A Backward Glance*. The other was from Chateaubriand's *Mémoires d'outre-tombe: "Je veux remonter le penchant de mes belles années."*

4. The autobiography (at age forty-six) of Negley Farson, journalist and travel writer, appeared in 1936.

5. George Santayana's novel *The Last Puritan* came out in 1935.

To Mrs. Royall Tyler

(Instructions after my death.)

(For Mrs. Royall Tyler)

May 23, 1936

Wherever I am buried, I wish, for the sake of my French friends, a funeral (or memorial) service, to be celebrated at the American Episcopal (pro-) Cathedral Church of the Holy Trinity, Paris.

I wish the service to be fully choral, & the following hymns to be sung:

"Lead, Kindly Light."

"Art thou weary."

"O Paradise."

I wish a *simple hearse*, with only two horses.

Friends to meet at the church.—

If it seems feasible, I should like to have as pall-bearers: Royall Tyler, Kenneth Clark, John Hugh Smith, Gaillard Lapsley, Robert Norton, Mr A. Boccon-Gibod, Mr Louis Metman, Mr Louis Gillet.

But if this complicates the arrangements, please do not suggest it.

I wish that Mrs. Royall Tyler, of 21 Quai de Bourbon, Ile St Louis, Paris, should have charge of all the arrangements, if the funeral & burial take place immediately, as I should prefer.—But if my niece Mrs. Max Farrand prefers to come from America, then I beg Mrs. Tyler to help her with the arrangements, as she helped me at the time of Walter Berry's death.—And I suggest that my friend John Hugh Smith will give them any aid they need.

I wish legal matters concerning my will to be attended to by Mr. B. H. Conner, 5 Avenue de l'Opéra, Paris & Mr Boccon-Gibod.

Edith Newbold Wharton

The above is written & signed by me. E.N.W.

May 23. 1936

Memorandum. May 23. 1936.

I. My will (French) is in the safe in my bedroom at the Pavillon Colombe, St Brice sous Forêt. (If not there, then in the hands of Maître André Boccon-Gibod, 22 rue Cambon, Paris.[)]

II. The keys of said safe are with my personal papers, jewelry, &c, in my bedroom at Pavillon Colombe, in the chiffonier by my bed, or in my bedroom at Ste Claire-le-Château, Hyères, Var, also in chiffonier.

III. Personal papers are also to be found in a small locked portfolio, marked E.W., which is always with the documents in one or the other of these chiffoniers.

IV. I wish to be buried at the Cimetière des Gonards, at Versailles, & have bought there a double plot, as near as possible to Walter Berry's grave. I wish a grave stone like his, with my birth & death dates (January 24, 1862—) & Ave Crux Spes Unica engraved under it.

The receipt for my burial plot will be found with my other papers.

v. Notify Mr. B. H. Conner of my death, or, in his absence, Mr Boc-con-Gibod.

vi. Cable to Mrs. Max Farrand (Trix—New York, cable address). Notify Gaillard Lapsley, Esqre, Trinity College, Cambridge. Notify Frederic R. King in New York.

Edith Newbold Wharton

Ms:WRT

To Jane Clark

Stanway,
Cheltenham.
Monday, July, 1936.

Dearest Jane—

I look back on my visit to your stately home (the Bedford) with unmixed enjoyment, & the wish that it might have lasted longer! Oh, for another prowl in the Lanes (I hope you went back to buy those two pink glass jars)—oh, for another good gossip in that friendly sitting-room. I don't know when I've had a better week-end.

I lunched en route at the Nicholsons, & after lunch E. M. Forster (why on earth did I call him Michael?)[1] came in to see me, looking spectrally ill, poor fellow.

So I didn't get away till 3.30, & for four long hours I toiled over lovely endless roads toward an elusive Gloucestershire. There has always been something fugitive about that region, & it takes longer to get to than any other point of the globe at an equal distance.

I staggered in, dog-tired, at 7.30, to learn that we were to dine in 15 minutes, on account of a village feast, so I participated in tweeds, surrounded by lovely visions in cloth of gold & rosy chiffon!

The party was very pleasant—Max Beerbohm[2] (& Mrs. ———, a pink-eyed friendly mouse), Wells,[3] Ld D. Cecil,[4] the Cynthia Asquiths,[5] Sybil C., Eddie Marsh,[6] & a wonderful dyed & spangled young lady (produced to pacify Hugo)[7] who did indifferent parodies of (to me) unknown actresses.

I'm always so amused by the inexhaustible English devices for avoiding rational intercourse.

Well, I've enjoyed it all, & Stanway is more incredibly beautiful than ever, & I'm glad of this sunset glimpse of it; but I see quite clearly that the Isle of Mull is much too far away for me to attempt it, & so I'm marking time for another day or two, before making plans for the rest of my holiday.

I got to the station with your umbrella just as the gates were closed! So sorry, but will bring or send it to London. I'll write tomorrow, with final plans.

Yr devoted
    Edith

Saluti to Kenneth.

Ms:KC

1. The close friends of the novelist E. M. Forster (1879–1970) called him by his middle name—Morgan.

2. Max Beerbohm (1872–1956), writer of uncommon wit and charm, was the author of a brilliant satirical novel (*Zuleika Dobson*, 1911), a group of fine short stories (*Seven Men*, 1919), and several collections of essays. He was also a professional drama critic and a noted caricaturist. EW first met him in the social whirl of December 1908. Beerbohm had been married since 1910 to the one-time actress Florence Kahn.

3. H. G. Wells (1866–1946), whose company EW had enjoyed intermittently since 1908, was the author most recently of *The Shape of Things to Come* (1933). *The Outline of History* had appeared in 1920, following several decades of scientific romances as well as realistic and comic novels.

4. David Cecil (born 1902) was known at this time as the author of *The Stricken Deer* (1929), a study of William Cowper, the eighteenth-century author of *John Gilpin*, and other poems.

5. Cynthia Asquith, daughter of EW's friend Lady Wemyss, was married to Herbert Asquith, the son of former Prime Minister Herbert H. Asquith.

6. Edward Howard Marsh (1872–1953), civil servant and energetic supporter of modern poetry and painting. His five volumes of *Georgian Poetry* (1912–1922) were extremely influential.

7. Viscount Elcho, the eleventh Earl of Wemyss.

To Mary Berenson

Pavillon Colombe
October 11, 1936.

Dearest Mary—So many thanks for your good letter. I am delighted that you are so much better, & all the reports I have heard about you during the Fitzharding St. furnace-frizzle have prepared me for this good news. Rex Nicholson, who arrived here yesterday, tells me you actually motored to Tallboys for lunch, & the Clarks also sent me good news of you. I am only sorry that your anxiety about Mrs. Russell's[1] health has saddened your visit. I wish I knew what people mean when they say they find "emptiness" in this wonderful adventure of living, which seems to me to pile up its glories like an horizon-wide sunset as the light declines. I'm afraid I'm an incorrigible life-lover & life-wonderer & adventurer.—But bodily suffering strikes at the roots of all these joys.—I'm very glad that Logan is better, & is to be with you. I should think Desmond MacC's admirable "testimonial" would give him great pleasure. It *is* nice, once in a way, to be understood!—

I am noting down at once "*Plaza—Oct 27*," & will come at any hour (up to 4.30) that is convenient. I am glad you are perching in Paris for a few hours, & will suit my time to yours.

So a quick aurevoir, & fondest greetings to you & Logan—

Yrs ever affly
    Edith

Poor Cagnola. What sad things always seem to be happening to him. He was devoted to that sister, I know. But perhaps she may be better, & he may be able to put you up, after all.

Ms:VT

1. Alys Russell, Mary Berenson's sister, had been married to the English philosopher Bertrand Russell.

To Gaillard Lapsley

Pavillon Colombe
November 1, 1936

Dearest Gaillard— It is so long since I have heard from you that I am beginning to fret; but I hope your silence means simply too much to do.

We have had a delicious month of Oct. here, to which the inevitable rains of "La Toussaint" have now put an end. I have been trying to make up my mind to leave my golden autumnal garden for the dreariness of a Paris hotel, but if the sun shows itself again (here it is, as I write!) I shall linger on till the 9th. Then the Crillon for a week or ten days, & then (so my Doctor promises me) I Tatti for a fortnight. B.B. is here, at the renovated Plaza, in splendid form, & receiving congratulations from every one on his own renovation. What a réclame for Valmyre, if only he were a fashionable Paris doctor! B.B. enjoyed his dinner with you greatly, & was enchanted with your quarters.

I have evoked them so often lately, in my various readings about Housman. You probably noticed that the reviewer in the Lit Supp. pronounced him, in private life, to be "prim & grim," & apologized for his use of the poetic vocabulary, which the Victorians &c.— Luckily Desmond MacC., in a really good article, made short work of the latter nonsense. I was tempted to deal with the "grim & prim" in a letter to the Supp., but as my offerings to Times & Supp. are always rejected, I refrained. But what an age of mental darkness we are living in! We know how many bottles of champagne & brandy "Jim" Mollison consumes after an ocean flight, but not what voices speak to the poets.

Poor Robert had a bad blow last week. He came home after a dinner, saw a light in his kitchen, & found Allison[1] unconscious on the floor. He got him to the Hôtel Dieu (it was past midnight, & that was the nearest place), & he died there the next day of an unsuspected tumour on the brain. It is a real heart-break to Robert, & all my servants, who were devoted to him, grieved deeply, the more so as they were all so indignant at his wife's cruel desertion last spring. His poor old father came over for the funeral, & I sent in all the household.

Is there any chance that you cd· pick me up at I Tatti, & motor (or train) back to Hyères? You will be grieved to hear that the dreadful fires have destroyed the Coudon close-up, & in fact most of the mountain, & re-destroyed the Esterel! Robert says it is by far the worst series of fires we have ever had, & undoubtedly incendiary—the first time he has ever thought this.

"Ethan Frome" has been revived, & is on the road. I hope it may succeed, for the earnings will be welcome. And there, I think you have my budget of news—except that I have had a lyrical letter from Jane Clark, written from the Blisses', & en route to stay with the Wideners —New York so beautiful, & every one "so polite"!! Dio mio—

Yrs ever affly
        E.

I had almost forgotten to ask if you can find out whom I must thank for Mr. Gow's excellent little sketch of Housman,[2] which has come addressed in an unknown hand, & with no bookseller's name attached. Could it be Dr. Stewart, I wonder?

What a pity he didn't make the book longer & include letters, &c. It is a highly civilized little work.

Ms: BL

1. Robert Norton's chauffeur; see following letter.
2. *A. E. Housman, a Sketch* (1936, with a list of his writings and an index to his classical papers), by Andrew G. F. Gow (1886–1978).

To Jane Clark

Pavillon Colombe
November 11, 1936

Dearest Jane— It was dear of you to find time, under the tidal wave of U.S. hospitality for a line of good news to the renegade of St Brice. I am so delighted that everything has gone so well, & that you have enjoyed it all; but I cd tear my hair at having forgotten to give you a word for Janetta & Arnold Whitridge.[1] You will have seen them, of course, at Yale; but they are almost the only friends under the centenarian level that I have left in America, & I shd have liked to give you a message for them. My wobbling head spun around to Harvard, where

Eric[2] lectured, & I situated Kenneth there, instead of at Yale. Hence these tears!

I'm very glad you have been to Dumbarton, & have seen the garden that my niece (Beatrix Farrand) made out of a wilderness—& the treasures amassed for your hosts by Royall Tyler[3]—I wish I cd see all that, & the Whistlers at Washington. I shall be amused to hear your Widener[4] reactions. These (I mean the W.s) are the people that my haughty ancestors (engaged in acquiring copies of Carlo Dolci, & the bad Domenichinos & Caravaggios) wouldn't have touched with a ten foot pole—if indeed they'd been there to touch; but of course they were not! Isn't it funny?—

Well, I'm counting eagerly the days till we meet—when, I wonder? I'm making such good progress that I've been given medical leave to go to I Tatti, so I shall trail after B.B. (who leaves Paris on the 15th) &, I hope, spend a fortnight there before going to Hyères. B.B. is in magnificent form, & every one is amazed at his rejuvenation! Nick tells me that he was perfectly delighted with Kenneth's letter from the steamer. Of course, feeling so much better gives him a different view of life & of his fellow-beings, & I'm so glad to see him growing so mellow.

You'll be sorry to hear that Robert's devoted chauffeur, Allison, dropped dead about a week ago, from an unsuspected tumour of the brain. Mercifully it happened in R.'s flat, & not in the car! Robert is very much broken up, & all my servants are in great grief.—I wrote to ask Miss Arnold when you were sailing, but she failed to give me a date, so I am sending this to Portland Place.

> Yr devoted
> Edith

Ms:KC

1. Arnold Whitridge (1894–), the son of EW's old friend Lucy Arnold and the grandson of Matthew Arnold, was Master of Calhoun College at Yale, and a sensitive literary scholar. EW had been a "witness" at his wedding in Paris many years earlier.

2. Eric Maclagan.

3. The creation of the gardens at Dumbarton Oaks—the vast estate in the Georgetown section of Washington, D.C., purchased in 1922 by Robert and

Mildred Bliss—was the greatest single achievement in the distinguished career of Beatrix Farrand as a landscape gardener. Since 1940, Dumbarton Oaks has belonged to Harvard University.

Royall Tyler, collaborating with his friends the Blisses, supervised the matchless collection of Byzantine art housed on the estate.

4. Joseph Early Widener (1872–1943), American financier and art collector, was the younger brother of the celebrated connoisseur George Widener, who went down in the *Titanic* in April 1912, along with his son, Harry Elkins Widener.

To Bernard Berenson

Sainte-Claire
January 12, 1937

Dearest B.B.,

This is just a flying line, first to thank you for your good letter, & secondly to tell you that Gillet proposes to come here for a brief holiday (three or four days) on Feb. 17 or 18, & that it wd be delightful if you & Nick could coincide with him—that is to say, if his visit cd fall somewhere, it doesn't matter where, within the circle of yours—

I'm very sorry que la source a tari (the Book-source) for the moment, but I'm so used to this break of continuity in my work that I can't take it very tragically in your case. It is probably just the tank filling up. A propos of which, in looking this morning through an old diary-journal I have a dozen times begun & abandoned, I found this: (Dec. 10. 1934.)

"What is writing a novel like?

The beginning: A ride through a spring wood.

The middle: The Gobi desert.

The end: Going down the Cresta run."

The diary adds: "I am now" (p. 166 of "The Buccaneers") "in the middle of the Gobi desert."—

Since then I've been slowly struggling toward the Cresta run, & don't yet despair of sliding down.—Meanwhile, Robert is reading us (in the intervals of political news on the wireless) Granville-Barker's "Hamlet."[1] But last night we made him break away & read us the 3 great—greatest—scenes in Esmond.[2] And great they are.

Gaillard leaves today, very grieved at missing you.—Do you know where Aubrey Waterfield is?³ I wanted to send him a line of sympathy when I heard that poor Mrs. Waterfield was condemned to six months of immobility in an English nursing-home, but I've no idea where he is. What pitifully bad luck pursues those unhappy people!

Best love to all the Tattisti—

Yr affte
      E.

We are keeping Mme de la Noüe on ice for you.

Please let me know yr arrival date as soon as you can, as everybody seems to want to come in February!

Ms:VT

1. Harley Granville-Barker (1877–1946), whose productions of Shakespeare and of Shaw had been especially notable, published five series of prefaces to Shakespeare's plays, beginning in 1927; EW here refers to his edition of *Hamlet*.

2. Thackeray's *The History of Henry Esmond, Esquire* (1852).

3. Aubrey Waterfield and the journalist Lina Waterfield (herself the niece of the formidable Janet Ross, the resident English genius in Tuscany) lived in a villa near Florence and were close friends of the Berensons.

To Bernard Berenson

Sainte-Claire
April 9, 1937

Dearest B.B.,

Alas, what shall we do? My vista of recovered health in the spring has been clouded over by *three* successive attacks of flu—in January, March, & now, a queer sort of relapse, which has left me as weak as a cat, after what seemed at first an ordinary snuffle-cold. It appears (this last visitation) to have been part of a mild epidemic here, all in the form of foolish little colds suddenly leaving one with cotton-wool legs. I have lost a week, nearly, of heavenly capricious spring weather, with a garden tuning up here & there like a symphony orchestra, & suddenly bursting into a glorious "tutti." But I'm used to invalidism now, & find it full of oases & hidden springs; & I should bear it all with equanimity except missing I Tatti, which I find intolerable.

I had made the most elaborate plans—or dreamed the most elaborate dreams—about getting to you by delicious slow stages, & then dawdling with you for a fortnight; but instead I've had to be content with lingering here, fighting one tidal wave of fatigue after another, & occasionally getting in a little work on "The Buccaneers" or a short story. In spite of everything I stick to my work, & so do you, I know—& how I long to hear those 10,000 words, which by now have become many more, I'm sure!

I have had very pleasant visitors—the dear delightful young Bill Tyler couple, with an enchanting "Yes" boy of 3 months,¹ always smiling, agreeing with people, & laughing with a round mouth when his father boxes with him—the nicest child I ever met. Also Steven Runciman, full of anecdotes about his father's visit to the White House—all of which I meant to bring you de vive voix this month—confound it!

My only consolation is that if you were not going away you wd be overrun with trippers. I like the autumn ever so much better, & shall now look forward to calling on you next November.

Meanwhile I am "planning" (as the U.S. papers say when they want to be really distinguished) to meet Elisina in Venice next month, take a look at the Tintorets, & go on [to] see that little corner still unfamiliar to me, Aquileia, Grado, Cividale, &c. Thence a slow crawl back to St Brice. I expect to go very slowly, & spend about a month between here & Pav. Colombe.

You will be seeing more sensational sights—& oh, what wd I give to meet you at Famagusta, with young legs & a young & tireless head, & relive our divine week there. If only I had seen you before your start! But by all means see Crete too—& don't fail, on the way from Candia to the Italian excavations on the other side of the island, to stop & picnic beside a stream smothered in blossoming oleander, with snow-covered Ida soaring in the blue above.

Oh me, how thankful I am to remember that, whether as to people or as to places & occasions, I've *always* known the gods the moment I met them. Oh, how clearly I remember saying to myself that day by the stream, as I looked up at the snow through the pink oleanders: "Old girl, this is one of the pinnacles—" as I did the last time I was at Compostela.*

I'm very sorry that Mary has been having a bad time again. Please ask her, with my love, to let me know her Viennese address, if she finally decides to go there, so that I can send her a note now & then, or a book, if any turns up.

I expect to leave for Italy at the end of this month if I'm well enough, to get to Pav. Colombe about June 8th or 10th.

Greetings to you all.

Edith

* A sort of "Nous l'avons eu, votre Rhin allemand" feeling, of inalienable ownership of beauty!

Ms:VT

1. Royall Tyler, the firstborn child of William Royall and Bettine Tyler.

To William R. Tyler

Sainte-Claire
May 16, 1937
Whitsunday.

Dearest Bill,

It was very dear of you to offer to come here for a few days—and what a comfort you would have been. But I thought when you made the generous suggestion that I was going to L. Johnston's for a few days, and then taking my happy way to the Veneto to meet your mother, and see Cividale and Parenzo and all the rest of it. But, alas, just after wiring you I went "Kaput"—partly, I think, because I lost two *very* old friends within a few days of each other—my little Linky,[1] and then dear Lady Wemyss, who has been with me here so lately. It would seem odd to most people that I should group them together, but *you* will know and understand.

During the last years of the Roman Empire the Emperors had a pas-

sion for human "curiosities," such as mermaids, fauns, centaurs, etc.—
There were professional collectors, and whenever one was found, he,
she, or it was shipped to Rome (for they mostly came from Egypt or
North Africa). Once they found a boy who *understood what the birds said*;
and I have always been like that about dogs, ever since I was a baby.
We really communicated with each other—and no one had such wise
things to say as Linky . . .

Well, I was down and out, and then came Lady Wemyss's death,—
a friend of 30 years. And I somehow slumped, and the Dr. said I'd better
give up Italy, and I knew, alas, that he was right.

I meant to motor back to Paris, or at least to Fontainebleau, while
the servants are opening St. Brice—but on reflection I decided that I
wasn't quite up to the chances of the road, so next Thursday, the 20th,
I go by train to Paris. I shall stay 2 days in Paris to see my oculist, then
go for a few days to the Château de Grégy, Brie Comte Robert, Seine-
et-Marne, to stay with my old friend Ogden Codman (Tel. 85 Brie Cte.
Robert). Do call me up, either at the Crillon, where I expect to arrive
early in the morning on the 21st, or else at Grégy if you are still in
Paris! It would be a joy to catch you there.

Please let me know if I sent you Linky's photo in Herc's pram.[2] It is
too lovely. I meant to—but I really collapsed when she died, and I am
only just collecting my wits.

Yours ever affectionately,
    Edoo.

How I wish I were 40 years younger, and had seen the Coronation![3]
What a great people.

What did Herc think of the show? And how are Betsy and he?

Ms:WRT

1. The Pekinese who had been with EW for eleven years. On April 16, the
day after Linky's death, EW wrote shakily in her diary: "Oh, my little dog,"
—before the line fell blank. To William Tyler the next day, she said: "I wish
she could have outlasted me, for I feel for the very first time in my life, quite
utterly alone and lonely."

2. The temporary nickname for the infant Royall was Herc, or Hercules.

3. The coronation of King George VI, following the abdication of his brother King Edward VIII.

To Matilda Gay

Pavillon Colombe
August 4 [1937]

Dearest Matilda,

I am just sending you this line by Elisina, to tell you how sorry I am not to be able to go with her to see you this afternoon. I should have been quite willing to risk the fatigue, but Elisina & my maid behaved so awfully about it that I had no alternative [but to] go on snoozing on the sofa; so I send you instead my best love & deepest sympathy by Elisina. How often in passing your gate, I have said to myself, "I must stop & give a hug to dear Walter Gay"—& I am happy to say that I have always done it until today, when, alas, it only half matters.[1]

This brings you my best love, & many many thoughts of my beloved W. G. under whose mauve poppies, given to me 18 years ago, I am now lying.

Please arrange with Elisina to come out some day to lunch, & meanwhile, believe me yr affte

Edith

Ms:WRT

1. Walter Gay had died at Le Bréau three weeks before.

Chronologies
Sources and Acknowledgments
Index

Chronologies

THE LIFE

1862   Edith Newbold Jones born on January 24 at 80 East Twenty-first Street, New York City. Third and last child of George Frederic Jones and Lucretia Stevens Rhinelander. Older brothers: Frederic, born 1846 and Henry ("Harry"), born 1850.

1866–1872   With family in Europe, traveling or residing in England, France, Spain, Italy, and Germany. Edith receives her first schooling in the languages and literatures of these countries.

1872–1875   Family returns to America, and begins to divide the year between a brownstone on West Twenty-third Street, New York, and Pencraig, the summer home in Newport, Rhode Island. Edith is given German lessons by Anna Bahlmann, the young governess of the Rutherfurd children in Newport. She comes to know Mary Cadwalader Jones, the wife (later divorced) of her brother Frederic. Their only child, Beatrix, is born in 1872.

1877   Edith completes a thirty-thousand-word novella, *Fast and Loose*, about an ill-starred young couple.

1878   *Verses*, a collection of twenty-nine poems by Edith Jones, printed privately in Newport at Lucretia Jones's expense. One of the poems published by William Dean Howells in the *Atlantic Monthly*.

Edith makes her social debut late in the year.

1882   George Frederic Jones dies in Cannes, in March. Edith re-
            ceives $20,000 in trust fund.

            August: Engagement announced in Newport between Edith
            Jones and Henry Leyden Stevens, young son of one of New
            York's most visible socialites. In October, the engagement
            is broken off.

1883   In Bar Harbor, Maine, during the summer, Edith meets Walter
            Van Rensselaer Berry, a Harvard graduate who is preparing
            for the bar. Later in the season, Edward Robbins ("Teddy")
            Wharton, thirty-three years old and a friend of brother
            Frederic, arrives and begins courtship. Teddy Wharton, whose
            interests run chiefly to hunting and fishing, lives with his
            family in Boston. He has only a modest income of his own.

1885–1888   Edith Jones and Edward Wharton married on April 29, 1885,
            in Trinity Chapel, New York. The Whartons move into
            Pencraig Cottage, a small house on Mrs. Jones's Newport
            estate. They spend the winter and spring of each year trav-
            eling in Europe, mostly in Italy. In 1888, EW inherits
            $120,000 on the death of her reclusive New York cousin
            Joshua Jones.

1889   The Whartons rent a small house on Madison Avenue, New
            York.

            Three poems by Edith Wharton accepted by New York pe-
            riodicals. One of them, "The Last of the Giustiniani," is
            taken for *Scribner's Magazine* by its editor, Edward L. Burlin-
            game.

1890   Burlingame accepts EW's story "Mrs. Manstey's View" for
            Scribner's. It is published in July 1891.

1891   EW purchases narrow house at 884 Park Avenue (as the
            address will soon become). A few years later, she purchases
            the twin adjoining house at 882, for the staff to live in.

1893   EW buys Land's End, a Newport property overlooking the
            Atlantic, for $80,000. She works with Ogden Codman, a
            Boston architect, remodeling and redecorating the interior.

Paul Bourget, the French man of letters, comes with his wife, Minnie David, for a stay.

1894–1895 EW suffers a protracted breakdown, after several years of intermittent fatigue and nausea. The chief symptoms are intense exhaustion, nausea, and profound melancholia.

1896–1897 EW collaborates with Ogden Codman on *The Decoration of Houses*, which is published by Charles Scribner's Sons in 1897.

1899 EW and Teddy Wharton spend four months in Washington, D.C., seeing much of Walter Berry and coming to know George Cabot ("Bay") Lodge.

In March, EW's first volume of stories, *The Greater Inclination*, is published by Scribners. It consists entirely of recently written stories, EW rejecting all those she had composed earlier.

1900 *The Touchstone*, a novella, published in *Scribner's*.

1901 June 1901: EW purchases 113-acre property in Lenox, Massachusetts. Construction begun by architect Francis V. L. Hoppin on The Mount, a house modeled on Christopher Wren's Belton House in Lincolnshire.

Crucial Instances, a second collection of stories, published by Scribners.

Lucretia Rhinelander Jones dies in Paris, age seventy-six. EW inherits trust fund worth $90,000.

1902 *The Valley of Decision*, EW's first novel, comes out in February. EW translates *Es Lebe das Leben*, a play by Hermann Sudermann.

Correspondence with Henry James begins.

September: The Whartons move into The Mount.

1903 EW tours Italy collecting materials for *Italian Villas and Their Gardens* (1904).

She sells Land's End for $122,500.

Sanctuary, a novella.

1904   EW's first automobile, a Panhard-Levassor, purchased in France.

In England, the Whartons visit Henry James and make a motor trip with him.

The Descent of Man, EW's third collection of stories.

In the summer and fall, houseguests proliferate at The Mount, among them Henry James and his friend Howard Sturgis.

1905   James visits at 884 Park Avenue. In Washington, the Whartons dine with President Roosevelt at the White House.

The House of Mirth published in October. By the year's end, sales have reached 140,000.

1906   EW is introduced by Paul Bourget into the Parisian literary and intellectual circles. Charles Du Bos translates *The House of Mirth*.

In October, the stage version of *The House of Mirth* by Edith Wharton and Clyde Fitch opens in New York and promptly fails.

1907   In January, EW rents the apartment of the George Vanderbilts at 58 Rue de Varenne in the Faubourg St. Germain section of Paris. It is the start of her transfer from America to France.

In March, EW and Teddy make a motor trip through France with Henry James.

In the spring, EW begins to see something of Morton Fullerton, forty-two-year-old Paris correspondent for the London *Times*, a student of Charles Eliot Norton and a disciple of Henry James. Fullerton visits The Mount in autumn.

The Fruit of the Tree published in October.

1908   Through the winter and into the spring, EW again rents the Vanderbilt apartment on the Rue de Varenne in Paris. She leads an unceasingly busy social life, much of it centered in the famous Faubourg salon of Comtesse Rosa de Fitz-James.

With ailing Teddy back in America at an Arkansas spa, the relationship with Fullerton develops into a passionate affair.

Henry James arrives for a two-week stay in April. EW also sees a good deal of Henry Adams.

At The Mount from late May through October.

In England during last two months, EW enjoys celebrity status and a hectic social whirl. She meets the leading political, literary, and social figures in the Edwardian world. At Stanway, the home of Lord and Lady Elcho, she comes to know John Hugh Smith and Robert Norton, both of whom become lifelong friends.

A Motor-Flight Through France in October.

1909   Teddy arrives in Paris in wretched condition; in April, he goes back to Lenox.

Artemis to Actaeon, a book of poetry, in April.

June: EW and Fullerton spend a memorable night together in London, and later a summer month in England.

In September, EW and Bernhard Berenson, the distinguished art critic and connoisseur, initiate their long friendship.

October: EW witnesses an airplane flying over the city of Paris, an historic first occurrence.

November: It is revealed that Teddy has embezzled $50,000 of EW's money and used it to buy a house in Boston for his mistress.

1910   In January, EW moves into another apartment on the Rue de Varenne, at No. 53.

Walter Berry leaves the International Tribunal in Cairo and decides to settle in Paris.

Teddy enters a Swiss sanatorium for treatment of nervous spells and depression.

EW and Teddy return to New York in October. Teddy leaves on world tour with family friend Johnson Morton. EW goes back alone to Paris.

1911   Unsuccessful effort by EW, with others, to secure Nobel Prize in literature for Henry James.

In June, EW is back at The Mount. Teddy, following the long trip, is physically well but psychologically unstable. The two have painful sessions, and EW says they should live apart.

Henry James, Gaillard Lapsley, and John Hugh Smith come for a visit; James in top form.

Ethan Frome published in September; reviews respectful if puzzled, sales disappointing.

In the fall, EW and Berry drive through central Italy and visit Bernhard and Mary Berenson at their Villa I Tatti outside Florence.

1912   Teddy Wharton back in Paris from February to May.

EW and Berry undergo a series of misadventures while visiting a Tuscan monastery.

In the summer, EW comes to England, visits Henry James, to his enjoyment and alleged terror, and takes him to Cliveden, the home of William Waldorf Astor and Nancy Astor.

The Reef published by D. Appleton & Company, the start of EW's relationship with that firm. Sales poor, reviews unenthusiastic.

1913   January: Estrangement from brother Harry, who accuses EW of snubbing his Russian-born fiancée.

March: Effort instigated by EW to raise $5,000 for a seventieth-birthday present for Henry James broken off when James angrily repudiates it.

April: EW's divorce from Teddy Wharton granted by decree of Paris tribunal.

EW and Berry make a tour of Sicily.

May: EW becomes acquainted with Geoffrey Scott, author of *The Architecture of Humanism* and soon to be one of her most valued friends.

August: EW drives across Germany with Berenson.

The Custom of the Country published in October by Scribners. Sales quickly rise to sixty thousand.

December: EW comes to New York for the wedding of her niece, Beatrix Jones, a highly successful landscape gardener, and Max Farrand, professor of history at Yale.

1914   In March, EW drives across Algeria and Tunisia with Percy Lubbock, gifted young English writer.

In July, EW and Berry spend three weeks wandering through Spain.

August 3: Germany declares war on France.

EW immediately establishes workroom for seamstresses thrown out of work in the wartime confusion.

In late August, she goes to England, calls on Henry James in Rye and takes the Wards' home, Stocks, for a season. On news of the Battle of the Marne, she makes urgent efforts to get back to France and succeeds in late September.

In November, she establishes the American Hostels for Refugees, to house and take care of some of the hordes of refugees pouring in from the ravaged battle areas. Elisina Royall Tyler, Florence-born, the wife of art historian Royall Tyler and a Paris friend since 1912, is the invaluable second-in-command. By the end of 1915, EW could report that the hostels had assisted 9,330 refugees, 3,000 on a permanent basis; that 235,000 meals had been served, medical care given to 7,700 persons, and jobs found for 3,400. Total cost to date was $82,000.

1915

From February onward, EW makes a series of visits to the front lines, delivering medical supplies and inquiring about needs. She gives Henry James long accounts of these trips. She also describes them in articles for *Scribner's* that become *Fighting France, from Dunkerque to Belfort* (November).

April: Organizes Children of Flanders Rescue Committee; 750 Flemish children cared for in six homes between Paris and the Normandy coast.

Forms a friendship with André Gide, a fellow worker for the hostels.

1916

Henry James dies on February 28. EW to Lapsley: "His friendship was the pride and honour of my life."

Made Chevalier of the Legion of Honor by the President of France.

In the spring, EW helps inaugurate a cure program for the *tuberculeux de guerre*, the fourth of her "rescue organisations."

The Book of the Homeless, edited by EW and with contributions by scores of distinguished writers, artists, and musicians, earns $15,000, all told, for the hostels.

Xingu and Other Stories, in October.

1917

EW's novella *Summer* runs in *McClure's* February–August. The inability of Charles Scribner to take it for *Scribner's Magazine* was one cause of EW's break with her old publisher.

September: Makes month-long tour of Morocco with Walter Berry, by official invitation. Stays with the Resident General, her friend General Lyautey.

1918   Inspired by arrival and performance of American troops, and by spectacular July Fourth parade in Paris.

Frederic Jones, EW's older brother, dies.

EW deeply saddened by death of young wartime friend Ronald Simmons.

Buys Jean-Marie, a villa in the village of St. Brice-sous-Forêt, about ten miles north of Paris.

The Marne published by Appleton.

1919   Leases Ste. Claire du Vieux Château above the town of Hyères on the Riviera, overlooking the Mediterranean.

In the summer, EW moves into Jean-Marie, which will soon be renamed Pavillon Colombe.

French Ways and Their Meaning, a collection of articles, published by Appleton.

1920   *The Age of Innocence*, serialized in the *Pictorial Review* (for $18,000), then published in October by Appleton. Excellent critical reception; sale of sixty-six thousand copies in six months.

In December begins what will be her annual wintering at Ste. Claire in Hyères.

In Morocco, published by Scribners.

1921   In Hyères begins a particularly treasured friendship with Philomène de Lévis-Mirepoix, a younger woman and future journalist and novelist.

In May, *The Age of Innocence* wins the Pulitzer Prize. EW learns later that the jury had voted for Sinclair Lewis's *Main Street* but had been overruled by the Columbia University board of trustees. She writes Lewis of her disgust at this event and invites him to St. Brice.

EW's novella, *The Old Maid*, turned down by several magazines because of its theme of illegitimate birth, purchased by *Redbook* for $2,250.

1922   EW's year-round schedule now firmly fixed: at the Pavillon Colombe from June to mid-December; at Ste. Claire from mid-December through May.

         Harry Jones dies.

         The Glimpses of the Moon, published in August by Appleton, sells more than 100,000 copies in America and England in six months.

1923   Film version of *The Glimpses of the Moon*, starring Bebe Daniels, Nita Naldi, and Maurice Costello, with dialogue by F. Scott Fitzgerald, opens in Washington in April to fine reviews.

         Charles Cook, EW's chauffeur since 1904, has a slight stroke and is forced to give up driving. He leaves the household.

         June: EW sails to New York, visits the Cuttings and the Maynards on Long Island, and goes on to New Haven, where she receives the first honorary degree bestowed upon a woman by a major university at Yale University's commencement. The entire visit lasts eleven days, and is EW's last visit to America.

         A Son at the Front published in September by Scribners, fulfilling an old contract.

1924   *Old New York*, a collection of four novellas, set in New York from the 1840s to the 1870s, published in boxed sets of four volumes by Appleton in May.

         EW awarded the Gold Medal, given annually for "distinguished service to arts or letters" by the National Institute of Arts and Letters; the second novelist (the first was Howells) and the first woman so honored.

1925   January: EW visited at Ste. Claire by William Gerhardi, talented and eccentric young English novelist who had been born in Russia of English parents. EW had praised his first novel, *Futility* (1922), and had pressed for its publication in the United States, with a preface by herself.

The Mother's Recompense, published in June by Appleton. Sales satisfactory.

In June, EW receives a copy of *The Great Gatsby* inscribed by its author, F. Scott Fitzgerald. On EW's invitation, Fitzgerald visits St. Brice; it is a memorably calamitous encounter.

The Writing of Fiction, a series of five essays, one of them a long appreciation of Marcel Proust, brought out by Scribners in the summer.

1926   EW charters the *Osprey*, a 360-ton steam yacht, for a ten-week cruise in the Aegean in March–June. Her guests include Margaret Terry Chanler, Robert Norton, and Logan Pearsall Smith.

Here and Beyond, a volume of stories, published by Appleton in the summer.

Twelve Poems printed by the Medici Society in London.

September: Travels with Berry in northern Italy.

1927   January: Walter Berry suffers a mild stroke, and comes down to Hyères to convalesce.

EW's novel *Twilight Sleep* published in June by Appleton; by August, it has replaced Sinclair Lewis's *Elmer Gantry* at the top of the best-seller list.

Magazine editors bid against one another for serial rights to EW's next novel.

Berry suffers another stroke on October 2 and dies on October 12, EW by his bedside the final three days. EW to Lapsley: "All my life goes with him."

1928   Effort to gain Nobel Prize for EW (Chief Justice Taft and Lord Balfour joining in the venture initiated by Robert and Mildred Bliss) fails when the award goes to Henri Bergson and the Sardinian writer Grazia Deledda.

Teddy Wharton dies on February 7, at age seventy-nine. "I am thankful to think of him at peace after all the weary agitated years," EW writes Robert Grant.

EW spends a summer's fortnight in England; visits Tintagel, legendary site of King Arthur's castle.

The Children, a Book-of-the-Month selection in September, earns EW $95,000.

The Age of Innocence, expertly dramatized by Margaret Ayer Barnes and with Katharine Cornell as Ellen Olenska, opens on Broadway in December and runs until the following June.

1929   Severe winter storms wreck the Ste. Claire gardens. On top of the shock caused by this disaster, EW is stricken with pneumonia and heart palpitations. She is unable to work for four months.

With an enormous effort, EW completes her long novel *Hudson River Bracketed* in October.

Awarded Gold Medal for "special distinction in literature" by the American Academy of Arts and Letters.

1930   First meeting with Kenneth Clark, sometime protégé of Berenson and art critic and historian of vast promise.

December: First meeting with the novelist Aldous Huxley and with the anthropologist Bronislaw Malinowski.

Certain People, short stories, published by Appleton.

1931   March: Kenneth and Jane Clark pay the first of many visits to Ste. Claire. Clark, at twenty-eight, is appointed keeper of the Ashmolean Museum in Oxford.

During a festive three weeks in England in July, EW encounters many of the leading Georgian figures, among them Desmond MacCarthy, H. G. Wells, Sacheverell Sitwell, Edward Marsh, Harold Nicolson, and David Cecil.

EW in closer touch with Morton Fullerton than for a number of years.

1932   *The Gods Arrive*, the sequel to *Hudson River Bracketed*, serialized by the *Delineator* after being rejected by several magazines because of its "central idea"—an out-of-wedlock pregnancy. On publication by Appleton, it has a good reception but notably poor sales.

Effects of the 1929 Wall Street collapse and the resulting economic depression begin to be felt by EW. At least one short story ("Joy in the House") turned down by all editors, and fees sharply reduced.

In May, EW visits Rome with Nicky Mariano, Berenson's librarian and companion and EW's friend of some years.

EW becomes godmother to the Clarks' infant son, Colin.

1933   *Ladies' Home Journal*, via its editor, seeks to reduce the fee for EW's memoirs, *A Backward Glance*. EW announces she will sue if agreement not kept. The full fee is paid.

Elise, EW's French maid of many years, dies in May. *Human Nature*, short stories, published by Appleton. Summer: EW attends Salzburg music festival.

Catharine Gross, EW's housekeeper and friend since 1884, dies in October.

1934   EW at work on *The Buccaneers*, a novel left incomplete at her death, and published in 1938 with EW's outline of the remainder of the story and a note by Gaillard Lapsley.

EW so incensed by what she considers the poor advertising of *A Backward Glance* that she asks Appleton-Century (as it now is) to release her from the contract for her next novel. The chairman of the board replies at length, rehearsing the long and profitable relationship, and EW stays with the firm.

In September, EW tours Holland and Scotland. In England, she is shown through the National Gallery by Kenneth Clark, who has been appointed director at the age of thirty.

1935   *The Old Maid*, dramatized by Zoë Akins, opens in New York in January, beginning a successful run. In May, it wins the Pulitzer Prize for drama.

In April, EW suffers a mild stroke and the temporary loss of sight in her right eye. By the end of the summer, she is back at work.

September: Minnie Jones, EW's sister-in-law, dies in London. EW goes to England to arrange for the burial.

1936   *Ethan Frome*, dramatized by Owen and Donald Davis, with Raymond Massey as Ethan, Pauline Lord as Zeena, and Ruth Gordon as Mattie Silver, opens in January. It runs for four months in New York, and goes on the road for a long tour. In her own words, EW is "blazing along several White Ways at a time." Income from her plays amounts to $130,000. Money troubles are over.

The World Over, short stories, published by Appleton-Century.

On visit to England, EW goes to house party at Stanway with Wells, the Max Beerbohms, Cynthia Asquith, and others.

1937   January 24: EW has her seventy-fifth birthday.

June 1: On visit to Ogden Codman's château, south of Paris, EW has a stroke. She is transported by ambulance to Pavillon Colombe.

EW dies on the evening of August 11. She is buried in the Cimetière des Gonards in Versailles, near to the grave of Walter Berry.

THE WRITINGS

1878   *Verses* (privately printed by C. E. Hammett, Newport).

1897   *The Decoration of Houses*, with Ogden Codman, Jr. (Charles Scribner's Sons: hereafter S).

1899   *The Greater Inclination*, short stories (S).

1900   *The Touchstone*, novella (S).

1901   *Crucial Instances*, short stories (S).

1902   *The Valley of Decision*, novel (S).

1903   *Sanctuary*, novella (S).

1904   *The Descent of Man and Other Stories*, short stories (S).

        Italian Villas and Their Gardens (Century).

1905   *Italian Backgrounds* (S).

        The House of Mirth, novel (S).

1907   *Madame de Treymes*, novella (S).

        The Fruit of the Tree, novel (S).

1908   *A Motor-Flight Through France* (S).

        The Hermit and the Wild Woman and Other Stories, short stories (S).

1909   *Artemis to Actaeon and Other Verses* (S).

1910   *Tales of Men and Ghosts*, short stories (S).

1911   *Ethan Frome*, novella (S).

1912   *The Reef*, novel (D. Appleton & Company: hereafter A).

1913   *The Custom of the Country*, novel (S).

1915   *Fighting France, from Dunkerque to Belfort* (S).

1916   *Xingu and Other Stories*, short stories (S).

1917	*Summer*, novella (A).
1918	*The Marne*, novel (A).
1919	*French Ways and Their Meaning* (A).
1920	*The Age of Innocence*, novel (A).
	In Morocco (S).
1922	*The Glimpses of the Moon*, novel (A).
1923	*A Son at the Front*, novel (S).
1924	*Old New York: False Dawn, The Old Maid, The Spark, New Year's Day*, novellas (A).
1925	*The Mother's Recompense*, novel (A).
	The Writing of Fiction, essays (S).
1926	*Here and Beyond*, short stories (A).
	Twelve Poems (The Medici Society, London).
1927	*Twilight Sleep*, novel (A).
1928	*The Children*, novel (A).
1929	*Hudson River Bracketed*, novel (A).
1930	*Certain People*, short stories (A).
1932	*The Gods Arrive*, novel (A).
1933	*Human Nature*, short stories (A).
1934	*A Backward Glance*, autobiography (Appleton-Century).
1936	*The World Over*, short stories (Appleton-Century).
1937	*Ghosts*, short stories (Appleton-Century; reprinted from other volumes).
1938	*The Buccaneers*, novel (Appleton-Century; posthumous and incomplete; with a scenario of the unwritten portion of the narrative by Edith Wharton, and a note by Gaillard Lapsley).

1968 *The Collected Short Stories of Edith Wharton* (Charles Scribner's Sons; includes twelve stories not previously collected).

Some Uncollected Articles

1902 "The Three Francescas," *North American Review*, July.

1910 "George Cabot Lodge," *Scribner's*, February.

1920 "Henry James in His Letters," *Quarterly Review*, July.

1927 "The Great American Novel," *Yale Review*, July.

1936 "Souvenirs de Bourget d'outre-mer," *Revue Hebdomadaire*, June 21.

1938 "A Little Girl's New York," *Harper's*, March.

Translations, Editions, Introductions

1902 *The Joy of Living*, translated from Hermann Sudermann's play *Es Lebe das Leben* by Edith Wharton (S).

1916 *The Book of the Homeless*, edited by Edith Wharton (S).

1922 *Futility*, by William Gerhardi, introduction by Edith Wharton.

1935 *Speak to the Earth*, by Vivienne de Watteville (Vivienne Goschen), with a preface by Edith Wharton.

1936 *Benediction*, by Claude Silve (Philomène de la Forest-Divonne), translated from the French by Robert Norton, foreword by Edith Wharton.
      Ethan Frome, a play by Owen and Donald Davis, introduction by Edith Wharton (S).

1939 *Eternal Passion in English Poetry*, selected by Edith Wharton and Robert Norton, with the help of Gaillard Lapsley (Appleton-Century).

Sources and Acknowledgments

THE LETTERS OF Edith Wharton are published with the kind permission of William Royall Tyler, the owner of the Edith Wharton estate. Our thanks are due as well to Gloria Loomis, the literary agent for the estate.

SOURCES OF THE LETTERS

BL: Beinecke Library, Yale University

The majority of the letters in this volume are taken from the Edith Wharton archives in Beinecke Library. We record with pleasure our gratitude to the Beinecke staff for its thoughtful, friendly, and wonderfully efficient help: to Ralph Franklin, the director; David Schoonover, the former curator of the American holdings; and for varieties of particular assistance to Patricia Middleton, Richard Hart, Steven Jones, Marcia Bickoff, and Ann Maru.

Richard Hart was responsible, in addition, for procuring most of the photographic illustrations. See picture credits.

FL: Firestone Library, Princeton University

Firestone houses the vast Scribners archives, including letters from EW to Brownell, Burlingame, Charles Scribner, and others. We are most grateful to Richard Ludwig, the former director, and to the Firestone Library staff for their cooperation.

HL: Houghton Library, Harvard University

Here are scores of letters from EW to Sara Norton, Charles Eliot Norton, Corinne Roosevelt Robinson, Barrett Wendell, John Jay Chapman, Morton Fullerton (1916 and later), and others. For the securing of them, we happily thank Rodney Dennis, the director, and his excellent staff: James Lewis, curator, Susan Halpert, Jennie Rathbun, and Melanie Wisner.

IO: Iris Origo

The letters to Beatrix Farrand were among the thirty-nine letters from EW included in a collection of documents contributed by Marchesa Iris Origo to R. W. B. Lewis when he was writing the biography of Edith Wharton. The collection consisted of memoirs and letters brought together by Percy Lubbock, Marchesa Origo's stepfather, when he in his turn was writing *Portrait of Edith Wharton* (1946). It is now in Beinecke Library, Yale. Our thanks go to Marchesa Origo for this second use of the letters.

KC: Kenneth Clark

The late Lord Clark placed 120 letters and postcards from EW to Kenneth and Jane Clark at the disposal of R. W. B. Lewis, when the latter was writing his biography of EW. We are particularly grateful to the heirs of Lord and Lady Clark for the use of a number of these documents in the present volume.

LA: Louis Auchincloss

The letters of Edith Wharton to various correspondents—in particular, for our purposes, to Mildred and Robert Bliss, to Eunice Maynard, and to Matilda Gay—were collected over many years by the distinguished novelist Louis Auchincloss. They are now in Beinecke Library, Yale.

We are grateful to Louis Auchincloss not only for our use of these

letters but also for his invariably quick, colorful, and informative response to a series of questions. In any enterprise devoted to Edith
Wharton, Louis Auchincloss is the most enjoyable of *confrères*.

UT: The Harry Ransom Humanities Research Center at the University of Texas at Austin

The research center is the home of the three hundred–odd letters from
EW to Morton Fullerton that came into public view in 1985 (see general
introduction), as well as of letters to William Gerhardi and several others. A visit to the center, to examine the Fullerton letters and select from
them, was among the most memorable of the editors' experiences in the
preparation of this volume.

For expert guidance and assistance on that occasion and at a number
of later moments, we are exceedingly grateful to Dr. Deckerd Turner,
the courteous director, and to Catharine Henderson, the ever-efficient
staff member.

At the time of the visit to Austin, Professor Alan Gribben, who was
composing a special Edith Wharton issue of the university's *Library
Chronicle* to introduce the Fullerton letters, gave valuable advice. His
own scholarly findings, as we have indicated elsewhere, are drawn upon
in our annotations.

We are also glad to express our thanks to our old friend Professor
Shelley Fisher Fishkin, of the UT American Studies faculty, for her
exemplary help in procuring for us further literary and photographic
materials from the research center.

VT: Villa I Tatti, Settignano (Florence), Italy

In the former home of Bernard Berenson—now the Harvard University
Center for the Study of Renaissance Art—are more than six hundred
letters from EW to Bernard Berenson, Mary Berenson, and Nicky Mariano, written between 1909 and 1937.

Our numerous hours-long visits to I Tatti in 1985–1986—to go through
this abundant collection and to make and Xerox our choices—comprise

perhaps the happiest chapter in the work for this book. For this, we have to thank in particular Professor Louise Clubb, the distinguished director, and Fiorella Superbi, the beautifully efficient archivist.

WRT: William Royall Tyler

Among the many letters and papers inherited by William Royall Tyler from his mother, Elisina Tyler (who came into their possession as Edith Wharton's residuary legatee), are some four hundred letters from EW to members of the Tyler family. These, with a mass of other documents, are now in the Lily Library at the University of Indiana in Bloomington, Indiana. We are grateful for access to these materials; but it may be repeated here that William Royall Tyler is the legal owner of *all* EW's letters and literary properties wherever they happen to be lodged.

It is a special pleasure, meanwhile, to acknowledge William Tyler's continuing help, always so graciously given, in the way of reminiscences and biographical information.

OTHER SOURCES

The letters to Elizabeth Cameron are copies of the originals in the National Gallery in Washington, and most kindly supplied (with many others) by Jerome Edelstein.

The letter to Morgan Dix (December 5, 1905), with the letter *to* EW from Dr. Dix, was procured from the Archives of Trinity Church Parish, New York, by Scott Marshall. Our thanks go equally to Trinity Church and to Mr. Marshall.

The letter to Pauline Foster Du Pont (September 23, 1874) is a copy of the original in the Eleutherian Mills Historical Library, in Greenville, Delaware, and part of a batch of EW papers presented to Beinecke Library, Yale, by the Historical Library many years ago.

The three letters to André Gide (1916, 1917, 1923) are transcriptions of the originals, made in 1969 by Professor Jacques Cotnam (Department of French Literature, York University, Toronto, Canada) for R. W. B. Lewis. The originals are in the literary section of the Bibliothèque Jacques Doucet in the University of Paris. The bureaucratic arrangements of the Bibliothèque Doucet and of these particular holdings make it extremely difficult for anyone to examine the Gide letters, and impossible for anyone to Xerox them. Several obvious minor errors of transcription have been corrected, but at least one wrongly transcribed proper name has had to be left as is. We are grateful nonetheless for the sturdy efforts of Anne Shullenberger (of the Yale American Studies Graduate Program) to break through the barriers. Our warmest thanks go to Nicholas Fox Weber, who looked carefully into the matter, in Paris, and apprised us of the technical obstacles involved.

The letter to Frederick Macmillan (May 29, 1909) is a copy of the original in the British Museum, supplied by Mary Pitlick to R. W. B. Lewis. We are grateful indeed to be able to use this letter.

INDIVIDUAL ACKNOWLEDGMENTS

I. Assistance in annotation

We are happy to record our gratitude for help in tracking down a number of EW's allusions and quotations. Most, though by no means all, of the individuals listed are members of the Yale University faculty.

Classical references: John Hollander, Matthew Munich, Ramsay MacMullen.

French: Peter Brooks, Georges May.

German: Liselotte Davis, Peter Demetz, Richard N. Lawson (*Edith Wharton and German Literature*, 1974).

Italian: Jaroslav Pelikan, Barbara Spackman.

Old Norse: Norman Keul (who provided an illuminating short course of instruction on the Eddas).

Russian: Robert L. Jackson.

History: For early twentieth-century American history, John Blum; for aspects of French social history before the first war, Alan Gribben.

II. Other particular acknowledgments

We thank the following for the mode of assistance indicated:

Kristin Lauer, for the dating of an EW short story, and for helpful suggestions about EW's female characterizations.

Judith McConnell, for supplying a photograph of Margaret Terry Chanler, and for cogent advice on out-of-the-way volumes of memoirs and the like.

Scott Marshall (in addition to giving us the Morgan Dix letter), for pictures of The Mount and for the friendliest kind of cooperation.

Mary Pitlick, for generously presenting us with a thick folder of documents relating to her own editorial venue with the letters of Edith Wharton—a venue long since given up, but deriving from her very substantial research for the biography of EW.

Alan Price, for putting together for us a docket of letters by EW during the war and drawing our attention, among them, to the letter to Private Victor Solberg (October 19, 1918); and for wise and informed help over an extended period of time.

Annette Zilversmit, for eloquent encouragement and support.

Nicholas Fox Weber (in addition to advice on the Gide letters), for exploring in considerable depth the whole complex matter of the letters to Morton Fullerton, and especially their reappearance in Paris and their sale there after many years of invisibility.

III. Hospitality

Visits by the editors to libraries in the United States and Italy were made much more enjoyable and sometimes even possible by the kindly hospitality of:

William and Jane Stott (Austin, Texas), Edward T. Cone (Princeton), Guido and Anne Calabresi (Florence), George White (for the use of the Matthiessen Room in Eliot House, Harvard, of which Dr. White is Keeper), Robert and Annaliese Geis (Florence).

The contributions to this volume of Nathaniel Lewis would have been virtually impossible without the extraordinary kindness and hospitality of his friend and teacher Charles Welles, who made a home for his one-time student within his own family home.

IV. Preparation of the manuscript

Before Nathaniel Lewis took over the task of copy-editing, the editors were fortunately able to enlist the services of Constance Berger, who provided immaculate typescripts of the early letters, and whose queries and comments were always as welcome as they were acute. At a slightly later stage, Bonney MacDonald, of the American studies graduate program at Yale, earned our warmest thanks by supplying excellent copies of a batch of letters to Morton Fullerton. We were also given skillful assistance at different moments by Andrea Majka and May Sansone.

V. Financial aid

R. W. B. Lewis is happy to express his gratitude to the Whitney Humanities Center at Yale, and its director Peter Brooks, for a travel grant to visit the University of Texas at Austin; and to Yale University, in particular Dean Keith Thomson of the Graduate School, for making possible a year's leave of absence in 1985–1986.

He is no less grateful to the American Council of Learned Societies, and its late director, John William Ward, for a grant-in-aid over six months in late 1985 and 1986.

VI. Publication

It was Charles Scribner III who first proposed an edition of the letters of Edith Wharton, and who invited the two of us to become editors. To Mr. Scribner, and to Susanne Kirk, our talented publisher's editor, we are very much beholden. We are no less so to Beth Greenfeld, who did an exemplary job of copy-editing; and to Sam Flores, the learned and cultivated reader of the galleys, whose knowledge of France and the French and of European cultural history in general proved invaluable to us.

VII. Credits

Our special thanks are extended to the following for providing photographs and permission to use them:

Endpaper letterheads:

Beinecke Library, Yale University: 884 Park Avenue, 58 Rue de Varennes, Pavillon Colombe

Berenson Archives, Villa I Tatti, Florence, Italy: Sainte-Claire le Château

Firestone Library, Princeton University: Land's End, Newport

Harry Ransom Humanities Research Center, the University of Texas at Austin: The Mount

Illustrations (specifically credited in captions):

Beinecke Library, Yale University

Berenson Archives, Villa I Tatti, Florence, Italy

Firestone Library, Princeton University

Houghton Library, Harvard University

Lenox Library Association, Lenox, Massachusetts

National Portrait Gallery, Smithsonian Institution

David Pickman

Harry Ransom Humanities Research Center, the University of Texas at Austin

William Royall Tyler Collection, Lily Library, University of Indiana

Index

NOVELS

PAVILLON COLOMBE
ST BRICE-SOUS-FORÊT (S&O)
GARE: SARCELLES
TÉLÉPHONE: ST BRICE-SOUS-FORÊT, 12

Tuesday 18th

Dearest Daisy,

I couldn't have ~~todo~~ this week, either, as the dentist "wants" (!) me every other day. But the weather seems...

April 9. 37.

SAINTE-CLAIRE LE CHATEAU
HYÈRES (VAR)
TÉL: 2-29

Dearest B. B.,

Alas, what s...

health i...

three

Feb. 2d
58 RUE DE VARENNE
1909

My dear Mr. John,

You...

Jan. 21st 1902

884 PARK AVENUE.

Dear Sally

A sharp attack of influenza has kept me